FRANK LLOYD WRIGHT
COLLECTED WRITINGS

FRANK LLOYD WRIGHT
COLLECTED WRITINGS

INCLUDING AN AUTOBIOGRAPHY

Volume **2**

1930‒1932

Edited by
Bruce Brooks Pfeiffer

Introduction by Kenneth Frampton

Rizzoli/New York in association with The Frank Lloyd Wright Foundation

CONTENTS

INTRODUCTION   5

A BIOGRAPHICAL SKETCH   10

1930
Poor Little American Architecture   15
  (unpublished)

1931
Modern Architecture, Being the Kahn Lectures
  (Lectures, Princeton University)
    1: Machinery, Materials, and Men   19
    2: Style in Industry   31
    3: The Passing of the Cornice   42
    4: The Cardboard House   51
    5: The Tyranny of the Skyscraper   59
    6: The City   60
Two Lectures on Architecture
  (Lectures, Art Institute of Chicago)
    In the Realm of Ideas   80
    To the Young Man in Architecture   90

1932
An Autobiography
  (Longmans, Green)
    Book One
      Family Fellowship   102
    Book Two
      Work   183
    Book Three
      Freedom   325

INDEX   381

First published in the United States of America in 1992 by
Rizzoli International Publications, Inc.,
300 Park Avenue South, New York, New York 10010
Copyright © 1992 The Frank Lloyd Wright Foundation
The drawings of Frank Lloyd Wright are copyright
© 1992 The Frank Lloyd Wright Foundation

Printed in Mexico
Designed by Harakawa Sisco Inc

Library of Congress Cataloging-in-Publication Data
Wright, Frank Lloyd, 1867–1959.
  [Selections,   1992]
  The collected writings of Frank Lloyd Wright/
    edited by Bruce Brooks Pfeiffer.
      p.   cm.
    Includes index.
    Contents: v. 1.   1894–1930—v. 2. 1931–1932.
  including a reprint of his 1932 autobiography.
  ISBN 0-8478-1548-X (HC : v. 2). —
  ISBN 0-8478-1549-8 (pbk.: v. 2)
    1. Wright, Frank Lloyd, 1867–1959—Philosophy. I.
  Pfeiffer, Bruce Brooks. II. Wright, Frank Lloyd,
  1867–1959. Autobiography.
  NA737. W7A35 1992
  720—dc20   91–40987
                                                   CIP

INTRODUCTION

At the mature age of sixty-three, Frank Lloyd Wright entered the 1930s in a state of involuntary retirement; while his private life had stabilized, he was virtually devoid of work, partially as a consequence of the 1929 stock-market crash. To add insult to injury, 1929 had also seen the publication of Henry-Russell Hitchcock's *Modern Architecture: Romanticism and Reintegration,* in which Hitchcock relegated Wright to the category of the New Tradition, along with such seemingly retarditaire architects as Ragnar Ostberg, the designer of the Stockholm Town Hall. Clearly this did not sit well with Wright, and the unpublished "Poor Little American Architecture" is the start of a rebarbitive relationship with Hitchcock that will assume an *ad hominen* character in 1932, before being repaired through the magnanimity of Hitchcock's critical acumen; namely, his 1943 *In the Nature of Materials* dedicated to Wright's work. Despite his refusal to be counted among the New Traditionalists, Wright will nonetheless affirm his perennial anti–avant-gardist stance when he writes, ". . . all that is valuable in either Tradition or Pioneering is Old in the New and New in the Old."

1930 will see Wright's Kahn lectures at Princeton University given under the rubric of "modern" rather than organic architecture. In the course of six sessions he will present a summation of his thought as this had evolved over the previous three decades. In the first two lectures addressed to the problem of arriving at an authentic environmental culture for a democratic, industrialized society, Wright will begin with a reformulation of his 1901 address "The Art and Craft of the Machine" and will go on in Semperian terms to decry our proclivity for the mass-production of cheap substitutions, at the level of both material and form. Wright is particularly scathing in this regard about the wholesale manufacture of fake antique furniture, expressly reproduced for the reassurance of a deracinated *arriviste* middle class that had lost its original identity. For Wright the "model" for an alternative machine-age culture lay in the Momoyama era of Japan, and to this end he stressed the standardized modularity of its architecture, its compatibility with nature, its respect for the intrinsic character of material, its integral ornamentation, and above all its elimination of insignificant form.

In his second lecture, entitled "Style in Industry," Wright will insist on the generic character of the term rather than on "styles" in an academic sense. He outlined a hypothetical program for a new school of industrial art that was eventually realized in much modified form in the Taliesin Fellowship. Wright modeled the first version of this program on the 1901 Darmstadt Kunstlerkolonie, even including the appointment of seven "elect" artists who would offer instruction in their respective crafts, treating with wood, glass, metals, textiles, and pottery, etc. While landscape and urbanism were to be added to this curriculum, architecture as such was inexplicably omitted. That such a school was already in the process of being inaugurated at Cranbrook, near Detroit, under the leadership of Eliel Saarinen, surely accounts for the subsequent friendly rivalry between Saarinen and Wright.

The Kahn lectures establish beyond any doubt that Wright was always well informed about what was happening in Europe, for apart from his familiarity with the Wiener Werkstätte and his appreciation for French Art Deco at its best, he also took full cognizance of the work of Le Corbusier, who was his nemesis in so many respects. Thus Wright's deprecation of the fake classical cornice in his third lecture parallels to the letter Le Corbusier's own antipathy to classical moldings, whereas in his next lecture, entitled "The Cardboard House," he will take issue with the form and substance of Le Corbusier's Purist villas, arguing all too knowingly that ". . . they are the superficial badly built product of this superficial new 'surface-mass' aesthetic, falsely claiming French painting as a parent." Equally opposed to Le Corbusier's Ville Contemporaine of 1922 as to his slogan "a house is a machine for living in," Wright will opt in his final lecture for the dissolution of cities and for the redistribution of the population over the countryside. This general thesis, echoing Soviet deurbanization theories of exactly the same period, will come to be fully elaborated in his Broadacre City of 1934. Categorically anti-Classic and pro-Gothic and discriminating in this broad opposition between the cult of the pictorial versus the tactility of architecture, Wright will argue that the figurative representational arts should be subsumed under the new arts of photography and film. In a similar vein he will predicate his antithesis of the bourgeois city on the universalization of power and information; prophetic in this regard about the ubiquitous triumph of electrification and television. Thus while Wright was anti–avant-gardist he was certainly not opposed to the process of modernization when this appeared to resolve the intractable problems of the epoch. As in his 1931 lecture "To a Young Man in Architecture," Wright saw the future in terms of an industrial process that could still be symbiotically inflected. As he put it in the first Kahn lecture, "The machine does not write the doom of liberty, but is waiting at man's hand as a peerless tool, for him to use, to put a foundation beneath a genuine democracy."

Started in 1927 at Olgivanna's urging, when Wright was already sixty-three, and first issued, as published here, in 1932 and again in amplified form in 1943, Wright's autobiography was by far the longest text he ever wrote. There is more than a hint in the opening lines of each of the three books from which the first edition is composed that Wright would have liked to have structured the whole thing about a seasonal thematic. The winter, spring, and summer sequence implies an autumn that did indeed come to pass for Wright, who would outlive the first edition by another twenty-seven years, before he finally succumbed at the age of ninety-two in the spring of 1959.

Much of the autobiography is given over to what Wright would call "friction, waste and slip," a period of almost twenty years, 1909 to 1928, when he was constantly pursued by women, lawyers, creditors, clients, press photographers, and newspapermen. The somewhat rambling record of this period, some of which, if we are to believe him, was dictated on the run, is as revealing for its asides as for its prejudices—not to mention the long discursive passages that from time to time interrupt the narrative with reflections of substance. However, the omissions too are revealing, since these imply various Freudian lapses, ranging from Wright's Oedipal relationship with his mother to his narcissistic habit of failing to give credit where credit was due. This even applies to the engineer Paul Mueller, without whom Wright could never have achieved his Prairie masterworks, from the Larkin Building to the Imperial Hotel in Tokyo. Although Mueller is sympathetically rendered throughout the text, he surely deserved as much if not more credit for the survival of the hotel in the 1923 Tokyo earthquake.

In one way or another the autobiography serves to confirm many key facts that one always suspected about Wright or of which one had been made aware by other writers, at other times—even by Wright himself. Thus one learns again of his youthful reading of Victor Hugo's *Notre Dame de Paris;* the famous phrase *ceci tuera cela* —"this will kill that"— with which Hugo alluded to the invention of movable type and to the concomitant rise of the media and the decline of architecture. Wright's reaction to this prophecy is somewhat ironic given that he was to become a media figure and to write more than any other architect, with the possible exception of Le Corbusier.

We are repeatedly reminded throughout of Wright's distance from European modernism, be it in art, music, or architecture. He even goes so far as to liken modern music to the discordant sounds produced at the musical evenings of his Oak Park family, and later he will compare the playful assembly of his daughter's colored building blocks to the abstract creations of modern art. In 1943 he will extend his critique of the European avant-garde by boldly proclaiming his antipathy to Le Corbusier and insisting elsewhere that the entire body of Cubism and Futurism was predicated on the Japanese print. In retrospect this seems a trifle perverse, given that he will later become Hilla Rebay's architect for Solomon R. Guggenheim's museum collection of non-objective art. Yet Wright was more anti–avant-garde than he was anti-modern, as we may judge from the House on the Mesa (1931) or Fallingwater (1935). Thus he will ironically depict himself as Americanizing Europe while the European modernists were busy Europeanizing America.

Wright constantly displays his background as a nineteenth-century romanticist, not to mention the Midwestern provincialism from which he could never quite escape. Indeed, the egocentricity of much of the text owes a great deal to Wright's "*lieber meister,*" Louis Sullivan, and above all to Sullivan's *The Autobiography of an Idea,* published in 1926. In that posthumous publication, as in Wright's autobiography, the "idea" turns out to be a retrospective view of the author himself as a predestined genius. That Wright elected to see his life in this way is suggested by the idealized account in Book One of his bucolic boyhood in Spring Green, Wisconsin; the Usonian agrarian idyll of the "God Almighty Lloyd-Jones's" to whom Wright was the prodigal son.

Wright, like Sullivan, was destined to assume the role of the redeeming genius perennially misunderstood by the "mobocracy," as Wright contemptuously referred to the American public in his gloss on Sullivan's ornament, *Genius and the Mobocracy,* of 1949. As we know, Wright, like Sullivan, believed in the emancipatory myth of American democracy and in the manifest destiny of the post-industrial machine age. However, going beyond Sullivan's technological rationalism and the romantic pathos of his compensatory symbolic ornament, Wright pursued nothing less than a totally new beginning, politically and otherwise. To this end he championed the Single Tax theory of Henry George. For Wright, electrification, mechanized agriculture, and Taylorized production were each portents favoring a totally new symbiotic synthesis with nature that on occasion he elected to call "organic plasticity." He saw this last as an infinitely extendable horizontal civilization, following the groundline of his mythical prairie. Wright believed, as few have either before or since, that architecture was a crusading cause on the behalf of human civilization rather than a mere profession. That this lifelong passion caused Wright to write of his work with unmatched elegance and conviction is evident from the following passage describing the 1923 Millard house in Pasadena, La Miniatura:

> La Miniatura happened as the cactus grown, in that region still showing what folk from the Middle-Western prairies did when, inclined to quit, the prosperous came loose and rolled down there into that far corner to bask in eternal sunshine.
>
> Near by, that arid, sunlit strand is still unspoiled desert. You may see what a poetic thing this land was before this homely mid-west invasion. Curious tan-gold foothills rise from tattooed sand-stretches to join slopes spotted as the leopard-skin with grease-bush. This foreground spreads to distances so vast—human scale is utterly lost as all features recede, turn blue, recede and become bluer still to merge their blue mountain shapes, snow-capped, with the azure of the skies. The one harmonious note man has introduced into these vast perspectives, aside from the long, low plastered wall, is the eucalyptus tree. Tall, tattered ladies, these trees stand with careless feminine grace in the charming abandon appropriate to perpetual sunshine, adding beauty to the olive-green and ivory-white of an exotic symphony in silvered gold and rose-purple. Water comes, but it comes as a deluge once a year to surprise the roofs, sweep the sands into ripples and roll boulders along in the gashes combed by sudden streams in the sands of the desert. Then—all dry as before.

Despite such lyrical evocations, invariably inspired by a strong feeling for natural landscape, the lasting fascination of Wright's autobiography stems unavoidably from its confessional character, with which he both reveals and conceals errors and omissions of his life. As he would put it with admirable candor:

> Listen to any man you meet and you will see that nothing is more natural than autobiography, and usually, nothing more tedious. Every man you meet is either intensely, modestly, offensively

or charmingly autobiographical. Women are less so. They have learned the wisdom that makes them natural biographers. Too often, ones.

Thus, Book Two, dedicated to Wright's apprenticeship in Chicago, displays his racial prejudices as much as it admits to his psychological dependency on the Prairie School as a whole, not to mention Daniel Burnham's generous offer to send Wright to the Ecole des Beaux Arts; an offer, needless to say, that Wright refused. Elsewhere his spunky character comes fully to the fore in the temerity with which he built the sixty-foot-high windmill tower Romeo and Juliet for his doting aunts in 1896, seven years after he had assisted them with the building of the Hillside Home School in 1887, when he was only twenty years old.

Despite his gratitude to Sullivan for his apprenticeship, "as a pencil in the hand of the master," many of Wright's own protégés are summarily eclipsed in this account, from Walter Burley Griffin, who was Wright's top assistant during the formative years of the Prairie Style, to Griffin's wife Marion Mahony, who was without doubt Wright's most brilliant delineator and to whom Wright sensibly first offered the management of his studio when he decamped to Europe with Mrs. Cheney in 1909. This convenient amnesia extends beyond his most intimate colleagues to such collaborators as Jens Jensen, the Chicago landscapist with whom he worked on the garden of the Avery Coonley house, and the Czech Antonin Raymond, who went with Wright to Tokyo to work on the Imperial Hotel. Even his own architect son John Lloyd is patronizingly presented as his father's faithful site architect. Of his eldest son, Lloyd Wright, we learn nothing at all, despite the fact that he helped his father in his Fiesole exile by drafting the illustrations for the Wasmuth volumes. Understandably enough, perhaps, Wright was more generous to his clients, to the men that trusted him, to the good old boys, and, for that matter, to his distinguished patrons of the opposite sex, such as the strong-willed Aline Barnsdall and the cultivated Mrs. George Millard. Above all he fully acknowledges Darwin D. Martin, who was a client and a loyal supporter throughout his life.

Strong women clearly played a major role in Wright's life: from his mother, who was a doting and willful presence until she died at the age of eighty-four in 1923, when Wright himself was already in his fifty-sixth year, to the hypersensitive and demanding Miriam Noel, who inadvisedly intervened in Wright's life soon after the tragic death of Mrs. Cheney and married him in 1923 after nine distressful years. Above all there is the radical feminist and ill-fated Mrs. Cheney, neé Borthwick, who was possibly the most intense passion of Wright's life. Notably, she is referred to, but never mentioned by name. Thus he will allude to her as a figure of fate, "who by force of rebellion as by way of love was then implicated with me," and later he will justify her unmarked Taliesin grave with the words: "Why mark the spot where desolation ended and began?" Destined to outlive him by twenty-six years was Olga Ivanova Milanov Hinzenberg, whom Wright met in 1924, when she was a soon-to-be divorcée and committed follower of Gurdjieff. After his marriage to her, in 1928, she succeeded in totally reorganizing his life and indeed his means of livelihood by starting the Taliesin Fellowship, subject to her spiritual guidance. At its best the Fellowship was a unique cultural institution capable of providing an ad hoc education as well as affording a unique form of apprenticeship; at its worst (and the experience varied), it was somewhat exploitative. Displaying a strength of a very different kind, there was also Wright's first wife, Catherine Tobin, who clearly was a source of nurture and much support during the first decade of Wright's Prairie practice, the years 1894 to 1909.

Of this formative period, the autobiography is reasonably forthcoming, except for certain masterworks such as the Larkin Building and the Avery Coonley and Robie houses, of which we learn little. We learn even less of his 24-story skyscraper designed for San Francisco in 1912, since it is inexplicably absent from the account. Needless to say he will expand at length on the virtues of the Prairie Style as opposed to what he regarded as the "monogaria," of the American suburb, including even that of his beloved Oak Park, with its carpenter's Gothic jiggerwork, "little painted cardboard lawns and candle snuffer roof," not to mention its pernicious practice of building basements, dormers, and bay windows and its fatal weakness for the Arts and Crafts decadence of English stockbrokers' Tudor—to which even he once succumbed in order to remain in practice in the Moore House built in Oak Park in 1895.

Amid the reiteration of Wright's organic Prairie principles, two things strike one particularly forcibly. The first is his aversion to the ornate portico of the average suburban house; an aversion that no doubt explains his preference for the half-hidden side entries of almost all his domestic works. The second is his mythical, one might even say personal, obsession with fire, of which he wrote: "It comforted me to see the fire burning deep in the solid masonry of the house itself. A feeling that came to stay." Of equal consequence in this regard is his direct admission, in all but Semperian terms, that he was "working away at the wall as a wall and bringing it towards the function of a screen." Part and parcel of this dematerialization was Wright's advocacy of the casement instead of the guillotine sash window, because it opened out and thereby dissolved the barrier between interior and exterior. Along with his deployment of the casement *en serie* was his preference for low, overhanging, gutterless eaves, which when painted white reflected light into the house interior and were attractive to him for their spontaneous generation of icicles in winter. Complimentary to all this was Wright's newfound sense of plasticity, what he referred to as "streamlining," which entailed the cantilever, the lateral penetration of space, and the elimination of fittings and all the other knickknacks, including artworks of dubious quality.

Following Wright's first meeting with his client Aline Barnsdall in 1915, Wright's sensibility began to be transformed by a confrontation with the Californian desert, that by virtue of its hot dry climate became the setting and the inspiration for such structures as the canvas-covered Ocatilla camp built in the Arizona desert in 1927. The same dry, earth-colored landscape led to his atomization of tectonic form first appearing as the textile concrete block mosaic of the Millard house, La Miniatura. From these two related but different structural approaches—one may think of them as framed dematerialization versus piled-up materiality—came Wright's obsession with hermetic screen walls built of tessellated concrete, copper, or glass or of a judicious mixture of these materials, as in Wright's National Life Insurance offices designed for the "business mystic" A. M. Johnson. It is of utmost significance that Wright conceived of himself as a weaver rather than a sculptor and that woven fabric would be the metaphor for all of his architecture, from the high point of the Prairie Style through to the textile block houses of the early 1920s and culminating in the "woven" masterpiece of his entire career, the S. C. Johnson Administration Building, completed for Hibbard Johnson, at Racine, Wisconsin, in 1938. This vast mushroom-columned, lily-pad hall Wright would see as "an inspiring place to work as any cathedral was a place to worship."

How Wright manages to write as much as he did and how, despite receiving major commissions in the mid-1930s, this literary output continued unabated until the last years of his life, remains something of a mystery. Wright's proclivity in this regard not only testifies to the quite exceptional range of his talent, but also to the soundness of the basic education that he received under the supervision of his ever-watchful mother. More important perhaps, given his subsequent resistance to formal education, it points to the scope of Wright's self-cultivation, ardently pursued throughout his life. From this surely came his extensive vocabulary, his sense of rhythm, and his remarkable command of metaphor and simile that accorded his texts a rich, if ornate, precision. In the second edition of his autobiography he cites the authors to whom he feels indebted. This list is revealing not only for its catholic scope but also for its idiosyncratic juxtapositions. Thus we find the Russian anarcho-socialist Peter Kropotkin close to the Danish Christian revolutionary theologian Nicolai Grundtvig, the late American social theorist Thorstein Veblen in the same line as the pioneering psychologist Arnold Gesell. Strangely enough, given the circumstances under which it was written, there is no mention of Gurdjieff. Despite his anarchic nature and his susceptibility to romance and mysticism, Wright's larger vision was politically radical. In this however, like Le Corbusier, he was inclined towards the totalitarian progressive right, rather than to the left.

FRANK LLOYD WRIGHT
A BIOGRAPHICAL SKETCH:
1930–1932

In 1930 Wright wrote and delivered two important series of lectures, one at Princeton University and the other at Chicago's Art Institute. Both were then prepared for publication and appeared as the books *Modern Architecture: Being the Kahn Lectures for 1930* (Princeton University) and *Two Lectures on Architecture* (Art Institute), respectively. These lectures, a summation of his ideas on architecture and the fine arts, focused on the key issues he addressed for the remainder of his life. The lectures also mark a turning point in the style and content of his writing. Some of the bitterness and sarcasm that permeates his earlier writings gives way to more positive and often visionary thoughts. For both lectures his audience was composed mainly of students, and he positioned himself more in the role of teacher than castigator, suggesting new directions for architecture in the United States.

In the spring of 1931 a comprehensive exhibition of the work of Frank Lloyd Wright, which had toured the United States during the preceding year, was on its way to the Stedelijk Museum in Amsterdam. This was the first major exhibition, composed of models, photographs, objects, and original drawings of Wright's work, to be seen in Europe. H.Th. Widjeveld, architect and contributing writer to *Wendingen*, a Dutch journal that Wright admired, took on the responsibility of organizing venues in Holland, Belgium, and Germany.

With these lectures completed and published, and with the exhibition on tour in Europe, the architect and his wife headed to Rio de Janeiro, passing out of the autumn of the north to the spring of the south. The trip was a pleasant contrast to—and a long-needed reprieve from—the difficulties that preceded it.

In 1922 Wright's first wife, Catherine, had finally granted him a divorce after thirteen years of separation, and he was able to marry Miriam Noel—who had been living with him since 1915. But the marriage was doomed from the start. In fact, after the first few years of their relationship it became apparent that their life together was to be turbulent and tragic. Miriam's addiction to alcohol and morphine intensified the outbursts of uncontrollable temper that raged and tore at her on practically a daily basis. Shortly after their marriage, in November 1923, they were separated; Noel finally leaving Wright in May 1924. A few months later Wright met Olga Ivanova (Olgivanna) Lazovich Hinzenberg, a Montenegren by birth who was educated in Czarist Russia and then in Fontainbleau-Avon, at the Gurdjieff Institute for the Harmonious Development of Man. They fell in love and instantly decided to live together—although each was waiting for a divorce. Hounded by debts accrued during the rebuilding of his home, Taliesin, which had burned in the summer of 1925, hounded by Miriam herself, who pursued them relentlessly and threatened them wherever they traveled, hounded by the press, which wallowed in typical tabloid sensationalism of the time, it was only their faith in each other that kept them going. There was little or no work coming to him. The scandal that broke, nationwide, over their self-chosen life-style and their arrest on charges of violating the Mann Act in Minneapolis in 1926 denied him the architectural commissions that should by rights have come his way. But by August 1928 both Wright and Olgivanna were free to marry. They managed to get Taliesin back, which had been taken over by the banks, and once again reestablished life in southwestern Wisconsin.

Brazil's warm climate and ocean bathing, the sites around Rio, and the luxurious Copacabana Palace Hotel gave the Wrights renewed energy. Landing in Rio, Wright joined the Finnish architect Eliel

Saarinen and Horacio Acosta y Lara, an architect from Uruguay, to form the panel of judges for an architectural competition. Their task, assisted by an advisory council, was to select the winning design from ten submissions for the Christopher Columbus Memorial Lighthouse. Wright was asked to represent North America; Saarinen, Europe; and Acosta y Lara, South America.

When the judging panel made its decision on the lighthouse design, Wright composed the following notes:

> Except in the employment of one great modern resource—light—among the ten designs submitted in this competition none express what previous civilizations with such resources as they had could not have better expressed. New resources in construction characterizing our twentieth century are absent.
>
> But, one design does take refuge in a directness, simplicity and force worthy of the great monuments of the ages. The design is symbolic but not to the point where symbolism has interfered with the simple beauty of the design as architecture. Its symbolism is integral.
>
> Seen from the air or from the ground the simple mass becomes an elemental feature, in character worthy of the courage of the great discoverer it commemorates.
>
> The whole has idea, unity and force and avoids the dull craze for altitude and the trite erection of the "post." In this design may be seen the fact that dignity of architectural conception is not bound up with "height." Construction is simple and cost probably within programme limitations. The jury unanimously awards to this design, by J. L. Van Gleave of Nottingham, England, the first prize in this competition.[1]

There came Wright's way many honors and accolades in Brazil, the most meaningful of which was a reception a group of architectural students put on for him. Dinners, banquets, honors, tours, and special receptions abounded:

> Olgivanna and I hardly touched the ground during our stay. We went from place to place with a grand set of fellows and their handsome wives. We weekended at Petropolis, bathed on the beach before the Copacabana, rode in the suburbs and along the marvelous Rio waterfront dominated by curious mountain silhouettes.[2]

By this time, the manuscript for his autobiography, which he completed at the end of December 1930, was in the hands of the printer and scheduled to come out the next year from Longmans, Green and Company, New York.

Back in the United States by November, Wright returned to Taliesin and immediately prepared to participate in another exhibition while the one touring Europe was being installed in Belgium.

Entitled *Modern Architecture: International Exhibition*, the exhibit ran at New York's Museum of Modern Art from February 10 to March 23, 1932. Wright was asked to contribute a selection of his work as part of the exhibition. Accordingly he sent to New York a large number of drawings, models, and photographs. But when he learned that the exhibition would include the work of Richard Neutra and Raymond Hood, he was furious and threatened to remove his contribution altogether. In a letter to his friend, the architectural critic Lewis Mumford, he explained his position:

> I have walked into another propaganda-trap, tho a trap not consciously so designed, and have pulled out at the risk of seeming ignoble or ungenerous.
>
> The enclosed letter will explain.

I consented to join the affair thinking I would be among my peers: I heard only of Corbusier, Mies et al.[3] I found a handpicked select group including *Hood and Neutra.*

One drives the flu-flu bird off the nest only to find the cuckoo there, it seems. Well, no great matter. No, but I want to explain the thing to you so you will not be ignorant of the reason for my stand.

As for exception to Neutra. It applies to a type I have learned to dislike by cumulative experience and to suffer from.

Neutra is the eclectic "up to date," copying the living.

Hood is the eclectic copying the dead, is now the improved eclectic, copying the living. I do not propose to "take the road" in fellowship eclecticism in any form! It is too late to compromise now.[4]

The letter Wright mentioned enclosing was written to Philip Johnson, director of the exhibition. Dated the same day, it offered Johnson an explanation for withdrawing:

It seems to me I see too much at stake for me to countenance a hand-picked group of men in various stages of eclecticism by riding around the country with them, as though I approved of them and their work as modern, when I distinctly do not only disapprove but positively condemn them.

I respect Corbusier, admire van der Rohe, like Haesler, and many good men not in our show if the list is as indicative as intended. Howe is respectable, and Lescaze, so far as I know, though a fledgling.

I could feel at home in a show including them and such younger men as were earnestly at work trying to build noble and beautiful buildings. . . .

But I am sick and tired of the pretence of men who will elect a style, old or new, and get a building badly built by the help of some contractor and then publicize it as a notable achievement. This hits not one man only, but a type of which you have chosen a willing and busy exponent in Neutra. You know my opinion of Hood and his tribe?

I am aware, too, of the ammunition this act of mine furnishes my enemies. Oh yes, I have so many! No man more.

But my eye is on a goal better worth trying for, even if I am called in before I reach it. If I am, I shall at least not have sold!

Believe me, Philip, I am sorry.[5]

Finally a compromise was met, through the intercession of Lewis Mumford, although not on terms fully satisfactory to the architect.

Your absence from Modern Museum's show would be calamity. Please reconsider your refusal. I have no concern whatever on behalf of the museum but am interested in your own place and influence. We need you and cannot do without you. Your withdrawal will be used by the low rascal Hood to his own glory and advantage. As for company, there is no more honorable position than to be crucified between two thieves. Please wire your okay.

Affectionately Lewis.[6]

Wright immediately wired back:

All right Lewis, your sincere friendship trusted I will stay in the New York show. The two exceptions I made were chiefly important because showing up the show as the usual politics and propaganda.[7]

The inclusion of his work alongside work that he actively condemned was basically repugnant to him, and he vowed, afterwards, never again to be "lumped in and hung out on the line" with architects with whose work he could in no way sympathize.

The exhibition catalog was authored by Philip Johnson and Henry-Russell Hitchcock, Jr. Hitchcock's essay on Wright's work would deal him another blow. He chronicled Wright's development vis-à-vis the rise of the International Style in Europe:

> There is an essential and insuperable difference between Wright and those architects throughout the world who work consciously or unconsciously in a single international style. At bottom they are classicists and he a romantic.
>
> But now conditions are changed. No young architect anywhere grows up in quite the isolation of Wright's youth. American architecture need not develop entirely in the footsteps of her great individual genius. A larger and newer world calls. The day of the lone pioneer is past, the advance may be on a more general front at last. Throughout the world there are others besides Wright to lead the way toward the future.[8]

Wright's reaction to this was anger and despair: the work he had begun was now turned around, after its initial influence in Europe, and had come back into the country as the one thing he despised in architecture, a "style." The protesting against useless, meaningless ornament in works such as the Larkin Building was twisted via the International Style to come out, in his mind, as blank, cold surfaces, metal piping, and steel skeletons rarely linked to or related to the landscape. Those to whom he referred in 1925 as "My European Co-workers" appeared to him now to have betrayed the art of architecture and turned it into another cliché.

He began his career with only Louis Sullivan to guide him, and in 1932 it was obvious that he still stood alone. He believed, deeply and convincingly, that he was building an architecture belonging to and expressive of an indigenous American culture; and he strongly resented the importation of the European cliché "surface and mass" onto the soil of the nation he loved.

An Autobiography, which he had started in 1926 and worked on intermittently for four years, was published in 1932 by Longmans, Green. Immediately it was reviewed in all the major newspapers across the country:

> Wright is concrete, intensely personal, but he is an intelligent and virile critic of the American scene. His book proves it. And that he possesses in a high degree that quality which marks genius, the ability to think straight, uninfluenced by the past or present ideas, no one can doubt. Get hold of his book and digest it. You will have to stand for some few oddities in the writing—the author is not a literary man and does not pretend to be—but the fiery passion for the beauty inherent in "rightness" that shines through his pages is something to which it is worthwhile to expose yourself.—*San Francisco Chronicle*, April 10, 1932

One thinks a little of Benvenuto Cellini, if only because of certain contrasts, as one reads this self-told story of the life and art of Frank Lloyd Wright. In both cases the artist is passionate, combative, impatient of control, completely single-minded in his art. In both cases we see the artistic expression, not as a serene unfolding but as struggle and combat. But since Cellini died, a new force, born in his own day, has come to fruition, even in esthetics. Frank Lloyd Wright has carried over into architecture the intense moral conviction which in other fields is known as Puritanism. In everything he says and does he is an artist. He is also a preacher. . . .It is inevitable and right that the architect should justify and explain himself as a man, though the ethics of Frank Lloyd Wright's domestic life are no part of his ethics as an architect. The domestic story he has told simply and unequivocally, so that no open-minded person will fail to understand. It has been unfortunate and tragic. But the passion of the man was needed to support the passion of the architect and the end, architecturally and humanly, has been happy.—*The New York Times Book Review*, April 3, 1932

The book will afford heart to all who have suffered for uncompromising devotion to principle, and especially to artists who have been disciplined for their originality, who have met misunderstanding and hostility to new beauty. It will shame those who have weakly gone down under pressure of material circumstance, comprising with the necessity of "making a living." To them it will say, Rebellion is better, is the man's way. But for the general reader, too, the volume cannot but prove stimulating, entertaining, even exciting. . . .Today he is one of the happiest men in America. We must judge him also one of the wisest and greatest. His "Autobiography" is one of the most trenchant and most beautiful books of our time. Artist and layman alike should read it, for entertainment and for stimulus to new faith, and perhaps just a little for punishment.—*The Saturday Review of Literature*, April 23, 1932

It was evident by this time that Wright was not simply an architect writing about architecture, but had taken his place as a powerful personality and had created an influential literary work.

1. Notes on Copacabana Palace stationery by Frank Lloyd Wright, October 1931. The Frank Lloyd Wright Archives.
2. Frank Lloyd Wright, *An Autobiography* (Duell, Sloan and Pearce: New York, 1943), p. 519.
3. The exhibition catalog, *Modern Architecture: International Exhibition* (New York: The Museum of Modern Art, 1932), lists the participation of the following architects: Frank Lloyd Wright, Walter Gropius, Le Corbusier, J.J.P. Oud, Mies van der Rohe, Raymond M. Hood, Howe & Lescaze, Richard J. Neutra, and Bowman Brothers. Among the patrons of the exhibition, those who contributed for the use of Wright material were Dr. Alexander Chandler, his client for the defunct San Marcos-in-the-Desert, his cousin and client Richard Lloyd Jones, and Mrs. Alice Millard, patron of houses in Highland Park and Pasadena.
4. Letter from Frank Lloyd Wright to Lewis Mumford, January 19, 1932. The Frank Lloyd Wright Archives.
5. Letter to Philip Johnson, January 19, 1932. The Frank Lloyd Wright Archives.
6. Telegram from Lewis Mumford to Frank Lloyd Wright, January 21, 1932. The Frank Lloyd Wright Archives. Quoted with the kind permission of Mrs. Sophia Mumford.
7. Frank Lloyd Wright to Lewis Mumford, January 21, 1932. The Frank Lloyd Wright Archives.
8. *Modern Architecture: International Exhibition*, p. 37.

POOR LITTLE AMERICAN ARCHITECTURE

In *1941 the noted architectural historian and critic Henry-Russell Hitchcock wrote:*

> *To the eyes of the time Wright did not, in the twenties, seem always at the forefront of architectural progress. But the eyes of the twenties were in many respects rather blind. In the next decade his reputation, particularly in America—Europeans continued through the twenties to publish new books on his work—rose again. At long last the prophet of modern architecture, so strangely misunderstood in the twenties, began to receive honor in his own country.* [1]

But a decade earlier Hitchcock himself was among the "blind," and his writings on Wright tended to balance praise with disparagement. Although investing Wright as the greatest architect of the first quarter of the twentieth century, he nonetheless regretted, for example, that such a "mediocre" structure as the Imperial Hotel should have withstood the 1923 earthquake, and he described Taliesin as a "triumph of the picturesque."

Fragments of this response of Wright's were published in On Architecture, *edited by Frederick Gutheim in 1940, but here it appears in its complete form and as Wright edited it. The article is a satirical attack on Hitchcock and at the same time a defense of Wright's own work. Wright's wife, Olgivanna, later remarked that she tried over the years to rid her husband of these sarcastic outbursts, both in print and in his public talks, once telling him:*

> *You have no right to tear anything down unless you are prepared to build up, in its place, something better. That is certainly a principle to which you have subscribed throughout your life in architecture, and you should keep the same standards in whatever you write or say.*

Ten years after this article was written, Wright and Hitchcock collaborated on the book In the Nature of Materials, *which followed the exhibition of the same title of Wright's work at The Museum of Modern Art in New York. Hitchcock wrote that the plan of the book was to "display as fully as may be the architectural work and projects of Wright, with particular emphasis on the expression of the 'Nature of Materials.'"* [2]

[Unpublished essay, 1930]

SAFELY TUCKED AWAY BY HENRY RUSSELL HITCHCOCK, IN my own little red square, as the greatest architect of the first one-quarter (to be precise) of the Twentieth Century, I cock an eye at him—wondering— (strange name that for a Frenchman!)

Nor do I know Russell Hitchcock. But not long since dropping into the offices of *The Architectural Record* on business concerning a book (I am, I believe, the last "prolific writer" on Architecture in the whole world, to attempt one), I casually picked up a black engraving of a man: hat, typical French Mansard; beard, French, although the young woman at the desk (her smile most engaging) volunteered that the actual color of the beard was not typically French.

That is how I learned what Henry Hitchcock looked like and all I know about him except that I have been told that Russell occasionally comes over from Paris to teach young ladies at Vassar what they should think about Architecture, and that he is addicted to photographs for criticism. So I am as qualified to write about him as he is to write about me. I know him by a black engraving I casually picked up and his aesthetics. He knows me by some bad photographs of my work, probably picked up as casually—bad because there have never been any other kind taken of my work and he knows me, too, perhaps—I doubt it—by some "pieces" I have tried to write. I doubt it because he doesn't seem to be the kind of man that would care to read anything anyone else wrote on his special subject.

Two things I gather. First: Mr. Hitchcock is a man of decided opinions. Second: he is the man to keep opinions right there where they are. In reading Mr. Hitchcock's book, therefore, one is inevitably concerned with Mr. Hitchcock's inveterate opinions. Fortunately for him, his recently achieved aesthetic needs no conception of Architecture. In his own opinion, certain of his opinions are prophetic and he wishes to keep them that way, that is all.

He is often suggestive and the snapshots— themselves but haphazard attitudes—illustrating his aesthetic sometimes catch the unfortunate subject unaware—in attitudes gratifyingly compromising. This, too, is good French school, because attitudes, especially if photographed, must be true? However, Truth in all this is not much worse off in this critic's work, nor better, than the run of critics leave her— fooled by photographs read as they run to be read on the run.

H.R.H., I suspect, will have occasion to change many of his attitudes, in fact, has already plenty of occasion to try the other foot, but how is he going to do it? He has written a book! And when a man writes a book—if he is, or hopes to be, a somebody—he is committed to stand there that way for life!

Architecture herself, will therefore have to carry Mr. Hitchcock out stark, as a stiff, and gently deposit him with other remains also refusing to compromise, preferring to compromise Her.

You see, what I have set down here is the same kind of criticism as his, that is to say, based upon similar foundations in fact. And yet I am somehow "had" by the idea that were I really to know Henry Russell Hitchcock, as with almost all my detractors, I should have to like him and would perhaps admire him. And probably were he some day to stop prowling around with photographs and so change his attitude long enough to actually see my work, he too would be in the same embarrassing position concerning both my work and myself.

It is useless to ask why men will strike attitudes and write about things they know only haphazard. But were they to write only about what they know—presses and publishers would go two-thirds out of business. Writers could then at best write only about themselves—which is what they do anyway, in one guise or another, or cleverly disguised—and there would be no reading at all except between the lines, which is what one must do with Mr. Hitchcock's book if he would get anywhere beneath or beyond attitudes.

No, I do not say no man should write about building who has not himself built something worth building. I do not believe that a man should drink a tub of dye to know what color it is. But it is my feeling that any man who writes about building should know something about building in particular, other than some aesthetic he may have imbibed abroad or at home and subscribed to as such. Unless he does know, and writing of bricks he has not got his hands into the mud of which the bricks are made (structural details are mud and often times very heavy going), I think he is going to do himself or others some foolishness before he goes very far.

I think Russell is running this risk. Either he is in danger—or we are. Fortunately, we are all very young and together can live down any consequences of the folly of fooling with photographs that may force its way into current literature. As current literature, I can see that this book on Architecture has proper qualifications, but as History, it is just about as valuable as any current betrayal in the name of an unpopular subject might possibly be.

To otherwise engage with the Hitchcock opinions impressively made up into this splendid book would be to charge just so many wooden windmills. Principles one may usually discuss with profit. But where to find him involved with one either in question or in point, worth an architect's time? I am an architect not interested in making masonry pictures or metal pictures in two dimensions. I am interested in an organic architecture. Mr. Hitchcock is not, nor is Mr. Hitchcock an architect at all. He is not yet interested in organic architecture because, for one reason, he does not know what it is; for another, because he knows he wouldn't like it anyway, if he did know what it was.

Certain phases of his book are delightfully facetious, especially where Monsieur divides his flock into New and Old "Traditionalists"; New and Old "Pioneers"—a systemic inversion, this, of qualities in perverted circumstances. No doubt the perversion or inversion is humorously intended—but this much is quite too much.

As a matter of fact, all that is valuable in either Tradition or Pioneering is Old in the New, or New in the Old.

Concerning our own American ideal, as a culture so intimately a matter of growth all the while as to make the continual destruction of the old by the new barbarous and unnecessary: from Monsieur not one word! No word, I suppose, because the ideal of an organic architecture would accomplish this unity by abolishing all attitudes and all "izers," "ists," "isms" and "istics." And partly for that reason I think, organic architecture is an ideal the French mind in general could not well grasp if it would, nor any other mind—like the Hitchcock mind for instance—too susceptible to its influences. We have had enough of the Parthenon and the Greek vase, but the French—never forgetting and never learning—are right there, their way, with both, yet. This new book is with them, and for them in doing the Machine Age that same "aristocratic" (they say it is aristocratic) way. But, neglected and beaten down to earth, American Architecture, though both little and young, conceives something deeper, conceives culture as more a part of the nature of the thing cultivated and so likely to live in future where all else has had to die in the past. This inner-concept of art as integral, of art as having no longer a separate and contrasted existence, is truly the highest form of aristocracy in Art the world has ever seen. But it is not pagan—no—nor needs a Latin aesthetic! It is more nearly of the Crusades maybe, somewhat more Teutonic, or decidedly Oriental perhaps, although why racial or national any longer in any sense?

At any rate it seems to me it is this concept which is alone truly Modern, because it is new in the thought of the world, and a concept in which the New and Old shall ever be as one. As for myself, this Hitchcock concession of twenty-five years—a quarter of a century—bores me. And I warn Henry right here and now that, having a good start, not only do I fully intend to be the greatest architect who has yet lived but fully intend to be the greatest architect who will ever live. Yes, I intend to be the greatest architect of all time. And I do hereunto affix "the red square" and sign my name to this warning. Even some ordinary bootlegger, these days, gets more than twenty-five years for far less.

1. Henry Russell Hitchcock, *In the Nature of Materials* (New York: Duell, Sloan and Pearce, 1942), p.xxix.
2. Ibid., p. 82.

MODERN ARCHITECTURE, BEING THE KAHN LECTURES

In May 1930 Wright delivered six lectures to undergraduate architecture students at Princeton University. In many ways these articles are a summation of all he had written from 1894 to 1930. But whereas most of his articles were written for general consumption, or—in the case of The Architectural Record articles—for the architecture profession, here he addressed a specific audience of young students. He always remembered the Princeton lectures with a fondness brought on by the students' enthusiasm. An audience of young people would forever after be his favorite. In 1952, when he was called to New York to address the Junior A.I.A., the date for his address was mistakenly set one day in advance of the actual engagement. Unknowingly, Wright walked into the Waldorf-Astoria grand ballroom expecting an audience of young men and women. To his surprise, he found himself in the company of the elder members of the same organization, the American Institute of Architects. They immediately welcomed him, as surprised as he by his appearance. With a twinkle in his eye, he said to this author, at the time a Taliesin apprentice, "Well, here we are, smack dab in the camp of the enemy!" When asked to say a few words to the assembled architects, he replied: "No, I am afraid you boys are over the hill; I'll come back tomorrow and talk to the youngsters."

The six Princeton Lectures cover a wide range of material, beginning with "Machinery, Materials, and Men" and followed by "Style in Industry." Wright continues with a description of how he began his work in residential architecture and how he created a new architecture ("The Passing of the Cornice") in opposition to the "Cardboard House." The last two lectures are concerned with the "Tyranny of the Skyscraper" and "The City." His words were prophetic of his vision for city planning, a vision that would materialize four years later as Broadacre City.

In the lecture "Style in Industry," he described the type of design centers that he professed the nation needed in order to nurture fine, free-minded, creative architects and designers. What he was describing later became the prospectus of a school he was planning to found, The Hillside Home School of the Allied Arts. His plans for the school proved too ambitious; the project was abandoned. But the following year, a much modified version of the same idea was put into operation as The Taliesin Fellowship.

[Published lectures, Princeton University, 1931]

Design for Coonley House carpet (Project). Riverside, Illinois. 1908. Watercolor on art paper, 5 x 7" (detail).
FLLW Fdn#0803.001

1: MACHINERY, MATERIALS, AND MEN

AN ARCHITECTURE FOR THESE UNITED STATES WILL BE born "modern," as were all the architectures of the peoples of all the world. Perhaps this is the deep-seated reason why the young man in architecture grieves his parents, academic and familiar, by yielding to the fascination of creation, instead of persisting as the creature of ancient circumstance. This, his rational surrender to instinct, is known, I believe, as "rebellion."

I am here to aid and comfort rebellion insofar as rebellion has this honorable instinct—even though purpose may not yet be clearly defined—nor any fruits, but only ists, isms, or istics be in sight. Certainly we may now see the dawning of a deeper insight than has for the past thirty years characterized so-called American architecture. In that length of time, American architecture has been neither American nor architecture. We have had instead merely a bad form of surface-decoration.

This "dawn" is the essential concern of this moment and the occasion for this series of "lectures." We, here at Princeton, are to guard this dawning insight and help to guide its courage, passion, and patience into channels where depth and flow is adequate, instead of allowing youthful adventure to ground in shallows all there beneath the surface in the offing, ready to hinder and betray native progress.

In this effort I suppose I am to suffer disadvantage, being more accustomed to saying things with a hod of mortar and some bricks, or with a concrete mixer and a gang of workmen, than by speaking or writing. I like to write, but always dissatisfied, I, too, find myself often staring at the result with a kind of nausea . . . or is it nostalgia?

I dislike to lecture, feeling something like the rage of impotence. With a small audience hovering over my drawing board, there would be better feeling on my part and a better chance for the audience. But a lecturer may, in fact must, make his own diversion, indulge his "malice" as he goes along, or get no entertainment at all out of the matter.

So here at my hand I have some gently malicious pamphlets or leaflets issued, as myth has it, by that mythical group to which careless reference is sometimes made, by the thoughtless, as the "New School of the Middle West." From these rare, heretical pamphlets, from time to time as I may have occasion, I shall quote. Among them are such titles as: "Palladio Turns in His Grave and Speaks," another, "Groans from Phidias"; the author's original title—it would be beside our mark to mention it—was suppressed by the group as just that much too much. One solitary "New School" scholar, himself having, under painful economic pressure, degenerated to the practice of mere architectural surgery—blaming Vitruvius for his degradation—wrote bitterly and much under the title of "Vitruviolic Disorders."

A number of these leaflets are given over by several and sundry of the "New School" to the ravages of the "Vignola"—an academic epidemic showing itself as a creeping paralysis of the emotional nature—creeping by way of the optic nerve.

During the course of our afternoons, from among these modestly profane references, we may have occasion to hear from a rudely awakened Bramante, an indignant Sansovino, a gently aggrieved Brunelleschi, perhaps even from robustious "Duomo" Buonarroti himself, all, plucked even of their shrouds, frowning up from their graves on their pretentious despoilers . . . our own American classicists. These time-honored Italians in these wayward and flippant leaflets, are made to speak by way of a sort of motorcar Vasari. His name deserves to be lost—and as certainly will be.

Unfortunately and sad to say, because their names and individualities are unknown to us, so close were they, as men, to the soil or to man—we shall be unable to hear from the ancient builders of "Le Moyen-Age," those dreamers in cloisters, guild-masters, gardeners, worshipers of the tree, or the noble stone-craftsmen of still earlier Byzantium, who were much like the cathedral builders in spirit. No—we shall hear from them only as we, ourselves, are likewise dreamers, gardeners, or worshipers of the tree, and by sympathetic nature, therefore, well qualified to understand the silence of these white men. And those human nature-cultures of the red mall, lost in backward stretch of time, almost beyond our horizon, the Maya, the Indian, and of the black man, the African, we may learn from them. Last, but not least, come the men of bronze, the Chinese, the Japanese—profound builders of the Orient—imaginative demons, their art of earth winging its way to the skies: dragons with wings, their fitting symbol. Of their art— much. The ethnic eccentricity of their work makes it safe inspiration for the white man, who now needs, it seems, aesthetic fodder that he cannot copy or reproduce. I am not sure but there is more for us in our modern grapple with creation, in their sense of the living thing in art, than we can find in any other culture. Profundity of feeling the men of bronze could encourage. Their forms we should have to let alone.

In order that we may not foregather here in this dignified atmosphere of Princeton without due reference to authority, we will go far back for our text on this, our first afternoon together. Go so far back that we need fear no contradiction. Go without hesitation, to Rameses the Great, to find that: "All great architecture"—Rameses might have used the hieroglyph for art instead of the one for architecture—*"All great architecture is true to its architects' immediate present,"* and seal it with the regal symbol. And in this connection comes the title of our discourse—the *Machinery, Materials, and Men* of our immediate present.

Long ago—yes, so long ago that the memory of it seems to join with recent echoes from Tutankhamen's ancient tomb—I passionately swore that the machine was no less, rather more, an artist's tool than any he had ever had or heard of, if only he would do himself the honor to learn to use it. Twenty-seven years old now, the then offensive heresy has been translated and published, I am told, in seven or more foreign languages, English excepted, which means said in seven or more different ways. But just what the seven different ways each exactly mean, I can have no idea. At the time, I knew no better than to make the declaration—it seemed so sensibly obvious in the vast cinder field in which I then stood—our enormous industrial Middle West.

Today, twenty-seven years later, the heresy has become a truism, at least "truistic," therefore sufficiently trite to arouse no hostility even if said in several or even seven different ways. And yet, a Pompeian recently come back and struggling for nourishment on French soil has reiterated one-quarter of the matter, made more stark, with signs of success right here in our own country. The reiteration reaches us across the Atlantic, more machine-made than the erstwhile cry in the cinder field, but with several important omissions—most important, at least, to us. Or perhaps, who knows, they may not really be omissions but evasions. First among these probable evasions is the nature of materials; second is that characteristic architectural element, the third dimension; and third, there is integral ornament. This neglected trinity, it seems to me, constitutes the beating heart of the whole matter of architecture so far as art is concerned.

Surface and mass, relatively superficial, however machine-made or however much resembling machinery, are subordinate to this great trinity. Surface and mass are a by-product, or will be when architecture arises out of the matter. If proof is needed, we shall find it as we go along together. . . .

Machinery, materials, and men—yes—these are the stuffs by means of which the so-called American architect will get his architecture, if there is any such architect and America ever gets any architecture of her own. Only by the strength of his spirit's grasp upon all three—machinery, materials, and men—will the architect be able so to build that his work may be worthy the great name "architecture." A great architecture is greatest proof of human greatness.

The difference, to the architect and his fellow artists, between our era and others, lies simply enough in the substitution of automatic machinery for tools, and (more confusing), instead of hereditary aristocracy for patron the artist now relies upon automatic industrialism, conditioned upon the automatic acquiescence of men and conditioned not at all upon their individual handicraftsmanship.

At first blush an appalling difference, and the more it is studied, the more important the difference becomes. And were we now to be left without prophet—that is, without interpretation—and should we, among ourselves, be unable to arouse the leadership of supreme human imagination—yes, then we should be at the beginning of the end of all the great *qualities* we are foregathered here to cherish: namely, the arts which are those great qualities in any civilization. This republic has already gone far with very little of any single one of these great *saving* qualities, yet it goes further, faster, and safer; eats more, and eats more regularly; goes softer, safer, is more comfortable and egotistic in a more universal mediocrity than ever existed on earth before. But who knows where it is going? In this very connection, among the more flippant references referred to as at hand, there is also heavy matter and I have here serious original matter, saved several years ago from the flames by a miracle. The first pages were blackened and charred by fire, of this original manuscript, first read to a group of professors, artists, architects, and manufacturers at Hull House, Chicago. To show you how it all seemed to me, back there, twenty-seven years ago in Chicago, I shall read into the record, once more, from its pages. Should its clumsy earnestness bore you, remember that the young man who wrote, should, in that earlier day, as now, have confined himself to a hod of mortar and some bricks. But passionately he was trying to write—making ready to do battle for the life of the thing he loved. And I would remind you, too, that in consequence he has been engaged in eventually mortal combat ever since.

Here is the manuscript. We will begin, twenty-seven years later, again, at the beginning of—

THE ART AND CRAFT OF THE MACHINE

No one, I hope, has come here tonight for a sociological prescription for the cure of evils peculiar to this machine age. For I come to you as an architect to say my word for the right use upon such new materials as we have, of our great substitute for tools—machines. There is no thrift in any craft until the tools are mastered; nor will there be a worthy social order in America until the elements by which America does its work are mastered by American society. Nor can there be an art worth the man or the name until these elements are grasped and

truthfully idealized in whatever we as a people try to make. Although these elemental truths should be commonplace enough by now, as a people we do not understand them nor do we see the way to apply them. We are probably richer in raw materials for our use as workmen, citizens, or artists than any other nation—but, outside mechanical genius for mere contrivance, we are not good workmen, nor, beyond adventitious or propitious respect for property, are we as good citizens as we should be, nor are we artists at all. We are one and all, consciously or unconsciously, mastered by our fascinating automatic "implements," using them as substitutes for tools. To make this assertion clear I offer you evidence I have found in the field of architecture. It is still a field in which the pulse of the age throbs beneath much shabby finery and one broad enough (God knows) to represent the errors and possibilities common to our time-serving time.

Architects in the past have embodied the spirit common to their own life and to the life of the society in which they lived in the most noble of all noble records—buildings. They wrought these valuable records with the primitive tools at their command and whatever these records have to say to us today would be utterly insignificant if not wholly illegible were tools suited to another and different condition stupidly forced to work upon them, blindly compelled to do work to which they were not fitted, work which they could only spoil.

In this age of steel and steam, the tools with which civilization's true record will be written are scientific thoughts made operative in iron and bronze and steel and in the plastic processes which characterize this age, all of which we call machines. The electric lamp is in this sense a machine. New materials in the man-machines have made the physical body of this age what it is as distinguished from former ages. They have made our era the machine age—wherein locomotive engines, engines of industry, engines of light or engines of war, or steamships take the place works of art took in previous history. Today we have a scientist or an inventor in place of a Shakespeare or a Dante. Captains of industry are modern substitutes, not only for kings and potentates, but, I am afraid, for great artists as well. And yet, man-made environment is the truest, most characteristic of all human records. Let a man build and you have him. You may not have all he is, but certainly he is what you have. Usually you will have his outline. Though the elements may be in him to enable him to grow out of his present self-made characterization, few men are ever belied by self-made environment. Certainly no historical period was ever so misrepresented. Chicago in its ugliness today becomes as true an expression of the *life* lived here as is any center on earth where men come together closely to live it out or fight it out. Man is a selecting principle, gathering his like to him wherever he goes. The intensifying of his existence by close contact, too, flashes out the human record vividly in his background and his surroundings. But somewhere—somehow—in our age, although signs of the times are not wanting, beauty in this expression is forfeited—the record is illegible when not ignoble. We must walk blindfolded through the streets of this, or any great modern American city, to fail to see that all this magnificent resource of machine-power and superior material has brought to us, so far, is degradation. All of the art forms sacred to the art of old are, by us, prostitute.

On every side we see evidence of inglorious quarrel between things as they were and things as they must be and are. This shame a certain merciful ignorance on our part mistakes for glorious achievement. We believe in our greatness when we have tossed up a Pantheon to the god of money in a night or two, like the Illinois Trust Building or the Chicago National Bank. And it is our glory to get together a mammoth aggregation of Roman monuments, sarcophagi, and temples for a post office in a year or two. On Michigan Avenue, Montgomery Ward presents us with a nondescript Florentine palace with a grand campanile for a "farmer grocery," and it is as common with us as it is elsewhere to find the giant stone Palladian "orders" overhanging plate-glass shop fronts. Show windows beneath Gothic office buildings, the office-middle topped by Parthenons or models of any old sacrificial temple, are a common sight. Every commercial interest in any American town, in fact, is scurrying

for respectability by seeking some advertising connection, at least, with the "classic." A commercial renaissance is here; the renaissance of "the ass in the lion's skin." This much, at least, we owe to the late Columbian Fair—that triumph of modern civilization in 1893 will go down in American architectural history, when it is properly recorded, as a mortgage upon posterity that posterity must repudiate not only as usurious but as forged.

In our so-called "skyscrapers" (latest and most famous business building triumph), good granite or Bedford stone is cut into the fashion of the Italian followers of Phidias and his Greek slaves. Blocks so cut are cunningly arranged about a structure of steel beams and shafts (whose structure secretly robs them of any real meaning), in order to make the finished building resemble the architecture depicted by Palladio and Vitruvius in the schoolbooks. It is quite as feasible to begin putting on this Italian trimming at the cornice and come on down to the base as it is to work, as the less fortunate Italians were forced to do, from the base upward. Yes, "from the top down" is often the actual method employed. The keystone of a Roman or Gothic arch may now be "set"—that is to say, "hung"— and the voussoirs stuck alongside or "hung" on downward to the haunches. Finally this mask, completed, takes on the features of the pure "classic," or any variety of "renaissance" or whatever catches the fancy or fixes the "convictions" of the designer. Most likely, an education in art has "fixed" both. Our Chicago University, "a seat of learning," is just as far removed from truth. If environment is significant and indicative, what does this highly reactionary, extensive, and expensive scene-painting by means of hybrid collegiate Gothic signify? Because of Oxford it seems to be generally accepted as "appropriate for scholastic purposes." Yet, why should an American university in a land of democratic ideals in a machine age be characterized by secondhand adaptation of Gothic forms, themselves adapted previously to our own adoption by a feudalistic age with tools to use and conditions to face totally different from anything we can call our own? The public library is again asinine renaissance, bones sticking through the flesh because the interior was planned by a shrewd library board, while an "art-architect" (the term is Chicago's, not mine) was "hired" to "put the architecture on it." The "classical" aspect of the sham-front must be preserved at any cost to sense. Nine out of ten public buildings in almost any American city are the same.

On Michigan Avenue, too, we pass another pretentious structure, this time fashioned as inculcated by the Ecole des Beaux Arts after the ideals and methods of a Graeco-Roman, inartistic, grandly brutal civilization, a civilization that borrowed everything but its jurisprudence. Its essential tool was the slave. Here at the top of our culture is the Chicago Art Institute, and very like other art institutes. Between lions, realistic—Kemyss would have them so because Barye did—we come beneath some stone millinery into the grandly useless lobby. Here French's noble statue of the republic confronts us—she too, imperial. The grand introduction over, we go further on to find amid plaster casts of antiquity, earnest students patiently gleaning a half-acre or more of archaeological dry bones, arming here for industrial conquest, in other words to go out and try to make a living by making some valuable impression upon the machine age in which they live. Their fundamental tool in this business about which they will know just this much less than nothing, is—the machine. In this acre or more not one relic has any vital relation to things as they are for these students, except for the blessed circumstance that they are more or less beautiful things in themselves—bodying forth the beauty of "once upon a time." These students at best are to concoct from a study of the aspect of these blind reverences an extract of antiquity suited to modern needs, meanwhile knowing nothing of modern needs, permitted to care nothing for them, and knowing just as little of the needs of the ancients which made the objects they now study. The tyros are taught in the name of John Ruskin and William Morris to shun and despise the essential tool of their age as a matter commercial and antagonistic to art. So in time they go forth, each armed with his little academic extract, applying it as a sticking plaster from without, wherever it can be made to stick, many helplessly knowing in their hearts that it should be a

development from within—but how? And this is an education in art in these United States. Climb now the grand monumental stairway to see the results of this cultural effort—we call it "education"—hanging over the walls of the exhibition galleries. You will find there the same empty reverences to the past at cost to the present and of doubtful value to the future, unless a curse is valuable. Here you may see fruits of the lust and pride of the patron-collector, but how shamefully little to show by way of encouraging patronage by the artist of his own day and generation. This is a temple of the fine arts. A sacred place! It should be the heart-center, the emotional inspiration of a great national industrial activity, but here we find tradition not as an *inspiring* spirit animating progress. No. Now more in the *past* than ever! No more now than an ancient mummy, a dead letter. A "precedent" is a "hangover" to copy, the copy to be copied for machine reproduction, to be shamelessly reproduced until demoralized utterly or unrecognizable.

More unfortunate, however, than all this fiasco, is the fiasco al fresco. The suburban house-parade is more servile still. Any popular avenue or suburb will show the polyglot encampment displaying, on the neatly kept little plots, a theatrical desire on the part of fairly respectable people to live in châteaux, manor houses, Venetian palaces, feudal castles, and Queen Anne cottages. Many with sufficient hardihood abide in abortions of the carpenter-architect, our very own General Grant Gothic perhaps, intended to beat all the "lovely periods" at their own game and succeeding. Look within all this typical monotony-in-variety and see there the machine-made copies of handicraft: originals; in fact, unless you, the householder, are fortunate indeed, possessed of extraordinary taste and opportunity, all you possess is in some degree a machine-made example of vitiated handicraft: imitation antique furniture made antique by the machine, itself of all abominations the most abominable. Everything must be curved and carved and carved and turned. The whole mass a tortured sprawl supposed artistic. And the floor-coverings? Probably machine-weavings of oriental rug patterns, pattern and texture mechanically perfect; or worse, your walls are papered with paper-imitations of old tapestry, imitation patterns, and imitation textures, stamped or printed by the machine; imitations under foot, imitations overhead, and imitations all round about you. You are sunk in "imitation." Your much-molded woodwork is stained "antique." Inevitably you have a white-and-gold "reception room" with a few gilded chairs, an overwrought piano, and withal, about you a general cheap machine-made "profusion" of copies of copies of original imitations. To you, proud proprietors, do these things thus degraded mean anything aside from vogue and price? Aside from your sense of quantitative ownership, do you perceive in them some fine fitness in form, line, and color to the purposes which they serve? Are the chairs to sit in, the tables to use, the couch comfortable, and are all harmoniously related to each other and to your own life? Do many of the furnishings or any of the window millinery serve any purpose at all of which you can think? Do you enjoy in "things" the least appreciation of truth in beautiful guise? If not, you are a victim of habit, a habit evidence enough of the stagnation of an outgrown art. Here we have the curse of stupidity—a cheap substitute for ancient art and craft which has no vital meaning in your own life or our time. You line the box you live in as a magpie lines its nest. You need not be ashamed to confess your ignorance of the meaning of all this, because not only you, but everyone else, is hopelessly ignorant concerning it; it is "impossible." Imitations of imitations, copies of copies, cheap expedients, lack of integrity, some few blind gropings for simplicity to give hope to the picture. That is all.

Why wonder what has become of the grand spirit of art that made, in times past, man's reflection in his environment a godlike thing? *This* is what has become of it! Of all conditions, this one at home is most deplorable, for to the homes of this country we must look for any beginning of the awakening of an artistic conscience which will change this parasitic condition to independent growth. The homes of the people will change before public buildings can possibly change.

Glance now for a moment behind this adventitious scene-painting passing, at home, for art in the nineteenth century. Try to sense the true conditions underlying all, and which you betray and belie in the name of culture. Study with me for a moment the engine which produces this wreckage and builds you, thus cheapened and ridiculous, into an ignoble record.

Here is this thing we call the machine, contrary to the principle of organic growth, but imitating it, working irresistibly the will of man through the medium of men. All of us are drawn helplessly into its mesh as we tread our daily round. And its offices—call them "services"—have become the commonplace background of modern existence; yes, and sad to say, in too many lives the foreground, middle distance, and future. At best we ourselves have already become or are becoming some cooperative part in a vast machinery. It is, with us, as though we were controlled by some great crystallizing principle going on in nature all around us and going on, in spite of ourselves, even in our very own *natures*. If you would see how interwoven it is, this thing we call the machine, with the warp and the woof of civilization, if indeed it is not now the very basis of civilization itself, go at nightfall when all is simplified and made suggestive, to the top of our newest skyscraper, the Masonic temple. There you may see how in the image of material man, at once his glory and his menace, is this thing we call a city. Beneath you is the monster stretching out into the far distance. High overhead hangs a stagnant pall, its fetid breath reddened with light from myriad eyes endlessly, everywhere blinking. Thousands of acres of cellular tissue outspread, enmeshed by an intricate network of veins and arteries radiating into the gloom. Circulating there with muffled ominous roar is the ceaseless activity to whose necessities it all conforms. This wondrous tissue is knit and knit again and interknit with a nervous system, marvelously effective and complete, with delicate filaments for hearing and knowing the pulse of its own organism, acting intelligently upon the ligaments and tendons of motive impulse, and in it all is flowing the impelling electric fluid of man's own life. And the labored breathing, murmur, clangor, and the roar—how the voice of this monstrous force rises to proclaim the marvel of its structure! Near at hand, the ghastly warning boom from the deep throats of vessels heavily seeking inlet to the waterway below, answered by the echoing clangor of the bridge bells. A distant shriek grows nearer, more ominous, as the bells warn the living current from the swinging bridge and a vessel cuts for a moment the flow of the nearer artery. Closing then upon the great vessel's stately passage the double bridge is just in time to receive in a rush of steam the avalanche of blood and metal hurled across it; a streak of light gone roaring into the night on glittering bands of steel; an avalanche encircled in its flight by slender magic lines, clicking faithfully from station to station—its nervous herald, its warning, and its protection.

Nearer, in the building ablaze with midnight activity, a spotless paper band is streaming into the marvel of the multiple-press, receiving indelibly the impression of human hopes and fears, throbbing in the pulse of this great activity, as infallibly as the gray matter of the human brain receives the impression of the senses. The impressions come forth as millions of neatly folded, perfected news-sheets, teeming with vivid appeals to good and evil passions; weaving a web of intercommunication so far-reaching that distance becomes as nothing, the thought of one man in one corner of the earth on one day visible on the next to all men. The doings of all the world are reflected here as in a glass—so marvelously sensitive this simple band streaming endlessly from day to day becomes in the grasp of the multiple-press.

If the pulse of this great activity—automatons working night and day in every line of industry, to the power of which the tremor of the mammoth steel skeleton beneath your feet is but an awe-inspiring response—is thrilling, what of the prolific, silent obedience to man's will underlying it all? If this power must be uprooted that civilization may live, then civilization is already doomed. Remain to contemplate this wonder until the twinkling lights perish in groups, or follow one by one, leaving others to live through the gloom; fires are banked, tumult slowly dies to an echo here and there. Then the darkened pall is gradually lifted and moonlight outlines the shadowy, sullen masses of structure,

structure deeply cut here and there by half-luminous channels. Huge patches of shadow in shade and darkness commingle mysteriously in the block-like plan with box-like skylines—contrasting strangely with the broad surface of the lake beside, placid and resplendent with a silver gleam. Remain, I say, to reflect that the texture of the city, this great machine, is the warp upon which will be woven the woof and pattern of the democracy we pray for. Realize that it has been deposited here, particle by particle, in blind obedience to law—law no less organic. That universe, too, in a sense, is but an obedient machine.

Magnificent power! And it confronts the young architect and his artist comrades now, with no other beauty—a lusty material giant without trace of ideality, absurdly disguised by garments long torn to tatters or contemptuously tossed aside, outgrown. Within our own recollection we have all been horrified at the bitter cost of this ruthless development, appalled to see this great power driven by greed over the innocent and defenseless—we have seen bread snatched from the mouths of sober and industrious men, honorable occupations going to the wall with a riot, a feeble strike, or a stifled moan, outclassed, outdone, outlived by the machine. The workman himself has come to regard this relentless force as his nemesis and combines against machinery in the trades with a wild despair that dashes itself to pieces, while the artist blissfully dreaming in the halls we have just visited or walking blindly abroad in the paths of the past, berates his own people for lackluster senses, rails against industrial conditions that neither afford him his opportunity, nor, he says, can appreciate him as he, panderer to ill-gotten luxury, folding his hands, starves to death. "Innocuous martyr upon the cross of art!" One by one, tens by tens, soon thousands by thousands, handicraftsmen and parasitic artists succumb to the inevitable as one man at a machine does the work of from five to fifty men in the same time, with all the art there is meanwhile prostituting to old methods and misunderstood ideals the far greater new possibilities due to this same machine, and doing this disgracefully in the name of the beautiful!

American society has the essential tool of its own age by the blade, as lacerated hands everywhere testify!

See the magnificent prowess of this unqualified power—strewing our surroundings with the mangled corpses of a happier time. We live amid ghostly relics whose pattern once stood for cultivated luxury and now stands for an ignorant matter of taste. With no regard for first principles of common sense, the letter of tradition is recklessly fed into rapacious maws of machines until the reproduction, reproduced *ad nauseam,* may be had for five, ten, or ninety-nine cents, although the worthy original cost ages of toil and patient culture. This might seem like progress, were it not for the fact that these butchered forms, the life entirely gone out of them, are now harmful parasites, belittling and falsifying any true perception of normal beauty the Creator may have seen fit to implant in us on our own account. Any idea whatever of fitness to purpose or of harmony between form and use is gone from us. It is lacking in these things one and all, because it is so sadly lacking in us. And as for making the best of our own conditions or repudiating the terms on which this vulgar insult to tradition is produced, thereby insuring and rectifying the industrial fabric thus wasted or enslaved by base imitation—the mere idea is abnormal, as I myself have found to my sorrow.

And among the few, the favored chosen few who love art by nature and would devote their energies to it so that it may live and let them live—any training they can seek would still be a protest against the machine as the creator of all this iniquity, when (God knows) it is no more than the creature.

But, I say, usurped by greed and deserted by its natural interpreter, the artist, the machine is only the creature, not the creator of this iniquity! I say the machine has noble possibilities unwillingly forced to this degradation, degraded by the arts themselves. Insofar as the true capacity of the machine is concerned it is itself the crazed victim of artist-impotence. Why will the American artist not see that human thought in our age is stripping off its old form and donning another; why is the artist unable to see that this is his glorious opportunity to create and reap anew?

But let us be practical, let us go now afield for evident instances of machine abuse or abuse by the machine. I will show you typical abuses that should serve to suggest to any mind, capable of thought, that the machine is, to begin with, a marvellous simplifier in no merely negative sense. Come now, with me, and see examples which show that these craft-engines may be the modern emancipator of the creative mind. We may find them to be the regenerator of the creative conscience in our America, as well, so soon as a stultified "culture" will allow them to be so used.

First—as perhaps wood is most available of home-building materials, naturally then the most abused—let us now glance at wood. Elaborate machinery has been invented for no other purpose than to imitate the wood-carving of early handicraft patterns. Result? No good joinery. None salable without some horrible glued-on botchwork meaning nothing, unless it means that "art and craft" (by salesmanship) has fixed in the minds of the masses the elaborate old hand-carved chair as ultimate ideal. The miserable tribute to this perversion yielded by Grand Rapids alone would mar the face of art beyond repair, to say nothing of the weird or fussy joinery of spindles and jigsawing, beamed, braced, and elaborated to outdo in sentimentality the sentiment of some erstwhile overwrought "antique." The beauty of wood lies in its qualities as wood, strange as this may seem. Why does it take so much imagination just to see that? Treatments that fail to bring out those qualities, foremost, are not *plastic,* therefore no longer appropriate. The inappropriate cannot be beautiful.

The machine at work on wood will itself teach us—and we seem so far to have left it to the machine to do so—that certain simple forms and handling serve to bring out the beauty of wood and to retain its character, and that certain other forms and handling do not bring out its beauty, but spoil it. All woodcarving is apt to be a forcing of this material likely to destroy the finer possibilities of wood as we may know those possibilities now. In itself wood has beauty of marking, exquisite texture, and delicate nuances of color that carving is likely to destroy. The machines used in woodwork will show that by unlimited power in cutting, shaping, smoothing, and by the tireless repeat, they have emancipated beauties of wood-nature, making possible, without waste, beautiful surface treatments and clean strong forms that veneers of Sheraton or Chippendale only hinted at with dire extravagance. Beauty unknown even to the Middle Ages. These machines have undoubtedly placed within reach of the designer a technique enabling him to realize the true nature of wood in his designs harmoniously with man's sense of beauty, satisfying his material needs with such extraordinary economy as to put this beauty of wood in use within the reach of everyone. But the advantages of the machines are wasted and we suffer from a riot of aesthetic murder and everywhere live with debased handicraft.

Then, at random, let us take, say, the worker in marbles—his gangsaws, planers, pneumatic chisels, and rubbing-beds have made it possible to reduce blocks ten feet long, six feet deep, and two feet thick to sheets or thin slabs an inch in thickness within a few hours, so it is now possible to use a precious material as ordinary wall covering. The slab may be turned and matched at the edges to develop exquisite pattern, emancipating hundreds of superficial feet of characteristic drawing in pure marble colors that formerly wasted in the heart of a great expensive block in the thickness of the wall. Here again a distinctly new architectural use may bring out a beauty of marbles consistent with nature and impossible to handicraft. But what happens? The "artist" persists in taking dishonest advantage of this practice, building up imitations of solid piers with molded caps and bases, cunningly uniting the slabs at the edge until detection is difficult except to the trained eye. His method does not change to develop the beauty of a new technical possibility; no, the "artist" is simply enabled to "fake" more architecture, make more piers and column shafts because he can now make them hollow! His architecture becomes no more worthy in itself than the cheap faker that he himself is, for his classical forms not only falsify the method which used to be and belie the method that is, but they cheat progress of its due. For convincing evidence see any public library

or art institute, the Congressional Library at Washington, or the Boston [Public] Library.

In the stonecutting trade the stone-planer has made it possible to cut upon stone any given molded surface, or to ingrain upon that surface any lovely texture the cunning brain may devise, and do it as it never was possible to do it by hand. What is it doing? Giving us as near an imitation of hand tooth-chiselling as possible, imitating moldings specially adapted to wood, making possible the lavish use of miles of meaningless molded string courses, cornices, base courses—the giant power meanwhile sneered at by the "artist" because it fails to render the wavering delicacy of "touch" resulting from the imperfections of handwork.

No architect, this man! No, or he would excel that "antique" quality by the design of the contour of his sections, making a telling point of the very perfection he dreads, and so sensibly designing, for the prolific dexterity of the machine, work which it can do so well that handwork would seem insufferably crude by comparison. The deadly facility this one machine has given "book architecture" is rivalled only by the facility given to it by galvanized iron itself. And if, incontinently, you will still have tracery in stone, you may arrive at acres of it now consistently with the economy of other features of this still fundamental "trade." You may try to imitate the hand-carving of the ancients in this matter, baffled by the craft and tenderness of the originals, or you may give the pneumatic chisel and power-plane suitable work to do which would mean a changed style, a shift in the spiritual center of the ideal now controlling the use of stone in constructing modern stone buildings.

You will find in studying the group of ancient materials, wood and stone foremost among them, that they have all been rendered fit for *plastic* use by the machine! The machine itself steadily making available for economic use the very quality in these things now needed to satisfy its own art equation. Burned clay—we call it terra cotta—is another conspicuous instance of the advantage of the "process." Modern machines (and a process is a machine) have rendered this material as sensitive to the creative brain as a dry plate is to the lens of the camera. A marvelous simplifier, this material, rightly used. The artist is enabled to clothe the steel structure, now becoming characteristic of this era, with modestly beautiful, plastic robes instead of five or more different kinds of material now aggregated in confused features and parts, "composed" and supposedly picturesque, but really a species of cheap millinery to be mocked and warped by the sun, eventually beaten by wind and rain into a variegated heap of trash. But when these great possibilities of simplicity, the gift of the machine, get to us by way of the architect, we have only a base imitation of the hand-tooled blocks, pilaster-cap and base, voussoirs, and carved spandrils of the laborious manhandled stonecrop of an ancient people's architecture!

The modern processes of casting in metal are modern machines too, approaching perfection, capable of perpetuating the imagery of the most vividly poetic mind without hindrance—putting permanence and grace within reach of every one, heretofore forced to sit supine with the Italians at their Belshazzar-feast of "renaissance." Yes, without exaggeration, multitudes of processes, many new, more coming, await sympathetic interpretation, such as the galvano-plastic and its electrical brethren—a prolific horde, now cheap makers imitating "real" bronzes and all manner of metallic antiques, secretly damning all of them in their vitals, if not openly giving them away. And there is electro-glazing, shunned because its straight lines in glass-work are too severely clean and delicate. Straight lines it seems are not so susceptible to the traditional designer's lack of touch. Stream lines and straight lines are to him severely unbeautiful. "Curved is the line of beauty," says he! As though nature would not know what to do with its own rectilinear!

The familiar lithograph, too, is the prince of an entire province of new reproductive but unproductive processes. Each and every one has its individualities and therefore has possibilities of its own. See what Whistler made and the Germans are making of the lithograph: one note sounded in the gamut of its possibilities. But that note rings true to process as the sheen of the butterfly's wing to that wing. Yet, having fallen into disrepute, the most

this particular "machine" did for us, until Whistler picked it up, was to give us the cheap imitative effects of painting, mostly for advertising purposes. This is the use made of machinery in the abuse of materials by men. And still more important than all we have yet discussed here is the new element entering industry in this material we call steel. The structural necessity which once shaped Parthenons, Pantheons, cathedrals, is fast being reduced by the machine to a skeleton of steel or its equivalent, complete in itself without the artist-craftsman's touch. They are now building Gothic cathedrals in California upon a steel skeleton. Is it not easy to see that the myriad ways of satisfying ancient structural necessities known to us through the books as the art of building, vanish, become history? The mainspring of their physical existence now removed, their spiritual center has shifted and nothing remains but the impassive features of a dead face. Such is our "classic" architecture.

For centuries this insensate or insane abuse of great opportunity in the name of culture has made cleanly, strengthy, and true simplicity impossible in art or architecture, whereas now we might reach the heights of creative art. Rightly used the very curse machinery puts upon handicraft should emancipate the artist from temptation to petty structural deceit and end this wearisome struggle to make things seem what they are not and can never be. Then the machine itself, eventually, will satisfy the simple terms of its modern art equation as the ball of clay in the sculptor's hand yields to his desire—ending forever this nostalgic masquerade led by a stultified culture in the name of art.

Yes—though he does not know it, the artist is now free to work his rational will with freedom unknown to structural tradition. Units of construction have enlarged, rhythms have been simplified and etherealized, space is more spacious, and the sense of it may enter into every building, great or small. The architect is no longer hampered by the stone arch of the Romans or by the stone beam of the Greeks. Why then does he cling to the grammatical phrases of those ancient methods of construction when such phrases are in his modern work empty lies, and himself an inevitable liar as well?

Already, as we stand today, the machine has weakened the artist to the point of destruction and antiquated the craftsman altogether. Earlier forms of art are by abuse all but destroyed. The whole matter has been reduced to mere pose. Instead of joyful creation we have all around about us poisonous tastes—foolish attitudes. With some little of the flame of the old love, and creditable but pitiful enthusiasm, the young artist still keeps on working, making miserable mischief with lofty motives: perhaps, because his heart has not kept in touch or in sympathy with his scientific brother's head, being out of step with the forward marching of his own time.

Now, let us remember in forming this new Arts and Crafts Society at Hull House that every people has done its work, therefore evolved its art as an expression of its own life, using the best tools; and that means the most economic and effective tools or contrivances it knew: the tools most successful in saving valuable human effort. The chattel slave was the essential tool of Greek civilization, therefore of its art. We have discarded this tool and would refuse the return of the art of the Greeks were slavery the terms of its restoration, and slavery, in some form, would be the terms.

But in Grecian art two flowers did find spiritual expression—the acanthus and the honeysuckle. In the art of Egypt—similarly we see the papyrus, the lotus. In Japan, the chrysanthemum and many other flowers. The art of the Occident has made no such sympathetic interpretation since that time, with due credit given to the English rose and the French fleur-de-lis, and as things are now the West may never make one. But to get from some native plant an expression of its native character in terms of imperishable stone to be fitted perfectly to its place in structure, and without loss of vital significance, is one great phase of great art. It means that Greek or Egyptian found a revelation of the inmost life and character of the lotus and acanthus in terms of lotus or acanthus life. That was what happened when the art of these people had done with the plants they most loved. This imaginative process is known only to the creative artist. Conventionalization, it is called. Really it is the dramatizing of an object—truest "drama." To enlarge upon this simple figure,

as an artist, it seems to me that this complex matter of civilization is itself at bottom some such conventionalizing process, or must be so to be successful and endure.

Just as any artist-craftsman, wishing to use a beloved flower for the stone capital of a column-shaft in his building must conventionalize the flower, that is, find the pattern of its life-principle in terms of stone as a material before he can rightly use it as a beautiful factor in his building, so education must take the natural man, to "civilize" him. And this great new power of the dangerous machine we must learn to understand and then learn to use as this valuable, "*conventionalizing*" agent. But in the construction of a society as in the construction of a great building, the elemental conventionalizing process is dangerous, for without the inspiration or inner light of the true artist—the quality of the flower—its very life—is lost, leaving a withered husk in the place of living expression.

Therefore, society, in this conventionalizing process or culture, has a task even more dangerous than has the architect in creating his building forms, because instead of having a plant leaf and a fixed material as ancient architecture had, we have a sentient man with a fluid soul. So without the inner light of a sound philosophy of art (the educator too, must now be artist), the life of the man will be sacrificed and society gain an automaton or a machine-made moron instead of a noble creative citizen!

If education is doomed to fail in this process, utterly—then the man slips back to rudimentary animalism or goes on into decay. Society degenerates or has a mere realistic creature instead of the idealistic creator needed. The world will have to record more great dead cities.

To keep the artist-figure of the flower *dramatized for human purposes*—the socialist would bow his neck in altruistic submission to the "harmonious" whole; his conventionalization or dramatization of the human being would be like a poor stone-craftsman's attempt to conventionalize the beloved plant with the living character of leaf and flower left out. The anarchist would pluck the flower as it grows and use it as it is for what it is—with essential reality left out.

The hereditary aristocrat has always justified his existence by his ability, owing to fortunate propinquity, to appropriate the flower to his own uses after the craftsman has given it life and character, and has kept the craftsman, too, by promising him his flower back if he behaves himself well. The plutocrat does virtually the same thing by means of "interests." But the true democrat will take the human plant as it grows and—in the spirit of using the means at hand to put life into his conventionalization—preserve the individuality of the plant to protect the flower, which is its very life, getting from both a living expression of essential man-character fitted perfectly to a place in society with no loss of vital significance. Fine art is this flower of the man. When education has become creative and art again prophetic of the natural means by which we are to grow—we call it "progress"—we will, by means of the creative artist, possess this monstrous tool of our civilization as it now possesses us.

Grasp and use the power of scientific automatons in this creative sense and their terrible forces are not antagonistic to any fine individualistic quality in man. He will find their collective mechanistic forces capable of bringing to the individual a more adequate life, and the outward expression of the inner man as seen in his environment will be genuine revelation of his inner life and higher purpose. Not until then will America be free!

This new American liberty is of the sort that declares man free only when he has found his work and effective means to achieve a life of his own. The means once found, he will find his due place. The man of our country will thus make his own way, and *grow* to the natural place thus due him, promised—yes, promised by our charter, the Declaration of Independence. But this place of his is not to be made over to fit him by reform, nor shall it be brought down to him by concession, but will become his by his own use of the means at hand. He must himself build a new world. The day of the individual is not over—instead, it is just about to begin. The machine does not write the doom of liberty, but is waiting at man's hand as a peerless tool, for him to use to put foundations beneath a genuine democracy. Then the machine may conquer human drudgery to some purpose, taking it upon itself to broaden, lengthen, strengthen, and deepen the life of the simplest man. What limits do we dare imagine to an art that is organic fruit of an adequate life for the individual! Although this power is now murderous, chained to botchwork and bunglers' ambitions, the creative artist will take it surely into his hand and, in the name of liberty, swiftly undo the deadly mischief it has created.

Here ends the early discourse on the art and craft of the machine.

You may find comfort in the reflection that truth and liberty have this invincible excellence, that all man does for them or does against them eventually serves them equally well. That fact has comforted me all the intervening years between the first reading of the foregoing discourse and this reading at Princeton . . . the last reading, for I shall never read it again. Tomorrow afternoon there will be—I am afraid—heavy matter also because the question of qualifying the "machine-made" in American industries by human elements of style will be, in detail, our subject. There may be matter more subjective and difficult but I do not know what it may be.

It will be necessary for us all to give close attention and considerable thought to the subject, "style in industry." We shall see that any hope of such style will mean a crusade against *the* styles.

2: STYLE IN INDUSTRY

Where certain remarks I have made concern nature and romance on the one hand, and the machine upon the other, I am accused of inconsistency—also in several or seven different languages. But if the word "nature," and the word "romance" too, are understood in the sense that each is used we can find little to correct, although the last analysis is never to be made.

The machine is that mathematical automaton or automatic power contrived in brass and steel by men, not only to take the place of manpower, but to multiply manpower—the brainless craftsman of a new social order.

Primarily the word "nature" means the principle at work in everything that lives and gives to life its form and character. All lives, so we may refer to the nature of two plus two equals four, if we like, or to the nature of tin, or to the nature of a disease or of the chromatic seventh. The word has nothing to do with realistic or realism, but refers to the essential *reality* of all things, so far as we may perceive reality. We cannot conceive life, we do not know what it is, but we can perceive the nature of its consequences and effects and so enter into creation with some intelligence. If we have occasion to refer to the visible world we will use the term "external nature." The word "organic" too, if taken too biologically, is a stumbling block. The word applies to "living" structure—a structure or concept wherein features or parts are so organized in form and substance as to be, applied to purpose, *integral*. Everything that "lives" is therefore organic. The inorganic—the "unorganized"—cannot *live*.

While we are at the, perhaps unnecessary, pains of explaining, let us say also what we should understand by romance. True romanticism in art is after all only liberalism in art, and is so understood, I believe, by all great poets. Romance is the essential joy we have in living, as distinguished from mere pleasure; therefore we want no narrow inventions, as preventions, to rise up from small minds and selfish hands, no intolerant "modes" to grow up in the modern world; it is to be our privilege to build upon new fertile ground. Yes, we are to build in the arts upon this great ground fertilized *by* the *old* civilizations—a new liberty.

We, so beset by educational advantages as are Americans, cannot say too often to ourselves or others that "toleration and liberty are the foundations of this great republic." We should keep it well in the foreground of our minds and as a hope in our hearts that liberty in art as well as liberty in society *should* be, and therefore *must* be, the offspring of political liberty.

Then to us all, so minded, let the artist come. He has a public. And as we have already seen in "Machinery, Materials, and Men," the artist now has both the making and the means. Let him arise in our industry. For a new people a new art!

Liberty, however, is no friend to license. So, for our text in connection with difficult "Style in Industry," for due reference to authority suppose we again go far back in history—again to avoid all contradiction—this time to the birth of old Japan—and there, to safeguard liberty, take for text, simply, "An artist's limitations are his best friends," and dedicate that text to Jimmu Tenno.

At least the ancient civilization of his slowly sinking stretch of pendulous island, arising from the sea in the snows of perpetual winter and reaching all the way south to perpetual summer, affords best proof of the text anywhere to be found. "Limitations," in this sense, were, I take it, those of materials, tools, and specific purpose.

In Jimmu's island perfect style in industry was supreme and native until Japan was discovered within range of our own Commodore Perry's guns. That Western contacts have destroyed this early style—if not the industry—only enhances the value of that early style. *Certainly,* the arts and crafts, as developed in Nippon during her many centuries of isolation in happy concentration, afford universal object lessons incomparable in style.

Industry and style there—before the "peaceful" commercial invasion by the West—were supremely natural. Nor in Jimmu Tenno's time was there anywhere to be found separate and contrasted existence between art and nature. Nowhere else in the world can we so clearly see this nor so well inform ourselves in considering this matter of style in our own native automatic industries. This notwithstanding the fact that our industries are conditioned upon automatic acquiescence of men instead of upon the craftsmanship of the man. By giving our attention to the ease and naturalness with which things Japanese originally achieved style, we may learn a valuable lesson.

Our industry must educate designers instead of making craftsmen—for our craftsmen are machines, craftsmen ready-made, efficient and obedient. So far as they go—mechanical power stripped clean. How to get these formidable craft-engines the work to do they may do well? Then, beyond mechanical skill, the cadences of form?

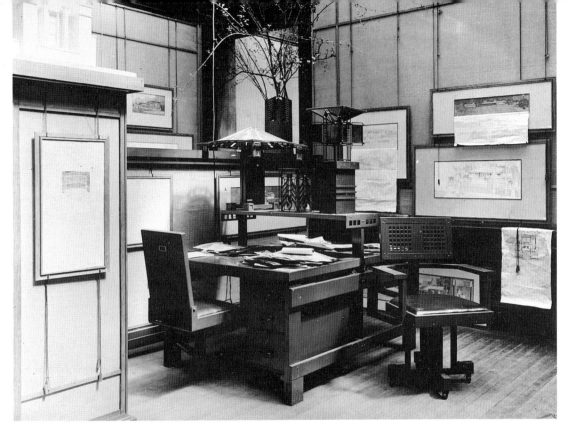

Larkin Desk at the Chicago Architectural Club Exhibition, Art Institute of Chicago. Chicago, Illinois. 1907. FLLW Fdn FA#0403.0068

The first answer will seem generalization beyond any immediate mark, for that answer is—by means of imagination. Imagination superior and supreme. Supreme imagination is what makes the creative artist now just as it made one then. And imagination is what will make the needed designer for industry now—no less than then or ever before. But, strange to say, it is of the true quality of great imagination that it can see wood as wood, steel as steel, glass as glass, stone as stone, and make limitations its best friends. This is what Jimmu Tenno's busy people proved so thoroughly well and what may be so useful to us to realize. Our machine-age limitations are more severe and more cruelly enforced than limitations were in this severely disciplined island-empire of Japan. Nevertheless, though more difficult in important ways, in other more important directions, we have marvelously more opportunity than ever Japan had.

Principles which made the art and craft of old Japan a living thing—living, that is, for old Japan—will work as well now as then. The same principles in art and craft either of the East or the West, wherever similar truths of being went into effect with some force in the lives of their peoples, need no change now. Secrets of cause and effect in work and materials in relation to life as lived are the same for the coming designer for machines as they were for the bygone craftsman designers. But when a man becomes a part of the machine that he moves—the man is lost.

We Americans, too, *do live*—in a way—do we not? But we differ. We do live and, notwithstanding all differences, our souls yet have much in common with all souls. The principles, therefore, on which we must work our modern style for ourselves will not change the way our interpretation and applications will utterly change. Results in American industry will be simpler, broader, more a matter of texture and sublimated mathematics as music is sublimated mathematics; therefore our designs will be more subjective than before. Our applications will be more generalized but our derivations not more limited than in the days of ancient handicraft.

Provided the limitations of any given problem

in the arts do not destroy each other by internal collision and so kill opportunity, limitations are no detriment to artist endeavor. It is largely the artist's business—all in his day's work—to see that the limitations do *not* destroy each other. That is to say, it is up to him to get proper tools, proper materials for proper work. Speaking for myself, it would be absurd if not impossible to take advantage of the so-called "free hand." To "idealize" in the fanciful sketch is a thing unknown to me. Except as I were given some well defined limitations or requirements—the more specific the better—there would be no problem, nothing to work with, nothing to work out; why then trouble the artist? Perhaps that is why "fairs" are so universally uncreative and harmful—the hand is too free, the quality of imagination, therefore, too insignificant.

No—not until American industrial designers have grown up to the point where they have known and made friends with the limitations characteristic of their job, will America have any style in industry. What are these limitations?

Automatic industrial fabrication is not the least of them. But—to reiterate from the matter of our first chapter, "Machinery, Materials, and Men"—the American designers' hope lies in the fact that as a consequence of the automaton, already machinery can do many desirable things, "by hand" prohibited or impossible. Now, mixed up with "Machinery, Materials, and Men," in our first chapter, was the word "plasticity" used as machine-aesthetic in modern designing for woodworking, stonework, metal-casting, and reproductive processes. Some practical suggestions were made to indicate how and wherein this new "aesthetic" which the machine has given to us may enable the artist to make new use of old materials, and new use of new materials instead of making abuse of both.

"Plasticity" is of utmost importance. The word implies total absence of constructed effects as evident in the result. This important word, "plastic," means that the quality and nature of materials are seen "flowing or growing" into form instead of seen as built up out of cut and joined pieces. "Composed" is the academic term for this academic process in furniture. "Plastic" forms, however, are *not*

"composed" nor set up. They, happily, inasmuch as they are produced by a *"growing"* process, must be developed . . . *created*. And to shorten this discourse we may as well admit that if we go far enough to find cause in any single industry like furniture for this matter of style, we will have the secret of origin and growth of style in any or in all industries. After getting so far, there would come only specialization in differences of materials and machinery in operation.

Repeatedly and freely too we are to use this word "style"—but if intelligently, what, then, is style? Be sure of one thing in any answer made to the question—style *has nothing to do with "the" styles!* "The great styles" we call them. "Styles" have been tattered, torn, and scattered to the four winds and all the breezes that blow between them as a form of mechanical corruption in industry, and yet, we have no style. The more "styles" in fact, the less style, unless by accident—nor anything very much resembling the stimulating quality. Our designers for various industries—still busy, unfortunately, trying to imitate "styles" instead of *studying the principles* of style intelligently—are at the moment jealously watching France as they see her products go from Wanamaker's on down the avenue and out along the highways of these United States as far as the Pacific Ocean. And yet, if you will take pains to compare the best of French products, say in textiles, with the products of the ancient Momoyama of Japan you will see the industrial ideas of old Japan at work in new French industry as direct inspiration. The French product is not Japanese and nearly all of the textiles are within the capacity of the machine; most of the product is good. But France, in all her moments of movement in art and craft, and no less at this "modern" moment in this "modernistic" particular, helps herself liberally if not literally from Japanese sources, and creditably. She it was who discovered the Japanese print by way of the de Goncourts. That discovery bore significant fruit in French painting. And there are more valuable brochures in the French language on the art of Japan in all its phases available for reference than in all other languages put together, the Japanese language included. France, the inveterate discoverer, must discover *l'esprit de l'art Japonais—à la Japon*, to her great honor be it said. Holland arrived at Nagasaki first, but France is probably further along today in profitable industrial results in present arts and crafts from the revelations she found when she got to Yedo by way of Yokohama than is any other country, Austria excepted—unless our own country should soon prove formidable exception.

This does not mean that France or Austria copies Japan or that America may do so. It does mean that France is, only now, beginning to do approximately well what Japan did supremely well four centuries ago in the great Momoyama period of her development—yes, about four hundred years ago!

Any principle is fertile, perhaps it is fertility itself! If its application is once understood in any branch of design, it will go on blooming indefinitely, coordinately, in as many different schools and schemes as there are insects, or in forms as varied as the flowers themselves, or for that matter be as prolific of pattern as the fishes or the flora of the sea.

We should, were we going into the matter at length, get to nature forms later on as the best of all references for the working of the principles we are here seeking, and I should have preferred to go to them at once as is my habit. But for the purposes of this hour I have preferred tradition because Japan has already done, in her own perfect way, what now lies for study before us. And I believe it well to know what humanity has accomplished in the direction we must take, if we are strong enough to profit by tradition—the spirit of principle—and leave traditions—the letter, or form—alone, as not our own. Even so, having finished with tradition, we will still have before us and forever, as an open book of creation, that natural appeal to the nature court of last resort.

Remember, however, that long before France rationalized and vitalized her industries, during the period when she was still sickened and helpless in the serpentine coils of l'art nouveau (derived from her own deadly rococo), you may find in the "Secession" of Middle Europe an application earlier than the present application by France of the vital principles we are discussing on behalf of our subject.

I came upon the Secession during the winter of 1910. At that time Herr Professor Wagner, of Vienna, a great architect, the architect Olbrich, of Darmstadt, the remarkable painter Klimt, of Austria, and the sculptor Metzner, of Berlin—great artists all—were the soul of that movement. And there was the work of Louis Sullivan and of myself in America. Many Europeans accounted for this Secession—their own early contribution to modern art—as a "Mohammedan renaissance." (It was natural by that time to believe in nothing but some kind of renaissance.) But later, when the Secession—though frowned upon by the royal academies—was in full swing in the products of the Wiener Werkstätte, seen today similarly in the products of French art and craft, we find the ancient art and craft of Japan's great Momoyama often approximated in effect.

Nothing at this "modern" moment could be more ungracious nor arouse more contumacious "edge" than thus looking the "gift horse" or the "modernistic" in the teeth. Nevertheless, I believe it valuable to our future to raise this unpopular issue.

Artists, even great ones, are singularly ungrateful to sources of inspiration—among lesser artists ingratitude amounts to phobia. No sooner does the lesser artist receive a lesson or perceive an idea or even receive the objects of art from another source, than he soon becomes anxious to forget the suggestion, conceal the facts, or, if impossible to do this, to minimize, by detraction, the "gift." And as culture expands, we soon, too soon, deny outright the original sources of our inspiration as a suspected reproach to our own superiority. This you may quite generally find in the modern art world. At this moment in our development Japan particularly is thus the "great insulted." Cowardly evasion seems unworthy of great artists or great causes, and certainly is no manner in which to approach great matter for the future. Ignorance of origins is no virtue, nor to keep fresh thought ill-advised concerning them. So let us pursue still further this quest as to what is style by digging at the root of this ancient culture where I imagine there was more fertile ground and the workman had severer discipline than he ever had anywhere else in the world. Thus we may interpret a ready-made record that is unique. Let us study for a moment the Japanese dwelling, this humble dwelling that is a veritable sermon on our subject, "style in industry."

It became what it is owing to a religious admonition. "Be clean!" "Be clean" was the soul of Shinto—Jimmu Tenno's own ancient form of worship. Shinto spoke not of a good man, nor spoke of a moral man, but spoke of a clean man. Shinto spoke not only of clean hands, but of a clean heart. "Be clean" was the simple cry from the austere soul of Shinto. Japanese art heard the cry, and therefore posterity has one primitive instance where a remarkably simple religious edict or ideal made architecture, art, and craftsmanship the cleanest, in every sense, of all clean workmanship the world over.

This simple ideal of cleanliness, held by a whole people, came to abhor waste as matter out of place, saw it as ugly—therefore as what we call "dirt."

Here you have a kind of spiritual ideal of natural, and hence organic, simplicity. Consequently all Japanese art with its imaginative exuberance and organic elegance (no fern frond freshly born ever had more) was a practical study in elimination of the insignificant. All phases of art expression in the Momoyama period were organic. There was no great and no small art. But there lived the profound Sotatsu, the incomparable Korin, the brilliant Kenzan, and their vital schools, as, later in the Ukiyoé, we find Kiyonobu, Toyonobu, Harunobu, Kiyonaga, Utamaro, Hokusai, and Hiroshige—a small student group gathered about each—all springing from the industrial soil thus fertilized by the school of the great Momoyama masters. Instinctive sense of organic quality qualified them as artists, *all*. Again, a kind of spiritual gift of significance. Here, as a saving grace in one civilization on earth, feeling for significance, simplicity in art was born, becoming soon an ideal naturally attained by organic means. Here, in this "plastic-ideal" *attained by organic means,* we touch the secret of great style. Wood they allowed to be wood, of course. Metal they allowed—even encouraged—to be metal. Stone was never asked to be less or more than stone.

Nor did the designer of that day try to make any thing in materials or processes something other than itself. Here is a sound first principle that will go far to clear our encumbered ground for fresh growth in "art in industry."

Also the modern process of standardizing, as we now face it on every side, sterilized by it, prostrate to it, was in Japan known and practiced with artistic perfection by freedom of choice many centuries ago, in this dwelling we are considering. The removable (for cleaning) floor mats or *tatami* of Japanese buildings were all of one size, 3' 0" by 6' 0". The shape of all the houses was determined by the size and shape of assembled mats. The Japanese speak of a nine, eleven, sixteen, or thirty-four mat house. All the sliding interior partitions occur on the joint lines of the mats. The *odeau*—polished wood posts that carry ceilings and roof—all stand at intersections of the mats. The light sliding paper *shoji* or outside wall-screens are likewise removable, for cleaning. The plan for any Japanese dwelling was an effective study in sublimated mathematics. And the house itself was used by those who themselves made it for themselves with the same naturalness with which a turtle uses his shell. Consider too that, "be clean"—"the simplest way without waste"—was dignified as *ceremonial* in old Japan. The ceremonies of that ancient day were no more than the simple offices of daily life raised to the dignity of works of art. True culture, therefore. Ceremonials, too, it seems, may be organic, integral though symbolic. For instance, what is the important tea ceremony of the Japanese but the most graciously perfect way, all considered, of serving a cup of tea to respected or beloved guests? Grace and elegance, as we may see—*of* the thing itself—organic elegance. Not *on* it Greek-wise as the "elegant solution." It was in easy, simple, spontaneous expression of nature that the Japanese were so perfect—contenting themselves with humble obedience to nature-law.

Naturally enough, disorder, too, in this "clean" house built by Jimmu Tenno's people is in the same category as dirt. So everything large or little of everyday use, even the works of art for humble and profound admiration, have appropriate place when in use and are carefully put away into safekeeping when not in use.

All designed for kneeling on soft mats on the floor you say? Yes—but the same ideal, in principle, would work out just as well on one's feet.

With this Shinto ideal of "be clean" in mind the Japanese dwelling in every structural member and fiber of its being means something fine, has genuine significance, and straightway does that something with beautiful effect. Art, for once, is seen to be supremely natural.

Yes—here is definite root of style in industry. Also in every other country and period where style developed as genuine consequence of natural or ethnic character, similar proofs may be found as to the origin of style.

Today, it seems to me, we hear this cry "be clean" from the depths of our own need. It is almost as though the machine itself had, by force, issued edict similar to Shinto—"be clean." Clean lines—clean surfaces—clean purposes. As swift as you like, but clean as the flight of an arrow. When this edict inspires organic results and not the mere picture-making that curses so-called "modernism," we will here find the basic elements of style in our own industry to be the same by machine as they were by hand back there in the beginning of the history of a unique civilization. To give this edict of the machine human significance, there is the command of the creative artist to keep a grip upon the earth in use of the architectural planes parallel to earth, and to make new materials qualify the new forms of the new methods, so that all is warmly and significantly human in the result. The human equation is the art equation in it all. "Clean," in human sense, does not mean "plain" but it does mean significant. Nor does it mean hard, nor mechanical, nor mechanistic, nor that a man or a house or a chair or a child is a machine, except in the same sense that our own hearts are suction pumps.

Style in our industries will come out of similar, natural, clean use of machines upon "clean" material, with similar, unaffected, *heart-felt* simplicity instead of *head-made* simplicity. The nature of both machine and material for human use must be understood and mastered so they may be likewise in

our case plastic interpretations by great imagination. We will learn how to use both machinery and materials, and perhaps men as well, in the coming century. But we must learn how to use them all not only for qualities they possess in themselves, but to use each so that they may be beautifully, as well as scientifically related to human purpose in whatever form or function we humanly choose to put them. Then let us take all as much further along beyond the implications of "be clean," as our superior advantages in aesthetics permit.

To get nearer to the surface. We started to speak of textiles: having during the discourse of our first chapter touched upon woodworking, stonework, and metalworking, let us now go back for a moment to the Rodier fabrics for an example of present-day, successful design for the loom. Textures, infinite in variety, are the natural product of the loom. Pattern is related to, and is the natural consequence of, the mechanics of these varying textures. Large, flat patterns involved with textures, textures qualifying them or qualified by them, picturesque but with no thought of a picture, as in this product, are entirely modern in the best sense. And I would emphasize for you, in this connection, the fact that the ancient art we have just been interpreting was never, in any phase of its industries, ruined by childish love of the picture. The "picture" sense in art and craft came in with the Renaissance, as one consequence of the insubordination of the arts that disintegrated architecture as the great art. And before we can progress in our own machine products as art, we, too, will have to dispose of the insufferable insubordination of the picture. Summarily, if need be. I should like to strike the pictorial death blow in our art and craft. Of course I do not mean the picturesque.

Because of this insubordination of the picture few tapestries except the "Mille-fleurs" (and then very early ones) exist as good textile designs on account of the complex shading essential to the foolish picture as designed by the undisciplined painter. The insubordination of painting, setting up shop on its own account, divorced from architecture (architecture being the natural framework and background of all ancient, as it will be of any future, civilization), has cursed every form of art endeavor whatsoever with similar abuses of the *pictorial*. *Toujours la peinture, ad libitum, ad nauseam*—the *picture*. We live in the pictorial age. We do not have child-like imagery in simplicity but are "childish" in art, and whatever form our great art and craft in future may take, one thing it will not be, and that thing is "pictorial." Even a Japanese print, the popular form of imagery illustrating the popular life of Japan in all its phases, as the French well know, never degenerated to the mere picture. Let us be thankful that the machine by way of the camera today takes the pictorial upon itself as a form of literature. This gratifying feat has, already, made great progress in the cinematograph. Let the machine have it, I say, on those terms and keep it active there and serviceable in illustration as well, for what it may be worth—and it is worth much. But let us henceforth consider literature and the picture as one—eliminating both from the horizon of our art and craft—and for all time.

Let us now, in passing, glance at glassmaking: the Leerdam glass products for which artists are employed to make designs upon a royalty basis, similar to authors writing for publishers, then the special art of Lalique, and finally, the great, clear plates of our own commercial industry, the gift of the machine . . . great glass sheets to be cut up and used with no thought of beauty, valuable only because of their usefulness.

Here again let us insist that the same principle applies to glass as to wood, stone, metal, or the textiles just mentioned. But how far variety may go can be seen in the range of the Holland product from the simple glass-blown forms of De Basle, Copius, and Berlage at Leerdam to the virtuosity of French pieces by the genius Lalique. Certain characteristics of glass are properties of these designs: a piece by Lalique, being specialized handicraft, is useful as indicating the super-possibilities of glass as a beautiful material. Concerning our own "commercial" contribution (contributions so far are all "commercial") to glass—glass, once a precious substance, limited in quantity, costly in any size—the glass industry has grown so that a perfect clarity in any thickness, quality or dimension up to 250

square feet from $1/8$" in thickness to $1/2$" thick, is so cheap and desirable that our modern world is drifting towards structures of glass and steel.

The whole history of architecture would have been radically different had the ancients enjoyed any such grand privileges in this connection as are ours. The growing demands for sunshine and visibility make walls—even posts—something to get rid of at any cost. Glass did this. Glass alone, with no help from any of us, would eventually have destroyed classic architecture, root and branch.

Glass has now a perfect visibility, thin sheets of air crystallized to keep air currents outside or inside. Glass surfaces, too, may be modified to let the vision sweep through to any extent up to perfection. Tradition left no orders concerning this material as a means of perfect visibility; hence the sense of glass as crystal has not, as poetry, entered yet into architecture. All the dignity of color and material available in any other material may be discounted by glass in light, and discounted with permanence.

Shadows were the "brushwork" of the ancient architect. Let the "modern" now work with light, light diffused, light reflected, light refracted—light for its own sake, shadows gratuitous. It is the machine that makes *modern* these rare new opportunities in glass; new experience that architects so recent as the great Italian forebears, plucked even of their shrouds, frowning upon our "renaissance," would have considered magical. They would have thrown down their tools with the despair of the true artist. Then they would have transformed their cabinets into a realm, their halls into bewildering vistas and avenues of light—their modest units into unlimited wealth of color patterns and delicate forms, rivaling the frostwork upon the windowpanes, perhaps. They were creative enough to have found a world of illusion and brilliance, with jewels themselves only modest contributions to the splendor of their effects. And yet somehow Palladio, Vitruvius, Vignola, seem very dead, far away, and silent in this connection; Bramante and Brunelleschi not so far, nor Sansovino, though we must not forget that the great Italians were busy working over ancient forms. There was Buonarroti. Where should he be in all this, I wonder?

The prism has always fascinated man. We may now live in prismatic buildings, clean, beautiful, and new. Here is one clear "material" proof of modern advantage, for glass is uncompromisingly modern. Yes, architecture is soon to live anew because of glass and steel.

And so we might go on to speak truly of nearly all our typical modern industries at work upon materials with machinery. We could go on and on until we were all worn out and the subject would be still bright and new, there are so many industrial fields—so much machinery, so many processes, such riches in new materials.

We began this discussion of art in industry by saying, "toleration and liberty are the foundations of a great republic." Now let the artist come. Well, let him come into this boundless new realm so he be a liberal, hating only intolerance and especially his own. As said at the beginning of this discourse, true romanticism in art is after all only liberalism in art. This quality in the artist is the result of an inner experience and it is the essential poetry of the creative artist that his exploring brother, tabulating the sciences, seems never quite able to understand nor wholly respect. He distrusts that quality in life itself.

But the sense of romance cannot die out of human hearts. Science itself is bringing us to greater need of it and unconsciously giving greater assurance of it at every step. Romance is shifting its center now, as it has done before and will do constantly—but it is immortal. Industry will only itself become and remain a machine without it.

Our architecture itself would become a poor, flat-faced thing of steel-bones, box-outlines, gaspipe, and handrail fittings—as sun-receptive as a concrete sidewalk or a glass tank without this essential *heart* beating in it. Architecture, without it, could inspire nothing, and would degenerate to a box merely to *contain* "objets d'art"—objects it should itself create and *maintain*. So beware! The artist who condemns romance is only a foolish reactionary. Such good sense as the scientist or philosopher in the disguise of "artist" may have is not creative, although it may be corrective. Listen therefore and go back with what you may learn, to live and be true to romance.

Again—there is no good reason why objects of art in industry, because they are made by machines in the machine age, should resemble the machines that made them, or any other machinery whatever. There might be excellent reason why they should *not* resemble machinery.

There is no good reason why forms stripped clean of all considerations but function and utility should be admirable beyond that point: they may be abominable from the human standpoint, but there is no need for them to be so in the artist's hands.

The negation naturally made by the machine, gracefully accepted now, may, for a time, relieve us of sentimental abortion and abuse, but it cannot inspire and recreate humanity beyond that point. Inevitably the negation proceeds upon its own account to other abuses and abortions, even worse than sentimentality. Again, let us have no fears of liberalism in art in our industries, but encourage it with new understanding, knowing at last that the term romanticism never did apply to make-believe or falsifying, except as it degenerated to the artificiality that maintained the Renaissance.

The facts confronting us are sufficiently bare and hard. The taste for mediocrity in our country grows by what it feeds on.

Therefore the public of this republic will, more than ever now, find its love of commonplace elegance gratified either by the sentimentality of the "ornamental" or the sterility of ornaphobia. The machine age, it seems, is either to be damned by senseless sentimentality or to be sterilized by a factory aesthetic. Nevertheless, I believe that romance—this quality of the *heart,* the essential joy we have in living—by human imagination of the right sort can be brought to life again in modern industry. Creative imagination may yet convert our prosaic problems to poetry while modern Rome howls and the eyebrows of the Pharisees rise.

And probably not more than one-fifth of the American public will know what is meant by the accusation, so frequently made in so many different languages, that the American is uncreative, four-fifths of the accused pointing to magnificent machinery and stupendous scientific accomplishment to refute the impeachment. So while we are digesting the nationalities speaking those same languages within our borders, such culture as we have in sight must assist itself with intelligence to materialize for Americans out of everyday common places—and transcend the commonplace.

So finally, a practical suggestion as to ways and means to grow our own style in industry.

The machine, as it exists in every important trade, should without delay be put, by way of capable artist interpreters, into student hands, for them, at first, to play with and, later, with which to work. Reluctantly I admit that to put the machine, as the modern tool of a great civilization, to any extent into the hands of a body of young students, means some kind of school—and naturally such school would be called an art school, but one in which the fine arts would be not only allied to the industries they serve, but would stand there at the center of an industrial hive of characteristic industry as inspiration and influence in design problems. Sensitive, unspoiled students (and they may yet be found in this unqualified machine that America is becoming) should be put in touch with commercial industry in what we might call industrial style centers, workshops equipped with modern machinery, connected perhaps with our universities, but endowed by the industries themselves, where the students would remain domiciled, working part of the day in the shop itself.

Machinery-using crafts making useful things might through such experiment centers discover possibilities existing in the nature of their craft, which the present industries know nothing about and might never discover for themselves. In such a school it would be the turn of the fine arts to serve machinery in order that machinery might better serve them and all together better serve a beauty-loving and appreciative United States.

Let us say that seven branches of industrial arts be taken for a beginning (a number should be grouped together for the reason that they react upon one another to the advantage of each). Let us name glassmaking, textiles, pottery, sheet metals, woodworking, casting in metal, reproduction. Each industry so represented should be willing to donate

machinery and supply a competent machinist and to a certain extent endow its own craft, provided such industries were certain of proper management under safe auspices, and assured of a share in results which would be directly theirs—sharing either in benefit of designs or presently in designers themselves, both adapted to their particular field.

Such experiment centers intelligently conducted could do more to nationalize and vitalize our industries than all else, and soon would make them independent of France, Austria, or any other country, except as instruction by international example from all countries would help work out our own forms. There is no reason why an experiment center of this character, each center confined to forty students or less, should not make its own living and produce valuable articles to help in "carrying-on." As compared with the less favorably circumstanced factories, and owing to the artists at the head of the group, each article would be of the quality of a work of art and so be a genuine missionary wherever it went.

Such a school should be in the country, on sufficient land so that three hours a day of physical work on the soil would insure the living of the students and the resident group of seven artist workers, themselves the head of the student group. There would remain, say, seven hours of each day for forty-seven individuals in which to unite in production. A well-directed force of this sort would very soon have considerable producing power. Thus belonging to the school each month there would be beautifully useful or usefully beautiful things ready for market and influence—stuffs, tapestries, table linen, new cotton fabrics, table glassware, flower holders, lighting devices, window glass, mosaics, necklaces, screens, iron standards, fixtures, gates, fences, fire irons, enameled metals for house or garden purposes, cast metal sculpture for gardens, building hardware. All sorts of industrial art in aluminum, copper, lead, tin. Practical flower pots, architectural flower containers on large scale, water jars, pots, and sculpture. Paintings for decoration suitable for reproduction and designs for new media—for process-reproductions. Modern music, plays, rhythm, designs for farm buildings; the characteristic new problems like the gasoline sta-tion, the refreshment stand, food distribution, town and country cottages and objects for their furnish-ings, and factories, too, of various sorts.

The station might broadcast itself. Issue brochures, illustrated by itself, of pertinent phases of its work. Devote a branch to landscape studies on conservation and planting and town planning. In short, the station would be a hive of inspired indus-try. Architecture, without hesitation or equivoca-tion, should be the broad essential background of the whole endeavor—again strong in modern life as it ever was in ancient times. It is logical to say that again it must be the background and framework of civilization. Such stations or centers could be al-coves in connection with standard university cours-es in the history of art, architecture, and archaeolo-gy. And it would not matter where the centers were located, were they sufficiently isolated in beautiful country. They should not be too easy of access.

No examinations, graduations, or diplomas. But so soon as a student worker showed special competence in any branch of industry, he would be available as teacher in the university or for a place in that industry, manufacturers who were contributors to the school having first right to use him or her. The body of inspirational talent and the trade ma-chinists should be of such character that outside stu-dents would enjoy and seek points of contact with the work going on at the school—helpful to them and to the school as well.

I believe the time has come when art must take the lead in education because creative faculty is now, as ever, the birthright of man—the quality that has enabled him to distinguish himself from the brute. Through tricks played upon himself by what he proudly styles his intellect, turning all experience into arrogant abstractions and applying them as such by systems of education, he has all but sterilized himself. Science has been tried and found to be only a body. Science, and philosophy, too, have known but little of those inner experiences of the soul we call art and religion.

This creative faculty in man is that quality or faculty in him of getting himself born into whatev-er he does, and born again and again with fresh pat-terns as new problems arise. By means of this facul-ty he has the gods if not God. A false premium has been placed by education upon will and intellect. Imagination is the instrument by which the force in him works its miracles. Now—how to get back again to men and cultivate the creative quality in man is the concern of such centers as here suggest-ed. What more valuable step looking toward the fu-ture could any great institution take than to initiate such little experiment stations in out of the way places, where the creative endeavor of the whole youth is coordinate with the machinery, and where the technique of his time is visible at work, so that youth may win back again the creative factor as the needed vitalizing force in modern life?

We know, now, that creative art cannot be taught. We know, too, that individual creative im-pulse is the salt and savor of the natural ego as well as the fruit and triumph of any struggle we call work. Civilization without it can only die a miser-able death. To degrade and make hypocritical this quality of the individual by imposing mediocrity upon him in the name of misconceived and selfish-ly applied democracy is the modern social crime. Too plainly we already see the evil consequences of sentimentalized singing to Demos—foolishly as-cribing to Demos the virtues of deity. Concentra-tion and sympathetic inspiration should be isolated and concentrated in experimental work of this kind in order to hasten the time when art shall take the lead in education, and character be a natural conse-quence. Were this to be put into effect on even a small scale in various units scattered over the surface of these United States, this indispensable ego might be strengthened and restored to a sanity compared to which "egotism," as we now know it in educa-tion, would only be a sickly disease of conscious-ness—highly improbable because manifestly absurd.

Thus given opportunity truly liberal, Ameri-can youth might soon become the vital medium through which the spirit of man may so appear to men in their own work that they might again see and realize that great spirit as their own.

This liberal opportunity to work and study is a practical suggestion for the growth of that quality of style in industry we have been seeking this afternoon.

Behind personality tradition should stand—behind tradition stands the race.

We have put tradition before personality—and made tradition as a fatal hurdle for race.

3: THE PASSING OF THE CORNICE

Instinctively, I think, I hated the empty, pretentious shapes of the Renaissance. When sixteen years old, I used to read the great "modern" of his day Victor Hugo. Reading his discursive novel, *Notre-Dame*, I came upon the chapter, *"Ceci Tuera Cela."* That story of the decline of architecture made a lasting impression upon me. I saw the Renaissance as that setting sun all Europe mistook for dawn; I believed Gutenberg's invention of the shifting types would kill the great edifice as architecture. In fact, as we all may now see, printing *was* the first great blow to art by the machine. I saw the lifeblood of beloved architecture slowly ebbing, inevitably to be taken entirely away from the building by the book, the book being a more liberal form of expression for human thought. This mechanical invention was to become the channel for thought—because more facile and more direct. In place of the art of architecture was to come literature made ubiquitous.

I saw that architecture, in its great antique form, was going to die. Ghastly tragedy—I could hardly bear the thought of the consequences.

About this time, too—catastrophe! As the new west wing of the old Wisconsin State Capitol at Madison fell, I happened to be passing in the shade of the trees that bordered the green park in which the building stood. Suddenly I heard the roar of collapse—saw the clouds of white lime-dust rise high in the air—heard the groans and fearful cries of those injured and not killed—some forty workmen dead or seriously hurt. I remember clinging to the iron palings of the park in full view of the scene, sick with horror as men plunged headlong from the basement openings—some seeming to be still madly fighting off falling bricks and timbers, only to fall dead in the grass outside, grass no longer green but whitened by the now falling clouds of lime. The outer stone walls were still standing. Stone basement-piers carrying the iron interior supporting columns had given way and the roof took all the floors, sixty men at work on them, clear down to the basement. A great "classic" cornice had been projecting boldly out from the top of the building, against the sky. Its moorings partly torn away, this cornice now hung down in places, great hollow boxes of galvanized iron, hanging up there suspended on end. One great section of cornice I saw hanging above an upper window. A workman hung, head downward, his foot caught, crushed on the sill of this window, by a falling beam. A red line streaked the stone wall below him and it seemed as though the hanging box of sheet-iron that a moment before had gloomed against the sky as the "classic" cornice, must tear loose by its own weight and cut him down before he could be rescued. The spectacle of that sham feature hanging there, deadly menace to the pitifully moaning, topsy-turvy figure of a man—a working man—went far to deepen the dismay planted in a boy's heart by Victor Hugo's prophetic tale. This terrifying picture persisting in imagination gave rise to subsequent reflections. "This empty sheet-iron thing . . . a little while ago it was pretending to be stone . . . and doing this, mind you, for the capitol of the great state of Wisconsin . . . what a shame!

"Somebody must have been imposed upon!

"Was it the state or perhaps the architect himself?

"Had the architect been cheated in that, too, as well as in the collapsed piers that had let the structure down? Or was it all deliberate and everybody knew about it, but did nothing about it—did not care? Wasn't this the very thing Victor Hugo meant?"

I believed it was what he meant and began to examine cornices critically. "Why was it necessary to make them 'imitation'? If it was necessary to do that, why have them at all? Were they really beautiful or useful anyway? I couldn't see that they were particularly beautiful—except that a building looked 'strange' without one. But it looked more strange when the roof fell in and this thing called the cornice hung down endwise and was 'thin.' But that was it. . . . No matter how thin it was, the great cornice put there regardless of reality, to make the building familiar. It had no other meaning. Well, then, Victor Hugo saw this coming, did he, so long ago? . . . He foresaw that architecture would become a sham? . . . Was it all now sham or was it just the cornice that was shamming? . . . And if they would lie about the cornice, or lie with it this way in matters of state, why wouldn't they lie about other parts of the building too . . . perhaps as a matter of taste?" And then came critical inquests held by the boy-coroner . . . the pilaster found to be another nauseating cheat. Others followed thick and fast, I remember.

It was early disillusionment and cruel, this vision of the lifeblood of idolized architecture ebbing slowly away, vividly pointed and finally driven home by the horror of the falling building, showing the sham architecture, a preposterous bulk, threatening to take the very life of the workman himself, his lifeblood already dripping away down the wall, just beneath. The poor workman became significant, himself a symbol. Both experiences, *"Ceci Tuera Cela"* and the wreck of the capitol by internal collapse, did something to me for which I have never ceased to be grateful. If the old order is to be preserved, regardless, it is not well for boys to read the great poets nor see classic buildings fall down.

Soon after this, Viollet-le-Duc's *Dictionnaire Raisonné de l'Architecture Française* fell into my hands by way of a beloved schoolteacher aunt of mine and the work was finished, ready for the master to whom I came some four years later, Louis H. Sullivan—Beaux-Arts rebel. I went to him, for one thing, because he did not believe in cornices.

Now if the "pseudo-classic" forms of the Renaissance had had more life in them they would have died sooner and long ago have been decently buried. Renaissance architecture, being but the dry bones of a life lived and dead, centuries before, the bones were left to bleach. For text, then, on this our third afternoon, our reference to authority is hereby inscribed to Moti, ancient Chinese sage.

This inscription: "In twilight, light of the lantern, or in darkness, worship no old images nor run after new. They may arise to bind you, or, being false, betray you into bondage wherein your own shall wither." (Twilight probably meaning partial understanding; lantern light, glamor; dark-

ness, ignorance.) Or another translation—Chinese is far from English: "Except in full light of day bow down to no images, cast, graven, or builded by another, less they, being false, betray and bind you powerless to earth." Still another: "Without full knowledge worship no images, lest being false they bind thee powerless to make thine own true."

And finally we have reached the title of the discourse—"The Passing of the Cornice," the image of a dead culture.

There was a Graeco-Roman feature advocated by the American Institute of Architects to finish a building at the top. This authentic feature was called the cornice. Not so long ago no building, great or small, high or low, dignified and costly, or cheap and vile, was complete without a cornice of some sort. You may see accredited cornices still hanging on and well out over the busy streets in any American city for no good purpose whatsoever . . . really for no purpose at all. But to the elect, no building looked like a building unless it had the brackets, modillions, and "fancy" fixings of this ornamental and ornamented pseudo-classic "feature." Cornices were even more significantly insignificant than it is the habit of many of the main features of our buildings to be. The cornice was an attitude, the ornamental gesture that gave to the provincial American structure the element of hallowed "culture." That was all the significance cornices ever had—the worship of a hypocritical theocratic culture. Usually built up above the roof and projecting well out beyond it, hanging out from the top of the wall, they had nothing in reason to do with construction—but there the cornice had to be. It had, somehow, became "manner"—something like lifting our hat to the ladies, or, in extreme cases, like the leg an acrobat makes as he kisses his hand to the audience after doing his "turn." The cornice, in doing our "turn," became our commonplace concession to respectable "form," thanks again to the Italians thus beset—and disturbed in their well earned architectural slumber.

But, have you all noticed a change up there where the eye leaves our buildings for the sky— the "skyline," architects call it? Observe! More sky! The cornice has gone. Gone, we may hope, to join the procession of foolish concessions and vain professions that passed earlier. Gone to join the corner-tower, the hoop skirt, the bustle, and the cupola.

Like them—gone! This shady-shabby architectural feature of our middle distance, the seventies, eighties, and nineties, has been relegated to that mysterious scrap heap supposedly reposing in the backyard of oblivion. Look for a cornice in vain anywhere on America's new buildings high or low, cheap or costly, public or private. You will hardly find one unless you are looking at some government "monument." Government, it seems, is a commitment, a rendezvous with traditions that hang on.

But for a time no skyscraper—yes, it is all that recent—was complete without the cornice. The Belmont Hotel and the Flatiron Building in New York City perhaps said the last word, took the last grand stand, and made the final grand gesture in behalf of our subject. For about that time the hidden anchors that tied the pretentious feature back on some high Chicago buildings began to rust off and let this assumption-of-virtue down into the city streets to kill a few people on the sidewalks below. The people killed, happened to be "leading citizens." But for "accident" what would modern American cities be looking like, by now? Cornices cost outrageous sums, cornices shut out the light below, but that didn't seem to hurt cornices, much, with us. Not until cornices became dangerous and pseudo-classic by way of the A.I.A. ("Arbitrary Institute of Appearances") and began to crash down to city streets—did the city fathers talk "ordinance" to the Institute. The learned architects listened, read the ordinances, and though indignant, had no choice but to quit. Observe the relief!

Nor dare we imagine they would have dared to quit the cornice on their own account!

Shall we see the stagey, empty frown of the cornice glooming against the sky again? Has this cultured relic served its theatrical "turn" or are appearances for the moment *too* good to be true? Periodic "revivals" have enabled our aesthetic crimes to live so many lives that one may never be sure. But since we've learned to do without this particular "hang-over" in this land of free progress and are getting

used to bareheaded buildings, find the additional light agreeable, the money saved extremely useful, and as, especially, we are for "safety first," we are probably safe from the perennial renaissance for some years to come. At any rate for the moment "the glory that was Greece, the grandeur that was Rome," ours by way of Italy, may cease turning in ancient and honorable graves. Oh Palladio! Vitruvius! Vignola! be comforted—the twentieth century gives back to you your shrouds!

Ye Gods! And *that* was the American architecture of liberty! Yes, it was unwarranted liberty that American architecture took.

We may well believe there is some subjective wave, that finally, perhaps blindly, gets buildings, costumes, and customs all together in effect as civilization marches on. At least it would so seem as we look about us, for in the umbrageous cornice-time immediately behind us, hats were extravagant cornices for human heads, just as the cornices were extravagant hats for buildings. And what about puffed sleeves, frizzes, furbelows, and flounces? Didn't they go remarkably well with pilasters, architraves, and rusticated walls? In fact, weren't they exactly the same thing? Even the skirts of the cornice-period were extravagant cornices upside down over feet. And there was the "train" trailing the floor on occasion, the last word in cornices. Nor was dinner in those days complete without its own peculiar "cornice." They called it "dessert." Many brave and agreeable men died of that less obvious "cornice," but "cornice" nevertheless.

And the manners of that period of grandomania! Were they not emulation of the "cornice" when really manner! And top-heavy too, with chivalry and other thinly disguised brutalities? Now? No hat brim at all. Just a close sheath for the head. Skirts? None. Instead, a pair of silken legs sheer from rigid stilted heel to flexing knees; something scant and informal hung round the middle from above. What would have barely served as underwear in the late cornice-days, now costume for the street. No "manner" in our best manners.

Study, by contrast, the flamboyant human and architectural silhouettes of the cornice-period just

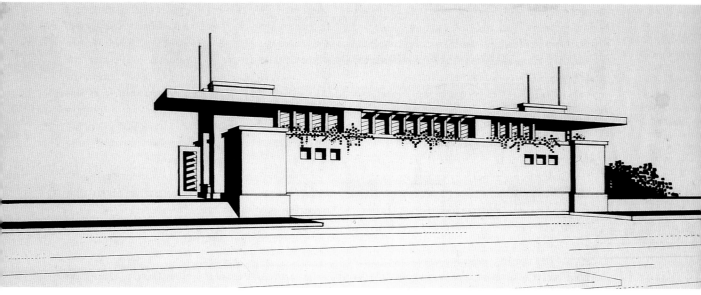

Yahara Boathouse (Project). Madison, Wisconsin. 1905. Perspective. China ink on tracing paper, 18 x 10". FLLW Fdn#0211.006

past with the silhouettes of today. After the comparison, be as grateful as it is in your nature to be—for escape, for even the *appearance* of simplicity.

Here comes "fashionable" penchant for the clean, significant lines of sculptural contours. Contrast these silhouettes in cars, buildings, clothing, hair dressing of today with those of the nineties. Even in the flower arrangements of the period of our "middle distance" and that of our immediate foreground you may see great difference. The "bokay" was what you remember it was. Now, a bouquet is a few long-stemmed flowers with artful carelessness slipped into a tall glass, or au naturel, a single species grouped in close sculptural mass over a low bowl. Consider, too, that modern music no longer needs the cornice. It, too, can stop without the crescendo or the grand finale, the flourish of our grandfathers, which was "classic." Yes, the cornice was "flourish" too. Curious! Jazz, all too consistently, belongs to this awakening period, to the youth that killed the cornice, awakening to see that nothing ever was quite so pretentious, empty, and finally demoralizing as that pompous gesture we were taught to respect and to call the "cornice." It had much—much too much—foreign baggage in its train, ever to be allowed to come back to America.

Should we now clearly perceive what the cornice really meant in terms of human life, especially of our own life as dedicated to liberty, we *would* be rid of cornices forever. Turning instinctively from the cornice shows our native instincts healthy enough. But we require *knowledge* of its fatality, where freedom is concerned, to insure protection from the periodic "aesthetic revival" that is successfully put over every few years just because of enterprising salesmanship and our own aimlessness. We must have a standard that will give us protection. If we know *why* we hate the cornice now, it may never rise again to ride us or smite us some other day.

Suppose, for the sake of argument, once upon a time we *did* live in trees, lightly skipping from branch to branch, insured by our tails as we pelted each other with nuts. We dwelt sheltered from the sun and rain by the overhanging foliage of upper branches—grateful for both shelter and shade. Gratitude for that "overhead"—and the sense of it—has been with us all down the ages as the cornice, finally become an emblem—a symbol—showed. Instinctive gratitude is of course fainter now. But whenever the cornice, true to that primeval instinct, was *real shelter* or even the sense of it, and dropped roof-water free of the building walls—

well, the cornice was not a cornice then but was an overhanging *roof.* Let the overhanging roof live as human shelter. It will never disappear from architecture. The sense of architecture as human shelter is a very fine sense—common sense, in fact.

But as soon as this good and innocent instinct became a habit, original meaning, as usual, lost by the time *usefulness* departed, the ancient and no less fashionable doctor-of-appearances took notice, adopted the "look" of the overhang, began to play with it, and soon the citizen began to view the overhang from the street, as *the* cornice. If ever "the doctor" knew or ever cared what meaning the overhang ever had, the doctor soon forgot. He became "cornice-conscious." The roof-water now ran back from the cornice on to the flat roof of the building and down inside down-spouts. But why should the doctor worry? Has the doctor of aesthetics ever worried about structural significances? No. So through him, although all had been reversed, this now obsession of the "overhead," for mere aesthetic effect, an aesthetic that had got itself into Greek and, therefore, into Roman life as art for art's sake, this arbitrary convention, became our accepted academic pattern. It was all up with us then—until now.

The net result of it all is that no culture is recognizable to us as such without the cornice. But just eliminate the troublesome and expensive feature from Greek and Roman buildings and see what happens by way of consequence. Then when you know what it meant in their buildings, just take that same concession to the academic artificiality of tradition from their lives and see, as a consequence, what happens to culture. You will see by what is lost, as well as by what is left, that the cornice, as such, originally was Graeco-Roman culture, and to such an extent that—pasticcio-Italiano—it has been our own "American pseudo-classic" *ever since.* Inasmuch as nearly everything institutional in our much over-instituted lives is either Roman or Graeco-Roman, we couldn't have had our chosen institutions without this cherished symbol. No, we had to do the precious cornice too. So we did the cornice-lie with the best of them, to the limit and far and away beyond any sense of limit at all.

Amazing! Utter artificiality become a more or less gracefully refined symbolic *lie,* the culture we Americans patterned and tried our best to make our own classic, too, and adored for a long, long time. Thomas Jefferson himself was blameworthy in that. George Washington no less so.

But pragmatic as the Romans were in all other matters, we may comfort ourselves a little, if there is any comfort in the fact that these same Romans, great jurists and executives, too, when it came to "culture," denied their own splendid engineering invention of the arch for centuries in order to hang on to the same cornice—or more correctly speaking, to hang the cornice on.

Not until the Roman doctors-of-appearances (their names are lost to us, so we cannot chastely insult them) could conceal the arch no longer, did they let the arch live as the arch. Even then, in order to preserve "appearances," the doctors insisted on running a cornice—in miniature—around over the arch itself and called the little cornice on the curve an archivolt. They then let the matter go at that. Yes, the noble arches themselves now had to have the cornices, and Renaissance arches have all had cornices on their curves for several centuries or more, in fact had them on until today. Roofs now have become flat or invisible. The roof-water ran back the other way. But here was the cornice, derived from and still symbolic of the overhanging roof, continuing to hang over just the same. Yes, it was now great "art." In other words, the cornice was secure as an academic aesthetic. No one dared go behind the thing to see how and what it *really* was. It no longer mattered what it was.

Another human instinct had left home and gone wrong, but civilization sentimentalized and made the degradation into prestige—irresistible. Professors taught the cornice now as "good school." Every building, more or less, had to defer to this corniced authority to be habitable or valuable. Only a radical or two in any generation dared fight such authority and usually the fight cost the radical his economic life.

But now you may look back, although the perspective is still insufficient, and see what a sham this undemocratic fetish really was, what an imposition it became, how pompously it lied to us about itself; realize how much social meanness of soul it hid and what poverty of invention on the part of the great architects it cleverly concealed for many centuries. And you may now observe as you go downtown that the worst is over. Only very sophisticated doctors-of-appearances dare use the cornice any more, and then the dead living dare use it only for monuments to honor the living dead; especially have they done so for a monument to Abraham Lincoln who would have said, with Emerson, "I love and honor Epaminondas—but I do not wish to be Epaminondas. I hold it more just to love the world of this hour, than the world of his hour."

Here the cornice, being by nature and derivation so inappropriate to the "great commoner," gave to the doctor his opportunity for final triumph. The doctor has now succeeded in using it where most awful—too insulting. When we see this, almost any of us—even the "best" of us—may fully realize why cornices had to die, for at least "let us desire not to disgrace the soul!"

Now, for some time to come, democratic governmental departments being what they are, it may be that America will continue to be-cornice her dead heroes, dishonor them by its impotence. But there is ample evidence at hand on every side that the "quick," at least, have shed the cornice. The sacred symbol is worn out—to be soon obliterated by free thought.

It is time man sealed this tradition under a final monument. I suggest as an admirable "project" for the students in architecture at Princeton a design for this monument, and by way of epitaph:

"Here lies the most cherished liar of all the ages—rest, that we may find peace."

For the first six thousand years of the world, from the pagodas of Hindustan to the Cathedral of Cologne, architecture was the great writing of mankind. Whoever then was born a poet became an architect. All the other arts were the workmen of the great work. The "symbol" unceasingly characterized, when it did not dogmatize, it all. Stability was an ideal—hence a great error of progress. What consecration there then was, was devoted to a conservation of previous primitive types.

According to the great modern poet, neglected now, quoted at the outset of this discourse—in the Hindu, Egyptian, and Roman edifices it was always the priest, . . . in the Phoenician, the merchant, . . . in the Greek, the aristocratic republican, . . . in the Gothic, the bourgeois. In the twentieth century—says our prophet—an architect of genius may happen, as the accident of Dante happened in the thirteenth, although architecture will no longer be the social art, the collective art, the dominant art. The great work of humanity it will be no longer.

But to Victor Hugo, when he spoke, architecture was the grand residue of the great buildings that wrote the record of a theocratic, feudalistic humanity, theologic, philosophic, aristocratic. Concerning that architecture his prophecy has come true. He foresaw democracy as a consequence, but did not foresee the consequences of its engine—the machine—except as that engine was symbolized by printing. He seems not to have foreseen that genius and imagination might find in the machine mightier means than ever with which to create anew a more significant background and framework for twentieth century civilization than was ever known before. Nor foreseen an architect who might create anew in genuine liberty—*for* great liberty—on soil enriched by the very carcasses of the ancient architectures. So let us take heart . . . we begin anew.

But instead of ourselves indulging in prophecy against prophecy, let us take hold of the cornice at the source from which it came to us, and take it apart—in order to see what the feature actually was. It may give us something useful in our own hard case. Perhaps we may find in it something valuable to the "modern"—in the sense that we ourselves are to be modern or die disgraced. Of course I visited Athens—held up my hand in the clean Mediterranean air against the sun and saw the skeleton of my hand through its covering of pink flesh— saw the same translucence in the marble pillars of the aged Parthenon, and realized what "color" must have been in such light. I saw the yellow-stained rocks of the barren terrain. I saw the ancient temples, barren, broken, yellow-stained too, standing now magnificent in their crumbling state, more a part of that background than ever they were when born—more stoic now than allowed to be when those whose record they were had built them—more heroic, as is the Venus of Melos, more beautiful without her arms. Like all who stand there, I tried to re-create the scene as it existed when pagan love of color made it come ablaze for the dark-skinned, kinky-haired, black-eyed Greeks to whom color must have been naturally the most becoming thing in life. I restored the arris of the moldings, sharpened and perfected the detail of the cornices, obliterated the desolate grandeur of the scene with color, sound, and movement. And gradually I saw the whole as a great painted, wooden temple. Though now crumbling to original shapes of stone, so far as intelligence went at that time there were no stone forms whatsoever. The forms were only derived from wood! I could not make them stone, hard as I might try. Nor had the Greeks cared for that stone quality in their buildings, for if traces found are to be trusted, and nature too, not only the forms but the marble surfaces themselves were all originally covered with decoration in gold and color. Marble sculpture was no less so covered, than was the architecture.

All sense of materials must have been lost or never have come alive to the Greeks. No such sympathy with environment as I now saw existed for them, nor had any other inspired them. No—not at all. These trabeated stone buildings harked back to what? A little study showed the horizontal lines of wooden beams, laid over vertical wooden posts, all delicately sculptured to refine and make elegant the resemblance. The pediments, especially the cornices, were the wooden projections of the timber roofs of earlier wooden temples, sculptured here in stone. Even the method of that ancient wood construction was preserved in more "modern" material, by way of the large, wooden beam ends that had originally rested on the wooden lintels, and by the smaller wooden beam ends that rested above those; even such details as the wooden pins that had fastened the beam structure together were here as sculptured stone ornament. Here then in all this fibrous trabeation was no organic stone building. Here was only a wooden temple as a "tradition" embalmed—in noble material. Embalmed, it is

true, with grace and refinement. But beyond that, and considering it all as something to be taken for itself, in itself, all was false—arbitrarily to preserve for posterity a tradition. Thought, then, in this life of the Greeks, was not so free? The grand sculptured stone cornices of their greatest building had originally been but the timber edges and projections of an overhanging roof that was intended to drop roof-water free of the walls. Elegant refinements of proportion were not lost upon me, but there was small comfort to see recorded in them—for evermore—that liberty had not gone very far in thought in ancient Greece. Here at this remote day, architecture had been merely prostitution of the new as a servile concession to the high priest of the old order. In the hands of the impeccable Greeks here was noble, beautiful stone insulted and forced to do duty as an imitation enslaved to wood. Well, at any rate, the beautiful marble was itself again falling back from the shame of an artificial glory upon its own, once more. Here too, then, in this triumph was tragedy!

Was all this symbolic—a mere symptom of an artificial quality of thought, an imposition of authority that condemned this high civilization of the Greeks to die? Their "elegant solutions" and philosophic abstractions beneath the beautiful surface—were they as sinister? Were they too as false to nature as their architecture was false? Then why had it all to be born, reborn, and again, and yet again—confusing, corrupting, and destroying, more or less, all subsequent chance of true organic human culture? Here it seemed was subtle poison deadly to freedom. Form and idea or form and function had become separated for the Greeks, the real separation fixed upon a helpless, unthinking people, whose tool was the chattel slave. By what power did such authority exist? In any case what could there be for democracy in this sophisticated abstraction, made by force, whether as intelligence or as power?

And then I thought of the beauty of Greek sculpture and the perfect vase of the Greeks . . . . Keats' "*Ode on a Grecian Urn*" came to mind. How different the sculpture and the vase were from their architecture—and yet the same. But Phidias fortunately had the living human body for his tradition.

He was modern and his works eternal. The vase was sculpture too, pure and simple, so it could be perfected by them. It would live and represent them at their best. And their great stone architecture—it, too, was beautiful "sculpture"—but it had for its architectural *tradition* only a wooden temple!

It should die: here today in our new freedom, with the machine as liberator of the human mind, quickener of the artist-conscience—it is for us to bury Greek architecture deep. For us it is pagan poison. We have greater buildings to build upon a more substantial base—an ideal of organic architecture, complying with the ideal of true democracy.

Democracy is an expression of the dignity and worth of the individual; that ideal of democracy is essentially the thought of the man of Galilee, himself a humble architect, the architect in those days called carpenter. When this *unfolding* architecture as distinguished from *enfolding* architecture comes to America there will be truth of feature, to truth of being: individuality realized as a noble attribute of *being*. *That* is the character the architecture of democracy will take and probably that architecture will be an expression of the highest form of aristocracy the world has conceived, when we analyze it. Now what architecture? Clearly this new conception will realize architecture as no longer the sculptured block of some building material or as any *enfolding* imitation. Architecture must now *un*fold an inner content—express "life" from the "within." Only a development according to nature, intelligently aimed-at purpose, will materialize this ideal, so there is very little to help us in the old sculptural ideals of the architecture Victor Hugo wrote about, so splendidly prophetic. And what little there is, is confined within the carved and colored corners of the world where and when it was allowed to be itself—and is underneath the surface, in far out-of-the-way places, hard to find.

But I imagine the great romantic poet himself would be first to subscribe to this modern ideal of an organic architecture, a *creation* of industry wherein power unlimited lies ready for use by the *modern mind,* instead of the *creature* of chisel and hammer once held ready in the hands of the chattel slave. An architecture no longer composed or arranged or

pieced together as symbolic, but living as upstanding expression of reality. This organic architecture, too, would be so intimately a *growth,* all the while, as to make barbarous the continual destruction of the old by the new. American architecture, though both little and young, therefore conceives something deeper and at the same time more vital than the great Parthenon or even the beautiful Greek vase: an architecture no longer symbolic sculpture but a true culture that will *grow* greater buildings and *grow* more beautiful belongings true to the nature of the thing and more at one with the nature of man. Radical, its roots where they belong—in the soil—this architecture would be likely to live where all else has had to die or is dying.

Being integral this art will not know contrasted and separate existence as art, but will be as much "nature" as we are ourselves natural. This should be the expression of any true democracy. Such an ideal is nowise pagan, more nearly of the Crusades maybe—but racial or national no longer except in superficial sense. It is only the method, the proper technique in which to use our resources with new sense of materials, that remains to be realized. This realization may truly be said to be modern: new in the thought of the coming world, in which the new and the old shall be as one.

Now comes the usual feeling that this discourse has all been too free in idealization, not intimate enough realization of a very simple matter. The discourse simply means that make-believe is played out; that it has no longer nor ever had genuine significance as art; that we are in a hard but hopeful case where any pretense fails to satisfy us. Something has happened in this new ideal of freedom we call America that is contagious and goes around the world. I don't even know that it belongs to us as a nation particularly, because we, being the thing itself, seem to realize it least. It is often so. Of that which a man is most, he usually speaks least unless he has to speak, and then he will tell you less than someone who is not so much the thing himself, but can see it a little apart, in perspective. We see then that in us is a deeper hunger—a hunger for integrity. For some such reason as this we are waking to see ourselves as the provincial dumping-ground for the cast-off regalia of civilization entire. We have been the village aristocracy of the great art world—"putting on" the style we took "by taste" from the pattern-books, or saw at the movies, or admired on postcards sent home by those who have "been abroad"—don't you know? It never occurred to us that we had greater and more coming to us *as our own* than any of the aristocracy of art we aped and imitated ever had. But now we are beginning to see that even Colonial was a "hangover," was a cornice, a nice, neat one, but the machine soon made it nasty-nice. *Ad libitum,* intoxicated by facility of "reproduction," we ran the gamut of all the "styles," the machine right after us to spoil the party. What, I ask you, in all history haven't we as a "free" people made free with in the name of art and architecture? We have acted like hungry orphans turned loose in a bakeshop.

And like the poor orphans, too, we have a bad case of indigestion now that would kill a less young and robust adventurer in that tasty, pasty, sugary realm we have known as art and decoration. The confectionery we have consumed—yes, but not digested, mind you—would have mussed up the sources from which it came beyond hope of any mortal recovery.

We are sick with it and we are sick of it. Some of us for that reason, and some of us because we are growing up. It was all bad for us—the machine made such "good taste" as we had, poisonous. Spanish was the latest acquired taste until "modernistic" got itself here by way of the Paris market with Madame. We will soon be no better satisfied eating that layer-cake than with the other cake-eating. It is all too modish, too thin, too soon empty—too illiberal, too mean. Our dyspeptic American souls hunger for realization, for a substantial "inner experience." Something more than a mere matter of taste, a taste for cake! All we've had has been predilection in this matter of taste, and we've tasted until we're so taste full that it is only a question of "where do we go from here?"

No wonder sensible Henry says "art is the bunk." He is right; all that *he* has known by that name is no more than what he says it is. And pretty

much all that all America knows, too, is likewise. The corruption of our own sources of power and inspiration shames or amuses us when we try to go deeper. But we are going deeper now, just the same. When we get the *meaning* of our shame we are disgusted—likely we turn from it all, but we come back to it again.

We have realized that life without beauty accomplished is no life; we grasp at anything that promises beauty and are somehow punished. We find that like the rose, it has thorns; like the thistle, it has defenses not to be grasped that way. The old canons have lost fire and force. They no longer apply. We are lost in the face of a great adversary whose lineaments we begin to see. Destruction of the old standards we see on every side. This new thing becomes hateful—but fascinates us. As we struggle, we begin to realize that we live on it, and with it, but still we despise and fear it—nevertheless and all the more because it fascinates us.

Well—we begin to glimpse this great adversary as the instrument of a new order. We are willing to believe there is a common sense. . . . A sense common to our time, directed toward specific purpose. We see an aeroplane clean and light-winged—the lines expressing power and purpose; we see the ocean liner, streamlined, clean, and swift—expressing power and purpose. The locomotive, too—power and purpose. Some automobiles begin to look the part. Why are not buildings, too, indicative of their special purpose? The forms of things that are perfectly adapted to their function, we now observe, seem to have a superior beauty of their own. We like to look at them. Then, as it begins to dawn on us that form follows function—why not so in architecture especially? We see that all features in a good building, too, should correspond to some necessity for being—the reason for them, as well as for other shapes, being found in their very purpose. Buildings are made of materials, too. Materials have a life of their own that may enter into the building to give it more life. Here certain principles show countenance. It is the countenance of organic simplicity. Order is coming out of chaos. The word organic now has a new meaning, a spiritual one! Here is hope.

With this principle in mind we see new value in freedom because we see new value in individuality. And there is no individuality without freedom. The plane is a plane; the steamship is a steamship; the motorcar is a motorcar, and the more they are and *look* just that thing, the more beautiful we find them. Buildings too—why not? Men too? Why not? And now we see democracy itself in this fresh light from within as an ideal that is consistent with all these new expressions of this new power in freedom. We see this adversary to the old order, the machine, as—at last—a sword to cut old bonds and provide escape to freedom; we see it as the servant and savior of the new order—if only it be creatively used by man! Now, how to use it?

Then—what architecture?

4: THE CARDBOARD HOUSE

"Inasmuch as the rivalry of intelligences is the life of the beautiful—O poet!—the first rank is ever free. Let us remove everything which may disconcert daring minds and break their wings! Art is a species of valor. To deny that men of genius to come may be the peers of the men of genius of the past would be to deny the ever-working power of God!"

Now what architecture for America?

Any house is a far too complicated, clumsy, fussy, mechanical counterfeit of the human body. Electric wiring for nervous system, plumbing for bowels, heating system and fireplaces for arteries and heart, and windows for eyes, nose, and lungs generally. The structure of the house, too, is a kind of cellular tissue stuck full of bones, complex now, as the confusion of bedlam and all beside. The whole interior is a kind of stomach that attempts to digest objects—objects, "objets d'art" maybe, but objects always. There the affected affliction sits, ever hungry—for ever more objects—or plethoric with over plenty. The whole life of the average house, it seems, is a sort of indigestion. A body in ill repair, suffering indisposition—constant tinkering and doctoring to keep alive. It is a marvel we its infestors do not go insane in it and with it. Perhaps it is a form of insanity we have put into it. Lucky we are able to get something else out of it, though we do seldom get out of it alive ourselves.

But the passing of the cornice with its enormous "baggage" from foreign parts in its train clears the way for American homes that may be modern biography and poems instead of slanderous liars and poetry-crushers.

A house, we like to believe, is *in status quo* a noble consort to man and the trees; therefore the house should have repose and such texture as will quiet the whole and make it graciously at one with external nature.

Human houses should not be like boxes, blazing in the sun, nor should we outrage the machine by trying to make dwelling-places too complementary to machinery. Any building for humane purposes should be an elemental, sympathetic feature of the ground, complementary to its nature-environment, belonging by kinship to the terrain. A house is not going anywhere, if we can help it. We hope it is going to stay right where it is for a long, long time. It is not yet anyway even a moving-van. Certain houses for Los Angeles may yet become vans and roll off most anywhere or everywhere, which is something else again and far from a bad idea for certain classes of our population.

But most new "modernistic" houses manage to look as though cut from cardboard with scissors, the sheets of cardboard folded or bent in rectangles with an occasional curved cardboard surface added to get relief. The cardboard forms thus made are glued together in box-like forms—in a childish attempt to make buildings resemble steamships, flying machines, or locomotives. By way of a new sense of the character and power of this machine age, this house strips and stoops to conquer by emulating, if not imitating, machinery. But so far, I see in most of the cardboard houses of the "modernistic" movement small evidence that their designers have mastered either the machinery or the mechanical processes that build the house. I can find no evidence of integral method in their making. Of late, they are the superficial, badly built product of this superficial, new "surface-and-mass" aesthetic falsely claiming French painting as a parent. And the houses themselves are not the new working of a fundamental architectural principle in any sense.

They are little less reactionary than was the cornice—unfortunately for Americans, looking forward, lest again they fall victim to the mode. There is, however, this much to be said for this house—by means of it imported art and decoration may, for a time, completely triumph over "architecture." And such architecture as it may triumph over—well, enough has already been said here, to show how infinitely the cardboard house is to be preferred to that form of bad surface-decoration. The simplicity of nature is not something which may easily be read—but is inexhaustible. Unfortunately the simplicity of these houses is too easily read—visibly an attitude, strained or forced. They are therefore decoration too. If we look into their construction we may see how construction itself has been complicated or confused, merely to arrive at exterior simplicity. Most of these houses at home and abroad are more or less badly built complements to the machine age, of whose principles or possibilities they show no understanding, or, if they do show such understanding to the degree of assimilating an aspect thereof, they utterly fail to make its virtues honorably or humanly effective in any final result. Forcing surface-effects upon mass-effects which try hard to resemble running or steaming or flying or fighting machines, is no radical effort in any direction. It is only more scene-painting and just another picture to prove Victor Hugo's thesis of Renaissance architecture as the setting sun, eventually passing with the cornice.

The machine—we are now agreed, are we not—should build the building, if the building is such that the machine may build it naturally and therefore build it supremely well. But it is not necessary for that reason to build as though the building, too, were a machine, because, except in a very low sense, indeed, it is not a machine, nor at all like one. Nor in that sense of being a machine, could it be architecture at all! It would be difficult to make it even good decoration for any length of time. But I propose, for the purposes of popular negation of the cornice-days that are passed and as their final kick into oblivion, we might now, for a time, make buildings resemble modern bathtubs and aluminum kitchen utensils, or copy pieces of well-designed machinery to live in, particularly the ocean liner, the aeroplane, the streetcar, and the motorbus. We could trim up the trees, too, shape them into boxes—cheese or cracker—cut them to cubes and triangles or tetrahedron them and so make all kinds alike suitable consorts for such houses. And we are afraid we are eventually going to have as citizens machine-made men, corollary to machines, if we don't look out? They might be face-masked, head-shaved, hypodermically rendered even less emotional than they are, with patent leather put over their hair and aluminum clothes cast on their bodies, and Madame herself altogether stripped and decoratively painted to suit. This delicate harmony, characteristic of machinery, ultimately achieved, however, could not be truly affirmative, except insofar as the negation, attempted to be performed therein, is itself affirmative. It seems to me that while the engaging cardboard houses may be appropriate gestures in connection with "Now What Architecture," they are merely a negation, so not yet truly conservative in the great cause which already runs well beyond them.

Organic simplicity is the only simplicity that can answer for us here in America that pressing, perplexing question, "Now What Architecture?" This I firmly believe. It is vitally necessary to make the countenance of simplicity the affirmation of reality, lest any affectation of simplicity, should it become a mode or fashion, may only leave this heady country refreshed for another foolish orgy in surface decoration of the sort lasting thirty years "by authority and by order," and by means of which democracy has already nearly ruined the look of itself for posterity, for a half-century to come, at least.

Well then and again, "what architecture?"

Let us take for text on this, our fourth afternoon, the greatest of all references to simplicity, the inspired admonition: *"Consider the lilies of the field—they toil not; neither do they spin, yet verily I say unto thee—Solomon in all his glory was not arrayed like one of these."* An inspired saying attributed to a humble architect in ancient times, called carpenter, who gave up architecture nearly two thousand years ago to go to work upon its source.

And if the text should seem to you too far away from our subject this afternoon—

"THE CARDBOARD HOUSE"

—consider that for that very reason the text has been chosen. The cardboard house needs an antidote. The antidote is far more important than the house. As antidote—and as practical example, too, of the working out of an ideal of organic simplicity that has taken place here on American soil, step by step, under conditions that are your own—could I do better than to take apart for your benefit the buildings I have tried to build, to show you how they were, long ago, dedicated to the ideal of organic simplicity? It seems to me that while another might do better than that, I certainly could not, for that is, truest and best, what I know about the subject. What a man *does, that* he has.

When, "in the cause of architecture," in 1893, I first began to build the houses, sometimes referred to by the thoughtless as the "New School of the Middle West" (some advertiser's slogan comes along to label everything in this our busy woman's country), the only way to simplify the awful building in vogue at the time was to conceive a finer entity—a better building—and get it built. The buildings standing then were all tall and all tight. Chimneys were lean and taller still, sooty fingers threatening the sky. And beside them, sticking up by way of dormers through the cruelly sharp, sawtooth roofs, were the attics for "help" to swelter in. Dormers were elaborate devices, cunning little buildings complete in themselves, stuck to the main roof slopes to let "help" poke heads out of the attic for air.

Invariably the damp, sticky clay of the prairie was dug out for a basement under the whole house, and the rubble-stone walls of this dank basement always stuck up above the ground a foot or more and blinked, with half-windows. So the universal "cellar" showed itself as a bank of some kind of masonry running around the whole house, for the house to sit upon like a chair. The lean, upper house walls of the usual two floors above this stone or brick basement were wood, set on top of this masonry-chair, clapboarded and painted, or else shingled and stained, preferably shingled and mixed, up and down, all together with moldings crosswise. These overdressed wood house walls had, cut in them—or cut out of them, to be precise—big holes for the big cat and little holes for the little cat to get in and out or for ulterior purposes of light and air. The house walls were be-corniced or bracketed up at the top into the tall, purposely profusely complicated roof, dormers plus. The whole roof, as well as the roof as a whole, was scalloped and ridged and tipped and swanked and gabled to madness before they would allow it to be either shingled or slated. The whole exterior was bedeviled—that is to say, mixed to puzzle-pieces, with corner-boards, panel-boards, window frames, corner-blocks, plinth-blocks, rosettes, fantails, ingenious and jigger work in general. This was the only way they seemed to have, then, of "putting on style." The scrollsaw and turning-lathe were at the moment the honest means of this fashionable mongering by the wood-butcher and to this entirely "moral" end. Unless the householder of the period were poor indeed, usually an ingenious corner-tower on his house eventuated into a candlesnuffer dome, a spire, an inverted rutabaga or radish or onion or—what is your favorite vegetable? Always elaborate bay windows and fancy porches played "ring around a rosy" on this "imaginative" corner feature. And all this the building of the period could do equally well in brick or stone. It was an impartial society. All material looked pretty much alike in that day.

Simplicity was as far from all this scrap pile as the pandemonium of the barnyard is far from music. But it was easy for the architect. All he had to do was to call: "Boy, take down No. 37, and put a bay window on it for the lady!"

So—the first thing to do was to get rid of the attic and, therefore, of the dormer and of the useless "heights" below it. And next, get rid of the unwholesome basement, entirely—yes, absolutely—in any house built on the prairie. Instead of lean, brick chimneys, bristling up from steep roofs to hint at "judgment" everywhere, I could see necessity for one only, a broad generous one, or at most, for two, these kept low down on gently sloping roofs or perhaps flat roofs. The big fireplace below, inside, became now a place for a real fire, justified the great size of this chimney outside. A real fireplace at that time was extraordinary. There were then "mantels" instead. A mantel was a marble frame for a few coals, or a piece of wooden furniture with tiles stuck in it and a "grate," the whole set slam up against the wall. The "mantel" was an insult to comfort, but the *integral* fireplace became an important part of the building itself in the houses I was allowed to build out there on the prairie. It refreshed me to see the fire burning deep in the masonry of the house itself.

Taking a human being for my scale, I brought the whole house down in height to fit a normal man; believing in no other scale, I broadened the mass out, all I possibly could, as I brought it down into spaciousness. It has been said that were I three inches taller (I am 5' 8½" tall), all my houses would have been quite different in proportion. Perhaps.

House walls were now to be started at the ground on a cement or stone water table that looked like a low platform under the building, which it usually was, but the house walls were stopped at the second-story windowsill level, to let the rooms above come through in a continuous window-series, under the broad eaves of a gently sloping, overhanging roof. This made enclosing screens out of the lower walls as well as light screens out of the second-story walls. Here was true *enclosure of interior space.* A new sense of building, it seems.

The climate, being what it was, a matter of violent extremes of heat and cold, damp and dry, dark and bright, I gave broad protecting roof shelter to the whole, getting back to the original purpose of the "cornice." The undersides of the roof projections were flat and light in color to create a glow of reflected light that made the upper rooms not dark, but delightful. The overhangs had double value, shelter and preservation for the walls of the house as well as diffusion of reflected light for the upper story, through the "light screens" that took the place of the walls and were the windows.

At this time, a house to me was obvious primarily as interior space under fine *shelter.* I liked the sense of shelter in the "look of the building." I achieved it, I believe. I then went after the variegate

bands of material in the old walls to eliminate odds and ends in favor of one material and a single surface from grade to eaves, or grade to second-story sill-cope, treated as simple enclosing screens—or else made a plain screen band around the second story above the windowsills, turned up over on to the ceiling beneath the eaves. This screen band was of the same material as the underside of the eaves themselves, or what architects call the "soffit." The planes of the building parallel to the ground were all stressed, to grip the whole to earth. Sometimes it was possible to make the enclosing wall below this upper band of the second-story, from the second story windowsill clear down to the ground, a heavy "wainscot" of fine masonry material resting on the cement or stone platform laid on the foundation. I liked that wainscot to be of masonry material when my clients felt they could afford it.

As a matter of form, too, I liked to see the projecting base, or water table, set out over the foundation walls themselves as a substantial preparation for the building. This was managed by setting the studs of the walls to the inside of the foundation walls, instead of to the outside. All door and window tops were now brought into line with each other with only comfortable head-clearance for the average human being. Eliminating the sufferers from the "attic" enabled the roofs to lie low. The house began to associate with the ground and become natural to its prairie site. And would the young man in architecture ever believe that this was all "new" then? Not only new, but destructive heresy, or ridiculous eccentricity. So new that what little prospect I had of ever earning a livelihood by making houses was nearly wrecked. At first, "they" called the houses "dress-reform" houses, because society was just then excited about that particular "reform." This simplification looked like some kind of "reform" to them. Oh, they called them all sorts of names that cannot be repeated, but "they" never found a better term for the work unless it was "horizontal Gothic," "temperance architecture" (with a sneer), etc., etc. I don't know how I escaped the accusation of another "renaissance."

What I have just described was all on the *outside* of the house and was there chiefly because of what had happened *inside*. Dwellings of that period were "cut up," advisedly and completely, with the grim determination that should go with any cutting process. The "interiors" consisted of boxes beside or inside other boxes, called *rooms*. All boxes inside a complicated boxing. Each domestic "function" was properly box to box. I could see little sense in this inhibition, this cellular sequestration that implied ancestors familiar with the cells of penal institutions, except for the privacy of bedrooms on the upper floor. They were perhaps all right as "sleeping boxes." So I declared the whole lower floor as one room, cutting off the kitchen as a laboratory, putting servants' sleeping and living quarters next to it, semi-detached, on the ground floor, screening various portions in the big room, for certain domestic purposes like dining or reading, or receiving a formal caller. There were no plans like these in existence at the time and my clients were pushed toward these ideas as helpful to a solution of the vexed servant-problem. Scores of doors disappeared and no end of partition. They liked it, both clients and servants. The house became more free as "space" and more livable, too. Interior spaciousness began to dawn.

Having got what windows and doors there were left lined up and lowered to convenient human height, the ceilings of the rooms, too, could be brought over onto the walls, by way of the horizontal, broad bands of plaster on the walls above the windows, the plaster colored the same as the room ceilings. This would bring the ceiling-surface down to the very window tops. The ceilings thus expanded, by extending them downward as the wall band above the windows, gave a generous overhead to even small rooms. The sense of the whole was broadened and made plastic, too, by this expedient. The enclosing walls and ceilings were thus made to flow together.

Here entered the important element of plasticity—indispensable to successful use of the machine, the true expression of modernity. The outswinging windows were fought for because the casement window associated the house with out-of-doors—gave free openings, outward. In other words, the so-called "casement" was simple and

more human. In use and effect more natural. If it had not existed I should have invented it. It was not used at that time in America, so I lost many clients because I insisted upon it when they wanted the "guillotine" or "double-hung" window then in use. The guillotine was not simple nor human. It was only expedient. I used it once in the Winslow House—my first house—and rejected it thereafter, forever. Nor at that time did I entirely eliminate the wooden trim. I did make it "plastic," that is, light and continuously flowing instead of the heavy "cut and butt" of the usual carpenter work. No longer did the "trim," so-called, look like carpenter work. The machine could do it perfectly well as I laid it out. It was all after quiet.

This plastic trim, too, with its running "backhand," enabled poor workmanship to be concealed. It was necessary with the field resources at hand at that time to conceal much. Machinery versus the union had already demoralized the workmen. The machine resources were so little understood that extensive drawings had to be made merely to show the "mill-man" what to leave off. But the "trim" finally became only a single, flat, narrow, horizontal wood band running around the room, one at the top of the windows and doors and another next to the floors, both connected with narrow, vertical, thin wood bands that were used to divide the wall surfaces of the whole room smoothly and flatly into folded color planes. The trim merely completed the window and door openings in this same plastic sense. When the interior had thus become wholly plastic, instead of structural, a new element, as I have said, had entered architecture. Strangely enough, an element that had not existed in architectural history before. Not alone in the trim, but in numerous ways too tedious to describe in words, this revolutionary sense of the plastic whole, an instinct with me at first, began to work more and more intelligently and have fascinating, unforeseen consequences. Here was something that began to organize itself. When several houses had been finished and compared with the house of the period, there was very little of that house left standing. Nearly every one had stood the house of the period as long as he could stand it, judging by appreciation of the change. Now all this probably tedious description is intended to indicate directly in bare outline how thus early there *was* an ideal of organic simplicity put to work, with historical consequences, here in your own country. The main motives and indications were (and I enjoyed them all):

First—To reduce the number of necessary parts of the house and the separate rooms to a minimum, and make all come together as enclosed space—so divided that light, air, and vista permeated the whole with a sense of unity.

Second—To associate the building as a whole with its site by extension and emphasis of the planes parallel to the ground, but keeping the floors off the best part of the site, thus leaving that better part for use in connection with the life of the house. Extended level planes were found useful in this connection.

Third—To eliminate the room as a box and the house as another by making all walls enclosing screens—the ceilings and floors and enclosing screens to flow into each other as one large enclosure of space, with minor subdivisions only.

Make all house proportions more liberally human, with less wasted space in structure, and structure more appropriate to material, and so the whole more livable. *Liberal* is the best word. Extended straight lines or streamlines were useful in this.

Fourth—To get the unwholesome basement up out of the ground, entirely above it, as a low pedestal for the living portion of the home, making the foundation itself visible as a low masonry platform on which the building should stand.

Fifth—To harmonize all necessary openings to "outside" or to "inside" with good human proportions and make them occur naturally—singly or as a series in the scheme of the whole building. Usually they appeared as "light-screens" instead of walls, because all the "architecture" of the house was chiefly the way these openings came in such walls as were grouped about the rooms as enclosing screens. The *room* as such was now the essential architectural expression, and there were to be no holes cut in walls as holes are cut in a box, because this was not in keeping with the ideal of "plastic." Cutting holes was violent.

Sixth—To eliminate combinations of different materials in favor of mono-material so far as possible; to use no ornament that did not come out of the nature of materials to make the whole building clearer and more expressive as a place to live in, and give the conception of the building appropriate revealing emphasis. Geometrical or straight lines were natural to the machinery at work in the building trades then, so the interiors took on this character naturally.

Seventh—To incorporate all heating, lighting, plumbing so that these systems became constituent parts of the building itself. These service features became architectural and in this attempt the ideal of an organic architecture was at work.

Eighth—To incorporate as organic architecture—so far as possible—furnishings, making them all one with the building and designing them in simple terms for machine work. Again straight lines and rectilinear forms.

Ninth—Eliminate the decorator. He was all curves and all efflorescence, if not all "period."

This was all rational enough so far as the thought of an organic architecture went. The particular forms this thought took in the feeling of it all could only be personal. There was nothing whatever at this time to help make them what they were. All seemed to be the most natural thing in the world and grew up out of the circumstances of the moment. Whatever they may be worth in the long run is all they are worth.

Now *simplicity* being the point in question in this early constructive effort, organic simplicity I soon found to be a matter of true coordination. And beauty I soon felt to be a matter of the sympathy with which such coordination was effected. Plainness was not necessarily simplicity. Crude furniture of the Roycroft-Stickley-Mission Style, which came along later, was offensively plain, plain as a barn door—but never was simple in any true sense. Nor, I found, were merely machine-made things in themselves simple. To think "in simple," is to deal in simples, and that means with an eye single to the altogether. This, I believe, is the secret of simplicity. Perhaps we may truly regard nothing at all as simple in itself. I believe that no one thing in itself is ever so, but must achieve simplicity (as an artist should use the term) as a perfectly realized part of some organic whole. Only as a feature or any part becomes an harmonious element in the harmonious whole does it arrive at the estate of simplicity. Any wild flower is truly simple but double the same wild flower by cultivation, it ceases to be so. The *scheme* of the original is no longer clear. Clarity of design and perfect significance both are first essentials of the spontaneously born simplicity of the lilies of the field who neither toil nor spin, as contrasted with Solomon who had "toiled and spun"—that is to say, no doubt had put on himself and had put on his temple, properly "composed," everything in the category of good things but the cookstove.

Five lines where three are enough is stupidity. Nine pounds where three are sufficient is stupidity. But to eliminate expressive words that intensify or vivify meaning in speaking or writing is not simplicity; nor is similar elimination in architecture simplicity—it, too, may be stupidity. In architecture, expressive changes of surface, emphasis of line, and especially textures of material, may go to make facts eloquent, forms more significant. Elimination, therefore, may be just as meaningless as elaboration, perhaps more often is so. I offer any fool, for an example.

To know what to leave out and what to put in, just where and just how—ah, *that* is to have been educated in knowledge of simplicity.

As for objects of art in the house, even in that early day they were the *bête noir* of the new simplicity. If well chosen, well enough in the house, but only if each was properly digested by the whole. Antique or modern sculpture, paintings, pottery, might become objectives in the architectural scheme and I accepted them, aimed at them, and assimilated them. Such things may take their places as elements in the design of any house. They are then precious things, gracious and good to live with. But it is difficult to do this well. Better, if it may be done, to design all features together. At that time, too, I tried to make my clients see that furniture and furnishings, not built in as integral features of the building, should be designed as attributes of whatever furniture was built in and should be seen as mi-

nor parts of the building itself, even if detached or kept aside to be employed on occasion. But when the building itself was finished, the old furniture the clients already possessed went in with them to await the time when the interior might be completed. Very few of the houses were, therefore, anything but painful to me after the clients moved in and, helplessly, dragged the horrors of the old order along after them.

But I soon found it difficult, anyway, to make some of the furniture in the "abstract"; that is, to design it as architecture and make it "human" at the same time—fit for human use. I have been black and blue in some spot, somewhere, almost all my life from too intimate contacts with my own furniture. Human beings must group, sit, or recline—confound them—and they must dine, but dining is much easier to manage and always was a great artistic opportunity. Arrangements for the informality of sitting comfortably, singly or in groups, where it is desirable or natural to sit, and still to belong in disarray to the scheme as a whole—that is a matter difficult to accomplish. But it can be done now, and should be done, because only those attributes of human comfort and convenience, made to belong in this digested or integrated sense to the architecture of the home as a whole, should be there at all, in modern architecture. For that matter about four-fifths of the contents of nearly every home could be given away with good effect to that home. But the things given away might go on to poison some other home. So why not at once destroy undesirable things . . . make an end of them?

Here then, in foregoing outline, is the gist of America's contribution to modern American architecture as it was already under way in 1893. But the gospel of elimination is one never preached enough. No matter how much preached, simplicity is a spiritual ideal seldom organically reached. Nevertheless, by assuming the virtue by imitation—or by increasing structural makeshifts to get superficial simplicity—the effects may cultivate a taste that will demand the reality in course of time, but it may also destroy all hope of the real thing.

Standing here, with the perspective of long persistent effort in the direction of an organic architecture in view, I can again assure you out of this initial experience that repose is the reward of true simplicity and that organic simplicity is sure of repose. Repose is the highest quality in the art of architecture, next to integrity, and a reward for integrity. Simplicity may well be held to the fore as a spiritual ideal, but when actually achieved, as in the "lilies of the field," it is something that comes of itself, something spontaneously born out of the nature of the doing whatever it is that is to be done. Simplicity, too, is a reward for fine feeling and straight thinking in working a principle, well in hand, to a consistent end. Solomon knew nothing about it, for he was only wise. And this, I think, is what Jesus meant by the text we have chosen for this discourse: "Consider the lilies of the field," as contrasted, for beauty, with Solomon.

Now, a chair *is* a machine to sit in.

A home *is* a machine to live in.

The human body *is* a machine to be worked by will.

A tree *is* a machine to bear fruit.

A plant *is* a machine to bear flowers and seeds.

And, as I've admitted before somewhere, a heart *is* a suction pump. Does that idea thrill you?

Trite as it is, it may be as well to think it over because the *least* any of these things may be, *is* just that. All of them are that before they are anything else. And to violate that mechanical requirement in any of them is to finish before anything of higher purpose can happen. To ignore the fact is either sentimentality or the prevalent insanity. Let us acknowledge in this respect, that this matter of mechanics is just as true of the work of art as it is true of anything else. But, were we to stop with that trite acknowledgment, we should only be living in a low, rudimentary sense. This skeleton rudiment accepted, *understood, is* the first condition of any fruit or flower we may hope to get from ourselves. Let us continue to call this flower and fruit of ourselves, even in this machine age, art. Some architects, as we may see, now consciously acknowledge this "machine" rudiment. Some will eventually get to it by circuitous mental labor. Some *are* the thing itself without question and already in need of "treatment." But "Americans" (I prefer to be more spe-

cific and say "Usonians") have been educated "blind" to the higher human uses of it all—while actually in sight of this higher human use all the while.

Therefore, now let the declaration that "all is machinery" stand nobly forth for what it is worth. But why not more profoundly declare that "form follows function" and let it go at that? Saying "form follows function" is not only deeper, it is clearer, and it goes further in a more comprehensive way to say the thing to be said, because the implication of this saying includes the heart of the whole matter. It may be that function follows form, as, or if, you prefer, but it is easier thinking with the first proposition just as it is easier to stand on your feet and nod your head than it would be to stand on your head and nod your feet. Let us not forget that the simplicity of the universe is very different from the simplicity of a machine.

New significance in architecture implies new materials qualifying form and textures, requires fresh feeling, which will eventually qualify both as "ornament." But "decoration" must be sent on its way or now be given the meaning that it has lost, if it is to stay. Since "decoration" became acknowledged as such, and ambitiously set up for itself as decoration, it has been a makeshift, in the light of this ideal of organic architecture. Any house decoration, as such, is an architectural makeshift, however well it may be done, unless the decoration, so-called, is part of the architect's design in both concept and execution.

Since architecture in the old sense died and decoration has had to shift for itself more and more, all so-called decoration is become *ornamental,* therefore no longer *integral.* There can be no true simplicity in either architecture or decoration under any such condition. Let decoration, therefore, die for architecture, and the decorator become an architect, but not an "interior architect."

Ornament can never be applied to architecture any more than architecture should ever be applied to decoration. All ornament, if not developed within the nature of architecture and as organic part of such expression, vitiates the whole fabric no matter how clever or beautiful it may be as something in itself.

Yes—for a century or more decoration has been setting up for itself, and in our prosperous country has come pretty near to doing very well, thank you. I think we may say that it is pretty much all we have now to show as domestic architecture, as domestic architecture still goes with us at the present time. But we may as well face it. The interior decorator thrives with us because we have no architecture. Any decorator is the natural enemy of organic simplicity in architecture. He, persuasive doctor-of-appearances that he *must* be when he becomes architectural substitute, will give you an imitation of anything, even an imitation of imitative simplicity. Just at the moment, he is expert in this imitation. France, the born decorator, is now engaged with Madame, owing to the good fortune of the French market, in selling us this ready-made or made-to-order simplicity. Yes, imitation simplicity is the latest addition to imported stock. The decorators of America are now equipped to furnish *especially* this. Observe. And how very charming the suggestions conveyed by these imitations sometimes are!

Would you have again the general principles of the spiritual ideal of organic simplicity at work in our culture? If so, then let us reiterate: first, simplicity is constitutional order. And it is worthy of note in this connection that 9 x 9 equals 81 is just as simple as 2 + 2 equals 4. Nor is the obvious more simple necessarily than the occult. The obvious is obvious simply because it falls within our special horizon, is therefore easier for us to *see*, that is all. Yet all simplicity near or far has a countenance, a visage, that is characteristic. But this countenance is visible only to those who can grasp the whole and enjoy the significance of the minor part, as such, in relation to the whole when in flower. This is for the critics.

This characteristic visage may be simulated—the real complication glossed over, the internal conflict hidden by surface and belied by mass. The internal complication may be and usually is increased to create the semblance of and get credit for simplicity. This is the simplicity-lie usually achieved by most of the "surface and mass" architects. This is for the young architect.

Truly ordered simplicity in the hands of the great artist may flower into a bewildering profusion, exquisitely exuberant, and render all more clear than ever. Good William Blake says exuberance is *beauty,* meaning that it is so in this very sense. This is for the modern artist with the machine in his hands. False simplicity—simplicity as an affectation, that is, simplicity constructed as a decorator's *outside* put upon a complicated, wasteful engineer's or carpenter's "structure," outside or inside—is not good enough simplicity. It cannot be simple at all. But that is what passes for simplicity, now that startling simplicity-effects are becoming the *fashion*. That kind of simplicity is *violent*. This is for "art and decoration."

Soon we shall want simplicity inviolate. There is one way to get that simplicity. My guess is, there is *only* one way really to get it. And that way is, on principle, by way of *construction* developed as architecture. That is for us, one and all.

5: THE TYRANNY OF THE SKYSCRAPER

Michelangelo built the first skyscraper, I suppose, when he hurled the Pantheon on top of the Parthenon. The Pope named it St. Peter's and the world called it a day, celebrating the great act ever since in the sincerest form of human flattery possible. As is well known, that form is imitation.

Buonarroti, being a sculptor himself (he was painter also but, unluckily, painted pictures of sculpture), probably thought architecture, too, ought to be sculpture. So he made the grandest statue he could conceive out of Italian Renaissance architecture. The new church dome that was the consequence was empty of meaning or of any significance whatever except as the Pope's mitre has it. But, in fact, the great dome was just the sort of thing authority had been looking for as a symbol. The world saw it, accepted and adopted it as the great symbol of great authority. And so it has flourished as this symbol ever since, not only in the great capitals of the great countries of the world, but, alas, in every division of *this* country, in every state, in every county, in every municipality thereof.

From general to particular the imitation proceeds, from the dome of the national Capitol itself to the dome of the state capitol. From the state capitol to the dome of the county courthouse, and then from the county courthouse on down to the dome of the city hall. Everywhere the symbol leaves us, for our authority, in debt to Michelangelo for life. Great success the world calls this and Arthur Brisbane called it great art. Many institutions of learning also adopted the dome. Universities themselves affected it until they preferred Gothic. Big business, I suspect, covets it and would like to take it. But to its honor be it said that it has not yet done so. Yes—this is success. Probably every other sculptor who ever lived would like to have done or to do the thing that Michelangelo did.

Yet, as consequence of a great sculptor's sense of grandeur in an art that was not quite his own, we may see a tyranny that might well make the tyrannical skyscraper of the present day sway in its socket, sick with envy, although the tyrannical dome is by no means so cruel as the tyrannical skyscraper. But the tyrannical dome *is* more magniloquent waste. How tragic it all is! It is not only as though Buonarroti himself had never seen the Grand Canyon, which of course he never could have seen, but it is as though no one else had ever seen it either, and monumental buildings therefore kept right on being domeous, domicular, or domeistic—on stilts because they knew no better.

Domed or damned was and is the status of official buildings in all countries, especially in ours, as a consequence of the great Italian's impulsive indiscretion. But no other individual sculptor, painter, or architect, let us hope, may ever achieve such success again, or architecture at the end of its resources may pass out in favor of something else.

It would be interesting to me to know what Buonarroti would think of it now. But it is too late. We shall never know except as we imagine it for ourselves.

We should have to ignore the cradle-of-the-race, Persia, even Rome itself, to say that the sculptor did more than appropriate the dome. The earlier Romans had already made fat ones thrusting against the building walls, and the domes of Persia, relatively modest, though seated deep in the building, were tall and very beautiful. Stamboul and Hagia Sophia, of course, make St. Peter's look like the scrap pile of reborn posts, pilasters, and moldings of the Graeco-Roman sort that it is.

But Buonarroti got his dome up higher than all others—got it out of the building itself up onto stilts! Ah! That was better. History relates, however, that a hurry-up call had to be sent in at the last moment for the blacksmith. A grand chain was needed, and needed in a hurry, too, to keep this monumental grandeur, up there where it was, long enough for it to do its deadly work. While they were getting this grand chain fastened around the haunches of the grand dome, in jeopardy on its stilts, our hero, the truly great sculptor, deeply, or rather highly, in trouble with architecture, must have known some hours of anguish such as only architects can ever know.

I can imagine the relief with which he crawled into bed when all was secure, and slept for thirty-six hours without turning over. This contribution "by the greatest artist who ever lived"—Arthur Brisbane said that is what he is—was our grandest heritage from the rebirth of architecture in Italy, called the Renaissance, and countless billions it has cost us to brag like that.

But all triumph, humanly speaking, is short-lived and we ourselves have found a new way to play hobbyhorse with the Renaissance—a way particularly our own—and now we, in our time, astonish the world similarly. We are not putting a dome up on stilts—no, but we are carrying the stilts themselves on up higher than the dome ever stood and hanging reborn architecture, or architecture-soon-to-be-born, all over the steel, chasing up and down between the steel-stilts in automatic machines at the rate of a mile a minute; until the world gasps, votes our innovation a success, and imitates. Another worldly success, but not this time empty in the name of grandeur. By no means; we are no longer like that. We are doing it for money, mind you, charging off whatever deficit may arise in connection therewith to advertising account. We are now, ourselves, running races up into the sky for advertising purposes, not necessarily advertising authority now but still nobly experimenting with human lives, meantime carrying the herd-instinct to its logical conclusion. Eventually, I fervently hope, carrying the aforesaid instinct to its destruction by giving it all that is coming to it so that it will have to get out into the country where it belongs—and stay there, for the city will be no more, having been "done to death."

Our peculiar invention, the skyscraper, began on our soil when Louis H. Sullivan came through the door that connected my little cubicle with his room in the Auditorium tower, pushed a drawing board with a stretch of manila paper upon it over onto my draughting table.

There it was, in delicately penciled elevation. I stared at it and sensed what had happened. It was the Wainwright Building—and there was the very first human expression of a tall steel office building as architecture. It was tall and consistently so—a unit, where all before had been one cornice building on top of another cornice building. This was a greater achievement than the papal dome, I believe, because here was utility become beauty by sheer triumph of imaginative vision.

Here out of chaos came one harmonious thing in service of human need where artist-ingenuity had struggled with discord in vain. The vertical walls were vertical screens, the whole emphatically topped by a broad band of ornament fencing the top story, resting above the screens, and thrown into shade by an extension of the roof-slab that said, emphatically, "*finished*." The extension of the slab had no business to say "finished," or anything else, so emphatically above the city streets, but that was a minor matter soon corrected. The skyscraper as a piece of architecture had arrived.

About the same time John Wellborn Root conceived a tall building that was a unit, the Monadnock. But it was a solid-walled brick building with openings cut out of the walls. The brick, however, was carried across openings on concealed steel angles and the flowing contours, or profile, unnatural to brickwork was got by forcing the material—hundreds of special molds for special bricks being made—to work out the curves and slopes. Both these buildings therefore had their faults. But the Wainwright Building has characterized all skyscrapers since, as St. Peter's characterized all domes, with

this difference: there was synthetic architectural stuff in the Wainwright Building, it was in the line of organic architecture—St. Peter's was only grandiose sculpture.

A man in a congested downtown New York street, not long ago, pointed to a vacant city lot where steam shovels were excavating. "I own it," he said, in answer to a question from a man next to him (the man happened to be me), "and I own it clear all the way up," making an upward gesture with his hand. Yes, he did own it, "all the way up," and he might have added, too, "all the way down through to the other side of the world." But then he might have thoughtfully qualified it by, "at least through to the center of the earth." Yes, there stood His Majesty, legal ownership. Not only was he legally free to sell his lucky lot in the landlord lottery to increase this congestion of his neighbors "all the way up," but he was blindly encouraged by the great city itself to do so, in favor of super-concentration. The city, then, gets a thrill out of "going tall"? Architects, advertising as wholesale "manufacturers of space for rent," are advocating tall, taller, and tallest, in behalf of their hardy clients. Inventive genius, too, properly invited, aids and abets them all together, until this glorious patriotic enterprise, space-making for rent, is looked upon as bonafide proof of American progress and greatness. The space-makers-for-rent say skyscrapers solve the problem of congestion, and might honestly add, create congestion, in order to solve it some more some other day, until it will all probably dissolve out into the country, as inevitable reaction. Meantime, these machine-made solutions with an ancient architectural look about them all, like the Buonarroti dome, are foolishly imitated out on the western prairies and in the desolate mountain states. In large or even in smaller and perhaps even in very small towns, you may now see both together.

Our modern steel Goliath has strayed as far away from native moorings as Tokyo, Japan, where it is almost as appropriate to that country as the cornice is appropriate to Abraham Lincoln, in our own.

This apotheosis of the landlord may be seen now as another tyranny—the tyranny of the skyscraper. It is true, so it seems, that "it is only on extremes that the indolent popular mind can rest."

Having established an approximate form for these lectures—a preliminary amble in the direction of the subject, then a reference to authority as text, then the discourse, and a conclusion to lay it finally before you, all in the good old manner of my father's sermons—let us keep the form, choosing as text this time: "Do unto others as ye would that others should do unto you." The attribution is universally known. But not so well known perhaps is the command by Moti, the Chinese sage: "Do yourselves that which you would have others do themselves."

The Tyranny of the Skyscraper

It has only just begun, but we may observe that Father Knickerbocker's village, to choose our most conspicuous instance, is already gone so far out of drawing, beyond human scale, that—become the great metropolis—it is no good place in which to live, to do good work in, or wherein even to go to market. This, notwithstanding the stimulus or excitation of the herd-instinct that curses the whole performance.

Nonetheless—in fact just because of this—the price of ground that happens to be caught in the urban drift as it runs uptown in a narrow streak—no doubt to rush back again—soars just because the lucky areas may be multiplied by as many times as it is possible to sell over and over again the original ground area—thanks to the mechanical device of the skyscraper. The ground area used to be multiplied by ten, it was soon multiplied by fifty, and it may now be multiplied by one hundred or more. Meantime, we patiently pass over wide, relatively empty spaces in the city to get from one such congested area to another such congested area, waiting patiently, I suppose, until the very congestion, which is the source of inflated values, overreaches itself by solution and the very congestion it was built to serve severely interferes with and finally curses its own sacred sales privilege. New York, even at this very early stage of the high and narrow, speaks of the traffic problem, openly confessing such congestion—though guardedly. And as con-

gestion must rapidly increase, metropolitan misery has merely begun. Yes—merely begun—for should every owner of a lot contiguous to or even already within the commercially exploited areas, not to mention those hopefully lying empty in between, actually take advantage of this opportunity to soar, all upward flights of ownership would soon become useless and worthless. This must be obvious to anyone. Moreover the occupants of the tall buildings are yet only about one-third the motorcar men that all will eventually emerge if their devotion to machine-made concentration means anything profitable to them.

So only those congestion-promoters with their space-manufacturers and congestion-solvers who came first, or who will now make haste, with their extended telescopes, uplifted elephant trunks, Bedford-stone rockets, Gothic toothpicks, modern fountain pens, shrieking verticality, selling perpendicularity to the earthworms in the village lane below, can ever be served. Nevertheless property owners lost between the luck, continue to capitalize their undeveloped ground on the same basis as the man lucky enough to have got up first into the air. So fictitious land values are created on paper. Owing to the vogue of the skyscraper, real estate values boom on a false basis, and to hold and handle these unreal values, now aggravated by the machine-made, standard solution, subways—sub-subways, are proposed, and super sidewalks, or super, super sidewalks, or double-decked or triple-decked streets. Proposals are made to set all the fair forest of buildings up out of reach of the traffic on their own fair stilts as a concession to the crowd. The human life flowing in and out of all this crowded perpendicularity is to accommodate itself to growth as of potato sprouts in a cellar. Yes—these super-most solutions are seriously proposed to hold and handle landlord *profits* in a dull craze for verticality and vertigo that concentrates the citizen in an exaggerated super-concentration that would have shocked Babylon and have made the tower of Babel itself fall down to the ground and worship.

"To have and to hold," that is now the dire problem of the skyscraper minded. Just why it should be unethical or a weakness to allow this terrific concentration to relieve itself by spreading out is quite clear. Anyone can see why. And to show to what lengths the landlord is willing and prepared to go to prevent it: as superior and philanthropic a landlord as Gordon Strong of Chicago recently argued—as the Germans originally suggested—the uselessness of the freedom of sun and air, claiming artificial ventilation and lighting now preferable, demanding that walls be built without windows, rooms be hermetically sealed, distribution and communication be had by artificially lighted and ventilated tunnels, subways, and super-ways. Here, on behalf of the landlord, by way of the time-serving space-maker-for-rent, we arrive at the "City of Night": Man at last and all so soon enslaved by, and his very life at the mercy of, his own appliances.

A logical conclusion, this one of Gordon Strong's, too, with its strong points—if the profits of exciting and encouraging the concentration of citizens are to be kept up to profitable pitch and the citizen be further educated and reconciled to such increased congestion as this would eventually put up to him. This patient citizen—*so much more valuable, it seems, if and when congested!* Must the patient animal be further congested or further trained to congest himself until he has utterly relinquished his birthright? Congested yet some more and taught—he can learn—to take his time (his *own* time especially, mind you), and watch his step more carefully than ever? Is he, the pickle in this brine, to be further reconciled or harder pushed to keep on insanely crowding himself into vertical grooves in order that he may be stalled in horizontal ones?

Probably—but in the name of common sense and an organic architecture, why should the attempt be made to so reconcile him, by the architects themselves, at least architects are yet something more than hired men, I hope. Else why should they not quit and get an honest living by honest labor in the country, preparing for the eventual urban exodus?

May we rightfully assume architecture to be in the service of humanity?

Do we not know that if architecture is not reared and maintained in such service it will eventually be damned?

The city, too, for another century, may we not still believe, was intended to add to the happiness, security, and beauty of the life of the individual considered as a human being? Both assumptions, however, are denied by the un-American false premium put upon congestion by the skyscraper-minded: un-American, I say, because for many years past rapid mobilizing, flying, motoring, tele-transmission, steadily proceeding, have given back to man the sense of space, free space, in the sense that a great, free, new country ought to know it—given it back again to a free people. Steam took it away. Electricity and the machine are giving it back again to man and have not only made super-concentration in a tight, narrow tallness unnecessary, but vicious, as the human motions of the city-habitant became daily more and more compact and violent. All appropriate sense of the space-values the American citizen is entitled to now in environment are gone in the great American city, as freedom is gone in a collision. Why are we as architects, as citizens, and as a nation, so slow to grasp the nature of this thing? Why do we continue to allow a blind instinct driven by greed to make the fashion and kill, for a free people in a new land, so many fine possibilities in spacious city planning? The human benefits of modern automobilization and teletransmission—where are they? Here we may see them all going by default, going by the board, betrayed—to preserve a stupid, selfish tradition of proprietorship. Is it because we are all, more or less, by nature and opportunity, proprietors? Are we proprietors first and free men afterward—if there is any afterward? At any rate, all these lately increased capacities of men for a wide range of lateral movement due to mechanicization are becoming useless to the citizen, because we happen to be sympathetic to the cupidity of proprietorship and see it not only as commercially profitable but as sensational.

Now, as a matter of course and in common with all Usonian villages that grow up into great cities and then grow on into the great metropolis, Father Knickerbocker's village grew up to its present jammed estate; the great metropolis grew up on the original village gridiron. New York, even without skyscrapers and automobiles, would have been crucified long ago by the gridiron. Barely tolerable for a village, the grid becomes a dangerous crisscross check to all forward movements even in a large town where horses are motive power. But with the automobile and skyscraper that opposes and kills the automobile's contribution to the city, stop-and-go attempts to get across to somewhere or to anywhere, for that matter, in the great metropolis, are inevitable waste—dangerous and maddening to a degree where sacrificial loss, in every sense but one, is for everyone.

Erstwhile village streets become grinding pits of metropolitan misery. Frustration of all life, in the-village-that-became-a-city, is imminent in this, the great unforeseen metropolis; the machine that built it and furnishes it forth also was equally unforeseen. Therefore it may not be due, alone, to this ever-to-be-regretted but inherited animal tendency of his race to herd, that the citizen has landed in all this urban jam. But that animal tendency to herd is all that keeps him jammed now against his larger and more important interests as a thinking being. He is tragically, sometimes comically, jammed. True, properly fenced, he jams himself. Properly fenced he may continue to jam himself for another decade or so, and cheerfully take the consequences. Strangely helpless for long periods of time is this Usonian, human social unit! But let us try to believe that—as Lincoln observed—not all of him for all of the time.

Now what does the human unit, so far in contempt in all this commercial bedlam, receive as recompense for the pains of stricture and demoralizing loss of freedom, for the insulting degradation of his appropriate sense of space? What does he receive beside a foolish pride in the loss of himself to his time, increase in his taxes, and increase in the number of handsome policemen at crossings?

A little study shows that the skyscraper in the rank and file of the "big show" is becoming something more than the rank abuse of a commercial expedient. *I see it as really a mechanical conflict of machine resources. An internal collision!* Even the landlord must soon realize that, as profitable landlordism, the success of verticality is but temporary, both in kind and character, because the citizen of the near future pre-

ferring horizontality—the gift of his motorcar, and telephonic or telegraphic inventions—will turn and reject verticality as the body of any American city. The citizen himself will turn upon it in self-defense. He will gradually abandon the city. It is now quite easy and safe for him to do so. Already the better part of him can do better than remain.

The landlord knows to his dismay that to sell the first ten floors of New York City is his new problem. The city fathers, too, now see that, except on certain open spaces, and under changed conditions where beautiful tall buildings might well rise as high as the city liked, the haphazard skyscraper in the rank and file of city streets is doomed—doomed by its own competition. In certain strategic locations in every village, town, or city, tall buildings, and as tall as may be, should be permissible. But even in such locations very tall buildings should be restricted to only such area of the lot on which they stand as can be lighted from the outside and be directly reached from a single interior vertical groove of direct entrance to such space. Normal freedom of movement may thus be obtained below on the lot area that is proprietary to the building itself. Thus all tall building would be restricted to the central portion thus usable of each private lot area, adding the balance of that area, as park space, to the city streets. There would then be no longer interior courts in any building.

All real estate in the rank and file and upon which the tall buildings will cast their shadows, and from which they must partly borrow their light, should in building stay down to the point where the streets will be relieved of motorcar congestion, whether that point be three, five, seven, or nine stories, this to be determined according to the width of the streets on which the buildings stand.

As for the widening of streets, the present sidewalk and curb might be thrown into the street as transportation area, and the future sidewalks raised to headroom above the present street level, becoming in skillful hands well-designed architectural features of the city. And these elevated sidewalks should be connected across, each way, at the street intersections and down, by incline, to the streets below at the same four points of street intersections. This would make all pedestrian movement free of automobilization and, crossing in any direction above the traffic, safe. Motorcars might be temporarily parked just beneath these elevated sidewalks, the sidewalks, perhaps, cantilevered from the buildings.

Parking space in front of all present shop windows would thus be provided and protected overhead by the elevated sidewalks. Show windows would become double-decked by this scheme. Show windows above for the sidewalks and show windows below for the roadbed. This practical expedient, for of course it is no more than an expedient—only expedients are possible—would put a show-window emphasis on the second-story sidewalk level, which might become a mezzanine for entrances to the different shops also.

Entrances could be had to stores from the roadbed by recessions built in the lower store front or by loggias that might be cut back into them. Such restraint and ordered release for tall buildings as here proposed might enhance the aspect of picturesque tallness and not leave further chaotic unfinished masses jamming into the blue. Such well-designed separation of transportation and pedestrians as this might save the wear and tear of citizens doing daily the stations of the cross on their way to work.

Since in the metropolis the gridiron is organic disaster, and to modify it much is impossible, why not, therefore, accept and respect it as definite limitation and ease it by some such practical expedient? Working toward such modifications as suggested would vastly benefit all concerned:

First—By limiting construction.

Second—By taking pedestrians off the roadbed and so widening it.

The upper sidewalks might be made sightly architectural features of the city. While all this means millions expended, it might be done; whereas to abandon the old cities may be done but to build new ones will not be done.

Various other expedients are now practicable, too, if they were to be insisted upon, as they might well be, in the public welfare—such as allowing no coal to be burned in the city, all being converted into electricity outside at the mines, and cutting down the now absurd automobile sizes of distinctly city carriers. All these things would palliate the evil of the skyscraper situation. But the danger of the city to humanity lies deeper, in the fact that human sensibilities naturally become callous or utterly damned by the constantly increasing futile sacrifices of time and space and patience, when condemned by stricture to their narrow grooves and crucified by their painful mechanical privileges. Condemned by their own senseless excess? Yes, and worse soon.

It seems that it has always been impossible to foresee the great city; not until it has grown up and won an individuality of its own is it aware of its needs. Its greatest asset is this individuality so hard won. The city begins as a village, is sometimes soon a town and then a city. Finally, perhaps, it becomes a metropolis; more often the city remains just another hamlet. But every village could start out with the plans and specifications for a metropolis, I suppose. Some few, Washington D.C. among them, did so and partially arrived after exciting misadventures.

But the necessity for the city wanes because of the larger human interest. That larger human interest? Is it not always on the side of *being,* considering the individual as related, even in his work—why not especially in his work?—to health and to the freedom in spacing, mobile in a free new country; living in and related to sun and air; living in and related to growing greenery about him as he moves and has his little being here in his brief sojourn on an earth that should be inexpressibly beautiful to him!

What is he here for anyway? *Life* is the one thing of value to him, is it not? But the machine-made in a machine age, here in the greatest of machines, a great city, conspires to take that freedom away from him before he can fairly start to civilize himself. We know why it does. And let us at this moment try to be honest with ourselves on another point, this "thrill"—the vaunted *beauty* of the skyscraper as an individual performance. At first, as we have seen, the skyscraper was a pile of cornice-buildings in reborn style, one cornice-building riding the top of another cornice-building. Then a great architect saw it as a unit, and as beautiful architecture. Pretty soon, certain other architects, so educated—probably by the Beaux-Arts—as to see that way, *saw it as a column,* with base, shaft, and capital. Then other architects with other tastes seemed to see it as Gothic—commercial competitor to the cathedral. Now the wholesale manufacturers of space-for-rent are seeing it as a commercial tower-building with plain masonry surfaces and restrained ornament upon which New York's setback laws have forced a certain picturesque outline, an outline pretty much all alike. A picturesqueness at first welcome as a superficial relief, but already visible as the same monotony-in-variety that has been the fate of all such attempts to beautify our country. Standardization defeats these attempts—the machine triumphs over them all, because they are all false. Principle is not at work in them.

The skyscraper of today is only the prostitute semblance of the architecture it professes to be. The heavy brick and stone that falsely represents walls is, by the very setback laws, unnaturally forced onto the interior steel stilts to be carried down by them through twenty, fifty, or more stories to the ground. The picture is improved, but the picturesque element in it all is false work built over a hollow box. These new tops are shams, too—box-balloons. The usual service of the doctor-of-appearances has here again been rendered to modern society.

New York, so far as material wealth goes, piled high and piling higher into the air, is a commercial machine falsely qualified by a thin disguise. The disguise is a collection of brick and masonry façades, glaring signs, and staring dead walls, peak beside peak, rising from canyon cutting across canyon. Everything in the narrowing lanes below is

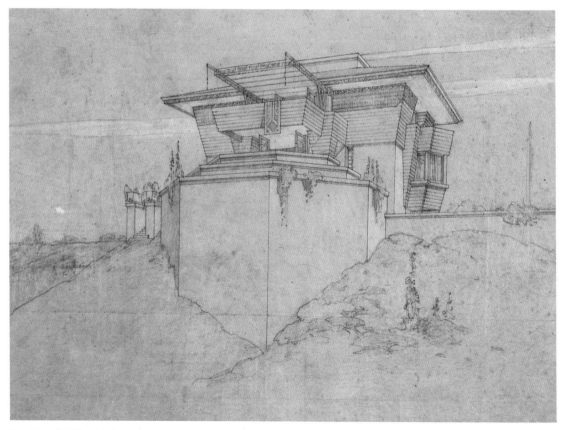

Mrs. Samuel William Gladney House (Project). Fort Worth, Texas. 1925. Perspective. Pencil and color pencil on tracing paper, 15 x 22".
FLLW Fdn#2502.001

"on the hard," groaning, rattling, shrieking! In reality the great machine-made machine is a forest of riveted steel posts, riveted girder-beams, riveted brackets, and concrete slabs, steel reinforced, closed in by heavy brick and stone walls, all carried by the steel framing itself, finally topped by water tanks, set-backs, and spires, dead walls decorated by exaggerated advertising or chastely painted in panels with colored brickwork.

What beauty the whole has is haphazard, notwithstanding the book-architecture which space-makers-for-rent have ingeniously tied onto the splendid steel sinews that strain from story to story beneath all this weight of make-believe. But the lintels, architraves, pilasters, and cornices of the pseudoclassicist are now giving way to the better plainness of surface-and-mass effects. This is making, now, the picturesque external New York, while the steel, behind it all, still nobly stands up to its more serious responsibilities. Some of the more recent skyscraper decoration may be said to be very handsomely suggestive of an architecture to come. But how far away, yet, are appearances from reality!

The true nature of this thing is prostitute to the shallow picturesque, in attempt to render a wholly insignificant, therefore inconsequential, beauty. In any depth of human experience it is an ignoble sacrifice. No factitious sham like this should be accepted as "culture."

As seen in "The Passing of the Cornice," we are the modern Romans.

Reflect that the ancient Romans at the height of their prosperity lied likewise to themselves no less shamefully, when they pasted Greek architecture onto their magnificent engineering invention of the masonry arch to cover it decently. The Romans, too, were trying to make the kind of picture or the grand gesture demanded by culture. The Roman arch was, in that age, comparable to the greatest of all scientific or engineering inventions in our own machine age, comparable especially to our invention of steel. So likewise, what integrity any solution of the skyscraper problem might have in itself as good steel and glass construction has been stupidly thrown away. The native forests of steel, concrete, and glass, the new materials of our time,

have great possibilities. But in the hands of the modern doctor-of-appearances they have been made to *seem* rather than allowed to *be*. Sophisticated polishing by the accredited doctor only puts a glare upon its shame. It cannot be possible that sham like this is really our own civilized choice?

But owing to the neglect of any noble standard such as that of an organic architecture, it is all going by default. All—sold.

Were it only strictly business there would be hope. But even that is not the case except as competitive advertising in any form is good business. Business ethics make a good platform for true aesthetics in this machine age or in any other.

No—what makes this pretentious ignorance so tragic is that there is a conscious yearn, a generosity, a prodigality in the name of taste and refinement in nearly all of it. Were only mummery dropped, temporary expedient though it may be in itself, space-manufacturing-for-rent, so far as that goes in the skyscraper, might become genuine architecture and be beautiful as standardization in steel, metals, and glass.

We now have reasonably safe mechanical means to build buildings as tall as we want to see them, and there are many places and uses for them in any village, town, or city, but especially in the country. Were we to learn to limit such buildings to their proper places and give them the integrity as standardized steel and glass and copper they deserve, we would be justly entitled to a spiritual pride in them; our submission to them would not then be servile in any sense. We might take genuine pride in them with civic integrity. The skyscraper might find infinite expression in variety—as beauty.

But today the great city as an edifice mocks any such integrity. Artists idealize the edifice in graphic dreams of gigantic tombs into which all life has fled—or must flee—or in which humanity remains to perish. Uninhabitable monstrosities? An insanity we are invited to admire?

From any humane standpoint the super-concentration of the skyscraper is super-imposition not worth its human price.

It is impossible not to believe that, of necessity, horizontality and the freedom of new beauty

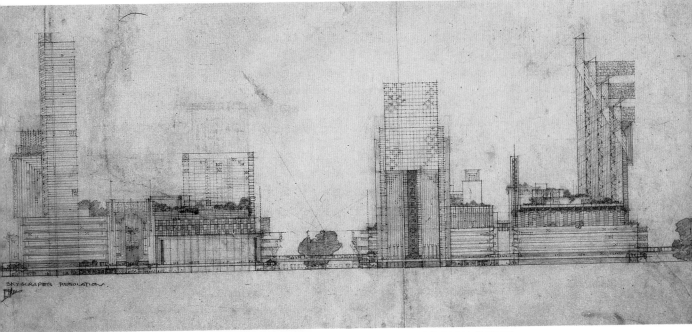

SKYSCRAPER REGULATION.

"Skyscraper Regulation" (Project). 1926. Elevation. Pencil on tracing paper, 35 x 20". FLLW Fdn#2603.001

will eventually take the place of opportune verticality and senseless stricture. And if these desiderata cannot be realized *in* the city, if they have no place there, they will take *the place of the city*. Breadth is now possible and preferable to verticality and vertigo, from any sensible human standpoint. Transportation and electrical transmission have made breadth of space more a human asset than ever, else what does our great machine-power mean to human beings? In all the history of human life upon earth, breadth, the consciousness of freedom, the sense of space appropriate to freedom, is more desirable than height to live with in the use and beauty that it yields mankind.

Why then, has commerce, the soul of this great, crude, and youthful nation, any pressing need further to capitalize and exploit the rudimentary animal instincts of the race it thrives on, or need to masquerade in the path picturesque, like the proverbial wolf in sheep's clothing, in New York City or anywhere else?

As for beauty—standardization and its cruel but honest tool, the machine, given understanding and accomplished technique, might make our own civilization beautiful in a new and noble sense. These inept, impotent, mechanistic elements, so cruel in themselves, have untold possibilities of beauty. In spite of prevalent and profitable abuses, standardization and the machine are here to serve humanity. However much they may be out of drawing, human imagination may use them as a means to more life, and greater life, for the commonwealth. So why should the architect as artist shirk or ignore humane possibilities to become anybody's hired man—for profit? Or if he is on his own why should he be willing to pay tribute to false gods merely to please the unsure taste of a transitory period, or even his own "superior" taste?

Today all skyscrapers have been whittled to a point, and a smoking chimney is usually the point. They whistle, they steam, they moor dirigibles, they wave flags, or they merely aspire, and nevertheless very much resemble each other at all points. They compete—they pictorialize—and are all the same.

But they do not materialize as architecture. Empty of all other significance, seen from a distance something like paralysis seems to stultify them. They are monotonous. They no longer startle or amuse. Verticality is already stale; vertigo has given way to nausea; perpendicularity is changed by corrugation of various sorts, some wholly crosswise, some crosswise at the sides with perpendicularity at the center, yet all remaining envelopes. The types of envelope wearily reiterate the artificial set-back, or are forced back for effect, with only now and then a flight that has no meaning, like the Chrysler Building.

The light that shone in the Wainwright Building as a promise, flickered feebly and is fading away. Skyscraper architecture is a mere matter of a clumsy imitation masonry envelope for a steel skeleton. They have no life of their own—no life to give, receiving none from the nature of construction. No, none. And they have no relation to their surroundings. Utterly barbaric, they rise regardless of special consideration for environment or for each other, except to win the race or get the tenant. Space as a becoming psychic element of the American city is gone. Instead of this fine sense is come the tall and narrow stricture. The skyscraper envelope is not ethical, beautiful, or permanent. It is a commercial exploit or a mere expedient. It has no higher ideal of unity than commercial success.

6: THE CITY

Is the city a natural triumph of the herd instinct over humanity, and therefore a temporal necessity as a hangover from the infancy of the race, to be outgrown as humanity grows?

Or is the city only a persistent form of social disease eventuating in the fate all cities have met?

Civilization always seemed to need the city. The city expressed, contained, and tried to conserve what the flower of the civilization that built it most cherished, although it was always infested with the worst elements of society as a wharf is infested with rats. So the city may be said to have served civilization. But the civilizations that built the city invariably died with it. Did the civilizations themselves die *of it?*

Acceleration invariably preceded such decay.

Acceleration in some form usually occurs just before decline and while this acceleration may not be the cause of death it is a dangerous symptom. A temperature of 104 in the veins and arteries of any human being would be regarded as acceleration dangerous to life.

In the streets and avenues of the city acceleration due to the skyscraper is similarly dangerous to any life the city may have left, even though we yet fail to see the danger.

I believe the city, as we know it today, is to die.

We are witnessing the acceleration that precedes dissolution.

Our modern civilization, however, may not only survive the city but may profit by it; probably the death of the city is to be the greatest service the machine will ultimately render the human being if, by means of it, man conquers. If the machine conquers, it is conceivable that man will again remain to perish with his city, because the city, like all minions of the machine, has grown up in man's image, minus only the living impetus that is man. The city is itself only man-the-machine—the deadly shadow of sentient man.

But now comes a shallow philosophy accepting machinery, in itself, as prophetic. Philosophers draw plans, picture, and prophesy a future city, more desirable, they say, than the pig-pile now in travail, their pictures reducing everything to a mean height—geometrically spaced.

In order to preserve air and passage, this future city relegates the human individual as a unit or factor to pigeonhole 337611, block F, avenue A, street No. 127. And there is nothing at which to wink an eye that could distinguish No. 337611 from No. 337610 or 27643, bureau D, intersection 118 and 119.

Thus is the sentient individual factor—the citizen—appropriately disposed of in the cavernous recesses of a mechanistic system appropriate to man's ultimate extinction.

This future city may be valuable and utilitarian along a line of march toward the ultimate triumph of the machine over man and may be accomplished before the turn finally comes.

Theatre for Aline Barnsdall (Project). Olive Hill, Hollywood, California. 1915–1920. Perspective. Watercolor and ink wash on art paper, 30 x 7". FLLW Fdn#2005.004

To me it is dire prophecy. Skull and cross-bones symbolize a similar fate. Let us prefer to prophesy, finally, the triumph of man over the machine.

For final text, then, for our final discourse:
"Except as you, sons-of-earth, honor your birth-right, and cherish it well by human endeavor, you shall be cut down, and perish in darkness, or go up in high towers—a sacrifice to the most high God. Look you well, therefore, to yourselves in your posterity. Keep all close to earth, your feet upon the earth, your hands employed in the fruit-fulness thereof be your vision never so far, and on high."
—*Attributed to some unheeded Babylonian prophet.*

What built the cities that, invariably, have died? Necessity.

With that necessity gone, only dogged tradition that is another name for *habit* can keep the city alive, tradition that has the vitality of inertia and the power of the ball and chain.

Necessity built the city when we had no swift, universal means of transportation and had no means of communication except by various direct personal contacts. Then the city became naturally the great meeting place, the grand concourse, the immediate source of wealth and power in human intercourse. Only by congregating thus, the vaster the congregation the better, could the better fruits of human living then be had.

In that day the real life of the city lay in the stress of individual ties and the variety of contacts. The electric spark of curiosity and surprise was alive in the street, in public buildings, in the home.

Government the city had—fashions and fads. But the salt and savor of individual wit, taste, and character made the city a festival of life: a carnival as compared with any city today.

And architecture then reflected this livelier human condition as it now reflects the machine. Nor had the common denominator then arrived in the reckoning.

The common denominator has arrived with the machine in Usonia. Machine prophecy such as

we have just referred to shows, if nothing else, that we are to deal with machinery considered as common-denominator salvation and in its most dangerous form here among us and deal with it soon, before it has finally to deal with our posterity as dominator. To deny virtue to the common denominator or to deny virtue to its eventual emancipator the machine would be absurd. But the eventual city the common denominator will build with its machines will not only be greatly different from the olden city or the city of today; it will be vastly different from the new machine-city of machine-prophecy as we see it outlined by Le Corbusier and his school.

What once made the city the great and powerful human interest that it was is now preparing the reaction that will drive the city somewhere, into something else. The human element in the civic equation may already be seen drifting or pushed—going in several different directions.

Congestion was no unmixed human evil until electricity, electrical intercommunication, motorcars, the telephone, and publicity came; add to these the airship when it lays away its wings and becomes a self-contained mechanical unit.

Accepting all these, everything changes.

Organic consequences of these changes, unperceived at first, now appear. Freedom of human reach and movement, therefore the human *horizon* as a sphere of *action* is, in a single decade, immeasurably widened by new service rendered by the machine. Horizontality has received an impetus that widens human activities immeasurably.

Therefore such need for concentration as originally built the city is really nearing an end. But these new facilities of movement gifts to us of the machine, have, for a time, only intensified the old activity.

We are really witnessing an inevitable collision between mechanistic factors. The struggle is on. Additional human pressure, thus caused, thoughtlessly finds release by piling high into the air. The thoughtless human tendency in any emergency is to stand still, or to run away. We do—stay right there and pile up, or run away from the collision, to live to fight again some other day. To meet this human trait of staying right where we are, the skyscraper was born and, as we have seen, has become a tyranny. But the skyscraper will serve, equally well, those who are to run away, because probably the tall building has its real future in the country. But the skyscraper is now the landlord's ruse to hold the profits not only of concentration but of super-concentration: in the skyscraper itself we see the commercial expedient that enables the landlord to exploit the city to the limit, and exploit it by ordinance.

So greater freedom to spread out without inconvenience, the most valuable gift brought by these new servants, electrical intercommunication, the automobile, telephone, airship, and radio, has been perverted for the moment into the skyscraper, and the gifts of the machine diverted to profit lucky realty.

Let us admit popular thrill in the acceleration, the excitement, directly due to these *new* mechanistic facilities. Temperatures run high. No one seems to know whether the excess is healthy excitement of growth or the fever of disease; whether it means progress or is only some new form of exploitation.

Forces are themselves blind. In all history we may see that the human beings involved with elemental forces remain blind also for long periods of time. But—saving clause—along with the forces released by our new mechanistic servants, there comes in our day an *ubiquitous publicity,* a valuable publicity that often succeeds in getting done in a month what formerly may have drifted a decade. We have already cut elapsed time in all forms of human intercommunication a hundred to one. To be conservative, what took a century in human affairs now takes ten years.

Fifteen years, an epoch.

Thirty years, an age.

So the reactions to any human activity, idea, or movement may control this great agency, and even in one lifetime show the people the wisdom or folly of the nature of any particular activity and call for correction before the affair is too far gone. Thus the fate of earlier civilization may be avoided by the dissemination of knowledge in ours. Educational influences thus brought to bear may avert disaster.

The traffic problem, as we have already seen in "The Tyranny of the Skyscraper," forces attention to tyrannical verticality. The traffic problem is new but increasingly difficult—if not impossible—of solution.

Other problems will call soon and call louder.

As we have seen, the gridiron, originally laid out for the village now grown to the metropolis, already is cause for sufficient economic waste and human pain to wreck the structure of the city. High blood pressure, in the congested veins and arteries that were once the peaceful village gridiron, is becoming intolerable.

The pretended means of relief provided by space-makers-for-rent—the skyscraper itself—is now rendering distress more acute. The same means of relief carried somewhat further, and long before the solution reaches its logical conclusion, will have killed the patient—the overgrown city. Witness the splitting up of Los Angeles and Chicago into several centers, again to be split into many more.

And yet in new machine-prophecy, the tyranny of the skyscraper now finds a philosophy to fortify itself as an *ideal!*

We see, by the prophetic pictures of the city of the future, how the humanity involved therein is to be dealt with in order to render the human benefits of electricity, the automobile, the telephone, the airship, and radio into herd-exploitation instead of into individual human lives.

And alongside these specific skyscraper solutions-by-picture of downtown difficulties there usually goes the problem of the tenement, the none-too-pretty picture of wholesale housing of the poor. The poor, it seems, are still to be with us and multiplied, in this grand new era of the machine. At any rate they are to be accepted, confirmed, and especially provided for therein as we may see in the plans. Catastrophe is to be made organic—built in.

That the poor will benefit by increased sanitation may be seen and granted at first glance. But not only are the living quarters of the poor to be made germ-proof, but life itself, wherever individual choice is concerned, is to be made just as antiseptic, if we trust our own eyes.

The poor man is to become just as is the rich man—No. 367222, block 19, shelf 17, entrance K.

But the surface-and-mass architecture that now proposes to extinguish the poor man as human, has already proposed to do the same for his landlord. Therefore why should the poor man complain? Has he not, still, his labor for his pains?

There he is, the poor man! No longer in a rubbish heap. No. He is a mechanized unit in a mechanical system, but, so far as he goes, he still is but two by twice. He has been cleaned up but toned down.

Nor can the poor in the modernistic picture choose anything aesthetically alive to live with, at least so far as neighbors or landlord can see it. Dirty rags have been covered with a clean cardboard smock.

The poor man is exhibit C—cog 309,761,128 in the machine, in this new model for the greater machine the city is to become.

Observe the simplified aspect!

This indeed, is the *ne plus ultra* of the *e pluribus unum* of machinery. This new scheme for the city is delightfully impartial, extinguishes everyone, distinguishes nothing except by way of the upper stories, unless it be certain routine economies sacred to a businessman's civilization, certain routine economies to be shared by the innovators with the ubiquitous numericals who are the "common denominator," shared with them by the nominators of the system as seen perfected in the picture. Shared fifty-fifty? Half to the initial nominator, half to the numericals? Fair enough—or—who can say?

The indistinguishable division of the benefits must in any case be left to the generosity of the initial nominators themselves, whoever they are. And who may say who they are?

But Humanity here is orderly. Human beings are again rank and file in the great war—this time industrial—a peaceful war. The rank and file of the common denominator this time is gratuitously officered by architecture, standardized like any army, marched not only to-and-fro but up and down. Up and down—even more—much more and more to come. The common denominator on these up-and-down terms would be no more alive without the initial nominator than the machine will be without the human brain. The common denomi-

nator itself has become the machine, come into its very own at last before the war is fairly begun.

"The Noble Duke of York, he had ten thousand men"—he made them all go ten floors up and ten floors up again. And none may know just why they now go narrowly up, up, up, to come narrowly down, down, down—instead of freely going in and out and comfortably around about among the beautiful things to which their lives are related on this earth. Is this not to reduce everyone but the mechanistic devisors and those who may secure the privileges of the top stories, to the ranks of the poor?

Well, the poor?

Why are they the poor? Is there mechanical cure, then, for shiftlessness—machine-made? Or are the thriftless those whom the machine age is to herd beneficially in the mass and cover becomingly with a semblance of decency in a machine-made utopia? Or are the poor now to be the thrifty, themselves thus turned poor in all senses but one?

The lame, halt, blind, and the sick are the only poor. As for the other poor—the discouraged, the unhappy—fresh air, free space, green grass growing all around, fruits, flowers, vegetables in return for the little work on the ground they require, would do more to abolish their poverty than any benefice mechanistic devisors can ever confer.

At present the urban whirl *is* common-denominator recreation; the urban crowd *is* common-denominator consolation; the dark corners of movie halls *are* the common-denominator retreats for recreation when those retreats are not far worse.

And the herd instinct that moves in the crowd and curses it is only the more developed by the mechanistic conditions in which the crowd swarms and lives. Millions are already sunk so low as to know no other preferment, to desire none. The common denominator—so profitable when congested—being further educated to congest, *taught* to be lost when not excited by the pressure and warmth of the crowd, turns Argus-eyed toward what—more whirl?

Yet many of the individuals composing the crowd, the best among them, know well that an ounce of independence and freedom in spacing under natural circumstances, is worth a ton of machine patronage, however disguised or distributed as sanitation or as "art."

A free America, democratic in the sense that our forefathers intended it to be, means just this *individual* freedom for all, rich or poor, or else this system of government we call democracy is only an expedient to enslave man to the machine and make him like it.

But democracy will, by means of the machine, demonstrate that the city is no place for the poor, because even the poor are human.

The machine, once our formidable adversary, is ready and competent to undertake the drudgeries of living on this earth. The margin of leisure even now widens as the machine succeeds. This margin of leisure should be spent with the fields, in the gardens, and in travel. The margin should be expanded and devoted to making beautiful the environment in which human beings are born to live, into which one brings the children who will be the Usonia of tomorrow.

And the machine, I believe—absurd as it may seem now, absurd even to those who are to be the first to leave—will enable all that was human in the city to go to the country and grow up with it: enable human life to be based squarely and fairly on the ground. The sense of freedom in space is an abiding human desire, because the horizontal line is the line of domesticity, the earthline of human life. The city has taken this freedom away.

A market, a countinghouse, and a factory is what the city has already become; the personal element in it all, the individual, withdrawing more and more as time goes on.

Only when the city becomes purely and simply utilitarian, will it have the order that is beauty, and the simplicity which the machine, in competent hands, may very well render as human benefit. That event may well be left to the machine.

This, *the only possible ideal machine* seen as a *city,* will be invaded at ten o'clock, abandoned at four, for three days of the week. The other four days of the week will be devoted to the more or less joyful matter of living elsewhere under conditions natural to man. The dividing lines between town and country are even now gradually disappearing as conditions are reversing themselves. The country absorbs the life of the city as the city shrinks to the utilitarian purpose that now alone justifies its existence. Even that concentration for utilitarian purposes we have just admitted may be first to go, as the result of impending decentralization of industry. It will soon become unnecessary to concentrate in masses for any purpose whatsoever. The individual unit, in more sympathetic grouping on the ground, will grow stronger in the hard-earned freedom gained at first by that element of the city not prostitute to the machine. Henry Ford stated this idea in his plan for the development of Muscle Shoals.

Even the small town is too large. It will gradually merge into the general non-urban development. Ruralism as distinguished from urbanism is American, and truly democratic.

The country already affords great road systems—splendid highways. They, too, leading toward the city at first, will eventually hasten reaction away from it. Natural parks in our country are becoming everywhere available. And millions of individual building sites, large and small, good for little else, are everywhere neglected. Why, where there is so much idle land, should it be parceled out by realtors to families, in strips 25', 50', or even 100' wide? This imposition is a survival of feudal thinking, of the social economies practiced by and upon the serf. An acre to the family should be the democratic minimum if this machine of ours *is a success!*

What stands in the way?

It is only necessary to compact the standardized efficiency of the machine, confine the concentration of its operation to where it belongs and distribute the benefits at large. The benefits are human benefits or they are bitter fruit. Much bitter fruit already hangs on the city-tree beside the good, to rot the whole.

An important feature of the coming disintegration of the Usonian city may be seen in any and every service station along the highway. The ser-

Cinema San Diego (Project). San Diego, California. 1915. Perspective. Watercolor on art paper, 15 x 19". FLLW Fdn#0517.002

FRANK LLOYD WRIGHT · ARCHITECT · San Diego

vice station is future city service in embryo. Each station that happens to be naturally located will as naturally grow into a neighborhood distribution center, meeting-place, restaurant, restroom, or whatever else is needed. A thousand centers as city equivalents to every town or city center we now have, will be the result of this advance agent of decentralization.

To many such traffic stations, destined to become neighborhood centers, will be added, perhaps, features for special entertainment not yet available by a man's own fireside. But soon there will be little not reaching him at his own fireside by broadcasting, television, and publication. In cultural means, the machine is improving rapidly and constantly.

Perfect distribution like ubiquitous publicity is a common capacity of the machine. This single capacity, when it really begins to operate, will revolutionize our present arrangement for concentration in cities. Stores, linked to decentralized chain service stations, will give more perfect machinery of distribution than could ever be had by centralization in cities.

Complete mobilization of the people is another result fast approaching. Therefore the opportunity will come soon for the individual to pick up by the wayside anything in the way of food and supplies he may require, as well as to find a satisfactory temporary lodging.

The great highways are in process of becoming the decentralized metropolis. Wayside interests of all kinds will be commonplace. The luxurious motorbus, traveling over magnificent road systems, will make intercommunication universal and interesting. The railway is already only for the "long haul" in many parts of the country.

A day's journey anywhere will soon be something to be enjoyed in itself, enlivened, serviced, and perfectly accommodated anywhere en route. No need to tangle up in spasmodic stop-and-go traffic in a trip to town or to any city at all.

Cities are great mouths. New York the greatest mouth in the world. With generally perfect distribution of food and supplies over the entire area of the countryside, one of the vital elements helping to build the city has left it forever, to spread out on the soil from which it came: local products finding a short haul direct, where an expensive long haul and then back again was once necessary.

Within easy distance of any man's dwelling will be everything needed in the category of foodstuffs or supplies which the city itself can now supply. The "movies," through television, will soon be seen and heard better at home than in any hall. Symphony concerts, operas, and lectures will eventually be taken more easily to the home than the people there can be taken to the great halls in old style, and be heard more satisfactorily in congenial company. The home of the individual social unit will contain in itself in this respect all the city heretofore could afford, plus intimate comfort and free individual choice.

Schools will be made delightful, beautiful places, much smaller, and more specialized. Of various types, they will be enlivening, charming features along the byways of every *countryside*. Our popular games will be features in the school parks, which will be really sylvan parks available far and near to everyone.

To gratify what is natural and desirable in the get-together instinct of the community natural places of great beauty—in our mountains, seasides, prairies, and forests—will be developed as automobile objectives, and at such recreation grounds would center the planetarium, the racetrack, the great concert hall, the various units of the national theater, museums, and art galleries. Similar common interests of the many will be centered there naturally, ten such places to one we have now.

There will be no privately-owned theaters, although there will be places for them along the highways. But good plays and other entertainments might be seen at these automobile objectives from end to end of the country in various national circuits—wherever a play showed itself popular or desired.

Such objectives would naturally compete with each other in interest and beauty, stimulate travel, and make mobilization a pleasure, not a nuisance— affording somewhere worthwhile to go. The entire countryside would then be a well-developed park—

buildings standing in it, tall or wide, with beauty and privacy for everyone.

There will soon remain the necessity for only shorter and shorter periods of concentration in the offices directly concerned with invention, standardization, and production. The *city of the near future* will be a depot for the factory—perhaps. Whatever it is, it will be only a degraded mechanistic servant of the machine, because man himself will have escaped to find all the city ever offered him, plus the privacy the city never had and is trying to teach him that he does not want. Man will find the *manlike freedom* for himself and his that democracy must mean.

Very well—how to mitigate, meantime, the horror of human life caught helpless or unaware in the machinery that is the city? How easiest and soonest to assist the social unit in escaping the gradual paralysis of individual independence that is characteristic of the machine-made moron, a paralysis of the emotional nature necessary to the triumph of the machine over man, instead of the quickening of his humanity necessary to man's triumph over the machine?

That is the architect's immediate problem, as I see it.

Measured over great free areas, the living interest should be educated to lie in the contact of free individualities in the freedom of sun, light, and air, breadth of spacing—*with* the ground. Again we need the stress of encountering varieties on a scale and in circumstances worthy the ideal of democracy and more a part of external nature than ever before seen—more so because of internal harmony. We want the electric spark of popular curiosity and surprise to come to life again, along the highways and byways and over every acre of the land. In charming homes and schools and significant public gathering places . . . architectural beauty related to natural beauty. Art should be natural and be itself the joy of creating perfect harmony between ourselves and the birthright we have all but sold.

We may now dream of the time when there will be less government, yet more ordered freedom. More generous human spacing, we may be sure, will see to that.

When the salt and savor of individual wit, taste, and character in modern life will have come into its own and the countryside far and near will be a festival of life—great life—then only will man have succeeded with his machine. The machine will then have become the liberator of human life.

And our architecture will reflect this.

Shirking this reality, vaunted "modernity" is still making another "picture," everywhere clinging to the pictorial—missing joy in merely seeking pleasure. "Modernistic" is attempting by fresh attitudinizing to improve the "picture." The "new movement" still seeks to recreate joy by making shift to improve the imitation, neglectful of all but appropriate gestures.

But even an improved imitation as a picture will soon be trampled down and out—because of the machine. No amount of picture making will ever save America now!

The artifex alone in search of beauty can give back the significance we have lost—and enable the republic to arrive at that great art, in the inevitably man-made concerns of life, which will be to the human spirit what clear springs of water, blue sky, green grass, and noble trees are to parched animal senses. For where the work of the artificer is a necessity, there the artist must be creatively at work on *significance* as a higher *form* of life, or the life of the human spirit will perish in this fresh endeavor that as yet is only a promise in this twentieth century.

The necessity for artistry that is laid upon us by the desire to be civilized, is not a matter only of appearances. Human *necessity,* however machine-made or mechanically met, carries within itself the secret of the beauty we must have to keep us fit to live or to live with. We need it to live in or to live on. That new beauty should be something to live *for.* The "picture," never fear, will take care of itself. In any organic architecture the picture will be a natural result, a significant consequence, not a perverse *cause* of pose and sham.

Eventually we must live for the beautiful whether we want to or not. Our industrial champion, Henry Ford, was forced to recognize this—

probably not connecting the beautiful with art, "the bunk." Just as he did in his industry, so America will be compelled to allow necessity its own honest beauty, or die a death nowise different from those nations whose traditions we accepted and idolized.

Unless what we now miscall culture becomes natively fit and is no longer allowed to remain superficial, this picture, which America is so extravagantly busy "pictorializing," can only hasten the end. The buttons, stuffs, dictums, wheels, and things we are now using for the purpose of the picture will smother the essential—the life they were falsely made to falsely conceal instead of to express. And this experiment in civilization we call democracy will find its way to a scrap heap into which no subsequent race may paw with much success for proofs of quality.

Suppose some catastrophe suddenly wiped out what we have done to these United States at this moment. And suppose, ten centuries thereafter, antiquarians came to seek the significance of what *we* were in the veins of us; in the ruins that remained, what would they find? Just what would they find to be the nature of this picture-minded pictorialization of life and its contribution to the wisdom or the beauty of the ages past or to come?

Would the future find we were a jackdaw-people with a monkey-psychology given over to the vice of devices—looking to devices for salvation—and discovering this very salvation to be only another and final device?

No? Just the same, they *would* find broken bits of every civilization that ever took its place in the sun hoarded in all sorts of irrelevant places in ours.

They would dig up traces of sacred Greek monuments for banking houses. The papal dome in cast-iron fragments would litter the ancient site of every seat of authority, together with fragments in stone and terra-cotta of twelfth-century cathedrals where offices and shops were indicated by mangled machinery—relics of dwellings in fifty-seven varieties and fragments of stone in heaps, none genuine in character, all absurdly mixed. They would find the toilet appurtenances of former ages preserved as classic parlor ornaments in ours. They would find a wilderness of wiring, wheels, and complex devices

of curious ingenuity, and—ye gods—what a collection of buttons! They might unearth traces of devices that enabled men to take to the air like birds or to go into the water like fishes, and they might find relics of our competent schemes of transportation, and a network or web of tangled wires stringing across the country, the relic of all our remarkable teletransmissions. But I think the most characteristic relic of all would be our plumbing. Everywhere a vast collection of enameled or porcelain waterclosets, baths and washbowls, white tiles and brass piping. Next would be the vast confusion of riveted steelwork in various states of collapse and disintegration where it had been imbedded in concrete. Where the steel was not so buried all would be gone, except here and there where whole machines—a loom, a Linotype, a cash register, a tractor, a dynamo, a passenger elevator—might be entombed in concrete chambers and so preserved to arouse speculation and curiosity, or to cause amusement as they were taken for relics of a faith in devices—a faith that failed! Of the cherished *picture* we are making, nothing of any significance would remain. The ruin would defy restoration by the historian; it would represent a total loss in human culture, except as a possible warning. A few books might be preserved to assist restoration, although the chemicalized paper now in use would probably have destroyed most of them utterly. Such glass and pottery as we make could tell but little except curious falsehoods. Certain fragments of stone building on the city sites would remain to puzzle the savant, for they would be quite Greek or quite Roman or quite Medieval Gothic, unless they were Egyptian or Byzantine. But mainly they would find heaps of a pseudo-Renaissance—something that never told, nor ever could tell, anything at all. Only our industrial buildings could tell anything worth knowing about us. But few of these buildings would survive that long—electrolysis and rust would have eaten them utterly, excepting those where steel was buried in concrete. Glass fragments would be found in great quantity, but the frames, unless they happened to be bronze, and all else would be gone. They would have no skyscraper to gauge us by. Not one of those we have built would be there.

Phi Gamma Delta Fraternity House (Project). Madison, Wisconsin. 1925. Perspective. Pencil and color pencil on tracing paper, 24 x 20". FLLW Fdn#2504.041

How and where, then, were it suddenly interrupted, would our progressive democratizing based upon picturizing the appliance, take its place in the procession of civilizations that rose and fell at appointed times and places? What architecture would appear in the ruins?

And yet—in all this attempt behind the significantly insignificant picture, may we not see culture itself becoming year by year more plastic? Are not some of our modern ideas less obviously constructed and more potent from within wherever we are beginning to emerge from the first intoxication of liberty? The eventual consequence of individual freedom is surely the elimination by free thought of the insignificant and false. Imprisoning forms and fascinating philosophic abstractions grow weaker as character grows stronger and more enlightened according to nature; this they will do in freedom such as we profess—*if only we will practice* that freedom. And, in spite of our small hypocrisy and adventitious reactions, let no one doubt that we really do yearn to practice genuine freedom to a far greater extent than we do, all inhibitions and prohibitions notwithstanding. Yes, we may see a new sense of manlike freedom growing up to end all this cruel make-believe. Freedom, in reality, is already impatient of pseudoclassic posture and will soon be sick of all picturizing whatsoever.

A common sense is on the rise that will sweep our borrowed finery, and the scene-painting that always goes with it, to the museums, and encourage good life so to live that America may honorably pay her debt to manhood by keeping her promises to her own ideal.

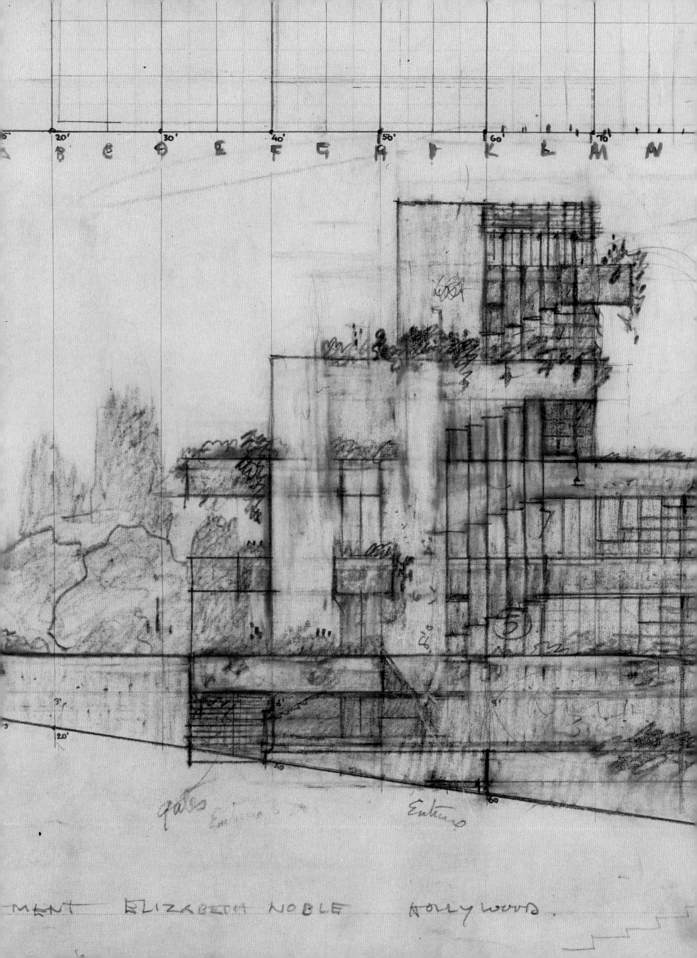

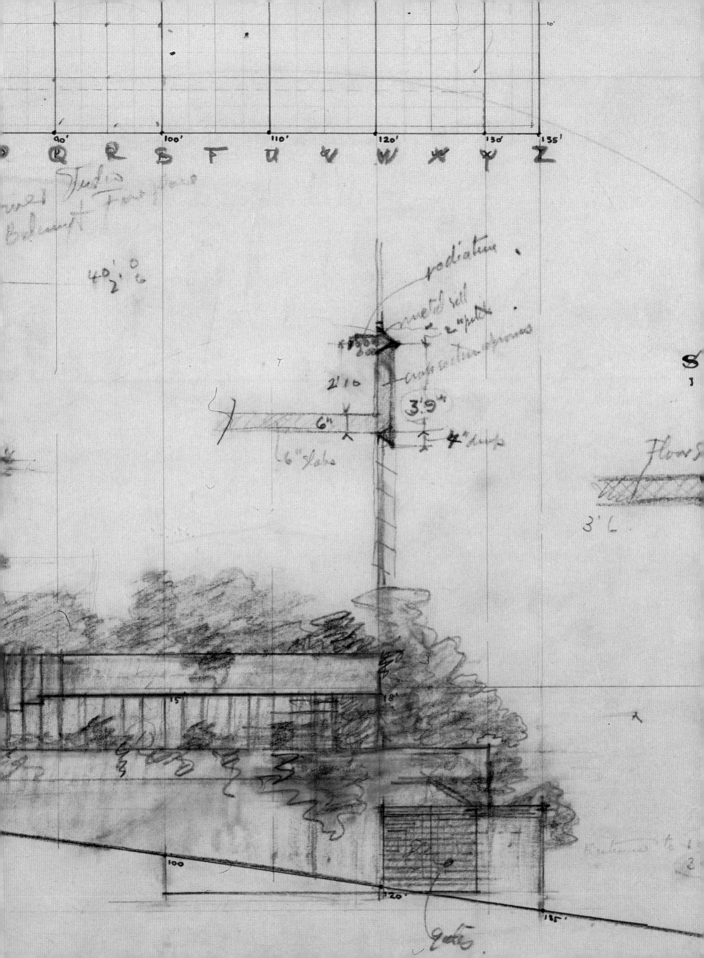

P Q R S T U V W X Y Z

90'   100'   110'   120'   130'   135'   10'

radiation

metal sill

2" pit

2'10

3.9"

6"

6" slab

4" deep

Floor S

3' L

15   18'

100

120'

135'

gate

TWO LECTURES ON ARCHITECTURE

Wright prepared two papers to be delivered at the Art Institute of Chicago on October 1–2, 1930, in connection with an exhibition of his work that was touring the country. In 1931 the lectures were issued as a book-pamphlet under the title Two Lectures on Architecture. When Wright wrote for Architectural Record—as well as for Progressive Architecture and The American Architect—he was speaking directly to professionals or students of architecture. But at the Art Institute the audience was varied, like the audiences who heard him speak in Chicago, Evanston, and Oak Park at the turn of the century. In the first address, "In the Realm of Ideas," he reiterates many earlier themes: how his work evolved, how he considered the design of the American home, how he looked at materials and machine methods. He writes with great clarity and succinctness and consequently is understandable to a nonprofessional audience.

The second address, as its title implies, was directly aimed at the "Young Man in Architecture":

Meantime, since all we have been talking about is a higher and finer kind of integrity, keep your own ideal of honesty so high that your dearest ambition in life will be to call yourself an honest man, and look yourself square in the face. Keep your ideal of honesty so high that you will never be quite able to reach it.

Later to appear in book form first in 1931 and then again in 1953, this stands as one of Wright's most inspired lectures. He warns, cautions, counsels, explains, and guides those youths who aspire to become architects. [Published lectures, The Art Institute of Chicago, 1931]

1. IN THE REALM OF IDEAS

THE IDEALIST HAS ALWAYS BEEN UNDER SUSPICION as performer, perhaps justly. The explorer Stanley wrote of a monkey caught and tied up overnight by a rope around his neck. The monkey gnawed the rope in two and departed, the knot still tied about his neck. Next morning found the monkey with the strange "necktie" trying to go home, but each approach to rejoin the tribe would bring wild cries from his fellows and such commotion—no doubt inspired by the Scribes—that the monkey "with something about him" now—would stop, dazed, pull at his "experience" a little, and think it over. Then he would move toward his fellows again, but such commotion would result that he would have to give it up. The Scribes had succeeded with the Pharisees. This kept up all day because the poor monkey kept on trying to come home, (to "tell the truth"?). Finally just before dark, the whole tribe, exasperated, rushed upon the suspected monkey . . . tore him limb from limb.

Monkey psychology? Of course, but our own tribe too, often destroys on similar suspicion the man who might impart something of tremendous importance and value to his tribe . . . such ideas as this poor suspect might have imparted, concerning how to avoid being caught and tied up, say, or if tied up, how to escape.

In our own tribe we have another tendency, the reverse side of this same shield, and that tendency, no doubt *inherited* too, hails the monkey with delight, puts on rope-ends likewise, makes them the fashion, soon ostracizing any monkey without the fashionable necktie.

And yet as similar experience ideas are not bad in their way, nor are ideas troublesome necessarily, unless they are great and useful ideas. Then, in earnest, the chattering, warning, prophesizing, and crucifying begin with the Scribes. Some form of murder is usually the result. In America we are now perfectly well used to ideas in the mechanical-industrial world. An inventor on that plane is practically immune and may safely come in with almost anything about him or on him and be acclaimed. We will try the thing though we are killed by thousands; we will scrap millions in the way of paper currency to put a shiny new dime in our pockets; as a result we get somewhere among commercial and mechanical lines.

But the absorbed idealist, egocentric inventor in the realm of the thought-built, has a hard time with us socially, financially, and, with peculiar force, morally. In addition to the instinctive fear for the safety of the tribe, in our form of social contract the man with an idea seems to have become an invidious reflection upon his many fellows who have none. And certain effects belonging naturally to the idealist, such as belief in himself as having caught sight of something deeper, wider, higher, or more important just beyond, mark him. He, all unsuspecting, will appear soon on the path as peculiar to his own individuality in ways the poor fool, less absorbed, would have realized as unimportant if true and have kept under cover. Ridicule from his many fellows, safely in the middle of the road, is always ready. And now it is only the incurably *young* person, in our country, who ever attempts to break through all down the line—and is laughed out of countenance, laughed out of a job, and eventually out of house and home.

But at the absorbed idealist the tribe has laughed wrong so many times that the prevailing middle-of-the-road egotists are getting sensitive on the subject. They should realize, as Carlyle reminded us—himself a perfectly good specimen of the absorbed egocentric—"Great thoughts, great hearts once broke for, we breathe cheaply as the common air." History will continue to repeat itself: the middle-of-the-road egotist will keep on breathing cheaply, and egocentric hearts will keep on breaking in the cause of ideas.

But our middle-of-the-road egotist is not so safe as he imagines. He may as well face the fact that just as commerce has no soul, and therefore cannot produce as life, so no inventive genius on the commercial or the mechanical plane can preserve him now. In a flood of carbon monoxide he is hellbound for somewhere and he does not know where. Ask him! He is trapped by the device, soon to be victimized, no doubt, by a *faith* in devices, now become a device in itself, and soon seen as a fool's faith that failed. Meantime, machine overproduction has made the statesman a propagandist for the poor, the banker a bulkhead, the salesman a divinity. Around each revolves a group of white-collar satellites as parasites while the workman himself continues to trip the lever or press the button of the automaton that is substitute for hundreds of workmen like him. Yes, for many reasons America, herself the great middle-of-the-road egotist, should be kind to her absorbed egocentrics. Russia killed off hers, and was compelled to import many before her tragic experiment could turn a wheel forward. America may also bankrupt herself, but America is

(Previous pages): **Elizabeth Noble Apartments (Project). Los Angeles, California. 1929. Elevation. Pencil and color pencil on tracing paper, 26 x 12".** FLLW Fdn#2903.001

likely to bankrupt life by commercial, political, and utensil machinery. No. No political device, no device of organization, no device of salesmanship, no mechanical device can help our country much further on beyond. Only ideas can help her now. Unhappily the word "ideas" and the word "egocentric" come naturally together in human affairs, and go together. Never mind; patience now with the "Nut"; toleration and a turn for the "Crank!"

Although egocentricity may develop egomania all too often and be only a folly, egotism, like other qualities of human nature, is bad only when it is poor and mean in quality, that is to say, pretentious, vain, and selfish; in a word, dishonest. We should realize, too, that *optimism* to the *idealist*, to the *realist pessimism*, are but the two sides of the same shield, both extremes of egotism.

But however all this by way of "setting the stage" may be, I am going to be direct and personal with you now in this matter of ideas.

What a man *does*, that he *has*; and I shall best show you respect by the self-respect that means hereafter talking out of my own experience. Nevertheless I shall try not to sing "but of myself," and so fail, and, like Pei-Woh, prince of Chinese harpists, I shall leave the harp to choose and, as he said, "know not whether the harp be I or I the harp. . . ."

An idea is a glimpse of the nature of the thing as more workable or "practical," as we say (we like that word "practical," but abuse it), than found in current practice or custom. An idea, therefore, is an act expressing in terms of human thought implicit faith in the character of nature, something for lesser men to build and improve upon.

A fancy or conceit trifles with appearances as they are. An idea searches the *sources* of appearances, comes out as a form of inner experiences, to give fresh proof of higher and better order in the life we live. Finally . . . AN IDEA IS SALVATION BY IMAGINATION.

Such ideas as I shall rehearse for you now belong to your immediate present, but instead of saying the "present," to be truthful, we should say, with Lao-tzu, your "infinite." Lao-tzu said two thousand five hundred years ago that the present

was "the ever-moving *infinite* that divides Yesterday from Tomorrow. . . ."

Suppose something you always took for granted as made up of various things, "composed" as artists say, suddenly appeared to you as organic growth. Suppose you caught a glimpse of that "something" as a living entity and saw it as no creature of fallible expediency at all but really a creation living with integrity of its own in the realm of the mind. Suppose too you saw this something only awaiting necessary means to be born as living creation instead of existing as you saw it all about you as miserable makeshift or sentimental, false appliance.

Well, something like this is what happened to Louis Sullivan when he *saw* the first skyscraper, and something like that, in architecture, has been happening to me ever since in various forms of experience.

Thus a single glimpse of reality may change the *world* for any of us if, from the fancies and conceits of mere appearances, we get within the source of appearances. By means of human imagination at work upon this source untold new life may find expression, for, with new force, ideas do actually fashion our visible world. A new order emerges to deepen life that we may become less wasted in anxious endeavor to go from here to somewhere else in order to hurry on somewhere from there. Any true conception as an idea, derived from any *original* source, has similar consequences in all the fields of our common endeavor to build a civilization.

As it worked with Louis Sullivan in designing the skyscraper, thus did going to the source work with me in building houses as the subsequent, consequent, flock of ideas that take flight from any constructive ideal put to work.

Here at hand was the typical American dwelling of 1893 standing about on the Chicago prairies. (I used to go home to Oak Park, a Chicago suburb, which denies Chicago.) That dwelling there became somehow typical, but, by any faith in nature implicit or explicit, it did not belong there. I longed for a chance to build a house and soon got the chance because I was not the only one then sick of hypocrisy and hungry for reality. And I will

Elizabeth Noble Apartments (Project). Los Angeles, California. 1929. Perspective. Pencil on tracing paper, 26 x 16". FLLW Fdn#2903.002

venture to say, at this moment ninety out of a hundred of you are similarly sick.

What was the matter with the house? Well, just for a beginning, it lied about everything. It had no sense of unity at all nor any such sense of space as should belong to a free people. It was stuck up in any fashion. It was stuck on wherever it happened to be. To take any one of those so-called homes away would have improved the landscape and cleared the atmosphere.

This *typical* had no sense of proportion where the human being was concerned. It began somewhere in the wet, and ended as high up as it could get in the blue. All materials looked alike to it or to anybody in it. Essentially this "house" was a bedeviled box with a fussy lid: a box that had to be cut full of holes to let in light and air, with an especially ugly hole to go in and come out of. The holes were all trimmed, the doors trimmed, the roofs trimmed, the walls trimmed. "Joinery," everywhere, reigned supreme. Floors were the only part of the house left

plain. The housewife and her "decorator" covered those with a tangled rug collection, because otherwise the floors were "bare"—"bare" only because one could not very well walk on jigsawing or turned spindles or plaster ornament.

It is not too much to say that as architect my lot was cast with an inebriate lot of criminals, sinners hardened by habit against every human significance, except one. (Why mention "the one touch of nature that makes the whole world kin"?) And I will venture to say, too, that the aggregation was at the lowest aesthetic level in all history: steam heating, plumbing, and electric light its only redeeming features.

The first feeling therefore was for a new simplicity, a new idea of simplicity as organic. Organic simplicity might be seen producing significant character in the harmonious order we call nature: all around, beauty in growing things. None insignificant. I loved the prairie by instinct as a great simplicity, the trees and flowers, the sky itself, thrilling by contrast. I saw that a little of height on the prairie was enough to look like much more. Notice how every detail as to height becomes intensely significant and how breadths all fall short! Here was a tremendous spaciousness sacrificed needlessly, all cut up crosswise and lengthwise into fifty-foot lots, or would you have twenty-five feet? Salesmanship parceled it out and sold it without restrictions. In a great new free entry, everywhere, I could see only a mean tendency to tip up everything in the way of human habitation edgewise instead of letting it lie comfortably flatwise with the ground. Nor has this changed much today since automobilization made it a far less genuine economic issue and a social crime.

I had an idea that the planes parallel to earth in buildings identify themselves with the ground— make the building belong to the ground. At any rate I perceived it and put it to work. I had an idea that every house in that low region should begin *on* the ground—not *in* it, as they then began, with damp cellars. This idea put the house up on the "prairie basement" I devised, entirely above the ground. And an idea that the house should *look* as though it began there *at* the ground put a projecting base-course as a visible edge to this foundation, where as a platform it was seen as evident preparation for the building itself.

An idea that shelter should be the essential look of any dwelling put the spreading roof with generously projecting eaves over the whole; I saw a building primarily not as a cave, but as shelter in the open.

But, before this had come the idea that the size of the human figure should fix every proportion of a dwelling—and, later, why not the proportions of all buildings whatsoever? What other scale could I use? So I accommodated heights in the new buildings to no exaggerated established order but to the human being. I knew the dweller could not afford too much freedom to move about in space at best; so, perceiving the horizontal line as the earthline of human life, I extended horizontal spacing by cutting out all the room partitions that did not serve the kitchen or give privacy for sleeping apartments or (it was the day of the parlor) prevent some formal intrusion into the family circle, like the small social

office set aside as a necessary evil to receive callers. Even this concession soon disappeared as a relic of barbarism.

To get the house down in the horizontal to appropriate proportion with the prairie, the servants had to come down out of the complicated attic and go into a separate unit of their own, attached to the kitchen on the ground floor. Closets disappeared as unsanitary boxes wasteful of floor space: built-in wardrobes took their places.

Freedom of floor space and elimination of useless heights worked a miracle in the new dwelling place. A sense of appropriate freedom changed its whole aspect. The whole became more fit for human habitation and more natural to its site. An entirely new sense of space values in architecture came home. It now appears it came into the architecture of the modern world. It was due. A new sense of repose in quiet streamlining effects had then and there found its way into building, as we now see it in steamships, airplanes, and motorcars. The "age" came into its own.

But more important than all, rising to greater dignity as an idea, was the ideal of plasticity as now emphasized in the treatment of the whole building. (Plasticity may be seen in the expressive lines and surfaces of your hand as contrasted with the articulation of the skeleton itself.) This ideal in the form of continuity has appeared as a natural means to achieve truly organic architecture. Here was direct expression, the only true means I could see, or can now see to that end. Here, by instinct at first (all ideas germinate), principle had entered into building as continuity that has since gone abroad and come home again to go to work, as it will continue to work to revolutionize the use and custom of our Machine Age. This means an architecture that can live and let live.

The word "plastic" was a word Louis Sullivan himself was fond of using in reference to his scheme of ornamentation, as distinguished from all other or any applied ornament. But now, and not merely as form following function, why not a larger application of this element of plasticity considered as *continuity* in the building itself? Why any principle working in the part if not working in the whole?

If form really followed function (it might be seen that it did by means of this concrete ideal of plasticity as continuity), why not throw away entirely the implications of post and beam? Have *no* beams, *no* columns, *no* cornices, nor any fixtures, nor pilasters or entablatures as such. Instead of two things, *one* thing. Let walls, ceilings, floors become part of each other, growing into one another, getting continuity out of it all or into it all, eliminating any constructed feature, such as any fixture or appliance whatsoever, as Louis Sullivan eliminated background in his ornament in favor of an integral sense of the whole. Conceive now that here the idea was a new sense of building that could *grow* forms not only true to function, but expressive beyond any architecture known. Yes, architectural forms by this means might now "grow up."

Grow up—in what image? Here was concentrated appeal to pure imagination. Gradually proceeding from generals to particulars, plasticity, now *continuity*, as a large means in architecture began to grip and work its own will. I would watch sequences fascinated, seeing other sequences in those consequences already in evidence. The old architecture, as far as its grammar went, began literally to disappear: as if by magic new effects came to life.

Vistas of a simplicity would open to me and harmonies so beautiful that I was not only delighted but often startled, sometimes amazed. I concentrated with all my energy on the principle of plasticity as continuity and a practical working principle within the building construction itself to accomplish the thing we call architecture.

Some years later I took continuity as a practical working principle of construction into the actual method of constructing the building. But to eliminate the post and beam, as such, I could get no help from the engineer. By habit, engineers reduced everything in the field of calculation to the post and the girder before they could calculate anything and tell you where and just how much. Walls that were part of floors and ceilings all merging together and reacting upon each other the engineer had never met, and the engineer has not yet enough scientific formulae to enable him to calculate for such continuity. Slabs stiffened and used over supports as cantilevers to get planes parallel to the earth, such as were now necessary to develop emphasis of the third dimension, were new. But the engineer soon mastered this element of continuity in these floor slabs. The cantilever became a new feature in architecture. As used in the Imperial Hotel in Tokyo it was one of the features that insured the life of that building in the terrific temblor. After that demonstration not only a new aesthetic, but (proving the aesthetic as sound), a great new *economic stability* had entered building construction. And, as further sequence of this idea that plasticity should be at work as continuity in actual construction, from laboratory experiments made at Princeton by Professor Beggs it appears that the principle of continuity actually works in physical structure as specific proof of the soundness of the aesthetic ideal. So the ideal of continuity in designing architectural forms will soon be available as a structural formula. Thus continuity will become a new and invaluable economy in building construction itself. Welding instead of riveting steel is a new means to the same end, but that is ahead of the story.

An idea soon came from this stimulating, simplifying ideal that, to be consistent in practice, or, indeed, if it was at all to be put to work successfully, this new element of plasticity must have a new sense as well as a science of materials. It may interest you to know, as it astonished me, there is nothing in the literature of the civilized world on that subject.

I began to study the nature of materials. I learned to see brick as brick, learned to see wood as wood, and to see concrete or glass or metal each for itself and all as themselves. Strange to say, this required concentration of imagination; each required a different handling and each had possibilities of use peculiar to the nature of each. Appropriate designs for one material would not be appropriate at all for any other material in the light of this ideal of simplicity as organic.

Had our new materials—steel, concrete, and glass—existed in the ancient order, we would have had nothing at all like ponderous "classic" architecture. No, nothing. Nor can there now be an organic architecture where the nature of these materials is ignored or misunderstood. How can there be? Perfect correlation is the first principle of growth. Integration means that nothing is of any great value except as naturally related to the whole. Even my great old master designed for materials all alike; all were grist for his rich imagination with his sentient ornamentation. All materials were only one material to him in which to weave the stuff of his dreams. I still remember being ashamed of the delight I at first took in so plainly "seeing around" the beloved master. But acting upon this new train of ideas soon brought work sharply and immediately up against the tools that could be found to get these ideas put into form. What were the tools in use everywhere? *Machines!*—automatic many of them, stone or wood planers, stone or wood molding-shapers, various lathes, presses, and power saws—all in commercially organized mills: sheet-metal breakers, presses, shears, cutting-, molding-, and stamping-machines in foundries and rolling mills—commercialized in the "shops": concrete-mixers, clay-bakers, casters, glass-makers, and the trades union—all laborers, units in a more or less highly commercialized greater union in which craftsmanship only had place as survival for burial. Standardization was already inflexible necessity, either enemy or friend—you might choose. And as you chose you became either master and useful or a luxury—and eventually a parasite.

Already machine-standardization had taken the life of handicraft in all its expressions. But the outworn handicraft as seen in the forms of the old architecture never troubled me. The new forms as expression of the new order of the machine did trouble me. If I wanted to realize new forms I should have to make them not only appropriate to old and new materials, but so design them that the machines that would have to make them, could and would make them well. But now with this ideal of internal order as integral in architecture supreme in my mind, I would have done nothing less even if I could have commanded armies of craftsmen. By now had come the discipline of a great ideal. There is no discipline, architectural or otherwise, so severe, but there is no discipline that yields such rich rewards in work, nor is there any discipline so safe

and sure of results as this ideal of "internal order," the integration that is organic. Lesser ideas took flight, like birds, from this exacting, informing ideal, always in the same direction, but further on each occasion for flight until great goals were in sight. You may see the "signs and portents" gathered together in the exhibition gallery.

But, before trying to tell you about the goals in sight, popular reactions to this new endeavor might be interesting. After the first house was built (it was the Winslow house in 1893), my next client did not want a house so different that he would have to go down the back way to his morning train to avoid being laughed at. Bankers at first refused to loan money on the houses, and friends had to be found to finance the early buildings. Millmen would soon look for the name on the plans when they were presented for estimates, read the name, and roll the drawings up again, handing them back to the contractor, with the remark "they were not hunting for trouble." Contractors often failed to read the plans correctly—the plans were so radically different—so much had to be left off the building.

Clients usually stood by, often interested and excited beyond their means. So, when they moved in, quite frequently they had to take in their old furniture. The ideal of organic simplicity, seen as the countenance of perfect integration, abolished all fixtures, rejected all superficial decoration, made all electric lighting and heating fixtures an integral part of the architecture. So far as possible all furniture was to be designed in place as part of the architecture. Hangings, rugs, carpets—all came into the same category, so any failure of this particular feature of the original scheme often crippled results—made trouble in this plan of constructive elimination.

Nor was there any planting done about the house without cooperating with the architect. No sculpture, no painting unless cooperating with the architect. This made trouble. No decoration, as such, anywhere; decorators hunting a job would visit the owners, learn the name of the architect, lift their hats, and turning on their heels leave with a curt and sarcastic "Good day"—meaning really

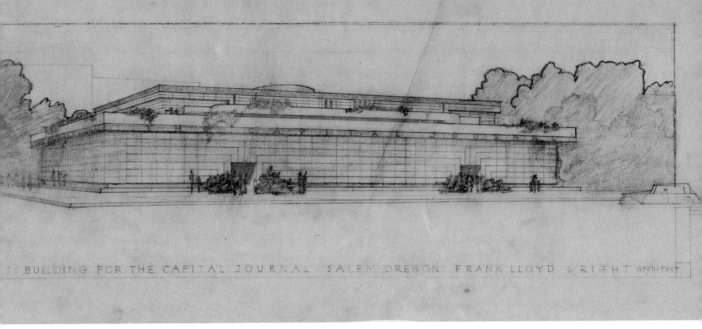

BUILDING FOR THE CAPITAL JOURNAL SALEM OREGON FRANK LLOYD WRIGHT architect

"Capitol Journal" Newspaper Plant (Project). Salem, Oregon. 1930. Perspective. Pencil and color pencil on tracing paper, 31 x 17".
FLLW Fdn#3101.001

what the slang "Good night" meant, later. The owners of the houses were all subjected to curiosity, sometimes to admiration, but they submitted, most often, to the ridicule of the middle-of-the-road egotist. There was "something about them too," now, when they had a house like that—"the rope-tie?"

A different choice of materials would mean a different scheme altogether. Concrete was coming into use and Unity Temple became the first concrete monolith in the world—that is to say—the first building complete as monolithic architecture in the wooden forms in which it was cast.

Plastered houses were then new. Casement windows were new. So many things were new. Nearly everything was new but the law of gravitation and the idiosyncrasy of the client.

But, as reward for independent thinking in building, first plainly shown in the constitution and profiles of Unity Temple at Oak Park, more clearly emerging from previous practice, now came clear *an entirely new sense of architecture*, a higher conception of architecture: architecture not alone as form following function, but conceived as space enclosed. The enclosed space itself might now be seen as the reality of the building. This sense of the

within or the room itself, or the rooms themselves, I now saw as the great thing to be expressed as *architecture*. This sense of interior space made exterior as architecture transcended all that had gone before, made all the previous ideas only useful now as means to the realization of a far greater ideal. Hitherto all classical or ancient buildings had been great masses or blocks of building material, sculptured into shape outside and hollowed out to live in. At least that was the sense of it all. But here coming to light was a sense of building as an organism that had new release for the opportunities of the Machine Age. This interior conception took architecture entirely away from sculpture, away from painting, and entirely away from architecture as it had been known in the antique. The building now became a creation of interior-space in light. And as this sense of the interior space as the reality of the building began to work walls as walls fell away. The vanishing wall joined the disappearing cave. Enclosing screens and protecting features of architectural character took the place of the solid wall.

More and more light began to become the beautifier of the building—the blessing of the occupants. Our arboreal ancestors in their trees are more likely precedent for us than the savage animals that holed in for protection. Yes, in a spiritual sense, a higher *order* is the sense of sunlit space and the lightness of the structure of the spider spinning as John Roebling saw it and realized it in his Brooklyn Bridge.

Inevitably, it seems to me, this sense of building is to construct the physical body of our Machine Age.

Our civilization is emerging from the cave. We are through with the fortification as a dwelling place. Feudal society, if not feudal thinking, is disappearing. With its disappearance will disappear the massive building that protected the might of its estate. With our new materials, steel, glass, and ferro-concrete with the steel always in tension, lightness and strength become more and more obvious as directly related to each other in modern building. The resources of the Machine Age confirm the new materials in this space-conception of architecture at every point. Steel-in-tension brings entirely new possibilities of spanning spaces and new aid in creating a more livable world.

Yes, already a sense of cleanliness directly related to living in sunlight is at work in us and working not only to emancipate us from the cavern but waking in us a desire for the substance of a new and more appropriate simplicity as the countenance of building construction: simplicity appearing now as a youthful clear countenance of truth. This reality is new. This sense of the reality as within, and with no exterior pretensions of architecture as something applied to construction, makes all the heavy pretentious masonry masses ornamented by brick or stone walls seem heavy, monstrous, and wrong, as in matter of fact they are utterly false in this age, as is, no less, the little-decorated cavern for a house.

Modern architecture is weary of academic make-believe. Architecture sees the airplane fly overhead, emancipated from make-believe, soon, when it lays its wings aside, free to be itself and true to itself. It sees the steamship ride the seas, triumphant as the thing it is, for what it is. It sees the motorcar becoming more the machine it should be, becoming daily less like a coach, more a freedom to be itself for what it is. In them all and in all utensils whatsoever, the Machine Age is seen more and more freely declaring for freedom to express the truths of being instead of remaining satisfied to be a false seeming. Modern architecture is profiting by what it sees and in five years' time you may look upon any sham-boxes with holes or slots cut in them for light and air as senile, undesirable.

A new sense of beauty seen in the Machine Age, characteristic of direct simplicity of expression, is awakening in art to create a new world, or better said, to create the world anew. No mind that is a mind considers that world inferior to the antique. We may confidently see it as superior. And, within the vision of this conception of architecture, see the very city itself, as a *necessity*, dying. The acceleration we are witnessing in the tyranny of the skyscraper is no more than the hangover of a habit. The very acceleration we mistake for growth heralds and precedes decay.

Decentralization not only of industry, but of the city itself is desirable and imminent. Necessity built the city, but the great service rendered to man as a luxury by the machine as seen in automobilization and electrification will destroy that necessity. Already internal collision of the mechanistic device of the skyscraper and of these more beneficent automobilization and electrical factors may be seen winning in the struggle between the greedy skyscraper and the fleet automobile—the city splitting up in consequence. This is only one of the more obvious evidences of disintegration.

In the growth of the great highways, natural, state, and county, and in the gradually extending servicing of the ubiquitous gasoline station, we see in embryo other advance agents of decentralization! Such new avenues and spreading centers of distribution and servicing mean eventually the disintegration and subordination of the centralization now seen in the city. The greatest service sentient man is to receive from the machine he has built in his own image, if he conquers the machine and makes the machine serve him, will be the death of urbanism! Hectic urbanism will be submerged in natural ruralism. And we shall see soon that the natural place for the beautiful tall building, not in its present form but in this new sense, is in the country, not in the city.

If the machine conquers man, man will remain to perish with his city, as he has before perished in all the cities the great nations of the world have ever built.

Mankind is only now waking to visions of the machine as the true emancipator of the individual as an individual. Therefore we may yet see the Machine Age as the age of a true democracy, wherein human life is based squarely on and in the beauty and fruitfulness of the ground: life lived in the full enjoyment of the earthline of human life—the line of freedom for man, whereby man's horizon may be immeasurably extended by the machine, the creature of his brain in service of his heart and mind.

So, we may see, even now, taking shape in the realm of ideas in architecture to express all this, a new significance, or we might fairly enough say: *significance as new*. Significance as new because in architecture for five centuries at least "significance" has been lost, except as an outworn symbolism was feebly significant, or except as a tawdry sentimentality had specious significance. This new significance repudiates the sentimentality of any symbol; looks the philosophic abstraction full in the eye for the impostor it usually is; reads its lessons direct in the book of creation itself; and despises all that lives either ashamed or afraid to live as itself, for what it is or may become because of *its own nature*.

A new integrity then? Yes, integrity new to us in America—and yet so ancient! A new integrity, alive and working with new means—greater means than ever worked before. A new integrity working for freedom—yours and mine and our children's freedom—in this realm, we have called, for the purpose of this hour together, "the realm of ideas."

2. TO THE YOUNG MAN IN ARCHITECTURE

Today the young man I have in mind hears much too much about new and old. Sporadic critics of the new take their little camera minds about (snapshot emulation by the half-baked architect) and wail, or hail the dawn. If by chance the novice builds a building the cackling, if not the crowing, outdoes the egg. Propagandists, pro and con, classify old as new and new as old. Historians tabulate their own oblique inferences as fact. The "ites" of transient "ists" and "isms" proclaim the modern as new. And yet architecture was never old and will ever be new. From architecture the main current, little streams detach themselves, run a muddy course to be regathered and clarified by the great waters as though the little rills and rivulets had never been. All art in our time is like that and we witness only the prodigal waste Nature sponsors when she flings away a million seeds to get a single plant, seeming in the meantime to enjoy her extravagance. Nature's real issue, no doubt, in the life of the mind is no less wasteful, and she may enjoy her extravagance in the million fancies for one idea, millions of celebrations for one thought, a million buildings for even one small piece of genuine architecture. Yes, she gives gladly a million for one now, because the species has declined five hundred years to the level of a commercially expedient *appliance*. The species itself, you see, is in danger. So be glad to see as evidence of life the babel of personal books, the dereliction of aesthetic movements—especially be glad to see the half-baked buildings by the novitiate.

But confusion of ideas is unnatural waste of purpose. Such confusion as we see means a scattering of aim nature herself would never tolerate. The confusion arises because there is doubt in some minds, fear in some minds, and hope in other minds, that architecture is shifting its circumference. As the hod of mortar and some bricks give way to sheet metal, the lockseam, and the breaker—as the workman gives way to the automatic machine—so the architect seems to be giving way either to the engineer, the salesman, or the propagandist.

I am here to assure you that the circumference of architecture *is* changing with astonishing rapidity, but that its *center* remains unchanged. Or am I here only to reassure you that architecture eternally returns upon itself to produce new forms that may live on forever? In the light of the new and with pain of loss, only now does America waken to see why and how art, conceived as a commercial expedient or degraded to the level of a sentimental appliance, has betrayed American life. Yes, that is one reason why the circumference of art, as a whole, is rapidly shifting. The circumference is shifting because hunger for reality is not yet dead, and because human vision widens with science as human nature deepens with inner experience.

The center of architecture remains unchanged because—though all unconfessed or ill-concealed—beauty is no less the true purpose of rational modern architectural endeavor than ever, just as beauty remains the essential characteristic of architecture itself. But today, because of scientific attainment, the modern more clearly perceives beauty as integral order; order divined as an image by human sensibility; order apprehended by reason, executed by science. Yes, by means of a greater science, a more integral order may now be executed than any existing. With integral order once established you may perceive the rhythm of consequent harmony. To be harmonious is to be beautiful in a rudimentary sense: a good platform from which to spring toward the moving infinity that is the present. It is in architecture in this sense that "God meets with nature in the sphere of the relative." Therefore, the first great necessity of a modern architecture is this keen sense of order as integral. That is to say the *form* itself in orderly relationship with purpose or function: the *parts* themselves in order with the form: the materials and methods of work in order with both: a kind of natural integrity—the integrity of each in all and of all in each. This is the exacting new order.

Wherein, then, does the new order differ from the ancient? Merely in this—the ancient order had gone astray, betrayed by "culture," misled by the historian. But the organic simplicity to be thus achieved as new is the simplicity of the universe, which is quite different from the simplicity of any machine, just as the art of being in the world is not the same thing as making shift to get about in it.

Internal disorder is architectural disease if not the death of architecture. Needed then, young man, by you who would become an architect, and needed as a very beginning, is some intellectual grasp, the more direct the better, of this radical order of your universe. You will see your universe as architecture.

An inspired sense of order you may have received as a gift—certainly the schools cannot give it to you. Therefore, to the young man in architecture, the word *radical* should be a beautiful word. Radical means "of the root" or "to the root"—begins at the beginning and the word stands up straight. Any architect should be radical by nature because it is not enough for him to begin where others have left off.

Traditions in architecture have proved unsafe. The propaganda of the dead which you now see in a land strewn with the corpses of opportunity, is no more trustworthy than the propaganda of the living. Neither can have much to do with organic architecture. No, the working of principle in the direction of integral order is your only safe precedent. So the actual business of your architectural schools should be to assist you in the perception of such order in the study of the various architectures of the world—otherwise schools exist only to hinder and deform the young. Merely to enable you, young man, to make a living by making plans for buildings is not good enough work for any school. Thus you may see by this definition of order that the "orders" as such have less than nothing at all to do with modern, that is to say organic, architecture. And, too, you may see how little any of the great buildings of the ages can help you to become an architect *except as you look within them* for such working of principle as made them new in the order of their own day. As a matter of course, the particular forms and details appropriate to them become eccentricities to you— fatalities, should you attempt to copy them for yourselves when you attempt to build. This much at least, I say, is obvious to all minds as the Machine Age emerges into human view, with more severe limitations than have ever been imposed upon architecture in the past, but these very limitations are your great, fresh opportunity.

Now, even the scribes are forced by inexorable circumstances to see old materials give way to new materials, new industrial systems taking the place of old ones, just as all see the American concepts of social liberty replace the feudal systems, oligarchies, and hereditary aristocracies: and by force of circumstances, too, all are now inexorably compelled to see that we have nothing, or have very

Prefabricated Farm Units (Project). 1932. Perspective. Pencil and color pencil on tracing paper, 26 x 13". FLLW Fdn#3202.007

little, which expresses, as architecture, any of these great changes.

Due to the very principles at work as limitations in our mechanical or mechanized products, today, you may see coming into the best of them a new order of beauty that, in a sense, *is* negation of the old order. In a deeper sense, a little later, you may be able to see it, too, as scientific affirmation of ancient order. But you, young man, begin anew, limited, though I hope no less inspired, by this sense of the new order that has only just begun to have results. Only a horizon widened by science, only a human sensitivity quickened by the sense of the dignity and worth of the individual as an individual, only this new and finer sense of internal order, *inherent* as the spirit of architecture, can make you an architect now. Your buildings *must* be new because the law was old before the existence of heaven and earth.

You may see on every side of you that principle works in this spirit of cosmic change today just as it worked since the beginning. Lawless you cannot be in architecture, if you are for nature. And do not be afraid, you may disregard the laws, but you are never lawless if you are for nature.

Would you be modern? Then it is the nature of the thing, which you now must intelligently approach and to which you must reverently appeal. Out of communion with nature, no less now than ever, you will perceive the order that is new and learn to understand that it is old because it was new in the old. Again, I say, be sure as sure may be that a clearer perception of principle has to be "on straight" in your mind today before any architectural ways or any technical means can accomplish anything for you at all.

As to these technical ways and means, there are as many paths as there are individuals with capacity for taking infinite pains, to use Carlyle's phrase. All are found in the field itself, the field where all that makes the America of today is active commercial issue. An architect's office may be a near corner of that field. A school in which modern machinery and processes were seen at actual work would be your true corner of that field. If only we had such schools, one such school would be worth all the others put together. But only a radical and rebellious spirit is safe in the schools we now have, and time spent there is time lost for such spirits. Feeling for the arts in our country, unfortunately for you, is generally a self-conscious attitude, an attitude similar to the attitude of the provincial in society. The provincial will not act upon innate kindness and good sense, and so tries to observe the other guests to do as they do. Fear of being found ridiculous is his waking nightmare. Innate good sense, in the same way, forsakes the provincial in the realm of ideas in art. By keeping in what seems to him good company, the company of the "higher-ups," he thinks himself safe. This self-conscious fear of being oneself, this cowardly capitulation to what is being done, yes, the architectural increment *servility* deserves—this is your inheritance, young man!—you inheritance from the time when the architect's lot was cast in between, neither old nor new, neither alive nor quite dead. Were this not so it would not be so hard for you to emerge, for you to be born alive. But as a consequence of the little modern architecture we already have, young architects, whatever their years, will emerge with less and less punishment, emerge with far less anguish, because the third generation is with us. That generation will be less likely to advertise to posterity by its copied mannerisms or borrowed styles that it was neither scholar nor gentleman in the light of any ideal of spiritual integrity.

It would be unfair to let those architects in between who served as your attitudinized or commercialized progenitors go free of blame for your devastating architectural inheritance. Where they should have led they followed by the nose. Instead of being arbiters of principle as a blessed privilege, they became arbiters or victims of the taste that is usually a matter of ignorance. When leisure and money came, these progenitors of yours became connoisseurs of the antique, patrons and peddlers of the imitation. So, with few exceptions, it was with these sentimentalized or stylized architects: "Boy, take down Tudor no. 37 and put a bay window on it for the lady"; or, solicitous, "Madam, what style will you have?" A few held out, all honor to them. A tale told of Louis Sullivan has the lady come in and ask for a Colonial house: "Madam," said he, "you will take what we give you."

Except in a few instances (the result of some such attitude as this), the only buildings we have to-

day approaching architecture are the industrial buildings built upon the basis of common sense: buildings built for the manufacturer who possessed common sense or buildings for residence built to meet actual needs without abject reference to the "higher-ups"—nor with foolish, feathered hat in hand to culture. These sensible works we possess and the world admires, envies, and emulates. This American common sense, is today the only way out for America. He is still the only architectural asset America ever had or has. Give him what he needs when he needs it.

To find out what he needs go whenever and wherever you can to the factories to study the processes in relation to the product and go to the markets to study the reactions. Study the machines that make the product what it is. To acquire technique study the materials of which the product is made, study the purpose for which it is produced, study the manhood *in* it, the manhood *of* it. Keep all this present in your mind in all you do, because ideas with bad technique are abortions.

In connection with this matter of "technique" you may be interested to know that the Beaux-Arts that made most of your American progenitors is itself confused, now likely to reinterpret its precepts, disown its previous progeny, and disinherit its favorite sons or be itself dethroned, since posterity is already declining the sons as inheritance: the sons who enabled the plan-factory to thrive, the "attitude" to survive in a sentimental attempt to revive the dead. Yes, it is becoming day by day more evident to the mind how shamefully the product of this culture betrayed America. It is beginning to show and it shames America. At our architecture, as "culture," quite good-naturedly the Old World laughs. Coming here expecting to see our ideals becomingly attired, they see us fashionably and officially ridiculous, by way of assumption of customs and manners belonging by force of nature and circumstances to something entirely different. They see us betraying not only ourselves but our country itself. But now by grace of freedom we have little otherwise to show to command dawning respect. No, young man, I do not refer to the skyscraper in the rank and file as that something nor does the world refer to it, except as a stupendous adventure in the business of space-making for rent—a monstrosity. I again refer you to those simple, sincere attempts to be ourselves and make the most of our own opportunities which are tucked away in out-of-the-way places or found in industrial life as homes or workshops. Our rich people do not own them. Great business on a large scale does not invest in them unless as straightforward business buildings where "culture" is no consideration and columns can give no credit.

American great wealth has yet given nothing to the future worth having as architecture or that the future will accept as such unless as an apology. In building for such uses as she had, America has made shift with frightful waste.

Though half the cost of her buildings was devoted to making them beautiful as architecture, not one thought-built structure synthetic in design has American great wealth, and even less American factotumized learning, yet succeeded in giving to the modern world. American wealth has been sold as it has, itself, bought and sold and been delivered over by professions, or the Scribes, to the Pharisees. So, young man, expect noting from the man of great wealth in the United States for another decade. Expect nothing from your government for another quarter of a century! Our government, too (helpless instrument of a majority hapless in art), has been delivered over to architecture as the sterile hangover of feudal thought, or the thought that served the sophist with the slave. That is why the future of architecture in America really lies with the well-to-do man of business—the man of independent judgement and character of his own, unspoiled by great financial success—that is to say the man not persuaded, by winning his own game, that he knows all about everything else.

Opportunity to develop an architecture today lies with those sincere and direct people, who, loving America for its own sake, live their own lives quietly in touch with its manifold beauties—*blessed by comprehension of the ideal of freedom that founded this country*. In our great United States, notwithstanding alleged "rulers" or any "benign" imported cultural influences, these spontaneous sons and daughters are the soul of our country; they are fresh unspoiled life and, therefore, they are your opportunity in art, just as you, the artist, are their opportunity. You will be their means to emerge from the conglomerate "in between."

And this brings us to the American "ideal." This American ideal must be in architecture what it is in life. Why obscure the issue by any sophisticated aesthetics or involution with academic formulae? The arts are only such media as we have for the direct expression of life reacting in turn with joy-giving force upon that life itself—enriching all human experience to come. The arts in America are on free soil, and therefore all-imperatively call for the creative artist.

The soul of that new life we are fond of calling American is liberty: liberty tolerant and so sincere that it must see all free or itself suffer. This freedom is the highest American ideal. To attain it, then, is inner experience, because there is no "exterior" freedom. Freedom develops from within and is another expression of an integral order of the mind in high estate. Freedom is impossible where discord exists either within or without. So, perfect freedom no one has, though all may aspire. But, to the degree freedom is attained, the by-product called "happiness," meaning, I suppose, innocent life, will be the consequence.

Very well, take the American ideal of freedom from the realm of human consciousness to our specific expression of that consciousness we call architecture. Could any decorator's shop, even if it were called a "studio," sell anything ready-made out of the world's stock of "styles" to do more than bedizen or bedevil this essential sentiment?—artificially dress it up for artificiality-making social occasion? No, it would be impossible to do more—architecture like freedom *cannot be put on*, it must be worked out from within.

Could any school of architecture inculcating the culture of Greece or Rome fit the case any better with current abstractions of ancient culture as dedicated to the sophist and the slave? No, ancient culture produced nothing to fit the case of an individual freedom evolved by the individual from within. And this is justification (is it?) for evolving nothing and going on with make-believe just be-cause make-believe is organized and therefore the decorator has it in stock, the plan-factory sells it, and the schools provide it. The present tendency in architecture which we style modern says emphatically "No" to this betrayal.

If we are determining ourselves as a free people (and we are), by what you build you will now say proudly "No" to further menial treason of this academic type.

Are we a free people? Of course not. The question that is important, however, is: do we have it in our hearts as it is written in our constitutional charter to be free? Is it sincerely and passionately our ideal to be free? Notwithstanding so much cowardly popular evidence to the contrary, I say it is our ideal. Those highest in the realm of freedom should build suitable buildings and build them now, for that spirit first, and for America to ponder. There is no longer any doubt in the mind that

eventually America will have a truly characteristic architecture—that much is already written for you on the vanishing wall and the disappearing cave.

Young man in architecture, wherever you are and whatever your age, or whatever your job, we—the youth of America—should be the psychological shock-troops thrown into action against corruption of this supreme American ideal. It will be for youth, in this sense, to win the day for freedom in architecture.

That American architecture cannot be imitative architecture is self-evident in spite of false standards. It is self-evident that neither architect who imitates nor architecture imitative can be free—the one is a slave, the other forever in bondage. It is as evident that free architecture must develop from within—an integral, or as we now say in architecture, an "organic" affair. For this reason if for no other reason, modern architecture can be no mode nor can it ever again be any "style." You must

Mrs. Samuel William Gladney House, Scheme #2 (Project). Fort Worth, Texas. 1925. Perspective, 29 x 20". FLLW Fdn#2508.002

defend it against both or senility will again set in for another cycle of thirty years.

Specifically then, you may ask, what is truly modern in architecture? . . . The answer is *power*— that *is* to say material resources—*directly applied to purpose*. Yes, modern architecture is power directly applied to purpose in buildings in the same sense that we see it so applied in the airplane, ocean liner, or motorcar. Therefore, it is natural enough perhaps for newly awakened architects to make the error of assuming that, beyond accepting the consequences of directness and integral character, the building of itself must resemble utensil-machines or flying, fighting, or steaming-machines, or any other appliances. But here is this essential difference (it makes all the difference) between a machine and a building. A building is not an appliance nor a mobilization. The building as architecture is born out of the heart of man, permanent consort to the ground, comrade to the trees, true reflection of man in the realm of his own spirit. His building is therefore consecrated space wherein he seeks refuge, recreation, and repose for body but especially for mind. So our Machine Age building need no more look like machinery than machinery need look like buildings.

Certain qualities, humanly desirable qualities, I am sure you may obtain by means of machinery or by intelligent use of our mechanized systems without selling your souls to factotums by way of a factorialized aesthetic. There is rather more serious occasion for becoming ourselves in our environment, our architecture becoming more human, our dwelling-places becoming more imaginatively fresh and original in order to overcome not only the "cultured tag" but the deadly drag of mechanical monotony and the purely mechanical insignificance that otherwise characterizes us and that will eventually destroy us. But the "ites" of the "ism" and the "ist" give signs of being so engrossed in a new machine-aesthetic that they will be unable to rise above themselves—sunk, and so soon, in the struggle for machine technique. Already hectic architects' "modernistic" and the decorators' "modernism" obscure the simple issue. I would have you believe that to be genuinely new, the man must begin to win over the machine, and not the machine win over the man by way of the man.

We have already observed that whenever architecture was great it was modern, and whenever architecture was modern human values were the only values preserved. And I reiterate that modern architecture in this deeper sense is novelty only to novitiates, that the principles moving us to be modern now are those that moved the Frank and Goth, the Indian, the Maya, and the Moor. They are the same principles that will move Atlantis recreated. If there is architecture on Mars or Venus, and there is, at least there is the architecture of Mars and Venus themselves, the same principles are at work there too.

Principles are universal.

If you approach principles from within you will see that many of the traditions we flattered to extinction by emulation never were even on speaking terms with principle, but were bound up with education by way of impotence or deadly force of habit, or what not? Modern architecture knows them now for impositions, and is gaining courage to cast them out, together with those who insist upon their use and administer them. This in itself you should gratefully recognize as no small value of the so-called "modern movement."

Goethe observed that death was nature's ruse in order that she might have more life. Therein you may see the reason why there must be a new, and why the new must ever be the death of the old, but this tragedy need occur only where "forms" are concerned, if you will stick to principle. It is because we have not relied on principle that the genius of the *genus homo* is now to be taxed anew to find an entirely new kind of building that will be a more direct application of power to purpose than ever before has existed in history. But again let us repeat that to secure beauty of the kind we perceive in external nature in the inflexible standardization that characterizes that power today, we must not dramatize the machine but dramatize the man. You must work, young man in architecture, to lift the curse of the appliance, either mechanical or sentimental, from the life of today.

But this modern constructive endeavor is being victimized at the start by a certain new aesthetic wherein appearance is made an aim instead of character made a purpose. The "new" aesthetic thus becomes at the very beginning old because it is only another "appliance." The French with all the delicacy and charm they seem to possess as substitute for soul, and with French flair for the appropriate gesture at the opportune moment, have contributed most to this affix or suffix of the appliance. Initiators of so many "art movements" that prove ephemeral, they recognize the opportunity for another "movement." The new world and the old world too had both already recognized a certain new order that is beauty in the clean-stripped, hard look of machines—had admired an exterior simplicity due to the direct construction by which automatons were made to operate, move, and stop. But certain aesthetes—French by sympathy or association—are trying to persuade us that this exterior simplicity *as a new kind of decoration*, is the appropriate look of everything in our Machine Age. French painting foolishly claims to have seen it first—foolishly because we saw it first in ourselves. But French modernism proceeds to set it up flatwise in architecture in two dimensions—that is to say, to survey it in length and breadth. Although these effects of surface and mass were already well along in our own country (two dimensions, completed by surfaces parallel to the earth, as a third dimension to grip the whole building to the ground), Paris nevertheless ignores this, with characteristic desire for "movement," and sets up characteristic machine-appearance in two dimensions (that is to say, in the surface and mass effects with which Paris is familiar), and architecture thus becomes decoration. You may see it in the fashionable shops while France contemplates a fifty-four million dollar building to propagandize her arts and crafts in the American field while America is busy making enough motorcars to go around.

A certain inspiration characterized the first French recognition, but uninspired emulation has become reiteration, and in the end nothing will have happened unless another "mode," another aesthetic dictum goes forth to languish as superficial fashion. Another "istic," another "ism" comes to

town to pass away—this time not in a hansom cab but in a flying machine!

Yes, America is young, so healthy it soon wearies of negation. The negation we have here is stranger to mysterious depths of feeling. It is protestant. The protestant is useful but seldom beautiful. When he ceases to protest and becomes constructive himself, some new protestant will arise to take his place and we may see this happening at the moment.

Yet for young America today a light too long diverted to base uses is shining again through all the propaganda and confusion. This light is the countenance of integral order, a more profound, consistent order than the world has fully realized before, wherein power is applied to purpose in construction just as mathematics is sublimated into music. By that light you may clearly see that, where there is no integral order, there is no beauty, though the order be no more obvious than mathematics in music is obvious.

Not so strange then that the novitiate takes the machine itself as the prophet of this new order, though you must not forget that although music is sublimated mathematics the professor of mathematics cannot make music. Nor can the doctor of philosophy nor the master of construction nor the enthusiastic antiquarian make architecture.

No rationalizing of the machine or factorializing of aesthetics can obscure the fact that architecture is born, not made, and must consistently grow from within to whatever it becomes. Such forms as it takes must be spontaneous generation of materials, building methods, and purpose. The brain is a great tool with great craft; but in architecture you are concerned with our sense of the specific beauty of human lives as lived on earth in relation to each other. Organic architecture seeks superior sense of use and finer sense of comfort, expressed in organic simplicity. That is what you, young man, should call *architecture*. Use and comfort in order to become architecture must become *spiritual satisfactions* wherein the soul insures a more subtle use, achieves a more constant repose. So, architecture speaks as poetry to the soul. In this Machine Age to utter this poetry that is architecture, as in all other ages, you must learn the organic language of the natural, which is *ever the language of the new*. To know any language you must know the alphabet. The alphabet in architecture in our Machine Age is the nature of steel, glass, and concrete construction, the nature of the machines used as tools, and the nature of the new materials to be used.

Now what language?

Poverty in architecture—architecture the language of the human heart—has grown by unnatural appropriation of artificiality, has grown wretched and miserable by the fetish of the appliance, whether by the appliance as mechanical or sentimental. Prevailing historical sympathy administered as standardized learning has confused art with archaeology. In this academic confusion we have been unable to cultivate the principles that grow architecture as a flower of the mind out of our own nature as flowers grow out of earth.

To make architectural growth, you must now perceive that the essential power of our civilization can never be expressed or even capitalized for long in any shallow terms of any factorialized or merely mechanized art. If you would be true to the center of architecture wherever the circumference of architecture may be formed you will see the machine as a peerless tool but otherwise you will see any machine as sterility itself. Engrossed in the serious struggle for the new technique, you may not override your love of romance, except such foolish abuse of romance as is our present sentimentality or senility—our barren lot long since past.

I assure you that at least enough has appeared in my own experience to prove to me that the power of the man with the machine is really no bar at all to tremendously varied *imaginative* architecture.

Nor does any mind that is a mind doubt that the worthy product of our own industrialism should and would give us more digestible food for artistic enjoyment, than the early Italian, Italian pasticcio, or the medieval ever gave us. But such artistic enjoyment should not, could not, mean that the Machine Age commonplaces were accepted as worthy. It would mean these commonplaces transfigured and transformed by inner fire to take their

places in the immense vista of the ages as human masterpieces. Such interpretation by inner fire as *character in the realm of nature* is the work of the young man in architecture.

Oh, America will have to go through a lot of amateurish experiments with you. We as Americans may have to submit to foolish experiments used in the American manner as quick-turnover propaganda. But we must be patient because architecture is profound.

Architecture is the very body of civilization itself. It takes time to grow—begins to be architecture only when it is thought-built, that is to say when it is a synthesis completed from a rational beginning and, naturally as breathing, genuinely *modern*.

America will factorialize and factotumize much more, and as many Americans will die of ornaphobia as of ornamentia by the wayside before any goal is reached. She will listen to much reasoning from all and sundry and will justly despise the poisonous fruits of most of the reasoning. She will see many little bands or cliques among you muddling about near-ideas, attempting to run with them and kick a goal for personal glory in what we already sufficiently know as modern movements. And you yourselves will see exploitation of perfectly good ideals by every shade of every imported nationality on earth when the women's clubs of America wake to the great significance to the family of this rapidly changing order in which we live and which they are only now learning to call modern from the midst of antiques. And then in characteristic fashion America will be inclined to mistake abuse of the thing for the thing itself and kick the thing out. As a characteristic abuse we have already seen pseudo-classic architecture stripping off its enabling cornices, entablatures, and columns, and fundamentally unchanged, hung up to us on a grand scale as modern. We will soon see more of it on a grander scale. But washing pseudo-classic behind the ears cannot make architecture modern.

One abusive formula that enables the plan-factory to modernize overnight is that all architecture without ornament is modern. Another agonizing formula that gives the decorator a break is that sharp angles cutting flat surfaces are modern. Never mind, we will accept anything, just so recurrent senility does not again become a new aesthetic.

Yes, modern architecture is young architecture—the joy of youth must bring it. The love of youth, eternal youth must develop and keep it. You must see this architecture as wise, but not so much wise as sensible and wistful, nor any more scientific than sentient, nor so much resembling a flying machine as a masterpiece of the imagination.

Oh yes, young man, consider well that a house is a machine in which to live, but by the same token a heart is a suction pump. Sentient man begins where that concept of the heart ends.

Consider well that a house is a machine in which to live but architecture begins where that concept of the house ends. All life is machinery in a rudimentary sense, and yet machinery is the life of nothing. Machinery is machinery only because of life. It is better for you to proceed from the generals to the particulars. So do not rationalize from machinery to life. Why not think from life to machines? The utensil, the weapon, the automaton—all are *appliances*. The song, the masterpiece, the edifice are a warm outpouring of the heart of man—human delight in life triumphant: we glimpse the infinite.

That glimpse or vision is what makes art a matter of inner experience; therefore, sacred and no less, but rather more, individual in this age, I assure you, than ever before.

Architecture expresses human life, machines do not, nor does any appliance whatsoever. Appliances only serve life.

Lack of appreciation of the difference between the appliance and life is to blame for the choicest pseudoclassic horrors in America. And yet our more successful "modern" architects are still busy applying brick or stone envelopes to steel frames in the great American cities. Instead of fundamentally correcting this error, shall any superficial aesthetic disguised as new enable this same lack of appreciation of the principles of architecture to punish us again this time with a machinery abstract which will be used as an appliance of another cycle of thirty years? If so, as between architecture as sentimental appliance and architecture as mechanical appliance or even the aesthetic abstract itself as an architectural appliance, it would be better for America were you to choose architecture as the mechanical appliance. But, then, organic architecture would have to keep on in a little world of its own. In this world of its own the hard line and the bare upright plane in unimaginative contours of the box both have a place, just as the carpet has a place on the floor, but the creed of the naked stilt, as a stilt, has no place. The horizontal plane gripping all to earth comes into organic architecture to complete the sense of forms that do not box up contents but imaginatively express space. This is modern.

In organic architecture the hard straight line breaks to the dotted line where stark necessity ends and thus allows appropriate rhythm to enter in order to leave suggestion its proper values. This is modern.

In organic architecture, any conception of any building as a building begins at the beginning and goes *forward* to incidental expression as a picture and does not begin with some incidental expression as a picture and go groping *backward*. This is modern.

Eye-weary of reiterated bald commonplaces wherein light is rejected from blank surfaces or fallen dismally into holes cut in them, organic architecture brings the man once more face to face with nature's play of shade and depth of shadow seeing fresh vistas of native, creative human thought and native feeling presented to his imagination for consideration. This is modern.

The sense of interior space as reality in organic architecture coordinates with the enlarged means of modern materials. The building is now found in this sense of interior space; the enclosure is no longer found in terms of mere roof or walls but as screened space. This reality is modern.

In true modern architecture, therefore, the sense of surface and mass disappears in light, or in fabrications that combine it with strength. And this fabrication is no less the expression of principle as power-directed-toward-purpose than may be seen in any modern appliance or utensil machine. But modern architecture affirms the higher human sensibility of the sunlit space. Organic buildings are the strength and lightness of the spiders' spinning, buildings qualified by light, bred by native character to environment, married to the ground. That is modern!

Meanwhile by way of parting moment with the young man in architecture—this he should keep—concerning ways and means:

1. Forget the architectures of the world except as something good in their way and in their time.

2. Do none of you go into architecture to get a living unless you love architecture as a principle at work, for its own sake—prepared to be as true to it as to your mother, your comrade, or yourself.

3. Beware of the architectural school except as the exponent of engineering.

4. Go into the field where you can see the machines and methods at work that make the modern buildings, or stay in construction directly and until you can work naturally into building-design from the nature of construction.

5. Immediately begin to form the habit of thinking "why" concerning any efforts that please or displease you.

6. Take nothing for granted as beautiful or ugly, but take every building to pieces, and challenge every feature. Learn to distinguish the curious from the beautiful.

7. Get in the habit of analysis—analysis will in time enable synthesis to become your habit of mind.

8. "Think in simples" as my old master used to say, meaning to reduce the whole to its parts in simplest terms, getting back to first principles. Do this in order to proceed from generals to particulars, and never confuse or confound them or yourself be confounded by them.

9. Abandon as poison the American idea of the quick turnover. To get into practice half-baked is to sell out your birthright as an architect for a mess of pottage, or to die pretending to be an architect.

10. Take time to prepare. Ten years' preparation for preliminaries to architectural practice is little enough for any architect who would rise above the belt in true architectural appreciation or practice.

11. Then go as far away as possible from home to build your first buildings. The physician can bury his mistakes, but the architect can only advise his client to plant vines.

12. Regard it as just as desirable to build a chicken-house as to build a cathedral. The size of the project means little in art, beyond the money matter. It is the quality of character that really counts. Character may be large in the little or little in the large.

13. Enter no architectural competition under any circumstances except as a novice. No competition ever gave to the world anything worth having in architecture. The jury itself is a picked average. The first thing done by jury is to go through all the designs and throw out the best and the worst ones so, as an average, it can average upon an average. The net result of any competition is an average by the average of averages.

14. Beware of the shopper for plans. The man who will not grubstake you in prospecting for ideas in his behalf will prove a faithless client.

It is undesirable to commercialize everything in life just because your lot happens to be cast in the Machine Age. For instance, architecture is walking the streets today; a prostitute because to get the job has become the first principle of architecture. In architecture the job should find the man and not the man the job. In art the job and the man are mates; neither can be bought or sold to the other. Meantime, since all we have been talking about is a higher and finer kind of integrity, keep your own ideal of honesty so high that your dearest ambition in life will be to call yourself an honest man, and look yourself square in the face. Keep your ideal of honesty so high that you will never be quite able to reach it. Respect the masterpiece—it is true reverence to man. There is no quality so great, none so much needed now.

AN AUTOBIOGRAPHY

In the summer of 1926, on the advice of his attorneys, Wright, Olgivanna Hinzenberg, her daughter, Svetlana, and their baby daughter, Iovanna—not yet a year old—fled from their home in Wisconsin and went into hiding in Minneapolis. They lived, under an assumed name, in a small cottage that some friends had secured for them (Wright admitted that he kept forgetting exactly what the assumed name was). Since his first meeting with Olgivanna in 1924, Wright had been hounded by his estranged wife, Miriam Noel. They had been separated for nearly two years, and Wright had asked for a divorce, but Miriam persistently threatened to take Taliesin and its contents from him. Soon the banks foreclosed on the mortgage and took possession of the building, including his art collections and architectural drawings.

In Minnesota Olgivanna urged Wright to start writing the story of his life. Her motive was direct and straightforward: she was convinced that the result of such a creative person being cast out of his home and studio and cut off from his architectural work would be a strenuous and frustrating existence, detrimental both to himself and to their relationship. She reminded him that he was now fifty-nine years old and had led a full and rich life establishing the roots of modern architecture—a story that would be of interest to many.

At first he resisted the idea, but she told him his words would be preferable to someone else's biography of him, and she also explained that in various published and unpublished articles he had begun to accumulate material that easily could be used in his autobiography:

> *"How will I tell about myself as a small boy on Uncle James' farm? That was such an important part of my upbringing," Wright asked.*
> *"Simply refer yourself as 'he,' and when you are done with that part of your boyhood and early youth, and arrive in Chicago to pursue your life in architecture, change the 'he' to 'I,'" she replied.*

Which is precisely what he did. He wrote the beginning chapters in longhand, someone was brought in to do the typing, and Olgivanna helped with the editing. She had a strong background in literature, from her years in Russia and in France. During her childhood in Russia she had an English governess, and thus at an early age she learned the language. And when she was studying with Gurdjieff in France, many of her colleagues and friends were literary people, including Jane Heap, Margaret Anderson, Alfred Orage, and Katherine Mansfield.

Work on the book was interrupted when Wright and Olgivanna were jailed in October 1926. Long, drawn-out legal battles followed. But by the end of 1930 enough material was assembled to consider publication. Initially, Wright had planned to title the work "From Generation to Generation," in deference to his Welsh relations and ancestors. But Olgivanna convinced him that the most direct title would be the best: "An Autobiography."

George Bye, acting as Wright's literary agent, suggested approaching Longmans Green publishers of New York, and their editor Frank Hill worked with Wright on the general outline and final drafts.

Wright designed the book, chose its size, layout, and typeface and designed the special graphics that preceded each "Book." The cover itself was an abstraction illustrating the first book's "Prelude." He sent the design to Hill with the following note in the margin of the drawing:

My dear F. H.:

You won't like this design at first—I have disobeyed instructions and altered my own suggestions somewhat. But you will like it much when you see it on the bookstands in contrast to other books. Where every cover is barking loud(like the samples you sent) no one hears (or sees) anything in particular. It is contrast that catches the eye or the ear—I am sure of this and I ought to know?
—FLLW

There are scholars and writers who maintain that in his autobiography Frank Lloyd Wright misconstrued facts, altered dates, and wrote incorrectly concerning the incidents in his life. They further maintain that he misrepresented himself in relation to his family, to his friends, and in particular to his clients. Certain uncontestable facts, on record as historic events, however, shape the general outline of Wright's book. He was descended from powerful, almost Druid-like Welsh characters. His time spent with Louis Sullivan cannot be denied, nor the influence he attributes both to Adler and Sullivan for his own development. His role as an architect in what he was creating, in the path of what he was pioneering, is certainly born out by history. The making of the great buildings he writes about, from the early concepts of what the American dwelling should be and how he built it to the Larkin Building, Unity Temple, Midway Gardens, and the Imperial Hotel, are all intriguing stories. His insightful and absorptive reaction to Japan while living and working there constantly reiterates his ongoing appreciation and reverent love of Japanese culture.

The tragedies that besought him—his home burned and his loved ones and friends murdered—are told in such a manner that it is evident that his ability to overcome great anguish reflects the fiber of his being.

Arguments and difficulties with clients, such as Aline Barnsdall, are unsurprisingly shaded with his point of view; it is for scholars to research and reveal the other side of the story. His accounts of the four women who figured most prominently in his life vary—as the women themselves did. He tells of his youthful romance with Catherine, his first wife, and the raising of a family of six children. Mamah Borthwick Cheney, by contrast, is portrayed as an almost ephemeral, mythical figure, too close, too precious, to be able to describe. He does not even mention her name. His memories of life with Miriam Noel suggest her strange and unpredictable nature, which finally dissipated into nervous frenzy, yet he does not go into lurid detail about the stormy life he endured with her. His meeting with Olgivanna seems a relief to all the disappointments, tragedy, and anxiety he experienced with the others—like coming upon a port in a storm or an oasis in the desert. Since the book was written with her directly at his side, and since the events of their meeting and living together were so close to the time the book was published, she figures in an especially romantic and endearing light. Indeed, the book ends with a story of an event in their life written in fact by Olgivanna.

In 1943, when he added to and expanded the 1932 edition of An Autobiography, *he glossed over, or excused, whatever importance readers might place upon the inconsistencies, the casualness of dates in the stories and narratives, be they accounts or legends, with the sweeping statement: "I said at the beginning that the real book was between the lines. It is true of any serious book concerned with culture."*[1]

But whatever its faults, a strong sense of poetry and drama permeates the entire opus. Some passages are so poetic, in fact, that the memory of them is both consuming and haunting. Of all his writings up to 1932, the style here is the most consistent. Above all, it is an engrossing and exciting book to read, because being comprised both of autobiography and of discourses on architecture it richly chronicles his ideas and work and presents an intimate, sometimes painful, view into his very complex character. [Published by Longmans Green, New York, 1932]

1. Frank Lloyd Wright, An Autobiography (*Duell, Sloan and Pearce, New York, 1943*), *p.561.*

BOOK ONE **FAMILY FELLOWSHIP**

PRELUDE

A light blanket of snow fresh-fallen over sloping fields, gleaming in the morning sun. Clusters of pod-topped weeds woven of bronze here and there sprinkling the spotless expanse of white. Dark sprays of slender metallic straight lines tipped with quivering dots. Pattern to the eye of the sun, as the sun spread delicate network of more pattern in blue shadows on the white beneath.

"Come, my boy," said Uncle John to his sister Anna's nine year old. "Come now, and I will show you how to go!"

Taking the boy by the hand he pulled his big hat down over his shock of gray hair and started straight across and up the sloping fields toward a point upon which he had fixed his keen blue eyes.

Neither to right nor to left, intent upon his goal, straight forward he walked—possessed.

But soon the boy caught the play of naked weed against the snow, sharp shadows laced in blue arabesque beneath. Leaving his mitten in the strong grasp, he got free.

He ran first left, to gather beads on stems and then beads and tassels on more stems. Then right, to gather prettier ones. Again—left, to some darker and more brilliant—and beyond to a low-spreading kind. Farther on again to tall golden lines tipped with delicate clusters of dark bronze heads. Eager, trembling, he ran to and fro behind Uncle John, his arms growing full of "weeds."

A long way up the slope, arrived at the point on which he had fixed, Uncle John turned to look back.

A smile of satisfaction lit the strong Welsh face. His tracks in the snow were straight as any string could be straight.

The boy came up, arms full, face flushed, glowing.

He looked up at his uncle—see what he had found!

A stern look came down on him.

The lesson was to come.

Back there was the long, straight, mindful, heedless line Uncle John's own feet had purposefully made. He pointed to it with pride.

And there was the wavering, searching, heedful line embroidering the straight one like some free, engaging vine as it ran back and forth across it. He pointed to that too—with gentle reproof.

Both stood looking back. The small hand with half-frozen fingers was again in its mitten in the older, stronger hand; an indulgent, benevolent smile now down on the shamed young face.

And somehow, there was something not clear.

Uncle John's meaning was plain—NEITHER TO

RIGHT NOR TO THE LEFT, BUT STRAIGHT, IS THE WAY.

The boy looked at his treasure and then at Uncle John's pride, comprehending more than Uncle John meant he should.

The boy was troubled. Something was left out.

PART ONE FAMILY

Back in Wales in the Victorian Era, there lived a hatter, stalwart maker of strange, black, high-pointed cones. The witches wore them when riding on their broomsticks. The Welsh wore them for hats. The hatter was proud of his work and peddled his hats at fairs. He would throw one down on the ground and, "stand on it!" he would say to anyone likely to buy.

On Sundays he preached, a firebrand of a man, questioning how man should be just with God, rejecting the answers most men, and women too, gave him.

He was tall, this Richard Jones, dark-eyed—an impassioned, unpopular Unitarian. The daughter of an old Welsh family, Mary Lloyd, heard him and fell in love with him.

"For there is the just man who perisheth in his righteousness, and there is the wicked man who prolongeth in his wickedness."

"But he that knoweth God and serveth him shall come forth of them all."

So she believed, and went away with him against her parents' will. If her wealthy family looked askance at her staunch man, what did it matter? She loved him and so trusted him.

Seven children they had, whose family name became now Lloyd-Jones.

Then his outspoken liberality offending conservative popular opinion made America seem a hope and a haven to the Unitarian, and he came with a delicate wife and seven to "the West." He came to find a farm where his stalwart strength might make a home and a place where he could work in a land where speech was free, because men were.

So the hatter-preacher, in his fifty-third year, became the Wisconsin Pioneer, with his Thomas, John, Margaret, Mary, Anna, Jenkin, and Nannie.

His little Nannie, dying on the way, was left behind in strange ground.

They came by canal-boat and lake-steamer to Milwaukee on the way to Ixonia, Wisconsin. Six years the pioneer couple lived there, where they invoked four more children, Ellen, Jane, James, and Enos, to join the little band, before they found the valley by the Wisconsin River.

"The Valley," they all lovingly called it in afterlife, and lovable it was, lying fertile between two ranges of diversified soft hills, with a third ridge intruding and dividing it in two smaller valleys at the upper end. A small stream coursing down each joined at the homestead and continued as a wider stream on its course toward the River. The lower or open end of the Valley was crossed and closed by the broad and sandbarred Wisconsin and from the hills you could look out upon the great sandy and treeless plain that had once been the bed of the mighty Wisconsin of ancient times.

When the virgin soil was broken by the grandfather and his sons, friendly Indians still lingered in the neighborhood.

By the eldest son, Thomas, a carpenter, a small house was built on a sloping hillside facing south. Balm-of-Gilead trees, Lombardy poplars were planted by the Mother and her brood around the little house and along the lanes: lanes fenced with oak-rails split in the hillside forests which clung to the northern slopes and hillcrowns.

The southern slopes were all too dry for wood, and bare except where rock ledges came through. The stables were roofed with straw like the old Welsh thatch. The small simple house, however, was "modern," clapboarded and shingled by Thomas and his brothers. The kitchen was a lean-to at the rear; an outside stairway led to a cool stone cellar beneath. A root-house was close behind, partially dug into the ground and roofed with a sloping mound of grass-covered earth.

Here in "The Valley," the family tree of Richard Lloyd-Jones, Welsh pioneer, with its ten branches and one scar, struck root in the America of his hope. It was now his haven.

Up to this time he had preached, even while

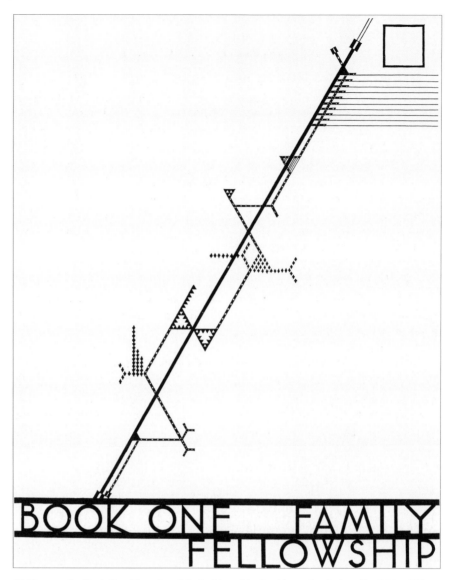

Divider page for "Book One," from the original edition of *An Autobiography*, designed by FLLW. 1932.

traveling on the ships or the canal boats or at the inns where the family stayed. Usually he was listened to with respect.

There was fervor, exaltation in him.

He read the Bible his own way with strong Welsh accent, but no one could mistake his meaning. It was often new to his lettered betters and would change their thought. He was Pioneer, not on the earth alone, but in mighty reaches of the spirit where the earth grows dim.

He had a Church during his years in Ixonia but again "where speech was free because men were" the Church proposed to "try him." He said,

"You need not. If I am intrusive, I will get out. I cannot quell my spirit."

He had for family crest, the old Druid symbol: "Truth Against The World." ⁄|\

Grandfather preached as Isaiah preached. "The flower fadeth, the grass withereth—but the word of the Lord, thy God, endureth forever." His children had to learn that chapter of Isaiah, the fortieth, by heart so they could recite it.

His grandson grew to distrust Isaiah. Was the flower any less desirable because it seemed to have been condemned to die that it might live more abundantly? As they all went to work in the fields, the grass seemed always necessary to life in the Valley, most of all when it "withered" and was hay to keep the stock alive in winter so the preacher himself might live.

The flowers have closed their eyes beneath the stars, opened to the sun, and dropped their seeds into the bosom of friendly earth these thousands of years away from that time of Isaiah and bid fair to be unfaded when the "word of our Lord," as Isaiah heard it, has been much modified in the mouth.

And was the earth not covered with forms of life, among them MAN himself, due to this very grass?

Might it not be before all, that this very grass and these flowers are, in themselves, in truth the very word of GOD?

There seemed base ingratitude in the boastful thunder of that hateful text.

When storms swept the Valley from bank to bank of its ranges of hills, now black against a livid sky—lashing the trees, drowning the helpless small things, in the destruction that was wrought and the wreck that followed, the boy would see Isaiah's "Judgment."

Ah yes! In this prophet Hell enlarged itself and opened "her" mouth without measure!

Woe! Woe! that word "woe" struck on the young heart like a blow—"O Woe unto them that are mighty to drink wine and mingle strong drink!" Nor was there to be pity on "the fruit of the womb."—Little children were to be trodden under foot.

Isaiah's awful Lord smote the poor multitudes with a mighty continuous smite, never taking away the gory, dreadful hand outstretched to smite more; never satisfied with the smiting he has already done.

And yet, according to Isaiah, were you willing to argue the matter, to reason with "Him" (none seemed to know whether Isaiah or His Lord was meant), your sins would be white as snow. Why?

Verily this Holy Warrior was a prophet making GOD in his own image. Turning his own lusts into virtues because they were on the side of pain instead of on the side of pleasure.*

What a curse to put upon the mind of a child! How much too much to thrash him! How much less than too little to lead him!

His grandson would see the stalwart figure, legs straight in stirrups, of this spiritual brother of Isaiah, his dreaded and beloved Welsh Grandfather, white-bearded and hoary-headed, sitting up straight upon his horse, "Timothy," like a Patriarch; stick with shepherd's crook hung over the left forearm, the Bible of his faith firm against his side under the upper arm, the bridle-reins in his other hand. And his grandson would see that he was thus able to whack his horse on the flank without losing his hold on the Book.

On weekdays grandfather believed in the gospel of hard work. Relentlessly he taught his children to add tired to tired and add it again, until the fountain of energy he himself was, working out through his offspring, began to cut away the forests and establish a human decency where the wilderness was. A human smile, where before had been the Divine Countenance.

The Indians, in passing, sometimes brought venison and laid it on his doorstep and he had tobacco for them.

For he smoked a pipe.

And this pipe was a great source of shame to his family in after years. Their one shadow of reproach to him. Though he was hard, and, should a child by some slip pour much more sorghum on his plate than intended, Grandfather would righteously make him eat it all ("his eyes should not be bigger than his stomach")—yet this cruelty they respected.

The pipe they could neither explain nor forgive.

After all, it was the little Grandmother who loved him and tempered his harshness. She taught him to smoke as a cure for his asthma.

The asthma he outgrew but his pipe stayed with him while he lived.

Grandmother's gentle spirit had welded together with their father's the strong wills of his ten children in a united affection that was never broken.

Some ten years in the new home and the

---

* In Chapter Four, Isaiah apportions seven women to take hold of every man and they were to feed and clothe themselves at that, if he would give them his name to purge them of any uncleanness in the matter. All that the seven who "took hold" of Isaiah were to ask was to be "Mrs. Isaiah."

Grandmother, carried out into the open air of the arbor the Grandfather had built for her with his own hands, passed painlessly away. As if he, too, were transported, Grandfather, the better part of his life now gone, got on his feet and led these children in prayer which they ever after remembered as the most beautiful they had ever heard.

Eleven years later, eighty-seven years of age, he lay down in his bed to sleep. In the night— painlessly—he, too, slipped away.

But not then was his spirit "quelled."

His "spirit" lived on now in a typical emigrant establishment on virgin American soil. A little Welsh clan, by himself set in this little corner of that enormous new ground dedicated to Freedom, and parceled out among all the breeds of the world, stayed there with the ground.

The ground! What does it not hold impartially in its depths, breadths, and beauty for the pioneer like Richard Lloyd-Jones, in league with the stones of the field, himself like the ridges of primeval rock that ribbed the hills in contrast to the verdure rolling over them. He planted a small world within the world that is again within other worlds, without end.

He did not consider the lilies—how they grew.

The little Grandmother was that to him.

All strong men drink cool, fresh water somewhere.

Beauty comes to them in some guise, sometimes in disguise.

His children, his flesh and blood, were like him but with something of the element added to them of the prayerful consideration for the lilies that was the gentle Grandmother's. Sympathy "for the flower that fadeth," gratitude for the "grass that withereth," came a step nearer to them in their mother.

"Mother's Pine" stands on the hillside lawn, a living child of hers. The little Grandmother planted it there. A small thing. Careless mowing in the yard severely injured it. They were going to pull it up and throw it away. "No, leave it to me," she said, and, bringing her sewing basket, knelt by the tree on the grass and covered the injury with pitch she called for. She sewed a firm canvas band over it, tight around the damaged trunk.

It is seventy-five feet tall today! Twice, the lightning struck it, but it is still a noble specimen of its fast disappearing tribe.

Occasional Lombardys, of which she was fond, stand isolated in clumps where once their ranks along the lanes up the hillsides were unbroken.

Balm of Gilead has scattered around the Valley to meet you in unexpected places.

And the Lilacs and Bouncing-Betty of her dooryard have colonized on their own along the roadsides in great masses good to see.

Willing worker in this intensive human-hive of work, song, and prayer in rural Wisconsin was the Sister Anna, whose boy, the grandson who doubted Isaiah, went in quest of weeds while his Uncle John preached a sermon to him with his feet, in the snow.

Sister Anna herself, fourth child of Richard and Mary, was five years old when the immigration from Wales took place. She walked with a free stride like a man, had much dark brown hair above a good, brave brow; a fine nose and dark, dreaming brown eyes. Much fire and energy gave her temper beneath a self-possession calm and gracious.

Education was Sister Anna's passion even while very young.

All this family was imbued with the idea of education as salvation.

Education it was that made man from the brute and saved him from the beast.

Education it was too (and that was her mistake) that unlocked the stores of Beauty and let it come crowding in on every side at every gate. Although she believed Education the direct manifestation of God to reach it, Sister Anna loved—Beauty.

Soon she became a teacher in the countryside, riding a horse over the hills and through the woods to and from her school each day. Old men in the neighborhood still speak of Sister Anna as their teacher, with admiration and respect.

Her school lay sometimes in one direction and sometimes in another, but always miles away. She walked when the horse was needed in the fields, but usually she rode, coming from the still shadows of the wood to the far prospect from the hilltops or overlooking the warm yellow-green sunshine on the meadow-stretches. All blazed with bewildering color in autumn, more beautiful than ever sleeping under wintry coverlets of snow, the shapes of the hills seeming like huge primeval monsters lying peacefully beneath them. Often she made those journeys after dark alone. Farmsteads were few and miles between.

And often it rained. She had to go just the same covered with a blue soldier's cape that had brass buttons and a hood. Bareheaded, otherwise, she went. She knew the ferns, the flowers, by name, the animals that, startled, ran along the road. There were berries by the roadside too, wild cherries, plums, and grapes. She might reach out and take them on the branches, hanging the branches to the saddle bow, eating from them as she rode.

How it happened that Sister Anna's ideals then are modern now, who can say, unless first-hand contact with Nature in the primitive struggle, and the rugged faith of the father ("at destruction and famine thou shalt laugh, neither shalt thou be afraid of the beasts of the earth for thou shalt be in league with the stones of the field") gave it to her. This "league with the stones of the field" must have given power to her imaginative vision.

The boy of this story was her first child.

Sister Anna came by him as the law prescribed—by marriage with a man who satisfied her ideal of "Education." A man from Hartford, Connecticut. A "circuit rider." A musician now going about the countryside near Lone Rock teaching folk to sing.

She was twenty-nine when she married him. Seventeen years her senior, the music-master was a product of "Education," one of a family of intellectuals to which James Russell Lowell belonged, and Alice and Phoebe Cary, from which distant branches he got his middle names.

He was William Russel Cary Wright, tirelessly educating himself, first at Amherst, then to practice medicine, soon found to be no genuine science.

Now "the law," but again—disillusioned.

He was just about to hear the "call" his preacher ancestors back to the days of the Reformation in England had all been hearing. And Sister Anna was the one to help him hear it. Soon after they were married, he too became a preacher.

He had his music still, which always consoled him, and music was his friend to the last when all else had failed.

When her son was born something happened between the mother and father. Sister Anna's extraordinary devotion to the child disconcerted the father.

The father never made much of the child, it seems.

No doubt his wife loved him no less but now loved something more, something created out of her own fervor of love and desire. A means to realize her vision.

The boy, she said, was to build beautiful buildings. Faith in prenatal influences was strong in this prospective mother. She kept her thoughts on the high things for which she yearned and looked carefully after her health.

There was never a doubt in the expectant mother's mind but that she was to have a boy.

Fascinated by buildings, she took ten full-page wood engravings of the old English Cathedrals from *Old England*, a pictorial periodical to which the father had subscribed, had them framed simply in flat oak and hung upon the walls of the room that was to be her son's.

Before he was born, she said she intended him to be an Architect.

In due course of nature, in a little inland town among the hills, Richland Center, Wisconsin, the father preaching and sometimes lawing, still teaching music, her son was born.

That meant invocation ceased and "Education" took hold.

When the boy was three with a baby sister a year old, the father was called to a Church at Weymouth near Boston.

About this time the father's father died at his home in Hartford, Connecticut, aged ninety and nine. He went upstairs to his room, wrote by candlelight a letter to each of his three sons, addressed each in his own handwriting, went to bed, and, like the mother's father, painlessly slept to final sleep.

Leaving the Lloyd-Joneses prospering in their Valley, the little family went east, nearer to the father's native place. Went on to activities still religious but to different scenes, a different atmosphere—that of a Boston suburb.

A modest, gray, wooden house near a tall white-brick church in drab old historic Weymouth.

The tall, handsome mother in that house with her boy and the little girl Jane, named after the mother's sister back there in the Valley. A donation party of the previous evening had left twenty-three pumpkin pies on the pantry shelves where there was nothing much else to eat after the party had gone away. The mother longing for the Valley for which she seemed always to pine.

BACH

At this time a nervously-active intellectual man in clerical dress seated at the organ in the church, playing. Usually he was playing.

He was playing Bach now. Behind the organ, a dark chamber. In the dark chamber, huge bellows with projecting wooden lever-handle. A tiny shaded oil lamp shining in the dark on a lead marker running up and down to indicate the amount of air pressure necessary to keep the organ playing.

A small boy of seven, eyes on the lighted marker, pumping away with all his strength at the lever and crying bitterly as he did so.

Streams of sound went pouring out into the Church against the stained glass windows "fortissimo" and the boy worked away for dear life to keep air in the bellows, knowing only too well what would happen to him should he give out. Then came a long-drawn-out, softer passage. It was easier to pump—The Vox Humana—far away beauty, tenderness, and promise in it stealing over boy-senses. He stopped, tears and all, entranced. Listening—breathless—he forgot, but suddenly remembered just in time to work away again with all his might to keep air enough for the Bach as

it broke into the sound-waves of triumphant, march-like progress. The heroic measures brought him back again to strength, and for a while he pumped away with fresh energy, hopefully. But as on and on the wondrous music went, more and more the young back and arms ached until again the tears began to flow. Would father never stop? He felt forgotten and he was. Could he hold out? Pulling all his energies together now. But despair gaining on him. Eye on that leaden marker. Should it ever drop, but it will . . . it will . . . for he can't . . . No . . . .

Just then the music ended abruptly. The stops knocked back into their sockets. The cover of the keyboard slammed down. His father called him. "Frank! . . . Frank!" There was no answer.

The figure of the father darkened the small doorway, took in the situation at a glance, took the boy by the hand, and led him home without a word.

When they got there his mother, seeing the state the boy was in, looked reproachfully at the father.

It was always so. The differences between husband and wife all seemed to arise over that boy. Mother always on the defensive, father taking the offensive.

And the boy grew afraid of his father.

His father taught him to play. His knuckles were rapped by the lead pencil in the impatient hand that would sometimes force his hand into position at practice time on the Steinway Square piano in the sitting room. But he felt proud of his father too. Everybody listened and seemed happy when father talked and Sundays when he preached the small son dressed in his homemade Sunday best, looked up at him absorbed in something of his own making that would have surprised the father and the mother more than a little if they could have known.

His pupil always remembered father as he was, when "composing," ink on his face and fingers. For he always held the pen crosswise in his mouth while he would go to and from the desk to the keyboard to try over the passage he had written. His face would soon be fearful with black smudges in the wrong place. Weird he was, to his observant understudy at those times.

Was music made in such heat and haste as this, the boy wondered?

How did Beethoven make his?

And how did Bach make his?

He thought Beethoven must have made most of his when it was raining, or just going to, or when the days were gloomy and the sun was soft with clouds. He was sure Bach made his when the sun shone bright and breezes were blowing as little children were happily playing in the street.

Father sometimes played on the piano far into the night and much of Beethoven and Bach the boy learned by heart as he lay listening. Living seemed a kind of "listening" to him—then.

Sometimes it was as though a door would open, and he could get the beautiful meaning quite clear. Then it would close and the meaning would be dim or far away. But always there was some meaning. And it was the boy's father who taught him to see a symphony as an edifice of sound!

At the Centennial at Philadelphia, after a sight-seeing day, mother made a discovery. She was eager about it now. Could hardly wait to go to Boston as soon as she got home—to Milton Bradley's.

The kindergarten!

She had seen the gifts in the Exposition Building. The strips of colored paper, glazed and "matte," remarkably soft, brilliant colors. Now came the geometric by-play of those charming checkered color combinations! The structural figures to be made with peas and small straight sticks: slender constructions, the joinings accented by the little green pea globes. The smooth shapely maple blocks with which to build, the sense of which never afterward leaves the fingers: so *form* became *feeling*. And the box with a mast to set up on it, on which to hang with string the maple cubes and spheres and triangles, revolving them to discover subordinate forms.

And the exciting cardboard shapes with pure scarlet face—such scarlet! Smooth triangular shapes, white-back, and edges, cut in rhomboids with which to make designs on the flat tabletop. What shapes they made naturally if only you would let them!

THE GIFTS

A small interior world of color and form now came within grasp of small fingers. Color and pattern, in the flat, in the round. Shapes that lay hidden behind the appearances all about.

Here was something for invention to seize and use to create. These gifts came into the gray house in drab old Weymouth, and soon made something begin to live there that had never lived there before.

Mother would go to Boston, take lessons of a teacher of the Froebel method, and come home to teach the children.[1]

When her housework was done, mother and the two children would sit at a low mahogany table with a polished top working away with these gifts.

Fra Angelico's bright-robed angels: some in red, some in blue, others in green. And one—the loveliest of all—in yellow, would come and hover over the table. From their golden harps simple rhythms were gently falling on child minds like flying seeds carried on the wings of the wind to fertile ground. Giotto standing in the shadow at the mother's elbow would have worn a smile beneath his Florentine cap; musing smile prophetic of seedtime and harvest other than his but eternally the same. Again—architecture.

His mother's son has been in Miss William's private school for some years, no doubt with the usual Snobbyists and Goodyites. For several years, the minister's son was kept in this fashionable school with the few little Lord Fauntleroys Weymouth afforded.

At this time the mystery that was girls began to intrigue a lively imagination. There was something, mysterious, between himself and the mystery. But he was so shy he never dared speak to a girl for fear of spoiling that something.

Next door across the white picket fence, peeking often between the white pickets and pink hollyhocks, was Nelly Pray. It was perhaps the hollyhocked fence that gave particular charm to Nelly.

But next door beyond the Pray's, probably Allan Hunt was a "bad boy." Son of a petted, languid, aristocratic mother and a wealthy father who smoked big, black cigars. It was Allan's ambition to smoke them too. In the glass cupola of the Hunt house "learning" began, and how long it lasted is out of memory. But the leaden, sunken sense of the scene, and all connected with it, remains. The novice slid backward down the attic stair believing himself dying, a trail of interior decoration all the way down, to go with the work of the capable inferior desecrators who had just finished the setting for this debacle.

Got the front door open, crawling along the sidewalk he got up the steps to the minister's house. Managed to pull the bell. The sight that mother saw may be imagined.

Let the delicate psychology of biological unfoldings in boys under eleven, important, but so much the same, stand as on record by able artists with a taste for psychological anatomy. In public schools the susceptible little animals encounter and learn things that mothers promptly unlearn and protect boys from. So well was this done with him that until marriage in his twenty-first year personal biological experience was exactly nothing at all.

This early period indicates this boy as adventuresome, none too likely to be good unless an imaginative game might be made of it.

The minister, returning from prayer meeting one summer evening, found a crowd of neighboring children gathered before the house on the sidewalk, and things usually stored in attics coming down from the small attic window by the hand of the minister's son, aided by his small sister. As each familiar thing fell into the crowd there would be a scramble. Free for all! The arms of many of the children already full.

A "donation party," you see? Only given this time by the minister himself by way of his own son.

And certain sophisticated boys bade the minister's son with the long curls on which rested a blue soldier's cap with a shiny black visor, a rather deciduous effect go down to Binney's, buy barley-candy, glass agates, and blood alleys to divide with them, and walk out as he invited Mr. Binney to charge them to the "town-pump." Binney promptly charged the barley-candy, glass agates, big and little, to his father. This went on about a month until

the bill came in, and the easy understudy in high-finance had reason to know who the "town-pump" really was.

But nothing much of this period remains very clear to the boy who dreamed as much as this lad did.

His imagination made a world for himself pretty much as he would have it, except where rudely intruded upon by forces that would and could have it otherwise.

Music he adored, and the gifts.

Meantime he was learning to play the piano. Going to his mother's kindergarten. Learning to paint and draw a little. Learning to sing a little. Reading much all the while. Playing alone usually for, boy-like, his sister he discounted. There would be an occasional excursion to Nantucket, or a clambake at Narragansett. What he was taught in school made not the slightest impression that can be remembered as of any consequence.

So he grew day by day.

For many of the early years of his life when the minister's son was told by his mother that he must not eat a certain thing, "for it would make him sick," he would always say, "Well! Let's see if it will then!"

For the first twelve years of his life he got a ginger cookie now and then, ginger bread with a glass of milk, molasses-candy, popcorn aplenty, but store-candies only when mother didn't know it. No pie. No cake—except at other houses as he grew older. Sometimes, driven to it in the bitterness of thwarted desire, he would hurl this withering sarcasm at his defenseless mother, "Huh! Bringing up your children on graham bread, porridge, and religion, are you?"

She, probably confirmed by the influence of the father's unhappy essay in medicine, distrusted doses and doctors.

Her idea of food was that everything in cooking should be left as simple as possible. The natural flavor heightened, but never disguised. Her brown bread, stews, baked dishes, roasted meats were delicious without sauces. The frying pan had no place in her sense of things. "Eat the skins of your baked potatoes," she would say. And if potatoes were boiled, it would be with jackets on, to enhance the potato-flavor. And she would slice the apples for pie or sauce without peeling a certain number of them. She believed the life-giving part of grains or fruit or vegetables was in the color the sun put into them. And that was concentrated in the skins.

The apple barrel from the Valley was open between meals or just before bedtime.

If she picked flowers, she would take the stems long, or the branches, and would arrange them not, as was the mode, in variegated bunches, but freely and separately—none too many together. And she always loved best a glass vase for them, showing the stems in water.

In the matter of clothes, she cared little for bright colors. She liked black or white or gray or purple with cream-colored or black lace at hands and throat, long, flowing lines.

She never believed in corsets and never wore them. She used to say that a beautiful head of hair was nature's most beautiful gift to mortals, and seldom wore more than a scarf on her own head unless she were on duty in her place as minister's wife.

When she read to her children, as she was fond of doing, it was from Whittier, Lowell, or Longfellow, or fairytales—Usually poetry.

The most beautiful thing in the world, she said, was a lovely mother nursing her baby.

Though living in this atmosphere of emphasis on the natural and though physically well made and strong, knowing little fear except shyness where his feelings were concerned, this boy was too much in the imaginative life of the mind. He preferred to read to playing with other boys—and no wonder! He would rather listen to music than eat his food. He liked to read, listen to music, draw, and make things rather than sleep. Above all he liked to dream by himself. And this dreaming he did, with encouragement, regardless of the taunt, "graham bread, porridge, and religion."

The mother saw which way her man-child was going. She was wise and decided to change it. And change it she did.

The eastern pastorate was wearing out by now. The father had been a Baptist in that land consecrated to Unitarianism. But Unitarianism in the air and the mother's Unitarianism of a more colorful kind at home, must have had its effect, for the preacher resigned—a Unitarian.

TRUTH AGAINST THE WORLD ‼

To the mother, accustomed to the free stride of her life in the country, the meticulous righteousness of a world now her world, the punctilio of her position, the hard-shell "godliness" of the provincial Baptist, and the consequent consecration of meanness, probably made every "donation party" an argument for going back home "out West."

The minister's pay was a pittance, of course, in keeping with the parsimony and poverty of the ideals of life—intolerance and infallibility—which it paid for.

The Unitarianism of the Lloyd-Joneses, a far richer thing, was an attempt to amplify in the confusion of the creeds of their day the idea of life as a gift from a divine source, one God omnipotent, all things at one with Him.

Unity was their watchword, the sign and symbol that thrilled them, the Unity of all things! This mother sought it continually. Good and evil existed for her people still, however, and for her. The old names still confused their faith and defeated them when they came to apply it. But the salt and savor of faith they had, the essential thing, and there was a warmth in them for truth, cut where it might! And cut, it did—this *truth against the world.* Enough trouble in that for any one family—the beauty of Truth! The family did not so well know the truth of Beauty. The valley-folk feared beauty as a snare for unwary feet, and the straight way their feet might mark in the snow be less admirable in their sight as an example for the irresponsible.

Now there was to come back to the valley from the East by way of Sister Anna and her preacher the "Unitarianism" that had been worked out in the transcendentalism of the sentimental group at Concord: Whittier, Lowell, Longfellow, yes, and Emerson, too. Thoreau? Well, Thoreau had always

seemed too smart, made them uncomfortable.

This poetic transcendentalism was to unite with their own richer, sterner sentimentality, with the results that will be seen.

The luxury of the Lloyd-Joneses was not laughter, but tears.

Until you had water in the eyes of them, you really hadn't got them.

Quick in emotional response to human need, sorrow or suffering, good deeds always thrilled them.

The little preacher-family in Weymouth were desperately poor in this scrabby, stony vineyard of the Lord. And but for the children of the mother and the music of the father, body and soul by this time would have been far apart.

Maginel, a frail little thing, was born in this lean period. She was, for months, handled carefully on a pillow. Her mother alone saving her by giving her own vital energy, manipulating and exercising her for hours.

She came to be added to the responsibilities of the preacher.

Salvage for the Mother: private schooling for her boy, the gifts, the household, and the transcendentalism of Concord that was reaching back to the Valley in letters she wrote and books she sent—the books of Channing, Emerson, Theodore Parker, and Thoreau.

Salvage for the Father: a strange Italian, looking like Paganini, came to play. Remenyi with his grotesque nose and eyes came too. Later in the West, to the house at Madison, came the handsome Ole Bull. And, always, there was the church organ in the quiet, deserted church.

So the preacher-father and teacher-mother came back West to a modest house on the shore of Lake Mendota, in Madison, forty miles from the valley. Education of the male child to begin in earnest.

But this child was to be saved from the "word of God" as it was thought to be, something written in mighty books or spoken by learned men from pulpits instead of the living, breathing thing it is: "The flower that fadeth, the grass that withereth."

ADDING TIRED TO TIRED

A letter to Sister Anna's beloved brother, James, brought him from the Valley to the modest town house by the blue lake.

He drove down leading a cow tied behind his wagon the entire forty miles, so that Anna's children might have good fresh milk.

There stood Uncle James, tall, strong, and brown with a great shock of waving brown hair on his handsome head, a thick brown beard on his face. When he smiled his eyes went nearly shut and witty wrinkles came to the corners of his eyes. His nephew trusted him at first glance.

The golden curls had been cut off. The mother wept as she cut them. Curls there still were, but shorter, their glory gone. This "going to work" of her boy was costing the mother something more than the shedding of the curls. It could be seen now.

Uncle James put his arm around his sister to comfort her. She whispered something to him the boy did not hear. He patted her shoulder, and laughed a reassuring laugh. How he always laughed! So clear! And ringing out so it always made you want to laugh too. He promised her something as he took the boy by the hand. "Ready now, Frank? We're going West. Going to make a farmer of you." The mother gathered the child in her arms and wept.

And he went. Went away from mother, books, music, city boys, and father, little Maginel and Jane, idle dreams, and city streets to learn to add tired to tired and add it again—and add it yet again. And then beginning all over again at the beginning to add it all up some more until it seemed to him he would surely drop.

A low attic bedroom lit by a single window in one of the whitewashed sloping walls, heated by a stovepipe running up through the floor and ceiling above from the room below.

Sharp rapping now on the stovepipe—loud. Again, sharper, louder. The boy rubbed his eyes, shocked by the banging outrage.

A voice below, "Four o'clock, my boy, time to get up."

How could it be?

He had just gone to bed! But he remembered soon and sleepily called, "All right, Uncle James—coming!"

He looked down at the things Uncle James had put there by the bed the night before, got up, and put them on. It was early spring and he shivered. Two pieces, a hickory shirt, blue-jean overalls with blue cotton suspenders. Coarse blue cotton socks and clumsy cowhide shoes, with leather laces. These last were worst. And there was a hat. That hat!

He, forthwith, hating hat and shoes, learned to do without both.

Uncle James was waiting for him at the foot of the stairs with that life-giving voice of his and his winning smile. After splashing water on his face from the basin on the bench—you got it by dropping a bucket into the cistern tied to a rope—he was ready. His uncle took him off to the barn. The strange smells sickened him, but he dutifully began milking as shown until his hands ached.

And that very morning he learned to look out for certain cows who, feeling you come in beside them, would lean over and crush the breath out of you against the wall of the stall. Beating them over the back with the milking stool only made them push harder.

Milking done, came breakfast. Potatoes, fried. Fried corn meal mush, fried pork, green cheese, and cornbread. Pancakes and sorghum. Buttermilk, glass of milk. Coffee or tea, but not for the boy.

No cream.

When Gottlieb "Munch"—red-faced, yellow-haired hired man—would pour sorghum over his big piece of fat pork, he would take the boy's appetite away.

After breakfast, helping Uncle James' wife, Aunt Laura, to feed the calves. Teaching the darned crowding, pushing, bunting things to suck the milk by holding the fingers in the pail for them to suck. A nasty business. And often a desperate calf would give the bucket a bunt and send milk flying all over him from head to foot, until, exasperated by the senseless bunting and pushing, he would lay about him with the pail to keep from being trampled down.

Aunt Laura would laugh then.

After this, carrying sticks of cordwood to the crosscut saw, pausing to run errands maybe, if your uncle saw you were getting the worst of it, and told you to. Then dinner. Boiled fresh beef, boiled potatoes, carrots, turnips, homemade bread and butter. Jam, pickles, prunes, sorghum, and honey and green cheese, or pie or cake. Tea or coffee, but not for the boy.

No cream.

Afternoon, holding the split oakrails while Uncle James nailed them to the fenceposts, hands full of slivers, going off to get the cows for the first time, at five. Home to supper at six. Fried potatoes, as regularly as the sun set. Homemade bread and butter. Cornbread, cornmeal mush and milk, honey, and homemade preserves. Fried salt-pork or smoked beef, "creamed." Milk.

No cream!

After supper, milking again.

In bed about half-past seven, too tired to move.

Again the outrageous banging on the stovepipe, almost before he had really fallen asleep.

It had begun—this business of "adding tired to tired, and adding it again—and adding it again."

And so, as it was that day with the eleven year old, it was next day and the day after and the day after that, until the clothes he drew on in the morning, to the violence of that rapping on the stovepipe, were sweat-stiffened. They went on stiff and stayed stiff until he limbered them up by working in them.

On Saturday night he got a bath by carrying soft water from the cistern, heating some of it on the stove. He threw the stark things aside for his city clothes on Sunday morning. And already in April, for the first years, he would begin to look forward to September seventeenth when school would begin for him. Longing for the time to come. How sore! If mother only knew.

She came before long. Seeing him, she clasped him to her and burst into tears. The boy wondered why she was so sad to see him.

And then, after she went away, work went on some four or five weeks and he began to wear down. His back ached so. His fingers were so stiff and sore, knees and elbows, feet, too. He was ashamed to let it be known, but one afternoon he decided to change it himself. Having a difficulty with Aunt Laura over the free use of a hammer he seldom put back in its place, he got it, threw it in the creek for good and all, and departed. He took a kitchen knife with him, intending to get home somehow, anyhow.

He started across the hill toward the river to find the ferryboat that would take him to Spring Green. He was footsore. Crestfallen, his legs stiff. Guilty, his back lame. Ashamed of running away, his hands bleeding in places.

Uncle James knowing what was good for the boy had given it to him until, well—here he was, running away from home or somewhere—what did he care where, if he couldn't go where he could find comfort?

His nephew adored Uncle James. Uncle James could do everything, and so well that the others liked to stop and watch him do it. Break colts to harness for the neighbors. Handle a kicking cow that Gottlieb, the "hired man," would be afraid to touch. Swing an ax with such ringing accuracy that the clean-cut chips whizzed furiously around your head as you tried to dodge them. Could run all the machines. Always knew how to fix what was the matter with them—and there was always something the matter with them. Was always laughing at the same time, and never afraid of anything. As the boy thought of him now he wanted to turn back and stick. But he was too sore in body and mind. So he limped along. The home by the blue lake and mother seemed very dear and all he wanted, but how far away!

As the road ran over the hilltop above Uncle Enos', soft, white sandrock cropped out in long, thin ledges beside it. Fascinated by whatever there is in sand that bewitches boys, he scraped away at it with his knife and took the soft piles of pure white in both his hands. To the right were pink ledges. He scraped those. To the left, yellow, and he scraped those. Put a layer of yellow over a layer of white, then pink and then white and, even in his misery, it occurred to him to cut through the pile

with his knife and take one half away and look at the color streaks in the section he thus made.

This diversion ruined his enterprise, though he did not know it. His anguish grew less, and he thought about going back before Uncle James came home and found him gone. But he had started something now, on his own. So he went on to the ferry.

He was sitting now on the barge-board of the old ferryboat, legs over the side in the flowing water, waiting for a start. He sat there for some time, watching the eddies marking the sand, along the shore. Then, feeling something, he looked up and saw Uncle Enos!

He liked Uncle Enos, mother's youngest brother.

Uncle Enos was fond of him. They had wrestled and played together often.

Word had gone out from Uncle James to look for the boy. It would soon be getting dark. Uncle Enos' instinct had been the right one. In a kindly tone he asked,

"Where are you going, Frank?"

No answer.

Tears. . . .

Uncle Enos took the boy by the hand and led him to the grass on the bank overlooking the river. The boy cried it out, telling his woes and his resentment.

"Yes, yes. I know, my boy. Work the soreness out by keeping right on working! You will grow stronger by keeping at it, no matter how it hurts. Soon you'll be so strong you'll like it, and you can do things like Uncle James. The only way to do. Just keep on when you are sore and tired and stiff and think you're discouraged. But you never are discouraged. No. . . . And by keeping on, still more, and again more, you'll see you can do most anything and never feel it too much." He gripped the biceps in the soft arm. "As much muscle as a blackbird's got in his leg," he said. Then stretching out his own arm, "Feel this"—and the boy felt his uncle's iron upper-arm with admiration. "Your muscles will be like that, Frank, if you keep on at it. Then you can laugh, too, like Uncle James, and never be afraid of anything. Work is an adventure that makes strong men and finishes weak ones."

"Aunt Laura? Well, Aunt Laura is a bit hasty. Not very well just now. Something is going to happen. You needn't mind her too much. Think of your mother and Uncle James. How disappointed they both would be if you went on with this. Shall we go back now?"

"Yes!"

Under cover of darkness, hand in hand, they made their way back. The boy went ruefully up to his bed in the attic.

Next morning—as though nothing at all had happened—the rapping on the stovepipe, perhaps not so loud, but relentless just the same.

And it began all over again.

Something Uncle Enos had said stuck in his mind: "Adventures make strong men and finish weak ones."

But Uncle Enos had said work was that adventure. The connection of adventure with work got lost in the impressionable mind for the time being. But later he was to find it.

The rebel ran away again before long. Got farther this time. Brought back by Uncle James himself unregenerate, he slipped to hiding in the strawstack as soon as they got inside the gate. All night he lay there hidden in the straw, not answering by any sign; listening to the anxiety and confusion in the dark, as one or the other of the household would call him from different directions, near or far away.

Thus, the truant took his revenge for the hurts that were his by hurting them. A reprobate element of character, this "eye for an eye, and a tooth for a tooth," worthy of Isaiah. That ulcerous mosaic-root of human misery had shown itself in him before.

He fell asleep. So glad were they to find him in the morning, fearing some evil had befallen him, that his punishment was in Uncle James's hand, and light. Aunt Laura, for the time being, stood aside.

That was the last of running away.

What Uncle Enos had said, and what Uncle James had said too, began to come true. Work was an adventure when you were fit for it. Yet there was a small boy's mind fixed upon that springwater stream flowing over the soft mud-bottom as it passed below the house. And whenever he could

get into that stream, his was "recreation," in building dams of sticks and stones across it, sailing his shoes along the banks, wading and playing in it tirelessly whether he might or might not. Fascination for a child . . . running water!

Whenever it rained, running out into the rain for a shower bath, naked, was irresistible. Mother had started it when he was several years old by taking off his clothes and setting him running out of doors in thunderstorms.

"Uncle James!"

How many million times his earnest young disciple's voice had called that name from first to last. The young novice's questions were so incessant, Uncle James finally hesitated to take him to town as he usually did the small legs dangling from the spring seat of the lumber wagon, just because he wanted a little peace!

The restless, inquisitive one, further was a simpleton, looking for a little white bird which no one could make him believe he would not see. He had seen blue ones, and bluebirds, they said, were for happiness. And he had seen many red ones: scarlet tanagers, yellow thistle-birds, and orioles. He had seen black, and black-and-red ones, and many colors mixed. Brown ones. But none all white. No, never one. Why was there no white bird? Uncle James would assure him that there were none in that region except doves and hens. But they wouldn't do. Much to his uncle's annoyance, he believed a white one existed. He continued to look for it just the same. But he never saw one, and has never seen one yet.

The boy dreamed now, again. Sitting a long time, never moving, a look on his face that Uncle James came to recognize, and he would call him, "Frank! Frank! Come back! Come back, Frank!" But the open sky was overhead, the woods surrounded the fields in which work was forever going on in a routine that was endless. Endless, the care of the animals: horses, cows, pigs, sheep.

His early lot was cast with the cows.

TO HER!
Cow! What a word! And cowbell!

Mary Lloyd Jones (the Grandmother).
FLLW Fdn FA#6301.0056

Richard Lloyd Jones (the Welsh pioneer) at age eighty-seven.
FLLW Fdn FA#6301.0016

William Russel Cary Wright (the Minister).
FLLW Fdn FA#6301.0015

Anna Lloyd Wright (the Minister's wife).
FLLW Fdn FA#6301.0014

The cows! My boy. The cows! Always the cows!

The cows were red in the Valley—Durhams—until Uncle James later got a black-and-white Holstein bull, envy of all the township. And the herd, from year to year, grew to black-and-white. In three years the cattle in the valley all changed from red to black-and-white.

And why is any cow—red, black, or white—always in just the right place for a picture in any landscape? Like a cypress tree in Italy, she is never wrongly placed. Her outlines quiet down so well into whatever contours surround her. A group of her in the landscape is enchantment.

Has anyone sung the song of the calf-bearing, milk-flowing, cud-chewing, tail-switching cow, slow-moving, with the fragrant breath and beautiful eyes, the well-behaved, necessary cow, who always seems to occupy the choicest ground anywhere around?

She is the dairy farm, the wealth of states, the health of nations.

How many trusties and lusties besides her lawful calf have pulled away at her teats these thousands of years, until the stream flowing from them would float fleets of battleships, drown all the armies the world has ever seen?

Oceans and oceans. All consumed by man and his beasts.

How the cow has multiplied the man!

And yet, so battened upon, she is calm, faithful, and fruitful.

As companion, she endures all—even indifference—contented.

But the Minnesingers down the ages have given small place to the cow in poetry or song except in the picture, in passing.

She is just a cow.

Yet, to go through the herd lying on the grass as the dew falls, all quietly chewing their cud in peace together, is to find a sweetness of the breath as it rises, a freshness of earth itself that revives something essential to life lying deep in the instincts of the human race.

Is the cow now mother to the man to such an extent that his "instinct" begins to be aware of her

The boy, at age three.
FLLW Fdn FA#6001.0002

in this exhalation from her nostrils?

And the dung that goes from her to the fields by way of sweating youths and men saturated and struggling in the heavy odor and texture of her leavings! This indispensable wealth that goes to enrich and bring back the jaded soil to a greenness of the hills and fertility to life itself—for man!

Yes, where her tribe flourishes, there is the earth, green, and the fields, fertile. Man in well-being and abundance.

She is Hosanna to the Lord! For where she is, "at destruction and famine man laughs," as he salts her, fodders her, beds her, milks her, and breeds her. And thus tended she contentedly eats her way from calfhood clear through to the digestive tract of humanity—her destiny. Her humble last farewell to man—the shoes upon his feet!

"Come, my boy, the cows," or that cry like an alarm of fire: "The cows are in the corn!"

Getting the cows back home and taking them out to grass again was his especial duty.

There were no fences about the woods in those days, few roads, even, and no cow-paths except near the farmsteads, so each time he went after them was an adventure.

Aunt Nell.
FLLW Fdn FA#6301.0010

Aunt Jane.
FLLW Fdn FA#6301.0009

Uncle Enos.
FLLW Fdn FA#6301.0020

Uncle James.
FLLW Fdn FA#6301.0011

They were usually far away over the hills.

The plaintive tinkle of that far-away cowbell!

How many small boys in the homes of the brave on these Usonian* grounds-of-the-free were, at that moment or for that matter have been at any moment since, listening to the measured tinkle of that far-away bell—anxiously hearkening, stopping to listen, hearing it again. This time—yes—nearer!

The tinkle of the cowbell has steadily called the boys of Usonia. And, in some form or other, calls and will call them always.

Now he went through the moist woods that in their shade were treasuring the rainfall for the sloping fields below, or to feed the clear springs in the ravines, wending his way along the ridges of the hills gay with Indian-pinks or shooting-stars, across wide meadows carpeted thick with tall grass on which the flowers seemed to float. The field lilies there stood above the grass like stars of flame. Wading the creeks, sometimes lost in the deep shade and deeper shadows of white-oak woods, he would go to find and bring home the cows.

He had to start early in order to get them home before dark, but sometimes it would be after dark before he brought them back. Sometimes he found them not at all!

It was his duty to help milk while the herd was standing in the yard, if very warm, or at the stanchions in the cow-stable roofed with straw, if cooler. At this milking, each milker would sit balanced on a one-legged stool, barehead against the warm flank of the cow, drawing away at the teats with a slow, rhythmical squeezing pull of the hands to the music that was the sound of the milk-streams striking into the foaming milk in the pail. Occasionally a gushing stream of warm milk caught in the mouth.

A trick learned from Gottlieb.

Everyone had to milk, even Aunt Laura, who wasn't very well.

The cows all had names like Spot, who broke into the granary, ate her fill of ground feed, drank all the water she could, and died—a glorious heroine's death in her tribe, no doubt.

The death of Spot was a blow, for she was a kindly old cow with a long tail. When the small adventurer was tired and the cows struck the dusty road toward the end of the home journey, he would come tagging along in the dust holding on to her tail. It was a help. There were other tails to hang on to and they served, but none so willing for the purpose as Spot's.

In these adventures alone abroad in the wooded hills to fetch the cows, he, barefoot, bareheaded urchin, was insatiably curious and venturesome. So he learned to know the woods from the trees above to the shrubs below and the grass beneath. And the millions of curious lives living hidden in the surface of the ground, among roots, stems, and mold. He was soon happy in such knowledge. As a listening ear, a seeing eye, and a sensitive touch had been given naturally to him, his spirit was now becoming familiar with this marvelous book-of-books, experience, the only known reading—The Book of Creation.

One small boy of eleven was learning to *experience* what he heard, touched, or saw.

There can be nothing so surpassingly beautiful in any cultivated garden as in these wild pastures.

Sunrise.

Sunset.

Night shadows so wonderfully blue, like blue shadows on snow.

The chokecherry with its pendent blooms and black clusters of cherries that puckered your throat.

Solid depths of shade.

Springs, a glittering transparency in the cool shadows.

Sunlight, aslant through the leaves on the tree trunks, splashing the ground beneath.

The white birches gleaming.

Wild grape in bloom festooning the trees and fences.

Sumach with its braided foliage and dark red berry-cones.

Herbs and dripping leaves in rain.

In the fields, milkweed blossoming, later scat-

*Usonia—Samuel Butler's appropriate name for the United States of America. Derived from the word "union." If the United States is "America," then Georgia is South America and New York is North America.

Frank Lloyd Wright's mother at age seventy-seven.
FLLW Fdn FA#6301.0013

Uncle Jenkin.
FLLW Fdn FA#6301.0024

tering its fleece on every breeze.

The sorrel reddening the fields far and wide.

The world of daylight and gold and orange passing through violet into deep blue or the dark purple of the night.

He would dawn now as freshly as the day. His studious experiences never ceased in the swarming insect life in the warm living breath of fern beds.

In the marvel of mosses. In leaf mold.

In the damp grasses beneath bare feet.

In the strange life going on in them.

There was the feel of mud between the toes and burning sand beneath the feet, the cool, fresh grass on the open slopes.

He knew where the lady's slippers grew and why, and where to find yellow ones and where those rare ones, white and purple, were hidden.

He could lead you surely to where jack-in-the-pulpit stood in the deep shade of the wood, to wild strawberries in the sunny clearings of the hills, to watercress in the cool streams flowing from hillside springs.

He knew where the tall, red lilies could be found afloat on the tall meadow-grass. And where nuts and berries abounded, there he would be.

The spot of red made by a lily on the green always gave him an emotion. Later, the red square as spot of flame-red, became the crest with which he signed his drawings, and marked his buildings.

Soon, his ear could tell what flew overhead. What sang, and where, and why. He studied, by the hour, the tumblebugs, black-beetles, the scarabs rolling their marbles of cow manure in the hot sun of the dusty road. Mysterious folk!

The anthills, busy cities; catkins cutting circles on the still water. He would go catching sleek frogs or poking stupid toads. Catching crazy grasshoppers. Listening at night to the high treble of the frog-song as it rose from the marshes. He delighted in devils' darning needles, and turtles, too. Their fascinating structure, color pattern, strange movements—curious about them all. He was studying unconsciously what later he would have called "style."

And there were enemies: skunks, snakes, and hornets.

How about killing a rattlesnake with nine rattles?

Blue racers now and then? Swift dull blue streaks shot through grass—if your eye was quick.

And bull-snakes, seven or eight feet long sometimes, although they should not be killed unless you saw them climbing trees to reach a bird's nest, and the mother and father birds crazy with fear.

Cleaning out nests of water moccasins by the creek, in one nest, seventeen of them! Sort of spoiled swimming to see *them* in the water, too.

And pretty garter-snakes, most everywhere, but not to kill. Gottlieb would catch one, pull out his shirt at the neck, drop the wriggling garter in, and when he shook his leg, the snake would drop out over his shoe—Ugh!

Mosquitoes were there in the warm months to pester the boy. Flies to torture the cows. Cut-grass and nettles and poison ivy. What that poison ivy could do to young blood and tender skin, and did do! And wasps and bumblebees. Hidden sticks and stumps to stub one's toes. There were always too many toes. Quicksand in the streams. And hornets' nests in the barn-rafters, their wonderful house-nests sometimes hanging from the bushes. The threat of terrible thunderstorms—the lightning. Always the lightning.

Cruel winds that seemed to be the enemy of every growing thing swept the valley sometimes. But he learned their value later.

"Wild Rose!" A legendary woman, gone wild, living in the hills in a hut and wandering about. He had not seen her. All seemed afraid of her and cautioned the boy.

Such, teeming in the sun, quiet under clouds, drenched with rain, were the then-time pastures of the cow. And the trees stood in it all like various, beautiful buildings, of more different kinds than all the architectures of the world. And the boy was some day to learn that the secret of all the human styles in architecture was the same that gave *character* to trees.

Work was hard and sometimes interfered with dreaming studies or studious dreams. At other times, the dreams went on undisturbed beneath or above the routine. These dreaming moments must have had their characteristic expression in him still for he would again and again, as before, hear Uncle James calling, "Come back, Frank! Come back!"

SUNDAY

Sundays were salvation for the "tired to tired" week.

The uncles and aunts, some of them graying, some white-haired now, would sit in the old-fashioned rocking chairs provided for them round the platform on which the pulpit stood. The pulpit on which the family bible lay was covered with a purple velvet cloth and, Sundays, was usually smothered in wild flowers brought by the children.

The "help" were included, too.

Sometimes the neighbors came.

But if Uncle Jenkin preached there was luxury of tears. Going gently to-and-fro as tears were shed and, unheeded, trickled down. His sermons always brought them to emotional state, but then, so did readings from the transcendental classics or the singing of the children. Tears, too, when all rose in strength and, in the dignity of their faith, straightened themselves to sing, "Step by step since time began we see the steady gain of man." The faltering, the falsetto, and the flat would raise that favorite hymn to the boarded ceiling and go swelling out through the open windows and doors and—to the young mind looking out toward them—seem to reach far away and fade beyond the hills. Surrender to religious emotion, fervent and sincere! There was true heart in the favorite hymn for all, and for all water in the eyes of them.

Uncle Thomas, who was poet of the group, had planted the fir grove beside the chapel so future Sunday picnics might have shade.

On the east side of the shingle-sided chapel with its quaint belfry opposite the fir grove was the churchyard where the simple white marble obelisk did reverence to the memory of "EinTad" and "EinMam." Grouped around that tall slender obelisk were the family graves.

Every Sunday, spring and summer of these youthful years, up to September fifth, the boy would put on his city clothes and go to these chapel gatherings.

It was his work to decorate the pulpit.

Early in the morning, while still cool, his cousins would go with him to get what flowers and branches he particularly wanted. Tremendous riches were within reach along the roads as the team jogged along and stopped, jogged and stopped, until the wagon box was piled high.

The result would be broad masses of bloom and verdure freely arranged, pretty much as they grew, only more so. The rostrum and pulpit, Sundays, were a gracious sight.

The little wooden chapel stands in fair repair in the valley. It is almost hidden by the sober, towering, green mass of Uncle Thomas' fir trees under which pine-board tables used to be bountifully spread for the young and old of a united family. Uncles and aunts, ten. With husbands and wives, eighteen. Girls and boys all told, forty. An audience with the neighbors and the help, usually about seventy-five. That is, unless something special was going on, like Uncle Jenkin's preaching, a wedding, a funeral, or a camp meeting. Then the whole countryside would be there.

This family chapel was the simple wooden temple in which the valley clan worshipped the images it had lovingly created and which, in turn, reacted upon the family in their own image.

Those sunny religious meetings were, in reality, family gatherings of the clan.

But in midsummer the meetings were an orgy of visiting divines and divinity. William C. Gannett, Henry M. Simmons, J. T. Sunderland, and Dr. Thomas of Chicago were family favorites. But from time to time there were many others. The visitors would come at preacher's vacation-time, and camp meetings, reunions, picnics, and birthday celebrations would greet them.

Uncle Thomas with his gentle, rather downcast mien was always for picnics. "Come now, girls," he would say to his sisters, "let us go for a picnic. Do not bother at all, a little graham bread, a little cheese, a drink of milk—let us all be together."

And preparations would begin.

All the children—they had begun to swarm by now—would be called in to help.

Soon the "graham bread, a bit of cheese, a drink of milk," would swell into roast pig, roast turkey. Maybe fresh corn-on-the-ear to be roasted. Roast chicken, delectably stuffed. Chicken, fried. Boiled ham, hard-boiled eggs. Sugared doughnuts. Turnovers. Cinnamon-covered Dutch rolls. Corn bread. White biscuits, brown bread and butter. Ripe tomatoes. And maybe fresh cucumbers whole to be peeled, eaten in the hand, like a banana with salt. All kinds of sandwiches and pickles. Fat and sugary green apple pies and pumpkin pie and green cheese and cream cheese. And sorghum and honey. Of course, homemade preserves that ran the gamut from strawberry to watermelon rind. Interesting pickles. All kinds of dark and light cookies, slabs of gingerbread. Each household's favorite frosted or layer or plain cake. Plums or berries might be thereabouts for the picking. Coffee would be made on the fire. Milk, buttermilk, and clabbered milk to drink would be set in the spring water. All in abundance until there was hardly anything left out that could or ever had gone into a Jones at one time or another and had pleased or profited him.

Pharaoh, no doubt, fared worse.

All this would go into baskets and each family go with its basket and children into the family wagon. The first wagon ready would draw up and wait for the others. All, dressed for the occasion would, soon after waiting for all to get together, go off in a procession large enough to have been the funeral of some prophet—even Moses himself.

But it was just a Lloyd-Jones picnic.

Bright-colored cloths would be spread on green grass in some cool selected spot—probably in the shade of beautiful trees, if possible always near a spring or stream. All the preparations would be gorgeously spread out. Swings would be hung from the trees for the children. After the feast the children would sing and speak "pieces." The boy's father would play the violin and sing leading the uncles and aunts in their favorite hymns. Some of the older ones knew songs in Welsh. They used to sing them in Wales. There would be "Esteddvod" then and there. The boy, the "modern" note, would give "Darius Green and His Flying Machine," or the "Wonderful One Hoss Shay." All—grownups and children too—would have something or other to speak or sing. But the hymn-singing—in concert of course—was the most satisfying feature of the day, unless it was Uncle Jenkin's preaching. All would join in, until the tears under those circumstances reached their best.

At a distance you would hear the harmonicas and jew's-harps of the hired men walking about by the banks of the stream with the hired girls. Preaching and psalm-singing hadn't the same delight in it for them as for the Lloyd-Joneses.

These sons and daughters of Richard Lloyd-Jones, Welsh pioneer, in his Valley had gone far toward making the kind of life for themselves he would have approved.

The united family already had its own chapel, its own gristmill (Uncle John's), owned and cultivated or pastured pretty much all the land in sight in the Valley and its branches.

Steadily Lloyd-Jones family life was growing in human welfare and consequences.

This spring and summer life of the Valley and of the city in fall and winter was now established. It was to last five years more for the boy, until he was coming sixteen. But the twelve year old now comes home in September to the modest brown-wood house by the blue lake in Madison where were mother, father, Jennie, and Maginel.

Madison is a beautiful city. From near or far away the white dome of the state Capitol on a low, spreading hill shone white in the sun between two blue lakes—Mendota and Monona. Two more, smaller and not so blue—Wingra and Waubesa—were flung on one side for good measure.

The State University stood on its own hill beside Madison: a collection of noncommittal, respectably nondescript buildings.

Its hill, too, was crowned by a dome—a brown and gold one.

Both domes were in debt for life to Michaelangelo. But it was no discredit. As anyone might see, they were doing the best they could. The young student saw both domes destroyed within a few years: the mortgage of time (not Michaelangelo's) on human fallibility—foreclosed.

The city was laid out as a sort of wheel with eight spokes radiating from the Capitol dome, one of the spokes hitting the campus below the University dome.

Madison was a self-conscious town. A city, but a city provincial beyond most villages. And the University gave it a highbrow air, the air, that is, of having been educated far beyond its capacity.

There were a few good residences—good for their day. The Vilas home, the best of them. These better places bordered on the lakes. As to the rest, it was Sun Prairie, or Stoughton, or any Wisconsin village of one to five thousand or more population on a somewhat larger scale.

The intelligentsia, as was proper, ruled in Madison. The University, their badge of brief authority.

There was influx and exodus of ambitious legislators from the various provinces of the State once a year, coming to immortalize their services by making more "laws."

The Capitol then wrested the honors from the University.

At all times, there was a feeble "town" and "gown" rivalry. But it never became exciting enough to attract much notice.

Monona and Mendota connected by the Yahara, how beautiful they were! Especially Mendota!

What play spaces!

The lakes saved the city and its population from the utter weariness of self-imposed importance in this provincial matter of intellectual respectability.

One "William C. Wright" had started a Conservatory of Music above some kind of store on Pinckney Street.

The Madison ward schools were, at that time, good. And at the Second Ward school—his ward—on the bank of the lake, near the music-master's home, his son found Robie Lamp. Red-headed Robie Lamp—"the cripple." Boyish enterprises grew out of the circumstance. More than ever shy, the boy had need of few friends but somehow always needed one intimate companion. He couldn't live, move, and have his being, so it seemed, without a heart-to-heart comrade. Even then.

Robie Lamp was fourteen years old.

Courageous, faithful Robie Lamp! How may it be with Robie now? His legs were taken away from him here because of human ignorance. His kind old mother and father let him lie too long in one position when, three years old, he lay ill with inflammatory fever. No fault of Robie's! Nor theirs!

They didn't "*know!*"

Was the lifelong struggle, lasting more than forty years, put upon him for what it was worth to his "Soul" as "they" say? Was the calamity an immortal mistake? Or was it only that he might be Robie to his comrade as the comrade knew him, and Robie knew his comrade? How does the account stand now? . . . And there is no answer.

Robie's legs were shriveled, and dangled dead as he moved along on crutches. He had a good large head well covered with coarse, bright-red hair. His face had the florid complexion and blue eyes of the Teuton. His arms and chest did the work of the legs that "went out on him"—to use Robie's "Pa's" phrase. So arms and chest were fine and strong, although his hips were withered and twisted. The arms were much stronger because the legs were helpless.

All there was of Robie was the splendid head, brawny shoulders, chest, arms and hands and—the Robie spirit.

Lamp was a good name for him, he was so effulgent. His well-earned nickname was "Ruby," but his eyes were turquoise ringed with white, clear and wide open.

The schoolboys teased the cripple—unmercifully.

Savagely, squat-on-the-ground, he would strike out at them, those powerful arms of his swinging the brass-shod crutches. The tormentors were careful to keep out of reach but enough of them together could get him, and in this autumn, when he comes in here, they would bury him in the leaves until he was all but smothered, wherefrom he would finally emerge, raging, sputtering, and crying.

Plucked up by his farm training of a season, the boy rescued him. Drove off the boys cruelly picking on him; got the crutches they had wisely thrown so far out of his reach; dusted him off; got him up on them and on his smile again. This was the first meeting with "Robie."

The boys were fast friends thereafter till Robie, forty-four, died in a little cream-white brick house with a quaint roof-garden filled with flowers that had been designed for him by this rescuer of his.

At the boy's home in Madison was the irascible, intellectual father, with his piano and violin, now—and more frequently—writing and reading in his study. The household was peaceful then. The father was trying to make his Conservatory go—preaching occasionally. The modern refinement of the home grew from the yearning, ambitious mother's hands: the new-laid white, waxed maple floors, the cream-colored net curtains hanging straight beside the windows, and partly over them, pictures (good engravings) hanging on the walls—framed in narrow maple-bands. The centers of the room floors were covered with India rugs—cream-colored ground with bright-colored patterns and border. Maple and rattan furniture. And everywhere, books. Simple vases were gracefully filled with dried leaves. A simplicity, yes—but not of soul.

The "son-of-his-mother," as might be expected, has ideas about fixing things up. He was coming along by way of architecture, whether he knew it or not. Sometimes he did know it.

The flat wooden door to his attic bedroom was marked in large loose letters, "SANCTUM," and it opened with a latch and a string. This attic room with its sloping sides was decorated with dried leaves and the pod-topped weeds we have seen in the snow; for all of Uncle John's "lesson," there they were. The woodcuts of the English Cathedrals, which the boy saw as soon as he opened his eyes to see anything, were on the walls and as many "things" as were not needed below. "Things" at this stage were just so many objects to compose—with which to "fix up effects" in the childlike desire to make "pictures" of everything—including himself.

There were his own drawings and some "oil paintings" he had made in the East, as disciple of Miss Landers, a friend of mother's who imagined oil painting a useful accomplishment for any architect.

"Oil paintings?" One invited your consideration of a cardboard cock-robin on a lead-pipe branch looking nowhere, on guard beside his wife's four speckled eggs. She had thoughtfully laid them in a cast-iron nest under a baby-blue sky. Another was a "landscape" with hairy tree and oilcloth water deep-sunk in a really fine plain-gold frame chosen by Miss Landers. This "painting" was committed in the bushy brush work of the "buckeye" of that period. The "buckeye," as you may remember, was profitably distributed about the villages for a dollar to two dollars each, or painted while you waited. A virtuosity and, sometimes because it was so slight, curiously effective. He always liked that frame.

But the paintings were Miss Landers' innocent crimes to which the innocent mother had allowed her innocent son to become an innocent party. Innocent yet indubitably crime. In due course suitably punished.

A certain earthenware churn—he stippled it with color and decorated it with plum blossoms scratched through the paint while it was fresh—was better. It was a later work and "untaught." Really a kind of "sgraffito" he afterward came to know.

But the son had given up this precocious "painting" by way of Miss Landers. He was learning now to play the viola in the orchestra his father was getting together from Madison pupils—boys and girls. Jennie played the piano.

Robie, too, was now taking violin lessons of the father. "Ma" and "Pa"' would always sit and listen while their Robie practiced. They saw in it a career for him perhaps.

A small printing-press with seven fonts of Devinne type, second-hand, was set up in the old barn at first and later a quite complete printing-office fixed up in the basement of the house. The boys grew to love the smell of printers' ink.

Books read together: *Hans Brinker*, Ruskin's *Seven Lamps of Architecture,* a gift from the Aunts Nell and Jane. Jules Verne's *Michael Strogoff, Hector Servadac.* Goethe's *Wilhelm Meister.* The *Arabian Nights* as always—Aladdin and his Lamp—forever, and many tales. Not much poetry. Whittier, Longfellow, Bryant. If they were not poets, at least they were poetic.

A seductive touch upon dreaming life were those enchanted and enchanting pages of the *Arabian Nights*!

And enchantment, no less, the tattered illiterature of thrills—the Nickel Library—secretly read. Hidden at the reading for hours. The culprit, appearing at mealtime—still elsewhere, absent-minded—would fail to answer in time. Mother would perhaps be anxious.

"What has happened to you, Frank? Are you feeling well?"

"Oh, Mother, I'm all right. I was just thinking."

"Thinking of what?"

"Oh, just how wonderful the lives of some people are—and what things happen to them. And we live along just the same every day. Nothing ever happens."

"Frank, what have you been reading?" Mother would ask, fixing him with her searching eyes.

He would come out with it, then he would lose that one too, and never know if they got the Scarlet-Rover in the ambuscade at the river-crossing or not.

IN MEMORIAM

Was the Nickel Library really bad? Why would Mother or Father or Teacher take the blood-and-thunder tales away and burn them, if they caught us with them? Greasy, worn and torn like old banknotes they would secretly circulate in exchange for a glass-agate or two. One would go from pocket to pocket until it would have to be patched together to be read, fragments maddeningly missing at critical moments. Stark, they were, with the horror of masks and corpses—dripping with gang-gore—but cool with bravery in the constant crash of catastrophe. The *bravery* thrilled. The daring hero, usually some lad like ourselves, triumphant all the time. Going down, only to come right-side up through scrambled Indians and half-caste cut-throats, carcasses, bowie knives, and cutlasses.

The movie requires no imagination.

The Nickel Library did. And (just like "the movies") all was utterly arranged in every detail to the perfect satisfaction of the girlish heroine, whose virtue, meantime, was tested and retested from every possible ambush, she too, at the critical moment emerging manhandled but unspotted—with style all the while!

Were "Nickel Libraries" taboo because of the binding and gagging of the law—perhaps? Because murdering dead-shots confounded "the service" and made monkeys of the police, showing the chief all mussed up beside the cool, intrepid lad of seventeen who got the chief's job in the end but scorned to take it away from the poor simp when he learned that, if he did, the chief's beautiful young daughter must forego a college education?

More likely, they were pernicious because virtue was so easily winner: because daring was so invariably successful.

But there you have the same fault in the Sunday-School Library with its Rollo Books or Dotty Dimple stories, Oliver Optic, or Louisa Alcott or *Black Bess* or *Uncle Tom's Cabin*. They were all just as badly "out of drawing."

That is it perhaps, "out of drawing" with the facts of life. But if that was the real reason, why didn't Mothers, Fathers, and Teachers get the emphasis on the distortion they preferred, by "forbidding" what they approved—and so have got it as avidly read?

No—there was a real difference: the Nickel Library was vivid!

Wouldn't you like to read one or two in the old style now, just to see how you would react? "Dead-eye Dick," "The Phantom Hand," "The Open Window or Who Stole the Cook," "Horrible Hank of Hell's-water," "The Terror of Deadman's Gulch."

And these boys lived many lives.

One with the lake.

One, typesetting, printing, and composing. Inventing, designing.

Another with music in the evenings and reading.

The girl-friends of the boy's sisters came in often to sing and play.

Gay evenings! The happy freshness of young lives; like the freshness of roses. Young, eager, happy voices, and clear-shining eyes. Jennie at her best centering the fun on the piano. She played well now and was always willing to play all the time. Gilbert and Sullivan lyrics were then not popular—they were the rage. Born of true lyrical genius that never failed to charm the singers who sang them and those who heard them no less. Nor did they ever fail to yield new effects in the experiments made with them. The "Mikado!" "Pinafore!" "Patience!" "Iolanthe!" "Pirates of Penzance!" No such musical gifts have come to life since. Because they have the genius of true Gaiety they will last for centuries. How could *they* have come out of the Victorian Era? All inhibited life has its release. Gilbert and Sullivan must have been Victorian "release."

These evenings were no concerts. They were happy riots. No one could tell where laughter left off and singing began. Nor where singing left off and laughter began.

Koko, as grotesque as ever his creators intended, came to life in all absurdity, in the general lyrical joy:

"The flowers that bloom in the spring, tra la!"—all the unreasoning joy of fresh life in that "tra la!"—"have nothing to do with the case; I've got to take under my wing, tra la!" . . . Mother sitting with Maginel in her lap, both laughing at the rest . . . Father's study door open to let in the fun.

The youth later in life sang the songs to his children, likes to sing them yet. As he has written these lines he has sung them to himself.

Then, at other times more seriously, all would take turns playing the piano to one another. The youth had many of Mendelssohn's "Songs without Words" "by heart"—"Consolation," "Confidence," "Gondolied," mother's favorites. And Beethoven's lovely "Minuet in G," which has lasted him all his life. And Schubert and Bach and Stephen Heller's Studies. He would have to be headed off by his sister from showing off in Czerny's Exercises for he, too, was "willing-to-play-all-the-time."

Musical education, however, stopped short for the youth when he entered the University and his father had gone. Somehow, the "undergraduate" got the unpardonable idea that being "musical" was "unmanly," and started in to harden up with the boys.

Naive perspectives were already opening outward into the world in many directions, but in one direction all the others were steadily converging: this direction encouraged in skillful ways by the mother. Her son was to be an architect. He was to get beautiful buildings built. Bridges and dams were fascinating him now. Any construction whatsoever would do to pore over. And he would make now what he called "*designs.*"

Both boys had real passion for invention. Both were banged, pinched, stained or marred or were "had" somewhere by the perpetual experimenting going on.

A water-velocipede was started to be called the "Frankenrob." Drawings made for a Catamaran that cost too much to happen. The boys made a cross-gun, bows and arrows, and long bob-sleds on "double-runners." They painted them—the joy of striping them in colors! They had them "ironed" according to design by the blacksmith. A new style newspaper—a scroll. Another kind of ice-boat. Fantastic new kinds of kites of colored paper.

Kites with fantastic tails. A water-wheel. Who could remember how many schemes were hatched, patched up, and scrapped during these winter-schooling periods of adolescence. And there was the excellent scroll-saw and turning lathe. The boys were perpetually making "designs." Drawings always. Always making drawings for fun. Especially by lamplight, evenings.

But—of the schooling itself? Nothing he can remember!

A blank! Except colorful experiences that had nothing academic about them. Like dipping the gold braid hanging down the back of the pretty girl sitting in front of him, into the ink-well of his school desk and drawing with it. Getting sent home in consequence.

There was the cruel torture of "speaking" once a month.

The mortification of the nickname "Shaggy" pursued him, earned by the still abundant curls that made any hat he put on his head seem deciduous.

Distant worship of several pretty girls. "Goodie" Storer, Carrie Jacobs, Floy Stearns. And Robie at this time began to contract his hopeless secret passion for little blue-eyed Etta Doyon next door. Golden curls and brown eyes, the boy then preferred. Ella Gernon had both to perfection!

Etta's younger brother Charlie, more innocent of heart, if possible, than the pair, wanted to come into the printing office with them.

Mr. Doyon was rich for that town and time, and Charlie was told that if his father would lend "the firm" two hundred dollars to buy a larger Model-Press and more type, they would let him in. Charlie got the money easily. And the "papers" were offered by Mr. Doyon and signed by the boys.

Such was the origin of the firm of "Wright, Doyon and Lamp, Publishers and Printers."

Charlie's share in the enterprise was "Capitalist."

All he had to do was to sit around and look as though he owned the whole thing and the boys too because they owed his father money. And he would "pi" the type when things went altogether wrong for him.

Is anything more pleasurable to the mind than unsullied paper? The studious comparisons and selection of "stock" in textures and colors of cards and paper?

Letters are works of art, or may be.

The choice of type—a range of choice to tease the most ample taste.

The absorbing mechanics of actual press work.

What room for space invention—"composing!"

A real toy—the press—for boys as well as for grown-up rich men.

And what *is* the fascination to the average man or boy of seeing his name in type, even on a business or visiting card? It is phenomenal! A secret is there of intense human interest.

But the schooling!

Trying to find traces of it ends in *none.*

What became of it?

What did it contribute to this consciousness-of-existence that is the boy?

It seems purely negative.

For that reason it may not have been positively harmful. It is difficult for one to say. You can't let boys run wild while they are growing. They have to be roped and tied to something so their parents can go about their business. Why not a snubbing post or—school, then? A youth must be "slowed-up," held in hand. Caged—yes—mortified too. Broken to harness as colts are broken or there would be nothing left but to make an "artist" of him.

But certain episodes were harmful and remain so to this day. "Speaking pieces," for instance. The "accomplishments" after all seem most devastating as one looks about.

OH SIR, I AM A WIDOW WITH CHILDREN

Mother had, on short notice, chosen the "piece." The several verses had no interest for the boy, but he took the piece because it was short. In learning it he procrastinated as though he sensed some evil in it.

"Frank, have you got your piece?"

"Yes, Mother!"

"Then let me hear it!"

He begins: "Oh sir, I am a widow with children," etc., etc., pretty nearly through, then getting stuck.

"I thought so," from Mother. "Go study it some more."

He studied it some more.

In a few days: "Now let's see if you are ready with your piece, Frank. Speak it for me!" He did, letter perfect.

No, it was not *long,* that "piece" beginning, unhappily, "Oh sir, I am a widow with children." But what or who wrote the hapless thing can no longer be remembered. It should have been "anonymous." Probably was.

The piece now learned by heart—time came to deliver.

Teacher walking back and forth in the back of the schoolroom, the better to hold her own over the speakers who went up to the front to "speak."

She called his turn now.

The hapless victim slid sidewise from his seat into the aisle and made his way to the platform.

The first line came straight and brave enough:

"Oh sir, I am a widow with children." But now, for the first time, the statement struck him as absurd.

He went hot. Felt utterly ridiculous. Game—he started again—"Oh sir, I am a widow with children" . . . hopelessly confused he stuck willing to let the affair go at that and quit.

But glancing up he saw the mortified glare of the teacher, who, at that time, happened to be his own Aunt Jane.

Gathering together everything he had left in him, the curly-head—yes, "Shaggy," once more started—"Oh sir, I am a widow with children." Before he could go on the school snickered.

That settled it.

He came to a fatal pause—a hole where the piece had been—then panic.

Oh—the anguish of that moment! Perspiration broke from him as he turned—absurd—undone, and somehow got to his seat.

Then the storm of unkind school-laughter broke.

The lost-one could see the shamed-crimson of his aunt's face without looking.

It was just time for afternoon recess.

In the school yard the boys ran after him mocking, "Oh sir, I am a widow with children." He saw the girls laughing at the mocking.

There was nowhere to hide. The fun followed wherever he went.

Thus it was that a fond mother innocently conspired with the "system" to ruin what prospect her son ever had of becoming a self-confident speaker. For to this day, the mortification of that collapse returns to overcome him whenever he steps upon a platform, or is set for public speaking.

But the "system" was vindicated by performances like Frank Wootton's, who could do a Shakespearean soliloquy as easy as bat a ball over the fence; do it with a roll and delivery to match any professional actor's. He was an idol in consequence. How the boy victim envied him the looks of admiration from the girls! He *was* somebody, *that* Frank!

At this period in the spring and summer life at the Valley were the country cousins of Frank, the city-boy—Dick, Tom, and Ed. The city-boy practiced on them too. They looked upon their cousin with confiding interest. He was fully conscious of their admiration.

He beguiled them and showed off for them, used them and fooled them and loved them sincerely.

This life-of-the-imagination in him wrought havoc with them.

One time, the four all day together in the fields. The young Aladdin suddenly got the idea of a "party." The party grew so real in his imagination, as he rubbed his lamp, that it became due for that very evening given by Mother at Grandfather's where she was then on a visit. It grew so real he began to talk about it to the boys and as he talked about it the party grew in his imagination. As the day wore on he built it up, touched it up here and there to his satisfaction. There were to be presents for Tom, Dick, and Ed. Things he knew they longed for. There were to be goodies of all sorts. And surprises were cleverly hinted at, to work up excitement. As he talked the possibilities grew until expectations were boundless. Three mouths were watering, his own no less.

When they all turned toward home, they could hardly wait for the party to come with the evening.

Tom, Dick, and Ed's parents had heard nothing of the party, but believed the boys—scrubbed them clean and dressed them up in their Sunday-best.

By this time the enthusiasm of invention had cooled in the boy and a certain uneasiness came uppermost in him as he remembered what he had done.

But he said nothing.

The invited guests came early. The mother in the middle of her work, received them, wondering—with "Hello boys! Why! Why are you all so beautifully dressed? Where are you going?"

"We've come to Frank's party."

"Party?" said his mother, and looked at her son! One look was enough. And she soon found from the guests they were expecting presents and goodies.

She rose to the occasion to her son's delight and gratitude.

Perhaps he knew she would, who knows!

Anyhow, she found something in the way of presents so there was only partial disappointment. She made molasses-candy, gave them popcorn and ginger-cookies, got father to play "Pop Goes the Weasel" on his violin and sing for them too. And sent them home in an hour or so—her precious son's reputation saved she hoped.

Now he was facing mother as to his idea of this party.

"Why did you want to fool your cousins, Frank?"

Indignantly, he denied wanting to *fool* them.

"Why did you promise them all those things when you knew they were not going to get them?"

"Well, why did they have to believe they were going to get them? It was fun to think about getting them, wasn't it? Why did they have to come to the party anyway? Couldn't they just let it alone?"

And mother understood.

Nobody else.

The time came a year or two later when the boy drove Pont (short for Pontius) and Pilate afield alone, on his own for the first time. That was a day for him!

The day before he had been only a boy on the farm.

Today he was a man among men.

To be a man is to do a man's work. The "job" in hand now was driving the "plankers" to smooth finally the harrowed fields for the marking of the rows before corn-planting. The whiffle-trees of Pont and Pilate were hitched to a clevis fastened to the planks at the middle of the side, dragging them crosswise along over the fields. You stood upright on the planks at the center or to one side as you wanted them to drag, and drove with short hold on the lines rather close up to the horses.

All went well. Home at noon as good as the best. In the afternoon, toward four o'clock, coming down the sloping field the planker caught on a rotten stump half-hidden in the ploughed ground. The jerk broke the top off the stump and the planker, thus suddenly released, jumped forward on to the horses' heels throwing the boy on to Pont's rump. Instinctively the lad grasped the breeching of each horse with his hands as they jumped, kicked, and started to run. The clinging boy was so close to Pont he was lifted each time the horse kicked. And Pont was kicking continually as he ran. Pilate running close but, fortunately, not kicking.

If he let go his hold on Pont's breeching, or the straps broke, the plankers would go over him. To hold on and hope nothing would break was the only hope.

There were no cries, no words, as the team came tearing down the side-hill, the boy rising and falling with the running kicks of the horse. Adolph Sprecher, the good-hearted hired man, at work elsewhere marking the field, saw the dangerous flight and with all his brawny might ran over the ploughed ground to head off disaster. Grabbed at the horses' heads, missed, and fell. Got up and fortunately as the breeching was pulling Pont's check-rein on one side causing him to run in a wide circle, he cut across and got him just in time.

The boy just promoted to man's work dropped on the planks and lay there to get the breath back into the body that crazy horse had kicked until he kicked the breath out of it. All that Pont-horse ever needed to indulge in similar performances was a horsefly on the job in earnest. Many a tussle the boy had with him from first to last.

Adolph Sprecher, for some time, could not believe the boy not seriously hurt. He was begged not to tell Uncle James. He agreed, but broke his promise. The fact was—the boy stuck for another hour's work, went home, and did his chores. Next morning, he was so stiff and black and blue and sore, he simply could not make it go. Then the story came out.

His Uncle James had sent him with hired man number two, with confidence in Adolph. And for some time after this he was sent out in company.

But he always liked best to be sent off alone—to be treated "like a man."

He was soon trusted and sent alone.

That summer he "bound" his station after the reaper.

In those days the reaper was a "rake-off Mc-Cormick," a bright red affair with a varnished wood grain-platform on to which bright blue, green, yellow, and red reels knocked the yellow grain as it was cut by the busy to and fro of the gleaming sickle. This machine, gaily painted, like a toy, would leave the bundles raked off neatly on the stubble behind, to be bound by four or five men spaced around the field as the crop of grain was light or heavy, and the bundles would be tossed aside out of the way of the horses as they made the next round.

Taking up a wisp of the grain-straw in the left hand for a band, dividing it in two parts, deftly twisting it together at the head and in the right hand—stopping and reaching under the bundle with the hand—lifting the bundle in the arms, bringing the ends of the band together over it, dropping it to the ground under the knee as the band would be pulling up sharply—twisting and tucking the ends of the band under tight with a thrust of the fingers and tossing the bundle away—bound!

The young harvester's fingernails would be worn to the quick and bleeding before the last band on the bundles of the season's grain was "tucked in."

There was the hauling of the grain in the ample grain racks that also served for hay racks. The pitching of the bundles with a long-handled, three-tined fork. And the stacking. The stacking was expert, entrusted to but few. Else the whole thing would come down. Sometimes it did "slide." There had already been hauling of the hay and the pitching of hay to the stack.

Aching muscles in the morning always had to be limbered up again by the first few hours of each day's work.

Soon he learned to endure the routine of continuous labor by finding in it a sort of singsong. "Hum-drum"—but for the imagination.

He would actually sing to the ever recurring monotonies. Hum them or whistle them to some sort of rhythm, when he was at it or in it or of it. Here is the secret of endurance for the imaginative.

Any monotonous task involving repetition of movement has its rhythm if you can find it and the task can soon be made interesting in that sense. The "job" may be syncopated by changing the accent or making an accent. Binding grain and shocking it, or pitching bundles to the wagon and racks. Pitching hay, hoeing, dropping corn with a checker. Cultivating corn as the green hills passed regularly four feet apart between the shovels—planted four feet apart each way.

All machinery, too, makes some recurrent noise, some clack or beat above the hum that can be made into the rhythm of song movement—a rhythm that is the obvious poetry in the mathematics of this universe—maybe.

The body in performing heavy-labors for hour after hour can get into a swinging rhythm with music to accompany it, to be whistled or sung aloud or kept in the mind.

Folk dances originate in this way, no doubt. Sacred dances, no less.

Walking after the plow, bare feet in the furrow, was an ideal opportunity for him to indulge this inner rhythm to outward movement.

This sense of rhythm, entering into monotonous repetition, naturally led to arrangements of sound to go with it—sometimes a song with words.

The idea—no, it could have been no idea. It was instinct, whatever it was to suit this naive release of the within to the work in hand. Work would be better done and no fatigue.

Milking was the perfect opportunity to make monotony into music. The sounds of the streams alternately shot by left or right hand into the pail, the tin giving back the rhythmic sound at first, this soon to be modified by the foaming of the milk in the pail—a kind of music! And usually, the boy sang to this rhythm while he milked. Gottlieb— his red face turned down and sideways, his yellow hair against the cow's flank—would sometimes sing with him. You see here, *within himself,* he had found release. He had found a way to beat "tired to tired." And Uncle James would not have to call, "Come back, Frank! Come back!" He would be satisfactorily active while he dreamed.

More significant than all also at this time was this sense-of-rhythm in him.

"Life" impelling itself to live?

Notwithstanding this release coming up in him, and out in him continuously, he was doing a man's work now on the farm and at the age of fourteen getting a man's pay—nineteen dollars a month and his board and clothes.

Uncle James was doing pretty well by him— because . . . .

THE HORSE

Now the amateur "hired man" had come to the knowledge of The Horse: of bits and bridling . . . saddling, haltering, harnessing. Eternal buckling and unbuckling. He knew whiffle-trees, neck-yokes, and whips; tugs, breechings, and collars; straps, hooks, bits; hoofs and fetlocks, withers and hocks . . . all man's part in the HORSE! He saw— PROCREATION. The rearing gorgeous pride of the Clydesdale STALLION with his noble head and quivering nostrils. Sleek, meek mares. The young colts, if unluckily male, forthwith sex-degraded to geldings and struggling against the inevitable without a sound.

The work horses: he was forever getting them up. Currying them. Brushing them. Getting them over, while getting the stables clean under them and behind them. Always this "cleaning up" to do behind them. Braiding their tails. Hitching them. Unhitching them. Switching them. Sometimes ditching them. Feeding them. Leading and coaxing them. Driving them. Riding them bareback or saddled before and after they were broken. Seeing Uncle James break them, sometimes himself all but broken by them. Getting thrown off them. Getting run-away-with by them. Getting run over. Getting kicked or stepped on. Getting angry and jerking a horse shamefully and feeling ashamed. Getting the horses shod. Putting the horses with alternate patience and exasperation to the plow, to harrows, seeders, markers, plankers and planters, cultivators and lumber-wagons. To sulkies, buggies, and logging-trucks. To milk-wagons, reapers, and turntables. To threshing-machines. Saws. Hayracks. Hayrakes. And there he would work the horses and take them away again to feed and water them, curry them, and bed them.

Getting these gaily painted accessories to the

horse greased, geared. Getting them to go. Getting the life-sized man-toys to stop.

Learning to swear in the style proper to the "hired man" . . . This amateur young master of the HORSE.

Noble excitement comes to the boy in this fellowship with the horse. Most respectable of all man's animal associates it is, and the most "romantic."

THE SOW

And the boy was daily hauling fodder and boiling something—pumpkins or something or other—for the hogs. The grunting boar with foaming mouth and ugly tusks. And the heavy brood sows, bellies almost dragging the ground—grunting. The clean, pink little pigs. Ringing their snouts at four months so they could never "root" and spoil the sod. Catching and holding unlucky young boars—screaming infernos of despair as they were degraded into barrows. Loading them all—eventually—into the rack and hauling them to market.

The boy was also perpetually running to get them out of the corn. Get them out of the garden. Get them out of the neighbor's fields. Getting them—well, always "*getting*" them out or "*getting*" them into—something, himself breathless and perspiring and oftentimes despairing.

And this business of getting the heavy sows off their own little pigs. He knew they were lying on them by the infernal heart-rending squeals.

Calling them, "P-o-o-i-g! P-o-o-i-g! P-o-o-i-g." The tenor of that call would do credit to opera.

Sickened as you assisted at butchering by seeing the knife stuck deep in the fat-throat and the hot blood gushing and steaming from the one marked for family "pork."

The smell of their yard—devastating! Desecration at all times, in all places. Utter degradation in smells. PROCREATION, too, of the Pig.

This unreconciled assistant to the HOG now knew these devastations full well.

THE COW

The boy was always afraid of the heavy-necked, bellowing Holstein Bull. Ring in his nose—"sex-slave"—but pride and terror of every farm just the same. And his first farm familiars—the Cows. Calling them—"So Boss! So-o Boss! So-o-o Boss!" A baritone call. For years and years—and years—would they never end?—the cows in from the pasture. Getting the cows into their proper places in the barn. Feeding them. Milking them in the morning. Milking them in the evening, eaten up by flies. Cruelly twisting their tails to make them stamp their hind legs and stand over to be milked. Getting the vile manure off their bags before milking them to keep the milk clean. Getting the lazy creatures up. Milking them weekdays. Milking them just the same on Sundays. Milking them—always milking them. Getting bare feet soiled—"cut," the farm-boys used to say—in the warm, fresh cow-flops, in the stable or in the lane. Always cleaning away at the stables. Always "cleaning up" to be done—never done till next time and soon. Getting the slow moving bovines out to pasture again. Getting the adventuresome ones out of the corn. Getting the whole tribe out of the grain. Getting hooked. Beating a cantankerous old one that would gore a young sister, the gored one bellowing agony, her head stretched out, big eyes bulging in terror rolled back until the whites were all that you could see. Fixing a "poke" on the neck of the "leader"—the one first to jump the fence and lead the others to glory—while it lasted. The boy seeing the torture of the poor adventurer punished for her innocent initiative as that adventurer in all skins in all ages is always punished in some form . . . secretly taking the cruel poke off again without permission. Getting reprimanded when next the cows were in the corn, but taking the cruel poke off again—just the same.

Feeding the calves. "*Sukem*-suke-suke-suke, suke-suke-suke-suke." Tenor again. Soprano preferred. Catching and tying the luckless bull calves while, bawling in fear, they were degraded into steers—or hauled to market for "veal" after six weeks of here-on-earth. Seeing a fine steer knocked in the head with a maul—dropped with a thud like lead, throat cut in a flash. Helping to strip off the heavy skin for leather and dress the steaming carcass for beef. The boy was getting the cows in, getting them out, day in and day out—summer after summer. Occasionally helping Uncle James to haul one out, when she got stuck in the mud of the creek. Haul the cow out with a team of horses hitched to a rope tied around her neck. No harm to her whatever.

PROCREATION of the cattle—in season.

Chased by the thoroughbred bull several times but never tossed. This "go-getter" of the Cow knew all this cow-business now habitually as the cattle themselves knew content—as they chewed their cuds.

THE HEN

And there was the Rooster with the scarlet comb. And there were the Hens. The boy hadn't so much to do with the fowls but there were always hundreds of chickens, all over the place. Crowing. Scratching. Clucking. Squawking as he would scatter grain for them. He would get up at night to look into the hen-house when a terrific squawking commotion there indicated a prowling enemy in their midst. It was given to him sometimes to catch and strike off the heads of superfluous young roosters when their turn came to be eaten, as it invariably came. Throwing the flapping convulsive fowl aside in its headless tumble over wood-pile and dooryard in frantic letting go of life. Eggs. Hunting eggs. Always getting eggs. Setting eggs. Sucking eggs as taught by Gottlieb. Chucking or ducking cross old hens who should have known better into the water-trough to cool maternal ardor. Or dropping them into the bottom of a barrel with water in it to let them "set" on that. Getting pecked by the lousy things. Getting covered with lice from them. This young fowler, admiring the Rooster and his brood but never liking them and their PROCREATION—perpetual.

He liked the guinea fowl with the raucous cry and the speckled gray plumage and form like a quail. The Peacock fascinated him—a spiritual element because in all this they seemed introduced for love of beauty—as ornament? How that element hovers over everything, this sentiment for beauty. Man cannot drive it entirely away! No—even when he domesticates the animals it will linger there.

THE HOE

And the Garden. A comparatively peaceful place the Garden—when not raided by unnatural domesticated enemies from over the none-too-good fence—the chickens, the little pigs, and some few extraordinary sows. To say nothing of natural enemies underground—grubs, worms, and the marching army of insects. Insects! Will they eventually win the battle and exterminate man?

Whosoever would sow must hoe.

And if he who hoes would reap—he must weed.

Weeding is an art, though the back breaks. The boy learned to twist his fingers around the weed-stems close to the ground and with a sidewise twist—thumb as a lever—bringing the narrow side of the hand to the ground—prying, you see—while pulling, he would get them out, roots unbroken, while the skin on his fingers lasted.

Thus the process would go on for hours a day, all the days the garden was young, until back and arms were stiff and fingers sore in the continued effort to clean the weeds out from between the plants known to be useful.

The boy hoed. He hoed lettuce. He hoed radishes, beets, carrots, parsnips, and turnips. Cabbages. Tomato plants. Hoed onions. Always he seemed to be hoeing in the season of early summer. Hoeing and weeding. Weeding and hoeing, until the palms of his hands were thick and hard—as shiny as the hoe handle—both like glass. And finally they would have to come and cut down the triumphant weeds with a sickle or scythe and burn them.

The wielder of the hoe would wonder why weeds couldn't be studied, possibilities found and then maybe cultivated. The "crop" eliminated. Perhaps the "crop" was weeds once upon a time just because the farmer didn't know what they were for. Tobacco was a weed once. And corn. And potatoes. And tomatoes were once thought to be poison. Cancerous. Yes, nearly everything was a weed once upon a time. Maybe sometime there would be no "weeds," then?

But meanwhile weeds always seemed fittest to survive in this unequal strife—in this contending, never-ending competition between Good and Evil, or whatever the competition was.

What vitality these "weeds" had!

Pusley, for instance. And Chess. And Pigweed. And Dock and Ragweed. Quack grass—king of them all. Canada thistle—the queen! Would the weeds become feeble, if they were cultivated, and the crops become as vigorous as weeds, if let alone to flourish on their own?

And yet, afield in June, he saw as the reward of toil, forethought, and some science, the sweeping acres of clover-bloom floating in perfume, heard the hum of busy bees as the tall, round spires of the timothy stood above, slender spires bending to the sweeping of the breeze. Soon there would be the large round cones of the yellow grain-stacks standing in the transparent stubble-fields in August, gathered together from the orderly ranks of yellow grain-shocks dotting the tawny stubble—in July green. The silvering rows on rows of haycocks in June to end in the purple haystacks tomorrow. In September would come the wigwam rows of Indian-corn-shocks; solid-gold pumpkins lying thick in the reddening sun over the fields between the wigwams.

And at the red barns, there the boy would be—handling the dangerous hayfork, choking in the dust of the great big hot haymows. He would be "tailing" on the straw-stacks, struggling to keep from being choked and buried alive in the chaff that fell from the end of the straw-carrier of the threshing machine, his features obliterated by grime and sweat and dust. And later there in the silos he would be putting away the alcoholic silage, his body dripping with sweat. Turning tedious grindstones under sickles, scythes, and axes. Turning the crank of the fanning-mill to the limit of endurance. Working the wood handle of the old green pump until his arms were numb.

And did wet weather bring a rest from all these labors? Except for digging post-holes and fencing—yes.

Someone should do the barbed-wire fence in song and story. It would be the story of our civilization. Together with the tin can, it has made man's "conquest" too easy? Enough.

On the farm there was always the glib Ax. The honest Bucksaw. And the persuasive Hammer. No farm could have a farmer without these. And, yes, almost forgotten, the tragic monkey wrench! Whose is that? What disorganization could be wrought with a monkey wrench? And what about the precious Jack Knife?

So it is that farmboy life is continually at the mercy of hoofs, horns, and blades. Gleaming plowshares, flashing scythes, poisonous stings and bites and briars. Boy-life is one continuous round of fatal ups and downs and disastrous ins and outs. Too dry! Too high! Too low! Too wet! Too hot! Too cold! Too soon! Too late! Drought and Frost—major enemies the farmer must learn to defeat or he will go down.

He must make constant demands upon refractory or dull tools. His world is a desperate "merry-go-round" of ill or happy contrivances painted bright red, poison green or red, white, blue, and gilt, fascinating to the farmer as toys are fascinating to children. Contrivances that will or will not work.

Main strength and awkwardness is the farmer's never-failing final resource in every end.

And—continually—this perpetual restless movement of perverse or willing perspiring, laboring animal-bodies strapped, tied to—and straining at those machines. Machines that would kill them if not managed. Machines that ploughed and dug, cut and piled and tore and ground and bound if you mastered them or killed you if you didn't—but gaily painted just the same. Machines all in some way dangerous, all rusting in vital spots and at some time or other all—damned!

Such is the amazing, endless category of "parts" every one necessary to the stupendous complex whole into which the boy on the "farm" was thrown—to survive if he could.

Thus the boy's encounter with the Cow, the Sow, the HEN! Served by the humbled HORSE—and himself. Meantime, all imposed upon by fascinating machines. The matter helped by them—perhaps. Who really knows?

PEACE! BEAUTY! SATISFACTION! REST!

Ah yes, the divine discontent of the Creative Spirit was havoc with all that, then and there—as things were. And as they are now. Anyone might have seen this and have avoided it if he could. But the boy didn't know. No one warned him.

He was unsuspecting.

So, fearlessly this human item lived the life of the imagination in all he did.

Sometimes when the day had been too hard, too tired to sleep he would get out of bed, sweaty jeans pulled on and rolled above his knees and barefoot and bareheaded slowly climb the path up the hill behind the house. Climb to the long, quiet ridge that ran along to the north high in the moonlight ornamented here and there with scattered hazel-brush and trees. Climbing to wander and look forward and "imagine," enjoy waking dreams in a high place.

Going over that ridge later in life, many times, he would wonder how a barefoot boy could negotiate that stony way in daylight not to speak of moonlight.

On either side of the ridge lay fertile valleys luminously bathed and gentled by the moon.

The different trees all made their special kinds of pattern when the moon shone on them and their favorite deep-dark silhouettes when it shone against them.

The flowers had no color, but their cups and corollas glistening with dew were like pallid gems.

The boy's feet and legs were wet with the cool freshness of the dews in the long grasses.

Broad, shallow mists, distilled from the heavy dews, floating in cool, broad sheets below were lying free over the tree-tops in long, thin, flat ribands.

All would be quiet except for the drowsy singing undertone of summer insects.

The ancient principle of moisture seemed to prevail there as a kind of light flooding over all.

The deep shadows held mysteries alluring and all-friendly.

There was no haste.

He could listen to music religiously as though it were the last strain he might ever hear and make more in the heart of his mind. Or he would hear the strains of Beethoven that had come to him from his father's playing as, early in life, in his bed he lay listening. Entranced, he would now be uplifted by it.

The intimate fairy princess would come near, she who was growing up somewhere preparing herself and looking forward, as dreamily, to him, listening too.

Sometimes fair and sometimes dark she was always beautiful as only adolescent boys can picture girlish beauty.

Great deeds would rise in him then. Unquenchable triumphs, until the evanescent scene would fade into many-colored achievements and boy-sized glory.

There was no feeling that the dreams could ever be desecrated by failure.

Out of character they arose into the mind as waking dreams, in magical, mystic, pale amber and amethyst nights, and settled quietly on the spirit to refresh a mortal weariness as the dew came upon the flowers that stood beside his naked legs.

Looking back now, the dreams seem not great. But then how he thrilled with them and walked in the tall dew-laden grass among moon-struck flowers as on air. Feeling no stones beneath his naked feet.

Half-consciously he would wander back, come down, and climb into bed again to sleep—deep sleep with no dreams at all.

After one thousand two hundred and sixty "todays" and "tomorrows" like those "yesterdays," the boy was coming sixteen.

Farm-days for him were over.

He was about to enter the University of Wisconsin.

Farm-days had left their mark on him in a self-confidence in his own strength called courage. Muscles hard. Step—springing. Sure-footed, and fingers quick as thought and *with* thought. Mind buoyant with optimism. Optimism that came through seeing sunshine follow clouds and rain—working out success succeeding failure. It had come to him self-consciously out of his daily endeavors as underlying sense of the essential balance of forces in nature. Something in the nature of an inner experience had come to him that was to make a sense of this supremacy of interior order like a religion to him. He was to take refuge in it. Besides, now seventeen, for several years the youth had been doing a man's work. He had learned how to do much and do much well, do most of it happily, feeling himself master where he would. That gave him a whip-hand.

He was afraid only of people.

That was the fearful unknown to him—"people."

Not to mention girls.

The sight of a "girl" would send him like a scared stag, scampering back into his wood.

But things were, by now, not so well at the small town house by the blue lake. There was no longer much agreement between father and mother.[2]

The father on this eve of the entrance of his son into the university was himself deep in learning to write SANSCRIT.

Mother for some years had been ailing.

Poverty pinched.

The youth would see her self-denial at table. See her eating only what the others did not want. Drinking her tea without sugar and not because she preferred it so: pretending to prefer the neck of the roast chicken so well you almost believed she did—when, rarely, a chicken from the small coop in the back yard would be killed and come to the table.

Provisions often arrived from the farm—potatoes, vegetables, barrels of apples.

The father's earnings were small and shrinking. Music wasn't much of a livelihood in Madison.

Irregular preaching there and in surrounding towns less so.

And he grew irascible over crosscurrents of family feeling.

The Joneses didn't much approve of Anna's privations. And he, being a proud man, resented their provisions.

The lad was his mother's adoration. She lived much in him. Probably that didn't help either.

For some disobedience about this time, the father undertook to thrash the young man. It had happened in the stable and the young rebel got his father down on the floor, held him there until his father promised to let him alone. He had grown too big for that sort of thing. "Father ought to realize it," said the boy, as he went into the home, white, shamed, and shaken to tell his mother.

The youth hardly had known himself as his father's son. All had gone well enough on the surface that was now broken. The son had sympathy for his talented father as well as admiration. Something of that vain struggle of superior talents with untoward circumstance that was his father's got to him and he was touched by it—never knowing how to show Father. Something—you see—had never been established that was needed to make them father and son. Perhaps the father never loved the son at any time. Memories would haunt the youth as they haunt the man. . . .

His father's son listening at the closed study door, hearing father walking—walking to and fro studying; reciting as he walked, practicing for readings he sometimes gave at churches. Experimenting with changes of intonation and accent, evidently reading the poem, book in hand, and occasionally trying over certain passages again and again. This time listening to —"The Raven." Measured footsteps, father's voice reciting . . .

> . . . *As of someone gently rapping*
> *Rapping at my chamber door.*
> *"'Tis some visitor" I muttered,*
> *"tapping at my chamber door.*
> *—Only this and nothing more."*

Interval:
Slowly walking

> *And the silken, sad, uncertain*
> *rustling of each purple curtain*
> *thrilled me—filled me—with*
> *fantastic terrors never felt before. . . .*

Silence . . .
Now

> *Darkness there and nothing more.*
> *Darkness there and nothing more.*
> *Merely this, and nothing more.*

Pause . . .
Footsteps, measured as before

> *Let me see, then what thereat is,*

and this mystery explore, and
this mystery explore—
'Tis the wind, and nothing more.
'Tis the wind, and nothing more.

Silence.
Walking faster . . .

"Prophet still if bird or devil! . . .
Prophet still if bird or devil! . . .

All quiet for a time and . . .

"Is there—is there balm in Gilead?
Tell me—tell me I implore
Quoth the Raven, 'Nevermore!'
Quoth the Raven, 'Nevermore!'
. . . Quoth the Raven . . .
And my soul from out that shadow
that lies floating on the floor
Shall be lifted—nevermore!
Shall be lifted" . . . and

the youth would tiptoe away to hear no more.

Sometimes, after all had gone to bed, he would hear that nocturnal rehearsal and the walking—was it evermore?—would fill a tender boyish heart with sadness until a head would bury itself in the pillow to shut it out.

At other times Father would recite "The Bells!" And that was lighter.

Oh the rapture that impels
To the singing and the ringing
Of the bells, bells, bells,
Of the bells, bells, bells, bells,
Bells, bells, bells—
To the rhyming and the chiming of the bells!
To the rhyming and the chiming of the bells!

Father must have loved "The Bells" for there would seem to be varying trials of intonation, the bells passing through all phases from their rhyming and their chiming to clamor and the clangor, and then "the melancholy menace of their tone, the moaning and the groaning of the bells! . . . bells! . . .

bells! The moaning and the groaning of the bells?"

One day when difficulties between father and mother had grown unbearable the mother, having borne all she could—probably the father had borne all he could bear too—said quietly, "Well, Mr. Wright"—always she spoke of him and to him so—"leave us. I will manage with the children. Go your way. We will never ask you for anything except this home. The savings of my earnings as a teacher have gone in this, and I have put into it so many years of my life.

"No—we will never ask you for help.

"If ever you can send us anything, send it. If you cannot we will do the best we can."

Who can know what, in the eighteen years preceding, led gradually and inevitably to the heart-break beneath simple words—quietly spoken?

Like some traveler taking the long road to some point where another road branches to the left or to the right, the turn is taken with nothing to mark it as an event, yet direction, destination, perhaps all of life—are changed.

Destruction, too, may wait on that turn.

All real crises in Life, are they not, finally, so simple?

And who may judge the silent changes gradually taking place in the human heart like organic changes taking place in trees or plants, and like them, when manifest as complete, to be accepted?

What folly to presume to rise against them with "No!"

Senseless hazard to encourage them!

What mischief to advise; what idiocy to "judge!"

The father was to disappear and never be seen by his wife or his children.

Quietly Judge Carpenter dissolved the marriage contract.

The mother's people all deeply grieved, shamed because of her disgrace.

She herself bowed down in grief. Although believing in the rightness of separation for her children's sake she had not believed in her heart—it seems—their father would take advantage of her offer to release him.

And, until he died fifteen years later, she never ceased to believe he would come back.

There was never a thought of another man in her life, nor thought of another woman in his.

Perhaps it was that their life together had worn its soul away in the strife of failure after failure added to failure. And an inveterate withdrawal on his part into the intellectual life of his studies, his books, and his music, where he was oblivious to all else.

The boy himself, supersensitive, became aware of "disgrace." His mother was a "divorced" woman. His faith in her goodness and rightness did not waver. Therefore there was "injustice" to her. Did this injustice to her serve some social purpose?

A wondering resentment grew in him. It became a subconscious sense of false judgment entered against himself, his sisters Jennie and Maginel innocent of all wrong-doing. His mother's unhappiness—was it a social crime? Why must she, as well as they, be punished? Just what had they all done?

He never got the heavy thing straight and just accepted it as one more handicap—grew more sensitive and shy than ever. And a little distrustful.

The mother was alone now with her son and his two sisters. She found a place for the budding architect with blue-eyed Allen D. Conover, Dean of Engineering at the University of Wisconsin, himself a competent civil engineer.

He had an office of his own and a private practice in Madison and probably really needed some boy to work for him. How can one be sure?

Professor Conover was a cultivated and kind man.

He allowed the youth to work for him afternoons so that he might have the mornings for classes. He gave him thirty-five dollars a month.

This arrangement left the freshman "free" to study evenings.

Architecture, at first his mother's inspiration, then naturally enough his own desire, was the study he wanted. But there was no money to go away to an architectural school. There were classes in engineering at the home university. That was the nearest to architecture within his reach.

So the youth was enrolled at the University of Wisconsin as a prospective civil engineer.

Fortunately too, by the limitation, he was spared the curse of the architectural education of that day as sentimentalized in Usonia with its false direction in culture and wrong emphasis on sentiment.

Every morning he walked to the University—a couple of miles away. After recitations there, he walked back down to the Conover office at noon to eat the lunch he carried. And after an afternoon's work done at the drawing-board he walked home again to eat his supper and to study. Robie Lamp and he were still chums though other associations now drew the youth away from "Robie" for Robert Lamp had not entered the university.

The retrospect of university years is mostly dull pain.

Thought of poverty and struggle, pathos of a broken home, unsatisfied longings, humiliations—a frustration.

There seemed little meaning in the studies, mathematics excepted. At least mathematics "worked." But mathematics was taught by Professor Van Velzer, an academic little man with side-whiskers, who had no feeling for romance in his subject. A subject rightly apprehended most romantic. Music itself is but sublimated mathematics.

Consequently the punctilio of the conscientious little professor opened for his pupil the stupendous fact that "two plus two equal four." It is unreasonable to suppose that a professor of mathematics should be a poet? Or a civil engineer be a creative composer of symphonies?

French? Miss Lucy Gay, a charming honest person whom everyone loved and respected, taught him that. He read the *Romance of the Poor Young Man, Le Cid,* etc.

English Composition was taught him by Professor Freeman. A handsome gentleman, deeply afflicted, so it seemed, by a strong expression of professional dignity.

The youth yearned to read and write his own language—yearned to speak it—supremely well. He had no chance under the pompous professor. His compositions were all marked "good," "thought excellent," when he already knew both to be dishwater. And barring the correction of gross grammatical errors which he seldom made anyway, what did he get from that "marking" business? Merely nothing, with less subtracted for pleasure or good-measure. English, to this day, remains more or less a mystery. He was never taught just why English is English—just what it is that makes it English as distinguished from all other languages and what its peculiar and individual resources are. What its limitations are and how they may be turned to advantages. He was left to find out for himself.

The hungry student read at this time, at home, Carlyle's *Sartor Resartus, Heroes and Hero Worship, Past and Present,* the father's calf-bound copy of Plutarch's *Lives,* Ruskin's *Fors Clavigera, Modern Painters, Stones of Venice,* gift of Aunt Nell and Jane, Morris' *Sigard the Volsung,* and Shelley, Goethe's *Wilhelm Meister,* a little of William Blake, *Les Miserables,* Viollet Le Duc's *Raisonné d'architecture.* But he doesn't know in the least what he read in the school course.

Professor Conover and Storm Bull were the engineers to whom he reported and who looked over his work in Stereotomy, Graphic-Statics, Analytical and Descriptive Geometry. All as painfully spread by him upon his drawing-board in the drafting room in the old dormitory on the hillside. But it was with Professor Conover in that practice of his the youth really learned most.

THE FRESHMAN PARTY

Charlie Ware saw May White, his cousin, explained the matter, the diffidences, etc., made the engagement after the formality of a call with the fool who was about to reverse the Biblical order and go fearfully in where the angels happily tread.

The morning of the party, a beautiful clear day, the freshman, chesty as a young cockerel, went for a walk. He ran into Charlie.

"Yes, but say, Charlie, I ought to know what I do at this party anyhow, and how do I or ought I to do it."

Said Charles, "Nothing much to know, man. Get May. Take her in. Dance a few dances with her. Keep off her toes. Then get some of the fellows to dance with her. There you are! Dance with some of the girls yourself. After the last dance—and you dance that with May—mind you—take May back to "Ladies' Hall."

But the freshman, somehow thought it good form to kiss the girl when you left her at the door after the party. It was more of this he had been thinking than anything else. Charlie laughed at this; "Oh," he said, "that's optional."

And so left the freshman in the air.

The class-party was to occur in Assembly Hall, next door to Ladies' Hall.

But a carriage was "good form," so carriage it was.

Dressed. White tie. Black suit. Patent-leather pumps. White gloves in hand. Bouquet for lady. Boutonniere for black coat. So far so good—far too good. He had an uneasy feeling himself that it was too good.

Got to Ladies' Hall, found May ready. May found her escort too embarrassed to say anything at all.

But May had been "informed." She got him safely back to the carriage.

No sooner started, May White and Frank Wright sitting at a respectful distance apart, than the carriage stopped at the Hall. Nothing whatever said.

The young couple got out and the amateur led the way to the entrance.

They got in only to find a crowd of the "fellows" inside chasing each other. No ladies in sight.

Blushing painfully, he realized he had brought May to the men's entrance. Helplessly he looked around. "Where was the women's dressing room, anyway?" May evidently didn't know either.

He went sick with shame.

Charlie Ware, from the other side of the room, took in the situation at a glance and rushed over, "Come with me, May!"

She straightway left the freshman stranded; standing out from the crowd, he felt, like the bull's-eye of a big target.

Some boy took pity on him and showed him where to stow his coat and hat. Then he went back to look for his unfortunate lady.

He couldn't find her.

Came the promenade.

No lady!

Came the first waltz.

No lady!

The waltz nearly over and he about to cut it all, when May's voice: "Why here you are! I waited a long time at the dressing-room door. Then I thought you didn't recognize me. You see, you don't know me very well so I came to find you."

He felt he should indignantly deny not knowing her among a thousand like her. But could only murmur—neither ever knew what!

They danced together. Charlie came when the dance was over and got May's programme filled. Got May's partner himself a dance or two for good measure—Charlie was what "Charlies" usually are. All of which went off without resistance or remarks from the green partner. Now he hung around and waited for that last dance with May, wondering if it was going to be expected of him to kiss her when he said "good night."

He couldn't picture it.

But although an amateur, he wanted not to be a duffer and disgrace Charlie.

So he made up his mind he would go through with it.

He felt he ought to tell May her dress was pretty and that she danced well. He really admired her dress and white shoes and the way she wore her hair.

All he could say was "We're having a good time, aren't we?"

"Are we?" said May—a bit miffed by now.

The pair got into the carriage after anxious moments when the escort would have given his college education to be well out of the affair forever.

But no more absurdities until "We had a good time, didn't we?"

"Did we?"

That kiss seemed far away from May!

Standing on the steps, time to say good-bye. . . "Well," he stammered—he felt miserably foolish—he felt . . . . "Thank you," said he, and ran to the waiting carriage leaving his lady to open the door for herself. He had faith that she got in. But he didn't know.

When he got home, he lit his lamp, took off the infernal togs he had so miserably betrayed. Threw them aside. Took *Sartor Resartus* to bed for consolation; but was inconsolable.

He went over the whole affair and made himself brilliant—irresistible.

He staged himself and played the part to perfection—too late!

It was the next term before he had the courage to try again. A nice town girl named Blanche Ryder took pity on him and asked him herself. Tactfully she saw him through.

About this time, a vivid tragic memory, that had its effect upon the incipient architect all his life long.

Passing by the new North-wing of the old State Capitol, he was "just in time" to hear the indescribable roar of building collapse and see the cloud of white lime dust blown from the windows of the outside walls, the dust-cloud rising high into the summer-air carrying agonized human-cries with it. The white dust-cloud came down to settle white over the trees and grass of the park. Whitened by lime dust, as sculpture is white, men with bloody faces came plunging wildly out of the basement entrance blindly striking out about their heads with their arms, still fighting off masonry and beams. Some fell dead on the grass under the clear sky and others fell insensible. One workman, lime-whitened, too, hung head-downward from a fifth-story window pinned to the sill by an iron-beam on a crushed foot, moaning the whole time.

A ghastly red-stream ran from him down the stone wall.

Firemen soon came. Crowds appeared as though out of the ground and men frantically tugged and pulled away at the senseless mass of brick and beams to reach the moans for help of the workmen lying dying beneath them. White-faced women, silently crying, went about looking for husbands, brothers, or sons.

A sudden movement of alarm and scattering of the crowd startled him, as someone pointed to a hand sticking out between chunks of brick-work on which the crowd itself was standing. After pulling away bricks and finally scarlet plaster, a mangled human being was drawn out—too late. One of the sobbing women knelt over it on the grass. And so it went all day long and far into the night.

The youth stayed for hours clinging to the iron fence that surrounded the park, too sick with the horror of it all to go away. Then he went home—ill. Dreamed of it that night and the next and the next. The horror of the scene has never entirely left his consciousness and remains to prompt him to this day.

Only outside walls were left standing. The interior columns had fallen and the whole interior construction was a gigantic rubbish-heap in the basement.

The huge concrete piers in that basement, on which rested the interior cast-iron columns supporting the floors and roof, had collapsed and let the columns down and of course that meant all the floors and interior walls as well.

Architect Jones, a good and conscientious architect, had made those piers so excessively large, the contractor thought it no sin to wheel barrows full of broken brick and stone into the hearts of them. They were found rotten at the core where the columns stood. Poor Architect Jones![3] He was now guilty of manslaughter—tried by a jury of his peers and condemned. He never built another building.

The University of Wisconsin had its beautiful situation on the hill by Lake Mendota, but the life of the University then was not as it is now. The herd of hungry students was less by many thousands. The buildings were few and badly furnished. Nor were the professors so distinguished. It was more as a modern high school is today only less sophisticated than the modern high school. It had the airs, dignitaries, and dignities. Thereby it assumed the pretentions of a university. And, all values being relative, it served then as it serves now.

There were few fraternity houses. The "Chi Psi" house could be called one.

Finally "rushed" by several Greek-letter fraternities for some unknown reason—for the youth was poor and his people obscure—he joined the Phi Delta Theta.

Phi Delta Theta held forth on the second floor of a store building on the west side of the Capitol Square overlooking the park. There was the mysterious initiation of course. Thrilling. The goat! The pool table. The fellows—and good fellows too. Ferd Geiger, Fred Simpson, Frank Bamford, Harry Butler, and others. Outside the fraternity for him, there was Louie Hanks, Jimmie Kerr, Eldon Cassidy, and George Thorpe. In the University classes there were Parman, Ostenfeldt, and Bob Spencer.

They were all good for him.

He got something out of them but not much for he was too shy, too interior to exchange much with them.

But, in love with the grand gesture and in common with the others—he got himself a black "mortar-board" with a beautiful red-silk tassel hanging "overboard": a pair of light-gray, skin-tight "pants"—in vogue then: "toothpick" shoes. And he dressed and acted the part with his hair still rather too long for it all. An incorrigible sentimentalist.

But his heart was never in this "Education." It never seemed to be for him. Where was architecture in all this?

"Education" meant nothing so much as a vague sort of emotional distress, a sickening sense of fear—of what he could not say. And the inner meaning of anything never came clear.

There was something embarrassing in the competitive atmosphere. Something oppressive and threatening in the life of rules and regulations. Both hampered him.

The weight grew lighter as the years of the "course" wore on but the cause of it—a mother's yearning that had put him into the meaningless competition—was too pitiful, too sad to think of.

Perhaps high-school days were best. For some reason they usually are best in most lives and during those high-school days, there was the life of the farm in the valley to go with his schooling. The one brightened and heightened the other.

So the University training of one Frank Lloyd Wright, Freshman, Sophomore, Junior, and part Senior was lost like some race run under a severe handicap, a race which you know in your heart you are foredoomed to lose: a kind of competition in which you can see nobody winning anywhere. Nor quite knowing why anyone should want to win. Just for the degree? Emulation? Just to be one of the countless many who had that "certificate"? A certificate from whom?

Things would start but nothing would seem to happen.

It wasn't like the farm.

Doctrine, it was. Perfunctory opinion administered the doctrine.

The professors seemed to him Doctorial.

He was being doctored in a big crowd and the doses never seemed to produce any visible effect at any vital spot whatever; and anyway, he didn't feel sick.

And Science Hall was in course of construction. So was the machine shop and chemical laboratory.

He didn't get into those new buildings.

His "course" didn't lead him into any shop at all, although he did get a beautiful red and white field rod and a fine transit into his hands and went surveying with his classmates. And there was the testing of materials. But finally he did get to work on the buildings themselves by the way of Professor Conover.

At that time Science Hall was being built by a Milwaukee architect out of Professor Conover's office, the professor being superintendent of buildings for the University. So the young sophomore got some actual contact with this construction.

He was entrusted with the working out of some steel clips to join the apex of the trusses of the main roof. . . . They wouldn't go together and the workmen, disgusted, left them hanging up there against the sky by the few bolts that would go in.

It was dead of winter—only the iron beams of the floors were in place in the floor levels below. All was slippery with ice but he went up there, climbing the lattice on the chords of the trusses to the very top, with nothing between him and the ground but that forest of open steel beams. Got the clips loose. Dropped them down.

That was educational?

The office work with Professor Conover was a great good for him. As he realized then and since.

Work that was truly educational.

But in the university, notwithstanding certain appearances, he was and remained outsider, yearning all the while for the active contact with the soil or for the tests of a free life of action—waiting for something to happen that never happened. Now he realizes that it never could have happened, for "they" were all there to see that it did not happen.

Reading Goethe only made matters worse, for action, again action and more action was his urge.

The boy already wondered why "Culture"—that was what the University stood for?—shouldn't consist in getting rid of the inappropriate in everything. Whereas "Education" as he encountered it, was as inappropriate as the rubbish wheeled by the contractor into the foundation piers of the Capitol. This he couldn't have told you then, but he felt it—as resentment.

But his "Classical" course whenever he compared it with the life on the farm seemed to him to be the *practice* of the inappropriate; so any human edifice reared on it—likely to fall down like the Capitol.

The gestures were here and they were fine enough but—how about *work*?

The feeling about this best period of youth, lasting three and one-half years, is not so much that it was wasted.

It probably wasn't wasted.

How foolish to say anything is wasted in the living of any life!

Because, were one thing different, all were different.

Perhaps the most insignificant of circumstances is ever essential to the most important.

So what weakness to regret any incident or any turning.

"Might-have-beens" are for the "Never-weres." Uncle James had said that.

Nature was organic even in Man's character-making, as in her other forms. His instinct was not to criticize her work, unless he could know her method and discern her ends: thanks to the farm.

But Man's puny mind and pusillanimous aims so affront "Nature" continually! He never knows what happens to him in consequence or because of his philosophy, his "wisdom," which is usually by way of abstraction—something *on* life and seldom *of* life.

And now, motoring to and from Taliesin—seeing masses of the ten or more thousand students increasingly thronging grounds and buildings of the University, overflowing into the University Avenue, comes the same feeling of unhappiness. Something tragic in it all: perhaps in a seeming futility or betrayal? The feeling is indefinable, but deep. A resentment against the mass product? Deeper than that. A conviction of betrayal.

Small wonder that we grow "old"? And so soon.

Now in his eighteenth year, dreaming architecture, seeing it more and more in everything, the feeling of depression regarding his one-two-thousand-five-hundredth share in the education afforded by the University of Wisconsin was growing unbearable.

Added to dissatisfaction with it and himself, there was a sense of shame in accepting the Mother's sacrifices for so little in return. True, he turned over his Conover stipend to her but the demands of "college-education" forever pressed in one mean form or another.

He had sold some of his father's books to meet some of them.

The father had taken with him nothing but his clothes and violin—his mother's beautiful gold Swiss watch had now gone to Perry, the pawn-broker, by way of her son.

He had made things evenings, or during holiday vacations, with his scroll-saw, and sold them to be used as "Christmas presents." Making these things was recreation, too, in a sense.

But his situation in "college" was all hopelessly inappropriate so far as he could see.

In spite of everything he was the heavy item of expense in that household. But for this miserable college-education mother and sisters could get along well enough for a while.

Mother would never consent to his giving up so near the time for graduation—only another winter and spring term? A sacred sacrifice she was making.

But the fall term of his senior-year was just ended.

Why go on with it?

For Mother's sake? Look at her. She was ailing and unhappy. Why not go to Chicago where Uncle Jenkin Lloyd-Jones was building a new church, himself in a great work, get work in some architect's office, really help her and be getting nearer architecture himself?

He would plead—"There are great architects in Chicago, Mother, so there must be great buildings too. I am going to be an architect. You want me to be one. I am nowhere near it here. Professor Conover is fine but he isn't an architect. Here in the university I am doing nothing but draw and draw and see professional generalities glitter, spending money we haven't got or you have to slave to get.

"Do you believe in it yourself, Mother? In your heart I mean? It isn't real you know, like the farm. Why won't you ask Uncle 'Jenk' why I can't begin to be an architect right now. Soon it will be too late. I was eighteen last June, remember."

And then, threatening: "I'll go anyway. It's time I put a stop to this foolish waste motion myself. You are willing to starve for it because all the Joneses, every one of them, is cracked about education. 'Education'? You sent me to the farm yourself for experience, didn't you? Well, it's experience I want now. You spoiled me, yourself, for this marking time. It's vicious I tell you! I was sick of it long ago. It's no good for me. Can't you see, Mother? It's no good."

Finally the mother, continually thus beset, did write to Uncle Jenkin. Came back from the great preacher the answer, "On no account let the young man come to Chicago. He should stay in Madison and finish his education. That will do more for him than anything else. If he came here he would only waste himself on fine clothes and girls."

Mother was hurt, and relieved too. Her son would graduate.

But for the son, that insulting letter settled it.

He intended to go. If there was no more sympathy or understanding of the pathetic situation there than that letter showed, well—he would show the writer of the letter something . . . some day.

A few days later he left. Seven dollars in his pocket, after buying the ticket—money got from old man Perry at the pawn shop for his father's—and his—favorite calf-bound copy of Plutarch's *Lives,* thumbed edges at the life of Alcibiades. A finely bound set of Gibbons' *Rome,* which he detested. Several other books from the father's library, and a mink collar that had been his mother's but fitted by her to his overcoat . . . !

Well. . . mother wouldn't know he had gone until he didn't come home tomorrow night. He had fixed it all up to deceive her that far ahead; and he would write to her from Chicago as soon as he had a job, and that wouldn't be long. . . .

He put University behind him; a boundless faith strong in him. A faith in what? He could not have told you. He got on the Northwestern train for Chicago—the Eternal city of the West.

Childhood! Boyhood! Youth! Ever-living parts of manhood—told, in perspective, against the warm indispensable background of Family.

The telling none the less faithful for having the equality of life in a fond dream? Now individual independence is to begin.

Beyond, waiting in the eternal shadows of experience—shadows cast by human life on the living field since time began—are untold events: events ready to meet the adventurer at every step, as he goes forward step by step with courageous faith to meet them.

There is a bravery of all Life in this voluntary break with background to stand against clear sky—all fear superfluous: Now this is my own earth! The song in the heart.

Here say good-bye to "the boy."

Henceforward, on my own, I am "I."

The sentimental son of a sentimental mother grown up in the midst of a sentimental family planted on free soil by a grandly sentimental grandfather . . . the Welsh pioneer.

INTERLUDE

It is seed time.

The field is brown with the unctuous brown of freshly turned earth.

The sowing has been harrowed home.

Life stirs at the root.

Sap rises to flow again into accustomed channels and course to new growth.

A faint tinge of green is already coming over the brown field. The wood is flecked with green and touched with delicate pink. The Bob-white has been calling the Spring these two weeks past. The boy, as he rakes the leaves and rubbish from the fresh green grass of the dooryard, wonders as he notices the plum trees the apple trees, the berry bushes, and flower beds show no sign of Spring. He goes over to the flower beds to rake off the clean cane-stalks holding down the dead leaves when . . .

"Frank! Let the flowers alone! Not safe to let them up yet."

A beautiful, warm, clear day.

A clear, high night. Stars. A slender moon in a clear sky when the boy went to bed.

Next morning Winter returning unexpectedly while he slept had spread a rime of thick, white frost afield.

The warm sun came out in the still morning and the tiny flecks of green, the pink and green tinge over the wood—went black.

Nipped in the bud!

"I thought so," said Uncle James, "I was afraid of it!" Let the Bob-white whistle another week. Keep the frost in the roots.

And the boy knew for the first time why "cover" was carefully spread over the berry and flower beds after the ground had been frozen deep, and was spread around over the roots of the fruit trees.

To keep the frost in the roots until safe for them to wake!

The young sentimentalist has recourse to the oracle. "Uncle James! Why don't the trees and flowers know when to come out?"

"Well, that's something I can't tell," said his uncle.

A vague fear settled over the spirit of the seeker after Truth. Was the Spring singing about something it knew so little about as to be set back like this?

Did Uncle James know more about "Spring" than Nature knew herself? No, of course not.

He just knew how to play some trick on the ground that would make the trees and flowers wait—make them feel it was still Winter when it wasn't Winter, so he could be sure to have lots of fruit. Well, it was just like making the cows have calves to get the milk, wasn't it? Like making the pigs have little pigs so you could eat them?

That didn't explain anything.

And that wasn't Nature at all.

Not the real thing, that was just how men got their living out of Nature. Just craft.

The boy wanted to know something deeper.

This sentimentalist in love with Truth!

Is there a more tragic figure on Earth—in any generation?

PART TWO FELLOWSHIP

Chicago. Wells Street Station: six o'clock in late Spring, 1887. Drizzling. Sputtering white arc-light in the station and in the streets, dazzling and ugly. I had never seen electric lights before.

Crowds. Impersonal, intent on seeing nothing.

Somehow I didn't like to ask anyone anything. Followed the crowd.

Drifted south to the Wells Street Bridge over the Chicago River. The mysterious dark of the river with dim masts, hulks, and funnels hung with lights half-smothered in gloom—reflected in the black beneath. I stopped to see, holding myself close to the iron rail to avoid the blind hurrying by.

I wondered where Chicago was—if it was near. Suddenly the clanging of a bell. The crowd began to run. I wondered why: found myself alone and realized why in time to get off but stayed on as the bridge swung out with me into the channel and a tug, puffing clouds of steam, came pushing along below, pulling at an enormous iron grain boat, towing it slowly along through the gap.

Stood there studying the river-sights in the drizzling rain until the bridge followed after and closed to open the street again. Later, I never crossed the river without being charmed by somber beauty.

Wondered where to go for the night. But again if I thought to ask anyone, there was only the brutal, hurrying crowd, trying hard not to see.

Drifted south.

This must be Chicago now. So cold, black, blue-white, and wet.

The horrid blue-white glare of arc-lights was over everything.

Shivering. Hungry. Went into an eating place near Randolph Street and parted with seventy cents, ten percent of my entire capital. As I ate, I was sure of one thing, never would I go near Uncle Jenkin Lloyd-Jones nor ask his help nor use his name.

Got into the street again to find it colder, raining harder.

Drifted south and turned left, shivering now in front of the Chicago Opera House on Washington Street, the flood of hard city lights made the unseeing faces of the crowd in the drizzle, livid, ghastly. Under a great canopy that made a shelter from the rain were enormous posters—"SIEBA"—Extravaganza by David Henderson, Grand Corps de Ballet. And there the dancers were, life-size almost, out on the sidewalk, holding color in the glare.

The doors were just open and a dollar let me go in where it was dry and warm to wait nearly an hour for the show to begin. During that waiting . . . went back to the home by the lake—to see the mother and Jennie and Maginel . . . wondered what they would feel when they knew I had gone for good . . . never to come back? But they were all coming to me in Chicago. There must be clean, quiet "home" places in Chicago near the lake, maybe. I wondered if they were anxious about me, hardly realizing I wouldn't be missed until tomorrow night. Saw Mother's sad eyes and pale face as she sat quietly—waiting. She seemed now always waiting and—a pang of homesickness already! But the orchestra filed out from under the stage.

Tuning up began, always exciting.

Then the florid overture.

I knew it wasn't good music—good music was not so sentimental (my father's term of contempt)—but I was glad to hear it.

The Henderson Extravaganzas in those days were duly extravagant. This one took the roof off an unsophisticated mind.

Went out after all was over, drifting with the crowd to Wabash Avenue. Cottage Grove Avenue cable cars were running there. My first sight of the cable car. So, curious, I got on the grip-car beside the gripman and tried to figure it all out, going south in the process until the car stopped and "all out!" That car was going to the barn.

Got on the one coming out headed north now. Not sleepy nor tired. Half resentful because compelled to read the signs pressing on the eyes everywhere. They claimed your eyes for this, that, and everything beside. They lined the car above the windows. They lined the way, pushing, crowding, and playing all manner of tricks on the desired eye.

Tried to stop looking at them. Compelled to look again. Kept on reading until reading got to be torture.

There were glaring signs on the glass shopfronts against the lights inside, sharp signs in the glare of the sputtering arc-lamps outside. HURRAH signs. STOP signs. COME ON IN signs. HELLO signs set out before the blazing windows on the sidewalks. Flat fences lettered both sides, man-high, were hanging out across above the sidewalks and lit by electric lamps.

Coming from extravaganza here was the beginning of phantasmagoria.

Supersensitive eyes were fixed by harsh dissonance and recovered themselves: reasoned and fought for freedom. Compelled again—until the procession of saloons, food shops, barber shops, eating houses, saloons, restaurants, groceries, laundries—and saloons, saloons, tailors, dry goods, candy shops, bakeries, and saloons, became chaos in a wilderness of Italian, German, Irish, Polak, Greek, English, Swedish, French, Chinese, and Spanish names in letters that began to come off, and get about, interlace and stick and climb and swing again.

Demoralization of the eye began: names obliterating everything. Names and what they would do for you or with you or to you for your money. Shutting your eyes didn't end it, for then you heard them louder than you saw them. They would begin to mix with absurd effect and you need take nothing to get the effect of another extravaganza. Letters this time. Another ballet, of A. B. C. D. E. F. G., L. M. N. O. P., X. Y. and Z the premier-danseuse, intervening in fantastic dances.

It would have been a mercy not to have known the alphabet. One pays a heavy toll for the joys of being "eye-minded."

Got to bed at the Brigg's House north on Randolph Street, wrapped a sheet around myself—

it seemed awfully like a winding sheet as I caught sight of it in the mirror—and slept.

A human item—insignificant but big with interior faith and a great hope. In what? Not yet could I have told you.

Asleep in Chicago.

A Chicago murderously actual.

Next day I began on Chicago.

My hand in my pocket after breakfast, I could feel sure of three silver dollars and a dime.

Took the city directory and made a list of architects, choosing names I had heard in Conover's office or that sounded interesting. All names, and missed the names of all names important to me. The name of the architect of my uncle's new church, "All Souls," I knew by heart—J. L. Silsbee, Lakeside Building, Clark Street, Chicago. But I wasn't going there. Tramped through street after street now seeing Chicago above the sign-belt.

And where was the architecture of the great city—The "Eternal City of the West"?

Where was it? Behind these shameless signs?

A vacant block would come by. Then the enormous billboards planted there stood up grandly, had it all their own way, obliterating everything in nothing. That was better.

Chicago! Immense gridiron of noisy streets. Dirty . . . heavy traffic crossing both ways at once, managing somehow: torrential noise.

A stupid thing, that gridiron: cross-currents of horses, trucks, streetcars, grinding on hard rails, mingling with streams of human beings in seeming confusion and clamor. But habit was in the movement making it expert, and so safe enough. Dreary—dim—smoked. Smoked dim and smoking.

A wide, desolate, vacant strip ran along the waterfront over which the Illinois Central trains incessantly pulled and ground, cutting the city off from the lake.

Terrible, this grinding and piling up of blind forces. If there was logic here who could grasp it?

To stop and think in the midst of this would be to give way to terror. The gray, soiled river, with its mists of steam and smoke, was the only beauty. That smelled to heaven.

Young engineer looking for work? Sam Treat

looked me over. "University man, eh!" The kindly intellectual face under a mass of gray hair smiled. "Sorry."

Caught a glimpse of a busy drafting room full of men as I came out.

Well!—there was Beers, Clay and Dutton. More tramping through brutal crowds that never seemed to see anything. Mr. Clay came out and looked me over—a twinkle of kindly humor in his black eyes. I have remembered that *he* seemed to see *me* and was amused. Why? Was it the longish hair again, or what? Took pity on me, maybe, for he asked me to call again in a few weeks if I found nothing. In a few weeks! And had just three dollars and ten cents!

Over now, to S. S. Beman in the Pullman Building way south on Michigan Avenue.

College "tooth-picks" made in vain if made for walking. Souvenir of sophomore vanity on right little toe raising Cain now. Perspiring freely. Found Mr. Beman "not in!" Foreman looked me over. I. K. Pond?

"University man? What college, Ann Arbor?"

"No, University of Wisconsin."

"No, nobody wanted at present, later perhaps—in a few months."

In a few months!

The famous Pullman Building had come into view. It looked funny—as if made to excite curiosity. Had passed the Palmer House, on the way down, that famous Chicago Pallazzo. It seemed curious to me: seemed like an ugly old, old man whose wrinkles were all in the wrong place owing to a misspent life. As I went on my way to W. W. Boyington's office I passed the Chicago Board of Trade at the foot of La Salle Street. Boyington had done it. This?—thin-chested, hard-faced, chamfered monstrosity? I turned aside from Boyington's office then and there.

Chicago architecture! Where was it? Not the Exposition Building, a rank, much-domed yellow shed on the lake front. No, nor the rank and file along the streets. The rank and file all pretty much alike, industriously varied but no variety. All the same thought or lack of it. Were all American cities like this one, so casual, so monotonous in their savage, outrageous attempts at variety? All competing for the same thing in the same way? Another

senseless competition never to be won?

So thinking, I got on toward Major Jenney's office. Mundie came out. He was President of the Chicago Architectural Club as I knew. "Ah, University man. Engineer?" "Yes." Had I any drawings? No? First time I had been asked for any drawings. "Why don't you come around to the Club meeting Saturday night? You might hear of something there. Bring some of your drawings along with you," he added.

Strange! I had not thought to bring any drawings with me. But some were in the bag, still checked at the Station. Mundie with his sunken eyes in an impassive frozen face was a little kindly warmth in the official atmosphere of the Chicago architect's office.

Too late to go to any more offices now. Got my bag to the Brigg's House not knowing where else to go, hungry. Asked for a cheaper room. Clerk sympathetic—one for seventy-five cents, almost as good. For supper, what twenty cents would buy at the bakery. I had found Kohlsatt's bakery-lunch. Tempting pastry piled high in plain sight, all that I had been denied or allowed to eat only occasionally, and things beside, I had never even dreamed of. A hungry orphan turned loose in a bake shop? Lucky I had little money.

To bed, dog-tired, not at all discouraged. On the whole everyone had been rather kind. Must be someone who needed me. Tomorrow, maybe.

Two days gone from home, Mother knew now! The thought of her was anguish. I turned away from it to action and repeated the performance of the day before in other offices, this time taking my drawings. Mundie was out. At five other offices, no success.

No lunch.

No supper.

During the day ten cents invested in bananas.

That night, a weird dream. Up in a balloon. Mother below frantically holding to the rope, dragged along the ground, calling Jennie and Maginel to help . . . all dragged along. I shouted down to hitch the end of the rope to something, anything, and make it fast. But it tore out of their helpless hands and I shot up and up and up—until I awoke with a sense of having been lifted miles to the strange ground of another world.

Awakened rudely to the fourth day. Got started again, pavement-sore, gaunt. Something had to happen today. Tired again, three more offices. Same result.

There was still Silsbee's office. He was building my uncle's "All Souls Church," but he needn't know who I was. After noon I went there. Liked the atmosphere of the office best. Liked Silsbee's sketches on the wall. Liked instantly the fine looking, cultured fellow with a fine pompadour and beard, who quietly came forward with a friendly smile.

Cecil Corwin.

"Hello!" he said as though he knew me. He looked the artist-musician. He had come through the gate in the outer office railing humming something from the "Messiah."

I smiled and said, "Do you sing?" He smiled too, looking at my hair-cut, or lack of it. "Yes . . . try to . . . Do you play?" "Yes . . . try to."

And I had found a kindred spirit.

He sat down by me in the outer office. His sleeves were rolled above the elbow. His arms were thickly covered with coarse hair, but I noticed how he daintily crooked his little finger as he lifted his pencil. He had an air of gentleness and refinement. I told him my trials.

"You are a minister's son?"

"Yes, how did you know?"

"Didn't know, something about you. I am one myself. The 'Old Man' (moving his head in the direction of Silsbee's private office) is one too. And there are two more here already, Wilcox and Kennard. If you come in here, there would be five of us."

We laughed.

"Well . . . could I by any chance come in?" I said anxiously. He looked me over. "I believe we could get along," he said. "Let me see your drawings."

He looked carefully at the sketches. "You made these just to please yourself?"

"Yes."

"You've got a good touch. Wait a minute." He took them and went in through a door marked "Private." Presently he appeared at the door with a tall, dark-faced, aristocratic-looking man, gold eyeglasses, with long gold chain, hanging from his nose. He stood in the door looking carelessly at me with a frown. It was Silsbee. "All right," he said, "take him on. Tracer's wages—$8.00."

And he turned and shut the door after him.

"Not much, but better than nothing," said Cecil. I agreed.

How far from my expectations, "$8.00." With my "experience" I should be able to earn three times as much. But no one thought much of my "experience." Cecil saw the disappointment following elation. "Had your lunch? No? Come with me." We went downstairs a block away to Kinsley's. Cecil insisted on a good portion of browned corned-beef-hash for me, and coffee.

"Thank you, no coffee. I don't drink it."

"Well then"—amused—"milk?" And ever since, when feeling hungry, nothing has tasted so good to me as browned corned-beef-hash.

"Got any money left?" he said abruptly.

"Oh, yes!"

"How much?"

"Twenty cents."

"Had anything to eat yesterday?"

This was getting rather too personal so I didn't answer.

"Come home with me tonight and we'll concertise with my new grand-piano."

It was Saturday. I was not to report for work until Monday morning.

So I got my bag from the Brigg's House and went home with Cecil. A nice home. Met his benevolent preacher father, a Congregational missionary. His mother had died some years ago but his sister, Marquita, looked after the father and her bachelor brother. She was "musical" too.

After a "musical" evening together, we went up to the room that was for me. Cecil found how anxious I was about things back home, gave me paper, pen and ink to write. I did.

And then: "Would you lend me ten dollars to send my Mother? I'll pay you back two dollars a week."

He said nothing, took a ten–dollar bill from his pocket and laid it on the table. I put it in the envelope and we took it to the nearest box to post it.

A load went off my heart.

I had a job.

But better still, I had a friend, and no mean one in any sense, as anyone could see.

Now I could go and see my uncle's new Church. Cecil himself had been looking after the building of it. I asked him about it.

"Would you like to see 'The Church,'" he said, with curious emphasis on "Church." "We'll run down to Oakwood Boulevard and Langley Avenue after dinner and have a look at it."

We went. Why the curious emphasis? I knew now. It was in no way like a Church, more like a "Queen Anne" dwelling. We used to say they were Queen Anne front and Mary Ann behind. And this was. But it was interesting to me. Again not beautiful, but . . . curious.

Taking advantage of the unexpected visit, Cecil went about looking after some details in the nearly completed building. I went along Oakwood Boulevard to look it over in perspective. Was standing back, looking over from across the street when a hand from behind took me firmly by the collar and a hearty voice like a blow, "Well, young man! So here you are."

I had recognized the voice instantly, Uncle Jenkin Lloyd-Jones! I was in for it.

"I've been expecting you, young fellow. Your mother wrote—distracted. I'll telegraph you're found."

"No!—Please." I said. "I wrote last night telling her I had a job and I sent her some money."

A job? "Where have you found a job?"

"Silsbee's office."

"Silsbee's? Of course. That was mighty good of him. Told him who you were I suppose?"

"No!" I said, "I didn't!" He looked suspicious. But got the point quickly. "All right," he said. Then Cecil came up and greeted him. "Where did you get hold of my young nephew?" said Uncle Jenkin.

"He's your nephew? I didn't know it," Cecil said in astonishment.

That proved my case.

"Well—where are you going to stay now?" asked the maternal uncle. I didn't know. "You're coming to stay near here where I can keep an eye on you. Tonight you must come and stay with us."

"No!" said Cecil, "he's going to stay with me tonight."

"All right then, Monday night."

Isn't the opening to "the way" usually as simple? Here the chance end of a sequence that like the end of twine in a skein of indefinite length, would unwind in characteristic events as time went on.

Frank Lloyd Wright and Cecil Corwin.
FLLW Fdn FA#6002.0009

Not at all as I had expected! It seldom is as much or at all as we expect it to be. But Cecil was already more in himself than I could have imagined. His culture similar to mine, yet he was different. And so much more developed in it than I.

I began to go to school to Cecil.

We were soon together everywhere.

Silsbee was doing Edgewater at the time, the latest attempt at "high-class" subdivision and doing it entirely for J. L. Cochran, a real-estate genius in his line.

Silsbee could draw with amazing ease. He drew with soft, deep black lead pencil strokes and he would make remarkable free-hand sketches of that type of dwelling peculiarly his own at the time. His superior talent in design had made him respected in Chicago. His work was a picturesque combination of gable, turret, and hip with broad porches quietly domestic and gracefully picturesque. A contrast to the awkward stupidities and brutalities of the period, elsewhere. He would come out to the draughting room as though we, the draughtsmen, did not exist, stand talking a moment with Cecil, one lank leg turning one long foot over sidewise, the picture of indifference or scorn as he stood on the other. He was grudging of words and shy of patience. All awed by him.

Not so Cecil.

The office system was a bad one. Silsbee got a ground-plan and made his pretty sketch, getting some charming picturesque effect he had in his mind. Then the sketch would come out into the draughting room to be fixed up into a building, keeping the floor-plan near the sketch if possible. The sketches fascinated me. "My God, Cecil, how that man can draw!"

"He can. He's a kind of genius, but something is the matter with him. He doesn't seem to take any of it or himself half seriously. The picture interests him. The rest bores him. You'll see. He is an architectural genius spoiled by way of the aristocrat. A fine education and family in Syracuse, but too contemptuous of everything."

And I did see. I saw Silsbee was just making pictures. And not very close to what was real in the building—that I could soon see, myself.

But I adored Silsbee just the same. He had style. His work had it too, in spite of slipshod methods. There was something finely tragic in his somber mien; authority in the boom of his enormous voice pitched low in his long throat with its big "Adam's apple." I learned a good deal about a house from Silsbee by way of Cecil.

Monday night I had gone to Uncle Jenkin to spend a few days at the parsonage. Interesting people came there to dine. Dr. Thomas, Rabbi Hirsh, Jane Addams, Mangasarian, and others. I enjoyed listening.

A letter had come from Mother. She wrote regularly every week. She seemed glad after all that I was at work. Told me to stay close to Uncle Jenkin. He was a good man beset by the countless trials of his position but would help me all he could. And I was not to worry about her.

She had sold Father's library and a few hundred dollars had come to her from her brothers, her small share in Grandfather's farm. If I got along and needed her she would sell the Madison place and come down and make a home for me. There were the usual anxieties about diet, warm underwear, companions.

"I would have you," she wrote, "a man of sense as well as sensibility. You will find Goodness and Truth everywhere you go. If you choose, choose Truth. For that is closest to Earth. Keep close to Earth, my boy: in that lies strength. Simplicity of heart is just as neccessary for an architect as for a farmer or a minister if the architect is going to build great buildings." And she would put this faith of hers in many different forms as she wrote on different subjects, until I knew just what to expect from her.

Always very brave she was, but I knew what she wanted—she wanted to come down to live with me. And as soon as I could earn eighteen or twenty dollars a week, I intended to have her come. Little Maginel was not yet very strong and Jennie had gone to teach school in the country.

I have always been fond of Uncle Jenkin's son, my cousin Richard. He was a good-looking, fair-haired, brilliant "city-guy," initiated and unabashed, his views of what went on around him keen and amusing. Richard had ambition, a certain affection but small reverence. He was a good specimen of minister's son. His mother was older than his father and more intellectual, I believe. She adored her son and never tired quoting him. He was quotable. I will say that for him, although Aunt Susan did "overdo" Richard, continually. Mothers have a habit of overdoing their sons.

His father found a boarding place for me at the Watermans', a block away on Vincennes Avenue. I got my clothes into a wheelbarrow one night late with Dick's help, and we started down the deserted Boulevard. It was so smooth I proposed to beat him the two blocks to the corner, I wheeling the barrow. We lit out. And I did beat him but in trying to turn to Vincennes, over went wheelbarrow, clothes, helter-skelter into the dirty street, myself following head first in a cruel slide as though shot out of a cannon, Dick tumbling after doing a cart-wheel into the wreck. A perfect success!

Both were scratched and scraped some, not hurt much. Laughing—we were always laughing—we gathered dusty underwear, ties, Sunday clothes, and shirts far and wide as the wind entered into the spirit of the thing and carried on . . . that Boulevard dust in my "things" as near permanent as any dye.

The Watermans' was a quiet, decent place. I saw Harry, a lad nearly my own age, once in a while. But they were all rather pessimistic folk saddened, it seemed to me, by something of a family nature. Did it follow me everywhere or did I see it because of my own experience?

Richard and I went about together. Richard—"Dick"—knew the ropes. "Dick" knew how to laugh. We would get to laughing and keep at it, the bait going to and fro between us until both were tired out.

And there was quite a social life going on at the church. Evening events, lectures, and meetings of one sort or another. Sociables. Browning classes. I got "Rabbi Ben Ezra" into my system about that time and the "Ring and the Book." Study classes of all kinds. All Souls had a circulating library, was a neighborhood-center in which were many activities intellectual, social, and literary. A kindergarten there too. The church was never closed.

My uncle's soul seemed a sort of spiritual dynamo that never rested.

His preaching, like Grandfather's, had force and fervor—and brains.

But I began to suspect him of sentimentality.

He was evidently becoming an active spiritual force in Chicago, his influence increasing rapidly.

Cecil was often taking me home and we went to the Apollo Club Concerts or other concerts wherever we could find them. And we went to the theaters sometimes. I had then, as now, a passion for the theater as for music.

The work in the office was easy for me and I soon made myself useful. We took on a new man about that time, a few months after I had entered—George Maher. He had asked Silsbee for eighteen dollars a week and got it as he had much "experience." After three months there I had been raised to twelve.

I soon found George was no better draughtsman than I was, if as good. And I made up my mind to try for a raise. If Silsbee could pay George eighteen, he could pay me twenty.

"The old man's here now—go in and talk to him," said foreman-and-friend, Cecil. I went in.

Silsbee looked at me and frowned. Evidently he knew what my being there meant.

"Well!"

"Mr. Silsbee, I can't get along on twelve dollars a week. Don't you think I can earn fifteen dollars a week at least—now?"

"You've just had a raise, Wright. No! Perhaps—the first of the year."

I was sure injustice was being done me. So then and there, I quit.

Mr. W. W. Clay of Beers, Clay and Dutton had interested me when I was "job hunting," and I went straight over to see him.

"One of Silsbee's men?" he asked. A man in Silsbee's office could usually draw and design in his style and was in demand by architects less capable in design.

"Yes sir."

"How much do you expect to earn?"

"Eighteen dollars."

He got up and went out with me to the foreman of the draughting room.

"Lockwood," said he, "take this young man on. We will pay him eighteen dollars a week. His name is Wright."

Cecil and I were still together noons and evenings. Mr. Clay, more than kind, seemed interested in me. But I soon found myself entrusted with work beyond me. Designing what I should be learning how to design.

I realized I had made a mistake in any long run. In a few weeks went in to tell Mr. Clay so. He was astonished.

"Aren't we good to you here, Wright? Isn't the work interesting?"

"Oh yes," I could truthfully say.

"Don't you like me?"

"Yes." And I really did.

"Well, out with it. What's the matter?"

I told him I didn't feel ready to "give out" designs. Wanted to learn how to make them. There was no one there skilled as a designer. I could learn very little.

"I see," he said dryly. He was hurt. I think he thought me a young cox-comb.

"What are you going to do?"

"I'm going back to Silsbee."

"Will he take you?"

"I don't know."

"Hadn't you better find out before you quit?"

"No."

"Why not?"

I had no answer.

"All right! Go out to Lockwood and tell him to give you your wages." But he thought that rather rough and went out with me himself. "Lockwood," he said gently, "give Wright his wages and let him out. Either he's got the big head or he's right. I don't know which." And he shook hands with me, the characteristic half-humorous look coming again into his eyes.

I went as straight back to Silsbee as I had left him. Told him the story. He smoked away without a word.

"You've quit already, have you?"

"Yes sir."

"What for?"

"Well, I didn't want it to look as though you were taking me away from Mr. Clay, if you let me come back."

He smiled that bitter smile of his, went to the door, and called "Corwin!" Cecil came. "Wright is coming back. His wages will be eighteen dollars." The Silsbee private office door closed behind me as I came out.

Cecil and I went dancing around the big table in the center of the room in a friendly tilt.

During these later months at Silsbee's Cecil and I were inseparable. Discussed everything in the heavens above, the earth beneath, and the waters thereof.

We would go to Madame Galle's, Italian table d'hôte, or various other cozy restaurants. Or, if we had a little money, to the "Tip-Top Inn" in the Pullman Building, then, as now, Hieronymus had made it Chicago's most delightful dining place.

Theodore Thomas was giving concerts in the old Exposition Building. We went there. In the rear of the audience were tables and refreshments in comfortable German style. I've never enjoyed any concerts more since.

They were just beginning to build the Chicago Auditorium. The papers were full of its wonders. Adler and Sullivan, the architects, were frequently

mentioned. I wondered how I had come to miss that firm in my search for work.

Usually I went to "All Souls," my uncle's church—mornings. Perhaps to dinner at the parsonage above on Sundays. I had noticed interesting people in the congregation but made no acquaintances, although a number of the people who knew me as "the pastor's nephew" asked me to come and see them or invited me without that formality to dine. But I didn't go. I preferred Cecil's company. If I couldn't have that I would find something to do.

From the library of "All Souls" I got two books you would never expect could be found there. Owen Jones' *Grammar of Ornament,* and Viollet le Duc's *Habitations of Man in All Ages.* I had read his *Dictionnaire,* the *Raisonné* at home, got from the Madison city library.

The *Raisonné* was the only really sensible book on architecture in the world, I believed. I got copies of it later for my sons. That book was enough to keep one's faith in architecture in spite of architects.

The Owen Jones was a reprint but good enough, as I read the "propositions" and felt the first five were "dead right." I didn't know about the others. It seemed these five were equally sound applied to human behavior. And they were. I got a packet of "onion skin," a delicate, strong, smooth tracing paper and traced the multifold designs. I traced evenings and Sunday mornings until the packet of one hundred sheets was gone and I needed exercise to straighten up from this "application."

I had been eager to learn to box while at the University. Had practiced a little with Jimmie Kerr who had a similar ambition. One of the items that rolled over the dusty Boulevard when, while moving I upset the barrow and Dick and myself was a set of boxing gloves. I used to "put on the gloves" with Harry Waterman. And I used to walk sometimes nearly forty blocks downtown to work. A number of times, out of carfare, I had walked the whole distance.

A PRETTY GIRL IN PINK

The Study Classes at All Souls had been busy with Victor Hugo's *Les Misérables* under the guidance of the Pastor. The students were to complete this study with a costume-party, all the characters or personages of the tale appearing as Victor Hugo designed them. The affair to be a sweeping one, music, dancing, and a supper. Therefore a large hall was hired somewhere near. I wasn't a regular member of the classes, but "Enjolras," young French officer, fell to my lot. My rôle was simple, so they said. All I needed was a pair of high-heeled, shiny black boots coming above the knee, clanking spurs, not to mention white, tight trousers, scarlet military jacket with stiff collar, gold braid, and epaulettes. And I would need a small red cap on my head. And I should have also, hanging alongside on a leather harness, a sword! I don't know where I got all the things—from some costumer's, I suppose. They were probably as correct as Victor Hugo himself sometimes wasn't. Cecil helped the great work on. When I was dressed and ready he said, "Maybe not anything like 'Enjolras,' Frank, but certainly 'something to look at.'"

I pulled out the sword, stuck it point down on the floor, and "made a leg." "You'll do," he said. "I almost wish I had agreed to come when your uncle invited me."

"Come on anyway!" I begged. But he wouldn't come. So putting on my cape-overcoat I buttoned it, sleeves hanging, to put the glory out and holding the sword by my side under the coat walked down the Boulevard to the hall. I went late not to be conspicuous.

The scene, after I had stowed my coat and opened the door to the hall, was really brilliant. There they were—happy "Misérables" all of them.

But my plan had worked out wrong, for coming late I *was* conspicuous.

The first dance over, the characters were standing around the sides of the large room regarding that large central area as I came upon it—an empty dancing floor! There were many groups of prettily dressed French peasant-girls and young yokels standing about. Marat I saw, terrible as he needed to be and perhaps wasn't. The best character there, seen at a glance, was my Aunt Susan, the Preacher's wife as the Abbaye. Suddenly a group of lasses in bright bodices, short skirts, and pretty caps

came rushing over the floor. In the lead Miss Emery. "Here you are at last," from her.

"Planning a dramatic entrance, you see," I said. And she turned to introduce me to the others.

The Emerys were wealthy parishioners of "All Souls" though they came to church but seldom. She was older somewhat than I. "Finished" in a fashionable Eastern school she spoke with pretty accent the broad "a." Too "pretty" to be natural and yet, somehow, peculiarly hers. It probably was hers, after all. . . .

Glad to be taken in hand I danced with a number of the church girls whom I knew slightly. But the infernal slab-sided sword was slung so low that if I took my hands off it, it got between my legs. If I took my mind off it, it got between my partner's legs with disastrous effects—some of them laughable.

I danced pretty well now no longer so shy with the girls as at the university, though I knew none. But that sword sank me. I tried a dozen schemes to control it for I wouldn't spoil the fine figure I was making by taking it off! I was going to hang on to that swinging, dangling, clanking thing if I mowed the legs off the whole *Les Misérables* tribe and broke up the party. Some of the girls entered into the spirit of the thing and were helpful holding on to it themselves while dancing or at psychological moments otherwise.

I went about with Miss Emery. Sat out a few dances with her or rather we went out into a silent, half-dark auditorium opening into the hall and walked and talked. I felt quite at home in her company. Was glad I came. But when I wasn't in trouble with that sword, she was.

Felt I was having a "bully" time. Outside the gathering, I could take off the superfluous weapon and let her take it. She seemed to like to hold it—probably felt safer when *she* had it.

At ten o'clock there came a lull in the evening. Refreshments were to be served. There was a general rushing about to restore the several units to their several parties. Rushing across the dancing floor to join Miss Emery's group, half-way over, a tall, pretty "peasant-girl" in pink, blonde curls dancing one way while she was rushing my way looking the other way, was upon me before I could avoid her. Striking her forehead square against mine she was knocked to her hands and knees. I myself "seeing stars," managed to pick her up. She was laughing it off bravely enough, still blinking. I saw the bump already reddening on her forehead as I led her over to her parents to apologize, but she wouldn't have it. "All her fault," she insisted. The parents were Mr. and Mrs. Tobin, and this was their Catherine. Her father called her "Kitty." I had noticed her in church, a gay-spirited, sunny-haired young girl of probably sixteen, with a frank, handsome countenance in no way common. I remembered her parents had asked me to dinner. They asked me again now for Sunday—tomorrow. I said I would come. I hoped the bump, now beginning to swell, would not be too painful.

I noticed they had left—soon after.

Next day, a bump on my own forehead.

The course of the party changed for me. At eleven o'clock, the hour for church parties to end, I saw Miss Emery into her carriage and walked home along the Boulevard alone.

Were the times such—an ancient oracle might have stretched a prophetic hand over that "crash." But nothing would have changed. What a lot of harm "oracles" have brought about in their time by subtle force of suggestion. Always irresponsible, I believe, or scheming.

Next morning, turned by the party toward Victor Hugo, I remembered a chapter in *Notre-Dame*. A chapter on architecture—"The Book Will Kill the Edifice," wherein the amazing Frenchman had disposed of the European Renaissance as "that setting sun all Europe mistook for dawn." When I got up I went over to the Church library.

Found a different translation. This chapter-heading, instead of using as in the original French, "*Ceci Tuera Cela*," was "The one will kill the other." Took it home and read it again instead of going to church.

Victor Hugo loved diffuse discussion in abstruse style. But this essay on the great edifice was one of the truly great things ever written on architecture. Again I felt its force. My own gathering

distrust was confirmed. Splendid writing. How modern the great romanticist must have seemed in his time! But this chapter was omitted from some editions of *Notre-Dame*, as I learned afterward in searching for it to initiate others.

Excited by the great poet into thinking about the difference between romanticism and sentimentality, I got started late, walking down Drexel Boulevard to the Tobin home in Kenwood at Kimbark Avenue near Forty-seventh Street. Late to dinner. Catherine opened the door for me—the "Les Misérables" bump most gone. It was easy to like Father Tobin. He carried everything before him in a bluff, hearty, easy way. Mother Tobin was very different. A fine looking, auburn-haired woman, evidently mistress of her nice new home, both beloved by their children—but the mother ruled.

Catherine was eldest, sixteen. Charlie and Robert were twins. They were twelve. And Arthur a pretty, affectionate boy of seven came and sat on my knee.

All were devoted to Jenkin Lloyd Jones, disposed to lionize his nephew.

Diffidence disappeared in this homely warmth like that I had lost since coming to the city. "Kitty," girlish and lovely, vivaciously adopted me at once. She was in the Hyde Park High School. Also one of Professor Tomlin's pupils in music. Evidently Catherine had pretty much her own way in that household although she seemed a sensible girl. Everything revolved around "Kitty." Not only was she accustomed to having her own way but having it without any trouble. I noticed at table she ate on her own particular plate with her own particular knife and fork and spoon. A hang-over from childhood. The idiosyncrasy seemed only natural. The dinner went off gaily. After dinner "Kitty" came in dressed to go out, tall laced boots, gloves and short plaid walking jacket. A "tam-o-shanter" topped her mass of ruddy curls.

She took me by the hand simply and said she was going to take me to see the new Kenwood houses. That meant to see some curious effects, because Kenwood was in process of becoming the most fashionable of Chicago's residence districts. So we went down the front steps hand in hand like children. She was one, although so tall and seeming to have such good sense. I was grown up pretty well in architecture, the thing that interested me in the sphere in which I lived and in which I was now getting to feel so "dead in earnest." But where people were concerned, I had nearly everything yet to learn, though plenty of assurance was waking in me to enable me to learn.

So more months went along until, after a year with Silsbee, coming twenty soon, and earning the necessary $18.00 per week I felt Mother should sell the Madison home by the lake and come to Chicago. Soon she did come.

The North Shore attracted me, but Mother was afraid of the raw winds of the lake for me and for Maginel too.

She didn't seem to want to be too near "All Souls" for some reason.

So we went to see Miss Augusta Chapin, a friend of Mother's in Oak Park. Again a preacher and this time a woman.

She was Oak Park's Universalist pastor. Miss Chapin was a thick set woman's woman of about forty, usually dressed in rustling black silk, a gold chain around her neck to hang a gold cross upon her breast.

She wore, alternately, a very kind or a very severe expression.

Miss Chapin and Mother fixed up some temporary arrangement whereby we were to come in to the red-brick on Forest Avenue with her for some time, to see if Oak Park was really the place to choose for a permanent home.

OAK PARK

Oak Park's other name was "Saint's Rest." There were so many too many churches for so many good people to go to, I suppose. Nevertheless, the village looked like a pretty solid, respectable place. The people were good people, most of whom had taken asylum there to bring up their children in comparative peace, safe from the poison of the great city.

The village streets were generously shaded.

It had a village government of its own, too, accounting for its subsequent growth to some extent.

"I remember" Superintendent Hatch, a kindly dark-faced man, driving about in an open buggy from school to school. My sister Jennie, now, owing to Miss Chapin's kind offices, was to be one of his teachers at the Chicago Avenue School.

"I remember" the old Scoville place, occupying a whole square of the town, the lean wooden house standing there shamelessly tall, to say the last word for the depravity characterizing the residence architecture of the period.

"I remember". . .

But to avoid too many recollections, the quiet village looked much like Madison to Mother. That settled it.

Opposite the red-brick on Forest Avenue and well within the center of the village was the Austin lot, another whole square competing with the Scoville square. This one untouched natural wildwood. A newly built all-shingle home in the entering mode, "Queen Anne," took the middle of a cleared space at the Lake Street front. To one side and to the rear of the house next to Forest Avenue stood an old-fashioned barn vertically boarded and battened. It had good proportion and an interesting rusty color where the festoons of vines let color through. Built in a much earlier period, being only a barn, it had been allowed to live. I liked the barn better than the Austin house. The old barn was honestly picturesque whereas the house had only elaborately tried to be so. But the Forest Avenue residents thought it outrageous that Mr. Austin, Oak Park's leading citizen, should leave this barn there on the best street in town.

Mr. Austin, a short, slow-moving solid Scotchman, carried his head well down in his shoulders on a short neck and wore a quizzical look on his short, bearded face.

This Austin wood-lot looked especially inviting to me in that aggregation of uninspired carpenter work: endless rows of drab or white painted wood houses set regularly apart, each on its little painted cardboard lawn. High front-steps went straight up to jigger-porches wriggling with turned balusters. All squirming with wanton scroll-work. And this prevalent porch-luxury was seldom of use, the roofs shut out the sun from the "parlors" and "sitting-rooms." These enemies of Mr. Austin's barn all had the murderous corner-tower serving as bay-window in the corner room. Where did that soul-destroying "motif" come from? The corner-tower never came from Earth.

This popular fetish—for it was more than a feature—was either rectangular across the corner or round or octagonal on it, eventuating above in candle-snuffer roofs, turnip domes, to corkscrew spires. I walked along the miles of this expensive mummery trying to get into the thinking processes of the builders but failed to get hold of any thinking they had done at all. The forms were utterly meaningless, though apparently much scheming and copying.

The houses were senseless; most of them looked equally comfortless. No more so in Oak Park than anywhere else; rather better, because here in Oak Park there were more trees and vines and wider shaven lots. Those who lived in this ambitious Eastlake mimicry were blissfully unaware of any losses or self-inflicted insults. And yet the monotonous iteration of the suburban-house parade like the sign-parade in Chicago streets compelled me whether I was willing or not.

The sign-parade—phantasmagoria—had at least a basis of meaning. This procession—monogoria—had none whatever. My father's complaints and criticisms of music came to mind. "Sentimentality" spoiled music for him in the making or the playing. Did it apply here?

As I walked and walked about, a helpless spectator, again a rank "outsider," it would seem a senseless reiteration. A monologue reciting in monotone . . . .

Nobody home! Nobody home! "They" stay here but they don't live here. We never knew life. But we are just as good as anybody's houses, just as good: just as good as "they" are—better, maybe.

Fooled? Maybe they are fooled. What do we care? Everybody is—everybody is! "They" are. We are. Everybody is. We suit them all. They suit us. Why should we mean anything if they don't mean anything?

We're as good as "they" are? We couldn't think if we would. They wouldn't think if they could.

They buy what thought there is in us ready made and what's in them, too. It's easier—maybe better? How do you know!

Houses are just like clothes aren't they? We're just clothes too, so we have to be "in fashion" don't we? Or we'll be laughed at! Won't we? Don't you see—boy? They'll be laughed at. What then?

Fools? Maybe—but fools on the laughing side.

Go get your hair cut, boy! We see you, just green! In on a load of poles? Ha! Ha!

Now, get in on the Fashion, Dunce!

Get in or get out!

Respect the respectable or move on—you!

What was the matter with me? More painful all this than the Chicago sign parade. More pitiful. This was "CULTURE." That was mongering. Here was tragedy, none the less so for being unconscious. Here was a mess. Were these meaningless monstrosities like the people whose houses they were—like the men and women who lived in them? Was all this waste what "they" *deserved*? Or had education been playing tricks with them—too. If "*they*" were so far wrong in this expression of themselves, so violent, so lacking in feeling and perception of the natural—what were their other institutions like if you looked them square in the face? Were "*they*" really right about anything at all above the alimentary canal and reproductive tract and weren't those being corrupted and spoiled in a confusion of ideals that ignored needs? Were they just sentimental about something? Else how could they take such horridly unnatural things into their lives? Didn't "they" want some real meaning in their buildings? Why were they all satisfied with pretentious attitudes and stupid gestures? Were they all sentimental instead of sensible?

I used to take these doubts to Cecil. For wasn't Silsbee doing the same thing in the pictures he made, only he did it as an artist?

Silsbee's houses were merely artistic then? Yes, that was all they were. For the lack of thought or what thought there was in them was just the same as this.

I began to be more than ever dissatisfied with Silsbee.

He seemed to me to be making matters worse. Making a lie or a vain boast more pretty, therefore making this shameful swindle easier.

Going by, I would sometimes lean on the Austin fence, an affair of dead oak tree branches with the bark on—therefore "rustic." As I was leaning there looking at the wood one Sunday morning, Mr. Austin came up and spoke to me. "Won't you come in?" he said. "You live next door? Young architect? Miss Chapin has spoken of you."

"I have wanted to go about a little in that 'oasis,'" I said, pointing to the wood. I asked him how he came to "let it alone" in the midst of all those harsh houses. He looked at me from under bushy eyebrows: "Don't you like their houses? Eh?"

"They want me to move my old barn there," looking toward it, "but"—eyes twinkling—"I like the looks of my barn better than I do their houses." He winked!

"I would rather live in it myself," I said.

"Come, let's look in it." And he led the way.

The old barn was fixed up inside, above, as a playroom or ballroom, being decorated now for a party to be given for his daughter Sophie who was returning from some fashionable finishing school.

Mr. Austin had turned his back on his new house to go to the old barn and never asked me what I thought of the house although next Sunday he asked me in to meet Mrs. Austin. The interior of the house was livable and homelike and I could say nice things about it. The exterior was never mentioned between us. It seems it was an old home with a new outside and so it looked. Mrs. Austin, a placid invalid, sat in a wheelchair by the window. There was a son Harry, away somewhere at college.

Getting back into the barn:

"Now what would you do with this room for an occasion?" he said. And I spontaneously made a few suggestions which happened to appeal to him—a decorative scheme of some sort I have forgotten. "Will you come over and help carry it out?"

Then he took me several blocks away to a lot at the corner of Forest and Chicago Avenues, a tangle-wood of all sorts of trees and shrubs and vines

belonging, he said, to a Mr. Blair, a Scotch landscape gardener who laid out Humboldt Park in Chicago for whom Mr. Austin had the greatest affection and respect. He never tired talking of the old gardener. I never met the gardener but I kept his lot in mind.

Mr. Austin got into the way of calling for me regularly Sunday mornings to go for a little walk.

I had found a quiet and, as circumstances proved, a staunch friend in Oak Park while he lived.

CLEAR WINE

Some months later Cecil and I as usual were talking over doubts that were gaining on me and making me less useful in the office.

"Frank, look out!" he would say. "Heresy in religion is bad enough, but nothing compared to heresy in fashion and culture.

"Read your Bible. Remember Jesus' instructions to his disciples?"

We happened to be at the Oak Park red-brick on a Sunday. I went after Miss Chapin's Bible. Cecil turned to Matthew and read: "Go ye not into the way of the Gentiles! And into any city of the Samaritans, enter ye not. And into whatsoever city or town ye enter inquire who in it is worthy. And there abide till ye go home. Behold, I send you forth as sheep in the midst of wolves. Be ye therefore, wise as serpents and harmless as doves. But beware of men, for they will deliver you up to the councils and they will scourge you in synagogues. And ye shall be brought before governors and kings for my sake for a testimony against them and the Gentiles." He put the book down.

"The Gentiles and Samaritans today, Frank, and the Pharisees, for that matter, are the people who are proud of those homes and satisfied with them. The architects who work for them are, literally, the 'scribes.' The 'professional men' of today are in much the same social relation to the people as the 'scribes' were to the Pharisees then."

He took the book up again. "Give not that which is holy unto the dogs, neither cast ye your pearls before swine". . . "swine" meaning those whose appetites for gain or fame or pleasure rule their judgment . . . "lest they trample them under their feet and turn again and rend you. Beware of the leaven of the Pharisees and of the leaven of Herod." He shut the book. Sat silent a moment. . . Then he said quietly, "Silsbee is right."

"Silsbee doesn't interfere with their beliefs or upset their ideas of themselves. He does the thing they have already accepted better than the others do it. That's all. And he is considered radical enough by them in consequence, and—God knows has enough trouble with them on that account."

Now I had waited, to be sure of what I wanted to say.

"But, Cecil, is Silsbee doing the best he can? I mean, could he do better if he would?"

"What does that matter if he's doing the right thing?"

"But he's not doing the 'right thing' if he is not doing as well as he knows and *all* he knows how to do."

"Why not?"

"Because if there is GOD he can be trusted to use the best he has made or he wouldn't have made it. If He *is, HE* can be trusted to make the modifications . . . not Silsbee. This GOD of our Grandfathers—the first thing he would put upon every member of creation, conscious or unconscious, would be just that thing . . . *to do the best he knew how to do.* Not as he was *told* to do it, but as he *saw* it for himself. Else what meaning has 'He'?"

Cecil laughed. "That mother of yours is going to have occasion to weep for you, Frank."

"Maybe, Cecil, but not on that account, not if she is Grandfather's daughter. And she is."

"Have you ever talked these things over with her?"

"No, because it's just coming clear to me now. I am not afraid of what she'll say, though."

"But *whom* are you going to build homes for? If you go against their wishes and try to give them what *you* think right and not what they think they want?"

"That's just where a wise creator comes in, Cecil. I won't need but one man in ten thousand to work for—even one man in a hundred thousand would keep me more than busy all my life, because that man will need me as much as I need him and

he will be looking for me. And I've been thinking about old Mr. Austin."

"Yes," said Cecil. "Look at his house!"

"Well, I am looking at it. He got the best architect he knew. It happened to be Fred Shock, of Austin and the old man did all he could with him and got disappointed. What he got isn't *his* own house and he knows it. He's one man in Oak Park I could work for on the basis of the best I've got in *me.* He's getting the modified Gospel, when he ought to have got it straight. If GOD is on the job and not loafing in heaven—*there* in Mr. Austin would be one client for me."

"Yes," laughed Cecil, "and all you'd need do, would be to find him and for him to find you." Sarcastically, "A simple matter as things are?"

"Well, I did find him and I could make others like him find me if I had anything to show them. I know what Mr. Austin needs and what he missed. And I believe he missed it because the "gospel is modified" as you suggest and yet you defend it and say it is the right thing. Man alive! Cecil, isn't making these modifications taking God away and sitting in his place? We are all given *choice* and left free to choose. We live or die as we are fit to do, and to the extent of our natures, only when *free to choose.* Not when somebody is allowing us to choose only what *they* think we want and cheating us out of what we might have, but for their interference. And only by such choice, can we fulfill the Law."

"What Law?" said Cecil. "That irreligious, inhuman survival of the fittest?"

"No," I said, feeling my way toward the proper answer. "No. The process of nature selection." I knew I had slipped . . . I tried again—"Well—no—*keeping the truest and best of which man is capable where men can use it."*

"If he can find it," said Cecil. "How are you going to put it in the show-window?"

"How do I know? That isn't my business either."

"Going to put that up to God?"—from Cecil.

"Why not?" I said. "And look here, old man Cecil, what's more—I see it now . . . that's just what's the matter, too, with the Gospel as preached today in churches: Jesus was doing the best he knew how. The truth was in him. He preached it. But *He,* the Nazarene Carpenter . . . I wonder if the carpenter wasn't the architect in those days . . . was modified by his disciples in the next place.

"The disciples were sincere enough and did the best they could but 'modified' him. Again the preaching was modified by the disciples of those disciples. Again it was 'modified' to suit the 'needs of mankind.' Not as Jesus or his Father saw those needs. No. But as your father and my father too saw them. Hadn't the sentiment of Jesus become sentimentality in his disciples? Where is there any 'clear wine to drink' on any such basis?"

"Who wants clear wine?" said Cecil. "The water-bottle stands beside the Chianti on the table and we use it unless we want the linings of our stomach corroded beyond repair."

"That won't do! I'm not talking about Chianti. That, you said, was made from the skins of grapes anyway. I am talking about Champagne or Mosel or Burgundy or Port—who wants water in real wine?"

"All watered at some time to some extent," said Cecil. And the discussion had fizzed out.

And now I began to wonder if, after all, my father's life had not been a sacrifice to sentimentality. I began to think about the matter and try to get it clear. What had the Lloyd Jones sentimentality done to him! What had it done to me—to them all? To Mother? What was sentimentality doing to the life of the world?

Next Sunday, it had begun with Catherine. I had sometimes taken her home from church evenings. One chilly evening, I tried to put my coat on her to keep her warm and she indignantly refused to let me. We compromised by walking with one arm each around the other to keep *both* warm. Sometimes her mother would let us go together to concerts in town. She began to wait for me to sit by her in church, and to wait with a vacant place by her side if I was late, and I would take her home after services, to the Sunday dinner to which I had become almost "a regular."

I told Mother about Catherine. She had already heard—from Uncle Jenkin probably. And, as now appeared, she had been anxious. The affair *was* conspicuous by now. Kitty Catherine had begun to fall off in her school studies. She was being teased by her schoolfellows a good deal. Young people at the church "took us for granted."

Cecil met her occasionally when she came to pick me up at the office. He thought her a gay, charming youngster. "She's awfully fond of me, Cecil."

"Well," he said, "so am I.

"So is your mother.

"So are your sisters.

"Maybe others would be too, if you gave them a chance. I don't see that *that* gives her any special claim on you, does it? You don't know any other girls at all, Frank. What do you know about women by merely knowing Kitty?"

He himself knew few girls and they were much older than I. Uninteresting, I thought. He was such an attractive person I often wondered why he didn't know more interesting ones.

"Why," I said, "does anyone have to know *many* if he finds himself at home with one?"

"Did you ever kiss one, except her?"

"How do you know I've kissed her?"

"I'm clairvoyant," he said, "didn't you know?"

"No, but . . ."

Cecil interrupted me: "Exactly; *but* . . . You are going into this thing heels over head. At home with her—*at home*"—he repeated excitedly. "Yes—that's what I was afraid of. Don't you know she's a child, *you're* a child? That before you can construct any family life you must know what women are?"

"So you mean I have to kiss and take women to study women before I know what I want? Is that what you are driving at? I can understand how a man might kiss a girl in a kind of game. But—how can a man take a girl he doesn't love and want to live with?"

He looked out of the office window, his gentle face drooped—didn't answer.

"Cecil, what is it? What's the matter, old man? I want to know."

"There's no use. Why talk? No one ever listened in this world—in these matters." Bitterly—

"No, not since time began. I see where you are going. And I, your best friend, can't stop you nor can anyone."

He was so in earnest and sad I really tried to understand the "danger." I sat trying to imagine and I couldn't. It all seemed beautiful and right to me not to have experimented, to have found the one I wanted and who wanted me without all that wiseacre evil-thinking.

I felt sorry for Cecil. He didn't know, of course he didn't. Look at the women he knew compared to the glowing Catherine! She was more of a woman than he thought too—no child at all. Really a very sensible girl. She wanted me to save money and had offered to take care of it for me and was doing it to some extent. And she was sensible and careful about things whereas . . . well . . . I wasn't there at all in that way—as anybody could see.

Then it flashed over me, "Look here, old man Cecil. Have you been talking to Mother about this thing?"

"No . . . She talked to me about it."

"What did she say?"

"You may ask her."

I was hurt. My mother talking over my own private affairs with my friend and saying nothing to me. I was ashamed of the situation and began to feel that both Catherine and myself had been betrayed. She seemed to need my care and protection, and feeling that had been merely warm and affectionate began to deepen in character.

"Well," said Cecil, "let's not quarrel. You couldn't manage an acquaintance with more than one anyway. You are a born 'soloist.' I know you! You'll have to go it alone in everything all through your life. Only don't go so desperately fast. You'll go far enough soon enough. Why try to put into a month what would last other fellows a year at least? I wish I had more of your sensibility and steam and you had more of my sense and laziness.

"Don't feel I'm unsympathetic, Frank, or that I am saying anything against Catherine. For all anybody knows she may be just the girl for you."

All the way to Oak Park that evening I was going over the scene I knew was coming with Mother.

How absurd and uncalled-for the whole thing was! There had been no thought of marrying or any talk of it between the principals in this affair.

We had just come together as I always imagined boys and girls did if they liked each other. There was no doubt Kitty and I had good boy and girl times and liked being together. It seemed only natural. Something wonderful about it. It had in no way interfered with my work. The reverse was true. Life seemed more complete and I richer in mind in consequence. I was more effective in my work.

I got home and sat silent at supper with Mother, the girls, and Miss Chapin. Mother's looks inquiring silently.

Upstairs in my room after supper she came in to see what had gone wrong with the day.

"What is it, my son?"

"Mother! why go around to Cecil about Kitty and me?"

She didn't even look surprised. "Why, indeed!" she said and smiled.

It didn't seem a smiling matter to me, so I burst out with—"What's all the anxiety and fuss over a perfectly natural thing all about anyway? It's making Nature monstrous. Where is the sense in it?"

"Frank, have you thought of the consequences to this young girl of your singling her out to the exclusion of all others?"

She had begun on the vulnerable spot. Her first shot went home. "No, of course I haven't. But isn't she the best judge of what that means to her? I don't see how I can judge for her. And if she can't, how about her father and mother?"

"Her mother's in trouble with her over this already. It seems beyond her control."

"So you went to see her mother too?"

"Yes . . . Catherine has been accustomed to having her own way, seems to be giving her mother trouble. She seems to be as unreasonable as you are."

"Well then, that proves, doesn't it that it's all right for her? So why all this worry, anxiety and anguish, curiosity and prying and praying and gossip, to make a perfectly natural thing scandalous? I don't get it at all. I've never seen you like this. It doesn't seem like you, Mother. You have always said, "If you have to choose between the good and the true, choose truth! And—God—Mother! What in this matter *is* Truth?"

"Don't swear, my son."

This was too much! "Swearing? What is the name of the supreme being for if not to be called upon in extremity? I *mean* it. I see—a conspiracy to force Catherine and me to give up everything fine and happy in our relationship and think of getting *married*.

"What a state of mind!

"Is only one thing possible in this world to boys and girls? Only one thing everyone sees, thinks, watches, and believes?

"Who made things so damned fearsome and artificial anyway?"

"Frank, you are swearing before your mother."

"'Damned' is swearing, too? Then how get along on the farm? 'Damned' is a wonderful, necessary word! How can you dispose of your feeling about contrary things without that word? What else have we got in English? Is 'damned' swearing just because all extremes are profane?"

"I see no use in talking to you, my boy, in your present frame of mind," said Mother.

"Just what old man Cecil said. Why, all of you are ready to weep, wring your hands, and wail!"

Mother quietly got up and left.

But she had "done it" just the same. "Have you thought of the consequences to this young girl of singling her out to the exclusion of all others?" It would seem something had been left out of my education. For that seemed just the natural thing to do. Evidently there was a game I had been born into of which I hadn't been taught the rules and regulations. That was how I scornfully felt about it. That game was "social."

But I didn't mean to hurt Catherine.

After this turmoil in family and among friends, I saw the object of all the contention but once. Something had been spoiled. Something we had to recover from. I felt a sort of pity for her and shame for myself as I said, "Catherine, everybody is anxious and unhappy about us. I feel I may be doing you harm by being with you so much. 'They' say so anyway."

"How perfectly ridiculous," she said. "I've had pretty nearly everything myself but an out-and-out spanking and if I can stand it, don't you think you can?"

"Of course, I can, if it were only a matter of that. But you see they are right in one thing. You don't know any boys but me and . . ."

"I do too, know dozens!" And she started to name them.

"No. You know what I mean.

"Anyhow, I'm not coming down here so often and I am going to keep clear in church."

"Well," this from her, "let them have their way for a while—I will write to you."

"Yes," I said, "there can't be harm in that."

A week later I learned by a note from her she had been sent to Mackinac for three months. Some relatives way off somewhere.

I began to see that in spite of all the talk about Nature "natural" was the last thing in this world they would let you be if they could prevent it.

Natural?

What did they mean when "they" used the word "nature"? Just some sentimental feeling about animals and grass and trees and out-of-doors generally—external nature?

But how about the nature of wood, glass and iron—internal nature?

The "nature" of boys and girls!

The "nature" of Law!

That was "nature," wasn't it? Wasn't nature in this sense the "nature" of God?

I had, somehow, always thought when I read the word "nature" in a book or used it in my own mind that it was meant that interior way. Not in an external way.

"Fools! They have no sentiment for nature. What they mean by nature is just sentimentalizing over the rudimentary animal. That's why all this confusion of ideas and these senseless rules—foolish regulations and unwise laws.

"What do *they* work them out from then? How do they really *know* anything at all?

"Look at Silsbee: his houses, I mean."

And now thrown more in on myself by

Catherine's being away, I brought the work in the office to bar to find it more than ever wanting in any true meaning to the life folk lived in it. It was all a kind of "fixing up"—some silly pose defying common sense. It aimed to be uncommon—unusual—pictorial. It was sheer ordinary sentimentality.

Wilcox, preacher's son number four, came excitedly in one day and leaned on my table. "Wright," he said, looking around to see that no one heard, "I know where you can get a good job if you want it."

"Where?"

"Adler and Sullivan."

My heart jumped. I had already formed a high idea of Adler and Sullivan. They were foremost in Chicago. Radical—going strong on independent lines. Burnham and Root their only rivals.

"How do you know, Wilcox?"

"Well, I've just been there myself. Sullivan turned me down. He's looking for someone to make the drawings for the interior of the Auditorium. I can't make them, but you can. I told him about you and he asked me to send you over to see him."

"You did, Wilcox? I . . ." Then I thought of Cecil. It would mean leaving his daily companionship.

I called him. Silsbee was away. We sat in his private office to talk.

"Go on, Frank," he said, "you've got pretty much all there is to get here; Sullivan is the coming man in the West. He may be just what you need. Anyway, no harm to try and we won't get lost."

I swept some of my work together and went over to the Borden Block, top floor.

"Would Mr. Adler do?" Mr. Sullivan was about to leave for St. Louis, Architects' Convention.

"No . . . Mr. Sullivan wanted to see me—it will only be for a moment."

"Name?"

"Wright."

The easy-natured old clerk came back, held the gate open, and I came in.

Mr. Sullivan was a small man immaculately dressed. His outstanding feature his amazing big brown eyes.

Took me in at a glance. Everything I felt, even to my most secret thoughts.

"Ah yes! The young man Wilcox mentioned. What have you there?" he said.

I unrolled the drawings on the table. He looked them over.

"You know what I want you for, do you?"

"Yes," I said.

"These aren't the kind of drawings I would like to see, but I have no time now. I'll be back Friday morning. Make some drawings of ornament or ornamental details and bring them back then. I want to look at them."

He looked at me kindly and saw me. I was sure of that much.

"Of course I will," I said eagerly and left.

The door to the big draughting room was open. There must have been twenty men or more as near as I could see at work there. Whatever the number was, I was going to make one more.

A large, tall, rather ungainly young man with a pointed head, black, bristling pompadour, and thin, black beard looked at me as I stood a moment in the door, his eyes a good deal like Mr. Sullivan's.

He looked too big for his age and the beard seemed out of place on his face. Evidently he was foreman.

"Looking for Mr. Adler?" he said.

"No," I said, "just looking at you." And I walked away before his astonished expression could change to anything else.

It was Paul Mueller, office foreman.

I went back to Cecil, elated.

"The job's mine."

"How do you know?"

"How does any one know anything? He *said*, I tell you, that I can do what he wants done. Making the drawings for him is just a formality."

"Just the same," said Cecil, "I'd make them as well as I could."

"Of course I will, but it will be all the easier and I'll do it better because I know I have the job."

Cecil gave it up. It was hopeless.

"What will Sullivan pay you?"

"Forgot to mention it, but I'll ask for $25.00. And it will be all right."

When I got to Oak Park that evening after telling Mother the good news I went to work on a drawing board in the room where I had "T" square and triangle; but I used them only for guide lines. I was going to show Mr. Sullivan what my freehand could do.

Some of Silsbee's own drawings of mantels and ornament I took, and drew them my own way directly and simply with clear definition. Not sentimental and "sketchy." Silsbee's way was magnificent, his strokes like standing corn in the field waving in the breeze. So I imitated his style in some few drawings just to show I could do that. Then I improvised some ornaments such as I had seen, characteristic of the Adler and Sullivan buildings. I had studied them a little since I learned of their work. It was three o'clock when I got to bed.

Next evening same thing until late.

Another evening I took the onion skin tracing of ornamental details I had made from Owen Jones, mostly Gothic, and made them over into "Sullivanesque."

Had a lot of things to show when Friday morning came and I got to Mr. Sullivan.

I took the work out in order:

First: "Imitations of Silsbee," I said.

"I see. You've traced Silsbee's drawings to show me?"

"They are not traced," I said. "I drew them. You see? They are not on tracing paper."

"But you might have transferred them."

I laughed. "Too much trouble."

He looked me over with that glance of his that "went through."

Second: "Imitations of Sullivan."

"Well! You couldn't have traced those. Not half bad". . . to himself, scratching his scalp with the sharp point of his lead-pencil. I noticed some white dandruff fell on the drawings. He blew it off.

Third: "Improvised Gothic from Owen Jones."

"Owen Jones? Who is he?"

I thought him joking. I said, "You know, *The Grammar of Ornament*."

He looked puzzled. "Anything like Raguenet?"

"I don't know Raguenet."[4]

"Oh, of course," he said, "I remember the book now. So you are trying to turn Gothic ornaments into my style just to please me, are you?"

"But you see how easy it is to do it," I said. And I saw I had displeased him. You see—unconsciously I had reduced his ornament to a mere sentimentality.

Fourth: "Here are some things, perhaps original—I don't know."

He was immediately interested. Said nothing. He was sitting on a high stool at his draughting board where he had been drawing. After looking them over he made no comment but drew aside the cover sheet from the board. I gasped with delight. "Oh!" I said, "and you asked me to show you mine?" I blushed with shame, felt like a duffer, as indeed I was in the light of this. He seemed to have forgotten me now and went on drawing. I was standing there thinking, if Silsbee's touch was like standing corn waving in the fields, Sullivan's was like the passion vine—in full bloom. I wondered what mine might be like if I developed one some day. I wanted to ask but, suddenly, "You've got the right kind of touch, you'll do," he said. "How much money have you been getting?"

"Not enough," I said.

"Well, how much is enough?"

"Twenty-five dollars."

He smiled, for I might have asked forty dollars and got it.

"All right, but you understand you've got to stick until the drawings for the Auditorium are finished. But I don't mean you are to work for that salary during all that time. We'll come to an arrangement after you take hold for awhile—can you come Monday morning?"

"I can come," I said, "for there is not much work at Silsbee's just now. And he'll be glad to let me go."

That was how I got into the Adler and Sullivan office and how I first met the master for whose influence, affection, and comradeship I have never ceased to feel gratitude.

Elated, I went back to Silsbee's and to Cecil. Cecil was glad and sad too—I could see.

"Go in and tell the old man," was all he said.

I went in.

"Mr. Silsbee."

"Well?" wheeling around from his desk.

"I haven't been doing very well for you or myself for some weeks."

"I've noticed it."

I was astonished. Didn't suppose he ever noticed anything much.

"I've asked Mr. Sullivan for a job."

"Did he give you one?"

"Yes, he gave me one that will last a long time, I believe."

"When are you going?"

"Next Monday, if you don't need me."

He thought a moment. "This doesn't seem up to your usual standard, Wright."

"You were away when the chance came. I was going to wait to come to you first, but I dreaded to wait for many reasons. The chance came unexpectedly . . . but if you needed me I would stay."

"No! I don't need you. I wanted to know your reason for falling down on your principles—that's all."

"Mr. Silsbee—I was so sure my usefulness here was ended and you would be relieved."

"But is that the point?"

"No. It's not the point at all. I am wrong. Dead wrong. I should not have gone to Mr. Sullivan without talking first with you. It's clear enough."

"Never mind, Wright. You may like it with Sullivan. Not my style, but maybe a genius, who knows?"

The interview was ended but I hated to leave it that way. No matter what I felt about Silsbee's shortcomings I adored him just the same and knew I left him like any tramp draughtsman when he had been really handsome toward me.

What could I say! I sat there.

Nothing to say at all.

I got out. If he saw my face, and I guess he did, he must have forgiven me. If he can see into my heart now, he will see what he saw in my face then.

I never saw Silsbee again.

LET THE DEAD BURY THEIR DEAD

Has every forward movement in human lives, as it is realized, its pang?

In this case—let us say—the cause of the pang was a fault of mine. I might have talked with Silsbee candidly at the proper moment and have quit with none.

I had taken too much for granted.

And yet, do the trees know a pang when the top branches float their leaves on the breeze and shut the sun from the branches below so those lower branches must die?

Do perennial plants suffer when in spring they rise through the dead growth of last year to greater glory and abundance this year?

Does the snake slough off its skin with a pang?

Does each stage of growth cost enough vital energy in suffering so that our span is measured—the allotment of life duration made—by the number of pangs we can sustain at each successive forward step or upward movement?

Do human beings die eventually of the pangs of growth?

If when we see a delphinium taller and more resplendent than the rest, a tree more superb than others, a human being in character and achievement outstanding from his fellows—are we to think: what magnificent resistance to suffering was there!

Let the dead bury their dead" was said by the gentlest, wisest, and most awful of men.

Growth, then, that it should have its pang, is this merely a human weakness or a human fault? Or is it the natural evil consequence of the so-called virtues which man in self-love is making for himself?

The fact that I now see I left Silsbee as I left college, as later, with anguish, I left home, may be the occasion of this homily. I see I left for the same reason, with the same suffering. The same hope. Already, then, I was obedient to a principle at work in me taking its toll to this hour, as I write.

Old as moral life is this urge to growth and its consequences! Listen to the Apostle Paul writing to the Philippians: "Brethren, I count not myself to have apprehended: but this one thing I do, forgetting those things which are behind and reaching forth to those things which are before."

And I was going to realize, "Do ye reject the commandment of GOD, that ye may keep your own traditions?" And to realize that traditions may be kept in the letter, after the spirit has fled, only by rejecting Him.

For Louis Sullivan had come to this understanding. He was at grips with the joys and sorrows of its affirmation—in action.

Monday morning. Some little time before nine o'clock in the draughting room of Adler and Sullivan. They then occupied most of the top floor of the old Borden Block, corner of Randolph and Dearborn Streets. Paul Mueller there, no one else, yet . . . "Where can I get you?" he asked in his idiom. He looked about. Fixed on one place. Changed his mind several times and finally landed me against the south wall between two large windows. Good place but surrounded by other tables. One of a crowd. Not like the studio atmosphere of Silsbee's. It might have been in the rank and file of any large business office where many clerks were working.

"I'll have Anton 'stretch' some boards for you," he said, calling the office cub. Said Anton, "How many?"

"Och! didn't I tell you? What you can find loose," he said excitedly with something of a German accent. "What you can find *loose, loose, LOOSE,*" he shouted. I could see Mueller was awkward, energetic, and emotional and under something of a strain. Too young, I was sure, to have any business with a beard. But that he was a hive of industry I could see too.

"What did Mr. Sullivan tell you to do?"

"He didn't tell me."

"Wait, then—wait till he comes. I've got enough to do without what he wants. He wants you for the designs anyway. My work is construction. I used to work for Tsilsbee myself. Yes, and Tsilsbee, he is a great designer." I loved the way he said "Tsilsbee" and wanted to hear him say it again. "Three years ago, Tsilsbee—he wanted an engineer. He took me. Then I came to Mr. Adler over here."

"How long have you been foreman?"

"More than a year."

"Like it?" I said.

"Och!" he said, "too much to do. What is it? Mr. Adler wants me . . . Yes, I like it."

I saw my question was stupid. The men were filing in by now and he went to his table by the entrance door where I had first seen him. He almost never sat down.

The office cub, "Tony," had found several boards "loose" with the manilla paper stretch in general use there. I laid one on my table delighting in the paper surface—a smooth untouched sheet of paper is one of the fairest sights—with my back to the room and I did not see the fellows as they filed in.

They were evidently a noisy crowd and chafed each other a lot as they settled down. A few remarks intended for me. But paid no attention. There was some discipline in the office apparently, for they were soon quietly at work. Tired of looking at the paper, I looked to the left. Got their names afterwards. Next table to mine Jean Agnas, a clean-faced Norseman. To the right Eisendrath—apparently stupid. Jewish. Behind me to the left Ottenheimer—alert, apparently bright. Jew, too. Turned around to survey the group. Isbell, Jew? Gaylord, no—not. Weydert, Jew undoubtedly. Directly behind, Weatherwax.

Couldn't make him out. In the corner Andresen—Swedish. Several more Jewish faces. Of course—I thought, because Mr. Adler himself must be a Jew. I had not seen him yet. I marked time, feeling alone in all that strange crowd, drawing on the margin of my "stretch." Had a notion to call up Cecil to say "hello" and hear his voice. But did not.

About 10:30 the door opened. Mr. Sullivan walked slowly in with a haughty air, handkerchief to his nose. Paying no attention to anyone. No "good mornings." No words of greeting as he went from desk to desk. Saw me waiting for him. Came forward at once with a pleasant "Ah! Wright, there you are," and the office had my name. And evidently, in Sullivan's unusually pleasant address, also my "number."

"Here," lifting a board by my table, "take this drawing of mine, a duffer I fired Saturday spoiled it. Redraw it and ink it in." And they all knew what I was there for. He wandered about some more in a haughty sort of way. He seemed to have no respect at all for anybody there except Mueller. My eyes had been following him when he was observable. Finally he stopped just behind me at Weatherwax's table.

"What the Hell do you call that?" in a loud voice, without even bending to look. I had turned my head to see the man flush and straighten up.

"What the Hell do you call that?" Mr. Sullivan repeated louder than before.

The whole room was now waiting for Weatherwax.

"What do I call it?" he said, evidently hot, as though struck by a lash. "Hell! It's a church, can't you see? *Christ!* What do you want?"

With trembling hands he was undoing the strings of his little black apron as he spoke. And with violence he threw his pencil down on the board, grabbed a leather case and deliberately walked out.

Sullivan, as though he had heard nothing, changing not a hair, looked a moment at the unhappy drawing, blew his nose into a fresh handkerchief, turned on his heel to the next table or two—I could see the cringing fear of him wherever he went—and walked slowly out of the room as he had come in without another word. There had been no sound from the draughting room during the episode. All were evidently used to something of the kind. When he had gone out there was a rustle and whispering and low talking which Mueller put down with warning looks.

My reaction to this was, "I'm afraid I won't last long here after all!" Evidently no one did where he was concerned. And then, "This is not the real Sullivan. I've seen a different one."

What was Dankmar Adler like?

Just before noon he opened the same door from which Mr. Sullivan had entered. A personality, short-built and heavy, like an old Byzantine church. He was not "gutty," just broadly and solidly built, one to inspire others with confidence in his power at once. I felt comforted.

He walked with deliberate, heavy-legged, flat-footed steps over to Mueller's desk, talking to him. The while his deep bass voice rumbled, he went about with his hands stuck under his coat-tails,

looking at drawings, a word of greeting occasionally. He would sit and make suggestions in a fatherly sort of way. He got to me. Looked at me pleasantly from his deep-set eyes under the bushy brows.

"Hello!"—kindly. "Sullivan's new man?"

"Yes sir!"

He sat down on the stool I had vacated to stand up to him. As he put one leg over the other, I noticed his enormous mannish feet. They spread flat like the foundations for some heavy building.

"Sullivan needs help, Wright. It's difficult to find anyone to 'catch on' to what he wants. I hope you will succeed!"

He got up abruptly almost as soon as he had sat down and, as though suddenly remembering something, he went heavily out among the draughting tables like a barge making its way between river craft. Dankmar was the name for him.

Thus began an association lasting nearly seven years.

Mr. Sullivan had been interested and interesting. His drawings a delight to work on and work out. His manner toward me markedly different from his manner toward the others. And mark me it did. I soon found my place in that office had to be fought for.

The work was going well. I could do it. The master was pleased. And I had got his permission to get George Elmslie over from Silsbee's to help me and incidentally make it a little less lonesome for me there. George wasn't a minister's son but ought to have been. He was coming over in a few days. This evident favoritism of the master together with my own natural tendency to mind my own business now coupled with a distaste for most of the Adler and Sullivan men had in the course of a few weeks set them on me. I was unpopular from that first day when I had been marked by his interest and respect. I was baited in various ways. My hair of course. My dress a bit too individual. There would be conversation behind me with unmistakable reference to me. Studied interference with my work. The gang had evidently combined to "get me," their phrase.

Mueller didn't see much of it. He was an innocent soul. It was all kept pretty well out of his way. And I couldn't say anything about it if I would. And I wouldn't if I could.

There was a back room devoted to blue-printing, where Isbell, Gaylord, and a few others would go at noon to eat their lunch and box a few rounds. Isbell was supposed to be pretty good if the aftermath of talk meant anything. And Gaylord was a candidate for pugilistic honors in the First Regiment at "The Armory."

They wanted me in to "box." Evidently the longish-hair, flowing tie, and rather good clothes gave them the idea I would be easy to eat up: a good spectacle.

I saw I would have to do something to square myself with that crowd and made up my mind.

I had boxed some. Had no doubt about my wind or strength or ability to stand punishment. But not much science. So, one noon, I went to see old Colonel Monsterry, who had a fencing and boxing academy near the old Athenaeum, and engaged for a course of twelve lessons, all twelve to be given in the course of two weeks. I told the old Frenchman I wanted to learn how to hit hard and stop body-blows. I could already take pretty good care of my head.

But why not the foils? "It is so much more a gentleman's game," he said.

"I'm not involved with gentlemen. I've got a battle on hand with a 'tough bunch,' and I want some rough training."

"All right," he said and handed me the gloves. I put them on and put up my guard. "No," he said, "college-boy! This way," and he put one hand down, the other in front like a feeler and provocative. "Now, look out." And he struck at me a number of times to see where I was. "Not so bad. Now I'm going to hit you," he said. "Go ahead." He did, and the jolt jarred me to the heels. If it was that easy to reach me I was far from that back room I thought. Took an hour. Felt wonderful as I got out from under the shower into my clothes and back to the office a half-hour later.

Meantime the nagging went on.

I had almost the two weeks of training. It wasn't a case of getting into condition—I knew. I was in better condition than either of the office stars.

The daily practice with the old Colonel had, by now, taught me all he knew. I don't think it was

much because he was a swordsman, not a boxer. But it might be enough. I could now take care of myself fairly well. I liked it and began to look forward with some pleasure to the event.

I looked at Isbell's heavy, prominent nose sometimes and thought—what a mark! He was a loud-voiced, blond-haired, conceited fellow, well-built, always keeping up a running fire of jibes and jokes when Mueller was out. Jaunty and undoubtedly strong. Gaylord was awkward and slow, but stronger.

About two months had gone by since I had entered the office and had steadily minded my own business. The taunting had grown, and was quite open now. As the noon rustle began just before the men went out, I turned to Isbell. "Boxing this noon?" He looked puzzled. "Sure. Coming in to look on?" "Yes, I might as well," I said.

"All right, why look on? Put on the gloves! we won't hurt you."

I hesitated. "You fellows must be pretty close to professionals, practicing all the time. But—well—all right, I will."

I saw the look of triumph, the winks passing between the office strong-men. The other members of the gang smiling, incredulous.

I went in alone, but they had their gang, six or seven of them. Coats, vests, and collars off. I drew on the gloves—dirty ones.

Isbell wanted the first "crack" at me and put on the gloves.

I knew nothing about his style but struck him—on the nose—just as he fairly got up his guard.

The blood came into his face and his blue eyes went hard and cold. He came after me hot and heavy and I saw he was just a "slugger."

I let him slug.

Stopped him, when I could, took it when I had to. Standing up to him and backing away, continually drawing him on.

He was breathing hard, rather white.

I had taken it easily.

The crowd so fresh at first, was flat now. Not just what they expected.

"Time!" called Gaylord. "Time? Not yet," I said. "This is a one-round contest," and I banged Isbell on the nose hard, this time with my left.

The blood came. First blood for me!

But no applause.

And now Isbell was out for blood, we rushed back and forth, crashed around the room, the fellows racing out of the way, knocking over everything that could come loose. Raging Isbell!

Again I got him "on the nose." He was a sight. My lip was cut and bleeding, but I sucked in the blood and swallowed it. I felt a wonderful lift, and still had the steam I started with.

"Izzy" was distinctly getting the worst of it. The gang saw it.

"Time!" said Gaylord. "Time, Hell," said I, "this is a one-round contest," and banged Izzy again on the nose, the organ abnormally large had begun to swell. This was too much for Billy Gaylord. "Here, Izzy, it's my turn now. Give me those gloves."

"Yes, it is your turn now," I said. I was waked up and felt nothing could ever stop me. I stood eagerly striking one glove into the open palm of the other while Gaylord put on the gloves.

He leaned way back, rocking back and forth, crouching low, weaving his arms in and out continually, crafty. I couldn't wait for him for my blood was up by now and while Billy had been comparatively decent, and I half liked him, this was a dirty trick. I was going to beat out of him all the hell there ever was in him, or die trying.

I stepped up to him like a flash and slapped him, down on the top of the head three times with all my might with my open glove. My foot was behind his and as he pulled back to recover, he went over backward among the gang. Got up red and angry. "That's a hell of a way to box. Two fouls," he said.

"Fouls, nothing," I said. "Who said this was a boxing-match? What are you doing in here before I finished with Isbell? Come on, foul me. DAMN you all, anyway. You wanted to get me in here to do me up and have a laugh. Now come and get it, take your gloves off, you coward." I threw mine away.

This wasn't what they looked for. The crowd interfered.

"Aw, pass him up, Billy. He's crazy-mad and wants to fight. It won't do in here. Let's fix it up for some other time."

"All right," I said. "You fix it! A fine sporting gang you are. If one of you can't win, you put another in on top of that one," and I went out, too excited to want anything to eat.

The afternoon was quiet. Ominously quiet.

I knew I had lost my case by getting "mad." If I had coolly taken Gaylord on, unfair as it was for him to follow Isbell, and good-naturedly made a good showing with him, it would have probably been all over in my favor. By getting angry and sailing into them I had made enemies of them all.

Then and there I made up my mind to live in that office to fire every one of "the gang," and I said so. Ottenheimer, the ringleader, an active, intelligent, little Jew was not present. He got the report from the gang next day and I heard him say, "Ooi, the God Damn Son of a Bitch. Leave him to me."

COMBAT

I might as well finish the story. I was now subjected to the refined cruelty of the taunts and innuendoes of their ringleader, Ottenheimer. Ottenheimer evidently had a drag with "the old man." That is to say, Mr. Adler. But it was easier to stand the isolation even though it had become downright enmity, now. I had George Elmslie at my side to talk to. He had come. I had him as a sort of understudy to help me in my work. George was a tall, slim, slow-thinking, rather anaemic but refined Scotch lad who had never been young. Faithful nature. Very quiet and diffident. I liked him and attached him. I couldn't get along without somebody. No, never.

We were both staying in to finish some work for the blue-printer one noon, some weeks after the boxing-bout that failed. Ottenheimer at the table behind me and over one to the left, staying in to study for Beaux Arts exams he was soon to take. He was whistling and jibing as was his habit. He had thrown my hat down the stair-well the day before. He was insolent always. Now especially so, ending with, "You're just a Sullivan 'toady' anyway, Wright. We all know it." I had stood, without flinching, far worse than that.

But it was "time" I laid down my pencil, swung around on the stool and looked at him. He sat at his table, a heavy-bodied, short-legged, pompadoured, conceited, red-faced Jew, wearing gold glasses. His face, now red as a turkey-cock's wattles. "I think I've had enough from you," I said. I got up and walked slowly over to him and without realizing he was wearing glasses, or hesitating, struck him square, full in the face with my right hand, knocking him from his stool to the floor, smashing his glasses. I might have blinded him forever.

With a peculiar animal scream—I've heard something like it since from a Japanese mad with *sake,* but never anywhere else—he jumped for the knife, a scratcher-blade with a long handle, lying by his board. Half-blinded, he came leaping for me with it.

I caught him, as he came, head down, under my arm. Got his head in chancery and was trying hard to put him out as with his free arm behind me he was stabbing away at the back of my neck and shoulders. But his head was too close—tight against my side, so, although the blood was running, I couldn't hit him hard enough. We struggled around like this, upsetting stools and overturning tables, George, white-faced and scared, looking on. I could feel the blood running down my back and legs into my shoes. They "cheeped" as though my feet were wet as I trod around in the struggle.

Finally, I wound my right hand in the back of his collar and with all the strength of despair, hurled him away from me. He went staggering, toppling backward across the draughting room to the opposite wall, struck with a heavy bang against the door leading to the next room, and went down—but not "out." He had dropped the knife near him. He got up on his feet again and with that same curious animal scream grabbed the knife and came on—a blood-thirsty beast. Quick as a flash, as he came toward me, I grabbed the long, broad-bladed maple "T" square on my board by the end of the long blade, swung it with all my might, catching "Ottie" with the edge of the blade beside his neck just above the collar. The cross-head snapped off: and flew clear down the length of the room.

The knife dropped from his hand as he wavered a moment. Then he wilted, slowly, into a senseless heap on the floor like a sail coming down.

My heart sank. "Good God! I've killed him, George! Get some water quick." George seemed paralyzed. It had all happened in a minute. "Wake up. Quick, man! Come on, George! Don't you see?"

Slow-moving George got back with some water in a dipper and I threw it in "Ottie's" face. No sign. "More, George" I threw more in his face—he sighed, opened his eyes. I stood there, waiting and trembling. "Are you badly hurt, Ottie?" No answer. Blinked—seemed to be "going out" again.

"Water!"

"No!. . . Quit. . . I'm all right"—from "Ottie."

He got up by degrees, stood white and shaking. "I'll pay you for this, Wright," he choked. "You'll get yours for this, you'll see!"

He went to his desk, shakily gathered up his instruments as I sat watching him, smiling—it was so good to see him move. I never saw Ottenheimer again.

He had intended to go to the Beaux Arts in Paris before long, and he went without ever coming back to the office.

The affair had taken place at noon, when everyone was out but George and Ottie and me.

My shoes were full of blood.

"George, call Cecil. I want to see how badly that wild little cuss cut me."

George called him. He happened to be in and came the five blocks in no time. He pulled off my coat and pushed my shirt down to the waist. "Man!" he said, counting, "you're stabbed on the shoulder blades in eleven places, to the bone, all of them. And lucky for you none on the spine. But near it on each side. I don't think any one of them is serious. Let's go over to Arthur's and get them dressed." Arthur was his brother, a physician.

Today I wear the welts of Ottie's fancy work on my shoulder blades. But not because I turned my back on him.

The disappearance of Ottenheimer broke the persecution for a time. Isbell had been laid off. Gaylord was now rather friendly to me.

Billy Gaylord was a rather decent chap on the whole. But there were sullen looks from Eisendrath and Weydert that I would surprise occasionally. I had them to deal with later. Nor did Mueller or Mr. Sullivan know about the feud until several years later after I had finally cleaned up the "gang" as will appear.

The Master's very walk at this time bore dangerous resemblance to a strut. He had no respect whatever for a draughtsman, as seen in the fate of Weatherwax, and as he more than once confided to me in later years. Nor, so far as I could see, respect for anyone else except "the big chief"—Dankmar Adler—whom he trusted and loved. And also Paul Mueller.

None of his contemporaries ever won from the meister much but contempt—except one, H. H. Richardson. Richardson he condescended to criticize. Also he was not so hard on "John"—John Wellborn Root—as on all the others. Evidently he liked him.

But Richardson at this time had a decided effect upon Sullivan's work as may be seen in the outside of the Auditorium Building itself, the Walker Wholesale, and other buildings. The effect is unmistakable although he seemed to hold Richardson in no very high esteem.

I believe the Master used to talk to me to express his own feelings and thoughts, regardless, forgetting me often. But I could follow him. And the radical sense of things I had already formed got great encouragement from him. In fact the very sense of things I had been feeling as rebellion was—in him—at work.

He was absorbed in what seemed extravagant worship of Wagner at the time, which I could not share, but which I could understand. It seemed too sentimental if not sensual. He would often try to sing the leitmotifs for me and describe the scenes to which they belonged as he sat at my drawing board. He adored Whitman, as I did. And, explain it how you can, was deep in Herbert Spencer.

Spencer's "Synthetic Philosophy" he gave to me to take home and read. The Master himself had just written "Inspiration." He read it to me. I thought it a kind of "baying at the moon." Again— too sentimental.

I never liked his writing in those early days. Challenged again by sentimentality. Yes, here was this inimical quality showing in him. What had been suspicion now began to ripen into rebellion against sentimentality in general.

Soon, the Auditorium finished, other work was going on—Pueblo Opera House (burned down), Salt Lake City Hotel, foundations laid, but never built. One of the office tragedies. I worked hard on them with him.

From the very beginning my "T" square and triangle were media of expression for my geometrical sense of things. But, at the time, Sullivanian ornament was efflorescence pure and simple.

Mr. Sullivan would still talk of John Edelman, for whom he had the greatest respect. He had known him in Paris and had visited him in New York. I conceived the idea that John Edelman had given him "direction" and was his most respected critic. I conceived a respect for John Edelman, knowing no more than this about him. I have drawings made by Louis Sullivan in Paris and dedicated to John Edelman.

Whenever the Master would rely upon me I would mingle his sensuous efflorescence with some geometric design, because I could do nothing else so well. And, too, that way of working seemed to hold the surface, give needed contrast, be more architectural; again—less sentimental. But I couldn't say this to him and I wasn't sure.

Often he would pick me up on this point— and try to bring me "alive," as he said, until I could make designs and drew them in his manner so well, that toward the end of his life he would mistake my drawings for his.

I became a good pencil in the Master's hand, and at a time when he sorely needed one. And because I could be this to him he had more Freedom now than he had enjoyed.

Healy and Millet were his comrades at this time. The three men had known one another in Paris. Sullivan spent much of his time in their company and in the company of Larry Donovan of "Yale and Towne."

About this time (I was now nineteen) I wanted to marry. I told him so.

"Who is the girl?"

"A young girl—in Hyde Park High School— Catherine, seventeen years old. I met her at 'All Souls Church.'"

"Ah-ha! So soon."

"They all think it too soon and object!"

"They would," he said.

"I have no visible means of support for another thing."

"No? Well . . . we can fix that up. How about a contract? Adler!" he called.

Adler came.

"Wright wants to get married—no visible means of support. What do you say to a five-year contract?"

"All right," said Adler. "You fix it, Sullivan!" And he went out in his usual manner of leaving—as though suddenly remembering something requiring immediate attention.

I turned to Mr. Sullivan with a new idea. "Mr. Sullivan, if you want me to work for you as long as five years, couldn't you lend me enough money to build a little house, and let me pay you back so much each month—taken out of my pay-envelope?"

Mr. Sullivan—it seemed—had some money of his own at the time. He took me to his lawyer, Felsenthal. The contract was duly signed, and then the Master went with "the pencil in his hand" to Oak Park to see the lot wanted. Mr. Austin, whose barn we have seen—owned it. A lovely old tangle-wood it was that you have already seen. It was on Forest Avenue.

He approved the lot and there was $3,500 left to build a small home on that ground Mr. Blair had planted, the old Scotch landscape-gardener, close friend of Mr. Austin's. After buying the ground from Mr. Austin that sum was left for the house.

"Now look out, Wright!" the Master said, "I know your tastes . . . no 'extras.'"

"No, none," I agreed.

But there was $1,200 more to be paid toward the end. I kept it dark, paid it in due course as best I could out of what remained of my salary.

The contract at that time made me the best-paid draughtsman in the City of Chicago, so Mr. Adler said, but all the same, the children that followed during those years made creditors a familiar sight—or was it the "tastes"?

To have both gratified, was what made the sleeves pull and the coat split across the back—

of course.

And the children grew up with similar "tastes" in an environment that invited the "tastes" to develop—and invited creditors to come. The havoc wrought by this matter of "taste!"

I had carved in the oak slab above the fireplace—in the living room—"Truth is Life!" A challenge to sentimentality. Soon after I thought: why did I not make it—"Life is Truth" and have it say what I meant?

But I could not alter it. It was "built."

It seemed to me an improvement over the challenge of Grandfather's "Truth against the World."

Now went along these early years of "master and apprentice." Louis Sullivan and myself. The apprentice, open-eyed, radical, and critical, but always willing. We had already moved to the top floor of the Auditorium tower, where I had a small room next to the Master and a squad of thirty draughtsmen or more under me to supervise in planning and detailing.

Mueller had the engineers and the superintendents, reporting to him, at the opposite end of the long row of windows to the north.

Adler and Sullivan now stood well to the forefront of their profession. Commercial work, chiefly office-buildings, theaters, and clubs, all came steadily in unbroken procession through the office.

Dankmar Adler had been Army engineer.

He commanded the confidence of contractor and client alike. His handling of both was masterful. He would pick up a contractor as a mastiff might pick up a cat—shake him and drop him. Some would habitually fortify themselves with a drink before they came up to see him.

All worshipped him.

He was a good planner, a good critic, but all for Sullivan. He always called him "Sullivan," never "Louis." In Sullivan's genius Adler had implicit confidence.

It seems he had taken Sullivan in as a draughtsman, when as a young man Sullivan returned from the Beaux Arts. Later Adler took Sullivan into partnership to be what was known even then as "designing partner." Architects all put the architecture on the outside—even in those days. So there was one man to make it—another man to "handle" it. But Adler and Sullivan were not quite like that.

Dankmar Adler was a Jew. Louis Sullivan was an Irishman. The clients all being Adler's clients, many objected to Sullivan. It did not matter. They *had* to take Sullivan or lose Adler.

In those days Sullivan's attitude and ego may be seen in the fate of Weatherwax. But I had, from the first, seen a different side of him, as I felt I would. He always loved to talk and I would often stay after dark in the offices in the upper stories of the great tower of the Auditorium looking out over Lake Michigan, or over the lighted City. Sometimes he would keep on talking, seeming to have forgotten me—keep on until late at night. And I would catch the last "suburban" for Oak Park.

As I have since reflected, he seemed unaware of the machine as a direct element in architecture, abstract or concrete. He never mentioned it. And he was interested in "the rule so broad as to admit of no exceptions." For the life of me I could not help, then or now, being most interested in the exception as proving any rule both useful and useless.

But this outpouring to a worshipful and sympathetic though critical listener soon enabled me to understand him. Like all geniuses he was an absorbed ego-centric—exaggerated sensibility, boundless vitality. This egotism of the absorbed ego-centric is more "armor" than character, more shell than substance. It is usually a defense for exaggerated sensibility—a defense become a habit. And with all his synthetic attitude and logical inclinations, his uncompromising search for principle, he was incorrigible romanticist. I have learned to see this as not inconsistent except as the romanticist degenerates to the sentimentalist. The beloved Master sometimes did sentimentalize. What rich nature does not at times? And when least suspecting itself would indignantly deny the "soft impeachment."

But during all this period with "Lieber Meister" when General Grant Gothic was the prevailing mode and Chicago itself was the center of the united fundamentalist-ugliness of the United States, his synthetic common-sense cut clean.

The romantic Richardson and the susceptible Root were beginning to appear, but the Potter Palmer Home on the Lake Shore Drive was still supreme. The Palmer Home, Palmer Hotel, and the Board of Trade were popular architecture. The Adler and Sullivan buildings stood clean and sharp by comparison. See their Borden Block, Gage Building, and others in Chicago wholesale district of this early period. At this earlier time John Edelman's influence may be seen in the ornament of those early buildings.

THE AUDITORIUM

The auditorium interior was the first *great* room for audience to really depart from various and curious prevailing traditions. In this room the magic word *plastic* was used by the Master in reference to his ornament. His ornament began to show the effects of this ideal. And it began to enter into the Auditorium building interior. Not consciously, I believe. Subconsciously.

Mr. Adler himself had invented the sounding-board in earlier theaters he had built. That is to say, the sloping surface extending above the proscenium opening into the audience-room. Owing to this simple invention no public hall built by Adler and Sullivan was ever acoustically bad. But see how the Master developed this "sounding board" into the concentric, elliptical arches as you may still see them in that great room for Opera. And while no advantage was taken of the arched elliptical form to carry the loads above, the inner shell itself being carried—suspended from the level trusses above it. Still the form was appropriate, suitable to its purpose, and prophetic.

The opening night of the great Chicago Auditorium was a gorgeous civic and social event to be remembered. Adelina Patti sang with a score of operatic stars. The great room for Opera was found to be perfect for its purpose. It was acknowledged to be the greatest building achievement of the period: and to this day, probably, is the best room for Opera, all things considered, yet built in the world. Adler and Sullivan's office was proud I can tell you.

With Silsbee, notwithstanding his purely sentimental drift, I had gained considerable light on the practical needs of the American dwelling. Adler and

Sullivan refused to build residences during all the time I was with them. The few that were imperative owing to social obligations to important clients fell to my lot out of office hours. They would, of course, "check up" on them in good time.

Also the Master's own home on Lake Avenue was one of these. As were his Southern house at Ocean Springs and the house next door for the Charnleys.

The city house for the Charnleys on Astor Street, Chicago, like the others, I did at home evenings and Sundays in the nice studio draughting room upstairs at the front of the little Forest Avenue home—now built. But this draughting room soon became two bedrooms for the children: the children that had been left out of the reckoning in the building of that house.

In the Charnley city-house on Astor Street I first sensed the decorative value of the plain surface—that is to say—of the flat plane as such. This may be seen in the placing of the single openings in the center of the plain wall-masses. These drawings for the Charnley house were all traced and printed in the Adler and Sullivan offices, but by preparing them for this purpose at home I helped pay my pressing building debts.

Other debts pressing toward the end of the five-year term, I accepted several houses on my own account, for Dr. Harlan, Warren McArthur, and George Blossom, and did not try anything radical, because I could not follow them up. I could not "follow up" because I did these houses out of office hours, not secretly. And the Master soon became aware of them. He was offended and refused to issue the deed to the Oak Park house now due, because, by now, the little house was paid for. But I had broken my contract by doing this "outside work," it seems. I had not realized there was such violation of any contract provision. So I protested. I asked the Master if I had been any less serviceable in the office lately.

"No," he said, "but your sole interest is here, while your contract lasts. I won't tolerate any division under any circumstances."

Louis Sullivan. FLLW Fdn FA#6700.0001

Dankmar Adler. FLLW Fdn FA#6700.0002

This seemed to me unjust. If I could work over hours at home for Adler and Sullivan and keep up my work in the office what harm in doing likewise for others to relieve my "necessities" now? All the same, I was wrong—I saw it, but angered now by what seemed the injustice of the beloved Master—it was the first time he had been harsh with me—I appealed to "the big chief"—Dankmar Adler.

Mr. Adler interceded, which more deeply offended the Master than ever, and—more offensively still—he refused to issue the deed.

When I learned this from him in none too kindly terms and with the "haughty" air now turned toward me, it was too much. I, too, threw my pencil down on my table now and I walked out of the Adler and Sullivan office . . . never to return. Within a few months my five-year contract would have expired. This five-year term added to the previous time would make more than six years with Adler and Sullivan.

Again "in the wrong." No less so than was my Master. Yes, more so. But—again, out "on my own"—to stay out.

Nor for more than twelve years did I see Lieber Meister again or communicate directly with him in any way. The deed to the home duly followed by Mr. Adler's hand. The Guarantee Building of Buffalo having just come into the office, the Transportation Building at the Columbian Fair had been the last important work in which I served as "apprentice."

Meantime as fellowship was taking its course in apprenticeship in the offices of Adler and Sullivan in the Auditorium Tower, let us go back to another fellowship—go back to the girl in the Hyde Park High School.

You have already had a more intimate glimpse of our first meetings, the struggle with the circumstance of family that led to the announcement to Lieber Meister and the plea for a house of my own.

Let us go back now to this other phase of fellowship—to the sunny-haired, tall, slenderly handsome high-school girl, now seventeen. The engaging Catherine.

She walks with a kind of light-hearted gaiety: mass of red curls, rather short, bobbing in the breeze. White skin. Cheeks rosy. Blue-eyed, frank, and impulsive. Generous to me.

"Kitty," idol of the Tobin household, still had pretty much her own way about everything and with everyone except White Grandma.

After the stabbing received as my share in the row at the office I had gone directly to her at Kenwood. There had been no mention of love—or marriage, no "proposal." Why talk about it? It was all a matter of course—so far as that went—sometime.

But Catherine, recently come back from the North where she had been sent, was quite changed. She was thinner and pale. Her blue eyes were not so happy now, her manner was less gay than usual. She would fall silent. Listless.

And I myself had felt, for some time past, we were in a false position. Catherine was doing nothing much in school. I knew Kitty was running the gauntlet there with the school-girls who knew of her attachment to me. I knew because I saw the drawing of a large-eyed kitten—with *"Perfectly Frank,"* the legend beneath the kitten. They had sent it to her from the school.

And at home, too, though holding her own with all but White Grandma, she *was* under her discipline. With no knowledge at all we had come to the boy and girl intimacy no longer satisfied with sheepish looks and perfunctory visiting or playing cards or talk or music.

Freedom is necessary to any beauty in any fellowship that is fellowship. Otherwise it becomes something else, mean and shameful by implication. It was shameful even to suspect we were being watched. Soon I decided to clear it all up.

The consequences of that announcement to Lieber Meister enabled a boy and girl courtship—lasting a year to end in marriage. Protests—sensible as well as sentimental ones still. They were there. But, withstanding all, marriage!

Young husband-to-be just twenty-one, the young wife-to-be not yet eighteen.

Wedding on a rainy day.[5] More resembled a funeral. The sentimentality I was learning to dread came into full flower. The heavens weeping out of doors—all weeping indoors. Mother of the groom fainting. Father of the bride in tears. Pastor performing—the now ceremonious uncle—affected likewise himself.

THE FIRST HOME

Off to the beloved Valley for the honeymoon.

A few weeks later, coming back to Oak Park, where the new house was being built, made possible by the contract with Adler and Sullivan. On the way across town from station to station, the first "meum" and "tuum."

The young husband wanted to carve mottoes in the panels of the doors of the rooms of the new house. The decided young wife with better sense, accustomed to having her own way, said "No, no mottoes." But the reason she gave was not good. "Didn't like mottoes."

I—new husband—lugging a heavy suitcase, tired by the useless effort to keep the thing off my legs, was surprised to find my superior "taste" in matters pertaining to my own work disputed. And I was caught red-handed in my own "sentimentality." It was forever claiming me and every time it did I would not only lose my face—but my patience. Find someone or something to "blame."

I put the suitcase down, wiped the sweat from my face, more indignant to be caught "sentimentalizing" than anything else. Picked it up again and refused the offer to take hold and help. Not in those circumstances. Thank you. We walked wide apart.

SIX CHILDREN[6]

The little new home.

The young husband seemed more interested in it than in his bride, so the young wife soon said to him.

No—no children were provided for, but they came. First came one within the year. A son—Lloyd. Then, two years later, another. A boy—John. The several grandmothers came in often to help and advise and keep domesticity working, right side up.

In two years more—another. A girl—Catherine II. Two years later, another. A boy, David. The grandmothers were kept pretty busy around there for years to come. And the several grandmothers agreed none too often.

This was something not in my reckoning. But just the same, two years later, another. A girl—Frances.

Five years went by and Llewelyn came.

The young husband found that he had his work cut out for himself. The young wife found hers cut out for her.

Architecture was my profession. Motherhood became hers.

Fair enough, but it was division.

The young architect's studio or workshop was within a few years built on Chicago Avenue. The young mother's home and kindergarten had continued and still kept on—on Forest Avenue.

The corridor through which the great sprawling willow tree grew and covered the house with its spreading green—connected the two establishments.

I knew only a few of the neighbors' names.

The young wife knew only a few of her husband's clients' names or what buildings he was building.

The handsome children were well born. They, each and all, were fine specimens of healthy childhood. They were curly-headed, blue-eyed, sunny-haired, fair-skinned like their beautiful mother. They all resembled her.

Every one of them was born, so it seemed, directly in his or her own right. You might think they had all willed it and decided it all themselves. They were seemingly endowed with the resistance and will of their father: inheriting all his perverse qualities. They inherited their mother's good looks.

That little home department soon became a lively place.

Things began to smash. Cries to resound. Shrieks. Quarrels and laughter. Someone or another or several or something in a pickle all the time. Destruction of something or other happening every minute, works of art and craft, crockery, toys. Then destruction of Mother's "Peace and Patience!" I, their legitimate "father," would hear all about it when I came in to be fed. And if I came in early to go to bed—which I seldom did.

The children were their mother's children and up to her except when the two young parents themselves made eight children all together at playtime. And early in the morning. Warren McArthur, friend and early client of mine and something of a wag, dining with us one Sunday, caught one of the children, and called to me—"Quick now, Frank. . . what's the name of this one?" It worked. The "father," surprised by the peremptory request gave the wrong name. Hard to believe—but true.

Sometimes pursuing a kind interest in my state someone would ask: "And are there children?"

The answer, "Yes—six" would leave the kindly interest wide-eyed—lips apart—wondering.

I am afraid I never looked the part. Nor ever acted it. I didn't feel it. And I didn't know how.

We two had a joint bank-account.

Man and wife drew checks until they began to come back N.S.F.—in red. Then we knew the money was gone.

Never mind! The first of the month was only two weeks off. There would be some more. Why worry?

The "father" in the architect took the children's future to heart in that I wanted them to grow up in beautiful surroundings. I intended them all to be infected by "a love for the beautiful." I then called it so in spite of growing prejudice against the sentimental.

So I built a beautiful large playroom for them all on the upper floor at the rear of the little house.

Before I could get it all paid for a benevolent sheriff came and sat in it all of one night. It was next morning before I could get the eighty-five dollars somewhere to send him on his way. I remember, to this day, that it was eighty-five dollars but I can't remember where I got it. Probably Wheaton, the old business clerk at Adler and Sullivan's advanced it on my pay. He did such things for me. Sometimes.

But the children didn't know about such things then. Never mind, they learned all about them later.

The playroom was a beautiful playroom and did its work well. The allegory at the end—the Fisherman and the Genii—from the *Arabian Nights*. The Genii, done in straightline pattern. A lesson to be drawn from the subject-matter by the children. I forgot what it was. Perhaps never to be "sentimen-

tal," curious, or there would be consequences!

The neighbors' children, too, came to kindergarten there. The home overflowed with children until one fell out of the window. Youngest son—Llewelyn. He was not hurt very much because his dress caught on the playroom window-sill and held him a moment.

There was little sickness but when there was, gloom settled over everything. A sick child and the place ceased to live until improvement came or the child well again. Fortunately little Doctor Luff lived only several doors away. And fortunately such sickness as came never lasted long. The six children were six happy, healthy-going institutions not to mention constitutions. And they all had their own way in the end. Always. They had about as much respect for their father as each had for the others. And at times, much later on in years, it was hard to tell which was father and son, whether by language, attitude, or age.

That household was pretty much children all the time—all together.

It was a double-barreled establishment. A three-ring circus on the one side. A stimulating excursion into the here and now on the other side. Both regardless. A good time had by all, until something or other would happen. As something or other always will and did. The establishments began to compete. The architect absorbed the father in me—perhaps—because I never got used to the word nor the idea of being one as I saw them all around the block and met them among my friends.

Is it a quality? Fatherhood? If so, I seemed born without it. And yet a building was a child. I have had the father-feeling, I am sure, when coming back, after a long time, to one of my buildings. That must be the true feeling of fatherhood? But I never had it for my children. I had affection for them. I regarded them as *with* me—and playfellows, comrades to be responsible for. But their wills were set alongside mine, never across or against mine unless I was trying to protect myself from them. Though I did have to take a hand in the upbringing of six-year-old Frances. I took her into the bathroom and punished her until her cries (Frances could cry enormously) were heard by all the next door neighbors. I had closed the door but forgot to close the window. Finished with it, she rushed out of the house, slammed the door, and went down the street to stay—"forever"—with Grandma. The unusual indignity outraged her and shocked and shamed me no less. She was always bringing in some dirty stray cat, or strange mangy dog, at large in the streets because no one wanted either, and adopting them with a passionate clinging—pathetic or ridiculous—according to the point of view. When her animals were turned out, Frances would stand stock-still, outraged, open her mouth wide and wail the wailing only Frances knew how to wail.

And if there is any meaner feeling man makes for himself than when he strikes a child, what may it be? The coward ninety-nine times out of a hundred is releasing vexation or a peevish resentment for upset "*authority.*"

"Spare the rod and spoil the child?" Another Mosaic root of human misery: the special invention—in self-defense—of that imposition called Fatherhood. "Fatherhood?" An institution I suppose in the interest of bigger and better domesticity.

These youngsters that grew up alongside my Coming of Age all now call me "Dad."

I wouldn't be surprised if they were to call me "Frank," nor ever would.

They often started to do it, too, when they were little. And their mother would treat it as a form of disrespect, and insist upon "Papa." Accent long on the first 'a' making a more offensive word "*paa*—pa" than even when accented on the last and it became "pa*paa.*" There is a stuffy domesticity about the sound applied to the male that was always intolerable to me.

"Father" is tolerable after fifty. "*Paa*pa" never!

I remember sitting on the terrace in front of the little Forest Avenue home waiting for Lloyd's mother to come home from Church. Two and a half year old Lloyd had been left with me. It was spring and I had turned on the revolving sprinkler to water the lawn. The two-year-old spied the revolving thing, and wanted it. "No, Lloyd," I said, "you can't have it—keep away or you'll get your new clothes all wet."

Unable to conquer desire himself, I assisted by gently leading him back to the steps. And I sat him down there in full view of the whirligig, out of the way of the water, but where he could see it and enjoy the whirl. A moment and he got up to go after it, regardless of warnings. Again I seated him. Again up and going. Threats now as to dire consequences. He seemed not to hear them. He was fascinated. Though seated again—up again and going. "Come back, young fellow!"

He was helpless to return. Again I got up and brought him back, angry by now myself. Should I punish him? Sunday, people coming home from church. So far as that went, yes, but what good?

By the time this thought got through my mind there he had got into the zone of the sprinkler and the lusty little red-headed fellow gasped and stopped a moment.

"Come back, Lloyd, or you'll be drowned," I called in a tone that might have blasted him where he stood. No sound from him. He went in farther. Drenched thoroughly, he gasped again, turned his face aside and stood his ground.

"All right," I thought, "maybe this *is* the best way." I sat down on the steps to watch the struggle.

His mother had dressed him freshly clean. He had looked nice. That was already a total loss.

He now shut his eyes, held his breath, and staggered in closer, to grab the coveted thing, his hand stretched out in the act.

Too much! . . . He was drenched and fell in the mud. Bawling lustily now but not giving an inch, he got up and turning his face aside stood there bawling loudly, angry himself.

He was a sight but there he was, only a few feet away from his desire, the water taking his breath, every time he turned to go forward.

"Come back, lusty boy," I said. "Can't you see you can't get it? Come back here!" Myself angry to see him so. He didn't know I called, apparently, because another totter brought him so close I thought he had the whirling thing, but no—he fell. Gurgling, bawling, and gasping he lay there for a moment, but rolled over again on to his hands and knees head down toward the whirling spray.

"All right," I cruelly thought, "Let's see what stuff he's made of!" And I let him lie there half-drowned, literally, to see what he would do. Features already obliterated, almost inarticulate with water and anger, still howling desire, he got up on his feet, fell forward, and clutched the coveted thing to him and rolled over on his back kicking and inarticulate with the water. I ran now and picked him up, mud from head to heels, gasping but hanging on to the whirligig, just in time to hear a piercing scream as his mother rushed at me, snatched him from me, and publicly reproached me, as she sobbed over the half-drowned infant. "My child," she sobbed. "My child!" And her beautiful spring costume was a sight—too.

All right. He was good stuff.

The hose was the cause of many a divertisement. Myself coming home one Sunday but not from church, the two boys, Lloyd and John, were playing the hose on the lawn already too wet. None too pleased I called, "Boys, put up that hose!" No inclination to put it up. "Lloyd! John! Put up that hose or I'll put you all up a tree and leave you up there." A challenge this. John had the hose and, at this, swung it around toward me. Just a little warning that's all. Now angry, I called—"Boys, PUT DOWN THAT HOSE!"

Nothing of the sort.

Both boys now took the hose and turned it on me. I had to get back a few strides. "Look here you . . ." but the neighbors were coming from church and some of them had stopped to see what would happen next. This "gallery" excited the boys and restrained me.

I walked around to flank them from the shrubbery.

They were waiting for me and wet me down.

"Boys, come on, be good sports—put down that hose" I coaxed now.

Not their idea of "sport."

"Let's see you get it!" said John, ringleader in the mischief this time. And they danced around and came toward me with it. I got back out of the water. The neighbors, by now a group on both sides of the street were laughing and enjoying the show at paternal expense. Paternal "authority" was getting a bad break. I was already wet, so I charged the pair. They turned the hose full on me and ran.

And so it went.

I took cold baths myself in the morning those days and I would fling the boys into a tub of cold water, drowning their yells which would lift the roof. Then after they were rubbed dry—putting one hand in my pocket and a boxing glove on the other, I would take them on, gloves on both their hands and both boys working together until they grew too big even to be handled with both my hands, gloved and free.

I gave to each child, early in his life, a musical instrument. To learn to play it was all I asked of their education.

Lloyd—Cello.
John—Violin.
Catherine—Voice.
Frances—Piano.
David—Flute.
Llewellyn—Guitar and Mandolin.

Their mother played the piano, reading. I played the piano a little myself, trying to improvise.

Later this incipient orchestra was presided over by Lloyd, conducting with the bow of his cello. He would reach out so quickly to rap the skull of the player of a wrong note that he could keep right on playing. And the howls and wails that mingled with the music gave a distinctly modern effect to every performance.

The connecting door to the Studio would open cautiously, when some rather important client would be in to go over the plans. And I would see curly heads and mischievous eyes challenging mine knowing I could do nothing about it in the circumstances.

There was a balcony around the draughting room reached from the corridor. The children always loved to get up there and peer down at the goings on, break out into a roar, and scamper back before unkind words could overtake them.

One day a fashionable, fastidious client from the North Side, Mrs. Aline Devin. Her first visit to the studio. Sitting together at the big central office table, facing the corridor—I was just about to show her plans to her for the first time—always a strained situation—when I saw the door open a little and saw

Catherine's curls, mischievous eyes, and dirty little face. A dirty little hand was on the door jamb.

I looked tons of "go away." But never fear. The door opened wide. In came Catherine, one stocking down over one shoe—largely chewing gum. Where did she get that gum? Gum was forbidden. The dirt was familiar.

She marched sidelong, perfectly conscious of the effect she was having on me, to the opposite side of the table. Her little jaws worked carelessly and freely while she regarded Mrs. Devin curiously—apparently unfavorably.

Then suddenly, stretching out her hand: "*Paa*pa! Mama wants a dime!"

I didn't have one. So I made merry over the "break," escorted Catherine II to the corridor door, and turned the key.

Fatal error.

There she was now up in the balcony above, looking down—freely chewing, as ever.

"*Paa*pa! Mama wants a dime!"

Her mother finally came to get the persistent creditor dunning me for the dime I didn't have.

I'll say Catherine made herself charming, if dirty—all the while.

Mrs. Devin was highly amused. And so must I have been, or worse, for I've never forgotten the moment.

Those children!

They are worthy a monograph, each.

Life and work went on in Oak Park for nineteen years.

Food, clothing, shelter, education, and amusement for my "six" were accomplished somehow, meantime. The eldest boys went from The Hillside Home School to College. The other boys from the Oak Park High School to universities. The girls went to private schools, Frances to Penn Hall and to Sophie Newcomb.

Catherine was sent to New York to study music. All had musical educations of a kind.

All seemed talented individuals, pretty much in their own right and happy only when they were on their own.

They knew how to be, even at that very early age.

So long as we had the luxuries the necessities could pretty well take care of themselves so far as we were concerned. We were seldom without our season tickets to the Symphony.

The children were always tastefully dressed, in expensive things. The best, I should say, that could be had. Their good looks made this an agreeable extravagance.

Catherine herself wore so well the clothes I designed for her it was always a temptation to get new dresses. Designing them was fun.

My love for beautiful things, rugs, books, prints, or anything made by Art or Craft kept the butcher, the baker, and the candlestick-maker waiting. Sometimes an incredibly long time.

GROCERIES

Our kind grocer, down at the corner, Mr. Gotsch, came around once, I remember, with a grocery bill for eight hundred and fifty dollars. How many months old I do not remember. But I remember the kindly way in which he sat down to plead his side of the case with me. He showed me how much cheaper he could serve me if I would pay his bill regularly.

"Then," I said, "you are charging me for giving me credit, are you?"

"Of course," he said, "I must. I have children of my own." And I knew them—nice children. He went on to say: "If I didn't protect myself I would soon be unable to give them even a small part of what you are pretty freely giving yours."

He didn't press the matter. He just showed me the folly of such neglect as mine. And I felt remorse, even though I *had* paid for my own neglect. I somehow got the money and paid him. I would resist the next adventure into art and craft, and perhaps for several months.

But this self-denial would not last. So always, the necessities were going by default.

It was my misfortune that everybody was willing to trust me. I don't know why they were willing, either, because I don't imagine my appearance or my way of life would appeal to a business man any more than my buildings appealed to the local bankers a little later on.

But I always found in those early days the merchants kind, indulgent to unbelievable extremes. And this, too, tended to make me dreadfully careless.

Only the banks would "N.S.F." us. So we came to distrust and despise banks. But they were really doing us the only favor they knew how to do.

I can imagine the feeling was cordially mutual in the course of time.

But the group of children, big and little, in the little gabled house on the corner with the queer studio alongside, had unusual luxuries, unusual advantages in education. And, eventually, though I never knew *how* nor quite *how much* they all "came to," I managed to pay for the necessaries plus delinquent tax—given time enough.

RENT

I remember the rent in the Schiller building when offices were opened there later. The rent would sometimes be seven or eight months behind. And I hear Mr. Dose, the manager of the building, say, when I would realize the enormity of the circumstances by being brought to book and would apologize and promise: "Never mind, Mr. Wright. You are an artist. I have never yet lost any rent owed me by an artist. You will pay me," said the heavy, severe-faced landlord.

And, of course, I did pay him. And after that, as regularly as I could. I don't believe anyone ever lost a penny either in rent or credit account in all those haphazard years. But, I believe, too, that it cost handsomely in the end to allow the necessities to drift. How much? Say twenty-five per cent. Perhaps it was worth it. Who knows?

I remember walking into a little thrifty, French investment broker's office one day and seeing on the wall, framed, this: "Spend what you earn." I told him I thought he was corrupting the youth of this country because no such motto would ever get anybody anywhere. "Make the motto read: 'Earn what you spend,' and you will have everybody working hard and to better purpose," I said. He would also have everybody to whom the youth owed money working on the youth, to make him work.

Nevertheless, always during those years there was a very real undertone of worry, a heavy drag of debt that fell to my share.

I believe no one, in our commercialized era, ever really forgets a money-obligation. It goes along with him wherever and as he goes. Pricking him sharply, from underneath, and coming to mind wakeful nights.

And I believe, too, while debt is stimulating to some, it is stultifying to others. It is just a question as to how much punishment, given a certain nature, one can stand.

The buying and selling of money has introduced a shopkeeping code into the shopkeeping ethics of modern life, itself more and more a kind of shopkeeping.

The secret information of the credit-detective systems, installment-buying finance companies and their ruses and extortions in re-financing—all this machinery takes a terrible toll from the man who goes in too deep, or lets his bills go by. We owe all these institutions to this tendency of youthful human nature to put off paying until tomorrow.

This simple human weakness has thus bred a whole school and a new type of money-shark. And the "system" with its teeth is in the lives of nearly everyone today. The victim of the type and the teeth will wake up some day to realize how costly these "monyana" moneymen are, and, by avoiding them, make them, too, go to work.

But what hope, while money may keep on working as something in itself to make all work useless?

We are getting in deeper than is proper here.

All that is to the economist?

Since we have reached the money-matter so unexpectedly, as a consequence of Family, Fellowship in mind it is time to go to WORK.

Come with me to the offices of one Frank Lloyd Wright, Architect, the offices at 1501 Schiller Building where the arches loop beneath the top story motif—the square mass of the top glooming against the sky. The Adler and Sullivan building now called the "Garrick."

It is late in the year Eighteen Hundred and Ninety-three. A fateful year in the culture of these United States. They are to go Pseudo Classic!

BOOK TWO **WORK**

THE FIELD

Midsummer sun floods the field of rippling grain. The swath of yellow stubble left by the reaper shows undertone of living green as the red-gold square of grain standing at the center of the field grows smaller each time the gaily painted reaper, pulled by the three white horses, cuts its way around.

The stubble field is lined by the big wheel of the reaper, patterned in regular order by grain-shocks. A man in a blue shirt is seen making the shocks. The bundles or sheaves of grain—six of them—he stands firmly, butt-end down, on the stubble and caps them by laying two bundles cross-wise over the grain at the top: the cap-bundles flattened and bent over the sides.

The entire field is become a linear pattern—a plan of routine. Work.

Coming along after the noisy reaper—red, blue, green, yellow, and white man-toy—its gay whirling reel and jerkily revolving rakes regularly sweeping the grain in regular piles on to the stubble behind are four more men, each man binding the bundles raked off on one side of the square of standing grain. Each must finish binding his side of the square before the reaper comes around again.

A certain rhythm in regular and patterned order everywhere established in this work of the harvest. Routine fitted to routine.

After the men comes the boy, barefoot, bare-headed, running to and fro in the stubble to pick up the bundles by the bands, and as many as he can carry at one time. He gathers eight together in each pile to be ready to the shocker's hand. The shocker is coming along behind the boy, grasping the bundles two at a time, and standing them up together.

The barefoot, bareheaded twelve year old, brown as a walnut, sits down on a bundle to rest a moment in the hot blaze of sun.

Nearby standing in the shadow of a shock is a brown stone jug filled with spring-water in which raw oatmeal has been sprinkled. He spies the jug, gets up, goes to the jug, uncorks the nozzle, slips two fingers through the stone handle, and manages to lift the jug, letting it drop over on to his forearm, as he has seen the men do. Head thrown back he takes a thirsty pull, water gurgling from the jug down his young throat. The jug set down in the shade again, he wipes the sweat from his tanned face and the water from his chin with the blue gingham sleeve of his forearm. He listens a moment.

The Meadow Lark!

He looks at his bleeding finger, nails worn down to the quick by the straw bands of the too many bundles already to his credit. Then, to carry on, he goes back a few steps, picks up the bundle on which he had been sitting. From the butt-end of the bundle a snake slips to the ground.

A rattler unwittingly bound into the sheaf a few moments before by one of the binders and tossed aside.

The rattler smoothly, swiftly coils in the stubble and—tail upended—rattles, darting a forked tongue—narrow hostile eyes, gleaming.

The barefoot boy starts back, his own eyes narrowing, too, at sight of the splendid enemy.

Instantly, clear consciousness of the whole scene comes full upon the boy, the golden blaze, the giddy whirl of the gay reaper, voices of the

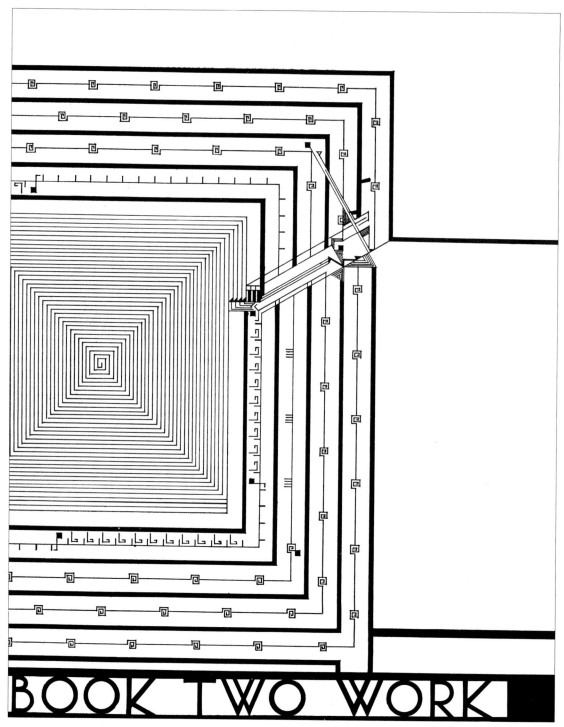

Divider page for "Book Two" from the original edition of *An Autobiography*, designed by FLLW. 1932.

men—one singing—the distant rattle of the sickle mingling with the immediate rattle of the rattler. All order process and golden. The beautiful brown embroidery of the golden body of the snake makes the reptile "belong." Some fascination holds the lad a moment. A sense of something predestined—lived before. To be lived again? Something in the far distant past comes near—as repetition?

It does not occur to the boy to run or call out. He stands eyeing the snake as narrowly as the snake eyes him. Yes—as hostile.

A three-tined pitchfork stands against the shock that shelters the stone jug. He leaps to the fork, and with a turn and thrust as swift as the darting tongue, pins the rattler to the ground. The piercing tines of the fork hold fast as the seething coils of the enraged serpent struggle to get free.

Now what?

He looks around him. His fingers slip again into the stone handle. With the bottom of the stone jug he flattens the evil-spitting head.

He picks up the gorgeous thing now, by the rattles—nine—and calls, "Adolph"—the binder nearest him.

The reaper come opposite, stops. His uncle drops off the driver's seat and comes toward him.

"See, Uncle James!"—from the now excited boy—"I've got him—nine rattles!"

"Why didn't you get away from him and let Adolph kill him?"

"Why?" the boy answers, missing the approval he felt earned.

"Why"—enough. "Next time you see one of those things you get out of the way. You are bare-footed, you might get worse than hurt."

But the boy holds the limp snake as much higher as he can, looking at its length.

Work goes on again.

The rhythm and routine of the harvest field as before. But something had happened to challenge for a moment the peaceful orderly field.

Work—the plan—interrupted by something not in the reckoning. Something ever a part of Life and ever a threat to the plan. Something that both-

ered the men who made the Bible. Is the Devil the only answer?

Then what Freedom?

WORK

The Columbian Fair had opened and closed its turnstiles to the crowd. Upon leaving Adler and Sullivan, Cecil Corwin and I opened offices on a tower-floor in the Schiller building, Chicago—a building that owing to Sullivan's love for his new home in the South had been more largely left to me than any other.

Accustomed to the view from a high place and feeling nearer Adler and Sullivan, I suppose, I wanted that space.

Cecil and I had a draughting room, each, either side of the central room for business. We used this central room in common. Defending this room was an anteroom or vestibule with the ceiling dropped down to the top of the doors. A straight-line glass-pattern formed this ceiling—glass diffusing artificial light.

The effect in the small anteroom was one of sunlight, no light-fixtures visible.

There was a large flat oak chest of drawers each side of the door with some of Hermon McNeil's Indian statuettes standing on them.

The walls were plain. At either end—two plain chairs. We liked to stand there and talk about the future—Cecil and I. And we would greet a coming client or linger there to talk with one leaving, enjoy the atmosphere, and end an interview.

The outside entrance door to this anteroom as well as the inner door to the business space itself was a single clear plate of glass bordered by the usual wood stiles and rails of the usual width. A single clear glass plate from side to side and top to bottom, with our names lettered on one side at the top of the plate-glass in the outside door in simple gold letters. On the inner door, "Private."

These single-panel plate-glass doors had style—were new. Anyone could see directly, not only into the anteroom from the elevator hall, but into the business-space as well, so we had a shade on each door to pull up from the bottom. But it was seldom used.

At the center of the business-space was a huge,

flat-topped table with four square chests of drawers for legs, leaving leg-space at the middle on four sides. Four comfortable chairs were placed one at the center of each side. We could thus sit each side with clients or contractors. This table was seven feet square and in the center was a glass globe usually filled with flowers from our small garden, but, sometimes by gifts from other gardens.

Sitting on this platform I could see directly out as anyone could see directly in.

This had various consequences.

I see one of the consequences as I write, in the yellow face and evil eyes of Shimoda, a Japanese draughtsman fired for cause and warned never to come back. The cause was speaking obliquely of a lady who got into the habit of leaving flowers in the glass globe on the big office table.

And yet, one noon, as I glanced up, there stood Shimoda.

A scared look came over the yellow face as I jumped to my feet. My time to be "out" so he was taken as much by surprise as I was. Probably he had come back with no worse intent than to see the boys, but I had warned him never to come back.

He turned to run, but I could open those two doors quickly by now, owing to much practice. Before he could get away I reached him. A well directed intimate kick landed him well down the half flight on the main public stair running from directly in front of the entrance door down on the half landing below. He lay there in a whimpering heap and I turned back into the office and sat down—waiting.

But not satisfied with this he carried the tale to my reverend uncle of All Souls Church. Described the event with enlarged details—my big riding boots—insinuating I had them on that morning for no other business and no other intention than to kill him.

"Very rough business for him," said "yerrow socks," as his familiars always called him.

And for this characteristic carrying of the tale I did the work more thoroughly next time he came—which strange to say he did some weeks later thinking I was out of town—by continuing the work on down from the landing to the floor below.

This finally settled it and Shimoda disappeared from the American scene, not very much worse for wear.

No, Shimoda was not a good Japanese.

To this clear plate with the small gold letters
        "Frank Lloyd Wright, Architect
          Cecil Corwin, Architect,"
came my first client.

You notice the order? By seniority Cecil should have been first but he wouldn't have it so.

And, you see, "opening an office" was all that simple.

Rent an office to your liking. Take out the door panels, all of them. Substitute a single beautiful clear plate of glass, then a novelty.

Sit down and letter your own name in the size and style preferred. Hesitate a moment becomingly—then add "Architect." Get a thrill out of this, as you regard it for a moment with none too adequate realization of the implication. Get a sign writer to put it all in gold leaf on the glass, and—there you are!

Another architect come to town.

How many of the boys in Usonia who have listened to the far-away tinkle of the cowbells, have had that same thrill—"professing" something or other—"opening an office"?

"Truth against the World" is a heavy standard. A flagrant banner. I had left it off the door. But it was sitting there inside.

Individual preferences are a compelling circumstance.

Babies are too.

Combine the several circumstances with the preferences and what have you? Or what has you, is fairer and better English.

W. H. Winslow of the Winslow Ornamental Iron Works had often been to Adler and Sullivan's office to consult with me about the work of that office. He now appeared to give me my first "job." I was to be the architect of his new home to be built at River Forest. I could hardly believe I had a "job"—it was difficult to believe the initiative I had taken was a reality. But I soon found it was.[1]

His house was to stand across the drive from

Frank Lloyd Wright and his family, on the porch of the Oak Park house. FLLW Fdn FA#6305.0048

Mr. Waller's own house in a park in River Forest.

Mr. Waller was the handsomest person and most aristocratic individual I had ever seen. He had become my friend. He much admired the Winslow house. The building of that house should have a story but it has none. Edward C. Waller and Daniel H. Burnham, the partner of John Root, were old friends. John Root had just died.

Mr. Waller brought about a meeting with "Uncle Dan," as they all called Dan Burnham—inviting Catherine and myself to meet Mr. and Mrs. Burnham at the Waller home. "Uncle Dan" had seen the Winslow house and straightway pronounced it a "gentleman's house from grade to coping."

After dinner Mr. Waller led the way to his cozy library. He wanted to show his friend some work I had done in it for him. And I saw him turn to lock the door after we were in—I wondered why?

Then the argument commenced which I have never forgotten.

Sitting there, handsome, jovial, splendidly convincing, was "Uncle Dan." To be brief, he would take care of my wife and children if I would go to Paris, four years of the Beaux Arts. Then Rome—two years. Expenses all paid. A job with him when I came back.

It was more than merely generous. It was splendid.

But I was frightened. I sat, embarrassed, not knowing what to say.

Mr. Waller got up, walked to and fro telling

me what a great opportunity it all was for me. I sat there trying to find the right words to say.

"Another year, and it will be too late, Frank," said Uncle Dan.

That was my cue.

"Yes, too late, Uncle Dan—it's too late now, I'm afraid. I am spoiled already.

"I've been too close to Mr. Sullivan. He has helped spoil the Beaux Arts for me, or spoiled me for the Beaux Arts, I guess I mean.

"He told me things too, and I think he regrets the time he spent there, himself."

Uncle Dan: "You are loyal to Sullivan I see, Frank, and that is right. I admire Sullivan when it comes to decoration. Essentially he is a great decorator. His ornament charms me. But his architecture? I can't see that. 'The Fair,' Frank, is going to have a great influence in our country. The American people have seen the 'Classics' on a grand scale for the first time. You've seen the success of the Fair and it should mean something to you too. We should take advantage of the Fair."

He went on: "Atwood's Fine Arts Building, Beman's Merchant Tailor's Building, McKim's Building—all beautiful! Beautiful! I can see all America constructed along the lines of the Fair, in noble 'dignified' classic style. The great men of the day all feel that way about it—all of them."

"No," I said, "there is Louis Sullivan, he doesn't. And if John Root were alive I don't believe he would feel that way about it. Richardson I am sure never would."

"Frank," he said, "the Fair should have shown you that Sullivan and Richardson are well enough in their way, but their way won't prevail—architecture is going the other way."

"But, it is essentially the uncreative way . . . isn't it?"

"Uncreative?—What do you mean uncreative? What can be more beautiful than the classic lines and proportions of Greek architecture. That architecture will never be surpassed. We should be taught by it, and accept its rules. Without a good education in the Classics, how can you hope to . . . succeed?"

"I know, yes—I know, Uncle Dan, you may be quite right but somehow it just strikes on my heart like . . . jail . . . like something awful. I couldn't bear it, I believe. All that discipline and time wasted again waiting for something to happen, that never could happen. I just can't see it as living. Somehow—it scares me."

I actually began to look for avenue of escape, the window was partly open.

Mr. Waller now interfered, manifestly provoked at my obstinacy, if not my stupidity, indeed.

"Frank, don't you realize what this offer means to you? As you choose now, remember, so you will go on all the rest of your life."

"Yes, Mr. Waller—that's just it," I said. "I know. They all do. I have seen the men come home from there all one type, no matter how much they were individuals when they went."

"Individuals? Great architecture *is* severe discipline," said Uncle Dan.

"Think of your future, think of your family," said Mr. Waller.

I felt the weight of the occasion.

I saw myself influential, prosperous, safe: saw myself a competent leader of the majority rule. That much faith I had in it all. There would be no doubt about it, with Daniel H. Burnham's power behind me, if I qualified, and there was no doubt in my mind but that I could qualify: it was all definitely "set," too easy and unexciting as I saw it. And it was all untrue. At the very best a makeshift.

This was "success" as I had dreamed of it then? Was it? Right here, within my grasp? I, too, had already seen the effect of the Fair. But I could not respect it, though I believed Uncle Dan spoke the truth. I did fear and believe it was going to *prevail* as he said. I would have given a good deal to know Lieber Meister's reaction to all this. But that was all over. I could not go to him now.

The two friends mistook my depression for a weakening in favor of the Beaux Arts.

"Well?" said both, smiling kindly—affectionately.

I felt like an ingrate. Never was the ego within me more hateful to me than at that moment. It stood straight up against the very roof of my mind.

"No, Mr. Burnham. No, Mr. Waller—I can't run away."

"Run away, what do you mean?" said Mr. Waller.

"Well, you see 'run away' from what I see as mine—I mean what I see as ours—in our country, to what can't belong to me, no I mean *us*, just because it means success. You see—I can't go, even if I wanted to go because I should never care for myself, after that."

I don't believe either of the two great friends believed me. They thought I must be showing off—I saw that by their expression, I thought. "It may be foolish, I suppose it is, somehow, but I'd rather be free and a failure and 'foolish' than be 'tied up' to any routine success. I don't see Freedom in it . . . that's all. Oh yes, I mean it, I really do. I'm grateful to you, both; but I won't go." I got up on my feet. Suddenly the whole thing cleared up before my eyes as only keeping faith with what we call "America."

"Thank you both," I said again. "I know how obstinate and egotistic you think me, but I'm going on as I've started. I'm spoiled, first by birth, then by training, and [this had now come clear under pressure] by conviction, for anything like that."

Mr. Waller unlocked the study door, opened it and stood aside—hurt I could see—to let me pass out. I helped Catherine on with her things, and we went home. I did not mention to her what had happened until long afterward.

The Winslow house had burst on the view of that provincial suburb like the Prima Vera in full bloom. It was a new world to Oak Park and River Forest. That house became an attraction, far and near. Incessantly it was courted and admired. Ridiculed, too, of course. Ridicule is always modeled on the opposite side of that shield. This first house soon began to sift the sheep from the goats in this fashion:

Mr. Moore, a lawyer on Forest Avenue near by my own house, was going to build. I had learned of this, and I had given up hope that he might ask me to build for him when, one day, sure enough—could I believe my eyes? I saw Mr. and Mrs. Moore standing outside the full-length clear-plate in the outer door of the Schiller Building Office.

I opened it—excited. The Moores came in and sat down.

"How is it, Mr. Wright," said Mr. Moore, "that every architect I know or have ever heard of, and some I never heard of, have come in one way or another to ask to build my house and you live almost across the street but I haven't had a word from you?"

"Did Mr. Patton come?" I asked. He was head of the American Institute of Architects, the A. I. A., at the time and lived in Oak Park.

"Yes, he was the first one to come. Why didn't you come?"

"I knew if you wanted me, you knew where to find me. And how did I know you wanted me? . . . .You are a lawyer," I said. "Would you offer yourself to someone whom you knew needed a good lawyer?"

"I thought that was it," he said.

"Now we want you to build our house . . . but . . . I don't want you to give us anything like that house you did for Winslow. I don't want to go down backstreets to my morning train to avoid being laughed at. I would like something like this," he said, and laid some pictures of English half-timber work on my table.

Three children were now running around the streets without proper shoes. How money was needed in that little gabled house! (I had been insulted several times by guesses as to whether the house was "sea-side" or "colonial.") None knew so little as I where money was coming from. Could I take Mr. Moore on? Could I give him a home in the name of English half-timber good enough so that I would not "sell out"? It was worth trying anyway. I tried it.[2]

They were delighted with the house, and so was everyone but me. Did I always resent the praise bestowed upon it because a mention of it made me think of my brave stand before Mr. Waller and Uncle Dan? But it was better to stand back and make way with a single house—wasn't it, than with a whole lifetime of them? Or was it?

So I consoled myself. At any rate it was the

Catherine Tobin Wright. FLLW Fdn FA#6305.0026

But, by the time an hour or so had passed I was quite likely to have made that client see why and how it was the wrong thing, especially now wrong, to build anything more like that in our own country, wrong in Usonia where men were free, and old enough to know that license, even in "taste," is not Freedom.

The offices in the Schiller (now the Garrick) saw the making of the Winslow plans; the plans for the Moore house. Mr. Baldwin, another Oak Park lawyer, had come in and laid a check for $350.00 on the table as a retainer. He had evidently heard from Mr. Moore. The Francis Apartments built for an estate, the Husser and Heller homes, the Lexington Terraces, the Wolf Lake Resort. A number of other buildings all characterized to a certain extent by the Sullivanian idiom, at least in detail. I couldn't invent the terms of my own overnight. At that time there was nothing in sight that might be helpful. I had no Sullivanian models, even, for any of these things.

A remark of Lieber Meister's had come back to me by way of my client Winslow: "Sullivan says, Frank, it looks as though you were going to work out your own individuality.". . . So he was interested in me still, was he?

Cecil had been working on some jobs of his own, Rush Medical College in particular. We were not partners. I did not see so much of him now for I was intensely busy, and meantime he had found some new intimates.

We sat talking in the business-office we used in common. He looked discouraged, I noticed.

"What's the matter, old man Cecil?"

"Not much, in general, Frank, except, in particular, I don't believe I'm an architect, that's all."

"What's the matter with 'Rush?' Don't you like it?"

He looked at me as he tilted gently back and forth in a gently creaking office chair—sadness and some whimsey in his look too.

"You know. Why ask me?"

"Because it's a fine piece of work."

"Is it architecture?" he said quietly.

"Well, it's better than ninety-nine out of a

one time in the course of a long career that I "gave in" to the fact that I had a family and they had a right to live—and their "living" was "up to me."

The tragedy of the binomial theorem!

Yes, I often had occasion to remember and regret "giving in" in the years immediately following.

I can look back now and see that young professional "architect." I soon left off the affix "architect" as beside the mark—sitting at that big platform—let's say the flowers were lilacs—listening to you expectantly. I suspect the ego in him invited or repelled you as you happened to be made yourself.

"You wish to build a house?" Oh? Like the one I built for Mr. Moore?

There is a feeling of disappointment that gets to you.

I hear myself saying, "But why like that house for Mr. Moore?" And the argument is on.

Anyone could get a rise out of me by admiring that essay in English half-timber. "They" all liked it and I could have gone on unnaturally building them for the rest of my natural life.

hundred architects are doing—better than their barbering and make-up. And, Cecil, you are only beginning. You have such fine feeling for proportion—you know it—and good taste, and . . . why are you looking at me, that way? You are worth more to any client than any architect I know." Again I asked, "What is the matter with you?"

"All right, I'll tell you, young fellow. I've found out there's no joy in architecture for me except as I see you do it. It bores me when I try to do it myself. There's the truth for you. You *are* the thing you do. I'm not and I never will be. And worse than all I'm not sure any longer, lately, that I want to be. There's joy in it for you—but there's obsession too, you live in your work. You will wake up some day and find that you can't do that, altogether, and then there'll be trouble, I foresee."

All this seemed to open a chasm where I thought all fair enough. I had lost sight of him. He had been lagging behind. Dear old Cecil.

After all was architecture everything?

But worse was coming.

"I'm going East, Frank. I'm interested with Dr. Buchanan—we're going into something together. You can take over my room and, as I see, you'll need it."

This was unbelievable. I reproached Cecil because I had an uneasy sense of having betrayed him and so—inclined to blame *him*. Never would I have believed this *of* him, was finding it hard to believe even *from* him.

I argued, pleaded. All of no use.

"I might as well make a clean breast of it, Frank. I don't want to go on seeing you do the things I can't do. Already I'm where I can do less than I could when we came in here together, and I really care less. Caring less, this isn't so difficult as you imagine it to be."

It flashed through my mind that I was right, this abnegation on his part was genuine discouragement due to my own neglect—and felt ashamed of myself. Why not take him in with me. But that was not what this meant. And I knew he wouldn't come.

But I said, "Why not join me Cecil—I need you to help me and maybe I could help you out of this. How do you know?"

"No, I'm not the man you need for a partner, Frank. I'm no business man at all. I despise 'business,' it's too gabby and grabby and selly for me—and I'm no architect. I know it now. You do need me for a friend, and I'll always be one. You are going to go far. You'll have a kind of success; I believe the kind you want. Not everybody would pay the price in concentrated hard work and human sacrifice you'll make for it though my boy. I'm afraid—for what will be coming to you," he added.

There was no bitterness in this, I could see that a load seemed to have slipped off his mind. He got up. His expression changed. He looked happy again.

I was miserable.

Cecil was something of a prophet.

Cecil went East and, God knows why—never have I seen him since.

That place in the Schiller Building soon seemed nothing at all without him. I had met Robert Spencer, Myron Hunt, and Dwight Perkins. "Dwight" had a loft in his new Steinway Hall building—too large for him. So we formed a group—outer office in common—workrooms screened apart in the loft of Steinway Hall. These young men, newcomers in architectural practice like myself, were my first associates in the so-called "profession" of architecture. George Dean was another and Hugh Garden. Birch Long was a young and talented "renderer" at this time and we took him into the Steinway loft with us.

I went with them to talk at Women's Clubs occasionally until they could all speak the language as well as I. But when they undertook to build, what a difference to me! So I decided to let them do the "speaking" and I would do the building.

About this time came the incipient Arts and Crafts Society at Hull House. And there I read the paper, protestant and yet affirmative—"The Art and Craft of the Machine."[3] Next day there was an editorial in *The Chicago Tribune* commenting on the fact that an artist had said the first word for the use of the Machine as an artist's tool. Jane Addams herself must have written it, I suspect. She sympathized with me as did Julia Lathrop.

But my thesis was overwhelmed by Professors Zueblin and Triggs and the architects and craftsmen present that evening. The Society went "handicraft" and then soon went defunct.

Never have I found support for radical ideas from architects or professors.

But there was nevertheless by now a certain cautious emulation on all sides. Soon it was like seeing one's own features distorted in an imperfect mirror. The emulation disturbed, when it did not anger me. At this time these young architects were all getting the gospel modified through me, never having known Sullivan themselves.

And I should have liked to be allowed to work out the thing I felt in me as architecture with no reflections or refractions or libelous compliments, until I had it all where I felt it really ought to be. But that was not possible. I was out in the open, to stay. Premature as it might be.

To this new Steinway Loft office came Ward Willets as client number one. And I did the stream-line house for him in Highland Park.[4] Others soon followed in this vein which was now really my own.

About this time "Romeo and Juliet," amateur engineering architecture—an idea of structure working out into architectural form—the future in embryo—got itself built.

These creations of ours! I see as we look back upon them, or as we look at them and try to re-create them, how we ourselves belong to them. And because it *was* the engineering-architecture of the future in amateur embryo, here is the tale.

ROMEO AND JULIET

At this time in the Valley were two matriarchal maiden sisters of "Sister Anna," my Aunts Nell and Jane.

Their buildings for the Lloyd Jones Sisters' Hillside Home School for boys and girls were designed by amateur me and built by Aunt Nell and Aunt Jennie in 1887 to mother their forty or fifty boys and girls. This school too, had for banner, or

crest, "Truth against the World." "The Aunts" built their school on the site of Grandfather's old homestead and added several other new buildings. And—the better to guard the development of this beloved school with a high aim, therefore with trouble ahead, its founders made a compact with each other never to marry.

Around about the Hillside Home School farm were the farms of their five patriarchal brothers, my uncles. They always referred to my aunts as "the girls" and with true clan-faithfulness watched over their sisters' educational venture and over them too. Anything "the girls" needed they got, if all the surrounding farms went to rack and ruin. That, at least, was the complaint the wives of some of the brothers used to make. Meantime the brothers were proud of their sisters and of the school. The boys and girls from a dozen or more states called them all "uncle" and the Lloyd-Jones Sisters Aunt Nell and Aunt Jennie no less than the legitimate nephews and nieces—some thirty or more of whom foregathered there to be "educated." Eventually the native nephews and nieces were all "educated" out of the beloved Valley—"by way of learning"—into white-collarites in the big cities.

The school prospered.

When working with architect Silsbee in Chicago and I had made the amateurish plans for the very first school buildings Cramer, the local contractor and "good enough architect too, around there," had built them. But inventing new construction to make itself beautiful as architecture was not a Cramer habit.

Now, a big reservoir on the hill above the school for a new water system had been scooped out in the white sandrock of the hilltop. The reservoir was finished and "the aunts" intended to erect a windmill over it. This was decided upon by the family gathering of the clan usually held to make such decisions concerning the school.

Said Aunt Ellen, or Aunt Nell—the managerial mind of the school: "Why not a pretty windmill tower in keeping with our school building instead of an ugly steel tower or, for that matter, the timber

"Romeo and Juliet." Taliesin, Wisconsin. 1896. FLLW Fdn FA#2501.0764 Photograph by John Amarantides

ones I have seen? I am going to ask Frank for a design."

"Nonsense, Nell," said the preacher-brother Jenkin, there on one of his frequent visits, "a steel tower like all the others is good enough. I never ride my horse in this countryside when I don't welcome the sight of one. They are practical and cheap."

The other brothers thought so too.

Sister Jane, emotional and the warmly humane mind of the school, disagreed with the brothers. She said: "The hill is visible from all over our several valleys. Something should be there to go with the school buildings. I agree with Nell. Let's ask Frank to send us a design."

The "meeting" grumbled. But when Nell put her foot down, all usually gave up quietly. She put her foot down now.

So Uncle James said, "Well, let's see what the boy will do, then."

The design came. A perspective sketch of the tower in the trees on the hill-top was included with the structural details. The sisters liked it and thought it becoming to the dignity of the beloved school.

To the uncles it looked expensive and foolish.

Cramer, builder "and good enough architect too, around there," was called in to take the drawings away with him to make an estimate. The "family" waited in vain for Cramer to come back. So brother James went, several towns away, to look for Cramer. James came back alone. "The brothers" got together to carefully consider the facts Uncle James had learned from Cramer.

"Cramer says it would be wasting time and money to build that tower. Blow down sure as Death and Taxes. Sixty feet high! Fourteen-foot wheel on top of that. Cramer says the thing is just a sort of big octagonal wood pipe, 4 × 4 posts each corner, boards nailed around, inside and outside, to the posts, then shingled all over on the outside. The whole thing is just like a barrel, only the staves run around across instead of up and down. There's a diamond-shaped part cutting into the octagon part, or barrel, to the very center and the outside half of

The Lloyd Jones sisters Jane and Nell, at the time of the building of "Romeo and Juliet." 1896. FLLW Fdn FA#6301.0026

the diamond makes a 'storm prow.' Frank named it 'storm prow' on the plan. The 'storm prow'" . . . laughter "looks like a big blade running up to the very top on the sou-wester side of the barrel. Up the center of this diamond-shaped part runs a big wood post six inches by six inches—runs up and out of the diamond to carry the big mill-wheel at the top. The boy wants a big stone foundation under the whole thing, eight big strap-bolts built into it, the straps to stick up out of the stone six feet alongside the posts, bolted to them.

"Cramer laughed. It looked crazy to him and he said we could tell the girls about it ourselves. Frank wants to try some experiment or other."

Anxious family gathering.

Aunt Nell: "Did Cramer positively say he knew Frank's tower would fall down?"

Uncle James: "Positively."

Uncle Jenkin: "To suppose such a thing could stand up there sixty feet high to carry a fourteen foot wheel in the storms we have in this region, why, Nell, it's nonsense. Trust Cramer. Why build something none of us ever saw the like of in our lives? Nor Frank, either, if I know him."

Aunt Jane: "Poor boy, what a pity his tower won't stand up. How can he know it will? I do not for the life of me see. Dear me! How he will be disappointed."

Aunt Nell said nothing, walked over to the window, and looked up at the hilltop. She may have seen the tower there among the trees, the wheel spinning; who knows? All she said was, "I'll telegraph Frank."

To all this seemed like temporizing with the devil. But there was nothing to do but wait. The telegram—"Cramer says windmill tower sure to fall. Are you sure it will stand? Signed Aunt Nell"—reached the young architect, now on his own in Chicago.

Came back the answer, "Build it."

Consternation now. In peaceful family relationships—war. Aunt Nell's work was cut out for her. It was clear to them all; she was going to build that foolish tower!

"That boy will be the ruination of his aunts."

This conviction settled firmly around there and became a slogan.

Cramer came now, himself, to argue and expostulate.

But with her back to the wall, Aunt Nell said, "Does the boy want to build anything that will fall down any more than we do? He has even more at stake. He says, '*Build it.*' Maybe he knows better than all of us? He would not be so confident unless he had his feet on something in this design."

Said Aunt Jane: "He is never willing to fully explain, but somehow *I do* believe he knows what he is about, after all."

"Cramer," said Aunt Nell, as she turned around to face the practical builder, "how much will it cost to build this tower just as it is planned?"

"Nine hundred and fifty dollars," he said.

"How much would a steel mill cost?"

"Two hundred seventy-five dollars," he said.

"Only six hundred and seventy-five dollars for all that difference," was her unexpected reaction. (This was in the country about 1896.) "Of course we are going to build it."

The anxious committee disbanded.

Dear Aunts Nell and Jane:

Of course you had a hard time with Romeo and Juliet. But you know how troublesome they were centuries ago. The principle they represent still causes mischief in the world because it is so vital. Each is indispensable to the other . . . neither could stand without the other. Romeo, as you will see, will do all the work and Juliet cuddle alongside to support and exhalt him. Romeo takes the side of the blast and Juliet will entertain the school children. Let's let it go at that. No symbol should be taken too far. As for the principle involved, it is a principle but I've never seen it in this form? NO. But I've never seen anything to go against it, either.

Yes, I could explain the way the storm-strains on the harmonious pair will be resolved into one another and be tuned into a pull on the iron straps built deep into the stone foundation. But, after all, for the life of this harmoniously contrasting pair, I am chiefly betting on the nails driven into the boards by the hammers of Cramer et al to fasten them to the upright cornerposts. We'll see that there are enough nails and long enough. Nails are not engineer-

*ing but they are "practice." Of course you will build it. I
will come out.*

Lovingly,
Frank

*N.B. Romeo and Juliet will stand twenty-five years
which is longer than the iron towers stand around there. I
am afraid all of my uncles themselves may be gone before
"Romeo and Juliet." Let's go.*

F.

Cramer, the local builder, good enough architect, too, around there, was sincere in his belief that "the thing" would fall down. "Sixty-foot post to the spring of the wheel," said he, shaking his head. "And a fourteen-foot wheel," he added—really dejected.

"It beats heck," said he, "the way those two old maids dance around after that boy. He comes up here with swell duds on, runs around the hills with the school girls and goes home. You wouldn't think he had a care in the world nor anything but something to laugh at."

"Well. . . ." He finally stopped grumbling and went to work.

Five gray-bearded uncles religiously kept away from the scene of impending disaster.

Two gray-headed, distinguished-looking maiden aunts, between whiles mothering their fifty-seven varieties of boys and girls, climbed to the hilltop, anxiously, to see what was going on.

Timothy, family friend and excellent old Welsh stone-mason, incorrigible in quaint misuse of the word "whateverr," had by now got up the stone foundation. Timothy, alone, gave them comfort. He knew well the aunts liked a good word for their nephew.

"The boys (meaning my uncles) don't know what's in the young man's head, whateverr. They'll be looking to him one of these days . . . whateverr. Could any wooden tower pull that stone foundation over?" And he built the rods in solider and deeper than they were called for . . . a staunch mason, and man too, that Welshman. Yes, and "whateverr."

As the frame went up into the air, the workmen were skittish at first, if the wind came up, and would come down.

But the wheel was finally "shipped" up there in the blue.

The tower swayed in the wind several inches as it should have done, but his "sway" made the men nervous. Some quit for one specious reason or another. It did look very far down to the ground when you were up in the little belvedere—named for Juliet. The tower lifted from the apex of the hill and from up there, you see, you looked all the way down the sides of the hill—vertigo was the consequence of this over-verticality.

I came out, once, to make sure all was going right and the boards were nailed to the corner uprights outside and inside. I knew I could count on Timothy for the anchorage.

It was all simple enough. You see, the wooden tower was rooted as the trees are. Unless *uprooted* it could not fall for it would not break, notwithstanding the "barrel" simile. Try, sometime, to break a barrel.

Romeo and Juliet stood in full view from five farm houses on five brotherly farms and Aunt Jane could see it from her sitting-room window. Several months after it was finished the first real "sou'wester" struck—in the night. As promptly as Aunt Jane's and Aunt Nell's, at sun up, the anxious faces of five gray-bearded farmer brothers all came to as many farm-house doors, shading their eyes to peer over at the new tower. It was still there. The Aunts promptly took their tower to heart—for granted. But the brothers kept on "peering." For "what was one storm, after all." A few years later Uncle Thomas, arch-conservative, died.

But year after year this little drama of unfaith—typical of scepticism directed toward the Idea everywhere on Earth—went on in the beloved valley. Storm after storm swept over. But each storm only left all nearer the conviction that the next must be the last. The uncles would shake their heads doggedly after coming to the door to look at the tower, each storm the tower weathered. Cramer, the builder, "and good enough architect too, around there," died ten years later. The

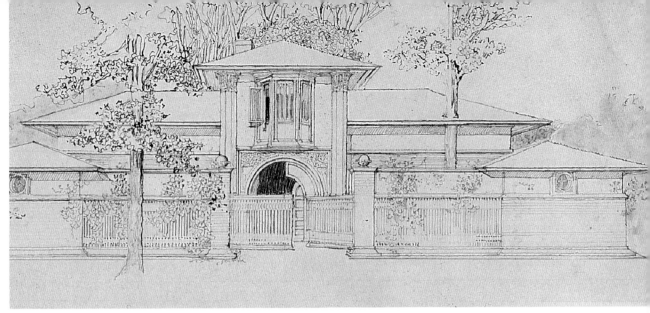

William Winslow Stable. River Forest, Illinois. 1893. Perspective. Sepia ink on art paper, 12 x 5". FLLW Fdn#9305.012

staunch Timothy, stone-mason, followed the builder to that mysterious "whatever" to which, during the English half of his long and simple lifetime, he had made quaint allusion.

Then Uncle James died. Heroic death, his. Three remaining brothers kept vigil. Uncle John, the miller, died some years later. In a few years— some twenty-five after the tower came to stand on the hill—both the Lloyd Jones sisters passed away to rest, their tower still standing. Uncle Philip, archsceptic, soon after moved away to the city, an old, old man. Some years further on, Uncle Jenkin died. But Uncle Enos, Sister Anna's younger brother, alone now, never failed true to the habit of that long vigil, to come to the door after a storm and shading his eyes with his hand peer over at the tower to see what damage it had suffered at last.

Now he too has moved away to the city where he can no longer see the tower.

Had the tower fallen at any time during that period, the unfaith would have found justification and uttered—judgment!

Now nearly thirty-five years have gone by since the windmill tower—"Romeo and Juliet"— took place on the hill in the sun overlooking the beloved Valley. I, the author of its being, hair getting white now as Aunt Nell's when before the tower was built she first walked to the window to see its wheel spinning there among the trees, look

over from Taliesin. Seemingly good as ever, the wooden tower that was an experiment still stands in full view. Shall I take it down, the faithful servant serving so well, so long? Or let it go until it falls just as I myself must do—though neither tower nor I show any signs of doing so. The tower is weather-beaten—my hair is gray. And one never knows. And when it falls, there will be those to say— "Well, there it is—down at last! We thought so!"

But . . . no. Romeo and Juliet shall live to crash down together.

About the time "Romeo and Juliet" came to stand on the hill as "Hillside" work had begun on the Middle Western prairies. The buildings were being built that came later to be known as "The New School of the Middle West."

A contract with the Luxfer Prism Co. of Chicago, as consulting engineer for making prism-glass installations in office buildings throughout the country, had enabled me to build the workroom— I then called it a "studio"—next to the little Oak Park dwelling-place built by means of my contract with Adler and Sullivan.

The old willow tree still stood in the corridor connecting the two buildings. I had succeeded in making the roof around the tree trunks watertight yet in a manner that would permit the tree to grow. The old tree gave us a grateful coolness in the studio in summer. And I liked the golden green mass of the great, sprawling, old willow above the amateurish buildings. If I could have covered the buildings all over with greenery, I would have done so. They were badly overdone.

Here, in this studio, I worked away with various boys and girls, some thirty or more from first to last, to get the houses built that now stand around the prairie and have influenced many of those built North, Northwest, Southwest, and West.

And soon, owing to this proximity to the draughting board, my own little children were all running around with thumbtacks in the soles of their shoes.

At last, my work was alongside my home where it has been ever since. I could work late and tumble into bed. Unable to sleep, because of some idea, I could get up, go downstairs to the "studio" by way of the connecting corridor and work.

As I had gone to and fro between Oak Park and my work with Adler and Sullivan in Chicago, here at hand was the typical American dwelling of the "monogoria" of earlier days standing about on the Chicago prairie. That dwelling got there somehow to become typical. But by any faith in nature, implicit or explicit, it did not belong there. I had seen that in the light of the conception of architecture as natural. And ideas had naturally begun to come as to a more natural house. Each house I built I longed for the chance to build another, and I soon got the chance. I was not the only one sick of hypocrisy and hungry for reality around there, I found.

What was the matter with the kind of house I found on the prairie? Well, now that the "monogoria" of my inexperience has become the clearer vision of experience—let me tell you in more detail.

Just for a beginning let's say, that house *lied* about everything. It had no sense of Unity at all nor any such sense of Space as should belong to a free man among a free people in a free country. It was stuck up however it might be. It was stuck on whatever it happened to be. To take any one of those so-called "homes" away would have improved the landscape and cleared the atmosphere. It was a box, too, that had to be cut full of holes to let in light and

air and an especially ugly one to get in and out of, or else it was a clumsy "gabled" chunk of roofed masonry similarly treated. Otherwise, "joinery" reigned supreme. You know—"Carpenter and Joiner" it used to read on the old signs. The floors were the only part of the house left plain and the housewife then covered those with a tangled rug-collection, because otherwise the floors were "bare"—bare, only because one could not very well walk on jigsawing or turned spindles or plaster-ornament.

It is not too much to say that as an architect my lot in Oak Park was cast with an inebriate lot of sinners hardened by habit against every human significance except one—why mention "the one touch of nature that makes the whole world kin"? And I will venture to say that the aggregation was the worst the world ever saw—at the lowest aesthetic level in all history. Steam heat, plumbing, and electric light were its only redeeming features.

The first feeling therefore had been for a new simplicity. A new sense of simplicity as "organic" had barely begun to take shape in my mind when the Winslow house was planned. But now it began in practice. Organic simplicity might be seen producing significant character in the harmonious order we call nature. All around was beauty in growing things. None were insignificant.

I loved the prairie by instinct as a great simplicity—the trees, the flowers, the sky itself, thrilling by contrast.

I saw that a little of height on the prairie was enough to look like much more—every detail as to height becoming intensely significant, breadths all falling short. Here was a tremendous spaciousness, but all sacrificed needlessly. All "space" was cut up crosswise and cut up lengthwise into the fifty-foot "lot"—or would you have twenty-five feet less or twenty-five feet more? Salesmanship cut and parceled it out and sold it with no restrictions. In a great, new, free country there was then, everywhere, a characteristic tendency to "huddle" and in consequence a mean tendency to tip everything in the way of human habitation up edgewise, instead of letting it lie comfortably and naturally flatwise with the ground. Nor has this changed, much, since automobilization made it stupid as an economic

AN AUTOBIOGRAPHY: BOOK TWO

measure and criminal as a social habit. I had an idea that the horizontal planes in buildings, those planes parallel to earth, identify themselves with the ground—make the building belong to the ground. I began putting this idea to work.

The buildings standing around there on the Chicago prairies were all tall and all tight. Chimneys were lean and taller still—sooty fingers threatening the sky. And beside them, sticking up almost as high, were the dormers.

Dormers were elaborate devices—cunning little buildings complete in themselves—stuck on to the main roof-slopes to let "help" poke heads out of the attic for air.

Invariably the damp, sticky clay of the prairie was dug out for a basement under the whole house, and the rubble stone-walls of this dank basement always stuck above the ground a foot or several—and blinked, with half-windows.

So the universal "cellar" showed itself above ground as a bank of some kind of masonry running around the whole house, for the house to sit up on—like a chair. The lean upper house-walls of the usual two floors above this stone or brick basement were wood and set up on top of this masonry chair. The wood walls were clapboarded and painted, or else shingled and stained. Preferably house walls were both sided and shingled and mixed, up and down, together or with moldings crosswise. These over-dressed wood house walls had cut in them or cut out of them, to be precise, big holes for the big cat and little holes for the little cat to get in or get out. Or for ulterior purposes of light and air. These house walls were be-corniced or bracketed up at the top into the tall, purposely, profusely complicated roof, dormers plus. The whole roof as well as the roof as a whole was ridged and tipped, swanked and gabled to madness before they would allow it to be either watershed or shelter. The whole exterior was bedeviled, that is to say, mixed to puzzle-pieces, with corner-boards, panel-boards, window-frames, corner-blocks, plinth-blocks, rosettes, fantails, ingenious and jigger work in general. This was the only way "they" seemed to have, then, of "putting on style." The scroll-saw and turning lathe were at that moment the honest means to this

fashionable mongering by the wood-butcher and to this entirely moral end.

Unless the householders of the period were poor indeed, usually the ingenious corner tower as seen in the monogoria eventuated into a candle-snuffer dome, a spire, an inverted rutabaga or radish or onion—or what is your favorite vegetable? Always elaborate bay-windows and fancy porches rallied "ring a round a rosie"—this imaginative corner fetish. And all this fetish the builders of the period could do, nearly as well, in brick or stone.

It was an impartial society. All materials looked pretty much alike to it in that day.

Simplicity was as far from all this scrap-pile as the pandemonium of the barnyard is far from music. But it was all easy enough for the architect. All he had to do was to call, "Boy, take down No. 37, and put a bay-window on it for the lady."

BUILDING THE NEW HOUSE

The first thing to do in building the new house was to get rid of the attic and therefore of the dormer, get rid of the useless "heights" below it. Next, get rid of the unwholesome basement, entirely, yes absolutely—in any house built on the prairie. Instead of lean, brick chimneys, bristling up everywhere to hint at "Judgment" from steep roofs, I could see necessity for one chimney only. A broad generous one, or at most, two, these kept low-down on gently sloping roofs or perhaps flat roofs. The big fireplace in the house below became now a place for a real fire, and justified the great size of this chimney outside. A real fireplace at that time was extraordinary. There were mantels instead. A "mantel" was a marble frame for a few coals. Or it was a piece of wooden furniture with tile stuck in it around a "grate," the whole set slam up against the wall. An insult to comfort. So the *integral* fireplace became an important part of the building itself in the houses I was allowed to build out there on the prairie.

Comforting to see the fire burning deep in the masonry of the house itself.

Taking a human being for my "scale" I brought the whole house down in height to fit a normal one—ergo, 5' 8" tall, say. Believing in no other scale than the human being I broadened the mass out all I possibly could, brought it down into spaciousness. It has been said that were I three inches taller (I am 5' 8½" tall) all my houses would have been quite different in proportion. Perhaps.

House walls were now to be started at the ground on a cement or stone water-table that looked like a low platform under the building, and usually was. But the house walls were stopped at the second-story window sill level, to let the bedrooms come through above in a continuous window-series under the broad eaves of a gently sloping, overhanging roof. For in this new house the wall as an impediment to outside light and air and beauty was beginning to go. The old wall had been a part of the box in which only a limited number of holes were to be punched. It was still this conception of a wall which was with me when I designed the Winslow house. But after that my conception began to change.

My sense of wall was not a side of a box. It was enclosure to afford protection against storm or heat when this was needed. But it was also increasingly to bring the outside world into the house, and let the inside of the house go outside. In this sense I was working toward the elimination of the wall as a wall to reach the function of a screen, as a means of opening up space, which, as control of building materials improved, would finally permit the free use of the whole space without affecting the soundness of structure.

The climate being what it was, violent in extremes of heat and cold, damp and dry, dark and bright, I gave broad protecting roof-shelter to the whole, getting back to the original purpose for which the cornice was designed. The underside of the roof-projections was flat and light in color to create a glow of reflected light that made upper rooms not dark, but delightful. The overhangs had double value: shelter and preservation for the walls of the house as well as diffusion of reflected light for the upper story, through the "light screens" that took the place of the walls and were the windows.

And at this time I saw a house primarily as liveable interior space under ample shelter. I liked the sense of "shelter" in the look of the building. I still like it.

Then I went after the popular abuses. Eliminated odds and ends in favor of one material and a single surface as a flat plane from grade to eaves. I treated these flat planes usually as simple enclosing screens or else I again made a plain band around the second story above the window sills turned up over onto the ceiling beneath the eaves. This screen band would be of the same material as the underside of the eaves themselves, or what architects call the "soffitt."

The planes of the building parallel to the ground were all stressed—I liked to "stress" them—to grip the whole to Earth. This parallel plane I called, from the beginning—the plane of the third dimension. The term came naturally enough: really a spiritual interpretation of that dimension.

Sometimes I was able to make the enclosing wall screen below this upper band of the second story—from the second story window sill clear down to the ground, a heavy "wainscot" of fine masonry material resting on the cement or stone "platform" laid on the foundation. I liked the luxury of masonry material, when my clients felt they could afford it.

As a matter of form, too, I liked to see the projecting base or water-table of masonry set out over the foundation walls themselves, as a substantial "visible" preparation for the building. I managed this by setting the studs of the walls to the inside of the foundation walls, instead of to the outside.

All door and window tops were now brought into line with each other with only comfortable head clearance for the average human being.

Eliminating the sufferers from the "attic" enabled the roof to lie low.

The house began to associate with the ground and become natural to its prairie site.

And would the young man in Architecture believe that this was all "new" then? Yes—not only new, but it was all destructive heresy—or ridiculous eccentricity. Stranger still all somewhat so today. But then it was all so *new* that what prospect I had of ever earning a livelihood by making houses was nearly wrecked. At first, "they" called the houses

William Winslow Stable. River Forest, Illinois. 1893. Perspective. Sepia ink on art paper, 12 x 5". FLLW Fdn#9305.012

"dress reform" houses, because Society was just then excited about that particular "reform." This simplification looked like some kind of "reform" to the provincials.

Oh, they called the new houses all sort of names that can not be repeated, but "they" never found a better term for the work unless it was "horizontal Gothic," "temperance Architecture" (with a sneer), etc., etc. I don't know how I escaped the accusation of another "Renaissance-Japanese" or "Bhutanese" from my complimentary academic contemporaries. Eclectics can imagine only eclecticism.

What I have just described was all on the *outside* of the house. But it was there, chiefly, because of what had happened *inside*.

Dwellings of that period were cut up, advisedly and completely, with the grim determination that should go with any "cutting" process. The "interiors" consisted of boxes beside boxes or inside boxes, called *rooms*. All boxes were inside a complicated outside boxing. Each domestic "function" was properly box to box.

I could see little sense in this inhibition, this cellular sequestration that implied ancestors familiar with penal institutions, except for the privacy of bedrooms on the upper floor. They were perhaps all right as "sleeping boxes."

So I declared the whole lower floor as one room, cutting off the kitchen as a laboratory, putting the servants' sleeping and living quarters next to the kitchen but semi-detached, on the ground floor. Then I screened various portions of the big room for certain domestic purposes, like dining or reading—receiving callers.

There were no plans in existence like these at the time, but my clients were pushed toward these ideas as helpful to a solution of the vexed servant problem. Scores of unnecessary doors disappeared and no end of partition. Both clients and servants liked the new freedom. The house became more free as "space" and more liveable too. Interior spaciousness began to dawn.

Thus an end to the cluttered house. Fewer doors; fewer window holes, though much greater window area; windows and doors lowered to convenient human heights. These changes made, the ceilings of the rooms could be brought down over on to the walls, by way of the horizontal broad bands of plaster on the walls themselves above the windows, colored the same as the room-ceilings. This would bring the ceiling-surface and color down to the very window tops. The ceilings thus expanded by way of the wall band above the windows gave generous overhead to even the small rooms.

The sense of the whole was broadened, made plastic, too, by this means.

Here entered the important new element of plasticity—as I saw it. And I saw it as indispensable element to the successful use of the machine. The windows would sometimes be wrapped around the building corners as emphasis of plasticity and sense of interior space. I fought for outswinging windows because the casement window associated the house with the out-of-doors, gave free openings, outward. In other words the so-called "casement" was simple, more human in use and effect, so more natural. If it had not existed I should have invented it. But it was not used at that time in the United States so I lost many clients because I insisted upon it. The client usually wanted the "guillotine" or "double hung" window in use then. The guillotine was neither simple nor human. It was only expedient. I used it once in the Winslow house and rejected it thereafter forever. Nor at that time did I entirely eliminate the wooden trim. I did make it "plastic," that is to say, light and continuously flowing instead of the prevailing heavy "cut and butt" carpenter work. No longer did "trim," so-called, look like "carpenter work." The machine could do it all perfectly well as I laid it out, in the search for "quiet." This plastic trim, too, enabled poor workmanship to be concealed. There was need of that trim to conceal much in the way of craftsmanship because machines versus the Union had already demoralized the workmen.

The machine-resources of the period were so little understood that extensive drawings had to be made merely to show the mill-man what to leave off. But finally the trim thus became only a single, flat, narrow horizontal band running around the room walls at the top of the windows and doors and another one at the floors. Both were connected with narrow vertical thin wood bands that were used to divide the wall-surfaces of the whole room

smoothly and flatly into color planes folded about the corners—exterior corners or interior corners—and the trim merely completed the window and door openings in this same plastic sense. When the handling of the interior had thus become wholly plastic instead of structural—a new element, as I have already said, had entered the prairie house architecture. Strangely enough an element that had not existed in architecture before, if architectural history is to be credited. Not alone in the trim but in numerous ways too tedious to describe in words, this revolutionary sense of the *plastic* whole, began to work more and more intelligently and have fascinating unforeseen consequences. Here was something that began to organize itself. When several houses had been finished, compared with the house of the period there was very little of that house left standing. But that little was left standing up very high indeed. Nearly everyone had endured the house of the period as long as possible, judging by the appreciation of the change. Now all this probably tedious description is intended to indicate in bare outline how thus early there was an Ideal of organic Simplicity put to work, with historical consequences, in this country.

Let me now put all this in clear outline for you. The main motives and inclinations were—and I enjoyed them all . . . and still enjoy them—

First . . . to reduce the number of necessary parts of the house or the separate rooms to a minimum, and make all come together as free space—so subdivided that light, air, and vista permeated the whole with a sense of unity.

Second . . . to associate the building as whole with its site by extension and emphasis of the planes parallel to the ground, but keeping the floors off from the best part of the site, thus leaving that better part for use in connection with the use of the house. Extended level planes or long narrow levels were found useful in this connection.

Third . . . to eliminate the rooms as boxes and the house itself as another boxing of the boxes, making all walls enclosing screens; ceilings and floors to flow the enclosing screens as one large enclosure of space, with minor or subordinate subdivisions only. And also to make all proportions more liberally human, eliminate waste space in structure, and make structure more appropriate to materi-

al. The whole made more sensible and liveable. Liberal *is the best word. Extended straight lines or stream lines were useful in this.*

Fourth . . . to get the unwholesome basement up out of the ground, entirely above it, as a low pedestal for the living portion of the home, making the foundation itself visible as a low masonry platform on the ground on which the building would stand.

Fifth . . . to harmonize all necessary openings to outside or inside with good human proportions and make them occur naturally, singly or in series, in the scheme of the whole building. Usually they now appeared as light screens—usually turning the corners—instead of walls, because chiefly the architecture of the house was expressed in the way these openings happened to such walls as were grouped about the rooms anyway. The room *was now the essential architectural expression. And there were to be no holes cut in walls anywhere or anyhow as holes are cut in a box, because this was not in keeping with the ideal of "plastic." Cutting holes was violence.*

I saw that the insensate, characterless flat surface, cut sheer, had geometric possibilities . . . but it has, also, the limitations of bare geometry. Such negation in itself is sometimes restful and continually useful—as a foil—but not as the side of a box.

Sixth . . . to eliminate combinations of different materials in favor of mono-material so far as possible, and to use no ornament that did not come out of the nature of materials or construction to make the whole building clearer and more expressive as a place to live in and give the conception of the building appropriate revealing emphasis. Geometrical or straight lines were natural to the machinery at work in the building trades then, so the interiors took on this rectilinear character naturally.

Seventh . . . to so incorporate all heating, lighting, plumbing that these mechanical systems became constituent parts of the building itself. These service features became architectural features. In this attempt the ideal of an organic architecture was at work.

Eighth . . . to incorporate as organic architecture, so far as possible, furnishings, making them all one with the building, designing the equipment in simple terms for machine-work. Again straight lines and rectilinear forms. Geometrical.

Ninth . . . eliminate the decorator. He was all "appliqué" and efflorescence, if not all "period." Inorganic.

This was all rational so far as the thought of an organic architecture went. The particular forms this thought took in the feeling of it all could only be personal to myself. There was nothing whatever at this time to help make them what they were.

But, all this seemed to me the most natural thing in the world and grew up out of the circumstances of the moment.

What the ultimate "forms" may be worth in the long run is all they are worth.

Now simplicity—organic Simplicity—in this early constructive effort, I soon found to be a matter of the sympathy with which such co-ordination might be effected. Plainness was not necessarily simplicity. That was evident. Crude furniture of the Roycroft-Stickley-Mission style, which came along later, was offensively plain, plain as a barn door—but never simple in any true sense. Nor, I found, were merely machine-made things in themselves necessarily simple. To "think," as the Master used to say, "is to deal in simples." And that means with an eye single to the altogether. This, I believe, is the single secret of simplicity: that we may truly regard nothing at all as simple in itself. I believe that no one thing in itself is ever so, but must achieve simplicity—as an Artist should use the term—as a perfectly realized part of some organic whole. Only as a feature or any part becomes harmonious element in the harmonious whole does it arrive at the state of simplicity. Any wild flower is truly simple, but double the same wild flower by cultivation, it ceases to be so. The scheme of the original is no longer clear. Clarity of design and perfect significance both are first essentials of the spontaneous born simplicity of the lilies of the field. "They toil not, neither do they spin." As contrasted with Solomon who "toiled and spun" and who, no doubt had put on himself and had put on his temple properly "composed" everything in the category of good things but the cook-stove. Solomon in his day was probably "fundamentalist" in his architecture—that is to say, "by book." He had "tastes" and may have been something of a functioneer.

SIMPLICITY

Five lines where three are enough is stupidity.

Nine pounds where three are sufficient is obesity. But to eliminate expressive words in speaking or writing—words that intensify or vivify meaning is not simplicity. Nor is similar elimination in architecture simplicity. It may be, or usually is, stupidity.

In architecture, expressive changes of surface, emphasis of line, and especially textures of material or imaginative pattern may go to make facts more eloquent—forms more significant.

Elimination, therefore, may be just as meaningless as elaboration, perhaps more often is so.

To know what to leave out and what to put in; just where and just how, ah, *that* is to have been educated in knowledge of SIMPLICITY—toward ultimate Freedom of Expression.

As for objects of art in the house—even in that early day they were "bêtes noires" of the new simplicity. If well chosen—well enough in the house, but only if each were properly "digested" by the whole. Antique or modern sculpture, paintings, pottery, might well enough become objectives in the architectural scheme, and I accepted them, aimed at them, assimilated them often. Such pre-cious things may take their places as elements in the design of any house, gracious and good to live with. But such assimilation is difficult. Better to design all as integral features.

I tried to make my clients see that furniture and furnishings not built in as integral features of the building should be designed as attributes of whatever furniture *was* built in and should be seen as a minor part of the building itself even if detached or kept aside to be employed on occasion.

But when the building itself was finished the old furniture they already possessed usually went in with the clients to await the time when the interior might be completed in this sense. Very few of the houses, therefore, were anything but painful to me after the clients moved in and, helplessly, dragged the horrors of the Old Order along after them.

Soon I found it difficult, anyway, to make some of the furniture in the "abstract." That is, to design it as architecture and make it "human" at the same time—fit for human use. I have been black and blue in some spot, somewhere almost all my life from too intimate contact with my own early furniture.

Human beings must group, sit, or recline, confound them—and they must dine, but dining is

Victor Metzger House (Project). Desbarats, Canada. 1902. Perspective. Watercolor on art paper, 39 x10". FLLW Fdn#0209.002

Remodeling for the C. Thaxter Shaw House. Montreal, Canada. 1906. Perspective. Watercolor on art paper, 15 x 8".
FLLW Fdn#0610.007

much easier to manage and always was a great artistic opportunity. But arrangements for the informality of sitting in comfort singly or in groups still belonging in disarray to the scheme as a whole: *that* is a matter difficult to accomplish.

But it can be done now and should be done because only those attributes of human comfort and convenience should be in order which belong to the whole in this integrated sense. About three-fifths of the contents of nearly every home could be given away with good effect to that home. But the things given away might go on to poison some other home. So why not destroy, at once, these undesirable things?

Human use and comfort should not be taxed to pay dividends on any "designer's" idiosyncrasy.

Human use and comfort should have intimate possession of every interior . . . should be felt in every exterior.

Decoration is intended to make Use more charming and Comfort more appropriate or a privilege has been abused.

As these Ideals worked away from house to house, finally freedom of floorspace and elimination of useless heights worked a miracle in the new dwelling place. A sense of appropriate freedom had changed its whole aspect. The whole became different, but more fit for human habitation, and more natural for its site.

It was impossible to imagine a house once built on these principles somewhere else. An entirely new sense of space values in architecture came home. Architecture taking the road to Freedom.

It now appears these new values came into the

architecture of the world. New sense of repose in quiet streamline effects arrived. The streamline and the plain surface seen as the flat plane, had then and there some thirty years ago, found their way into buildings as we see them in steamships, aeroplanes, and motorcars, although still intimately related to building materials, environment, and the human being.

But, more important than all beside, still rising to greater dignity as an idea as it goes on working, was the ideal of plasticity. That ideal now began to emerge as a means to achieve an organic architecture. (Plasticity may be seen in the expressive flesh-covering of the skeleton as contrasted with the articulation of the skeleton itself.) If "form" really "followed function"—as the Master declared[5]—here was direct means of expression to that end. The only true means I could see then or can see now to eliminate the separation and complication of joinery in favor of the flow of expressive continuous surface. Here—by instinct at first all ideas germinate—a principle entered into building that has since gone around the world. In my work this idea of plasticity may now be seen as "continuity."

In architecture, plasticity is the expression of a thought. The thought taken into structure throughout, will re-create in a badly "jointed," distracted world the entire fabric of human society. This magic word "plastic" was a word that *Lieber Meister*, Louis Sullivan, was himself fond of using in reference to his idea of ornamentation, as distinguished from all other, or applied ornament. But now, why not the larger application in the structure of the building itself in this sense?

Why a principle working in the part if not living in the whole?

If form really followed function—it did by means of this ideal of plasticity—why not throw away the implications of post or upright and beam or horizontal entirely? Have no beams or columns piling up as "joinery." Nor any cornices. Nor any "features" as *fixtures*. No. Have no appliances of any kind at all, such as pilasters, entablatures, and cornices. Nor put into the building any fixtures whatsoever as "fixtures." Eliminate the separations and separate joints. Classic architecture was fixation-of-the-fixture. Entirely so. Now why not let walls, ceilings, floors become *seen* as component parts of each other, their surfaces flowing into each other to get continuity in the whole, eliminating all constructed features just as Louis Sullivan had eliminated background in his ornament in favor of an integral sense of the whole. Here an ideal began to have consequences. Conceive now that an entire building might grow up out of conditions as a plant grows up out of soil, as free to be itself, to "live its own life according to Nature" as is the tree. Dignified as a tree in the midst of nature.

A CULTURAL IDEAL

I now propose that ideal for the architecture of the machine age, for the ideal "American" building. Grow up in that image. The TREE.

But here is pure appeal to the imagination for I do not mean to suggest the imitation of the tree.

PLASTICITY

Proceeding, then, step by step from generals to particulars, plasticity as a large means in architecture began to grip me, and work its own will. I would watch its sequences fascinated, seeing other sequences in those consequences already in evidence: the Heurtley, Martin, Heath, Thomas, Tomek, Coonley, and dozens of other houses.

The old architecture, so far as its grammar went, began literally to disappear.

As if by magic new architectural effects came to life—effects genuinely new in the whole cycle of architecture owing simply to the working of this principle. Vistas of inevitable simplicity and ineffable harmonies would open, so beautiful to me that I was not only delighted, but often startled. Yes, sometimes amazed.

I have since concentrated on plasticity as physical continuity, using it as a practical working principle within the very nature of the building itself in the effort to accomplish this great thing called architecture.

Every true aesthetic is an implication of nature, so it was inevitable that this aesthetic ideal should be found to enter into the actual building of the building itself.

But later on I found that actually to eliminate the post and beam, as such, in favor of structural continuity, that is to say, making the two things one thing instead of allowing them to remain two separate things, I could get no help from engineers. By habit, the engineer reduced everything in the field of calculation to the post and the beam resting upon it before he could calculate and tell you where and just how much for either. Walls that were made one with floors and ceilings all merging together and reacting upon each other, the engineer had never met, and the engineer has not yet enough scientific formulae to enable him to calculate for such continuity. Floor slabs stiffened and extended as cantilevers over centered supports, as a waiter's tray rests on his upturned fingers, such as I now began to use in order to get planes parallel to the earth to emphasize the third dimension, were new, as I used them, but the engineer soon mastered this element of continuity in the floor slabs, with such formulae as he had. The cantilever became a new feature of design in architecture. As used in the Imperial Hotel at Tokio it was one of the features of construction that insured the life of that building in the terrific temblor of 1922.⁶ So, not only a new aesthetic but, proving the aesthetic as sound, a great new economic, scientific "stability" derived from steel in tension was now to enter into building construction. As a further scientific sequence of the aesthetic ideal of plasticity I perceive from recent laboratory experiments made at Princeton by Professor Beggs that the aesthetic or artistic ideal of plasticity is valuable, practical means to be put to work as "continuity" in building-construction itself. Thus I find further proof of the validity of the aesthetic ideal which I had already felt and employed in Architecture at this much earlier time. Soon experiments will make available the necessary formulae. And structural continuity working as the physical body of continuity in building design, will be new, invaluable economy, stablizing construction itself. Just as welding instead of riveting steel is also new means to that same end. But all this is getting too far ahead of our story.

THE NATURE OF MATERIALS

From this early ideal of plasticity another ideal came. To be consistent in practice, or indeed if as a principle it was to work out in the field at all, I found that plasticity must have a new sense as well as a science of materials.

The greatest of the materials, steel, glass, ferro or armored concrete, were new. Had they existed in the ancient order we would never have had anything at all like "classic architecture."

And it may interest you, as it astonished me, to learn that there is nothing in the literature of the civilized world on the nature of materials in this sense. So I began to study the nature of materials, learning to "see" them. I now began to learn to see brick as brick, learned to see wood as wood, and to see concrete or glass or metal each for itself and all as themselves. Strange to say, this required great concentration of imagination. Each material demanded different handling and had possibilities of use peculiar to its own nature. Appropriate designs for one material would not be appropriate at all for another material. At least, not in the light of this ideal of simplicity as *organic plasticity*. Of course, as I could now see, there could be no organic architecture where the nature of materials was ignored or misunderstood. How could there be? Perfect co-relation is the first principle of growth. Integration, or even the very word "organic" itself, means that nothing is of value except as it is naturally related to the whole in the direction of some living purpose. My old Master had designed for the old materials all alike; brick, stone, wood, iron wrought or iron cast or plaster—all were grist for his rich imagination with his sentient ornamentation.

To him all materials were only one material in which to weave the stuff of his dreams. I still remember being ashamed of the delight I at first took in thus seeing—thanks to him, too—so plainly around the beloved Master's own practice. But *acting* upon this new train of ideals brought work sharply up against the tools I could find to get the ideas into practical form. What were the tools in use everywhere? Machines—automatic, many of them. Stone- or wood-planers, molding shapers, various lathes, and power-saws, all in commercialized organized mills. Sheet-metal breakers, gigantic presses, shears, molding and stamping machines in the sheet-metal industry, commercialized in "shops." Foundries and rolling-mills turned out cast-iron and steel in any imaginable shape. The Machine as such had not seemed to interest Louis Sullivan. Perhaps he took it for granted. But what a resource, now, that rolling or drawing or extruding of metal. And more confusion to the old order, concrete-mixers, form-makers, clay-bakers, casters, glass-makers, all organized in trades unions.

The unions themselves were all units in a more or less highly commercialized union in which craftsmanship had no place except as survival-for-burial: standardization already become inflexible necessity. Standardization was either enemy or friend to the architect. He might choose but, I felt, as he chose he became master and useful or he became a luxury and eventually a parasite. Although not realized then, at all, nor yet completely realized by the architect, machine standardization had already taken the life of handicraft in all its expressions. But for this outworn expression as it appeared in our country as pseudo-classic architecture I had never had any respect and my old Master had less

than none. Academic architecture had not troubled me much either before or after I had met him. But the new architecture as an expression of the new order of the machine did begin now to trouble me. If I was to realize new buildings I should have to have new technique. I should have to so design the buildings that they would not only be appropriate to materials, but so the machine that would *have* to make them could make them surpassingly well. But with this ideal of integral order now supreme in mind I would have done nothing less than this, even could I have commanded armies of craftsmen. Because, by now, I had come under the discipline of a great ideal. There is no discipline so severe as the perfect integration of true co-relation in any endeavor. But there is no discipline that yields such rich rewards in work, nor any discipline so safe and sure of results. Why should human relations be excepted?

The straight line, the flat plane were limitations until proved benefits by the machine. But steel-in-tension was clearly liberation: steel, the spider. Set the spider spinning his web, to enmesh glass, the perfect clarity to protect internal space.

Lesser ideas flew in flocks, like birds from this

Darwin D. Martin House. Buffalo, New York. 1904. FLLW Fdn FA#0405.0025. Photograph by John Reed

fertile central ideal—flying always in the same direction—but further on each occasion for flight until great goals were in sight.

But before telling you about the goals now in sight, some of the reactions to this endeavor, as I met them along the road to Freedom, new thirty years ago but now called modern, might be interesting.

REACTIONS

After the Winslow house was built in 1893 and Mr. Moore did not want a house so "different" that he would have to go down the back way to his morning train to avoid being laughed at, our bulkheads of caution—blindly serving Yesterday—our bankers, at first refused to loan money on the houses. Friends had to be found to finance the early buildings. When the plans were presented for estimates, soon mill-men would look for the name on them, read the name and roll the drawings up again, hand them back to the contractor with the remark—they were "not hunting for trouble." Contractors often failed to read the plans correctly. The plans were so radically "different" simply because so much nonsense had to be "left off" the building. Numbers of small men "went broke" trying to carry out their contracts. This made trouble. Fools would come walking in where angels were afraid to tread and we had the worst of the contracting element to deal with. The clients usually "stood by," excited, often interested beyond their means. So when they "moved in" they had to take their old furniture in with them. This was tragedy, because the ideal of an "organic simplicity" seen as the countenance of perfect integration, abolished all fixtures, rejected all superficial decoration, made all lighting and heating apparatus architectural features of the house. So far as possible all furniture too was to be designed by the architect in place as a natural part of the whole building. Hangings, rugs, carpets—all came into the same category. So this particular feature—gone wrong—often crippled results, made trouble. Nor was there any planting to be done about the house without co-operating with the architect. This made trouble. No sculptures, no painting unless co-operating with the architect.

This made trouble. Decorators hunting a job would visit the owners, learn the name of the architect, lift their hats with exaggerated courtesy and turning on their heels leave with a curt and sarcastic "Good Day"—meaning really what the slang "Good Night" meant some time ago. The owners of the houses were all subjected to curiosity. Sometimes to admiration. More often they submitted to the ridicule of the middle-of-the-road egotist.

Each new building was a new experience. A different choice of materials would mean a different scheme altogether. Concrete was just then coming into use. Unity Temple at Oak Park became the first concrete monolith in the world. That is, the first total building designed for and completed in the wooden forms into which it was poured as concrete. Even plastered houses were then new. Casement windows nowhere to be seen. So many things were new. Nearly everything, in fact, but the law of gravitation and the personal idiosyncrasy of the client.

The Larkin Building and the Buffalo dwellings of D. D. Martin and W. R. Heath soon came to the Oak Park Workshop.

THE PROTESTANT

The Larkin Building was the first emphatic protest in architecture—yes—it was the first emphatic outstanding protestant against the tide of meaningless elaboration sweeping the United States, as Uncle Dan, calling it a different name, had prophesied it would. The United States were being swept into one grand rubbish heap of the styles so far as creating an architecture was concerned.

The Larkin Administration Building[7] was a simple cliff of brick hermetically sealed to keep the interior space clear of the poisonous gases in the smoke from the trains that puffed along beside it.

It is perhaps tedious to go into details of this structure here. The story of the Larkin Building might well take its place beside the others but that story is already so many times written in the various architectural books and journals of Europe as well as in our own country that there is no need to write it again.

It is enough to say that, in masonry material—brick and stone—the Larkin Administration Building in terms of the straight line and the flat plane was a genuine expression of power directly applied to purpose in architecture in the sense that the liner, the plane, or the car is so. And fair to say that it had profound influence upon European architecture for this reason.

The character as well as the opportunity for beauty of our own age were both coming clear to me at that time. In fact I saw then as now that they are one. I saw our own great chance in this sense still going to waste on every side. Rebellious and protestant as I was myself when the Larkin Building came to me, I was conscious also that the only way to succeed as either rebel or protestant was to make architecture genuine and constructive affirmation of the new Order of the Machine Age. And I worked to get that something into the Larkin Building, interested now also in the principle of *articulation* as related to that Order. But not until the contract had been let to Paul Mueller[8] and the plaster-model of the building stood completed on the big detail board at the center of the Oak Park draughting room did I get the articulation I finally wanted. The solution that hung fire came in a flash. And I took the next train to Buffalo to try and get the Larkin Company to see that it was worth thirty thousand dollars more to build the stair towers free of the central block, not only as independent stair towers for communication and escape, but also as air intakes for the ventilating system. It would require this sum to individualize and properly articulate these features as I saw them.

Mr. Larkin, a kind and generous man, granted the appropriation and the building as architecture, I felt, was saved.

This entire building was a great fire-proof vault: probably the first really fire-proof building. All the furniture was made in steel and built into place—even the desks and chairs. The wastepaper baskets were omitted. I never had a chance to incorporate them later—or design the telephone I had in mind as the office had already arranged for both.

Magnesite was a new material then. We experimented with it—and finally used it—throughout the interior. And I made many new inventions. The hanging partition. The automatic chair-desk. The wall water closet were several among them. All were intended to simplify cleaning and make operation easy. The new architecture was practical or it was only another sentimentality, to further demoralize the country.

The top-lighted interior created the effect of a great official family at work in day-lit, clean airy quarters, officered from the central court. The top-story was a restaurant and conservatory, the ferns and flowers seen from below. The roof was a recreation ground paved with brick.

The officers appreciated the building in practice but it was too severe for the "fundamentalist" tastes of the Larkin family. They were distracted, too, I imagine by so many *experiments,* some of which delayed the completion of the building. A few minor failures annoyed them—and made them think the whole might be, queer?

They never realized the place their building took in the thought of the world—for they never hesitated to make senseless changes in it in after years. To them it was just one of their factory buildings—to be treated like the others. And I suppose from any standpoint available to them, that was all it was. In architecture they were still voluntary pall-bearers for the remains of Thomas Jefferson.

Now Unity Temple came into the studio at Oak Park—let us again say workshop instead of studio.

Several invitations to submit work in competition had come in by this time. But no matter how promising the programme nor how many promises were made, I steadily refused to enter a competition. I have refused ever since.

COMPETITIONS

The world has gained no building worth having by competition because: (1) The jury itself is necessarily a hand-picked average. Some "constituency" must agree upon the "jury." (2) Therefore the first thing this average does as a jury, when "picked" is to go through all the designs and throw out the best ones and the worst ones. This is necessary in order that the average may average upon something average. (3) Therefore any architectural competition will be an average upon an average by averages in behalf of the average. (4) The net result is a building well behind the times before it is begun to be built.

This might seem democratic if mediocrity is the democratic ideal in architecture. No. Competitions are only opportunity for inexperienced Youth to air their proficiency with the "project."

Moreover, to further vitiate the objective every architect entering any competition does so to win the prize. So he sensibly aims his efforts at what he conceives to be the common prejudices and predilections of the "jury."

Invariably the man who does this most accurately wins the competition.

A competition was first thought of for Unity Temple, but the idea abandoned and the commission given to me after much debate among the committee.

Committee decisions, too, are seldom above mediocre unless the committee is "run" by some strong individual. In this case the committee was so "run" by Charles E. Roberts—inventor. He was the strong man in this instance or Unity Temple would never have been built.

Let us take Unity Temple to pieces in the thought of its architect and see how it came to be the Unity Temple you now see.

DESIGNING UNITY TEMPLE

Had Doctor Johonnot, the Universalist pastor of Unity Church, been Fra Junipero the "style" of Unity Temple would have been predetermined. Had he been Father Latour it would have been Midi-Romanesque. Yes, and perhaps being what he was, he was entitled to the only tradition he knew—that of the little white New England Church, lean spire pointing to heaven—"back East." If sentimentality were sense this might be so.

Unity Temple (interior). Oak Park, Illinois. 1904. FLLW Fdn FA#0611.0016

But the pastor was out of luck. Circumstances brought him to yield himself up "in the cause of architecture." The straight line and the flat plane were to emerge as the cantilever slab.

And to that cause everyone who undertakes to read what follows is called upon to yield. It should only be read after studying the plans and perspective of Unity Temple. Constant reference to the plan will be necessary if the matter is to come clear.

Our building committee were all "good men and true." One of them, Charles E. Roberts, a mechanical engineer and inventor, enlightened in creation.

One, enlightened, is leaven enough in any Usonian lump. The struggle . . . it is always a struggle in architecture for the architect where "good men and true" are concerned—began.

First came the philosophy of the building.

Human sensibilities are the strings of the instrument upon which the true artist plays . . . "abstract". . . ? But why not avoid the symbol, as such? The symbol is too literal. It is become a form of Literature in the Arts.

Let us abolish, in the art and craft of architecture, literature in any "symbolic" form whatsoever. The sense of inner rhythm, deep planted in human sensibility, lives far above other considerations in Art.

Then why the steeple of the little white church? Why *point* to heaven?

I told the committee a story. Did they not know the tale of the holy man who, yearning to see God, climbed up and up the highest mountain—up and up on and to and up the highest relic of a tree there was on the mountain too? Ragged and worn, there he lifted up his eager perspiring face to heaven and called on "God." A voice . . . bidding him get down . . . go back!

Would he really see God's face? Then he should go back, go down there in the valley below where his own people were—there only could *he* look upon God's countenance.

Was not that "finger," the church steeple, pointing on high like the man who climbed on high to see HIM? A misleading symbol perhaps. A perversion of sentiment—sentimentality.

Was not the time come now to be more simple, to have more faith in man on his Earth and less anxiety concerning his Heaven about which he could *know* nothing. Concerning this heaven he had never received any testimony from his own senses.

Why not, then, build a temple, not to GOD in that way—more sentimental than sense—but build a temple to man, appropriate to his uses as a meeting place, in which to study man himself for his God's sake? A modern meeting-house and good-time place.

Build a beautiful ROOM proportioned to this purpose. Make it beautiful in this *simple* sense. A *natural* building for natural Man.

The pastor was a "liberal." His liberality was thus challenged, his reason piqued, and the curiosity of all aroused.

What would such a building be like? They said they could imagine no such thing.

"That's what you came to me for," I ventured. "I can imagine it and will help you create it."

Promising the building committee something tangible to look at soon—I sent them away, they not knowing, quite, whether they were foolish, fooled, or fooling with a fool.

That ROOM it began to be that same night.

Enter the realm of architectural ideas.

The first idea—to keep a noble ROOM in mind, and let the room shape the whole edifice, let the room inside be the architecture outside.

What shape? Well, the answer lay, in what material? There was only one material to choose as the church funds were $45,000, to "church" 400 people in 1906. Concrete was cheap.

Concrete alone could do it. But even concrete as it was in use at that time meant wood "forms" and some other material than concrete for outside facing. They were in the habit of covering the concrete with brick or stone, plastering and furring the inside of the walls. Plastering the outside would be cheaper than brick or stone but wouldn't stick to concrete in our climate. Why not make the wooden boxes or forms so the concrete could be cast in them as separate blocks and masses, these separate blocks and masses grouped about an interior space in some such way as to preserve this desired sense of the interior space in the appearance of the whole building? And the block-masses be left as themselves with no "facing." That would be cheap and permanent.

Then, how to cover the separate features and concrete masses as well as the sacrosanct space from the extremes of northern weather? What roof?

What had concrete to offer as a cover shelter? The slab—of course. The reinforced slab. Nothing else if the building was to be thoroughbred, meaning built in character out of one material.

Too monumental, all this? Too forthright for my committee I feared. Would a statement so positive as that final slab over the whole seem irreligious to them? Profane in their eyes? Why?

The flat slab was direct. It would be "nobly" simple. The wooden forms or molds in which concrete buildings must at that time be cast were always the chief item of expense, so to repeat the use of a single one as often as possible was desirable, even necessary. Therefore a building all four sides alike looked like the thing. This, in simplest terms, meant a building square in plan. That would make their temple a cube, a noble form.

The slab, too, belonged to the cube by nature. "Credo simplicitas."

That form is most imaginative and "happy" that is most radiant with the "aura" or overtone of superform.

Geometric shapes through human sensibility have thus acquired to some extent human significance as, say, the cube or square, integrity; the circle or sphere, infinity; the straight line, rectitude; if long drawn out . . . repose; the triangle . . . aspiration, etc.

There was no money to spend in working on the concrete mass outside or with it after it was once cast.

Good reason, this, if no other, for getting away from any false facing. Couldn't the surface be qualified in the casting process so this whole matter of veneered "Façade" could be omitted with good effect? This was later the cause of much experiment, with what success may be seen.

Then the Temple itself—still in my mind—began to take shape. The site was noisy, by the Lake Street car tracks. Therefore it seemed best to keep the building closed on the three front sides and enter it from a court at the center of the lot.

Unity Temple itself with the thoughts in mind I have just expressed, arrived easily enough, but there was a secularist side to Universalist church activities—entertainment—Sunday school, feasts, etc. . . .

To embody these latter with the Temple would spoil the simplicity of the room—the noble ROOM—in the service of MAN for the worship of GOD.

So finally I put the space as "Unity House," a long free space to the rear of the lot, as separate building to be subdivided by movable screens, on occasion. It thus became a separate building but harmonious with the temple—the entrance to both to be the connecting link between them. That was that.

To go back to the Temple itself. What kind of "square room." How effect the cube and best serve the purpose of the audience room?

Should the pulpit be put toward the street and let the congregation come in and go out at the rear in the usual disrespectful church fashion so the pastor missed contact with his flock? And the noise of street cars on Lake Street come in?

No. Why not put the pulpit at the entrance side at the rear of the square Temple entirely cut off from the street and bring the congregation into the room at the sides and on a lower level so those entering would be imperceptible from the audience? This would make the incomers as little a disturbance or challenge to curiosity as possible. This would preserve the quiet and dignity of the room itself. Out of that thought came the depressed foyer or "cloister" corridor either side leading front the main entrance lobby at the center to the stairs in the near and far corners of the room. Those entering the room in this way could see in to the big room but not be seen by those already seated within it.

And when the congregation rose to disperse here was opportunity to move forward toward their pastor and by swinging the wide doors open beside the pulpit, let the flock pass out by the minister and find themselves directly in the entrance loggia from which they had first come in. They had gone into the depressed entrances at the sides from this same entrance to enter the big room. But it seemed more respectful to let them go out thus toward the pulpit than turn their backs upon their minister to go out as is usual in most churches. This scheme gave the minister's flock to him to greet. Few could escape. The position of the pulpit in relation to the entrance made this reverse movement possible.

So this was done.

The room itself—size determined by comfortable seats with leg-room for four hundred people—was built with four interior free-standing posts to carry the overhead structure. These concrete posts were hollow and became free-standing ducts to insure economic and uniform distribution of heat. The large supporting posts were so set in plan as to form a double tier of alcoves on four sides of this room. Flood these side-alcoves with light from above: get a sense of a happy cloudless day into the room. And with this feeling for light the center ceiling between the four great posts became skylight, daylight sifting through between the intersections of concrete beams filtering through amber glass ceiling lights, thus the light would, rain or shine, have the warmth of sunlight. Artificial lighting took place there at night as well. This scheme of lighting was integral, gave diffusion and kept the room space clear.

The spacious wardrobes between the depressed foyers either side of the room and under the auditorium itself, were intended to give opportunity to the worshippers to leave their wraps before entering the worshipful room. And this wardrobe would work as well for the entertainments in the long room to the rear because it was just off the main entrance lobby.

The secular hall—Unity House—itself, was tall enough to have galleries at each side of the central space—convertible into class-room space.

A long kitchen connected to each end of the secular space was added to the rear of Unity House for the Temple "feasts."

The pastor's offices and study came of them-selves over the entrance lobby the connection between the two buildings. The study thus looked down through swinging windows into the secular hall—while it was just a step behind the pulpit.

All this seemed in proper order. Seemed natural enough.

Now for proportion—for the "concrete" expression of concrete in this natural arrangement—the ideal of an organic whole well in mind.

For observe, so far, what has actually taken place is only reasoned *arrangement*. The "plan" with an eye to an exterior in the realm of ideas but "felt" in imagination.

First came the philosophy of the thing in the little story repeated to the trustees. All artistic creation has its own. The first condition of creation. However, some would smile and say, "the result of it."

Second there was the general purpose of the whole to consider in each part: a matter of reasoned arrangement. This arrangement must be made with a sense of the yet-unborn-whole in the mind, to be blocked out as appropriate to concrete masses cast in wooden boxes. Holding all this diversity together in a preconceived direction is really no light matter but is the condition of creation. Imagination conceives here the PLAN suitable to the material and the purpose—seeing the probable—possible form.

Imagination reigns supreme, when now the *form* the whole will naturally take, must be seen.

And we have arrived at the question of *style*.

But if all this preliminary planning has been well conceived that question in the main is settled. The matter may be intensified, made eloquent, or modified and quieted. It cannot much change. Organic is this matter of style now. The concrete forms of Unity Temple will take the character of all we have so far done, if all we have so far done is harmonious with the principle we are waking to work. The structure will not put forth its forms as the tree puts forth branches and foliage—if we do not stultify it, do not betray it in some way.

We do not choose the style. Style is what this is now and what we *are*. A thrilling moment this in any architect's experience. He is about to see the countenance of something he is invoking. Out of this sense of order and his love of the beauty of life—something is to be born maybe to live long as a message of hope and joy or a curse to his kind. *His* message he feels. None the less is it "theirs," and rather more. And it is out of love and understanding such as this on the part of an architect that a building is born to bless or curse those it is built to serve.

Bless them if they will see and understand. Curse them and be cursed by them if either they or the architect should fail to understand. . . .This is the faith and the fear in the architect as he makes ready—to draw his design.

In all artists it is the same.

Now comes to brood—to suffer doubt and burn with eagerness. To test bearings—and prove assumed ground by putting all together to definite scale on paper. Preferably small scale at first. Then larger. Finally still larger-scale studies of parts.

This pure white sheet of paper! Ready for the logic of the plan.

T square, triangle, scale—seductive invitation lying upon the spotless surface.

Temptation!

"Boy! Go tell Black Kelly to make a blaze there in the work-room fire-place! Ask Brown-Sadie if it's too late to have baked Bermudas for supper! Then go ask your mother—I shall hear her in here—to play something—Bach preferred, or Beethoven if she prefers."

An aid to creative effort, the open fire. What a friend to the laboring artist, the poetic-baked-onion. Real encouragement to him is great music.

Yes, and what a poor creature, after all, creation comes singing through. About like catgut and horsehair in the hands of Sarasate.

Night labor at the draughting board is best for intense creation. It may continue uninterrupted.

Meantime reflections are passing in the mind—"design is abstraction of nature-elements in purely geometric terms"—that is what we ought to call pure design? . . . But—nature-pattern and nature-texture in materials themselves often approach conventionalization, or the abstract, to such a degree as to be superlative means ready to the designer's hand to qualify, stimulate, and enrich his own efforts. . . . What texture this concrete mass? Why not its own gravel? How to bring the gravel clean on the surface?

Here was reality. Yes, the "fine thing" is reality. Always reality?

Realism, the subgeometric, is however the abuse of this fine thing.

Keep the straight lines clean and significant, the flat plane expressive and clean cut. But let texture of material come into them.

Reality is spirit . . . essence brooding just behind aspect!

Seize it! And . . . after all, reality *is* supergeometric, casting a spell or a "charm" over any geometry, as such, in itself.

Yes, it seems to me, that is what it means to be an artist . . . to seize this essence brooding just behind aspect. These questionings arising each with its train of thought by the way, as at work.

It is morning! To bed for a while!

Well, there is Unity Temple at last. Health and soundness in it, though still far to go.

But here we have penciled on the sheet of paper, in the main, the plan, section and elevation as in the drawings illustrated here, all except the exterior of "Unity House," as the room for secular recreation came to be called.

To establish harmony between these buildings of separate function proved difficult, utterly exasperating.

Another series of concentrations—lasting hours at a time for several days. How to keep the noble scale of the Temple in the design of the subordinate mass of the secular hall and not falsify the function of that noble mass? The ideal of an organic architecture is severe discipline for the imagination. I came to know that full well. And, always, some minor concordance takes more time, taxes concentration more than all besides. To vex the architect, this minor element now becomes a major problem. How many schemes I have thrown away because some one minor feature would not come true to form!

Thirty-four studies were necessary to arrive at this as it is now seen. Unfortunately they are lost with thousands of others of other buildings. The fruit of similar struggles to coordinate and perfect them all as organic entities—I wish I had kept.

Unity House looks easy enough now, for it is right enough.

But this "*harmony of the whole*" where diverse functions cause diverse masses to occur is no light affair for the architect—nor ever will be if he keeps his ideal high.

Now observe the plans and the elevations, then the model or photograph of the building. See, now, how all that has taken place is showing itself *as it is* for what it is.

A new industrial method for the use of a new material is improved and revealed. Roof slabs—attic walls—screen walls—posts and glass screens enclose, as architecture, a great room.

The sense of the room is not only preserved—*it may be seen as the soul of the design*. Instead of being built into the heart of a block of sculptured building material, out of sight, sacrosanct space is merely screened in . . . it comes through as the living "motif" of the architecture.

The grammar of such style as is seen here is simply and logically determined by the concrete mass and flat layer formation of the slab and box construction of the square room, proportioned according to concrete-nature—or the nature of the concrete. All is assembled about the coveted space, now visibly cherished.

Such architectural forms as there are, each to each as all in all, are cubical in form, to be cast solid in wooden boxes. But *one* motif may be seen, the "inside" becoming "outside." The groups of monoliths in their changing phases, square in character, do not depart from that single IDEA. Here we have something of the organic integrity in structure out of which issues character as an aura. The consequence is style. A stylish development of the square becoming the cube.

Understanding Unity Temple one may respect it. It serves its purpose well. It was easy to build. Its harmonies are bold and striking, but genuine in melody. The "square," too positive in statement for current "*taste*," the straight line and the flat plane uncompromising, yes. But here is an entity again to prove that architecture may, if need be, live again as the nature-of-the-thing in terms of building material. Here is one building rooted in such modern conditions of work, materials, and thought, as prevailed at the time it was built. Single-minded in motif. Faithful in form.

Out of this concentration in labor will come many subsequent studies in refinement—correction of correlation, scale tests for integration. Overcoming difficulties in detail, in the effort to keep all clean and simple as a whole, is continued during the whole process of planning and building.

Many studies in detail yet remain to be made, to determine what further may be left out to protect the design. These studies seem never to end, and in this sense, no organic building may ever be "finished." The complete goal of the ideal of organic architecture is never reached. Nor need be. What worthwhile ideal is ever reached?

But, we have enough now on paper to make a perspective drawing to go with the plan for the committee of "good men and true" to see. Usually a committee has only the sketch to consider. But it is impossible to present a "sketch" when working in this method. The building as a whole must be all in order before the "sketch," not after it.

Unity Temple is a complete building on paper, already. There is no "sketch" and there never has been one.

Hardest of an architect's trials, to show his work, first time, to anyone not entirely competent, perhaps unsympathetic.

Putting off the evil contact as long as possible—letting all simmer. The simmering process, too, is valuable. There is seldom enough of it.

What hope to carry all through? The human ground for hope is gone over carefully again and again—wakeful nights. Already the architect begins to fear for the fate of his design. If it is to be much changed he prefers to throw it all away and begin all over again.

No—not much hope except in Mr. Roberts.

Why not ask him to see the design and explain it to him first? This is done. He is delighted. He *understands!* He is himself an inventor. And every project in architecture needs this one intimate friend in order to proceed. Mr. Roberts suggests a model. The model is soon made.

All right; let the committee come now. They do come—all curious. Soon confounded—taking the "show-me" attitude.

At this moment the creative architect is distinctly at disadvantage as compared with his obsequious brother of the "styles." His brother can show his pattern-book of "styles," speak glibly of St. Mark's at Venice or Capella Palatine, impress the no less craven clients by brave show of erudite authorities—abash them.

But the architect with the ideal of an organic architecture at stake can talk only principle and sense. His only appeal must be made to the independent thought and judgment of his client. The client, too, must know how to think from generals to particulars. How rare it is to go into court where that quality of mind is on the bench! This architect has learned to dread the personal idiosyncrasy—offered him three times out of five—substitute for such intelligence.

But, we try and we use all our resources, we two—the inventor and myself—and win a third member of the committee at the first meeting. Including the pastor, there are now four only left in doubt.

One of the four openly hostile—Mr. Skillin. Dr. Johnnot, the pastor, himself impressed but cautious—very—and tactful. He has a glimpse of a new world.

There is hope, distinctly hope, when he makes four as he soon does and the balance of power is with us.

We need three more but the architect's work is done now. The four will get the others. The pastor is convinced. He will work! So doubt and fears are finally put to sleep—all but Mr. Skillin's. Mr. Skillin is sure the room will be dark—sure the acoustics will be bad. Finally the commission to go ahead is formally given over his dissent and warnings. Usually there is a Mr. Skillin in Usonia on every building project.

Now, who will build the Temple? After weeks of prospecting, no one can be found who wants to try it. Simple enough—yes—that's the trouble. So simple there is nothing at all to gauge it by. Requires too much imagination and initiative to be safe. The only bids available came in double, or more, our utmost limit. No one really wanted to touch it. Contractors are naturally gamblers but they usually bet on a sure thing—as they see it.

Now Paul Mueller comes to the rescue, reads the scheme like easy-print. Will build it for only a little over their appropriation—and does it. He takes it easily along for nearly a year but he does it. Doesn't lose much on it in the end. It is exciting to him to rescue ideas, to participate in creation. And together we overcame difficulty after difficulty in the field, where an architect's education is never finished.

This building, however, is finished, to be opened on a Sunday.

I do not want to go. Stay at home.

When the church was opened the phone began to ring. Listened to happy contented voices in congratulation. Finally weary, I take little Francie by the hand to go out into the air with her to get away from it all. Enough.

But just as my hat goes on my head, another ring, a voice, Mr. Skillin's voice— "Take back all I said. . . . Light everywhere—all pleased."

"Hear well?"

"Yes, see and hear fine—see it all now."

"Glad."

"Good-bye." At last the doubting member was now sincere in praise and a "good sport" besides.

Francie got tossed in the air. She came down with a squeal of delight.

And that is how it was and is and will be.

Now, even though you are interested in architecture this story is more or less tedious and meaningless to you, as you were fairly warned it would be at the beginning, without close study of the plans and photographs as it is read. I have undertaken here, for once, to indicate the process of building on principle to insure character and achieve style, as near as I can indicate it by taking

Unity Temple to pieces. Perhaps I am not the one to try it.

As for the traditional church as modern building! Religion and art are forms of inner-experience—growing richer and deeper as the race grows older. We will never lose either. But I believe religious experience is outgrowing the church—not outgrowing religion but outgrowing the church as an institution. Just as architecture has outgrown the Renaissance and for reasons human, scientific and similar. I cannot see the ancient institutional form of any church building as anything but sentimental, or survival for burial. The Temple as forum and good-time place—beautiful and inspiring as such—yes. A religious edifice raised in the sense of the old ritual? No. I cannot see it at all as living. It is no longer free.

Of course what is most vitally important in all that is to be explained cannot be said at all. It need not be, I think. Here in this searching process may be seen work, as the boys in the studio would crowd around and participate in it. As you too, perhaps, may see certain wheels go around. Certain hints coming through between the lines may help someone who needs help in comprehending what a building really means.

This brief indication of the problem of building out of the man will not clear up the question as to what is style much either. But a little by way of suggestion, I hope.

Man's struggle to illumine creation is another tragedy.

About this time Mr. and Mrs. Avery Coonley came to build a home at Riverside, Illinois.

Unknown to me they had gone to see nearly everything they could learn I had done before coming.

The day they finally came into the Oak Park workshop Mrs. Coonley said they had come because, it seemed to them, they saw in my houses "the countenances of principle." This was to me a great and sincere compliment. So, I put the best in me into the Coonley house. I feel now, looking back upon it, that building was the best I could then do in the way of a house.

The story of this dwelling, most successful of my houses from my standpoint, is not included here as the description of the ideals and the nature of the effort at this time heretofore given at some length all applies directly and particularly to this characteristic dwelling.

KUNO FRANCKE

Kuno Francke, Roosevelt exchange-professor in aesthetics at Harvard, came out to the Oak Park workshop from Chicago. He had seen the new type house standing about on the prairies, had asked the name of the architect, time and again, getting the same name for answer.

A German friend, finally, at the German professor's request, brought Francke and his charming wife to Oak Park for a short visit. Kuno Francke stayed all day, came back the next day.

He, too, as had Mr. Waller and Uncle Dan, wanted me to go to Europe, wanted me to go to Germany to stay and go to work.

"I see that you are doing 'organically,'" he said, "what my people are feeling for only superficially. They would reward you. It will be long before your own people will be ready for what you are trying to give them."

I had always loved Germany, Goethe, Schiller, Nietzsche, Bach—the great architect who happened to choose music for his form. Beethoven and Strauss. And Munich! This beloved company—were they not Old Germany? And Vienna! Vienna had always appealed to my imagination. Paris? Never!

It would be wonderful to go!

I had resisted up to this time, only dreaming of Europe.

Earlier C. R. Ashbee of the London Arts and Crafts movement who was lecturing in America, representative of the Natural Trust for planes of historic interest and natural beauty, had come to see me. He had stayed, too, to urge a not dissimilar "mission" upon me. He was made to see the future I saw in the United States. Now to make Kuno Francke see it. . . . I tried the same argument, not dissimilar to the one used with "Uncle Dan."

"But, where will you be when America gets around to all this?" said the Herr Professor of Aesthetics. "Do you expect to live one hundred years longer, at least?"

"Oh no, but I hope to live long enough to see it coming," I said. "America is going fast. This country is a free country!" I boasted. And I told him the story of the Chicagoan at the Ashbee banquet who stood Ashbee as long as he could and got up on his indignant feet to say that Chicago wasn't much on Culture now, maybe, but when Chicago *did* get after Culture, she'd make Culture hum! We laughed the usual laugh and that was that.

Soon after this inspiring visit came a proposition from Germany—from the publisher Wasmuth in Berlin—to publish a complete monograph of my work if I would send over the material.

This proposal of the German publisher, was, I think, one net result of Kuno Francke's visit to the Oak Park workshop—though I never really knew.

I had written the above when word by way of a news-clipping falling on my desk this morning told me that Kuno Francke is dead.

THE CLOSED ROAD

This absorbing, consuming phase of my experience as an architect ended about 1909. I had almost reached my fortieth year: weary, I was losing grip on my work and even interest in it. Every day of every week and far into the night of nearly every day, Sunday included, I had "added tired to tired" and added it again and yet again, as I had been trained to do by Uncle James "on the farm" as a boy. Continuously thrilled, too, by the effort that now seemed to leave me up against a dead wall. I could see no way out. Because I did not know what I wanted, I wanted to go away. Why not go to Germany and prepare the material for the Wasmuth Monograph? . . . I looked longingly in that direction.

Afternoons after four o'clock I had been in the habit of riding Kano, my young black saddle horse, named after the Japanese Master, over the prairies north of Oak Park sometimes letting him run wild as he loved to do, sometimes reining him in and reading from a book usually carried in my

pocket, for I've always loved to read out-of-doors—especially Whitman.

Ever since boyhood, horseback riding, swimming, dancing, skating, and omnivorous reading. Always music—hungry. Motoring just that much added—or was it deducted—had come along to interfere with these recreations, a little. The motorcar brought a disturbance of all values, subtle or obvious, and it brought the disturbance to me.

Nevertheless, changing work to recreation and recreation to work as I might, the intensity of the effort, unrelenting concentration, giving up the best and deepest in me to an ideal I loved better than myself, had done something to me that reacted upon that very effort.

Everything, personal or otherwise, bore down heavily on me. Domesticity most of all. What I wanted I did not know. I loved my children. I loved my home. A true home is the finest ideal of man, and yet . . . to gain "freedom " asked for a "divorce." It was, advisedly, refused. But these conditions were made: Were I to wait a year, divorce would be granted. The year went by and contrary to promises legal freedom was still refused by Catherine and all concerned in the promise. So there remained to me in the circumstances only one choice—to take the situation in hand and, on my own, work out the best life possible for all concerned. I could not keep my home because, to keep the ideal high, well . . . these three necessities have emerged from the sense of struggles precipitated at this time. I will set them down here, as a means to honest life, instead of intruding any personal details of my own experience.

SOCIOLOGICAL (A "TRACT")

First: Marriage not mutual is no better, but worse than any other form of slavery.

Second: Only to the degree that marriage is mutual is it decent. Love is not property. To take it so is barbarous. To protect it as such is barbarism.

Third: The child is the pledge of good faith its parents give to the future of the race. There are no illegitimate children. There may be illegitimate parents—legal or illegal. Legal interference has no function whatever in any true Democracy where these three fundamentals are concerned except as follows.

Concerning the three foregoing conclusions:

First: Legal marriage is a civil contract between a man and a woman to share property and together provide for children that may spring from that marriage. So, in this respect legal marriage is subject to the legal interpretations and enforcements of any other contract. But legal marriage should be regarded as no mere legal license for "sexual relations." That relation should not, as the law now makes it, be the shameless essence of legal marriage in any such legal respect

Second: Love, so far as laws can go to protect it, is entitled to the benefit of hands-off and the benefit of the doubt . . . unless degraded to a matter of commerce. So degraded, it should be subject to the laws that govern any other degraded traffic.

Love should be its own protection or its own defeat—if it is to grow strong.

Third: The child being the pledge given to Society by Love, it is the duty of the state to make and enforce laws that protect the substance of the pledge. The substance of the pledge is that, provided by its parents, every child born shall have good shelter, good food, good treatment, and an open door to growth of body and mind. Added to this the child should have whatever in addition the circumstances of its birth may present to it—the most desirable of all being love. *But this latter can be no concern of the Law's.*

What I have tried to set down here with clarity in the foregoing conclusions was working in my mind during that miserable year of probation and demoralization. Then it was working more or less clearly, as right: any man's right to live.

The denial of the "right" worked against reconstruction more than anything else and invited, if indeed it did not insist upon, destruction.

Turning my work, plans, draughtsmen, and clients over to a man whom I had just met, Von Holst, a young Chicago architect, and making the best provision I could for my family for one year, I broke with all that was as it was.

Deliberately for a time I broke with all family connections though never with such responsibilities as I felt to be mine in that connection, or that I could humanly—yes—humanly discharge.

Resolutely, with the same faith as when I took the train for Chicago leaving home and college, I went out into the unknown to test faith in Freedom, test faith in life as I had already proved faith in work.

I faced the hazards of change and ruin inevitably involved in every inner struggle for objective freedom.

Objective struggle for inner freedom I have since learned is a far deeper and more serious matter, never finished, on this earth. Rebellion went its way volunteer in exile.

IN EXILE

In ancient Fiesole, far above the romantic city of Cities in a little cream-white villa on the Via Verdi.[9]

How many souls seeking release from real or fancied domestic woes have sheltered in Fiesole!

I, too, sought shelter there in companionship with her who, by force of rebellion as by way of Love, was then implicated with me.

Walking together up the hill road from Firenze to the older town, all along the way the sight and scent of roses, by day. Walking arm in arm, up the same old road at night. Listening to the nightingale in the deep shadows of the moonlit woods . . . trying to hear the songs in the deeps of life: pilgrimages to reach the small solid door framed in the solid blank wall toward the narrow Via Verdi itself. Entering, closing the medieval door on the world outside to find a wood fire burning in the small grate. Estero in her white apron, smilingly, waiting to surprise Signora and Signore with, ah—this time as usual the incomparable little dinner, the perfect roast fowl, mellow wine, the caramel custard—beyond all roasts or wine or caramels ever made I remember.

Or out walking in the high-walled garden that lay alongside the cottage in the Florentine sun or arbored under climbing masses of yellow roses. I see the white cloth on the small stone table near the little fountain, beneath the clusters of yellow roses, set for two. Long walks along the waysides of the hills above, through the poppies, over the hill fields to Vallombrosa.

The waterfall there finding and losing its sound in the deep silence of the pine wood. Breathing, deep, the odor of the great pines—to sleep at the cloistered little mountain-inn.

Back again, hand in hand, miles through the sun and dust of the ancient winding road, an old Italian road, along the stream. How old! And how thoroughly a road.

Together, tired out, sitting on benches in the galleries of Europe, saturated with plastic beauty, beauty in buildings, beauty in sculpture, beauty in paintings until no "chiesa," however rare, and no further beckoning work of human hands could draw or waylay us any more.

Faithful comrade!

A dream in realization ended?

No, woven, a golden thread in the human pattern of the precious fabric that is Life: her Life built into the house of houses. So far as may be known—forever!

Mamah Borthwick Cheney. FLLW Fdn FA#6700.0006

FOLLOWING VOLUNTARY EXILE AT FIESOLE: SOCIOLOGICAL CONSEQUENCES

"Publicity" now pursued me wherever I went.[10] Concerning that persecution all I have to say until a later portion of this book, I will try to set down clearly as three corollaries drawn from my own experience. At this time I was pursued and exploited by "publicity" together with all those I loved and was trying to respect while I was making a desperate effort to re-establish a better life for us all on a fairer basis.

Corollary One: Since all publicity in the United States is privately owned any exploitation damaging or insulting to any individual in respect to the three fundamentals before stated should be seen as demoralizing.

Corollary Two: No publicity exploiting these profoundly personal matters should be marketed for profit, but such publicity be limited to the purview of the laws unless crime or perversion harmful to all three interests be proved to exist. The burden of proof should be put upon the exploiter not upon the exploited.

Corollary Three: These three human interests are more sacred than any property interests whatsoever.

How can any social structure deliberately interfering with the three conclusions or neglecting these three corollaries, hope to endure, as free?

The passions have all contributed to the progress of Life. Sacrifice began as selfishness and even love began as lust. And still so begins.

Legislation can be no friend to moral growth except by the "hands off" or the "stand back, please" that allows the individual in the purely private and deeply personal concerns of his own life, to "do or die" *on his own*.

But I, too, believe that for any man to have found no lasting relationship in love in this brief life is to suffer greatest waste.

Flogging, ridicule, nor censure are needed to make such waste socially exemplar and effective.

Anyone not blinded by fear or eager to play the part of a wrathful Jehovah may see this.

How the laws of our government are continually used as weapons of blackmail or revenge because the government stays in the sex-business as the government has gone into the liquor business—by way of prohibition and punishment—is obvious enough.

Naturally, laws will be abused where they interfere with life and try to assume responsibility which they have no business to assume in any decent society.

Only where culture is based upon the building of character by freedom-of-choice will we ever have the culture of true Democracy.

Such exaggeration of government must continually resist continual exploitation of itself either as a weapon or a tool in the hands of unscrupulous or passionately vindictive individuals seeking public redress for private and personal wrongs.

Thomas Jefferson, most intelligent founder of our Republic, declared: "That Government is best Government that is least Government."

The sense of all this as fundamentally right and the same faith that characterized my forefathers from generation to generation—I suppose—carried me through the vortex of reactions, the deep anguish, and terrible waste of breaking up my home and work at Oak Park to go forward with the building of Taliesin. Work, life, and love to be transferred to the beloved Valley.

Taliesin was the name of a Welsh Poet. A druid-bard or singer of songs who sang to Wales the glories of Fine Art. Literally the Welsh word means "shining brow." Many legends cling to the name in Wales.

Fiesole, Italy. 1910 [photograph by FLLW].
FLLW Fdn FA#7109.0013

Fiesole, Italy. 1910 [photograph by FLLW].
FLLW Fdn FA#7109.0003

Fiesole, Italy. 1910 [photograph by FLLW]. FLLW Fdn FA#7109.0012

And Richard Hovey's charming masque "Taliesin" had made me acquainted with his image of the historic bard. Since all my relatives had Welsh names for their places, why not for mine? . . .

TALIESIN

This hill on which Taliesin now stands as "brow" was one of my favorite places when I was a boy, for pasque flowers grew there in March sun while snow still streaked the hill sides.

When you are on its crown you are out in mid-air as though swinging in a plane, as the Valley and two others drop away leaving the tree-tops all about you. "Romeo and Juliet" stands in plain view to the southeast, the Hillside Home School just over the ridge.

As "the boy" I had learned the ground-plan of the region in every line and feature.

Its "elevation " for me now is the modeling of the hills, the weaving and the fabric that clings to them, the look of it all in tender green or covered with snow or in full glow of summer that bursts into the glorious blaze of autumn.

I still feel myself as much a part of it as the trees and birds and bees, and red barns, or as the animals are, for that matter.

So, when family-life in Oak Park in that spring of 1909, conspired against the freedom to which I had come to feel every soul entitled and I had no choice would I keep my self-respect, but go out, a voluntary exile, into the uncharted and unknown deprived of legal protection to get my back against the wall and live, if I could, an unconventional life—then I turned to the hill in the Valley as my Grandfather before me had turned to America—as a hope and haven—forgetful for the time being of grandfathers' "Isaiah." Smiting and punishment.

Architecture, by now, was mine. It had come by actual experience to mean to me something out of the ground of what we call "America," something in league with the stones of the field, in sym-

Taliesin I. Spring Green, Wisconsin. 1911. FLLW Fdn FA#1104.0004

pathy with "the flower that fadeth, the grass that withereth," something of the prayerful consideration for the lilies of the field that was my gentle grandmother's. Something natural to the change that was "America" herself.

And it was unthinkable that any house should be put *on* that beloved hill.

I knew well by now that no house should ever be *on* any hill or *on* anything. It should be *of* the hill, belonging to it, so hill and house could live together each the happier for the other. That was the way everything found round about it was naturally managed, except when man did something. When he added his mite he became imitative and ugly. Why? Was there no natural house? I had proved, I felt, that there was, and now I, too, wanted a *natural* house to live in myself. I scanned the hills of the region where the rock came cropping out in strata to suggest buildings. How quiet and strong the rock-

ledge masses looked with the dark red cedars and white birches, there, above the green slopes. They were all part of the countenance of southern Wisconsin.

I wished to be part of my beloved southern Wisconsin and not put my small part of it out of countenance. Architecture, after all, I have learned, or before all, I should say, is no less a weaving and a fabric than the trees. And as anyone might see, a beech tree is a beech tree. It isn't trying to be an oak. Nor is a pine trying to be a birch although each makes the other more beautiful when seen together.

The world has had appropriate buildings before—why not more appropriate buildings now than ever before? There must be some kind of house that would belong to that hill, as trees and the ledges of rock did; as Grandfather and Mother had belonged to it, in their sense of it all.

Taliesin I. Spring Green, Wisconsin. 1911. FLLW Fdn FA#1104.0009

Yes, there must be a natural house, not natural as caves and log-cabins were natural but native in spirit and making, with all that architecture had meant whenever it was alive in times past. Nothing at all that I had ever seen would do. This country had changed all that into something else. Grandfather and Grandmother were something splendid in themselves that I couldn't imagine in any period houses I had ever seen. But there was a house that hill might marry and live happily with ever after. I fully intended to find it. I even saw, for myself, what it might be like and began to build it as the "brow" of the hill.

It was still a very young faith that undertook to build it. But it was the same faith that plants twigs for orchards, vineslips for vineyards, and small whips that become beneficent shade trees. And it did plant them, too, all about!

I saw the hill crown back of the house, itself a mass of apple trees in bloom, the perfume drifting down the valley, later, the boughs bending to the ground with the red and white and yellow spheres that make the apple tree no less beautiful than the orange tree. I saw the plum trees, fragrant drifts of snow-white in the spring, in August loaded with blue and red and yellow plums, scattering over the ground at a shake of the hand. I saw the rows on rows of berry bushes, necklaces of pink and green gooseberries hanging to the under side of green branches. Saw thickly pendent clusters of rubies like tassels in the dark leaves of the currant bushes. The rich odor of the black currant, I remembered and looked forward to in quantity.

Black cherries. White cherries.

The strawberry beds, white, scarlet, and green over the covering of clean wheat-straw.

I saw abundant asparagus in rows and a stretch of sumptuous rhubarb that would always be enough. I saw the vineyard on the south slope of the hill, opulent vines loaded with purple, green and yellow grapes, boys and girls coming in with baskets filled to overflowing to set about the rooms, like flowers. Melons lying thick in the trailing green, on the hill slope. Bees humming over all storing up honey in the white rows of hives beside the chicken yard.

And the herd that I would have! The gentle Holsteins and a monarch of a bull—a glittering decoration of the fields and meadows as they moved. The sheep grazing the meadows and hills, the bleat of the little white lambs in the spring.

The grunting sows to turn the waste to solid gold.

I saw the spirited—well-schooled horses, black horses, and white mares with glossy coats and splendid strides, being saddled and led to the mounting-block for rides about the place and along the country lanes I loved—the best of companionship alongside. The sturdy teams ploughing in the fields. The changing colors of the slopes, from seeding time to harvest. I saw the scarlet comb of the rooster and his hundreds of hens—their white eggs. The ducks upon the pond. The geese—and swans floating in the shadow of the trees upon the water.

I saw the peacocks Javanese and white on the walls of the courts. And from the vegetable gardens I walked into a deep cavern in the hill—the root-cellar of my grandfather—and saw its wide sand floor planted with celery, piled with squash and turnips, potatoes, carrots, onions, parsnips, cabbages wrapped and hanging from the roof. Apples, pears, and grapes stored in wooden crates walled the cellar from floor to roof. And cream! All the cream the boy had been denied. Thick—so lifting it in a spoon it would float like an egg on the fragrant morning cup of coffee or ride on the scarlet strawberries.

Yes, Taliesin should be a garden and a farm behind a workshop and a home.

I saw it all, and planted it all, and laid the foundation of the herd, flocks, stable, and fowls as I laid the foundation of the house.

All these items of livelihood came back—improved—from boyhood.

And so began a "shining brow" for the hill, the hill rising unbroken above to crown the exuberance of life in all these rural riches.

There was a stone quarry on another hill a mile away, where the yellow sand-limestone, when uncovered, lay in strata like the outcropping ledges in the façades of the hills.

The look of it was what I wanted for such masses as would rise from the slopes. The teams of neighboring farmers soon began hauling it over to the hill, doubling the teams to get it to the top. Long cords of this native stone, five hundred or more from first to last, got up there, ready to hand, as Father Larson, the old Norse stone mason working in the quarry beyond blasted and quarried it out in great flakes. The stone went down for pavements of terraces and courts. Stone was sent along the slopes into great walls. Stone stepped up like ledges on to the hill, and flung long arms in any direction that brought the house to the ground. The ground! My Grandfather's ground: It was lovingly felt as part of all this.

Finally it was not so easy to tell where pavements and walls left off and ground began. Especially on the hill-crown which became a low-walled garden above the surrounding courts, reached by stone steps walled into the slopes. A clump of fine oaks that grew on the hilltop stood untouched on one side above the court. A great curved stone-walled seat enclosed the space just beneath them and stone pavement stepped down to a spring or fountain that welled up into a pool at the center of the circle. Each court had its fountain and the winding stream below had a great dam. A thick stone wall thrown across it, to make a pond at the very foot of the hill, and raise the water in the Valley to within sight from Taliesin. The water below the falls thus made, was sent, by hydraulic ram, up to a big stone reservoir built into the higher hill, just behind and above the hilltop garden, to come down again into the fountains and go on down to the vegetable gardens on the slopes below the house.

Taliesin, of course, was to be architect's workshop, a dwelling as well for young workers who came to assist. And it was a farm cottage for the farm help. Around a rear court were to be farm buildings, for Taliesin was to be a complete living unit, genuine in point of comfort and beauty, from pig to proprietor.

The place was to be self-sustaining if not self-sufficient and with its domain of two hundred acres, shelter, food, clothes, and even entertainment within itself. It had to be its own light-plant, fuel yard, transportation and water system.

Taliesin was to be recreation ground for my children and their children perhaps for many generations more. This modest human programme in terms of rural Wisconsin arranged itself around the hilltop in a series of four varied courts leading one into the other, courts together forming a sort of drive along the hillside flanked by low buildings on one side and by flower gardens against the stone walls that retained the hill-crown on the other.

The strata of fundamental stone-work reached around and on into the four courts, and made them. Then stone, stratified, went into the lower house walls and on up into the chimneys from the ground itself. This native stone prepared the way for the lighter plastered construction of the upper-wood-walls. Taliesin was to be a combination of stone and wood as they met in the aspect of the hills around about. The lines of the hills were the lines of the roofs. The slopes of the hills their slopes, the plastered surfaces of the light wood-walls, set back into shade beneath broad eaves, were like the flat stretches of sand in the river below and the same in color, for that is where the material that covered them came from.

The finished wood outside was the color of gray tree-trunks, in violet light.

The shingles of the roof surfaces were left to weather, silver-gray like the tree branches spreading below them.

The chimneys of the great stone fireplaces rose heavily through all, wherever there was a gathering place within, and there were many such places. They showed great rock-faces over deep openings inside. Outside they were strong, quiet, rectangular rock-masses bespeaking strength and comfort, within.

Country masons laid all the stone with the quarry for a pattern and the architect for teacher.

They learned to lay the walls in the long, thin, flat ledges natural to it, natural edges out. As often as they laid a stone they would stand back to judge the effect. They were soon as interested as sculptors fashioning a statue. One might imagine they were, as they stepped back, head cocked one side, to get the effect. Having arrived at some conclusion, they would step forward and shove the stone more to their liking, seeming never to tire of this discrimination. They were artistic for the first time, many of them, and liked it. There were many masons from first to last, all good, perhaps Dad Signola, in his youth a Czech, the best of them until Philip Volk came. He worked away five years at the place as it grew from year to year, for it will never be finished. And with no inharmonious discrepancy, one may see each mason's individuality in his work at Taliesin to this day. I frequently recall the man as I see his work.

At that time, to get this mass of material to the hilltop meant organizing man and horsepower. Trucks came along years later. Main strength and awkwardness directed by commanding intelligence got the better of the law of gravitation by the ton, as sand, stone, gravel, and timber went up into appointed places. Ben Davis was commander of these forces at this time. Ben was a creative cusser. He had to be. To listen to Ben back of all this movement was to take off your hat to a virtuoso. Men have cussed between every word, but Ben split the words, artistically worked an oath in between every syllable. One day Ben with five of his men was moving a big rock that suddenly got away from its edge and fell over flat, catching Ben's big toe. I shuddered for that rock, as, hobbling slowly back and forth around it, Ben hissed and glared at it, threatening, eyeing, and cussing it. He rose to such heights, plunged to such depths of vengeance, as I had never suspected, even in Ben. No "Marseillaise" or any damnation in the mouth of Mosaic prophet ever exceeded Ben at this high spot in his career as cusser. William Blake says exuberance is beauty. It would be profane, perhaps, to say that Ben at this moment was sublime. But he was.

And in "Spring Green"—the names in the region are mostly simple like "Black Earth," "Blue

Mounds," "Lone Rock," "Silver Creek," etc.—I found a carpenter.

William Weston was a natural carpenter. He was a carpenter such as architects like to stand and watch work. I never saw him make a false or unnecessary movement. His hammer, extra-light, with a handle fashioned by himself, flashed to the right spot every time, like the rapier of an expert swordsman. He, with his nimble intelligence and swift sure hand, was a gift to any architect.

That William stayed with Taliesin through trials and tribulations the better part of fourteen years. America turns up a good mechanic around in country places every so often. Billy was one of them.

Winter came. A bitter one. The roof was on, plastering done, windows in, the men working inside. Evenings, the men grouped around the open fire-places, throwing cord-wood into them to keep themselves warm as the wind came up through the floor boards. All came to work from surrounding towns and had to be fed and bedded on the place during the week. Saturday nights they went home with money for the week's work in pocket, or its equivalent in groceries and fixings from the village. Their reactions were picturesque. There was Johnnie Vaughn, who was, I guess, a genius. I got him because he had gone into some kind of concrete business with another Irishman for partner, and failed. Johnnie said, "We didn't fail sooner because we didn't have more business." I overheard this lank genius, he was looking after the carpenters nagging little Billy Little, who had been foreman of several jobs in the city for me. Said Johnnie, "I built this place here off a shingle." "Huh," said Billy, "that ain't nothin'. I built them places in Oak Park right off'd the air." No one ever got even, a little, over the rat-like perspicacity of that little Billy Little.

Workmen never have enough drawings or explanations no matter how many they get—but this is the sort of slander an architect needs to hear occasionally.

The workmen took the work as a sort of adventure. It was adventure. In every realm. Especially in the financial realm. I kept working all the while to make the money come. It did. And we kept on inside with plenty of clean soft wood that could be left alone, pretty much, in plain surfaces. The stone, too, strong and protective inside, spoke for itself in certain piers, and walls.

Inside floors, like the outside floors, were stone-paved or if not were laid with wide, dark-streaked cypress boards. The plaster in the walls was mixed with raw sienna in the box, went on to the walls "natural," drying out tawny gold. Outside, the plastered walls were the same but grayer with cement. But in the *constitution* of the whole, in the way the walls rose from the plan and the spaces were roofed over, was the chief interest of the whole house. The whole was all supremely natural. The rooms went up into the roof, tent-like, and were ribanded overhead with marking-strips of waxed, soft wood. The house was set so sun came through the openings into every room sometime during the day. Walls opened everywhere to views as the windows swung out above the tree-tops, the tops of red, white, and black oaks and wild cherry trees festooned with wild grape-vines. In spring, the perfume of the blossoms came full through the windows, the birds singing there, the while, from sunrise to sunset—all but the several white months of winter.

I wanted a home where icicles by invitation might beautify the eaves. So there were no gutters. And when the snow piled deep on the roofs and lay drifted in the courts, icicles came to hang staccato from the eaves. Prismatic crystal in pendants sometimes six feet long, glittered, between the landscape and the eyes inside. Taliesin in winter was a frosted palace roofed and walled with snow, hung with iridescent fringes, the plate-glass of the windows delicately fantastic with frosted arabesques. A thing of winter beauty. But the windows shone bright and warm through it all as the light of the huge fire-places lit them from the firesides within and streams of wood-smoke from a dozen such places went straight up toward the stars.

The furnishings inside were simple and temperate. Thin tan-colored flax rugs covered the floors, later abandoned for the severer simplicity of the stone pavements and wide boards. Doors and windows were hung with modest, brown checkered fabrics. The furniture was "home-made" of the same wood as the trim and mostly fitted into the trim. I got a compliment on this from old Dan Davis, a rich and "savin'" Welsh neighbor, who saw we had made it ourselves. "Gosh-dang it Frank," he said, "Ye're savin' too, ain't ye?" Although Mother Williams, another neighbor, who came to work for me, said, "Savin'? He's nothin' of the sort. He could 'ave got it most as cheap ready-made from that Sears and Roebuck. . . . I know."

A house of the North. The whole was low, wide, and snug, a broad shelter seeking fellowship with its surroundings. A house that could open to the breezes of summer and become like an open camp if need be. With spring came music on the roofs for there were few dead roof-spaces overhead, and the broad eaves so sheltered the windows that they were safely left open to the sweeping, soft air of the rain. Taliesin was grateful for care. Took what grooming it got with gratitude and repaid it all with interest.

Taliesin's order was such that when all was clean and in place its countenance beamed, wore a happy smile of well-being and welcome for all.

It was intensely human, I believe.

Although, thanks to "bigger and better publicity," among those who besieged it Saturdays and Sundays from near and far came several characteristic ladies whose unusual enterprise got them as far as the upper half of the Dutch door, standing open to the living room. They couldn't see me. I was lying on a long walled-seat just inside. They poked in their heads and looked about with ohs and ahs. A pause. In the nasal twang of the more aggressive one "I wonder" . . . "I wonder, now, if I'd like living in a place like this as much as I would living in a regular home?"

The studio, lit by a bank of tall windows to the north, really was a group of four studies, one large, three small. And in their midst stood a stone fireproof vault for treasures. The plans, private papers, and such money as there was, took chances anywhere outside it. But the Taliesin library of Genroku embroidery and antique colored woodblock prints, all stayed safely inside. But, as work and sojourn overseas continued, Chinese pottery and sculpture and Momoyama screens overflowed into the rooms where, in a few years, every single object used for decorative accent became an "antique" of rare quality.

If the eye rested on some ornament it could be sure of worthy entertainment. Hovering over these messengers to Taliesin from other civilizations and thousands of years ago, must have been spirits of peace and good-will? Their figures seemed to shed fraternal sense of kinship from their places in the stone or from the broad ledges, where they rested.

For the story of Taliesin, after all, is old: old as the human spirit. These ancient figures were traces of that spirit, left behind in the human procession as Time went on, and they now came forward to find rest and feel at home. So it seemed as you looked at them. But they were only the story within the story: ancient comment on the New.

The New lived for itself for their sake as, long ago, they had lived, for its sake.

The storms of the north broke over the low sweeping roofs that now sheltered a structure in which hope purposefully lived at earnest work. The lightning in this region, always so crushing and severe, crashed and Taliesin smiled. Taliesin was minding its own business, living up to its own obligations and to the past it could well understand. But the New failing to recognize it as its own, still pursued and besieged, traduced and insulted it. Taliesin raged, wanted to talk back—and smiled. Taliesin was a "story" and therefore had to run the gauntlet. It made its way through storm and stress, threats and slanderous curiosity to its happiness for more than three years and smiled—always. No one feeling the repose of its spirit could believe in the storm of publicity that kept breaking outside because a kindred spirit—a woman—had taken refuge there for life.

Gradually creative desire and faith came creeping back again. Taliesin began to come alive and settle down to work.

Chicago business offices were now in the Orchestra Hall Building, though the workshop was still at Taliesin. A number of buildings went out from that office. The neighborhood playhouse of Mrs. Coonley was among them, and the Midway

Gardens Plaisance, near the Chicago University. As the Gardens were a product of the first re-establishment associated in my mind with the tragedy of Taliesin and new in so many ways, here is the story of that adventure.

THE TALE OF THE MIDWAY GARDENS

In the fall of 1913 Young Ed Waller's head got outside the idea of the Chicago Midway Gardens and he set to work. First on me, one day when I had come in from the workshop, now in order, at Taliesin I. We had been at work out there in the Valley some two years.

Said Ed: "In all this old town there's no place to go but out nor any place to come to but back that isn't bare and ugly, unless it's cheap and nasty. I want to put a garden in this wilderness of smoky dens, car-tracks, and saloons."

This sounded like his father, whom you have seen in the experience with Uncle Dan in the library of the house at River Forest.

"I believe Chicago would appreciate a beautiful Garden-Resort. Our people would go there, listen to good music, eat and drink: you know, an outdoor garden something like those little parks 'round Munich where German families go.

"The dance craze is on now, too, and we could have a dancing floor inside somewhere for the young folks. Yes, and a place outside near the orchestra where highbrows could come and sit to hear a fine concert, even if they wanted to dine at home.

"The trouble is the short season. We could fix that by putting up a winter-garden on one side, for diners, with the big dancing floor in the middle. And to make it all sure as to money we would put in a bar—the "affliction" had not yet befallen—that would go the year around. We would run the whole thing like an entertainment on a grand scale—Pavlova dancing—Max Bendix full orchestra playing—music outdoors starting at seven o'clock. Between orchestral numbers a dance-orchestra striking up, back there in the winter-garden,

so the girls could get the boys to dance. Matinees several days a week. People up on balconies and all around over the tops of the buildings. Light, color, music, movement—a gay place!

"Frank, you could make it unique." He went on: "I know where I can get the ground. Down on the south-side just off the Midway. The old Sans Souci place. Been on the rocks for years. Stupid old ballyhoo. It's just big enough, I think. About three acres. You'll get paid for your drawings anyway."

All Ed didn't know was where he could get the money. But, he said, that was the easiest part of it. "*He* would fix that."

"What do you think of the idea?" said he.

Well, Aladdin and his wonderful lamp fascinated me as a boy, but now, I knew the enchanting young Arabian was just a symbol for creative desire, his lamp intended for another one—imagination.

I sat listening, myself "Aladdin." Young Ed? The genii. He knew apparently where all "the slaves of the lamp" could be found. Well, this might all be necromancy but I believed in magic. Had I not rubbed my lamp with what seemed wonderful effect, before this?

"When you get back to the office, send me a survey of the old Sans Souci grounds. Then come back Monday, Ed," I said. "You'll see what . . . you'll see."

He did. The thing had simply shaken itself out of my sleeve. In a remarkably short time there it was on paper—in color. Young Ed gloated over it.

"I knew it," he said. "This is it."

Paul Mueller, it was, whom we both desired as "slave of the lamp." Paul-the-builder got interested in the scheme, and with accustomed energy started to make the dream reality. His "organization," as he called it, of partners, foremen, workmen skilled and workmen unskilled, all belonged to various departments of the great big Chicago-building-contractor known as "The Union." Mueller rented slaves from the Union by making the usual terms. But himself, as usual, was the organization so far as it went in getting the Midway Gardens built.

Railing design, Midway Gardens. Chicago, Illinois. 1913. Pencil and color pencil on tracing paper, 31 x 33" (detail). FLLW Fdn#1401.081

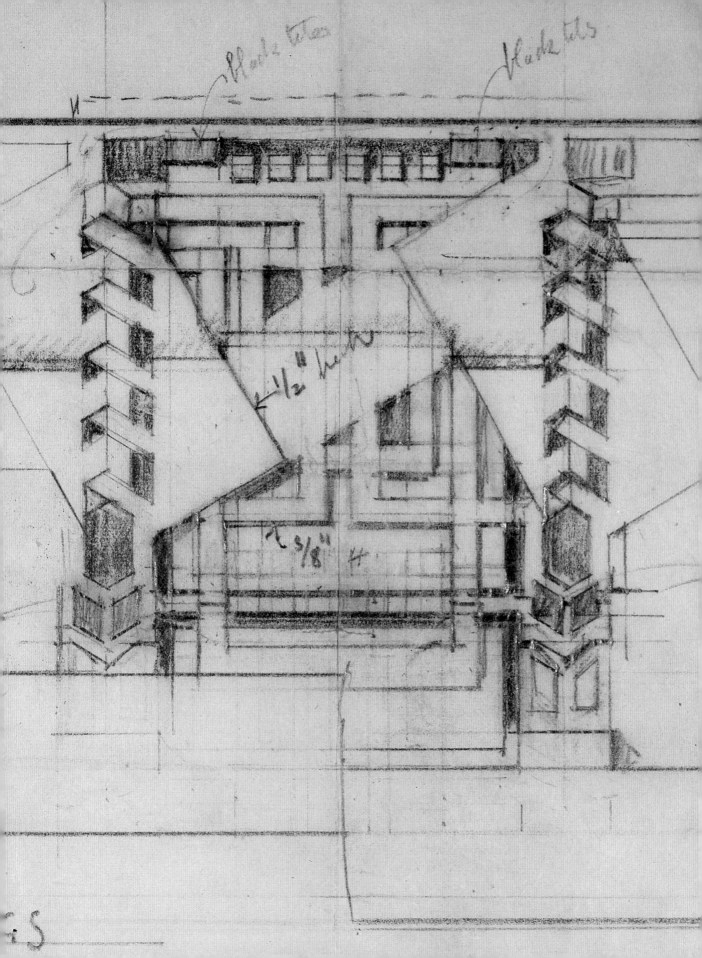

Nor could Young Ed wait for any process very long. He was very young. His Genius started all this on the fly and kept it flying.

In another several days old Sans Souci's several acres had begun to boil. The Union on the job with watchful, jealous eye.

Soon all of old Sans Souci left in sight was a rusty old steel-tower standing up in one corner of the lot. Laborers started to wreck it but the Union raised its hand. The rickety old tower was iron, therefore consecrated to the steel-workers. Skilled steel-workers only should dare demolish it. This meant a thousand or so wasted but no time to argue—the Union knew that too. Skilled steel-workers took the thing down.

Mueller, slave-driver, stood up six feet two inches tall in all this commotion madly shouting through a megaphone to five points of the compass all at the same time, giving directions to seemingly insane activity.

Excavators, steam shovels, wagons, dumping materials, and trucks hauling dirt away, barrows, mules, more trucks, concrete mixers, derricks, gin poles, mud, water, and men. Cement-bags, sand, brick, beams, timber came piling up into great heaps. Masons, hod-carriers, brick layers, plasterers, carpenters, steel workers all found the proper thing to do at the proper time because capable foremen were correctly reading the architect's blue-prints in the little board-shanty that had now taken the place of the consecrated iron tower. "Paul F. P. Mueller & Co., Builders" was the legend painted in big black letters across the edifice.

You know without being told where the blue-prints came from. And Young Ed, genius of this hubbub—and expected to pay for it—hovered over it all, excited. To date, it was the time of his life.

In Ed's office was a cultivated chap, Charlie Matthews. Artistic, music-mad Charlie. He too went off his head over the scheme for the Midway Gardens. Got others into a state of mind to buy stock in the enterprise. And while this frenzied army of workmen were busy—Ed and Charlie and their friends were busy too, trying to raise money. But, as subsequently appeared, there was only about sixty-five thousand dollars in hand to meet the three hundred and fifty thousand to be paid. No one knew that at the time unless it was Ed. And I doubt if even he did. Anyhow, that is about all the real money there ever was with which to build the Midway Gardens.

But, all unaware of that fact, the Gardens were well above ground, rapidly moving up toward the blue overhead. Even Chicago weather permitted, entering into the conspiracy, if there was any conspiracy outside the Union. I knew of none except the conspiracy to get the Midway Gardens done in ninety days, get the diners seated, dinner on the table, and the music playing. And the date of opening was May 1, 1914.

The Midway Gardens were planned as a Summer-Garden: a system of low masonry terraces enclosed by promenades, loggias and galleries at the sides, these flanked by the Winter-Garden. The Winter-Garden also was terraced and balconied in permanent masonry without and within. This Winter-Garden stood on the main street, opposite the great orchestra shell. The Bar, "supporting feature," as Ed intended, was put on the principal corner. Ed argued that a bar should be right across a man's path, a manifest temptation. That boy knew a lot about human weaknesses—among other things. This "bar" as manifest temptation, was going strong when nation-wide "affliction" befell.

At the extreme outer corners of the lot toward the main street were set the two tall welcoming features, topped by trellises to be covered with vines and flowers, ablaze with light to advertise the entrances to both summer and winter gardens.

The kitchen, of course, as stomach is to man, was located beneath and at the very center of the building scheme, short tunnels leading direct to the Gardens for quick service, stairs leading straight up into the winter-garden terraces above it. A waiter could with reasonable ease get direct to all the various terrace levels, balconies, and roofs. And they were legion.

"Quick service and hot food," said John Vogelsang; John was to regale the inner man, interior-decorate him, while Max Bendix charmed his ears, the Gardens charmed his eyes, and altogether charmed the dollars out of popular pockets into the Midway Garden coffers. "Quick service and hot food are the secret of contented diners."

John knew, for he was a Chicago *restaurateur* and a success at the time he was talking.

So, after getting the kitchen located and connected up we made all the kitchen arrangements "according to John."

But the orchestra shell became a bone of contention.

Out of a good deal of experience in such matters with Adler and Sullivan—they designed the Chicago Auditorium and twenty-six other successful opera houses—I had designed the shell, sure it would work out.

Here is where Charlie Matthews' knowledge of music came in, because Charlie, having been a director himself, was appointed committee of one to see this important feature a success. As anyone knows, acoustics are "tricky" unless you know them to be simple and scientific. This was little known then. So the first thing Charlie did was to run around the United States interviewing musicians.

Each musician wanted it different from the others and all wanted it different from the way I had it.

I wouldn't change it. Then Charlie got mad and called in experts. The experts were all agreed that the open sides that I wanted in order to distribute the sound well to the sides of the Gardens were a mistake. Charlie said "change it."

I said, "No, not just for that. Give me a better reason."

Said Charlie, unbecomingly heated, "Hell, Frank, do you think you are the only one in the world who knows anything about orchestra-shells?"

"No, Charlie," I said, trying to keep my case in court, "but about this particular orchestra shell, utterly yes. I am sure I do."

A little later Ed's voice on the phone—"Say, Mr. Architect, are you sure that shell will be all right?"

"Perfectly sure, Ed."

"Then go ahead and build it. Don't change it for anybody." And I knew "anybody" meant Charlie.

You see, in regard to this shell, I was in the position the Union was in toward the Gardens. Success to the dictator lay in this matter of *time*, for the thing had to be done without delays.

All this conflict did make me a little anxious. But, had I shown it, all would have been "up" with the shell, and just because it is impossible to build anything more than one way at a time. Had I lost my nerve I should have had to build it six different ways at least at the same time and then after all probably tear it down.

So I proposed something that made friends with Charlie. The shell was cupped well out above over the orchestra, rising with no complex curves from a wall behind the musicians, a wall about nine feet high. The sides were only partially closed and those open sides being the chief contention, I proposed to make the sides at this point swinging doors that could be swung to if it proved necessary. If not, they were there as features to carry the programme-numbers, etc., signs in electric lights.

This expedient restored harmony.

The Midway Gardens, meantime, were fast growing up out of chaos. Long, low, level lines and new rectangular masonry forms were taking definite shape. They could be seen now, far enough along to make one wonder what in the world was coming?

At the time the Midway Gardens were designed, 1913, L'Art Nouveau was dying in France where it originated and gasping wherever else it happened to have "caught on." Various experiments in the "abstract" in painting and sculpture were being made in Europe exciting the aesthetic vanguard and insulting the rank and file.

But the straight line, itself an abstraction, and the flat plane for its own sake, had characterized my buildings from the first hour I became building-conscious on my own account.

Never interested in "realism," I was already dissatisfied with the realistic element in any building. Like *Breaking Home Ties* in painting, The Rogers' Groups in sculpture, or *Liberty* covers today, the work of the period was flat on its stomach to the "realistic." Or else the buildings were the usual dull and vulgar imitations of the old styles, false and imitative. I admired nothing going on in architecture at the time this design for the Midway Gardens became due to happen.

I clearly saw my trusty T Square and aspiring triangle as means to the Midway Garden end I had in view.

I meant to get back to first principles—pure form in everything; weave a masonry-fabric in beautiful pattern in genuine materials and sound construction, bring painting and sculpture to heighten and carry all still further into the realm of the Lamp in the same *Spirit.*

Yes, why not have the whole Gardens as consistently a unit for once in a century as anything in music Max Bendix could find to play in them? That early kindergarten experience with the straight line; the flat plane; the square; the triangle; the circle! If I wanted more, the square modified by the triangle gave the hexagon—the circle modified by the

Frank Lloyd Wright Studio Residence, Goethe Street (Project). Chicago, Illinois. 1913. Perspective. Pencil and color pencil on tracing paper, 9 x 26". FLLW Fdn#1113.004

straight line would give the octagon. Adding thickness, getting "sculpture" thereby, the square became the cube, the triangle the tetrahedron, the circle the sphere. These primary forms and figures were the secret of all effects, not merely efflorescent or fluorescent, which or that were ever got into the architecture of the world. As by now, I could see. Were they not especially so in the time and place in which Aladdin rubbed his wonderful lamp?

Why then, not go back to the "source," bring form alive again in my own way, making a chime to the tune of imagination in Chicago?

Forms could be made into a festival for the eyes no less than music made festival for the ears, I knew. And this could all be genuine building, not scene painting.

Yes, but how about the Chicago audience? Would Chicago be able to "see"? Chicago was far behind in judging qualities in either form, sound, or color. The "Arts" were yet to come to Chicago. A painting still had to be a picture; and the more the picture could be mistaken for the real object, the better Chicago liked the work.

Sculpture the same way. That too had to look real, and if it could seem so to the touch, why, that was greatest sculpture.

Would Chicago respond to adventure into the realm of the abstract in the sense that I wanted to go into it? Did Chicago know what "abstraction" meant anyway? Perhaps not. Certainly not.

I didn't argue these things with anyone but myself. I kept still about them.

After all, what did these subjective matters signify to others?

Fortunately, human beings are really childlike, in the best sense, when directly appealed to by simple, strong forms and pure, bright color. Chicago was not sophisticated. Chicago was still unspoiled. So probably all this would go straight to the Chicago heart.

The straight line, square, triangle, and the circle were set to work in this developing sense of abstraction by now my habit, to characterize the architecture, painting, and sculpture of the Midway Gardens.

Most places of the kind I had seen at home or

Ravine Bluffs Bridge. Glencoe, Illinois. 1915. Perspective. Watercolor on art paper, 18 x 24". FLLW Fdn#1505.001

abroad were developed as a cheap sentimental, erotic foolishness—scene painting. In the Midway Gardens there was to be no eroticism. No damn'd sentimentality. There was to be permanent structure. The human figure might come into the scheme but only to respect the architecture, being dominated by the sense of the whole. The human "figure" should be there humbly to heighten the whole effect.

The human figure? Sprites of these geometrical forms themselves. They alone might come to play and to share in the general geometric gaiety. How far I would let them out of their geometric shells I found when I designed the terminal figures for the piers in the winter-garden exterior and interior and elsewhere, and called in young Ianelli from Los Angeles and dear old Dicky Bock from the woods.[11]

How far these ideas would go in flat color, I determined when I handed the general schemes for color-decoration to William Henderson and Jack Norton of the Art Institute, and Jerry Blum of the Orient.

Here in the Midway Gardens painting and sculpture were to be bidden back again to their original places and to their original offices in architecture, where they belonged. The architect, himself, here master of them all. (Making no secret of it whatever.)

But artists are very sensitive beings in their own right. In modern times they are become unaccustomed to sitting in the orchestra to play a mere part in an architect's "score," so to speak. The incumbent "altogether" means less to them than it did to their ancient progenitors. As an obligation it grinds on them. They "lose face," as the Orientals say, when they regard it. But I am glad I got them in anyway. About their feelings later, I am not so sure.

I've taken you into confidence in this explanation while these thoughts were taking visible novel effect in brick and concrete there in the Gardens. The work was going on night and day.

My son, John, helped superintend. I, myself, sometimes slept at night on a pile of shavings in a corner of the Winter-Garden when worn out. John would keep going.

"Look here, Wright," said the exasperated Mueller to me one day. "What's this you got here—this young bull-dog that he is. He follows me around and around. Every little while he sticks his teeth in the seat of my pants and I can't get away from him. Can I pull over everything that goes wrong in this work? Can I? Not if I get these Gardens finished up, already some day, I can't. Take him off me!"

But that sounded good to me and I didn't "take him off." John was in it all up to his ears. His "teeth" were serviceable.

We had built a couple of wooden shanties for the modeling of the sculpture. Dicky Bock and Ianelli were working away in them with helpers and a female model. This model was the mysterious object of continuous and extensive male curiosity. Although unable to read, she carried a volume of Ibsen's Plays coming and going. Scientifically she had reduced her garments to "one piece" plus shoes, stockings, gloves, and hat so she could "slip on" and "slip off" easily. Her Mona Lisa smile is evident in the figure pieces of the Gardens. (Thanks to Ianelli.)

While the Sculpture was going on in the shanty the "painters" were working on wooden scaffolds within the buildings of the Gardens. "The painter boys" had got some of their Art Institute pupils to help them, among them an accomplished girl, Catherine Dudley.

A plug-ugly stuck his head in the door of the modeling shanty one day. "The Union again for about the seventh time, on various pretexts."

"Say, what about it? What about that skirt y' got up there doin' paintin'? She ain't no artist, 's she? "

"Sh' is," I said, "and clever."

"Aw, come on. Sh' is just one o' them too good lookin' society dames. Say," he went on, lowering his head and sticking out his jaw, "you get that 'skirt' off'a there or these Gardens, maybe, they'll *never* open. See? And them other three guys yu' got out there a-paintin' with smockkies on a-smokin' don't look to me like no artists neither. Get cards for them, too."

"Artists? Man," I said, "they are. And so good, they're teachers at the Art Institute." (I thought that should impress him.) "Go and ask."

"Naw. I'm askin' nobody. Cards f'r 'em, see? Get 'em."

He glanced at the sculptors Bock and Ianelli. The curtains had hastily been drawn across the model.

"What yu got in there behind that curtain?"

"Now look here. Going pretty strong, aren't you? What business have you got in here, anyway?"

"Business?" he said. "I'll show you what business I got 'n here. Ye're hid'n' men out on me that ought to be 'n the Union, Scabs, see?"

He gave the sculptors a dirty look.

"Where's their cards?"

"Don't need cards. They're Artists, too—sculptors. Can't you see they look that way?" (I couldn't resist this.)

"Naw, n' more'n the carvers and modelers we got in the Union. Not's much," he said. "They got to get their cards or this show don' go on."

I called Dicky down from the scaffold where, before this ugly break, he had been working on the model for the four big capitals for the great piers of the Winter-Garden and took him aside.

"Dick, this looks funny to me. The Union is bad enough, God knows, but this fellow's drunk. Got any money in the bank, Dicky?"

"About seven dollars, I guess."

"Fine! Got your check book, Dicky?"

"Yes."

"Look here, rough-boy. How much for these two great Artists?"

"Thirty-five a piece."

"Seventy dollars?"

"Seventy."

"All right. Dick, give the Union a check for seventy dollars."

"Name?"

He got the check, turned, gave another dirty look at the curtains which, just then, parted. Hatted, gloved, volume of Ibsen under her arm, Mona Lisa stepped forward into view, eyes properly downcast.

The "ugly" grinned. "Yeah! I see," said he, and laughed himself out of the door.

"My God," said Dicky. "When that thug finds out there's no money back of that check, he'll come back here and—hands up."

"Let's see if he will," I said.

The Union had held up the work a half dozen times on one pretext or another, but no issue made of this matter. The artists per se, as such, carried on. No help from the "Union."

The Gardens, owing to high pressure and night-shifts, were nearly done. The electric needles that I made out of wrought-iron pipe, punctured to let the lamps through thickly at the sides, now stood delicately up into the sky and irradiated the whole place for night work.

Seen from afar, they were good advertisements for the Gardens—but not good enough for John Vogelsang. No, not for John. He had secretly started a campaign for a great big electric sign above it all with "MIDWAY GARDENS" blazing on it in colored lights. I discovered him and fought him, I won for awhile but, eventually—some time after the opening—he did get it up there. The first blow to the scheme.

We didn't have any money to color the walls, as intended, by inlaying scarlet and green flash-glass in the relief patterns made of concrete.

We had no money to finish the sky-frames on the four towers of the Winter-Garden intended to be garlanded with vines and flowers like the tops of the welcoming features, nor to plant the big trees at the corners of the Gardens. I mean that we had nothing at all that even promised money. Even the "stage money" was all gone. Gay colored balloons

of various sizes in great numbers were to have flown high above the scene, anchored to the electric needles and tower features. We couldn't get those. They wouldn't have cost much, but that little was too much.

Money troubles, now. Anxiety. Anger. But still hopes and active promises aplenty.

Mueller stood in the breach with his young partner, Seipp, and carried on, else the Midway Gardens would never have opened at all. We all had faith that when opened, the Gardens themselves would settle the financial question the first season.

And then, one noon, while I was eating a late luncheon in the Winter Gardens came the terrible news of tragedy at Taliesin that took me away from the Gardens and from all creative activity for a time.

Meantime the Gardens, though unfinished, had opened in as brilliant a social event as Chicago ever knew.

No, they were not finished, yet, nor were they ever finished. The decorations in the entrance-features remained to be done. Certain other things all about.

But the atmosphere aimed at was there. In a scene unforgettable to all who attended, the architectural scheme of color, form, light, and sound came alive with thousands of beautifully dressed women and tuxedoed men. This scene came upon the beholders as a magic spell. All there moved and spoke as if in a dream.

Chicago marveled, acclaimed, approved. And Chicago went back and did the same again and again and again. It was "Egyptian" to many, Maya to some, Japanese to others. Strange to all. It awakened a sense of mystery and romance in them all to which each responded with what he had in him to give.

And for the remainder of the season, Chicago, the unregenerate, came to rendezvous with Beauty and the coffers of Ed's company began to fill. It looked as though such a success could not be a failure for anyone concerned.

I returned when this popularity was at its height—still dazed, trying to realize it myself. The acoustics were all anyone could hope for, thanks to a perfect orchestra shell. Even Charlie was silent.

But the unfinished final touches so significant and telling in any work of art were lacking. This hurt and marred my sense of the thing as a success.

But these were days of tragedy. War soon broke out. Chicago unnaturally excited, the course of normal life everywhere was soon upset.

The Gardens opened the following season, in financial difficulties, but promising enough, if the second season equaled the first. Pavlova danced, the orchestra was superb.

But the safe was robbed while the creditors were not yet half paid. Dissension in the management now.

The Edelweiss Brewing Company took advantage of this stupid confusion, virtually chaos, to buy the Gardens for a song. They brought their beer to the Gardens—the beer was good—but they brought no imagination and only beer-garden management. The Gardens were never "beer" gardens in the sense that the Edelweiss then knew. The Midway Gardens fell into hands beneath their level and languished in consequence. The Edelweiss tried to "hit them up"—hired someone to come in, paint the concrete, stencil the plain surfaces, and add obnoxious features out of balance. The whole effect was cheapened to suit hearty Bourgeois "taste." A scheme that had been integral now became "decorated" in the meanest and worst popular sense. Where had been integral materials, here was raw red, dead white, and bad blue *paint*. Another "world's fair" effect.

And then the "affliction" befell. The Nation went dry.

That was the final blow to the misdirection already befallen the Gardens.

Because the country went dry, all the more reason for the sort of thing the Midway Gardens originally represented; the greater the need of gaiety in beauty, beauty in gaiety; the greater the need of some artistic rendezvous for the great city—some stimulating beauty to drink, managed with imagination.

But the Midway Gardens had sunk to the level of the "beer garden" without the beer. No imagination on that level to bring it back into its own.

The once distinguished Gardens languished now dreaming of past glory—of possibilities untouched, of a life different from this one of the Chicago gridiron—as sometimes does a beautiful woman who has once known honor, position, homage, but—dragged down by inexorable circumstance to—only shame.

It went from this bad to much worse. The place "changed hands" as they say of saloons, or used to say, in Chicago. These new hands carved it up and over into a dance hall. The Gardens themselves were flooded for a skating rink. "They" carried it all to the mob. For this "they" bedizened the interiors, still more rouged its cheeks, put carmine on its lips, and decked it out in gaudy artificial flowers.

"They" painted the chaste white concrete sculpture in more irrelevant gaudy colors, stenciled more cheap ornament on top of the integral ornament, wrecked the line and mass of the whole—until all semblance of the original harmony utterly vanished. Yes, a distinguished beautiful woman dragged to the level of the prostitute is now its true parallel. I have often thought "Why will someone, in mercy not give them the final blow and tear them down?"

Now they have been destroyed to make room for a filling station and auto-laundry. I am thankful. The contractor who removed the building found them so solidly constructed that he lost more on the contract than the contract was worth.

The Midway Gardens, once fascinating mistress, dragged down from heights of beauty and high purpose to belong to the filthy discord all around, it had so proudly scorned in its youth—now as cheap and low as any. The remnant of beauty and style still visible here and there, long having served to intensify shame.

We say of many a woman, not old, "You may see she was very beautiful once—but now!" And the relic of that beauty serves only to make the sense of ugliness tragic and hard to bear.

The Midway Gardens, still young, were such tragedy as this.

Strange fate! The Midway Gardens are, just now, new in the thought of the world.

What they might have been had the Gardens found in Chicago a true mate and help meet? They would be still more wonderful, covered with the climbing ivy which the scheme craved with a natural hunger. Arching trees massed about the walls, the little significances in the empty places that had longed for them all those years and that would have been like a happy glint in the eyes. The whole solidly built place would now be polished, mellowed, enriched by years of good care, hallowed by pleasant associations—a proud possession for any great city.

Is there no Chicago honor for such love as made the Midway Gardens an oasis of beauty in the wilderness of smoky dens, car tracks, and saloons? This "resort" Young Ed knew Chicago needed and believed Chicago wanted?

When the Midway Gardens were nearly finished, my son, John, and I sleeping there at night in a corner, on a pile of shavings, to keep track of the night work now necessary to finish the Gardens on time—at noon, as we were sitting quietly eating our lunch in the newly finished bar, came a long distance call from Spring Green. Taliesin was destroyed by fire. But no word came of the ghastly tragedy itself. I learned of that little by little on the way home on the train that evening.

Thirty-six hours earlier I had left, leaving all at Taliesin, living, friendly, and happy. Now a blow had fallen like the lightning stroke. In less time than it takes to write it, a thin-lipped Barbados negro, who had been well recommended to me as an ideal servant, had turned madman, had taken the lives of seven, and set the house in flames. In thirty minutes the house and all in it had burned to the stone work or to the ground. The living half of Taliesin—violently swept down in a madman's nightmare of flame and murder.[12]

The working half remained.

Will Weston saved that.

He had come to grips with the madman whose strength was superhuman; slipped from his grasps and his blows. Bleeding from the encounter he ran down the hill to the nearest neighbor to give the alarm, made his way back immediately through the cornfields only to find the deadly work finished and the home ablaze. Hardly able to stand, he ran to where the firehose was kept in a niche of the garden wall, past his young son, lying there in the fountain basin, one of the seven dead, got the hose loose, staggered with it to the fire and with the playing hose stood against destruction, himself, until they led him away.

The great stone chimneys with their fireplaces were now gaping holes, and stood blackened there above the Valley against the sky.

She for whom Taliesin had first taken form and her two children . . . gone. A talented apprentice, Emil Brodelle, the young son of William Weston, the gardener, David Lindblom, a faithful workman, Thomas Brunker—this was the human toll taken by madness. The madman was discovered hidden in the fire-pot of the steam boiler, in the smoking ruins of the house. He was taken to the Dodgeville jail. Refusing meantime to utter a word, he died there some days later.

There was a primitive burial in the ground of the family chapel. The men from Taliesin dug the grave, deep, near grandfather's and grandmother's grave. A funeral service could only be mockery. The undertaker's offices—his vulgar "casket" seemed to me profane. So I cut the garden down and filled to overflowing with the flowers a strong, plain box of fresh, white pine. I had my own carpenters make it.

My boy, John, helped me to lift the body and let it down to rest among the flowers. The flowers that had grown and bloomed for her. The plain box lid was pressed down upon the flowers and fastened home. Then the plain, strong box was lifted by my workmen and placed on our little spring-wagon, filled, too, with flowers—waiting hitched behind Darby and Joan . . . we made the whole a mass of flowers.

Since Taliesin was first built the faithful little sorrel team had drawn us along the Valley roads and over the hills, in spring, summer, autumn, and winter, almost daily.

Walking alongside the wheels, I drove the horses along the road to the churchyard, where no bell had tolled. No people were waiting. John followed. Ralph and Orrin, two young "Hillside" cousins were waiting at the chapel gate. Together we lowered the flower-filled and flower-covered pine box to the bottom of the new-made grave. Then I asked them to leave me there alone.

I wanted to fill the grave myself . . .

The August sun was setting on the familiar range of hills. I felt, dimly, the far-off shadows of the ages, struggling to escape from subconsciousness and utter themselves . . . then—darkness . . . I filled the grave—in darkness—in the dark.

No monument marks the spot where "Mamah" was buried.

All I had to show for the struggle for freedom of the past five years that had swept most of my former life away, had now been swept away.

Why mark the spot where desolation ended and began?

ALONE

I remained in what was left of Taliesin I, in the little bedroom back of the undestroyed studio workshop. Working to get work started on Taliesin II.

No one seemed near to me.

The gaping black hole left by fire in the beautiful hillside was no less empty, charred and ugly in my own life.

The tragedy that resulted in the destruction of Taliesin I had left me in strange plight.

From the moment of my return to that devastating scene of horror I had wanted to see no one and I would see no one but the workmen.

For the following week there was no one on the hill at night but myself and the watchman who sat on the steps to the court with a gun across his knees, because the whole countryside was terrified by the tragedy, not knowing what to expect.

Those nights in the little back room were black, filled with strange unreasoning terrors. No moon seemed to shine. No stars in the sky. No frog-song from the pond below. Strange, unnatural silence, the smoke still rising from certain portions of the ruin.

Unable to sleep, I would get up, numb, take a cold bath to bring myself alive, go out alone on the hills in the night, not knowing where. But I would come safely back again with only a sense of black night and strange fear, no beauty visible. Grope how I might—no help from that source. And I would grope my way to bed.

Strange! Instead of feeling that she, whose life had joined mine there at Taliesin was a spirit near, that too was utterly gone.

After the first anguish of loss, a kind of black despair seemed to paralyze my imagination in her direction and numbed my sensibilities. The blow was too severe.

I got no relief in any faith or in any hope. Except repulsion, I could only feel in terms of rebuilding—get relief only by looking toward rebuilding—get relief from a kind of continuous nausea.

That relief in habitual action was all I had. The only color life had for me. And in music. They had thrown my piano out of the window to save it and, legs broken, it was blocked up by the studio fireplace. I would sit there and try to play.

But everything else had been swept away or lurked in the strange oppression of some darkened forbidding room in which strange shadows moved.

At that time, as I looked back I saw the black hole in the hillside, the black night over all. And sinister shadows. Days strangely without light would follow the black nights. Totally—Mamah was gone.

This is not fanciful word painting. It is what happened. Gone into this blackness of oblivion for several years to come was all sense of her whom I had loved as having really lived at all.

This was merciful? I believe the equivalent of years passed in the course of weeks, in my consciousness. Time ceased to exist. Days passed into nights, numb to all but the automatic steps toward rebuilding.

The routine of the day's work, eating the three meals a day that were brought to me, this went on by sheer force of habit. And I began to go down. Physically I sagged. Boils (I had never had any in my life before) now broke out over my back and neck. I lost weight. Finally I got back to my little home at 25 Cedar Street and lived there alone, except for an Irish caretaker.

I had never needed glasses, but now I had to have them.

These now came between me and my work.

Nature is as merciful as she is cruel. Any faculty overtaxed becomes numb. The real pain comes when healing begins. In this the spirit seems subject to the same laws as the senses.

A horrible loneliness began to clutch me, but I longed for no one I ever loved or that I had ever known. My mother was deeply hurt by my refusal to have her with me. My children—I had welcomed them eagerly always—but I did not want them now. They had been so faithfully kind in my extremity. I shall never forget.

But strange faces were best and I walked among them.

I do not understand this any better now than I did then. But so it was. Months went by, but they might have been, and I believe they were, for me, a lifetime.

Perhaps new consciousness had to grow as a green shoot will grow from a charred and blackened stump?

But the fact remains—until many years after, to turn my thoughts backward to what had transpired in the life we lived together at Taliesin was like trying to see into a dark room in which terror lurked, strange shadows—moved—and I would do well to turn away.

I could see forward but I could not see backward.

It looked for some time as though I might not be able to see at all.

It was this fear that, like a lash, made me get to work upon myself none too soon.

Waves of publicity had broken over Taliesin again. The human sacrifice at Taliesin seemed all in vain. Its heroism was ridiculed . . .mocked. Its very heart, struck from it at a blow, was profaned by a public sympathy almost harder to bear than the public curiosity had been.

"Tried and condemned," they said. Was this trial for heresy too? Was this trial at some judgment seat, like Grandfather's, to quell a spirit that would not be quelled?

And this unconventional believer in the Good, the True, the Beautiful, as work and life and love, in the midst of all three thus all but struck down?

Some months before, sitting on the stone terrace overlooking the valley below, I saw one of the finest cows of the countryside, Maplecroft, Holstein thoroughbred worth several hundred ordinary cows, standing beneath an oak tree two other cows beside her, comparatively worthless. A lightning flash there below simultaneous with a stunning crash. The two walked away from beneath the tree unharmed, but Maplecroft lay there dead by stroke of lightning. Why peerless Maplecroft?

Why Taliesin?

Many willing answers to "Why Taliesin" were publicly made by "good men and true." "They" now had a text on which to preach. But no preaching more reasonable than that the unconventional gathers enmity of the conventional until, charged beyond the containing point, explosion in some form, obvious or occult, follows. But did this apply to Maplecroft's "unconventionality"? Hers consisted in being thoroughbred. Did the envy or displeasure of ordinary numbers attract destruction to her?

Nonsense!

So the rage that grew when I felt the inimical weight of human censure on my soul began to fade away and finally took refuge in the idea that Taliesin should live to show something more for its mortal sacrifice than a charred and terrible ruin on a lonely hillside in the beloved Valley.

There is release from anguish in action. Anguish would not leave Taliesin until action for renewal began. Again, and at once, all that had been in motion before at the will of the architect was set in motion. Steadily, again, stone by stone, board by board, Taliesin the II began to rise from the ashes of Taliesin the first.

Where scenes of horror had identified the structure with ugly memories, all changed. An open stone-floored loggia looked up the Valley to the Lloyd-Jones Chapel. This beautiful stone loggia to take the place of the scene of the tragedy.

Taliesin II. Spring Green, Wisconsin. 1914–1915. FLLW Fdn FA#1403.0003

A guest unit was added to the West, with a great fireplace, for my mother and aged aunts. I intended to bring them home to Taliesin now.

There was to be no turning back nor stopping to mourn. What had been beautiful at Taliesin should live as a grateful memory creating the new, and, come who might to share Taliesin, they would help in that spirit.

I believed it.

As a consequence of the publicity given the terrible tragedy hundreds of letters had come to me from all over the country. I tied them up together into a bundle and burned them unread.

TALIESIN II

More stone, more wood, more work, and more harmonious use of them all. More workmen, more sacrifice, more creative work on my part and efforts to find and earn the necessary money.

Another fall, another winter, another spring, another summer, and late in 1915, Taliesin the II stood in the place of the first. A more reposeful and finer one. Not a "chastened" Taliesin. No, rather up in arms declining the popular Mosaic-Isaian idea of "punishment" as unworthy the sacrifice demanded and taken there. Demanded? By whom? Taken? For what? And the sentimental or superstitious or profane answers, answered nothing.

But something was coming clear, through the brutalizing Taliesin had received. Something—no, not rebellion—now—but conviction. Purpose lifted the crown of the head higher. Made the eye see clearer. The tread that faltered for a moment in sorrow and confusion became elastic and more sure as work came alive again.

The German Monograph published by Wasmuth had duly appeared in beautiful format. The work was a success in Germany. Darwin D. Martin helped me to control the sale of the book in America but the copies reserved for that purpose went up in smoke when Taliesin burned. Some thirty copies only were saved.

Now came relief, a change of scene as . . . promptly . . . I was called to build the Imperial Hotel in Tokio, Japan.

A commission including the Japanese architect, Yoshitaki, and the intelligent manager of the Imperial Hotel, Aisaku Hayashi, had gone around the world to find an architect. Reaching the Middle West, they saw the "new" houses.

They were immediately interested in them. Such buildings, though not at all Japanese, would look well in Japan, they thought. So they came to the reconstructed Taliesin, Taliesin II, to see me. Taliesin itself impressed them. Said Hayashi-san, "I am taken back to Jimmu Tenno's time." He fell in love with the place as did his gentle wife, Takako.

Hayashi's young Takako-san was a beautiful presence at Taliesin, at this time, with her exquisite Japanese wardrobe. I regret so few pictures have been preserved for others. Very quiet and reserved in her manner, she was very frankly curious about our foreign ways—especially our manners. One evening at dinner she said, "Wrieto-san, what means 'goddam'?"

"Goddam?" I wondered where she got that.

"Oh, Takako-san, 'goddam' is a polite word for 'very.' You might say it is a 'goddam fine evening,' or 'it is goddam fresh butter.' Or after dinner you say to your hostess, 'Thank you for your goddam good dinner.'"

"O, O!" she said. ("O" was her invariable English exclamation.) "O, I see. Please, Wrieto-san, pass me the goddam fresh butter." And she goddam'd her way through the dinner to a running accompaniment of laughter. Afterward she turned to her host and with perfect naiveté, thanked him for the "goddam good dinner."

Was she wiser than she seemed? I wondered if she didn't know all the time what the laughter meant. Hayashi, whose laughter had joined in, wouldn't enlighten me.

Then and there in the workroom that had escaped destruction I made a preliminary plan according to Hayashi-san's general requirements. The little commission after a week at Taliesin went back to Tokio. Some months later an official invitation came to come to Tokio. I went as soon as I could. I was eager to go. Again now I wanted to get away from the United States. I still imagined one might "get away" from himself. In spite of all my reasoning power and returning balance I was continually expecting some terrible blow to strike. The sense of impending disaster would hang over me, waking or dreaming. This fitted in well enough with the sense

of earthquake, from the actuality of which I should have to defend the new building. But I looked forward to Japan as a refuge and rescue. The lands of my dreams—Japan and Germany.

During the years at the Oak Park workshop, Japanese prints intrigued me and taught me much. The elimination of the insignificant, a process of simplification in art in which I was engaged, beginning with my twenty-third year, found collateral evidence in the print. Ever since I discovered the print Japan has appealed to me as the most romantic, artistic country on earth. Japanese art, I found, real-

Taliesin II. Spring Green, Wisconsin. 1914–1915. FLLW Fdn FA#1403.0033

Aisaku Hayashi and his wife at Taliesin. c.1915.
FLLW Fdn FA#1509.0049

ly did have organic character, was nearer to the earth and a more indigenous product of native conditions of life and work therefore more nearly "modern" as I saw it, than any European civilization alive or dead.

I had realized this during a first visit in pursuit of the Japanese print made in 1906.

A SONG TO HEAVEN

Now again, as the ship's anchor dropped in Yokohama Bay, I was to have my earlier feeling deepened, intensified. Imagine, if you have not seen it, a mountainous, abrupt land, the sea everywhere apparently having risen too high upon it, so all gentle slopes to the water's edge are lost. It is morning. Pure golden skies are seen over far stretches of blue sea dotted in the distance by flocks of white sampan sails—white birds at rest on the blue water.

Imagine, if you can, sloping foothills and mountainsides all "antique" sculpture, carved, century after century, with curving terraces. The culti-

vated fields rising tier on tier to still higher terraced vegetable fields, green dotted. And extending far above the topmost dotted fields, see the very mountaintops themselves corrugated with regular rows of young pine trees pushing diagonally over them: "reforestation." The Imperial Government's share in the pattern everywhere visible.

Look at the clusters of straw-thatched villages nesting in the nooks of the mountainous land like birds nesting in trees. Or clinging, like the vegetation itself to steep slopes.

Turn about, and look at the ruddy-bronze naked bodies of fishermen gleaming red in the sun as they go sculling by in flat sampan. Turn again and see the toilers in the fields, animated spots of true indigo-blue, spots that live in the landscape like the flowers and birds. The birds strangely without song. Few of the flowers with perfume but so boldly made, so brilliant and profuse as to seem artificial.

Glance, as you go ashore for the first time, into the village streets, at the swarms of brightly clad, happy children, babies thrust into the bright kimonos on their backs. The child is the Japanese treasure of treasures. Observe the silhouette of the clothed female figures—young or old—a simple swelling curve from nape of the neck to white heels as they all go clogging about with short scraping steps on white feet thrust into tall wooden clogs.

These white feet will tell the story of the dwelling ancient Shinto religion built there in that land of the living as a matter of everyday life and everywhere! The feet, white, cotton clad, are more significant in the telling of that tale than anything else.

And the men and women so care for the very young and the very old, it is said their country is the paradise of old age and of childhood. Old age a qualification not a disqualification in Japan. A proof of civilization lacking in our own?

All these patient human beings from the very young to the very old, like one great family, seem humbly resigned to loving one another and respecting one another as they clog along over damp bareearth streets, feet made white with "tabi" and kept white. The significant tabi are merely a soft-fitted white-cotton low sock-shoe. When going out the tabi are thrust into the wooden geta or clogs. The geta are a sort of detachable wooden stilted hoof to be left outside on the dirt or stone pavement of the entry to the dwelling as the "white-feet" leave and step up inside onto spotless *tatami*. The removable sections of firm, padded straw-matting of their house floors are called *tatami*.

So clean are these straw mats of the floors that I have seen women, men, too, kneeling on the long side-benches of the railway trains to Tokio—facing the car windows, sitting on their feet in a posture which left the bottoms of their feet nicely put together underneath them toward you. And, as anyone might see, the very bottoms of their feet were spotless white.

Be clean! "Be clean" was the soul of Shinto, the ancient religion of Japan. Shinto spoke, not of a good or a moral man—but of a clean man. Spoke of clean hands—of a clean heart.

And the Shinto religion finally made the Japanese dwelling the cleanest of all clean human things. Clean too, in a spiritual sense. The sense that abhors waste as matter out of place. Therefore dirt. Therefore ugly.

As the centuries went by, every Japanese home, whether of the coolie or of the aristocrat, has been worked out in this "be clean" spirit as a temple.

Becoming more closely acquainted with things Japanese, I saw the native home in Japan as supreme study in elimination—not only of dirt but the elimination, too, of the insignificant. The Japanese house fascinated me and I would spend many hours taking it to pieces and putting it together again. I saw nothing meaningless in the Japanese home and could find very little ever added in the way of ornament because all "ornament," as we call it, they get out of the way the necessary things are done or by bringing out and polishing the beauty of the simple materials used in making the building. Again a kind of "cleanliness."

I had found this one country on earth where simplicity, as natural, is supreme.

The floors of these Japanese homes are all made to live on—to sleep on, to kneel and eat from, to kneel upon soft silken mats and meditate upon or on which to play the flute, or "make love."

Nothing is allowed to stand long as a fixture upon the sacred floors of any Japanese house. Everything the family uses is designed to be removed when not in use and put into its proper place. It is so made. Beautiful to use upon it only when appropriate and at the right moment. Even the partitions dividing the floor spaces into rooms are made removable for cleaning.

And strangely enough, I found this ancient Japanese dwelling to be a perfect example of the modern standardizing I had myself been working with. The floor mats, removable too for cleaning, are all three feet by six feet. The size and shape of all the houses are determined by the mats. The sliding partitions all occur at the point lines of the mats, and they speak of a nine, sixteen or thirty-six mat house, as the case may be.

The simple square, polished wooden posts that support the ceilings and roof all stand at the intersections of the mats. The sliding paper *shoji*, or outside screens that serve in place of windows and enclose the interior room spaces—they are actually the outside walls. All slide back into a recess in the walls and they are removable too.

The wind blows clean beneath the floors. The sloping tiled roofs are padded with clay under the heavy curved roof tiles and above the beautiful, low, flat, broad-boarded ceilings to make a cool overhead.

The *benjo* or earth-closet is made in the garden and set well away from the "devil's corner," and as if to prove to me that nearly every superstition has a basis of sense, that corner I found to be the one from which the prevailing breezes blow. Semi-detached from the house the *benjo* is reached, under shelter, on polished plank floors. Beside it always stands a soft-water cistern, perhaps made of some hollowed-out natural stone or a picturesque garden-feature made or set up out of various natural stones. Or it may be a great bronze bowl brimming with water. A delicate little bamboo dipper lies across the pool of water to be lifted by the little housemaid who will pour clean water over the hands of the master or of his guest as either leaves the *benjo*. Another libation to the Shinto God of Cleanliness. A little confusing at first to the foreign guest?

245

And the kitchen? Go down several steps to find that, for it is tiled flat with the ground and so goes high up into the rafters. It is like a cool, clean, well ventilated "studio." Its simple appointments are of polished concrete or stone. And it is hung with a collection of copper kettles and lacquer-ware that would drive a Western "collector" quite off his head.

And the bathroom! This is a good-sized detached pavilion, too, again flush with the ground and floored with stone or tiles pitched so water thrown from a bucket will drain away. Over the stone floor is a slat-floor of wood on which to stand in bare feet. The built-in tub is square and deep, to stand in. It is heated from beneath.

I have often been soaped and scrubbed before I was allowed to be tubbed. And then I might step in and cook the germs off me to any extent I was able to stand up to. Yes, the Shinto bath is a fine and religious thing as is everything else about the establishment. And bathing is perpetual. It has been made easy. The Japanese man or woman may loosen the girdle and slip all the garments off together in one gesture or put them on again the same way. In costume too, see simplicity, convenience, repose—their bodies as easily kept clean as their houses. Shinto will have it so. I found it wholly convenient and wore the native costume in the Japanese inn or dwelling.

And for the pleasure in all this human affair you couldn't tell where the garden leaves off and the garden begins. I soon ceased to try, too delighted with the problem to attempt to solve it.

Here is a house used by those who made it with just that naturalness with which a turtle uses his shell. It is as like the natives as the polished bronze of their skin, the texture of their polished hair or the sly look in their slant and sloe eyes.

Belonging to this domestic establishment, this "domestication of the infinite," there is everywhere to be seen a peculiar concentration on the part of "Ochsan," the kindly faced housewife. And as yet, on the part of her coy daughters O Kani-san and O Hisa-san. As they all go about their domestic tasks, in their minds must be some religious consecration to what they do, or in their hearts maybe.

"The simplest way with no waste." That is daily "Shinto" ceremonial in Japan. You may see this in the most dignified and valued of all Japanese ceremonials—their tea ceremony. All cultured Japanese women, rich or poor, must learn to properly perform the tea ceremony as laid down by the celebrated master-aesthete, Rikkyu. A master too, of flower arrangement, as I tried to learn it. This high tea ceremony came simply out of the science or art of most gracefully and economically getting a cup of tea made and reverently served to beloved or respected guests. Such reverent concentration as this "tea" ceremonial carries the ideal of "be clean" to such heights—and lengths—as weary us. We have not the spirit of it and we cannot stand it—very long. But in this ceremony the very sense of "be clean" becomes, as I have already said, the spiritual attitude that not only abhors waste as matter out of place—therefore dirt—but places disorder of any sort in the same category.

That attitude the West finds unbearable, because this practical application of their ancient Shinto religion would see most of our domestic arrangements tumbled out of the windows into the street, a rich harvest for some junk man. If Christian houses were ever treated by Christians to proper spiritual interpretation such as Japanese interpretation of "Shinto" the resulting integrity of spirit would immediately bankrupt our cherished "pictorial homes." Even if, yes especially *if* such interpretation did not enrich the soul of the West.

And how our good "taste" reacts upon and poisons them. For by contact with us they have suddenly seen how difficult and unnecessary such painstaking integrity is: seeing how such discipline as theirs is no necessary part of temporal authority or power and affluence as they discover it to be in the great West.

There is spiritual significance alive and singing in everything concerning the Japanese house. A veritable song. It is in unison with their "heaven."

It interested me to see the Japanese gratify the desire for "fine" things—as something added unto them. The desire is natural to them as it is to us. But they have a little recess in even the most humble houses always devoted only to appropriate Fine Art entertainment. They call the little treasure-alcove the *Tokonoma*. A single rare painting will be hung against the quiet-toned plaster walls of the *Tokonoma*. A single "cultured" flower arrangement in a beautiful vase will be set beside the painting or *Kakemono* in the *Tokonoma*. One fine piece of sculpture too, or some abstract form in fine material on a polished lacquer surface will be set below that. Three arts are thus brought together so we may see and admire the individual taste of the owner of the house. Never is the trinity without true cultural reference to some poetic significance of the day, occasion, or season. Literature, too, would be nearby, represented by some poet's profound saying in fine writing, framed and hung—usually on the "ranma," above the interior *shoji*, or sliding screens. All these things, however fine, must be "appropriate." They must be in "season." And they must take the rank of the masterpiece in whatever art.

These objets d'art, being precious, will be carefully wrapped in silk, boxed in safe and charming boxes, put back into the "go down" as the occasion or mood changes and they become less appropriate. Other fine things will then be brought out from time to time from among the household treasures of which, usually, there are very many. Cultivated people, the Japanese lavish loving care on beautiful things. To them beautiful things are religious things and their care is a privilege.

All—in their houses—designed for kneeling on soft mats? Of course. But the same significant integrity, or integrity made significant, would work just as well on one's feet—for us—as it worked for them on their knees.

We of the West couldn't live in Japanese houses and shouldn't. But we could live in houses disciplined by an ideal at least as high and fine as this one of theirs if we went about it—for a century or two.

I am sure the West needs sources of inspiration, for once, it can't copy. And the West can copy everything easier than it can "copy" Japanese things for domestic uses.

Isn't real barbarism merely ignorance of principle? Isn't barbarism trusting, merely, to instinct? Which is just what all our "taste" does or is? In-stincts such as ours, demoralized by opulence, are none the less barbaric because they have intellect they don't use, or a past culture they sentimentally abuse. More dangerous and offensive to life, such demoralization, I should say.

On tortured knees I have tried to learn some of these lessons from the Japanese. I have participated in this "idealized" making of a cup of tea that follows the Japanese formal dinner, trying to get at some of these secrets, if secrets they are. I have been eventually bored to extinction by the repetition of it all and soon would avoid the ordeal when I could see an invitation coming. And I freely admit, such discipline is not for us. It is far too severe. Yes, far too severe! We are not yet "civilized" enough to go that far in idealizing anything in life, not to mention environment. Or capable of making "living" into ceremony except, occasionally. For the moment. Our joys and sorrows come and go otherwise. Our recreations are mainly—different. And I become painfully aware of our crudity in the cultured Japanese environment. Their thumbs fold inward as naturally as ours stick up and out. Their legs quietly fold up beneath them where—when off our feet—ours must stick out and sprawl. It could be said that our civilization is founded upon the silken leg, the shapely thigh, and the high heel. Theirs upon the graceful arm, the beautifully modeled breast and the expressive hand. The finely molded leg rising from the shapely shoe indicates our heaven. The finely modulated breast and arm and expressive hand indicate theirs. There is a difference.

No matter, the difference happens to be only an idiosyncracy of nationality. Their simple dwelling is still exemplary for us by way of showing true Culture in this matter of environment which in any true civilization must be considered Fine Art.

The truth is the Japanese dwelling owing to the Shinto ideal "be clean" is in every bone and fiber of its structure honest. And in its every aspect sincerely means something fine and straightway does it.

It seemed to me as I studied the "song" that we of the West are cut off from the practical by so many old, sentimental, Christian expedients? We are too busy elaborately trying to get earth to heaven instead of seeing this simple Shinto wisdom of sensibly getting heaven decently to earth?

In the morning land I found this simple everyday singing of the human spirit, this "song to heaven" of ancient Shinto religion to be the every day dwelling place of the Japanese people. But I see that "song" as truly a blossom of interior nature as trees and flowers and bees are that blossoming. And I have learned much from the singing as I could hear and see it on my reverent knees, as Baron Kuki—poor lonely Baron, celebrated for his cuisine—or as some other Japanese gentlemen would send for me to come and dine. And the solemn "tea ceremony" as laid down by Rikkyu, would inevitably follow the twenty-four or more artistic courses of a formal Japanese dinner.

All this had settled as experience in my thought of Japan. And the question of modern architecture seemed more involved with Japanese architecture in principle than with any other. So in the circumstances—frustration and destruction behind me—I turned hopefully and gratefully to life in Japan once more. But as nature and character—both are fate—would have it, I had not come alone.

Months after the catastrophe at Taliesin came a short letter expressing sympathy in kind terms that understood suffering, evidently, from a developed artist-intelligence. I somehow thought it from some fine-spirited, gray-haired lady-mother who had suffered deeply herself. I spoke of the note to my mother. And, for some reason, now, I acknowledged it with a few grateful words. A reply asking if the writer might come to see me. She was a sculptress. She said life had crashed for her with much the same sorrow as mine. A luckless love affair. And she gave me some helpful suggestions as to thought. The philosophy, not so new, but neglected by me and needed now.

I wrote, appointing a time at the Orchestra Hall office. She preferred to come after office hours.

That was how Miriam Noel appeared.

She was the reverse of everything I had expected. I was—frankly—astonished. I could not connect the letters with her appearance. But as she sat opposite me at the office desk, when she spoke, I understood how she could have written them.

She was a Parisian by adoption and preference. Brilliant. Sophisticated, as might be seen at a glance. She had evidently been very beautiful, was so distinguished still. A violet pallor. A mass of dark red-brown hair. Clear seeing eyes with a green light in them. Carriage erect and conscious—her figure still youthful. She was richly dressed in the mode, a sealskin cape and cap. On her small hands were several rings. Around her neck she wore a gold chain with a jeweled cross—a monocle, too, suspended on a white silken cord, with which she played as she talked. She laid a cigarette case upon the office table. I lit for her the cigarette she took from it—not caring to smoke myself. In her left hand had been a small, black, limp book. She laid it on the desk. It was a copy of "Science and Health" by Mary Baker Eddy. Her latest study in psychology.

"How do you like me?" she said.

A trace of some illness seemed to cling to her in the continuous shaking of her head, slight but perceptible, as she looked at me, waiting for an answer to her simple question.

"I've never seen anyone like you," I said.

Her two daughters were married. Her son a traveling man. She had no one, she said—"nowhere to go and no desires." "Her health"—it might be seen and as she said—"had been broken by the tragedy of the luckless love affair."

Finally she had been driven out of Paris along with the other Americans by the declaration of war. She was now staying for a time in Chicago with one of her married daughters. She had heard of me in Paris from the Horace Holleys—had read of the terrible tragedy. It had touched her, and she apologized for being so bold as to write and offer her help.

Here she was. Outside the routine of my work I had scarcely spoken since the tragedy to anyone but my mother.

Drowning men—they say so—clutch at straws.

Here was no straw but enlightened comradeship, help, light to see by. Salvation maybe from blackness—blindness.

Miriam Noel. FLLW Fdn FA#6700.0005

And began the leading of the blind by the blind.

How do sentimental people ever manage to live at all? By hypocrisy? I have often asked the most sentimental person I ever knew—myself. And I am sure the answer is yes—hypocrisy. The hypocrisy of oneself—with oneself—which is the foundation of hypocrisy toward others.

Now, on the way to Tokio. The brilliant Miriam alongside.

Again, for the third time there stood Fujiyama, venerable, white hooded, inviolate against a golden sky. After the usual half sea-sickness that made every hour that would slowly go by on board wearily be counted as one hour nearer this landing, at dawn the "Empress of China" rides at anchor in Yokohama harbor. The engines stilled at last—the soft tread of the Chinese boys, keeping step with the silence.

The remembered beauty of the earlier experiences comes to refresh the jaded senses. The *jinrikisha* rolls off the dock to familiar sights.

But here we have come, two years after the second crossing. High work to be done. Foundation tests completed, the building of the Imperial Hotel is to begin and to continue in earnest the better part of four years.

Contrary to the popular superstition concerning voluntary, open relationships between grown-up independent men and women, there is usually a high ideal of life on both sides. There must be a sincere attempt to be true to each other and meet life's demands upon a higher plane of excellence than is ordinary and so, a more exacting code of ethics continuously makes demands upon integrity and personal quality of both man and woman. Comradeship makes constant demands that legal marriage may and does dispense with. Especially upon the woman does a voluntary relationship make these difficult demands. The woman brave enough or foolish enough to honestly go into one has that relationship alone to live by and to live for. Because she will, owing to environment and circumstances, be cut off from society in ways hard to bear at first and harder to bear as time goes on.

A developed interior life of no mean character is the condition of any success whatever, even temporarily, in any unconventional life a man and a woman may undertake to live openly together.

I was still "illegitimate."—That is to say, still unable to get my legitimate freedom from the marriage contract with Catherine. No arguments availing. So, any woman interested in me, caring enough for me to live with me, would be compelled to take that step into unconventional life or go under cover. Tragedy in these circumstances is double the similar tragedy in legal marriage, because the relationship is not only utterly defenseless, but mercilessly assailed and failure generally welcomed by Society.

I had never in my life learned to hide and if I had learned I should have declined any partnership on those terms because unconscious hypocrisy is bad enough. But conscious hypocrisy is a sure and swift corrosion of the soul.

No coward ever did creative work, I believe.

Equivocal conduct hurts ten times more those who practice it than those it is practiced upon. Secrecy and hypocrisy both do something to the character never to be repaired. And while the hypocrisy of others is hard to bear, it is better to *bear* it than to *be* it.

It is not the honest living of any life that endangers society, is it?

Aren't the *pretended* lives the rotten threads in the social fabric?

I am sure that, while marriage in true sense is only for those who do not need it, yet, it is so difficult to live long above it without the protection it gives that only coarse character or rare virtue can ever hope to survive without the legal formality of marriage.

The management of the Imperial had allowed me to build a modest little nook for myself in the new temporary annex. The hotel had built this annex from my plans, to take care of the increase in guests while the New Imperial was building. The annex was just finished.

The windows of this little apartment looked out to the south over the Japanese Garden and the apartment itself was connected to the hotel for complete service. I had a Japanese boy for my own uses. And the mystery of Tokio was all around. Tokio is much like London in many respects, there is so much room in it for surprises. A dingy street outside and palaces within the humble doors, casual gates and quiet entrance ways.

In this nook in Tokio was a small living room with a fireplace—fire always burning—a balcony filled with dwarf-trees and flowers, a bedroom with balcony and bath, a small dining room where meals were served from the hotel. All on the main floor of the apartment.

A narrow stair led up from the entrance way to a commodious studio-bedroom built as a penthouse above the roof. I slept there and had set up my drawing board there where I could work, disturbing no one, and could tumble into bed when tired out.

Into these quarters we now went. And for a time a peaceful, mutually helpful, relationship. There was a small grand piano—our friends in Tokio were all capable of making good music. There was much good reading, study, rambles through Tokio by night, motor trips sometimes, usually, on Sunday, by day. These recreations together with the few friends always faithful in such cases because they understand the situation and respect the characters involved, made up the world

we lived in. We knew a good many interesting, some charming, Russians in Tokio, among them the talented Polish Count and Countess Lubiensky, Princess Tscheremissinof, Count and Countess Ablomov, the Ivanoffs, Olga Krynska, a talented pianist and linguist, the Japanese Hani's of the wonderful little "School of the Free Spirit." I built a school building suitable to their purpose—one of the rare experiences of my life.

The clairvoyant Miriam, herself, for many years had been the victim of strange disturbances. Sometimes unnatural exaggeration, mental and emotional, spoiled life entirely for days at a time. I had hunted causes. Yes . . . I had looked into myself, too.

That, nervously, she had suffered wreck, was true. Strange disabilities began to appear in her. All would go happily for days. Then strange perversion of all that. No visible cause. An unnatural exaggeration of emotional nature grew more and more morbid. More violent the mystifying reactions until something like a terrible struggle between two natures in her would seem to be going on within and tearing her to pieces. Then peace again for a time and a charming life.

This undertow of strange—often weird—disturbance with happy intervals lasted during the construction of the Imperial Hotel. But the outbreaks grew more destructive as the years went by. Domestic drama increased at the expense of good sense and domestic peace. Misery and disquiet not only ran alongside the grueling effort on the building of the Imperial, but everywhere life itself went, now went various galling disturbances.

But there was the quest for Japanese prints. And the mysterious, wonderful Yedo to explore. Exploring Yedo in pursuit of the print. The print is more autobiographical than you may imagine. If Japanese prints were to be deducted from my education I don't know what direction the whole might have taken.

The gospel of elimination preached by the

Frank Lloyd Wright's apartment, Imperial Hotel Annex. Tokyo, Japan. 1916. FLLW Fdn FA#1604.0007

print came home to me in architecture as it came home to the French painters who developed "Cubisme" and "Futurisme." Intrinsically it lies at the bottom of all this so-called "modernisme." Strangely unnoticed, uncredited.

To go into Yedo in quest of prints with me, therefore cannot be imposing upon your time and credulity. We should all have a little knowledge of origins? Whether we have originality or have no originality?

I am aware that Japanese prints are uninteresting to the general reader. However this is *Auto*biography and so I may take liberties a biographer would avoid in fear of losing his reader.

THE ANCIENT JOURNAL OF JAPAN

The pursuit of the Japanese print became my constant recreation while in Tokio. A never failing avocation in fact. The adventures and excursions would take place at night or sometimes call for a journey by day to distant places, in search of them. Endless the fascination of this quest. Some said obsession.

The place this democratic art of Japan took in my life at this time could be compared to nothing else in my life unless to music. To that I might listen when I could. To the antique colored wood engraving I could go when I would.

Japanese prints!

Otherwise snow, moon, mist and flower. Twilight. Dawn. Evening. Fujiyama, Samisen, O Hisa-san—Fireflies—Fireworks—Geisha—Sumidagawa—Tokaido, Hokaido, Yoshiwara.

Academic art in Japan despised and rejected this spirit child of Japanese life as academic art usually rejects the spirit child. But at this distance we may see how this art of the colored wood engraving interpreting the old life of the ancient capital, Yedo, suffered no loss of quality as "greatest art," because it was in the street—popular and cheap.

All Japanese writing and painting, except the print, was what is called "classical." That is to say it was modeled on Chinese culture just as so much of our own art is modeled upon Greek and Roman culture. But by frequenting the Imperial Theatre I learned that the "classical" art of Old Japan celebrated heroism in war or loyalty to state or family or clan; mainly in Chinese style, but that "love" in our sense was "taboo." In the Japanese Classics "beauty," too, as we use the word was of light significance to the Japanese. Our term "art" they contemptuously named "*bijitsu*"—"sleight of hand"—on a par with jiujitsu. So all that brings us knowledge of the ancient popular life of that unique civilization and now keeps it on record for them or for us was left to the "Japanese prints."

France first found the print. Other countries followed her lead. But America owns the finest collections in the world.

In 1730 the art of printing from woodblocks was new in Japan. The ancient craft of color printing came into full development and flowered from about 1755 to 1800 to enable the work of these "popular" artists to become popular. And by this simple means hand-printing was release for work of the eye and hand as the machine releases to the streets similar work in the United States today.

So why is it not reasonable to say that working away in ancient Yedo to cheapen and broadcast the production of great artists a century or more ago, was the equivalent of our machine? In this wood engraving and "hand-printing" of theirs this product may be seen as journalistic as the product is seen at work in New York streets as I write, and to much the same end. After we have taken the print from the machine to the hand it was accomplishing pretty much the same thing.

"The well-springs of human activity are few— variety infinite."

Goethe might have specified as the "few"— self-preservation, hunger, and sex. Were self-preservation extended to include one's fellow-men, hunger to include aspiration, and sex to include love, we would see the basic motives of New York life now, as they were then in Yedo. The same. And we would finally find in spite of the complexity and confusion we have brought upon ourselves by machine, how little we have really changed except in loss of sensibility and desire for significance.

Truthfulness and elegance in human quality characterized this humble matter of popular printing in Yedo. It was true to the life of the period and reflected life—*interpreted*.

It would be foolish to say that the mere human-quality in anything is Art. But "Art" is what makes that quality "beautiful" in whatever we do. Come with me on a journey within this journey in search of the print. Let us see Yedo as the prints saw it and as Yedo saw the prints.

YEDO

Like Rome, Yedo was "The City of the Seven Hills." All ancient advertising medium of the limitless city—the "illuminated sign" is ancient!

But here, "advertising" does not repel the eyes—the characters, so beautiful in themselves, are "ideographs" and appropriate to the eye.

The first stories, shops; all the second stories of the buildings lining the sides of the swarming streets are dwelling-places. The sliding paper closure of the openings is protected by vertical wooden slats in geometrical patterns. These screens are becoming luminous from within as in daylight they were luminous from without. Charming silhouettes are cast upon the screens by the light within and play to and fro as human figures pass. The plaintive twang plucked from Samisen strings in these upper rooms by an ivory blade in the hands of the shop-keeper's daughter, Hirani-san or Nobu-san—maybe, is heard, coming through the picture.

It all looks—*just like the prints!*

The lower stories of the buildings lining the labyrinth of wide and narrow streets are all shops wide open from side to side. The shops are ingeniously crammed to overflowing with orderly array of curious or brilliant merchandise: seven famous places celebrated by the prints.

The quiet but gay life of the ancient-modern capital is aware of Toyonobu, Harunobu, Shunsho, and Shigemasa. Utamaro, Hokusai, and Hiroshige are soon to come. Commodore Perry has not yet insisted upon international "cooperation," no Hollanders have arrived. Will Adams, hardy Englishman stranded there, the only "Westerner" to have seen this land of mist, moon, snow, flower—and woman.

This hardy, shipwrecked sailor is there now as much because he wants to be as because the shoguns will not allow him to leave. Through him, only, does this singular culture, developing in complete isolation learn anything at all of Western ways. And by way of the print alone does the West know anything of Eastern ways at this time.

Enormous, populous area is fascinating Yedo, channeled with wide bare-earth streets humanly swarming their interminable length, beaten down hard by traffic, lined both sides with blue-gray tile-roofed two-story buildings. A gigantic village that is one of the greatest cities in the world. Several millions of people are already there. They are coming along in crowds pulling or pushing at loaded carts, others peddling, strolling or bargaining along the shopfronts. Queer little horses drawing loads so balanced just behind on two great cart wheels that they help push the cart along. Strange hump-backed horses are led through the throngs by their masters, no drivers. Big black bullocks, a turquoise head-dress wound about big black horns, come slowly laboring along, head down, sullenly drawing enormous loads of logs or merchandise. And sprinkled throughout the moving masses of sober-robed people, hand carts, back-boxes and horses, picturesque strollers and heaving bullocks, innumerable gaily clad children are playing. The children seem to have the right of way, gaily dressed as flowers in the sun.

Scarlet and gold shuttered-cabinets, the kago, blinds drawn, occasionally go by, slung to long black beams carried on the shoulders of naked-legged coolies, two coolies in front, two in the rear.

A mystery is everywhere maintained—as privacy.

Weird figures wander by as from another world.

Notwithstanding this tremendous activity, brooding quiet is over all as though some enchantment wrought the scene. Yet, a pleasant gaiety in ease and quiet gives assurance of repose and intimate human contentment.

Dusk is falling. Glowing vistas of the softly brilliant globes or cylinders, red-paper lanterns patterned with strange characters in white or black, begin to glow in the twilight. There are rows countering on rows along the streets and always there are clusters of the beautiful things or a simple large one on every building. Some hang above the street high on bamboo poles. Light, here beguiles the eyes and evidently here too is the ancient advertising medium of the limitless city. The "illuminated sign" is ancient.

Life in Yedo is familiar to the teeming streets. All the charming children seem to be playing there. Exuberance, here, is ordered beauty.

Heard over all as running accompaniment to this festival for the eyes is the ceaseless crescendo and diminuendo of the measured, scraping sound made by innumerable geta in the graveled street of the thronging city to an obligato of far-off cries—like animals calling. The ripple of soprano laughter and the reassurance of glad voices near by.

Laughter in Yedo—always laughter. Always the scraping clogs. Always the weird calls of street vendors. Always the snatches of strange animal cries. Japanese music seems an animal cry. At night—the mysteries of Silence. Or song-like night sounds that might be—but are not—made by the wind.

The nasal twang of Samisen strings punctures the sense of it all at intervals, and the sweet wail of flutes comes like lovely colored ribbons of sound from the private gardens behind the shops.

See family affection, true contentment. The

night life of Yedo is "Industry" even until midnight, wherever there is light to see by.

The scene is pervaded by quiet movement. Wherever the fascinating red and white paper lanterns glow, deep shadows hover round about them in friendly fashion for Yedo is not bright at night. It is subdued like some modern society-woman's red-shaded drawing-room, and the streets are as orderly, mannerly, and clean.

The human figures in this scene are not "dressed" but simply robed. So they may be, as simply, unrobed.

Outside, the life of Yedo swarms!

But, within, it all reposes. So kindly, glowing, humane and homely. And yet, at night, behind all the glow-worm lights and gently swinging lanterns with their mysterious messages and the lambent flambeaux of the open shops there is undergrowth of dark and mystery. This group of sinister black-robed, double-sworded figures, some with black hoods, swords that make all other swords innocuous, that pass again: gallant strides, reckless swagger. Such "side" and *style* as would make Fifth Avenue gasp. Adventurous Samurai abroad! Here comes a group of enormous, bulky, brutal-figures but with kindly faces. Long black hair brushed back high from the foreheads—giant strong-men followed by several attendants and shuffling, adoring crowds. The bulk of several Japanese in any one of these: here are the Sumo or professional wrestlers bred for that purpose alone and for centuries. When famous, the Sumo, too, are celebrated by the prints. To inbreed human beings for a special purpose as we breed race horses! Yes, they did it.

We see graceful elegant figures, faces concealed by huge bell-shaped head-cover of woven straw, going about with short-swords stuck in their belts. The *Komuso*, or aristocratic street adventurers.

We are, at this moment hungry—*O-cha* and *Sake*? Tea houses are everywhere. This one, by Tokyo-Bay, is inviting because it is thickly hung with gay red-paper lanterns. Especially fine, the entrances curtained with blue hangings patterned with the huge white *mon* of the keeper's household. We push through the hangings and find a stone-paved lobby level with the street and enter to find,

looking down at us from the matted floors just beyond the entrance, a smiling group of pretty Japanese girls on their knees bowing low and bowing lower—rising eager to take us by the hand and lead us in. Our shoes?—Well—we will take them off, step up in stocking feet on to the clean, fresh-smelling straw mats of Yedo floors.

Now look about and see for the first time what severe simplicity of form and beautiful materials left clean for their own sake can do for a house interior. Enter a scene of shifting color and quick movement. No noise but silvery laughter. All clean for soft white-shod feet. How can anything human be so polished and clean? Sliding screen partitions moving aside beneath great carved wood open panels cross the matting and make the general space into separate rooms at will.

As we pass by the rooms we glimpse charming sights. Guests robed in silks, fan in hand, heads gleaming with polished black. Ah! you see—in everything inimitable, imperishable style! *Black,* as in itself a property, is revelation here.

Pass, now, through building after building, separate buildings joined together with narrow open-sided corridors. The polished plank floors creak underfoot as crickets creak, as we tread on them. Glimpse little courts, as you go, filled with strange plants and flowers in graceful pots. Little cages of fireflies hang to the posts, as post by post we pass along the open corridors against the outside dark. Finally all will open along one entire roomside to an enchanted scene. The Japanese garden! Samisen notes coming from all directions like pervasive insect notes in a summer field. We hear the tender wail of flutes more distinctly as though a door had opened. See a landscape in which moon-lanterns are glowing under spreading pine trees as high moonlight streams over all; soft light from pendulous lanterns gleams on the still water, glances from the cool plashing of gently falling water; the sound of water falling gently from on high over great black stones mingles with the samisen and flutes; thin silver streams cascade down piles of fantastic rugged rock, half hidden in dark masses of sonari; flowers and blooming shrubs are massed about the rocks and tree trunks; in the background bloom—moonlit jewels—to the water's very edge.

It seems an ancient countryside, that garden. Or an empire. But it may be, yes, it must be, small. How small would be unbelievable!

And come here from another, noisier, more vulgar world—we kneel on somber silken cushions, subdued, entranced—looking humbly upon this life of perfect art.

Now a work of art, quite as marvelous as all the scene enters it. Fashioned as she is upon the head, hand, and breast instead of upon the leg as she would be fashioned in the West, she enters with modest mien, smiles sweetly, bows gracefully again and again to the floor. Gently she asks what the most honorable gentlemen will be pleased to have her unworthy self bring to them, this most tender of evenings, for their good pleasure? Black heads meantime are moving everywhere and gleam over smooth oval powder-whitened faces punctuated by lips of living scarlet, scarlet to match the sake cups.

Black! The science and the art of "black" in everything. Decorous black eyes slyly slant at you from every direction as little artful beings noise-lessly move swiftly about, grace and refinement in every feature of every movement. What may we say—gracious enough? For what might we ask? Crudely, but with a smile, we say, simply, "*Gohan.*" Leaving all to them.

Soon, kneeling as we now are on flat sober-colored silken cushions, we, too, like the other honored guests we have seen are surrounded by black, beautiful bowls of many sizes and small scarlet lacquered sake cups set forth in orderly array. The array accented by saki bottles, each bottle an individual piece done in relief by some famous artist-potter.

Take the clean pine twin-sticks in your fingers, break them apart—the *hashi* are fresh and for use but once—do your best with the steaming rice—such rice is cooked only in Japan, as the cover is lifted from the big black lacquered bowls. The pretty maid fills and refills our smaller red bowls from the large black one. The perfectly done fish on the Nabeshima china on the trays will please you.

Savory fish-soups in the delicately lacquered patterns of the covered golden bowls may not. You are not accustomed to fish-soup? Curiously designed sweets on the painted, gaily decorated stands are disappointing, not sweet as we know sweet. Meantime distant drums have been beating beneath the other sounds—beating, as we now become aware, in strange, secretly frustrated rhythms. The ear strives and fails to catch the rhythms—syncopated like nothing so much as raindrops falling from the eaves on hollow metal. Then, tired of eating, or the attempt to eat, the little *musume* bring in pretty woven baskets, in each a steaming wet towel wrung dry and offer it in a separate basket to each of us to refresh our hands and faces, gently regarding us with shy amusement the while. The *musume* break into gales of laughter as we groan and awkwardly stretch our legs to take kinks out of them, or with legs asleep, fall to our knees again in attempt to rise after sitting so long on our heels. The sake had nothing to do with it.

All the while, to and fro in the corridors, Geisha parties noiselessly undulate to and fro, Samisen in hand, faces crimsoned slightly at the temples, otherwise foreheads and cheeks whitened to brilliant-scarlet lips. Yes, then, except the more reddened cheeks, even as in New York today. Just as Harunobu, Kiyonaga and Utamaro, Shunsho and Shigemasa faithfully recorded it, that the world might never lose it. Again exclaim—"It is all just like the prints!"

Picturesque family parties you glimpse, pass and see for yourself how elegant an aesthetic feature of life the fan may be. A fine lady plays the *Koto*, its graceful length laid upon the expanse of matting. She kneels over it and caresses it. Then say—as you will—"such gentleness!" "Such good sense in elegant simplicity!" With what disciplined beauty Japan has mingled the uses and purposes of everyday life! Mingled? No. *Made* the necessities of life beautiful. This is a civilization, you will say, feeling it all too good to be true and that there must be some sinister side to the picture, lurking out there in the dark! May be! This is the East you know! And the skepticism of the West looks warily about.

Now we have seen nothing, yet, immoral.

Unless such exquisite grace and beauty in everything everywhere must be immoral. Of course it is. Ugliness being a kind of virtue in the West, beauty must be immoral in the East. But it all seems so innocent, naive, and charming.

But this will be different. Now we are going to see the Oriental Courtesan.

Is she immoral in this land of the rising sun? No! Only unmoral. We can understand the difference better now that we are here.

But can what is naturally sordid be made beautiful?

Probably not—we shall see.

We climb into a sitting posture, knees up to chin, crammed into the kago, glancing as we passed along into miles of open shop-fronts, many of them "news" shops, that is to say shops full of "prints." We pass peddlers, pilgrims with jangling-staffs, carrying slender cabinets on their backs filled with trays. The trays were sometimes filled with exquisite prints of every sort by popular artists of popular favorites to be sold in public places: the animated news-stands of the period. These peddlers were "news boys."

Actor-prints, too, we see displayed at the theaters on every side in great variety. Pictures of gorgeous *Oiran* or Courtesans and their *Komuso* or little pupils we see posted in bathhouses and certain shops.

"Advertising" was active then as now, it seems. But the artist's individuality never suffering on account of it. Why?

But suddenly ahead looms a great black gate, directly in front of the gateway a great group of cherry trees in full bloom like drifted pink snow seen now, in the light of innumerable red and white lanterns. And just inside the gate we come upon the *Oiran* or Yoshiwara procession the prints prepared us for. A procession that now seems prepared for us.

In the center of each group of the elaborate pageant slowly moves a gorgeous feminine creature exaggerated by resplendent robes and extravagant head-dress. She is slowly moving with feminine traits deliberately exaggerated, undulating with stately artificiality on white-clad feet thrust into high black-lacquered clogs. Her face is plastered dead-white, lips painted the limit of scarlet. The only animate human thing in the ensemble of gorgeous robes, impassive face, and black and gold head-dress is the pair of sly black eyes. They move in the white mask and regard you for one brief, seeing moment—with mischief in their depths. With measured tread and artificial graces she moves on in slow, stately pomp, surrounded by other creatures as feminine but far less gorgeous. And just behind her—the gorgeous *Oiran*—come two *Komuso*, plaintive little creatures, wonderfully dressed, made likewise in little. And being as stately as small editions can be. Such splendors as you can only call barbaric, are before you. It is beyond us to describe them otherwise. The procession centering about and behind the barbaric queen, too queenly for any but barbarism, moves slowly to the gate, herself now softly flecked by falling petals of the cherry blossoms. Other gorgeous *Oiran* are coming, surrounded by groups of dancing colored lanterns.

As the procession turns to go back again, like gray moths hovering about some glittering flame, sober-robed men follow "the Queen" in groups, fascinated. Surely such splendor must dazzle duller lives and seem like an apparition of heaven—to them.

Others come along the two avenues that run each side, the blossoming cherry trees massed between them. Individuality marks each *Oiran* and her group, in spite of the conventional style that seems imposed upon all. Here, as the high black-lacquered clogs scrape slowly over the roadway now pink with fallen cherry-flower petals, is ceremonial glorification of something we of the West have never been allowed to understand.

Here in the Orient, it appears, a woman is raised to nth power as symbol among men. You will understand that these creatures are not "women" but Woman, aggrandized, Institutionalized. Demoralized? No. *Professionalized* on a plane that here seems to carry a premium in place and

Polychrome mural for the Imperial Hotel. Tokyo, Japan. 1916–1922. Pencil and color pencil on tracing paper, 36 x 33" (detail).
FLLW Fdn#1509.005

preferment. A compelling power made artistic and deliberately cultured. Not yet awakened to "moral" discrimination, so, not sinful. Was there pride, think you, in doing surpassingly well this pleasuring of men? Was there conscientious sense of the value of the office—and a real ambition to deserve well of the luxury and opportunity to shine resplendent as the object of man's desire?

Judging from the poetic inscriptions on the prints that advertise and celebrate the *Oiran*—Yes.

The social or natural power at this stage of Japan's culture had placed this premium of *"woman"* upon these women—in all extravagance. If exuberance is beauty, here it was. Here artists like Utamaro lived and "designed" that popular series of prints wherein woman was made symbol of almost everything and it was here in the Yoshiwara that he enjoyed and criticized and was enjoyed and criticized. Here in the Yoshiwara of Yedo literati of the times came to remember, to forget. Here the Samurai in black masks came seeking release and Romance and in the intoxication of a freedom they could never otherwise know, laid their swords aside.

Here were the social graces and fine arts of music, poetry, dancing, running accompaniment to conviviality on no bestial plane. The "moral" element that could make it bestial was lacking. As it was with Philosopher and Hetira in Greece, so probably, it was here.

All this, then, knew nothing, could know nothing of its own degradation.

If we can look at it similarly we may see the beauty it had. If we bring to it the eyes of a mind confirmed in assumption of the "unclean," then we see only that.

But in the artist's celebration of this life as we find it illustrated in the Yedo daily journal, we see proof not of vice but proof of innocence, although were New York journalism to publish similar chronicles of similar life, today, police would confiscate the editions and close the editorial offices because moral progress has now left it all to the sordid and mean or to the abject animal.

But as the prints show it to us we may see that love of life and beauty was the poetic theme running like a thread of fine silk in all that Yoshiwara life of the Yedo courtesan. There was elemental romance in it. It would not be so now in the degradation that remains of the institution as it exists in Japan and as it has always been in the West. No. It would be money. And therefore no romance except the fortuitous romance of luck.

And we find it all so recorded in the most exquisite piece of illustrated magazine making in this world—a graphic journalistic report by Shunso and Shigemasa called the "Beauties of the Little Green Houses," showing, as it does, the elegance of these lives of "filles de joie" of Japan a century or more ago.

But elemental romance is what this Journal of Yedo contains for all time.

So, while the conception of the great hotel grew, and when later the building itself began to rise, Yedo was a presence always, at times even a window through which I looked on my own work, a road by which I saw it. Yet I must not linger more with this great heart of Japanese life, but pass to the telling of the building of the New Imperial Hotel at Tokio.

WHY THE GREAT EARTHQUAKE DID NOT DESTROY THE IMPERIAL HOTEL

From infancy, as a sort of subjective contemplation, the minds and hearts of the Japanese are fixed upon the great calm mountain God of their nation—the sacred Fujiyama brooding in majesty and eternal calm over all. They deeply worship as the mountain continually changes moods, combining with sun and moon, clouds and mist in a vast expression of elemental beauty the like of which in dignity and repose exists nowhere else on earth.

It is not too much to say that the "sacred mountain" is the God of old Japan: Japan the Modern Ancient.

And yet the dreaded force that made the great mountain continually takes its toll of life from this devoted people, as the enormous weight of the deep sea beside their tenuous island, the deepest sea in the world, strains the earth-crust opening fissures in the bottom of the great valley in which it rests and the sea rushes down to internal fires to become gas and steam expanding or exploding internally causing earth convulsions that betray the life on the green surface.

Great wave movements go shuddering through the body of their land spasmodically changing all overnight in immense areas. Whole villages disappear. New islands appear as others are lost and all on them. Shores are reversed as mountains are laid low and valleys lifted up. And always flames! The terror of it all invariably faces conflagration at the end.

Trained by these disasters of the centuries to build lightly on the ground—the wood and paper houses natural to them may be kindled by any spark. When fire starts it seldom stops short of several hundred homes and usually thousands, or complete destruction. So, when the earthquake is violent, fire finishes the terrible work.

The dead, not swallowed up, are buried, and once more *"Shikata-ga-nai"* ("it can not be helped"), goes patiently on as before. Naturally the earth-waves seem fate and unconquerable. A force useless to combat by strength alone, for it is mightier than any force at man's command. *"Shikata-ga-nai!"* This stoicism I have seen and lived with four years or more while preparing to meet this awful force by building on ground which the seismograph shows is never for a moment still—prepare to meet it by other means than rigid force.

The "foreigner" with the advent of Commodore Perry came to share Japanese joys and sorrows and soon a building was needed to shelter the "foreign" element in Tokio, the capital of Japan.

A social clearing house became necessary to official Japan, as a consequence of the new foreign interest in them, because, for one reason, no foreigner could live on the floor. The need steadily increased. At that time the Mikado took it upon himself to meet the need, and asked the Germans to build one of their characteristic national wood and plaster extravaganzas for the purpose.

That wretched marvel grew obsolete and the need of another, a great one, imperative. The Imperial household, this time, proposed to share the task of providing the new accommodation with the capitalists of the Empire, ship owners, cement manufacturers, bankers, tobacco interests, etc., and I, an "American," was chosen to do the work.

No "foreigner" yet invited to Japan had taken off his hat to Japanese traditions. When foreigners came, what they had back home came too, suitable or not. And the politely humble Japanese, duly impressed, took the offering and marveled. They tried to do likewise in their turn.

And yet, Japanese fine-art traditions are among the noblest and purest in this world, giving Chinese origins due credit.

It was my instinct not to insult them. The West has much to learn from the East—and Japan was the gateway to that great East of which I had been dreaming since I had seen my first Japanese prints—and read my first "Laotze."

But this terrible natural enemy to all building whatsoever—the temblor!

The terror of the temblor never left me while I planned the building nor while, for more than four years, I worked upon it. Nor is any one allowed to forget it—sometimes awakened at night by strange sensations as at sea, strange unearthly and yet rumbling earth-noises. Sudden shocks, subsidence—and swinging. Again shock after shock and upheaval, jolting back, and swinging. A sense of the bottom falling from beneath the building, terror of the coming moments as cracking plaster and groaning timbers indicate the whole structure may come crashing and tumbling down. There may be more awful threat to human happiness than earthquake—I do not know what it can be.

The Japanese turn livid, perspiration starts on them, but no other sign unless the violence becomes extreme, then—panic. I studied the temblor. Found it a wave-movement, not of sea but of earth—accompanied by terrific shocks no rigidity could withstand.

Because of the wave movements, deep foundations like long piles would oscillate and rock the structure. Therefore the foundation should be short or shallow.

There was sixty to seventy feet of soft mud below the upper depth of eight feet of surface soil on the site. That mud seemed a merciful provision—a good cushion to relieve the terrible shocks.

The office force building the Imperial Hotel, Tokyo. Endo-san stands behind Wright's helmet; Hayashi-san, general manager, is in front of Wright; Paul Mueller is beside Hayashi. 1922. FLLW Fdn FA#1509.0050

Why not float the building upon it? A battle ship floats on salt water.

And why not extreme lightness combined with tenuity and flexibility instead of the great weight necessary to the greatest possible rigidity?

Why not, then, a building made as the two hands thrust together palms inward, fingers interlocking and yielding to movement—but resilient to return to original position when distortion ceased? A flexure—flexing and reflexing in any direction.

Why fight the quake?

Why not sympathize with it and out-wit it?

That was how the building began to be planned.

The most serious problem was how to get the most carrying power out of that eight feet of cheese-like soil that overlay the liquid mud. During the first year of plan making, I made borings nine inches in diameter eight feet deep and filled them with concrete. Arranged to test the concrete pins thus made. Got carloads of pig iron and loaded the pins until they would drive into the ground. Kept the test figures of loads and reactions. Took borings all over the site to find soft pockets. Water stood in the holes two feet below the surface, so the concrete had to go in quickly as the borings were completed. Later, tapered piles were driven in to *punch* the holes and pulled out—the concrete thrown directly in as soon as the pile was out of the way.

This data in hand—the foundation plan was made to push these concrete pins, in, two feet on centers each way over the entire areas on which the wall footings were to spread. The strength of the whole depth of eight feet of top soil was thus brought to bear at the surface. That was simple.

But here was a compressible soil that might take a squeeze under the broad footings to add to the friction of the pins. Experiments showed the squeeze could safely be added to the friction.

This meant a settlement of the building of five inches the building itself driving the piles that much deeper. This was economy but dangerous and more complicated.

But finally the building was computed pound by pound and distributed according to "test data" to "float" below the grade of the ground surface—and it did. With some few slight variations it stayed level there.

This foundation saved hundreds of thousands of dollars over the foundations then in use in Tokio. But had the owners of the Imperial superficially known what was contemplated something might have happened to prevent it. "Rumor" nearly did prevent it. Here, however, was the desired shock-absorber, a cushion, pins, and all to be uniformly loaded and put to work against the day of reckoning.

Now how to make the flexible structure instead of the foolish rigid one? Divide the building into parts.

Where the parts were necessarily more than sixty feet long, joint these parts clear through floors, walls, footings and all, and manage the joints in the design. Wherever part met part, through joints also.

So far, good sense, and careful calculation.

But a construction was needed where floors would not be carried between walls because subterranean disturbances might move the walls and drop the floors.

Why not then carry the floors as a waiter carries his tray on upraised arm and fingers at the center—*balancing* the load. All supports centered under the floor slabs like that instead of resting the slabs on the walls at their edges as is usually the case.

This meant the cantilever, as I had found by now. The cantilever is most romantic—most free—of all principles of construction and in this case it seemed the most sensible. The waiter's tray supported by his hand at the center is a cantilever slab in principle. And so concrete cantilever slabs continuous across the building from side to side, supported in that way, became the structure of the Imperial Hotel at Tokio.

Roof tiles of Japanese buildings in upheavals have murdered countless thousands of Japanese, so a light hand-worked green copper roof was planned. Why kill any more?

The outer walls were spread wide, thick and heavy at the base, growing thinner and lighter toward the top. Whereas Tokio buildings were all top heavy. The center of gravity was kept low against the swinging movements and the slopes were made

an aesthetic feature of the design. The outside cover-hangs of the cantilever slabs where they came through the walls were all lightened by ornamental perforations enriching the light and shade of the structure. The stone everywhere under foot in Tokio was a workable light lava weighing as much as green oak. It was "sacrilege" to use this common material for the aristocratic edifice. But finally it was used for the feature material and readily yielded to any sense of form the architect might choose to indicate. And the whole structure was to be set up as a double shell, two shells an exterior of slim cunning bricks, and an interior one of fluted hollow bricks raised together to a convenient height of four feet or more. These shells were to be poured solid with concrete to bind them together.

The great building thus became a jointed monolith with a mosaic surface of lava and brick. Earthquakes had always torn piping and wiring apart where laid in the structure and had flooded or charged the building. So all piping and wiring was to be laid free of construction in covered concrete trenches in the ground of the basements independent even of foundations. Mains and all pipes were of lead with wiped joints, the lead bends sweeping from the trenches to be hung free in vertical pipe shafts, from which the curved lead branches were again taken off, curved, to the stacks of bath-rooms. Thus any disturbance might flex and rattle but could not break the pipes or wiring.

Last but not least there was to be an immense reservoir or pool as an architectural feature of the entrance court—connected to the water system of the hotel and conserving the roof water.

Thus the plans were made so that all architectural features were practical necessities, and, the straight line and flat plane were respectfully modified in point of style, to a building respectful to the traditions of the people to whom the building would belong. The *nature* of the design too, I wanted to make something their intensive hand methods could do well because we didn't know what machinery could be used. It was impossible to say how far we could go with that. Probably not very far.

Finally the plans were ready.

No estimates could be had.

It was all so unfamiliar, no commercial concern would touch it. Nothing left but to abandon the whole or organize to build it ourselves. The Imperial Hotel and its architect and builder.

The language was a barrier. The men and methods strange.

But the "foreign" architect with eighteen or twenty architectural students from the Japanese universities, several of whom were taken to Wisconsin during the plan-making period, and one expert "foreign" builder, Paul Mueller of Chicago, two "foreigners," all else *native,* we organized with the hotel manager, Hayashi-san, as general manager. We had already bought pottery kilns in Shizuoka and made the long slim cunning bricks of a style and size, never made before, for the outside shell. They were now ready to use.

We had also made the fluted hollow-bricks for the inside shell, the first in the Empire. We bought a fine lava-quarry at Oya near Nikko for the feature-material and started a flood of dimension stone moving down to the site in Tokio—a stream that kept piling into the building for four years. The size of the hole left in the ground at Oya was about like the excavations for the Grand Central Terminal.

We had a hundred or more clever stone "choppers" beating out patterns of the building on the greenish, leopard-spotted lava, for that period.

On an average we employed about 600 men continually for four years. As a large proportion of them came from the surrounding country they lived round about in the building as we built it. With their numerous families there they were—cooking, washing, sleeping.

And we tried faithfully—sometimes frantically and often profanely—to teach them how to build it, half-way between our way and their way.

We tried the stone-planer with the stone cutters. It was soon buried beneath the chips that flew from their busy stone-axes. Tried derricks and gin-poles and hoists. They preferred to carry heavy loads and enormous stones up inclined planes on their shoulders. We tried to abolish scaffolding and teach them to lay brick from the inside. Not to be done. They lashed tapering poles together in cunning ways as for centuries and clung with prehensile toes to the framework.

How skillful they were! What craftsmen! How patient and clever. So instead of wasting them by vainly trying to make them come our way—we went with them their way. I modified many original intentions to make the most of what, I now saw was naturally theirs. The language grew less an obstruction. But curious mistakes were perpetual. It is true that the Japanese approach to any matter is a spiral. Their instinct for attack in any direction is oblique and volute. But they made up for it in gentleness and cleverness and loyalty. Yes the loyalty of the retainer to his Samurai. They soon educated us and all went pretty well.

The countenance of the building began to emerge from the seemingly hopeless confusion of the enormous area now covered by the building materials of its terraces and courts and hundreds of families. And the workmen grew more and more interested in it. It was no uncommon thing to see groups of them admiring and criticizing too as some finished portion would emerge—criticizing intelligently.

There was a warmth of appreciation and loyalty unknown in the building circles of our country. A fine thing to have experienced.

The curse of the work was the holiday. There were no Sundays but a couple of holidays every fortnight instead, and it took a day or two to recover from most of them. So the work dragged.

And the rainy season! The Japanese say it rains up from the ground as well as down from the sky—in Tokio.

We did succeed in abolishing the expensive cover-shed of tight roof and hanging matting-sides under which most buildings are built in Japan. We congratulated ourselves until we found they knew their climate better than we did. Had we protected them from the rain and burning sun the buildings would have been finished about seven months sooner—besides making all more comfortable and so more efficient.

A few more such "successes" would have been enough.

The "directors" met regularly for a couple of

years and began to complain.

Rumors reached them from the English (the English love the Americans in Tokio) and "Americans" (why are "Americans" invariably so unpleasant to one another abroad?) to the effect that the architect of their building was mad. In any earthquake the whole thing would tumble apart—and the whole building would sink out of sight in the mud beneath. There was room enough for it in that cushion of mud.

Where all had been pleasant enthusiasm things began to drag. The loyalty of my own office force never for a moment wavered, but manager Hayashi was daily hectored and censured.

At this crucial time it became apparent that three and a half million yen more would be necessary to complete and furnish the work. Things looked dark.

By now a small army was working away in the lower stories of the building as it was completed. As soon as one portion was built it became a hive of frantic industry. The copper features and fixtures and roof tiles were all made there; the interior wood work and furniture—the upholstery and many other things went on in the vast interior spaces as soon as the floors slabs covered them over.

I had brought examples of good furniture from home and took them apart to teach the Japanese workmen how to make them according to the new designs which made them all part of the structure. They were fine craftsmen at this. Rug designs had gone to Pekin. The rugs were being woven there to harmonize with the interior features of the great rooms and the guest rooms.

We were about two-thirds of the way over with the building itself. The foreigners had no way of keeping track of costs or finding out much about them in detail. So things had gone on for several years.

The crash came.

The directors were called together.

Baron Okura was chairman of the board—representing, besides his own interests, the interest of the Imperial Royal Household, sixty percent, besides ownership of the ground. There was also,

Asano-san—a white-haired Samson of the shipping interests, a powerful man with shaggy white brows and piercing eyes. Murai of the tobacco interests—a peacemaker and with pleasant ways, always. Wakai, the banker, as broad as he was long with a beard that reached below the table when he stood up. Kanaka and half a dozen others.

Baron Okura had rather sponsored me from the beginning. He was in trouble now.

The meetings had been held in the old hotel building and were pleasant social affairs with refreshments.

This one was not. It was black. A long time, it had been threatening. The Baron, a black-haired youth of eighty—a remarkable man regarded as one of the astute financial powers of the Empire—sat at the head of the table. I sat on his left. On his right sat his cultivated secretary, a Harvard graduate, who was interpreter. It doesn't matter where the others were. They were there and all talking at once. I answered leading questions without end. The foundations. Always the foundations—and the money. The money!

The Baron was patient and polite—for some time. His lower lip had a trick of sticking out and quivering when he became intense. This personal idiosyncrasy of his was evident now.

Suddenly he rose—leaned forward, head thrust forward, angry, hissing, pounding the table with both fists—extraordinary conduct for him.

The crowd went back and down as though blown down by the wind.

There was silence—the Baron still standing looking over toward me. Not knowing what it was all about I instinctively rose. The interpreter rose, too, and said, "The Baron says that if the 'young man' (all things are relative) will himself remain in Japan until the building is finished, the Baron will himself find the necessary money and they could all go to" whatever the Japanese word is for the place they could go to.

Although homesick by now and sick besides I reached out my hand to the Baron. The compact was made. The meeting was over. The directors filed out red and angry to a man, instead of happy to have the responsibility lifted from them.

Was it Pericles who enacted some such role as the Baron's when the Parthenon was building?

And the building of the new Imperial went on.

But now every director became a spy. The walls had ears. Propaganda increased. My freedom was gone. I worked under greater difficulties than ever. But my little band of Japanese apprentices was loyal and we got ahead until another storm broke.

"Why not," said the directors to the Baron, "eliminate the pool and save 40,000 yen?" The Baron saw sense in this and sent for me. His mind was made up. No arguments took effect. I told him via interpreters that it was the last resource against the quake. In disaster, the city water would be cut off, and the window frames being wood in the 500 foot building front along the side street where wooden buildings stood, fire could gut the structure even though it withstood the quake. I had witnessed five terrible fires in Tokio already—walls of flame nothing in any degree inflammable could withstand.

No matter. The pool must come out. No, I said, it is wrong to take it out and by such interference he would release me from my agreement and I could and would go home, with no further delay. And I left his office. But I did not leave Tokio and the pool went in to play its final part in the great drama of destruction that followed two years later.

Another year and I could go home. The Tokio climate, so moist and humid summer and winter, depressing except in fall and early spring, together with the work and anxiety were wearing me down.

But now came a terrible test that calmed troublesome fears and made the architect's position easier.

The building construction was about finished. The architect's work-room had been moved to the top of the left wing above the promenade entrance. It was nearly noon. The boys in the office, reduced to ten, were there, and workmen were about. Suddenly with no warning a gigantic jolt lifted the whole building, threw the boys down sprawling with their drawing boards. A moment's panic and hell broke loose as the wave motion began. The structure was literally in convulsions. I was knocked down by the rush of workmen and my own boys to save their own lives. It is a mercy there were not more workmen in the roof space beyond or I should have been trampled out. As I lay there I could clearly see the "ground swell" pass through the construction above as it heaved and groaned to hideous crushing and grinding noises. Several thunderous crashes sickened me but later these proved to be the falling of five tall chimneys of the old Imperial left standing alone by the recent burning of that building.

At the time it seemed as though the banquet hall section, invisible just behind the workroom, had crashed down.

Only one faithful assistant stayed through this terrible ordeal. Endo-san, loyal right-bower—white to the teeth—perspiring. Otherwise the building was utterly deserted. We got up shaking to the knees and went together out onto the roofs. There across the street were crowds of frightened work-men. They had thrown down their tools and run for their lives, even those working in the courts. There they all stood strangely silent, pasty-faced, shaking. A strange silence too was everywhere over the city. Soon fires broke out in a dozen places—bells rang and pandemonium broke—women dragging frightened children ran weeping and wailing along the streets below.

We had just passed through the worst quake in fifty-two years. The building was undamaged. A transit put on the foundation levels showed no deviation whatever. The work had been proved.

Hayashi San, when reports of the damage to the city and none to the building came in, burst into tears of gratitude. His life had barely been worth living for more than a year, so cruel were the suspicions and harassing the doubts.

The year passed. The building was now so nearly complete there was no longer pressing need for the presence of the architect.

Another wing remained to be finished but it was a duplication of the one already done and furnished. So I could go home with a good conscience. My clients headed by the Baron, were generous, added substantial proof of appreciation to my fee, and I was "farewelled" at a champagne luncheon by the Baron and his directors; at a tea house entertainment by the building organization itself, all with unique expressions of esteem; by the workmen at another characteristic entertainment—all as usual in such matters.

The day of sailing came. To get to my car I had to pass from the rear through the new building to the front. All was deserted and I wondered. Arrived at the entrance courts, there all the workmen were, crowding the spaces, watching and waiting. Already there had been gratifying evidence of appreciation—I thought, but here was the real thing. This could have happened nowhere but in Japan. Here was the spirit of the old Japan I had tried to compliment and respect in my work.

As their architect came out they crowded round, workmen of every rank from sweepers to foremen of "the trades," laughing, weeping, wanting awkwardly to shake hands—foreign fashion. They had learned "aw-right," and mingled it now with *"arigato"* and *"sayonara, Wrieto-san."*

Too much, and "Wrieto-san" broke. They followed the car down along Hibiya way to the station, running, shouting, *"Banzai, Wrieto-san, banzai!"*

The dock at Yokohama, eighteen miles away, was reached by train, to find that sixty of the foremen had paid their own way down from Tokio to shout again and wave good-bye, while they faded from sight as the ship went down the bay. Such people! Where else in all the world would such touching warmth of kindness in faithfulness be probable or possible?

Two years later—1924—in Los Angeles. News shouted in the streets of terrible disaster. Tokio and Yokohama wiped out! The most terrible temblor of all history!

Appalling details came day after day. Nothing human it seemed could have withstood the cataclysm.

Too anxious to get any sleep, I tried to get news of the fate of the New Imperial, Shugio, Endo, Hayashi, the Baron, and the hosts of friends I had left over there. Finally, the third night, about two in the morning, the telephone bell rang. The "Examiner" wished to inform me that the Imperial Hotel was completely destroyed. My heart sank, but I laughed, "how do you *know?*" They read the despatch, a list of Imperial University, Imperial Theatre, Imperial Hospital, Imperial this and Imperial that. "You see," I said, "how easy it is to get the Imperial Hotel mixed with other Imperials? I am sure if anything is above ground in Tokio it is that building. If you print its destruction as 'news' you will have to retract."

Their turn to laugh and hang up the receiver.

Ten days of uncertainty and conflicting reports, for during most of that time direct communication was cut off.

Then a cablegram:

Sept. 13. 1923. Olive Hill Studio Residence B 1645 Vermont Ave Hollywood Calif Following wireless received from Tokio today Hotel stands undamaged as monument of your genius hundreds of homeless provided by perfectly maintained service congratulations signed Okura Impeho

For once good news was news, and the Baron's cablegram flashed around the world to herald the triumph of good sense.

Both the great Tokio homes of the Baron were gone. The splendid museum he gave to Tokio and all its contents destroyed. The building by the American architect, whose hand he took and whose cause he sponsored, was all he had left in Tokio—nor could love nor money now buy it or buy a share of stock in it.

When the letters began to come and nearly all the friends were found to be safe, the news most gratifying to the architect was the fact that after the first great quake was over, the dead rotting in unburied heaps, the Japanese in subsequent shocks had come in droves, dragging their children into the courts and onto the terraces of the building, praying for protection by the God that had protected that building as the wall of fire driving a great wail of human misery before it, came sweeping across the city toward the long front of the building: the hotel boys formed a bucket line to the big pool, water there the only water available anywhere, and kept the window sashes and frames on that side wet to meet the flames that came leaping across the narrow street.

The last thought for the safety of the New Imperial had taken effect.

Following the construction of the Imperial Hotel, I lingered in Los Angeles aided by my son Lloyd working on the new unit-block system.

Experience with the "Imperial" had made all probable experience to come—tame. When I first came back, I really took little interest in such prospects as would present themselves for solution from time to time.

No appetite for less than another Imperial Hotel, I suppose. Or, perhaps, satiated, exhausted by such incessant demands upon my resources as that experience represented.

I had been standing for the better part of four years in the thick of creative effort, domestic infelicity, perplexities and finally the characteristic serious illness that attacks men of the north in that humid lowland of the Pacific. My aged Mother, now eighty years old, hearing my condition was desperate had crossed the Pacific to be near. The fact that she came blew the remnant of my relationship with Miriam back across the Pacific in insane fury.

Luckily the Japanese made much of Mother—old age is a qualification in Japan. And, toward the end of her life, she enjoyed many happy and remarkable experiences, one of them a gratifying appearance at the Emperor's Garden Party, where she looked a queen, though happier than a queen usually looks.

For this occasion, I took pleasure in getting her dressed. A small silver-gray sunshade. A small violet bonnet like a close crown over her beautiful gray hair. A long purple cloak hanging from her shoulders over a simple silver and gray dress.

Shugio was immensely kind to her, taking her about. All my friends in Tokio came often to see her and took her to various occasions. I think she had no lonely hours in Tokio. Some four months later, though, having met with a painful accident while driving to Miyanoshita, she got back again to America, much the better for her heroism.

During the four years past I had commanded, under circumstances both trying and gratifying, the building of one of the great buildings on the beaten path around the world; building it directly out of the architect's office. I would make a design in the morning. Looking out of the office windows a few days later I might see it executed there in the yard.

In the building of the Imperial, the architect was again master of the combined activities of painter, sculptor, engineer, and an entire industrial line of activity in the crafts.

Strange! Expert handicraft had come to the beck and call of an architect who had devoted much of his effort to getting buildings built by machine and true to modern mechanical processes.

A world in itself began to take shape in that transition building, created spontaneously as any ever fashioned by the will of a creator in Le Moyen Age. Most of the plans I had prepared were thrown away and my presence on the work enabled such changes to be made in the work itself as I required. This work had been completed by the hand of one architect. In ancient times such was seldom the case, the work on any great building continuing from the architect of one generation to the architect of the next generation.

Here now, in Hollywood, I was still dreaming of the great edifice, not long since completed, living over again the romance of the one thousand and nine days and nights in Tokio—once Yedo.

This building, too, the Imperial Hotel of Tokio—as architecture was Romance. Again taken away from the task I had set myself—years ago.

But to have taken the straight line and the flat plane of the machine-age to Japan, regardless of Japanese nature would have been to crucify Japan's best life. Japan's fine traditions deserved, at least, respect, it seemed to me. I had taken the straight line and flat plane there, but, regardful.

While making their building modern in the best sense, I had still left the building their own, and today it is sympathetic consort to the palace buildings standing across Hibiya Park above the moat with no feature much, if at all, like them.

I wanted to show the Japanese how, as architecture, their own conservation of space and honest clean use of materials might take place indoors for them upon their feet, instead of upon their knees.

I wanted to show them how to use our new civilizing agents, plumbing, electric light, heating by electricity, without outrage to the building, making all a practical part of the building itself. Mechanical systems an advantage not a detriment to culture.

I wanted to show the Japanese how to make the same co-ordination of furnishing and building, on their feet, they had already so successfully and beautifully made for themselves on their knees.

I wanted to show them how to build an earthquake-proof building with masonry materials.

This last had been a severe drain that strained such resources as I had to the utmost.

When all was done I wanted the building to look "at home" in their own land, no unworthy associate of the noble native buildings in view across the palace-moat, one that would stand there no less richly imaginative than their own buildings wherein the Old was in the New as the New was in the Old.

In short, it was my desire to help Japan make the transition from wood to masonry and from her knees to her feet without too great loss of her own great accomplishments in civilization.

So here you may see a "transition building" again.

I wonder if all buildings are not transition buildings in some sense if they are really great buildings? And always will be?

Heraclitus would say so, of course. But, Heraclitus was stoned for a heretic and a fool in the streets of Athens, like so many other men we worship as *of* Greek Civilization—when, really, they were *in spite* of it.

Yes, let shame say, I had again been captured by Romance living in the life of a unique people, hoping to leave them my sense of themselves, for what it might be worth to them.

During the building of the Imperial Hotel the building of a home for Aline Barnsdall was going forward. She called the house Hollyhock House

before it was born. I called it a "California Romanza." This time, frankly, a holiday.

I had met Miss Barnsdall shortly after the tragedy at Taliesin while I was still in Chicago at the Cedar Street house. Henry Sell[13] brought her to see me, in connection with a project for a theatre in which she was interested in Los Angeles. Her very large, wide open eyes gave her a disingenuous expression not connected with the theatre and her extremely small hands and feet somehow seemed not connected with such ambition as hers.

Later I made the preliminary studies for this theatre she intended to build in Los Angeles. And now coming home from the land of Laotze and Tao, Zen, and Bushido, I went to work for the Christians in Hollywood for a time.

There stood Hollyhock House on Olive Hill.

It had been, with great difficulty, partly owing to my absence in Japan, finally completed.

Several other projects are by now presenting themselves for solution. But meantime here is the minor strain of the story of Aline Barnsdall's

HOLLYHOCK HOUSE IN HOLLYWOOD

Architecture is a greater art than music. If one art can be said to be "greater" than another. I believe one can only say it for the sake of argument. Nevertheless I have secretly envied Bach, Mozart, and the great music-masters. After concentration on creation they lifted an ivory baton or perhaps merely gracefully significant hands, and soared into execution of their designs with the alert obedience of a hundred or more kindred, willing hands and minds: the orchestra. And that means a thousand fingers quick to perform every detail of the general effect the master precisely wanted on instruments whose effects were definitely understood.

What a resource! That resource is comparatively modern.

And I never hear the brave chords of, say, at the moment, Tchaikowsky's concerto for pianoforte—baton in the hand of a Stowkowsky—that I don't get such a glorious lift myself that nothing really matters. I could conquer, and do conquer for the moment, any realm of the imagination to the everlasting glory of the race, though the symphony is,

"Hollyhock House" for Aline Barnsdall. Los Angeles, California. 1917. FLLW Fdn FA#1705.0163. Photograph by John Geiger

pretty well, all over in that first movement. Bach is invariably inspiration, even information, to me.

What facility great masters of music were afforded by various forms moving according to their mood, from fugue to sonata, from romanza to concerto, or proceeding from them all to the melodic grandeur and completeness of the symphony.

I suppose it is well no architect has got such facility nor can ever get it. Consequences to the country are bad enough—facility such as it is.

As a small boy long after I had been put to bed I used to lie and listen to my father playing Beethoven—for whose music he had passion—playing far on into the night. To my young mind music spoke a language that stirred me strangely and, as I have since learned, music is the language—

beyond all words—of the human heart. The symphony, as my father first taught me, is an edifice of sound. Just as I now felt that architecture ought to be symphonic.

So, when called upon by Aline Barnsdall—her metier the theatre—to build a house for her in Hollywood, why not make architecture stand up and show itself on her new ground, known as Olive Hill, as Romance?

A bit sentimental, Miss Barnsdall had pre-named the house for the Hollyhock she loved for many reasons, all of them good ones, and called upon me to render her favorite flower as a feature of Architecture how I might.

Unlike many "patronesses of the arts," Miss Barnsdall wanted no ordinary home for she was no ordinary woman. If she could have denied she was one at all, she might have done so. But the fact claimed and got her continually, much to her distress and the confusion of her large aims. If any woman ever hitched her wagon to a star, Aline Barnsdall hitched hers thereto. And so far as Hollyhock House and the building of the New Theatre that was to carry her "Art of the Theatre" a generation or two ahead of itself were concerned—at the moment—she chose her architect as that bright and particular star.

Now, these words, "poetry," "romance," are by now red rags or reproachful tags to those hopelessly confused house-owners who helplessly drift and continue to happen to architects as clients. Romance is—no wonder!—something clients would rather not hear about.

Because nearly all the good people who spoke the language and sought the "romantic" in good faith when they became "clients" drew baleful prizes in this lot-lottery of Los Angeles, fell ill of the "plague"—sentimentality—infected by the systematically "tasteful" architects who stick to that region. An exception found his way there, long ago, in Irving Gill. But his antiseptic simplicity did not please the fashionable.

So, this hectic quest for sentimentality in architecture in our beloved country has wasted billions of dollars, done spiritual harm more or less violent to millions of otherwise pretty good people. For that reason perhaps it would be better to say, as said of Taliesin, that Hollyhock House was to be a natural house, naturally built; native to the region of California as the house in the Middle West had been native to the Middle West.

Suited to Miss Barnsdall's purpose, such a house would be sure to be all that "poetry of form" could imply, because any house should be beautiful in California in the way that California herself is beautiful.

Yes, our word "romance" is now utterly disreputable, rather escape from life than any realization of ideal of life. Either by inheritance or as evil consequence, this loose attempt at "illusion" is now what is the matter with the word. "Romance" lies loose in the heart, askew in the mind, something fanciful, unlike life. Unlifelike. Results, at best, are exotic. At worst, idiotic. Romance in the United States is a sickly simpering mask for a new life.

It attempts to escape from the deadly pressure of the facts of life in a machine age, into a "beyond" each poor earthworm fashions as he may, for himself, and for others, if and as he can.

But none ever do escape except to arrest and imprisonment on still harder terms. Moronic in Moronia.

But, in music, "romanza" is only free form or freedom to make ones own form. A musicians sense of proportion is all that governs him in the musical romanza: the mysterious remaining just enough, "haunting," in a whole so organic as to lose all evidence of how it was made, in harmonies of feeling expressed as "sound." Now translate "sounds and the ear" to "form and the eye," romanza seems reasonable enough, in Architecture?

Moreover, for the sake of our argument, living rooms, bedrooms, kitchens, and bathrooms are no more poetry-crushers in this connection than are the organs and functions of a lovely woman a bar to "romance" in any popular sense . . . if you will think this over.

So we may use this word romanza, derived from the word romance, as a word to typify a house free in form that takes what is harmonious in the nature of the doing and the purpose and with honest sentiment (not false sentimentality) brings all *significantly* out into some enchanting visible "form."

Well, no master of an orchestra, I have to conquer a hard-boiled industrial world stewed in terms of money and persuade or please idiosyncratic, sometimes aristocratic clients, in order to render any romanza whatever or achieve even a modicum of integrity in any building. My lot was cast with a hod of mortar and some bricks or a concrete-mixer and a gang of workmen, the "Union," and the Machine. And last, but not least, the client as "medium of *expression.*" Ah—the "client"!—Curious term for the singular victim. The victim often reacting upon and victimizing any artist-architect who "professes" Architecture as the architect in turn, more often, reacts upon and victimizes his client.

Yes, I know, by now, that in every worthwhile human being of either sex there is the potential artist yearning for realization. And I know architects are only in the his or her hand of the so-yearning to enable them all, somehow, to realize this secret ambition of their inmost souls—and upset the balance for both themselves and their architect if not held true.

Of course, we are speaking of the considerable human being. Many humans care no more about the whole matter than the horse seems to care about his stable if the stall is roomy enough and the fodder where and when it belongs.

But here in Hollyhock House were met circumstances and opportunity. The situation didn't look equivocal, at all.

Nevertheless, these oblique remarks are prompted by trying to remember now, the circumstances—many of which I have tried to forget—of this holiday adventure in Romanza.

Miss Barnsdall turned this beautiful site, Olive Hill, over to me as a basis on which we were to go to work together to build under the serene canopy of California blue.

We went to work—or I did. My "client," I soon found, had ideas and wanted yours, but never worked much nor for long at a time, possessed by a wanderlust that made me wonder, sometimes, what she wanted a beautiful home for—anyhow or anywhere. Later, however, I came to see that *that* was just *why* she wanted one.

A restless spirit—disinclined to stay long at any time in any one place as she traveled over the face of the globe, she would drop suggestions as a warplane drops bombs and sails away into the blue. One never knew where or from whence the bombs would drop—but eventually they dropped.

To add to this discomfort, the fates picked me up and were dragging me to and fro over the Pacific for four or five years, to build the Imperial Hotel at Tokio. I would hear from her when I was wan-

dering about in the maze of the Imperial Hotel in Japan while she was in Hollywood. She would get my telegrams or letters in Spain when I eventually got to Hollywood. And I would hear from her in New York while I was in Chicago or San Francisco. Or, hear from her from some remote "piney" mountain retreat in the Rockies when I was seasick out on the Pacific Ocean. During the building of Hollyhock House there was no radio, only the telegraph. So Hollyhock House had mostly to be built by telegraph so far as client and architect had anything to do with it or each other until it was all too late.

Now, with a radical client, like Aline Barnsdall, a site like Olive Hill, a climate like California, an architect himself head on for Freedom, something had to happen—even by "proxy." This "Romance" of California had to "come out." I couldn't play it, more's the pity perhaps. And yet, there would have been no Hollyhock House if I could. To "play" it would have been the only alternative.

Sublimated mathematics is Music?

Well—mathematics in co-ordinated "Form" is architecture. I would still use the straight line and the flat plane. I had become accustomed to using them. But would use them here together with a third mathematical element clearly defined—*integral-ornament*, modifying or emphasizing both elements to allow suggestion, proper scope, and appropriate rhythms to enter: these, I offer as component parts of the California Romanza.

Would Aline Barnsdall be happy with the outcome of all this for a house? Probably not, but happier. Why not? She was neither neo, quasi, nor pseudo. She was as near American as any Indian, as developed and traveled in appreciation of the beautiful as any European. As domestic as a shooting star.

Conscience troubled me a little—that "voice within" said, "What about the machine crying for recognition as the normal tool of your age?"

Well, my critics, one does, often, weary of duty. Even of privilege—while young. I again told the voice to "go to" for a time.

Hollyhock House was to be another holiday.

"Residence B" for Aline Barnsdall. Los Angeles, California. 1920. FLLW Fdn FA#2003.0016. Photograph by John Geiger

The architect's plans joyfully traveled the upward road of poetic form and delighted Miss Barnsdall. I could scarcely have keyed the "romanza" too high for her, I found, had I made it a symphony.

But my "client" was in a hurry and I was urgently needed in Tokio. If we accomplished more than the preliminary plans themselves in the way of actual building, we would have to amplify the sketches into plans as best we could, making such added notes and details as we went along as would suffice to get the building properly built. The manner of work being what it is, this was not unseasonable.

My own son Lloyd introduced the "Union" in the person of a contractor—Robertson. By all evidence obtainable Robertson should have been competent "concert meister" with the sympathetic aid of my untried superintendent Schindler. But, while Robertson could read the average score, he couldn't read this one very well as it turned out and the superintendent didn't. Rudy was too smooth ever to learn how to be serious, which was why I liked him. But that was bad for the house. Soon, seriously enough, I would hear of trouble clear away across the Pacific.

Robertson said it was all because the plans were so hastily prepared. Only partially true. Every contractor will say that and *always—in any circumstances*—it will be partly true.

But he knows the allegation plausible alibi for him because every contractor has seen it, times without number, take effect. But the truly unreliable contractor never fails to use it with excellent results so far as he is concerned which is mostly all he cares about.

This is all in his day's work. The contractor is seldom "contractor" for anyone's health but his own and never precisely for that. The drawings were sufficiently complete. But details were being constantly added to educate the contractor as his grasp fell short.

Now, *the* penalty (one of the many, probably) for being feminine, with extremely small hands and feet, rich, alone, and mundane, is to have an entourage of "friends." Employees, to justify themselves as *friends,* undertake to guard the feminine employer's financial interest in such manner that they will look "faithful" until the employer rudely awakens. As employers do.

Collectively this insurance-brigade knew about as much about this building, Hollyhock House, as Sodom knew of Sanctity. Unless checked they could only insure defeat. Here enters at the psychological moment the perennial feature of the eternal triangle, Architect, Owner, Contractor. All too often the Owner at first sign of trouble with the Architect takes refuge in the Contractor. And this is what now happened.

My client had by now been angered by certain failings of her architect. They got tangled up with his virtues, among them one difficult to untangle

and that one, most offensive at this time, was a distinct failure to regard the mere owner of a work of art in hand like the romanza as of ultimate importance in the *execution* of the design. There were forthright refusals to allow her to take the life of the work itself by thoughtless changes suggested by these cerebratious guardians without reference to the architect's opinion. This was the consequence and the challenge to combat.

So, building about half done—a fortuitous decision. "They" should build the house. This is where I should have left Hollyhock House forever. But do you know the feeling of a sentimental architect for his creation? You love your child? Well, so does he. I couldn't go and leave the work to them entirely.

On the eve of sailing again for the ninth time, on the Pacific as far as Tokio, I consented to hang on by way of my affable superintendent, plainly seeing nevertheless that my client as well as I would finally have to take the consequences of her insurance, and eventually, conspiracy. Now this on my part was utter weariness, utter weakness, or utter cowardice.

And it might have some moral effect upon the prospects of other paternal architects and other self-willed clients to tell of the consequent griefs of the owner's administration when driven to unseemliness and hasty acts by their employer's fiats from long distance. And to speak in detail, for example, of the makeshifts the insurance brigade employed "to save money!" Makeshifts usually cost more than the real thing. And to dramatize, as warning to other architects, some of the architect's own serious mistakes, among these his unjust treatment of a naturally resourceful, forceful, and now aroused and suspicious client.

But enough. Ownership on Olive Hill in Los Angeles took whip hand of "art" by way of her own insurance brigade, with the best intentions and all the justification there was. And that was myself.

Shades of Beethoven and Bach—"Romanza" did I say? Rude awakening.

And yet—all too aware of the fact—a poetic idea was to be born. It had to conquer this stubborn, suspicious, mean, possessive old world—all of its refractory materials in between—in order to appear at all on that hill. Now, the subtraction of this treacherous pack of detractors clambering over the whole.

My client's own momentum—it was considerable—had wantonly cut the ground from beneath herself and her architect by making him alien, angered, dazed, and puzzled by all this. The only salvation any client ever has in such circumstances is to trust the architect, no matter what he is, if foolish enough to have employed him in the first place. And the client must uphold his hands no matter how quixotic and foolhardy it may seem—by advice of council—at the time being, to do so.

I am foolishly telling all this in detail to try to show that once started building along any unusual characteristic scheme, no timid owner has any other salvation, nor ever had or ever will have, in the agonizing triangle, this infernal A. I. A. invention of client, architect, and contractor. However fearful any owner, it will inevitably appear that the real interests of owner and architect were one and indivisible all the time and were so at all essential points. But the contractor, by no fault of his, sits there as born enemy of both architect and owner. Except as his moral worth may rise superior to the very nature of his office. Usually it is necessary from the start to defeat the contractor's advices to the client. He, the contractor, is, by the very nature of the *characteristic* building, himself the novice. But he will never openly admit his novitiate.

Nevertheless from out of this confusion, from this welter of misunderstanding and misapplied heat and fury, enough to have consumed the work out of hand finally resulting in violence . . . a shape appeared, inviolate.

A strangely beautiful "form" crept into view. Even the quarreling pack began to see it. Something had held all this diversity in adversity together enough to enable new significance to adorn the hill crown. Was it the marks on paper that this quarreling was all about, these traces of a design that, no matter how abused, *would* show itself in spite of friction, waste, and slip?

No, but anyhow, and *somehow,* by way of the downright brutality, insolence, and persistence of the architect and the client's desire, though both architect and client were torn to tatters—"Form" got into the building itself in spite of folly.

This it is that seems to me the miracle as I saw Hollyhock House on its hill now. And it is the miracle.

But, even at this distance, I am sure I exaggerate all this warfare just as any parent, fearful for the well-being of an infant, would exaggerate. I am underestimating the fine quality of Miss Barnsdall herself, who really desired a beautiful thing in her heart and, capable of loving it, kept coming back to it again and again, fending off her own organization and really seeing beyond the barrage of petty strife, in which, partly owing to her own timidity, she was continually involved. Or, well, but what does it all matter now? As you have read between the lines I was chiefly to blame, myself. I flouted my client—unable to understand her as I now see.

Like it or leave it. There stands Hollyhock House in Hollywood—conceived and desired California Romanza. No, not so domestic as the popular neo-Spanish of the region. But comfortable to live in well, with all its pride in itself. Yes, a very proud house is Hollyhock House.

But, why should all Usonian houses, so called, when they are anything but Usonian, be of so called domestic mold, when all Usonian people are not so? Why should Aline Barnsdall live in a house like Mrs. Alderman Schmutzkopf, or even like Mrs. Reggie Plasterbuilt's pseudo-Hacienda on the Boulevard-Wilshire. Individuality is the most precious thing in life, after all—isn't it? An honest democracy must believe that it is. And the thing Usonia is going to fight, tooth and nail, to preserve, as things are going, if the fashionable standardizing we have seen everywhere on the surface has any meaning beneath the eclectic's latest mode—the so called "international style."

Again and again within my limited experience the "fashionable" thing is ever the outworn carcass of the early tomorrow. If you would have your house "fashionable," be sure it is on its way out of luck even as it is being built.

In any expression of the human spirit it is principle manifest as character that alone endures.

And individuality is the true property of such character. No . . . not one house that possessed genuine character in this sense but stands, safe, outside the performance of the passing show.

Hollyhock House is such a house.

And Aline Barnsdall, finally, came back. She stayed in her house longer at a time than she ever stayed anywhere before. She planted greenery and color around it, some more, and she cared for it and tried to correct some of the mistakes that grew out of initial mistakes in the struggle of client and architect to build it mainly by proxy.

Some of them she couldn't correct, but took all now in good part as the sunshine began to build up the green round about it. Loving pines because of the mountain carpets they made, she planted pine-groves behind on the hill and great masses of the Eucalyptus to enclose the pines. Planted great carpets of brilliant flowers for ground cover beside and in front of the house like the carpets woven in Austria for the inside. She brought "home" a few choice objets d'art from Europe to add to others builded into the walls of the rooms themselves, and to go with the furniture that was made part of the house-design itself.

It looked for a time as though she would become a valuable Hollywood institution, and do more beautiful things there. Next, perhaps make the dream of her life come true, the New Theatre, by now already planned and seen in a new white plaster model.

Up there on Olive Hill above hillsides furrowed with rows of grey-green olive trees, the daughter of one of America's pioneers had constructed a little principality, her very own, free to live as queen.

There was nothing like it anywhere in the world.

She—the second generation—came and went. In her consciousness was a new sense of home to be handed on to the third generation, to her "Sugar-top."

Above all friction, waste, and slip, Aline Barnsdall had, so far, succeeded.

And then, as the little queendom grew in beauty and importance, yes, even as the ideas that built it—on holiday—grew likewise in significance around the world she began to feel alone in the possession of it—became more lonely because of it than she had felt without it.

Artists came and admired it.

Hollyhock House became known as a work of fine art in the various ateliers of the continent where she would go every summer. Europeans came and saw in it something of the higher harmony of the spirit of man. The newer "protestant" felt—perhaps justly, who knows—that the architect had indulged himself, again, regardless of the task with the machine he had set himself. But this Romanza in California was just another phase of the greatest of the arts—Architecture. Call that phase something else. Call it poetry. Call it what you like, if you do not want to call it architecture, as I shall call it, still.

They said in Hollywood, Aline Barnsdall was a Bolshevik—a "parlor Bolshevik," said some. They rather sneered, did some of these little people living in names—those to whom names were ideas and ideas names—at one whose ideas were "proletariat" and hard, while living soft herself like a princess in aristocratic seclusion unrivalled by other princesses who lived merely in the traditional and therefore in more or less hackneyed style. She now lived above commonplace elegance, like any princess, but matchless in style all her own. So far as that went, she lived in an atmosphere rare as "poetic." Herself a pioneer this daughter of the pioneer lived up to integral romance when all about her was ill with pseudo-romantic in terms of neo-Spanish, lingering along as quasi-Italian, stale with Renaissance, dying or dead of English half-timber and Colonial.

Well, no one may say what moved her finally. The motives of human deeds lie so deep-buried beneath seemingly irrelevant debris or are mixed in the tangled threads of feeling in the depths of the human heart. She made up her mind to give it all away: the precious hill-top by now sought by every realtor of the realm as a prize, she determined to give away. Together with its ideal buildings.

And she gave it all away, as it stood. Even the

faithful Japanese cook, "George"—he went along, too.

And she gave it, most wisely, to the class most needy in the United States, most abjectly mendicant at this time, owing to the triumphant march of the Machine. But not, be it said, to the most grateful. She gave it to the artists of California, to be the home of their California Art Club. She restricted the gift so that the house should not be touched or altered for fifteen years. By that time, she said, what she felt to be its real riches, its imaginative Californian "Form," would have had its suggestive way with them. So far as she herself was concerned, it might then go on its way to destruction.

Out there where everything, almost, is speculation and soon or late for sale, and where—perhaps just because of that—so few of the many having riches have ever given anybody anything culturally worthwhile, the wandering daughter of the pioneer bequeathed her enjoyment in her home, her faith in its beauty regardless of its faults, gave it wearing the Los Angeles realtor's tag of a "million dollars." This she did to help up to the level of life again, if possible, struggling artists, stranded in an era they may never survive.

Hollyhock House as it now disintegrates listens to these artists as they chide, complain, and admonish. As they admonish it and each other so it admonishes them. And perhaps—as its donor meant it should do—goes along with their personal issues into fresh life in new key, looking gratefully toward her whose home it was. Yes, and whose home it still truly is to a greater extent than ever; because, since without her it never could have been, her spirit is manifest in it, to all.

Meantime, Hollyhock House, as near finished as it would ever be, here I was looking around me in Los Angeles—disgusted. There they were busy with steam-shovels tearing down the hills to get to the top in order to blot out the top with a house in some "style," some aesthetic insanity or other.

The eclectic procession to and fro in the ragtag and cast-off of the ages was never going to stop—so it seemed to me. It was Mexico-Spanish now. Another fair, in San Diego this time, had set up Mexico-Spanish as another mode, for another run for another cycle of thirty years.

This mode was busy making these pretty pictures thus—and anywhere at all. Making pretty pictures cheap, getting "art and decoration" in to prettify the little plastered caverns. They made them "comfortable" by piling up pillows and stuffing them with "overstuffed" upholstery.

During all these years I had been at work out there in Anglicor no reality could be seen in any building where the house owners or the builders were themselves "art-conscious" or where they were socially "amenable" for that matter.

The desert of shallow effects. All curiously alike in their quite serious attempts to be original or "different." More "plain surface" was in sight—always a relief. But the same old thought, or lack of thought was to be seen everywhere. "Taste"—the usual matter of ignorance—had moved toward simplicity a little, but thought or feeling for integrity had not entered into this architecture. All was flatulent or fraudulent with a cheap opulent taste for tawdry Spanish medievalism. What would such taste for effects be tomorrow? Some other inane reaction with the same significant insignificance. Undoubtedly.

Soon began the gnawing of the old hunger for reality. Romance, I saw as no escape from reality. I had, not yet, descended to make believe. Could I go deeper now?

Always the desire to get some system of building construction as a basis for architecture was my objective—my hope. There never was, there *is* no architecture otherwise, I believe.

What form?

Well, let the form come. Form would come in time if a sensible, feasible system of building-construction would only come first.

The concrete block? The cheapest (and ugliest) thing in the building world. It lived mostly in the architectural gutter as an imitation of "rock face" stone.

Why not see what could be done with that gutter-rat? Steel wedded to it cast inside the joints and the block itself brought into some broad, practical scheme of general treatment then why would it not be fit for a phase of modern architecture? It might be permanent, noble, beautiful. It would be cheap.

There should be many phases of architecture as modern.

All that imagination needed to make such a scheme feasible was a plastic medium where steel would enter into inert mass as a tensile strength. Concrete was the inert mass and would take compression. Concrete is a plastic material—susceptible to the impress of imagination. I saw a kind of weaving coming out of it. Why not weave a kind of building? Then I saw the "shell." Shells with steel inlaid in them. Or steel for warp and masonry units for "woof" in the weaving. For block-size—say manhandled units weighing 40 to 50 pounds—all such units or blocks for either weaving or shells to be set steel-wound and steel-bound. Floors, ceilings, walls all the same—all to be hollow.

I had used the block in some such textured way in the Midway Garden upper walls. If I could eliminate the mortar joint I could make the whole fabric mechanical. I could do away with skilled labor. I believed I could and began on "La Miniatura."

Lightness and strength. Steel the spider, now spinning a web within the plastic material to be wedded to it by inner core of cement.

Hollow wall-shells for living in! The "shell," as human habitation. Why not?

Another phase of the concept of architecture as organic and yet the same.

The straight line, the flat plane, now textured, the sense of interior space coming through the openings all to be woven as integral features into the shell. The rich encrustation of the shells visible as mass, the true mass of the architecture. Here, a legitimate feature of construction.

Decoration asserts the whole to be greater than any part and succeeds to the degree that it helps make this good.

Genuine "mass" in this sense will always be modern. A pity were the United States to have one arrow to its bow, or neglect indigenous riches at any point.

I drew my son Lloyd into this effort.

THE ALTER EGO

Meantime some of the young men who had begun their architectural careers with me were at work out here—in the midst of popular falsification in this land of the realtoresque as substitute for the picturesque. What were they doing to modify popular meanness and qualify imitative Usonia? There were many such—fifty or sixty—young men working in the United States or Europe or Japan as architects by now. They had come to me from all parts of the world to enter into my work. Not so much as students; I am no teacher. No, they came more as apprentices, beginning with no pay—except their living at Taliesin—or with small pay if more competent to help. As they grew helpful they received a small salary in keeping with the work done, or to be done in the office or in the garden, over and above their living.

In the studio at Oak Park, inasmuch as all had to shift for themselves, all received a nominal sum—the equivalent of board and lodging at the beginning.

With the exception of some six or seven I have never had reason to complain of their enthusiasm for their work or of their loyalty to me. But, of their loyalty to the cause—yes. And, after all, were they not taken on in that cause?

This process of natural selection on their part had its advantages and some disadvantages. Never going out of my way after the material I really needed, but always taking those who wanted to come to me—I do make some sacrifices of "efficiency" for sympathetic co-operation, oftentimes not so efficient as it should be. I am fond of the flattery of young people. They indulge me, and I indulge them. It is easy for them and for me to do this. But they do get the idea that when the master's back is turned that to draw his ideas in his own way —does make those ideas and his way, theirs. Something, later on, they must do to justify them in this "reflection." So this type of alter ego soon becomes a detractor. I am in his way, unless I will good-naturedly let him trade on, or in, me.

But the individuality of my work has never swerved from first to last. It steadily grows on its own center line. The system, or lack of it—I have never had an office in the conventional sense—has become fixed habit, and works well enough because I stay directly with it in every detail, myself. When I go away there is usually trouble, and sometimes treachery. No. There was never "organization" in the sense that the usual architect's office knows "organization." Nor any great need of it so long as I stood actually at the center of the effort. Where I am, there my office is. My office is "me." And therein is a great difference between my own and current practice. A severe and exacting limitation.

And it was always hard to turn a boy down. An instance:

Sunday morning at the Oak Park studio. Had worked late the night before. I was called, "A boy in the studio to see me." I got up and went down. There, standing by the big detail table in the center of the draughting room . . . a small boy, face covered with adolescent pimples, blushing furiously. Wanted to be an architect—liked my buildings, believed he would like to build that kind.

Name?

Frank Byrne—young Irish lad.

Where working?

Montgomery-Ward's.

What doing?

Wrapping packages.

Getting how much?

Ten dollars a week.

A good preparation for architecture, I observed. Common school only? Studied at home? A little.

Rather sudden, isn't it—getting into architecture right off the reel like this?

Yes—he thought so, too.

What did he think he could do for me to earn ten dollars a week . . . knowing nothing about draughting?

Well, he could be office-boy—sweep the floors, wash the windows—anything. But, I said, we have already several boys doing that. His face fell.

There was something touching and fine too, in this straightforward break in the direction of his ambition, that appealed to me. Such breaks always do. It looked as though there might be something in this boy. He stood there, pale now. I didn't need him. I didn't want him, but there he was, he was young—unspoiled—how know what might be in him?

All right, I said—come in.

He stayed four years and turned out better than many who had many years the "start" of him in every way. He was my first "Catholic." The "Catholic" helped him when he got out on his own.

This episode might stand as typical, although many apprentices were "architects" and college graduates. A number of cultivated European architects joined the work at Taliesin. But all on the same basis, whatever their qualifications. The apprentices—when they qualified—would stay from two to ten years.

The same formula was impressed upon all: not to imagine they were coming to school. They were coming in to make themselves as useful to me as they could. I was an architect at work. They would see work going on under their eyes and would be taken into the work as far as they could go. Their living was assured meantime but they would get much or little else from their experience as they were able. It was all up to them. The discussions in the studio—pro and con—schemes and sketches for buildings, in general and in detail were made by myself in the midst of the studio-group, each man or boy taking over finally, as he could, whatever I assigned to him to do. Some would soon drop out—unable to stand the too great freedom—abusing it. Some would take it and go away with it to sell it as their own. Others would thrive on it. But a fine loyalty characterized all but very few as they were with me in full freedom of their own choice—entirely on "their own."

How about them? What have they accomplished?

Well . . . the architectural world into which they emerged was commercialized and fashionably if not fatuously inclined toward the great styles. The profession of architecture itself—because it yet has no basis of principle—is commercialized by the functioneer, professing the practical but exploiting "taste." I have had occasion to reproach some of my young men for what seemed to me "selling out"—going with the current of commercial degeneration. The usual answer was "we have to live."

Why? I have said. I don't see why anyone "has" to live. At any rate not as a parasite at the expense of the thing he loves. Why not try something else—where a "living" might be had honestly—fairly to all concerned?

Some identified themselves with other movements: "It is so hard to stand alone." Others became competitors, the "also-ran" and no less.

Nevertheless, I know only too well the weight of opposition they have all encountered and I am inclined to sympathize with all of them. It should be easier for them now and is so though many of us must still be ground up and buried before it will be easy enough. Many of my boys are giving a good account of themselves, Middle-West, North-West, South-West, and West.

But current life mocks most of our effort, breaks it to fragments, if it can, to save a few pieces for future reference as Life goes on its way.

Principle alone is defense and refuge—from chaos and utter defeat.

This digression because several young men were at this time doing good work in California on their "own"—when the work on La Miniatura was going forward. The block experiments had been made and I was ready to start on La Miniatura—the first block house.

LA MINIATURA

La Miniatura happened as the cactus grows, in a region that still shows what folk from the Middle-Western prairies did when, inclined to quit, the prosperous came loose and rolled down into that far corner to bask in eternal sunshine.

Nearby that arid, sunlit strand is still unspoiled—to show what a poetic thing it was before this homely invasion. Curious tan-gold foothills rise from the tatooed sand-stretches to join slopes spotted as the leopard-skin, with grease-bush.

This foreground spreads to distances so vast—human scale is utterly lost as all features recede, turn blue, recede, and become bluer still to merge their blue mountain shapes, snow capped, with the azure of the skies.

The one harmonious note man has introduced into these vast perspectives, aside from the long, low plastered wall, is the eucalyptus tree. Tall, tattered ladies, these trees stand with careless feminine grace in the charming abandon appropriate to perpetual sunshine, adding beauty to the olive-green and ivory-white of an exotic symphony in silvered gold and rose-purple.

Water comes, but comes as a deluge once a year to surprise the roofs, sweep the sands into ripples and roll the boulders along in the gashes combed by sudden streams in the sands of the desert—then—all dry as before.

No, not all, for man has caught and held the fugitive flood behind great concrete walls in the hills while he allows it to trickle down by meter to vineyards, orchards, and groves. And—yes—to neat, shaven lawns two by twice. Little "lots" just like those "back home" in the Middle West. Those funny and fixed little features—the homes—stand above the lawns wearing as many curiously unvaried expressions of the same fixed face as there are people looking out of the windows at each other.

The newcomer from the fertile Midwestern prairies came here to make sunshine his home. But at first his home did not know how to bask any more than he himself did. Shirt-sleeves were his limit and his home had no shirt-sleeves nor anything at all "easy" about it.

No indeed, that home of his was still as hard and self-assertive as the sticks he made it out of: as defiant as ever it was in the snows back there at home at zero. This Yankeefied house looked even more hard in perpetual sunshine where all need of its bristling defenses had disappeared.

Nor when the sunshiners turned to the planting of their places was the result much better. They could easily grow in that sunshine all kinds of strange plants and trees. They did so, as a neat, curious little "collection"—all nicely set out together on the clipped lawns of little town-lots.

And the Porch and the Parlor had come along with the pie and the ice-water, the rocking chair,

Alice Millard House, "La Miniatura." Pasadena, California. 1923. Block construction (in progress). FLLW Fdn FA#2302.0001

and the chewing gum with the appropriate name.

But before long Fra Junipero and Father La Tour would begin to have incidental influence, for it appeared that the Italo-Spanish buildings of the early missionaries own "back home" had just happened to be more in keeping with California.

This Southern type of building had already given shelter from a sun that could blister the indiscreet in Spain or Mexico as it was able to do now in Southern California. So it came to pass that the old Catholic Missions as buildings lived long enough to transform and characterize the Middle-Westerner's home in California at this late day although the actual mission was rejected as being far from midwestern spiritual conviction.

So sunshiners fell to copying Fra Junipero's buildings, copying his furniture, copying his gardens and style. Fell to buying his antiques. But tho' invading Middle West had fallen it still clung in toto to its hard-straw hat, English coat, trousers

and boots, and other customs in general.

As a concession to climate however, the Middle Westerner himself occasionally did put on a shirt with a soft collar and forgot his hat. But when he "dressed" not one iota would he budge. And he looked in his "Fra" surroundings as the Fra himself or a silken Spaniard would have looked in little midwestern parlors. Only for the Fra it would be plus—for the sunshiner it was minus.

By now Spain, by way of despised Mexico, had gradually moved up into the midst of this homely invasion. The plain, white-plastered walls—so far so good—of the little pictorial caverns gleam or stare through the foliage in oases kept green by great mountain reservoirs. A new glint of freshness, a plainness as refreshing foil for exotic foliage.

There are cool *patios,* too, for the Joneses and Smiths. Luxurious haciendas for the richer Robinsons. Arched loggias and vine-covered pergolas. Loose, rude Spanish-tiled roofs give back the sun-

Alice Millard House, "La Miniatura." Pasadena, California. 1923. FLLW Fdn FA#2302.0006

shine stained pink. Adzed beams or rude beam-construction real or imitated, are covered by gay stretched awnings.

California has retraced the first steps of an earlier invasion by priests who came there from a climate more like California climate than that of the Middle West. But the Californians of today—née Iowan, Wisconsinian, Ohioan—have yet nothing to say for themselves in all this except acquired taste for the Spanish antique, to go with the missionaries' house. Nevertheless, the town-lot on the gridiron; the modern bathroom; the incorporation of the porch and the kitchenette with the cozy breakfast-nook: all these prize possessions of his own "back-home" are now "features" of the "mission" style. Such is progress. To have and to hold while seeming to *be*. But California—given to drink—smothers the whole in eucalyptus and mimosa arms as she gently kisses all with roses. Thus are buried the mistakes of the decorative picturizing architect, whose art and decoration have entirely taken the place of architecture, there.

Here then, at some length, is the pictorial background against which La Miniatura, the little studio-house, stands—the flourishing sentimentality into which it was born.

All true building in our land of the free and home of the brave is a soul-trying crusade just as Fra Junipero Serra's mission that failed was a crusade. But his building that succeeded was not high adventure because he just brought it with him from "back home" and just because, too, and solely—he had none other to bring.

No, that building of his was no high adventure, in this sense, for it, too, was the nearest he could get done, by primitive means, to what he, too, had "back home."

Not so La Miniatura. This little building scientifically and afresh began to search for what was missing in all this background. And what was missing? Nothing more or less than a distinctly genuine expression of California in terms of modern industry and American life—that was all.

Few out there seemed to miss anything of the sort, but La Miniatura desired to be justly considered *architecture*. Mrs. George Madison Millard from those same Midwestern prairies near Chicago was the heroine of its story: Mrs. Millard, slender—energetic—fighting for the best of everything for everyone. Be it said she knew it when she saw it. Got it if she could.

The Millards had lived in a dwelling I had built for them fifteen years ago at Highland Park near Chicago. I was proud to have a client survive the first house and ask me to build a second. Out of one hundred and seventy-two buildings this made only the eleventh time it had happened to me. I was glad to add to these "laurels."

Gratefully I determined she should have the best in my portfolio. That meant, to begin with, something that belonged to the ground on which it stood. Her house should be a sensible matter entirely—an interpretation of her needs in book-collecting for book-collectors. Should she have one of those gun-nite Spanish blisters with a paper roof—decorator's supply company's Spanish-decorations pasted on it? She should not, nor anything of the scene-painting the San Diego Exposition had started and subsequent born-imitators sponsored. No, she should have a real home. Mrs. Millard, artistic herself, with her frank blue-eyed smile didn't fully know that she was to be lightly but inexorably grasped by the architectural fates and used for high exemplar, though she probably suspected it. I don't know why houses have so much grief concealed in them, if they try to be anything at all and try to live as themselves. But they do. Like people in this I suppose.

Gradually I unfolded the scheme of the textile block-slab house gradually forming in my mind since I got home from Japan. She wasn't frightened by the idea.

We would take that despised outcast of the building industry—the concrete block—out from underfoot or from the gutter—find a hitherto unsuspected soul in it—make it live as a thing of beauty—textured like the trees. Yes, the building would be made of the "blocks" as a kind of tree itself standing at home among the other trees in its own native land.

All we would have to do would be to educate the concrete block, refine it, and knit it together with steel in the joints and so construct the joints that they could be poured full of concrete after they were set up and a steel-strand laid in them. The walls would thus become thin but solid reinforced slabs and yield to any desire for form imaginable. And common labor could do it all.

We would make the walls double of course, one wall facing inside and the other wall facing outside, thus getting continuous hollow spaces between, so the house would be cool in summer, warm in winter, and dry always. Inside, the textured blocks—or plain ones—would make a fine background for old pictures, fine books, and tapestries. Outside—well, in that clear sunshine, even the eucalyptus tree would respect the house and love it for what it was. Instead of a fire-trap for her precious book-collections and antiques she would have a house fire-proof. I talked this idea over with her, and the more she listened to it the more she liked it. I made some tentative plans.

I forgot to mention that Alice Millard had just ten thousand dollars to put into the house—might get two thousand more, probably not. Bankers were Yesterday, out there too, and hostile to ideas as everywhere. The greater the idea the greater banker-animosity. So the whole scheme must be excessively modest. For instance, Alice Millard wanted only an unusually large living-room with a great fireplace, a beautiful balcony over it from which her own sleeping-room might open. That bedroom should be roomy too, with dressing room, another balcony in that, and a bath, of course. One for the balcony would be nice to have.

Then there must be a good sized guest-room that might be an office when not in use otherwise, and a bath. Two baths of course. And a dining room, not so small either—little parties—with pantry, kitchen, servants' bedroom, store-rooms, and baths. Making three baths of course. My client's tastes were good. She did not want cheap woods. She did not want, of all things, cheap hardware. She abominated poor workmanship and knew it when she saw it. She never failed to see it. There was to be nothing shoddy about that house. And a garage was to be thrown in as integral feature of the whole just for good measure. She would be glad to have all this permanent, have it fire-proof, and have it beautiful for $10,000.00. (The first sum mentioned.)

One day after the plans were ready she came enthusiastically to say: "I've found just the man to build our 'thoroughbred' house. I've been talking with him and went with him to see a house he's just finished for a friend of mine. It cost her less than he said it would. He gave her lots of little extras and never charged for them. He was so good and efficient they scarcely needed an architect at all. Let's go and see the house."

Here the other leg of the "triangle" showed its foot once more—its toes at least and ingratiating smile. But I could not refuse to go—yet. And so—we went.

That house was not badly done, a lot for the money, almost as much as Alice Millard wanted. I talked with the contractor, and she even went so far as to say, by now, she wouldn't have anyone else build her house anyway. "I feel," said she, "we can trust him 'utterly.'"

Now, she had been just as uncompromising about her architect. I understood her regard for her contractor. But here was already familiar and pretty slippery ground.

"How do you like him?" said she, brightly, but as I could see, anxiously.

"Well," I said, "a woman's intuition is valuable even in these matters. He does seem intelligent. He has had a good deal of independent experience. He likes this block-slab idea and volunteers to take the contract without any profit . . . for the sake of experience, as he says. Therefore he is a volunteer. Since you won't have anyone else build for you anyway, I am inclined to take him at face-value."

She sighed with relief.

She felt now quite safe. I had no good reason to oppose her ultimatum. But—I wish I had felt as safe as she. In honesty, I should add to this that I knew of no one else in that region, anyway, who could, or would, make such sacrifices for her, or for me.

Some material supply-men recommended him highly. I called them up. We got the god-father to the idea.

Here the familiar A. I. A. villain enters the piece

in disguise, with Alice Millard's ultimatum for my flimsy excuse. But I knew just how staunch her faith could be and dreaded any attempt to change it. Had she not disregarded the warnings of her friends and consented to the loss of some life-long friendships that she might embark with me in this innocent challenge to their ways and what they approved?

He began well. They all do.

You see I explain this in detail to show how every idea even as the "Romanza" enters and encounters life, as does a new-born child, pretty much as things happen to be—to take all when and where it comes. The idea then begins to grow up, to work like yeast in these haphazard conditions and may survive and become important or dwindle and die as the child may. It is at every moment up to the author of its being to defend it. He has to save its life —continually.

Here's for confession: let's see how good for the soul—in this affair.

Let's call this builder-fellow god-father of our idea. I could add appropriate adjectives to the word god and to the word father. But you do it.

Alice Millard trusted the gift and felt she needed him, I am ashamed to say this. Trusted him. Out there where, as I learned, no one ever thinks of trusting anyone or anything. And because everything and everyone is too much "on the surface" or too recent or too something or other.

I didn't know this at the time.

But I've hardly ever trusted anyone since, nor has Alice Millard . . . scarcely even me.

As you may see by now, architect and client were by nature incorrigibly young. Firmly believing in Santa Claus. They were encouraged by Mrs. Millard's builder to believe they could accomplish their "mission," for eleven thousand some odd dollars. That was the contractor's estimate. Unhesitating, he signed a contract.

Why should he not sign a contract?

Or sign anything at all?

Meantime we had rejected the treeless lot originally purchased by Mrs. Millard as my eye had fallen on a ravine near by in which stood two beautiful eucalyptus trees. The ravine was reached from the rear by Circle Drive. Aristocratic Lester Avenue passed across the front.

No one would ever want to build down in a ravine out there I believed. They all got out on to the top of everything or anything to build and preferably in the middle of the top. It was a habit. I considered it a bad habit. But because of this idiotsyncracy of the region we could get this lot very cheap. We got it at half-price—and it was better than the best at full-price.

We would head the ravine at the rear on Circle Drive with the house . . . thus retaining the ravine at the front toward Lester Avenue as a sunken garden. The house would rise tall out of the ravine gardens between the two eucalyptus trees. Balconies and terraces would lead down to the ravine from the front of the house. The neighbors on either side liked this idea as we left the entire front of the lot next their homes for a garden.

We began to build. Soon the builder grew in Mrs. Millard's estimation. Well over life-size. He settled full in the saddle. I could not fail to see this with some alarm and chagrin. It is not pleasant for an architect to see his client clinging to a contractor as safe insurance against what might prove to be too single-minded devotion to an idea on the part of her architect. Her friends had got that far with her? Or perhaps it was her nature. But she would not have admitted this, so I admit it for her here with wrinkles at the corners of my eyes. The architect has not infrequently in this region—for some peculiar reason, perhaps the climate—to endure this rivalry for the confidence and esteem of his client, I have learned from others. But what is this "something" about a contractor or builder that inspires confidence in the client—especially if the client be a woman? Of course, it is easy to believe that *he* is, before all, "practical." It is easy to believe that he is the man who really builds the building, in spite of the troublesome architect? He knows clapboards and shingles and so he must know concrete blocks, etc. etc. Always, to the woman client, the appeal of this "practical" man seems irresistible. Woman is far more objective than man— more susceptible to the obvious.

Still smiling, though I will say I resented this rivalry, I cheerfully did nothing about it. Let me admit, if less cheerfully, that *I could* have done nothing about it anyway, had I wanted to. So I helped along, every day on the ground myself, as best I might. I made more studies and details until finally we got the flasks and boxes made in which to make the blocks; got the right mixture of sand and gravel and cement, which we carefully chose; and so varied it that the blocks would not all be the same color. The "builder" had picked up some relations of his in Los Angeles to make them. We had no skilled labor, and the builder's relatives set the blocks, carrying them up ladders on their shoulders to their scheduled places in the walls. You see, this model house had to be clumsily home-made, as might be, for the price was very low. A good deal would have to be "put up with" on that account. Otherwise everything went along according to design—smoothly enough.

And, by now, that house represented about as much studious labor over a drawing board and attention to getting construction started as the Cathedral of St. John the Divine in New York City; certainly more trouble to me than any the architect had with the Woolworth Building.

Inventive effort was all "thrown in."

The house was by now, to me, far more than a mere house. Yes—Mrs. Millard's friends were right. Her architect had gone deep into his idea with concentration upon it amounting to passion. The blocks began to take the sun and creep up between the eucalypti. The "Weaver"—dreams regarding their effect. Came visions of a new Architecture for a new Life—the life of romantic, beautiful California—the reaction upon a hitherto unawakened people. Other buildings sprang full-born into mind from that humble beginning in bewildering variety and beauty. Gradually all complications, and needless expense of the treacherous and wasteful building system of a whole country all went by the board. Any humble cottage might now live as architecture with the integrity known only in former ages. The machine should be no longer bar to beauty in our own. At last, here I grasp near end of great means to a finer "order." Standardization *was* the soul of the machine, and here the architect was taking it as a

principle and "knitting" with it. Yes, crocheting with it a free masonry fabric capable of great variety in architectural beauty. And, I might as well admit it—I quite forgot this little building belonged to Alice Millard at all. Palladio! Bramante! Sansovino. Sculptors—all! Here was I the "Weaver." What might not now grow out of this little commonplace circumstance?

The "Weaver" concentrated on other studies and drawings to carry the idea further. Yes, argued the "Weaver"—is any one smiling?—have not all great ideas in Art had an origin as humble? At last: a real building-method beginning in this little house; here was a "weaving" in building that could not go wrong for anyone: a prohibition by nature, of affectation, sham, or senseless extravagance. Integrity in architecture in the realm prostitute to the expedient. Mechanical means to infinite variety was no longer an impractical dream! Thus I—already far beyond little La Miniatura!

But to come back again to the story, how lucky to have found the intelligence in a client to go through initial steps with me—go along with comprehension and faith complete in her contractor—some in me—no matter what anybody said. For that is what she did!

Thus the home got well above the second-story level and Alice Millard to Europe for the summer. She paid her builder herself before she left without a word to me. No vouchers asked. She wrote me she had done this. Under the circumstances existing between us all by this time, to ask for vouchers from him would have been to look a regal gift-horse in the teeth. . . This was the final blow to my self-esteem. But I was above it—or beneath it—by now!

I drove over daily to carry on, but no builder. I chafed, complained, and drove to and fro to find him. Finding him I got promises. Finally Mrs. Millard's builder came to me for more money, explaining that if he got it he could forge ahead. I gave him some more money myself—he didn't forge ahead. Mrs. Millard did when she came back with renewed enthusiasm for the whole thing and found so little done. The idea had grown on her too. Doubt crept into our triangle. I investigated "her" builder—well, our builder by now and . . .Well—let's have it over, if no one ever trusts me to build a house again:

I finally found him building a new house for himself way off somewhere. Tile floors throughout. New furniture. Grand piano. Strange. But we investigated some more. Found everything absolutely all right because everything was in his wife's name.

We were about halfway through: money two-thirds gone. Some of it, maybe, gone into tile-floors? New furniture? Grand piano? Why harrow with details? The builder now quit, angered by my own angry ungrateful attitude in the whole matter. Mrs. Millard was left in deep water with her inventive architect. And I must say her architect made me especially tired myself at this juncture just as he is making you now, for much the same reasons too. I believed her friends justified in their opposition to this architect. They could now all enjoy their "I told you so" with me.

Here in this tragi-comic situation is where my client rose and made herself the heroine of this piece.

"We are going to finish that building," she said, "if it takes every cent I've got in the world or can get to do it. It's going to be beautiful—and while it's not going to be so well-built as I hoped—I know something worthwhile is coming out of that block-pile there in the yard." That was that. And better than I deserved.

Somewhere, sometime, a prospective client asked me how much I could build a ten-thousand-dollar house for. I said I didn't know but supposed it could be built for about what it would be worth with something fine thrown in that money couldn't pay for. That home cost $18,000. The owner admitted it was worth it. It looked as though Alice Millard's $11,500 studio house would beat this now. And I knew she couldn't stand it. So I wrote home to see if my credit could be strained to go into it with her to that extent. By submitting to a collection of financial humiliations it could be. I deserved to be fined enough money to finish the house and I so fined myself with the six thousand available. Saying nothing about that at the moment we went ahead.

Now we were adrift among the Monyana men who were all in demand in a busy place well over-sold and badly under-built. I knew no one but the Hollyhock House crowd and they wouldn't do. They had already done. There were heart-rending trials of faith and friendship as one slippery human agency after another was seized from among the flotsam and jetsam of Monyana-land and put to work. I knew my client was avoiding her best "friends." It is the least one can do when in trouble.

And I knew Alice Millard's heart was breaking. But she stood up to everything with a brave smile. With never-failing energy she again kept bringing in new builders with assumed cheerfulness. She could find them when no one else could find them. But they kept fading away until I found one who promised well. This man of mine put the final work into place and was no better than the rest. All told, I should say, worse.

And here we were facing deficits and duns, ridicule, threats, liens, insult. More liens. Finally lawsuits, or anything else they had around there. And that region is particularly rich in all such active ingredients I found. Lucky I had that six thousand ready.

The lawsuit was brought by our builder himself. I never knew just what the fellow wanted or expected until the judge fined him $500 and costs. For his effrontery—I guess. And "fired" him. That cleared the matter up a little, although I still believe he brought the suit just because he couldn't refrain from trading a little further on the beautiful credulity he had found where he was concerned. It really was very beautiful?

Well, the little studio-house was there, battered up a little, patched somewhat, but—believe it or not—not so badly built after all. Alice Millard had some grief over it—her standards were high and Monyana men are not so good because they don't get much pay. But she had joy in the building now. She had fought a good fight.

Having taken so much trouble with it from first to last, I had a fool's pride in it myself, of course. And how, with the added terrace walls, balconies, and other things, it could have been built even for the sum it had now cost, I couldn't see—though we knew some of the money had been—well, perhaps not—wasted.

We rested. Enjoyed installing the books and other things especially appropriate, which its tasteful owner with her usual discrimination had picked up in Italy. We sat at the teatable in the afternoon, a blazing fire in the charming fireplace. The interior was all either of us had dreamed of, if you didn't go looking hard for nicked edges or something like that where the Monyana men had run into one another with the blocks or fallen down with one. Its owner with her taste for fine materials and workmanship would stop in the midst of enjoying the general result—to point to a mechanical defect as though shot through the heart. Nevertheless, she enjoyed a triumph—satisfaction goes far in seeing one's desires established on earth by means of what had been, less than ten months before, only an idea.

The ravine had become a lively little garden, a pool reflecting the block mass and the trees.

The whole mass and texture of the home made the eucalyptus trees more beautiful, they in turn made the house walls more so.

And the appropriate but expensive garden terraces, balconies, and roof gardens that had come to join the original inexpensive programme of interior rooms made the whole so naturally a part of that ravine that no one could even think of that building anywhere else or regret what the additional features cost. A miracle had come to pass. The old ravine—for half price—one used to take away the street water—had been converted, before our very eyes through all confusion and treachery, into a complete living home with infinite charm. Oh yes—it had charm! There was a quality living and holding all together through friction, waste, and slip that so blessed the result, for such is an Idea.

La Miniatura. New-born entity where before—emptiness.

But the Gods will allow no creative effort of man's to go untested. The Japanese themselves believe them jealous, purposely leaving some glaring fault in a conspicuous place to placate them. The Monyana men had done this in many places, but we had not done so. And just for that came a cloudburst concentrating on that ravine. In every fair-weather region it is always the unexpected that happens? No one in fifty years saw the culvert that now took the street water away below the basement of the house, overflow. But the heavens opened wide, poured water down until it got to the level of the pretty concrete dining-room floor, determined to float the house if the thing could be done. You see—the flood had mistaken the house for another Ark of another Covenant, but this time, failing utterly to float it, the flood left a contemptuous trace of mud on the lower terraces, put out the fires in the sub-basement, burying the gas heaters beneath solid mud, and went away. And Mrs. George Madison Millard's spirit, faith, and pride went out with the fires. She wept.

A man does not weep. Instead he curses—strong language has ever been to man what tears are to woman.

Soon we got this fixed up by the city of Pasadena. But even this was not to be enough to add to what had already been. Depths of misery were yet to be plumbed.

Cyrano de Bergerac, high-adventurer, after a lifetime of triumphs as idealist, was inadvertently knocked on the head by a flower-pot. It fell from a window sill above him—as, rapier in scabbard, he passed below: and I've always believed there was only a common red geranium in that pot.

La Miniatura's hard fought and all but won idealism was now to share a like fate. Yes—let no one imagine that because this region is "perpetual" sunshine the roof is any more negligible a feature of house-happiness than "back there" in rain and snow and ice. The sun bakes the roof for eleven months, two weeks, and five days, shrinking it to a shrivel. Giving the roof no warning whatever to get back to normal the clouds burst. Deluge the unsuspecting roof surfaces with a downpour.

I knew this and I knew there are more leaking roofs in Southern California than in all the rest of the world put together. I knew that the citizens come to look upon water thus in a singularly ungrateful mood. I knew that water is all that enables them to have their being there. But let any of it through on them from above unexpectedly in their houses and they go mad with it. It is a kind of phobia. I knew all this and had seriously taken precautions in the details of this little house to avoid such scenes as result from negligible roofs.

The details were perfect, and proved so to everyone's dissatisfaction. But what of it? What defense when the roof chooses to leak? Our builder had lied to me about the flashing under and within the coping walls—that's all. I had cautioned him concerning this, when called away to Tahoe. Not until I had safely escaped to Taliesin did the roof decide to leak. Saying nothing to me, not wishing to hurt my feelings, Mrs. Millard deliberately invited somebody, if not everybody, in to talk it over and fix up the roof. The roof was easy to fix for there would be no rain for another year. I feel that in confessing this shameful incompetence I am, somehow, making light of the matter. But really I am doing penance. But maybe I am only making a bad matter worse. However that may be, Mrs. George Madison Millard's spirit, though dampened, was not one made to be broken even by this last trial. Enough of "left-handed" confession.

The strength of her determination, the real courage of her faith in La Miniatura has lived to laugh at that trial too. Yes, we two laugh about it all now. But not then.

And sometimes, when I think what La Miniatura would have gained for the future of our Architecture and my own petty fortunes had the Gods not been jealous of it and given the local A. I. A., Mrs. Millard's private secretaries, her confidential advisors, realtors, inferior desecrators, convincing contractors, roofers, loafers, lawyers, plumbers, tourists, butchers, grocers, rooters, and servants—all working for the "I told you so" brigade, this last fatal chance to assassinate it because it "leaked." This fatal chance, I curse still. These publicists had all the while been roosting a la window sill—à la flower pot—to get the satisfaction of this final "knock." We ourselves survived the untoward circumstances—yes. The house was mainly all

right all the time. But not so for them, because—at bottom—La Miniatura had insulted them all by what it aspired to be. "They" had no wish to survive anything at all.

Well—Cyrano is dead. La Miniatura is not dead. It is still too young to die. And, as La Miniatura, first born of California, itself takes its place in the esteem and affectionate admiration of our continental judges in architecture across the sea—the process that built it now in use over there too, as here—and the humble building gives to architects another simple means to establish an indigenous tradition instead of aping styles from abroad. Thus, it appears in this shameful and perhaps too light recital of too serious woes that no creative impulse as idea ever does or ever can choose its hour, choose its means, or control its ends once started. The idea starts, and, if really an idea, soon shows itself so much bigger than the puppets it plays fast and loose with, that they take, miserably or thankfully as may in them be, whatever they happen to get and go their way. If they become ungratefully troublesome they may get into court, be fined $500 and costs by the judge, and "fired." But inevitably as the sun shall also rise, after some reactions and some bad days there will come to the seeker for integrity something beyond fashion, beyond price, beyond cavil.

That reward is the only atonement for the privilege of ever being able to build a house at all?

So, La Miniatura stands against the blue sky between loving eucalyptus companions in spite of all friction, waste, and slip—triumphant as idea. Friction, waste, and slip did not destroy—and cannot now. Alice Millard lives in it. She says she would have no other house she has ever seen. She fought for it and won—whoever may think she lost. So it is her home in more than ordinary sense. It is the reward anyone has a right to enjoy in any sincere high-adventure in building.

Seeking simplicity in the spirit in which it was sought in La Miniatura, you shall never fail to find beauty—though contractors do betray, workmen botch, all friends backslide, bankers balk, the jaws of heaven open wide to hitherto unsuspected deluge, and all the Gods—but one—be jealous.

As for me—probably living too long as a hermit—and reading only in the book of creation—I have got things sadly out of drawing—because I would rather have built this little house than St. Peter's at Rome.

Months before La Miniatura was finished, improvements and changes were made in block technique. Other block houses began to grow up now in that equivocal region on the "block system" as the "first" was being completed. The Storer house was one. The Freeman house another. And then the "Little Dipper," kindergarten for Aline Barnsdall, which she destroyed, half-way. And she employed my superintendent of Hollyhock House himself—by the way, he was ready—to turn it into a garden terrace.

The Ennis house was fifth of the block-shell group. I had drawn my son Lloyd into this effort and after completing the plans and details for this latter house I entrusted it to Lloyd to build—and went back to Taliesin.

Some one hundred and seventy-nine buildings, large and small, had been built from my own hand by now, known as this work of mine. About seventy more had life only on paper: the most interesting and vital "stories" might belong to these children of imagination were they ever to encounter the field. Say, the Lake Tahoe Project, the Doheny Ranch Project, and others.[14]

Such stories of actual buildings as are included here are typical in some way of success or failure—of certain phases of the whole group although the building of many was untroubled and a delight.

Many another building as I see might have served here, as well or better: say, the Winslow house at River Forest; the Hillside Home School buildings, the first "Dampfer House" . . . that is to say the Robie house down by Chicago University—now belonging to the Congregational Church. The Coonley house at Riverside. The Martin house at Buffalo. The little "School of the Free Spirit" in Tokio. The interesting Fukuhara Country House at Hakone, it parted in two during the great earthquake—the great living-room at the front following the rock-cliff on which it stood down the mountainside some thousands of feet into the valley below—all being in the bedrooms behind, no one harmed. The establishment of the Bitter Root Community in Montana—and many others.

It would be worth while to tell the story of the house for Henry Allen at Wichita, Kansas. Henry was as colorful a client as all outdoors. And of the new home I did not build for William Allen White because Will had an animal fear of being turned out of the old one.

I would like to tell of the home at Peoria for Francis Little, himself an intelligent builder and manager of civic gas plants for John R. Walsh. Mr. Little retired and sold the house to Bob Clarke. And—amusing to me—tell of the second and especially the third home I built for him on the shore of Lake Minnetonka, Minnesota. I liked that house much and the Littles more. The amusing story of how I got the Hotel and Bank block to build at Mason City, Iowa. And of the Aeroplane house, the Submarine, the Coach and Four, the Polar-star, and Perihelion. The Dana House at Springfield—dear old Mother Lawrence—salt-risen bread, blackberry preserves, and the way we kept faith with the old homestead. Especially of the lifelong interest and loyalty of Darwin D. Martin and the building of the several houses—under fire from Mrs. Martin—who finally joined us. Of the help of the inventive Charles E. Roberts at Oak Park.[15]

Many come trooping to mind, as children troop into school at the ringing of the bell after recess. And I can say, truthfully enough, if not modestly, that not one building, great or small, but was the working out of some idea, the practical demonstration of some principle at work and for that reason "as of record" not one has been lost. Although many have been torn down to make way for changes in the city. A number of the dwellings have "changed hands"—as the advertisement used to read—because of the rapidly shifting changes in the lives of the people for whom they were built in a young and rapidly changing country. Two were bought back again by the same people who built and sold them, because they could feel "at home" in no other. And especially I should like to tell the story of "the house that was never built." It was, of course, the best house I ever built.

Kaleidoscopic! These social-shifts demanded and taken by the restless to and fro of our artificial, hectic, economic life in the United States. What European would understand it any more than the people of these United States understand it themselves?

But there have now been "stories" enough. In Hollyhock House and La Miniatura I have wilfully taken those experiences in which I was most at disadvantage owing to the vicious triangle, by way of Time, Place, and Circumstance and by way of my own fault—to show how all creative effort in the direction of any Ideal is continually at the mercy of human nature—and trivial but characteristic circumstances. But I should retract that last statement. Where creative effort is involved there are no trivial circumstances. The most trivial of them may ruin the whole issue. Eternal vigilance is the only condition of creation in architecture.

Certainly it is only fair to include one's mistakes and errors of judgment—or any characteristic failings that had at any time relation to results as a whole in presenting architecture as essentially "human stuff."

During the two years passed in the beautiful Southwest, building conditions there had seemed to me to be a shallow sea of cheap expedients. Every effort made there was afloat on the surface and "for sale." I felt that were I to stay longer I too would be knocked down cheap to the highest bidder—if any. Desire for depth, for quality that is genuine seemed to be all in the future. Everybody and everything was "getting by."

So coming home to Taliesin once more I continued work on preliminary plans for the cantilever glass office building begun several years before— plan-making now to go forward for Mr. A. M. Johnson, the President of the National Life Insurance Company, who had offered to "grub-stake" me with $20,000 to prospect in his behalf with this structural idea as I had already laid it before him a year or two before.[16]

Cantilever construction was one of the principal features that brought the Imperial safely through the great quake. Mr. Johnson was interested to see how the cantilever principle so successful there could be adapted to skyscraper requirements. How would it all work out in a great office building for the site on Water Tower Square, Chicago?

The idea attracted the insurance man. He kept saying, "Mr. Wright, now remember!"—with his characteristic chuckle—"I want a Virgin. I want a Virgin." The studies finally in presentable order, I took them to him. He took them to his house and put them in his own bedroom. The glass of one of the drawings, the color perspective, one day being broken by the maid, he put the drawing in his car, took it to the framer, waited until it was fixed, and brought it back home himself. He was intensely interested in ideas, I believe, though not himself the kind of man inclined to build much. He seemed rather of the type, called conservative, who, tempted, will sneak up behind an idea, pinch it behind, and invariably turn and run. There is this type of man bred by our capitalistic system, not the captain, but the broker and the banker.

I believe that a good part of this is due to the fact that so soon as an idea attracts a man of that kind—all the agencies he is connected with or definitely knows react for him. The engineers will shake their heads—the rental expert will shake his—the banks will hang out the "busy" sign. The architects will all stand together and ridicule the idea—until— the "business" man who had a moment of illumination and some genuine desire for initiative is, by sheer weight of the circumstances in which he has himself taken root, pushed back—where he belongs, or is quite lost. Such is the conservative and the conservatism that battens and fattens on the capitalistic enterprise of the true captains—and turns the vision of real men into the perquisites of the parasite. To this type of conservative nothing much happens, either way. He is the middle-of-the-road egotist. The middle of the road is the place for him. He will have plenty of company there. Such as it is.

But here Mr. Johnson was, just the same, paying a round sum to see how an idea would work out in his behalf.

A. M. Johnson was a strange mixture of the fanatic, the mystic, Shylock, the humanist. And withal extraordinarily intelligent.

His back had been broken in a railway accident. By sheer strength of intelligent will, he survived, with but a slight stoop in the way of his walk.

We took a trip into Death Valley, together where he and Death Valley Scotty had made a place in which to live. He drove his own car, a Dodge. I rode beside him and Nature staged a show for us all the way.

A convert of Billy Sunday, famous for his religious activities, or rather his activities in religious matters, he was a fundamentalist and controversialist of no mean order. Religiously we were at the poles apart.

But he grub-staked me in search of an Idea!

There are no pigeonholes in nature, human or otherwise, in which to put anyone.

A singular trait of Mr. Johnson's was this lifelong friendship for Scotty.

Scotty was suspected of having gold mines on a location known only to him. But A. M. Johnson was Scotty's gold mine, I suspect.

THE GLASS SKYSCRAPER

A lot of approximately 300' x 100' facing to the south.

Sheet-copper and glass were the mediums I chose for the thin pendent wall-screens to be carried by the other edges of the cantilever slabs, and to avoid the prejudice I saw in my client's mind against excessive glass surfaces I decided to make the exterior area of this project about $^1/_4$ of copper and $^3/_4$ of glass. Sheet metal—copper—would therefore characterize this building as much as the glass.

At work upon this scheme—the metal and glass house, the metal and glass service station—brother to the car and the plane—seemed near at hand. And I made tentative structures of the standardized filling station.

I began to speculate on all these things. In various ways to design them seeing them all as definite and appropriate architecture.

For the Machine-age should have a great many types. It should have at least as many types as

there are materials and methods of construction: all genuine. All might become characteristic as architecture. But now, what forms? I had not gone directly into steel-construction before.

So these plans for the insurance building were an opportunity to devise a more practical solution of the skyscraper problem than current, because the advantages offered by modern materials and methods add up most heavily in their own favor where they can go farthest—either up and down or crosswise.

So standardization here might come completely into its own, because standardization is in the nature of both sheet-metal process and concrete as a material. Here, again it is the life of the Imagination awakens life within the very limitations of the architect's problems.

Now, exterior walls, as such, disappear—instead are suspended, standardized sheet-copper screens only slightly engaged with the edges of the floors. The walls themselves cease to exist as either weight or thickness. Windows become in this fabrication a matter of units in the screen fabric, opening singly or in groups at the will of the occupant. All the outside glass of the building may be cleaned from the inside with neither bother nor risk. The vertical mullions (copper shells filled with non-conducting mastic) are large and strong enough only to carry from floor to floor and the mullions project much or little as more or less light is wanted. Much projection enriches the shadows. Less projection dispels the shadows and brightens the interior. These protecting mullions which are really blades of copper act in the sun like the blades of a blind.

The unit of two feet both ways is small because of Mr. Johnson's fear of "too much glass." In this instance the unit is emphasized on every alternate vertical with additional emphasis on every fifth to enlarge the metal areas and create a larger rhythm. There is no emphasis on the horizontal units to catch water or dust. The edge of the various floors are beveled to the same section as is used between the windows where engaged with the wall screen. It appears in the screen as such horizontal division occurring naturally on the two-foot unit lines. The floors themselves, however, do appear, at intervals, in the recessions of the screen in order to bring the concrete structure itself into relief in relation to the screen as well as in connection with it, weaving the two elements of structure together.

Thus the outer building surfaces become opalescent, iridescent, copper-bound glass. To avoid all interference with the fabrication of the light-giving exterior-screen the supporting pylons are set back from the lot line, the floors carried by them thus becoming cantilever-slabs. The extent of the cantilever is determined by the use for which the building is designed. These pylons are continuous through all floors and in this instance exposed as pylons at the top. These pylons are enlarged to carry electrical, plumbing, and heating conduits which branch from the shafts, not in the floor slabs, but into piping designed into visible fixtures extending beneath each ceiling to where the outlets are needed in the office arrangement. All electrical or plumbing appliances may thus be disconnected and relocated at short notice with no waste at all in time or material.

Being likewise fabricated on a perfect unit system, the interior-partitions may all be made up in sections, complete with doors, ready to set in place, and designed to match the general style of the outer wall-screen.

These interior partition units thus fabricated may be stored ready to use, and any changes to suit tenants made overnight with no waste of time and material. Mr. Johnson was an experienced landlord and all this simplicity appealed to him. Again the kind of standardization that gives us the motor car.

The increase of glass area over the usual skyscraper fenestration is only about ten per cent (the margin could be increased or diminished by expanding or contracting the copper members in which the glass is set), so the expense of heating is not materially increased. Inasmuch as the copper mullions are filled with insulating material and the window openings are tight, being mechanical units in a mechanical screen, this excess of glass is compensated.

The radiators are cast as a railing set in front of the lower glass unit of this outer screen-wall, free enough to make cleaning easy.

The walls of the first two stories, or more, may be unobstructed glass suspended from the floor above. The dreams of the shop-keeper in this connection thus fully realized.

The connecting stairways necessary between floors are here arranged as a practical fire-escape forming the central feature, as may be seen at the front and rear of each section of the whole mass, and though cut off by fire-proof doors at each floor, the continuous stairway thus made discharges upon the sidewalk below without obstruction.

The construction of such a building as this would be at least one-third lighter than anything in the way of a tall building yet built—and three times stronger in any disturbance, the construction being balanced as the body on the legs, the walls hanging as the arms from the shoulders, the whole heavy only where weight insures stability.

But of chief value as I see it is the fact that the scheme as a whole legitimately eliminates the matter of "masonry architecture," that now vexes all such buildings and takes away from field construction, all such elements of architectural "exterior" or interior either—architecture in this scheme now becoming a complete shop-fabrication. Only the most complicated part of the building need be assembled in the field.

The shop in our mechanical era is ten to one economically efficient over the field, and will rapidly increase over the field in economy and craftsmanship in future as it has done in the past.

Here, the mere physical concrete construction of pylons and floors is non-involved with any interior or exterior. Easily rendered indestructible, it is made entirely independent of anything hitherto complicating it and mixed up with it in our country as "architecture." In the skyscraper as practiced at present so-called "architecture" is expensively involved but is entirely irrelevant. In this design "architecture" is entirely relevant but uninvolved.

Also the piping and conduits of all appurtenance systems may be cut in the shop, the labor in the field reduced to assembling only. No "fitting." Screwing up the joints is all that is necessary in heating, lighting, or plumbing.

Thus, literally, we have a shop-made building in all but the interior supporting posts and floors, which may be reinforced concrete or concrete-masked steel.

In this design, architecture was frankly, profitably, and artistically—why not?—taken from the field to the factory. A building is here standardized as any mechanical thing whatsoever might be, from a penny-whistle to a piano, and it is dignified, imaginative, practical. The economic advantages are enormous and obvious.

There is no unsalable floor space in this building—nothing at all created "for effect," as may be observed.

There are no "features" inside or outside manufactured merely "for architectural effect."

To gratify Mr. Johnson, the landlord, his lot area was now salable to the very lot-line itself and on every floor, where ordinances do not interfere and demand that they be reduced in area as the building soars.

What architecture there is in evidence here is a light, trim, practical, commercial fabric—every inch and pound of which is "in service." There is every reason why it should be beautiful. But it was best to say nothing about that to Mr. Johnson as things were now. And I said very little about it.

The present design was worked out for this lot three hundred feet by one hundred feet. The entrance courts are open to the south.

There is nothing of importance to mention in the general disposition of the other necessary parts of the plan. All is quite as customary.

The aim in this fabrication employing the cantilever system of construction was to achieve absolute scientific utility by means of the Machine. To accomplish—first of all—a true standardization which would not only serve as a basis for keeping the life of the building true as architecture, but enable me to project the whole, as an expression of a valuable principle involved, into a genuine living architecture of the present.

I began work upon this study the winter of 1920, the main features of it having been in mind ever since the Imperial in 1917. I had the good fortune to explain the scheme in detail and show the developed preliminary drawings to "liebermeister," Louis H. Sullivan, some time before he died.

Gratefully I remember—and proudly too, he said—"I have had faith that it would come. This is the architecture of Democracy. I see it in this building, Frank. It is genuine. It is a work of Art. I knew what I was talking about all these years—you see? I could never have done this building myself, but I believe that, but for me, you could never have done it."

I know I should never have reached it, but for what he was and what he himself did.

This design is dedicated to him.

During this period, building the Imperial Hotel and the block buildings in Los Angeles, life, of "legal" necessity—legal divorce still denied and so no legal protection—remained unconventional. Voluntarily—in exile.

Taliesin had become refuge to the misfortune of the unfortunate. Miriam.

Life when resumed at Taliesin II, had changed. There were no longer carefree walks over the friendly hills, nor swimming in the river below. No horse-back riding along the country lanes. Nor coasting and skating or happy sleighing in winter. No freedom, no singing. Involuntarily, all intention otherwise, life seemed paralyzed by subtle poison. Taliesin—it seemed—had encountered disintegration from within.

And, fortunately, the life that had entered Taliesin II as new, soon left it. Went to Japan.

Only caretakers and one faithful apprentice, William Smith, stayed there. Restlessly, during the following years Taliesin languished and called in vain, rewarded each year by a visit of several months from the land on the other side of the globe.

Dust settled on the heads of the ancient gods at rest upon the broad ledges.

Taliesin had been calling all these years, and I looking forward to the time when it should come alive again for me and all those I loved. Now I came back. Miriam and I had been married several months before. But instead of improving with marriage, as I had hoped, our relationship became worse.

With marriage she seemed to lose what interest she had in life at Taliesin and become more than ever restless and vindictive. Finally under circumstances altogether baffling—she left to "live a life of her own." To oppose her now in the slightest degree meant violence.

She went first to Chicago. Even now I would not give up hope or effort to make good a human relationship gone so wrong. Suffering and sacrifice had already entered on both sides. Shame, too—an unfamiliar moral cowardice, kept me from acknowledging defeat although by nature and equipment unfitted for the task I had undertaken. But the circumstances being more than ever violent, I consulted Dr. William Hixon, a famous psychiatrist of Chicago now at Geneva. A tardy consultation, long dreaded and deferred.

Convinced by his observations that the struggle of the past six years had been hopeless from the beginning and that Miriam, all along, had been a danger not only to herself but especially to anyone with whom she might live in close association, I agreed to arrangements to end the relationship, modifying, somewhat, the terms dictated by herself. She had returned to Los Angeles. Dr. Hixon had said that the only hope for a longer freedom for her lay in letting her "have her head." To oppose her would only be to burn her up more quickly.

The final arrangements were made by Judge James Hill.

I stayed on at Taliesin.

Young people had come from all over the world attracted by Taliesin's fame abroad as "American," to share its spirit; to learn what message the indigenous United States had for Europe. And, evenings, after good work done, the piano, violin, and cello spoke there the religion of Bach, Beethoven, and Handel. William Blake, Samuel Butler, Walt Whitman, and Shelley often presided, evenings. Carl Sandburg, Edna Millay, and Ring Lardner, too, had something to say or sing. And life in the hills revived for the little cosmopolitan group —eager to know this "America," for Taliesin was at work quietly Americanizing Europe while American architects Europeanized America.

But peace even for these gentle seekers from afar was not to last, for long. There were but eleven months of growing good will. The living things of Art and Beauty belonging now to the place as the eye to the face, become like Taliesin's own flesh, each and all were a loneliness and sorrow. Occasionally a living thought would go over them as they stood dignified but neglected. Taliesin dreamed, meditated, worked, and slept.

The primeval fire-places sent streams of light and warmth into the house but it no longer seemed to live. Dissension and discord had shamed the lifting walls and friendly ceilings.

A hope only, lived wishing to bring back happiness.

ISAIAH

Then about a year after Miriam and I had finally separated,[17] one evening at twilight as the lightning of an approaching storm was playing and the wind rising I came down from the evening meal in the little detached dining room on the hill-top to the dwelling on the court below to find smoke pouring from my bedroom. Again—there it was—Fire!

Fire, fanned by that rising storm, meant a desperate fight. My heart was sand as I realized all had gone from the place for the evening but two besides myself. Mel, the driver, and Kameki, a Japanese apprentice.

I called them to bring water. And water came to the constant cry of "Water" for two hours. I thought I had put the fire out when an ominous crackling above the ceiling indicated fire in the dead space beneath the "roof." The alarm went out again, and again the people of the countryside turned to fight flames at Taliesin.

The wind blew the flames—beneath the roof surfaces to break out above in a dozen places. "Let us save what we can of the things inside," they cried.

"No, fight . . . fight. Fight the flames. Save Taliesin or let all go," I shouted, like some dogged, foolish captain on the bridge of a sinking vessel doomed to all eyes but his.

More water. Water! was the cry as more men came over the hills to fight the now roaring sea of devastation. Whipped by the big wind, great clouds of smoke and sparks drove straight down the lengths of Taliesin courts. The place seemed doomed now—even to me. That merciless wind! How cruel the wind may be—as cruel as fire itself.

But on the smoking roofs, feet burned, lungs seared, hair and eyebrows gone, thunder rolling as the lightning flashed over the lurid scene, the hill-top long since profaned by crowds of spectators standing silent there—I stood—and fought—Isaiah?

I could not give up the fight, because now it was a fight to save the work rooms. But everyone else had given it up. Taliesin as a whole, they said, was gone.

And Destruction had reached to the work rooms—had begun to take hold of them too—water gone, human energy gone. Men were lying about the roofs to recover strength and breath to keep on fighting.

Suddenly a tremendous pealing roll of thunder and the storm broke with a violent change of wind that rolled the mass of flame up the valley. It re-coiled upon itself—as the rain fell hissing into the roaring furnace. The clouds of smoke and sparks were swept the opposite way—as by some gigantic unseen hand, that awed the spectators. It seemed like superhuman Providence.

The living half of Taliesin—gone—again.

Plate glass windows lay, crystal pools in ashes on hot stone pavements.

Smoldering or crumbled in ashes, priceless blossoms-of-the-soul in all ages—we call them works of Art—lay broken, or had vanished utterly.

Another savage blow struck.

Left to me out of most of my earnings, since Taliesin I was destroyed, all I could show for my work and wanderings in the Orient for years past, were the leather trousers, burned socks, and shirt in which I stood, defeated, and what the workshop contained.

But Taliesin lived where I stood! A figure crept forward from out the shadows to say this to me. And I believed what Olgivanna said.

The lightning had struck again, and—is human carelessness and fallibility all the wrath of God there is? The fire had originated in a house-telephone that had given trouble as it stood by the head of my bed. Again searching causes, I wondered. Everything of a personal nature I had in the world, beside my work, was gone. But . . . this time—how thankful—no lives lost except those images whose souls belonged and could now return to the souls that made them—precious works of Art.

Yes . . . poor trustee for posterity, I had not protected them. But they should live in me, I thought. I would prove their life by mine in what I did. And I said so to the suppliant figure standing on the hilltop in the intense dark that now followed the brilliant blaze.

And that lurid crowd! During the terrible de-struction it had stood there all about on the hill-top lit by the flames. Some few sympathetic, others, half-sympathizing, convinced of inevitable doom. Some sneering at the fool who imagined Taliesin could "come back" after all that had happened be-fore. Others stolidly chewing tobacco—entertained.

Were they the force that had struck again? Were they "Isaiah"?

Well—counselled by the living—there was I alive in their midst, key to a Taliesin nobler than the first if I could make it. And I had faith that I could build another Taliesin!

A few days later clearing away the debris to re-construct I picked up partly calcined marble heads of the Tang-dynasty, fragments of the black basalt of a splendid Wei-stone, Sung soft-clay sculpture and gorgeous Ming pottery turned to the color of bronze by the intensity of the blaze. The sacrificial offerings to—whatever Gods may be.

And I put these fragments aside to weave them into the masonry—fabric of Taliesin III that now—already in mind—was to stand in place of Taliesin II. And I went to work.[18]

Again after confusion, destruction, desolation, at work again in the workshop at Taliesin. Out in the fields—walking. Swimming in the river. Driv-ing over the hills. Skating in winter.

Appetite for creation still lagging . . . a little, but coming alive again. Hunger not far away.

Meantime just before the destruction of the first Taliesin, Lieber Meister and I had again come together.

Things had not been going so well with him since the separation from Dankmar Adler shortly after that triumphant disaster, the Columbian "Fair."

The Guarantee Building, Buffalo, had just come into the office when I left. It was the last building built under the Adler and Sullivan partnership.

To go back many years into Adler and Sullivan history . . .

Owing to the nature of creative work, Adler and Sullivan, Architects, made no money. Their work cost them as much, often more, than they received for it, although they were paid as well as any architects . . . probably better than most. Depression following the Columbian Fair therefore hit Adler and Sullivan hard. At this psychological moment Crane, of the Crane Company, came along as tempter to offer Adler $25,000 a year to sell Crane Elevators. Adler, in a fit of despondency, accepted. Some money had to be earned by someone. Sullivan was left alone, resentful.

The clientele had been mostly Adler's, as Sullivan now found out. And Louis Sullivan soon faced the fact that he was where he must take what was left to him from the Adler connection and start to build up a practice anew. Only one Adler and Sullivan client stayed with the lonely Sullivan: Meyer of Schlesinger and Meyer employed him to design his new retail store building on State Street.

Meantime it seems, as I got the story, a curious mishap had befallen Crane's new lion. He went to New York to sell Crane Elevators for the new Siegel Cooper Building. The opposing bidder, Sprague Electric, simply pulled out a report Adler, the architect, made concerning their elevator for use in the Auditorium Building some years previous. It gave the Electric everything—including the Siegel Cooper work.

Mr. Adler came home. Some words from Crane. The "lion" was unused to being talked to in that tone of voice, especially from one who had hitherto come to him for justice, or favors.

The result of the interview was a check to Adler for a year's salary and a canceled contract.

All now hoped to see the two partners together again. But no, the Master was resentful still—and the big chief had had enough.

About this time Mr. Adler was at the Union League Club, and called for me. I went to talk things over with him. As yet I had not communicated with Mr. Sullivan, nor had I seen him since leaving. The old chief seemed morose. He had been greatly worried by the risks he had taken to please his clients in certain features of the Auditorium Building, the addition to the height of the tower to please Sullivan—the addition of the banquet hall over the trusses . . . spanning the Auditorium to please Ferdinand Peck et. al. Movement had not yet stopped. The tower was settling and taking down the adjoining portions of the building.

I noticed a great change in him.

He spoke bitterly of Sullivan, who had published the Guarantee Building with Adler's name deleted from the plans.

"But for me, Wright, there would have been no Guarantee Building!"

"Yes," I said. "But I am sure the omission was not Sullivan's fault. Probably the publisher's. Why don't you make sure?"

"I'm sure enough," he said.

I tried him out concerning Sullivan. Told him there was such general disappointment over the separation—believed they needed each other—and if ever two men did, they did—had done such great work together—the depression couldn't last—and many private arguments for resuming the old relationship.

"No, Wright," thrusting out his bearded chin in characteristic fashion, "I am going to keep my office in my hat so far as I can—there's nothing in the big office with its big rent and big salary list. I'll do the few buildings I can do, and instead of earning $50,000—keeping $1,000—I'll earn, by myself, $5,000 and keep $2,000."

And looking at me sharply under his honest, shaggy eyebrows: "Take this from me, do you do the same."

"No architect on that individual basis ever needs a partner," he added.

I saw something that had lived between the two men, who so needed each other, was burning up or burnt out.

We walked over to the several small rooms he had taken on the Wabash Avenue side of the Auditorium—while Sullivan was still carrying on in the tower. It seemed a heartbreaking situation to me.

But I still believed they would come together, and said so when I left. Worry and disappointment had already done something to the grand old chief. This was no way of life for him.

In a short time he was dead.[19]

Some seven years later the Master and I met again. He had gone from bad to worse. The Auditorium management had refused to carry him further in the splendid tower offices, and offered him two rooms below near by those Adler had occupied on the Wabash Avenue front.

Later even these were closed to the Master.

He had called me over long-distance. Luckily I was able to re-instate him. But habits engendered by his early life in Paris had made havoc with him. He had "gone off," as they say, frightfully.

He was much softened though, and deepened too, I thought. He gently called me "Frank." I always loved the way the word came from him. Before that it had always been "Wright."

His courage was not gone. It would never go. The eyes burned as brightly as ever. The old gleam of humor would come into them and go. But the carriage was not the same. The body was disintegrating.

I remember sitting on his desk and noticing that it was littered with his papers. There were photographs, too, of the small bank-buildings he had been doing. These showed only remnants of his great genius as it had flashed from him in the Wainwright Building in the old days in the tower. He was leaning heavily now, I could see, on George Elmslie who was still with him at the time these were done.

Lieber Meister was, by now, safe in an armchair, life-member at the Cliff Dwellers club. It is one of the virtues of that organization that it did this for him. I had corresponded with him while in Japan, and from Los Angeles. Whenever I got to Chicago I took a room at the Congress for him, next mine.

He was staying at the old Hotel Warner way down on Cottage Grove Avenue, an old haunt of his with little else to recommend it. He had taken great pride in the performance of the Imperial Hotel. Had written two articles concerning it for the "*Record*." "At last, Frank," he said, "something they can't take away from you." (I wonder why he thought "they" couldn't take it away from me? "They" could take anything away from anybody, if not by hook, by crook.)

Several Architects in Chicago had befriended him, had been kind to him. Gates of the American and Lucas, Hottinger, and others of the Northwestern Terra Cotta Company especially so. But he was no more tolerant of his contemporaries in architecture now than ever before. Rather less so.

He had for many years been compelled to see great opportunities for work he could do so much better—as to make comparison absurd—going to inferior men, just because his personal habits had given provincial prejudices a chance to "view with distrust or dislike" where the matters involved were no concern of theirs nor directly connected with his efficiency as an architect. Ignorance, provincial, quotidian was his implacable enemy. A Genius? That term damned him as it was intended to do.

Beware . . . Finance! Tiptoe to safety!

But now his efficiency was actually impaired by himself. He had increasingly sought refuge from loneliness—frustration—and betrayal, where and as so many of his gifted brothers have been driven to do since time immemorial.

Had opportunity opened, even this late in his life it might have saved him for years of remarkable usefulness. But popular timidity and prejudice encouraged by jealousy had built a wall of ignorance around him and the wall blinded his country and wasted him. At times his despondency would overcome his native pride and natural buoyancy. Even his high courage would give way to fear for his livelihood. Then all would come clear again. For a while.

He was caustic when he chose, was the old Master. When he was in a bitter mood, a dozen or so of his hard-boiled contemporaries would come tumbling from their perches on high, top side down, inside out. His blade could cut and flash as it cut.

He was writing *The Autobiography of an Idea* at this time. Occasionally he would read chapters to me. He loved to write and now, completely shut off from his natural medium of expression, he turned to writing. Soon he was again the Master. The book meant much to him now . . .

He had visited Taliesin some years before. But it proved rather a strenuous experience for him. At this time, two years later, his breath was shorter still and after several cups of the strong coffee he loved too much, his breath was so short he would take my arm to walk—even slowly.

He was sinking. I continued to see him oftener than every week if I could.

Some months passed and a telephone call to Taliesin came from the Warner. I went, and found the place up in arms against him. He had fallen very sick. Violent "spells" came over him now more and more often. I made peace with the manager of the Warner—after raising Cain over the condition I had found his room in. The manager was really devoted to Sullivan as he said he was, but at his wits' end. We got a nurse finally who would stay. His devoted comrade, the little henna-haired milliner who understood him and could do most anything with him, was in the hospital at the time.

"Don't leave me, Frank," he begged." Stay."

And I stayed. He seemed to be himself again toward evening. We talked about the forthcoming book, *The Autobiography of an Idea.* He hoped there might be some income in it—for him.

He had everything to make him comfortable, and that evening late after he had fallen asleep, I went back to Taliesin again with a promise from the nurse to call me if I was needed.

In town a few days later, I went to see him again.

He seemed better. There—at last—the first bound copy of the *Autobiography* just come in, lying on the table by his bed. He wanted to get up, I helped him, put my overcoat round his shoulders as he sat on the bed with his covered-up feet on the floor. He looked over at the book. "There it is, Frank." I was sitting by him, my arm around him to keep him warm and steady him. I could feel every vertebra in his backbone as I rubbed my hand up and down his back to comfort him. I could feel his heart pounding. His heart, the physician said, was twice its natural size owing to the coffee and bromide he had become addicted to.

"Give me the book! The first copy to you. A pencil!" He tried to raise his arm to take the pencil; he couldn't lift it. Gave it up with an attempt at a smile.

And I have never read the book. All I know of it are the chapters he read to me himself. I could not read it.

Oh, yes, his courage was still there. And he cursed a little—gently enough. The eyes were deeper in their sockets, but burning bright. He joked about the end he saw now, and cursed—under his breath. For the first time, I think, he would admit to himself that the end was near. But to me he looked as though he were better, notwithstanding the helpless arm. But he seemed indifferent, didn't want to talk about it either way. Life had been pretty hard on him. Such friends as he had could do little to make up for the deep tragedy of his frustration as an architect. Only a year or so before in solitude he had made the beautiful drawings for the *The System of Architectural Ornament*, his hand shaking as with palsy until he began to draw. And these drawings show little falling off either in style or execution from his best at any time. His ornament was his inextinguishable gift, to the last. I had passed through many situations with him that had looked worse than this one. I put him back to bed again—covered him up—and sat there beside him on the edge of the bed, while he fell asleep. Another crisis had apparently passed. He seemed to sleep well, to breathe deeply enough and easily once more. The nurse had stepped out for a moment. An imperative call had come from Taliesin. I left a note for the nurse to be called immediately if there was any change in him for the worse.

At Taliesin, anxiously I listened for the telephone. No call coming I felt reassured.

The day after the next I learned of his death from the newspapers and a long-distance call from Max Dunning. He had died the day after I left.

Several architects, warm-hearted little Max Dunning, one of them, happened to come just at the end to see him and had taken charge.

I was not sent for.

The Master had nothing in the world he could call his own but the complete new outfit of clothes it had been one of the pleasures of my life to see him in some months before—these and a beautiful old daguerreotype of his lovely mother, himself and his brother, aged about nine, seen standing on either side of her.

Knowing he was dying he gave this prized possession of his to the nurse to give to "Frank."

I should have liked to keep the warm muffler he had worn about his neck . . . but . . . sentimentality. What use? He was gone!

Nor did anyone think to advise me concerning any of the arrangements. His tardy friends picked his body up, planned an ordinary funeral at Graceland, at which Wallace Rice spoke, and which I attended. Later they designed a "monument" for him . . . a slab of ornament designed for his grave in his own vein! They caused this to be designed by George Elmslie, the young understudy I had brought over to Sullivan from Silsbee's because the Master wanted me to train someone to take my place in case anything should happen to me. He had taken my place when I left, and stayed with the Master ten years or more. But to me, who had understood and loved him, this idea of a monument to the Master was ironic. There was nothing to be done about it worth doing. It was their own best thought for the man now, and no monument is ever more than a monument to those who erect it.

These monuments! Will we never make an end of such banality or such profanity?

What great man ever lived whose "memory" has not been menaced, traduced, made ridiculous, or insulted by the monument "they" erected to themselves in his name when he was dead! Abraham Lincoln comes to mind. How many monuments are made by those who, voluntarily or not, never did anything but betray the thing the great man they would honor loved most who were "charitable" when he was in need; officious when he died.

THE MASTER'S WORK

The New in the Old and the Old in the New is, ever, principle.

Principle is all and single the reality Louis Sullivan loved. It gave to the man stature and gave to his work significance.

His loyalty to principle was remarkable as a vision when all around him poisonous cultural mists hung low, to obscure or blight any bright hope of any finer beauty in the matter of this world.

As "the name of God has fenced around all crime with holiness" so in architecture the "pseudo-classic" during his lifetime perpetually invented skillful lies to hide ignorance or impotence and belie creation such as Louis Sullivan's.

That his great work was done in this age is marvel enough. That it could *be* at all under the terrible shop-keeping circumstances we call Democracy, that so mocked his own fine sense, was prophetic. And for his country—I should say—the greatest and best suggestion of its own hidden virtue.

The buildings he has left with us for a brief time are the least of him. In the heart of him he was of infinite value to his country, the country that wasted him, wasted him not because it would: but because it could not know him.

Any work, great as human expression, must be studied in relation to the time in which it insisted upon its virtues and got itself into human view.

So it should be with the work he has left us.

Remember, if you can, the contemporaries of his first great building, the Chicago Auditorium. The calm, noble exterior of that great stone building. The beautiful free room within, so beautifully conceived as a unit. Its plastic ornamentation, quiet in its deep cream and soft gold scheme of color.

Its hectic contemporaries were the Pullman Building on Michigan Avenue, W. W. Boyington's "Board of Trade," the hideous Union Station, and other survivors in the "idiom" of that insensate period of General-Grant Gothic.

Outside the initial impetus of John Edelman, in his early days, H. H. Richardson, the great emotional revivalist of Romanesque, was one whose influence the Master felt. And John Root, another fertile rival of that time who knew less than the Master but felt almost as much, sometimes shot very straight indeed. But they were his only peers. And they were feeling their way as he was *thinking* and feeling his way, to the New.

Dankmar Adler, master of the plan and master of men was his faithful partner. Adler's influence was great and good, for he was himself a great builder. He was also a manager of men, a fine critic.

The Auditorium Building is largely what it is, physically, owing to Dankmar Adler's good judgment and restraining influence.

Compare the imaginative plastic richness of the inspired interior of the Auditorium with the cut, butt, and slash of the period. Compare it with the meaningless stiffness and utter awkwardness that brutalized those buildings. For all their ambitious attitudes and grand gestures they were sterile. His contemporaries belonged to a world to which the sense of the word "plastic" had not been born except in the Monadnock, a solid-walled brick building by John Root. And that was masonry wall with holes in the wall. That the word "plastic" got itself understood at all in relation to architecture then, is doubtful—even by Sullivan himself. Root's was not a synthetic mind, nor was Richardson's as was Louis Sullivan's.

Back of that first really great though tentative building, "The Auditorium," was deepening knowledge, a tightening grasp on essentials. Much in this great effort got away from Sullivan as I have reason to know. It wore the man out. But the interior is good enough yet to be the most successful room for Opera in the world. I think I have seen them all.

His genius burst into full bloom with the impetus the success and fame of that great enterprise brought to him and to his brother in arms, Dankmar Adler.

The Getty Tomb was a work that soon followed, as did the Wainwright Building in St. Louis to greater purpose.

The Getty Tomb in Graceland Cemetery was a piece of sculpture, a statue, a poem, addressed to the sensibilities as such. It was architecture in a detached and romantic phase—a beautiful burial casket—"in memoriam" to Getty. But really memorial to the architect whose work it was.

But—when he brought the drawing board with the motive for the Wainwright Building outlined in profile and in scheme upon it and threw it down on my table, I was perfectly aware of what had happened.

This was Louis Sullivan's great moment, his greatest effort. The skyscraper as a new thing beneath the sun, an entity imperfect, but with virtue, individuality, beauty all its own—was born. Until Louis Sullivan showed the way tall buildings never had unity. They were built up in layers. They were all fighting tallness instead of accepting it. What unity those false masses that pile up toward the New York and Chicago sky have now is due to the master mind that first perceived the tall building as a harmonious unit—its height triumphant.

The Wainwright Building cleared the way for these tall office building effects. And to this day, the Wainwright remains the master key to the skyscraper so far as a skyscraper is a matter of architecture.

The masculine "Wainwright" and its sister the Guarantee Building of Buffalo were architecture living again. A true service was here rendered humanity because some proof of the oneness of spirit and matter came clear. That proof was awaited by the machine-age as the inevitable service of the artist-architect.

The Transportation Building at the "Fair" cost the Master most trouble of anything he did. He got the great golden doorway straight away, but the rest hung fire. I had never seen him anxious before, but anxious he was then. How eventually successful that beautiful intrusion into a pseudo-classic collection of picture-building was, shows how little cause he had for anxiety.

But the Transportation Building was no solution of the works of the world as was the

Wainwright Building. It too was a picture-building. But a picture-building with rhyme and reason, above all with individuality, not a mere pose of the picturesque. It was itself a remarkable circumstance and entertainment as scene painting. That is all it was intended to be. It was a thing created for itself alone. Almost any other "exterior" would have served the purpose as well.

Only the interior of the Chicago Auditorium, the pictorial Transportation Building, for what it was worth, the Getty Tomb, the Wainwright Building are necessary to show what great reach the creative activity had that was Louis Sullivan's genius. The other buildings he did are all more or less on these stems. Some grafted from them. Some grown from them. But all relatively inferior in point of the quality which we must finally associate with the primitive strength of the thing that got itself done or born regardless and "stark" to the idea.

As to materials: the impress of the Master's imagination gripped them all pretty much alike. As to relying upon them for beauties of their own, he had no need, no patience. All materials were stuff to bear the stamp of his imagination and bear it they did—cast iron, wrought iron, marble, plaster, concrete, wood, pretty much alike. In this respect he did not live up to his principle. He was too rich in fancy, too exuberant to allow anything to come, for its own sake, between him and the goal he desired. Where his work fell short, in this respect, whether he realized it or not, it fell short of his own ideal.

I see his richest individual quality and his sense of principle more clearly articulated by him in that feature of his work that was his sensuous ornament—as I see the wondrous smile upon his face. His system of ornament was something complete in itself—unique. It had personal, appealing charm. So very like and so very much—his own. His ornament, as he did it, will be cherished long because no one in ancient or modern times has had the quality to produce out of himself such a gracious, beautiful response, so lovely a smile evoked by love of Beauty.

The capacity for love—ardent, true, poetic—was great in him, as his system of ornament in itself, alone, would prove. His work in this was esoteric.

It is none the less precious for that?

Do you realize that here is no body of culture evolving through centuries of time a scheme and "style" of plastic expression but an individual working away in the poetry-crushing environment of a more cruel materialism than any seen since the days of the brutal Romans? An individual who, in this, evoked the goddess that whole civilizations strove for centuries to win—and wooed her with this charming interior smile—all on his own in his brief lifetime.

Is this perhaps to show us that the time may come when every man may have that precious quality called style for his very own?

Then I ask you where on earth are the others?

Ah, that erotic supreme adventure of the mind that was his ornament!

Often I would see him, his back bent over his drawing-board intent upon—what? I knew his symbolism. I caught his feeling as he worked. A Casanova on his rounds? Beside this sensuous master of adventure with tenuous, vibrant, plastic form, Casanova was a sensual duffer, Boccaccio's imagination was no higher than a stable-boy's. The soul of Rabelais alone could have understood, and he would have confessed himself—the duffer! How often have I held the Master's cloak and sword while he adventured into this realm within, to win his mistress. While he wooed the mistress I would woo the maid. Those days!

This aesthetic caress of "form" that was his own is something complete in itself and should be sacred to him. Treasured high for its own sake as we treasure sculpture, painting, or great writing. Take his principle who will and none may do better. But try the wings nature gave to you; do not try to soar with his. Eros is a fickle god and hard to please.

Genius the Master had, or rather genius had him. Genius possessed him. It reveled in him. He squandered it. And the lesser part of him was squandered by it. He lived—I know. He lived, and compared to what came to him in his life-time from his own effort, the effort itself being a fine interior quality of his life, I imagine the great successful careers, were—all of them—relatively lifeless—exterior.

The effect of any genius is seldom seen in its own time. Nor can the full effects of genius ever be traced or seen. Human affairs are flowing. What we call life in everything is plastic, a becoming, in spite of all efforts to fix it with names, and all endeavors to make it static to man's will. As a pebble cast into the ocean sets up reactions lost in distance and time, so does any man's genius go on infinitely forever. For genius is an expression of principle. Therefore in no way does genius ever run counter to genius!

We may be sure the intuitions and expressions of such a nature as his in the work to which he put his hand, no less than the suggestion he was himself to kindred or aspiring natures, is more conservative of the future of our country than all the work of all the schools of all the time combined with all the salesmanship of all the functioneers.

H. H. Richardson, great emotionalist in architecture that he was—elected to work in "a style," the "Romanesque." The Master dug deeper and made style for himself out of the same stuff the Romanesque was made from—yes, and the Gothic too.

A pioneer of this greater type was Louis Sullivan. So Louis Sullivan's performance was direct contrast to the leadership of such a man as Stanford White. White's mind was that of the connoisseur. His gift was exoteric. He was an eclectic. We owe to him and to his kind the eclectic army of "good taste" in the United States that smothered the practical in applied expedients. But his kind are now, in whatever terms they state their work, a popular retreating army, now, whose beauty-worship is excited and contented with the beauty of the painted lady, the lip-stick, paste, and rouge.

What does it matter if the army entrenched or retreating fails to see such loyalty to tradition as was Louis Sullivan's as wholly complete? His loyalty was as much greater than theirs, as the spirit transcends the letter.

Why is the vision of such a mind as the Master's mind lost in competitive confusion of near-ideas, selfish ambitions?

Why at the beginning of the Twentieth Century is culture itself nowhere sane or fertile except where and as sterile imitation is made safe commercial expedient of the hour?

Such culture is not nor ever was for long. Look backward toward Rome. Why should free men as slaves to the expedient emulate the fate of Rome?

Yes, my great master's works, as to form, except his ornament as something, *sui generis,* precious in itself, will die with him. It is no great matter.

A way-shower needs no piles of perishable granite, no sightly shapes behind him to secure his immortality or make good his Fame. It is to be his fortune that in the hearts of his fellows his service was real. The boon to us of the pioneer's journey on this earth in the narrow span of life and opportunity so grudgingly measured out to him by his own people in his own time is beyond question. The work of this pioneer was the work of a man for men. Sincere proof of his humanity—for humanity.

Many faults may be justly laid to him. Many.

Never mind! They are, all, the rough edges of the real thing. And what he said and did even more than the way he said it or did it will always repay painstaking study—if it is free study.

But the more the pedantic mind studies his word or his work the more the study will end in hostility. Such hostility never more than entertained and amused the Master though it all but bore him down. Such hostility to ideas as individual and to individuals as idea, as makes the provincial mind what it is—is found out on the farm, in the small town, on Main Street, but no less and more harmfully it is found in the seats of the mighty, in Church, New York, or Hollywood.

The hypocrite instinctively fears and therefore hates—the radical.

And whatever Louis Sullivan the man was, Louis Sullivan the architect was radical in the same sense as the ideal man who was the consummate radical of our human experience. Even that Man-of-men whom we have built up out of our own heart of hearts, would not yet be allowed to live among us. Nor any man at all like him. Then how could any master similarly moved toward an ideal live among us and "succeed"?

Unsuccessful pilot! Not long ago weary, in a despondent moment, he said to me—"it would be harder now to do radical work, more difficult to get radical work accepted, than it ever was."

"People have stopped thinking!"

"The inevitable drift toward mediocrity, in the name of Democracy has set it. I see it so."

No, my Master, it is not so. There is never an inevitable, contrary to life. The torch flung to your master-hand from the depths of antiquity, from the heart of this human world—kept alight and held aloft for twenty years, at least, by you—shall not go out. It has ever been flung from hand to hand and never yet—since time began for man—has it gone out.

My mother gone. At eighty-three years of age.[20]

The Master gone before his time.

Three beloved homes gone. The first—at Oak Park, stood for nineteen years. The second, Taliesin, withstood five years. The third, Taliesin II, stood eleven years.

Now the fourth home built by my own hands, a new home built out of a battered and punished but still sentimental self in the same quest—Life!

And help came from the deeps of Life with understanding ready for any sacrifice: the sympathy that makes the real friend. Olgivanna. Yes, a woman is, for man, the best of friends. If only the man will let her be one.

The idea that had come to Life with Taliesin II was, by now, conviction.

And the idea was, simply, that any man had a right to three things if he will be honest with all three. Could I be honest with them all?

The man's life?

The man's work?

The man's love?

I set to work again. Another spring of coordinate effort, more in love with life than ever. Another summer. Another autumn. Another win-

ter and, early in 1925, another chance to live and work in another Taliesin.

Taliesin III, if ruefully, none the less proudly took its place where the ashes of Taliesin I and Taliesin II and the life lived in each, had fallen.

The limestone piers, walls, and fireplaces of Taliesin II had turned red and crumbled in the fire, but I saved many stones not destroyed, so dyed by fire, and built them together with the fragments of great sculpture I had raked from the ashes into the new walls adding a richness to them unknown before.

Whereas the previous buildings had grown by addition, all could now be spontaneously born.

Taught by the building of Taliesin I and Taliesin II, I made forty sheets of pencil studies for the building of Taliesin III.

Still in debt for the second, no discretion whatever could detain me from beginning work on the third.

Waves of "publicity," this time neither ribald nor unkind, had broken over ruins. After all, even newspaper folk are kind, when they understand.

The frustration of the life of the past seven years had ended in the destruction of everything the frustrated life had touched.

I sought comfort in that thought as one fine thing after another would rise out of its ashes and reproach me with a shameful sense of loss.

And now, again, more and better building materials. More and, by this time, better trained workmen. More intelligent planning and execution, more difficulties in ways and means. More patience. Deeper anxiety. More humility.

Yet—in the same faith moving man forward.

Taliesin's radiant brow though now marked by shame and sorrow should come forth and shine with serenity unknown before. In this third trial, granted by Life itself, the new Life itself helped build the walls and make them more noble than before.

After many years, deep sorrows, trials, and defeats, Taliesin III was refreshed by the gift of a little new soul long desired to bring back to Taliesin something it had not found, or, finding, had lost.

No doubt Isaiah still stood there in the storms that muttered, rolled, and broke again over this low spreading shelter. The lightning played and crashed above. But the happy friendliness sheltered there was ready for any sacrifice if only Taliesin might come to Life to give one more proof of quality.

But the Mosaic Isaiah with eyes aslant where the beautiful would show its face or the lovely dare to lift its head with curly locks or black abundant tresses—was waiting there behind the hills to strike, should life at Taliesin rise from its ashes a third time.

Had the angry prophet struck twice? He could strike again?

And human obliquity going hand in hand with "bigger and better publicity" conspired with the ruthless prophet, self-appointed agent of an angry Jehovah, to do the "righteous" work, this time not by death and fire but by madness.

Taliesin, gentler prophet of the Celts, and of a more merciful God, tempted to lift an arm to strike back, suffered in silence, and waited.

The insulting hue and cry of "punishment" reached the doors of public officials. Some of them were moved by it. Knowing only the hue and cry they added their blows to give richness to the hue, adding insult to the injury of the cry until the sovereign insult in the gift of its own people, those who should have protected it and many of whom would have protected it had "Isaiah" not blinded them—was put upon Taliesin.

Taliesin raged and wanted to strike back, but again held his arm. Strike at what?

Like Isaiah—at little children and women, torn in the streets and bleeding?

Instead Taliesin turned to work. Work is defense against Isaiah. At least, Life was no longer betrayed *within* sheltering walls, however it might be beset from without by any wrathful jealous prophet.

And this stood firm now while newspaper-men, editors, reporters, camera-men, publishers, lawyers, petty officials, federal, state, county, local officials, lawyers in Washington, lawyers in Minneapolis, lawyers in Chicago, lawyers in Milwaukee, lawyers in Madison, lawyers in Baraboo, and in Dodgeville and Spring Green, newspaper-men

everywhere, judges, commissioners, prosecuting attorneys, process servers, sheriffs, jailors, justices of the peace, federal immigration officers, police officers, Washington officials, senators and congressmen, governors—has "Authority" anything else?—did their worst. And that is, their best.

The "row"—the Japanese word *yakamashii* would do better—finally ended by the interference of friends and clients to save Taliesin from wreck and myself for more work there.

Yes . . . Isaiah is the vengeful prophet of an antique wrath. Taliesin is a nobler prophet and he is not afraid of him. The ancient Druid Bard sang and forever sings of merciful beauty. Wherever beauty is, there Taliesin sings in praise of the flower that fadeth, the grass that withereth. Taliesin loves and trusts—man.

And now, standing where and how Isaiah, the Jew, may stand in this third and nobler construction in the name of Taliesin—Taliesin the Celt humbly declares not only an architecture on Usonian soil for a conscious United States but declares and for the same reason the right of every aspiring man, so long as the man shall be as honest as he knows how to be with all three, to his life, his work, and his love.

But, to leave the abstract figure, to be homeless and without work when life and work have become synonymous terms and be powerless to protect either; home and work and loved-ones at the mercy of the exploitation of irresponsible insane fury by bigger and better publicity, is the bottom of the vulgar pit any man may dig for himself by his own acts in our United States of America. Not the least of my trials was to see the weakness and helpless exaggeration of a hostile woman incited to destroy herself and destroy all that had ever touched her, to make "copy" for those who neither cared for her nor for anything she cared for—except "news."

And "news" is bad tidings. If the tidings do not exist as "bad" . . . they may be made bad.

And the trials by heartless, vulgar imposition that followed in the wake of self-inflicted "failure," are always harder to bear—yes, always—than those

Taliesin III. Spring Green, Wisconsin. 1925. FLLW Fdn FA#2501.0017

Taliesin III. Spring Green, Wisconsin. 1925. FLLW Fdn FA#2501.0008

failures we cannot trace to our own fault.

For three years I had self-inflicted failure to bear, as open secrets became open sores by way of the scandal of the "press" and finally the depth of outrage and humiliation and falsification.

But never have I been allowed to bear any failure alone. So I remember and record and leave the rest to Life. At least sensational distortion and exaggeration will here meet quiet fact for the first time.

With this extraordinary excitement a fine sense of the dignity and human-value of our institutions got to Olgivanna the figure that crept forward out of the shadow cast by the lurid flames destroying Taliesin the II.

I was sorry that she should see this obnoxious phase of American life first. I explained all these gratuitous performances of the public character in this charivari.

I explained that we had been betrayed into seeming disrespect of the established order, and took the blame upon myself as I should. Olgivanna took it all with suffering—but without resentment. And we stood our ground.

Born in Montenegro of people not unlike my own Welsh forbears, her upbringing had much in common with my own. At the age of nine she had gone to her married sister, at Batoum in the Caucasus, in order to have the advantages of an education in Russia. Her father was the chief justice of Montenegro for nearly thirty years. During the latter years of his life he was blind. He never saw the little daughter that used to lead her father by the hand through the streets of Cettinje. He was still chief justice for many years while blind. Her mother was the daughter of "Vojevoda" Marco—Balkan general to whom popular credit went for preserving Montenegro's independence. For Montenegro, like Wales and the country of the Basques, was a mountainous little country whose people were never conquered.

Olgivanna herself had grown up in a patriarchal family in an official society with a mind and will of her own.

When we first met I considered myself free, in the circumstances, as did she. Though she never had and never has met Miriam Noel, she knew as much about the circumstances as I did. We both knew that only the final signature to divorce that ended my separation from Miriam Noel, a separation begun more than a year before I met Olgivanna, was to be added. That signature *was* added soon.

But these facts were not news. The term "Montenegrin Dancer" was invented by the fancy of the more sensational reporters. They wrote their "stories" on that and implied character according to their devices.

I play the piano, but that doesn't make me a pianist? Olgivanna dances, but only as a feature of the training at the Gurdjieff Institute at Fontainebleau. This institution, too, came in for a measure of low suspicion and implication in order to complete the desired picture.

Unexpectedly, thus, came the public charivari.

And I managed to get Olgivanna to Hollis, safe with her brother Vladimir and his wife. Love and protection around her. A great change from the humiliation and misery of the last fortnight. Her people insisted on my coming to stay at Hollis too. I would go back to town with Vlada in the morning, to roam the streets of New York alone. I didn't care to see anyone for fear of revealing our whereabouts.

It was then I began to write. I tried to write some impressions of the big city. "In Bondage" was one. "The Usonian City" another.

Olgivanna did not improve as rapidly as she should. The weather was cold and disagreeable. After Christmas at Vlada's I began to wonder where we would go, and hit on Porto Rico. A long shot. But it would be warm at least. And it was. Porto Rico was now a possession of the United States of America. We would need no difficult passports. As a matter of fact, anywhere we went in the United States we were likely to splash more muddy water over the dam.

So, still incognito we took the boat for what remained of Atlantis. We put up at a pleasant inn—the "Coamo"—far down the island. The Coamo

Frank Lloyd Wright. 1928. FLLW Fdn FA#6004.0031

Olgivanna Hinzenberg. 1928. FLLW Fdn FA#6103.0006

had natural hot-sulphur springs piped into enormous old Spanish stone baths in which we could go and swim. At night we went under mosquito nets, but had to make constant war on the pests. The days and nights were sultry and oppressive until we would drive to the mountains. The air there was delightful. These old mountain roads of Spanish Porto Rico are remarkable.

The primavera were in bloom, enormous white tree trunks, white limbs loaded with brilliant scarlet bloom lying in great high drifts, in the beautiful landscape. Roads covered with falling scarlet. Such splendor.

We hung Iovanna in a basket in front of the tonneau from the cross ribs of the top of the open car. She was comfortable swinging there.

We would have our lunch put up at the Coamo and explore the islands every day. Slight showers would fall frequently but soon would clear away.

Porto Rico is beautiful but Porto Ricans are

pitiful. They seem small, fine featured remains of a highly civilized race. Gentle, apathetic. Poor beyond belief. The "Americans" had already "bought in" the sugar-plantations. Most all of them were in the hands of capital from the "States."

Wages were seventy cents a day. And no "raise" in sight, as it would affect the price of sugar.

Evidence of poverty spoiled the beautiful place for Olgivanna. She was touched by the sight of so many ill-fed, mournful-eyed children, and frail-looking women with sorrowful faces. The men were no better.

So poor the Portoricans were! We remember a man coming down to the Coamo on a peaked little horse, from miles away, carrying a small chicken covered with a red handkerchief to sell this one chicken to the hotel. To get a little money. These sights were everywhere.

So, after two months we said goodbye to the beautiful island with the romantic history—why not a fragment of Atlantis?—and returned to Washington where the first signs of spring were beginning to appear.

Iovanna had her airing every morning in the sunshine at the foot of the native Capitol. The faithful Alma never left the baby out of her sight, nor did the mother leave either out of her sight.

By this time Olgivanna was a shadow. The kind proprietor of the hotel, solicitous, asked if there was not something especial he might prepare for her. She ate so little.

These peregrinations had to cease. The anxieties were too great. We needed a home.

And so, braving the persecution, we returned to Taliesin to take the consequences.

Anything was better, and safer than this equivocal, dangerous, expensive and difficult migration from place to place.

I remember, in this connection, the time when and the circumstances by which I was soon thereafter forced to leave Taliesin because I had legally lost it. A bank by formal process asked me to get out. The drain of the two fires and lost collections at Taliesin, the years of forced inaction, wasteful legality, many lawyers—all left me finally at the mercy of rented money and its machine process. That process is interesting to me because it shows how, when legal machinery goes wrong, it is no better or worse than the intelligence that drives it. It is like any other cherished man-toy—strapped to the animals on the farm.

Some time before that finality came, however, I had, against my will, taken my lawyer's advice to take Olgivanna and Iovanna and Svetlana from Taliesin and go away again—this time to entirely lose ourselves for three months at least, and leave him to work out the situation now so complicated through the advantages taken, on every side . . . of my own indiscretion.

"Go away," said Levi Bancroft, "and I'll have your situation straightened out in three months. Publicity will then quiet down. There will be no further excuse for such performances as have been staged by Miriam Noel and the press.

"So long as there is any objective she will perform for them and you will be good for their headlines and 'stories.' They will get the authorities 'stirred up,'" said Levi. "The minor official of our country is owned by the newspapers because he gets or loses his office pretty much as they are with him or against him; more often than he gets it any other way.

"Newspapers, to get the story, will put the officials in a position where they will have to act to arrest you. And Olgivanna, too.

"Think it over."

"They are working on the cupidity and weakness of an irresponsible woman with nothing to lose except her appetite for publicity and revenge. They will stop at nothing. She can't. There is nothing there to stop with."

"She overturned her arrangements with you after she had agreed to them and signed them because they made her see she had a good chance to put you where you would have to give her everything you had left in the world.

"And now if you don't give it to her she thinks, and is probably so advised by her lawyers, that she can take it anyway. It isn't and won't be their fault if you have a cent to your name."

I listened knowing it all to be too true. I had seen something of "publicity" years ago. Taliesin, 1911. I had now seen the shameless manner in which the poor woman had been exploited by her lawyers and the press and had every reason to believe such exploitation would continue.

When I had walked out of the Dane County Court rather than blacken the character of two women—I found I would have to do this in order to get a divorce—I left the woman posing as the "outraged wife" and her lawyers free to attack and confiscate everything I owned. I now owed the Bank of Wisconsin a round sum of forty-three thousand dollars—owing to the building of Taliesin III, the loss a second time of the collections I had made in China and Japan, and the plans upset in work by previous and present storms of publicity.

In the circumstances Judge Hill and Levi Bancroft, both my lawyers, said, "Go to the bank. The president is your friend. He will be glad to help you in order to protect himself.

"Give the bank a blanket mortgage on everything you have. Don't leave out anything. Cover your plans, collections, drawing instruments, your tools in the studio and on the farm. Write it all in. Do this until we can get time to turn around against this enterprise."

"A man who has a lawyer and yet takes his own advice has a fool for a client," is a lawyer's maxim. Judge Evan Evans handed it to me.

Jim, and they don't make them any better than Jim, took me to the bank and explained the situation.

"All right," said the bank, "we'll help."

Jim had to catch his train and left me in the president's office at the Bank of Wisconsin.

An hour at the bank for papers to be drawn up by the bank's attorney. "Here," said the bank, "sign here." I did. A check for fifteen hundred dollars was handed to me, and I had nothing else in the world except by sufferance, or on honor of this bank.

This was the situation now at Taliesin.

Levi touched upon it. "The bank will look after things for you while you are gone.

"Everything is in their hands and they'll do that to protect themselves."

"But I have a feeling, Levi, that if I turn my back on this fight and hide or run away as you suggest, I'll lose what I have been fighting for. It isn't my conviction nor my style. I don't know how to carry on along those lines. I already regret what I had done with the bank."

I pleaded, "Why not let me stand up to this business and fight it out? Use me. I am all right—morally—much as it looks the other way. You know it. Why not allow me the courage of my convictions—and to stand by?"

Said Levi, "You forget, Frank. There is your child. There is where they have you. And Olgivanna can't stand any more of this. She is under a terrible strain."

"I know," I said. "But so long as we are all together, that can't matter so much as if we were separated."

"Well," impatiently, "you'll all be together—the way I suggest. Think it over."

I did. And I refused.

Levi wouldn't give up. Olgivanna thought it wise to go. And by appeals on behalf of Olgivanna and the child—Levi won. One had to respect his forceful sincerity. As a lawyer, he was right enough. And his uprightness has never been questioned.

My little family and I set out in the Cadillac for somewhere.

Why not go to Minneapolis? Minnetonka was beautiful. The Thayers were there. It was September.

That was not what Levi wanted. He was thinking of Canada.

But I knew if Olgivanna left the country in the circumstances I would have a hard time ever getting her back again.

I wasn't going that far. Together we might stand—divided we would surely fall.

So we drove up the Mississippi along the river and over it at LaCrosse into Minneapolis.

We didn't know at the time that we had by doing so committed a federal crime. We should have got out and walked across the line and we should have committed no crime.

We found a charming cottage at Minnetonka owned by Mrs. Simpson. I persuaded her that she needed a vacation and to let us take it as it stood for three months—the time Levi had specified—letting her accounts stand as they were. We to be her guests in her absence.

We were the Richardsons or something. We kept forgetting to remember who we were.

We stowed the Cadillac with the Victoria top away in the Simpson garage as too conspicuous for our purpose and took to the cleaver's sail boat on the lake and walks in the countryside. We were in hiding. It was for the first time in my life. The Thayers were in on the secret. And soon their friends, the Devines.

I had already begun this book at Olgivanna's earnest solicitation and was working away on the first two portions in Mrs. Simpson's cottage with Maude Devine coming in afternoons to do the typing.

Well, we learned from the newspapers before long that we were "fugitives from justice." A nice

Olgivanna and Iovanna. 1926. FLLW Fdn FA#6401.0006

Frank Lloyd Wright and Iovanna. Minneapolis, 1926. FLLW Fdn FA#6401.0007

legal phrase for sensational consequences.

It seems the father of Svetlana, from whom Olgivanna had been divorced, making common cause with the lawyer of the persecution—was taken to Taliesin a few days after we had left there.

Finding us gone and Svetlana, too, he was taken by the common lawyer to the county seat of Baraboo to swear out a warrant of arrest for the "abduction" of his nine-year-old daughter.

The devices of the law are devious resources, more useful to the unscrupulous than to the conscientious. Not for nothing are lawyers "inventive."

But we knew no better than to keep on in hiding. So we were cautious and really seemed incognito. It was hard to take the business as serious, knowing what was at the bottom of it and back of it all.

So we went on living and I kept on working at this book.

My son John came down to get instructions about clearing up certain details of work at Taliesin. And we settled down. To what? We didn't know.

I had made a fatal error.

Flight had given color to the low accusations.

And courage, too, to the persecution they called "prosecution."

The implications fed to the public by the press gained life-like color.

Six weeks went by.

The lawyer son of Mrs. Simpson had come down from Minneapolis on some pretext, to look for his fishing tackle. In his mother's attic he said it was.

I saw him sizing us up intently—but dismissed him from my mind. Olgivanna saw him too and worried. "Never mind," I said. "He is his mother's son. She is a lady."

We had just dined. The baby had been put to bed. Svetlana was asleep in her bed on the porch. Maude Devine was typing away on the book. Fire burned in the grate. All was warm and cozy on a late September evening.[21]

About half past nine o'clock. A rude knock on the door of the living room toward the street.

I went to the door and opened it.

A dozen or more rough looking characters—led by Miriam Noel's lawyer—now mutual with Svetlana's father—and accompanied by members of the press, several of whom I had seen, somewhere, before.

They all shouldered their way into the room and surrounded us.

"You are all under arrest," said the heavy-handed one, the bigger sheriff—there were three of them each of a different size and type.

Olgivanna shows her quality in any emergency.

She got up and asked them to kindly step out into the next room. I opened the glass door and they all did exactly as they were bid—a little ashamed. They could still watch through the glass door, however, and so were content to stay.

They recovered after finding themselves there and the heavy-handed lawyer said loudly with a swagger, "Well, here they are . . . at last. Now, where's the kid?"

He opened the door to the bedroom and went in. I went in after him. He jerked the blanket from the sleeping infant and laughed, "Yeah!—here it is!"

The sheriffs each took an arm, all I had, and said, "No violence. Take it easy. Take it easy."

To the sheriffs' credit, be it said, they moved him out.

Olgivanna opened the door and came in. "We must make the best of it, Frank." And I saw that I was only making scene for "copy." The usual circus.

"Please take it quietly," she said.

I did.

Of course it was a "frame up." The "mother's son" had found his information profitable. Cameras were already set up around the house—to illustrate the "story."

The horror of such impotence as mine!

I pleaded with the valiant sheriff to take me and leave the mother and children where they were with a guard over them until morning. The trap had been sprung late, after ten o'clock—and, having pretended to call up his superior at Minneapolis (it would have spoiled the story to leave them behind that way) he came back to say it was impossible to get him.

He agreed to leave my little family in custody where they were. And I went out in the face of the puffing flashlights, got into his car, and was driven down to the sheriff at the county jail in Minneapolis.

His name was Brown.

Brown was a man of some parts in the Hennepin County community. A sheriff, but serving as a patriot without pay to clean up the Baptist belt and make it moral. A reporter volunteered that he had himself in the newspapers a few days before handcuffed to two thugs—to show "the people" how serviceable a sheriff they had.

He had heard of us only as he had read the newspaper views of the case.

Well . . . I argued with him, in vain I pleaded with Brown—at length and with reason I pleaded to leave the nursing mother and the two children at the cottage until morning. I would go to jail willingly if he would be merciful to them.

"I give you my word, Mr. Wright, I couldn't do that not even for my own brother."

There was a sense of duty for you. They said he would accept no salary either.

"Nor for your own mother, I suppose," I said . . . again at wit's end. "Well . . . then let me call my little family and tell them what to expect, and what to do in the circumstances. I want to call them long distance," I said.

"No need," he said, "they are all here. In any case you are not allowed outside communication."

They had been brought to jail in the car following the one that brought me.

The crowd was busy doing the daily stuff. In the next room they were word-painting the "volunteer" as a hero. A reward for his "playing up" to their game, I suppose.

Coming to me, now, was the sovereign insult a free country has to offer one of its sons.

If only I were alone! Olgivanna!—And the children!

My sin had been done two by two. And that can never be paid for—one by one. Not in a *free* country such as ours.

So I went up in the elevator with the distinguished republican jailor, Brown.

And Brown turned me in.

"They" searched me. Took away my money. All but the small change. Entered my family pedigree on the jail record of Hennepin County. And with business-like hospitality, representing Minneapolis, whose dishonored guest I was now, Brown, a little dubious I thought, said "good night."

A warden took me down a long corridor along brutal heavy animal cages built tier on tier within a great empty space arched over by a high trussed roof. The clang of the gates he opened and shut, as he went, echoed and reverberated behind us in space.

He clanged our way to the far end where the "better element" of jaildom, the highswindlers and bootleggers were kept.

All was quiet.

They were asleep. He opened the little door of a cell a little longer than I am tall, a little narrower than I am long, a soiled mattress on one side and a dirty water closet at one end: the government allotment of squalor for manhood on such terms as had fallen to my lot.

I went in.

The warden said "good night."

My country! To one of your own free sons this "good night!"

The ponderous door of the animal cage slammed shut and automatically shot its heavy steel bolt. My first sensation was suffocation.

But I reached up and took hard hold of the cold iron bars to keep my mind clear and tried to hold on to my sense of humor. It could save me now.

Then I turned and used up the three steps in one direction—there the filthy water closet. Again suffocation.

Scarcely able to breathe I sat down on the mattress. Saw it stained. Was it blood? Whose and how?

I looked above. The polished steel ceiling. I could reach up and touch it.

Where was Olgivanna? Where were the children? I had begged for information.

"Let me send a note to their mother?"

Said Brown, "No, it's against the rules."

This was a machine made Brown. Brown the driver—by rote and routine or . . . wreck, of this machine, a jail.

Intelligence? Outside.

Humanity? Outside.

Life, love, work, honor? Outside.

Cut down? Cut off!

Inside Brown's machine was the impotence of hate. The damnation of idleness. Insulting fears and low suspicion.

Dung and dishonor!

Man's cruelty to man!

The blackest mark in all of human life is man's deep distrust of his fellow man! The deepest chasm dug by himself across his own future.

Every Usonian citizen, good or bad, as a feature of his education, should be condemned to spend two nights in one of his own jails.

Let the good, the obedient, the wary-wise sense the endless repeat of a monotonous "forever" they call a jail and keep to defend their goodness, their obedience, their wisdom.

Impotent, I cursed.

Again on my feet to measure my length against the bars; head back and I could breathe.

Footsteps along the corridor.

The warden-watch reaching the end of his beat . . . my cell.

He looked in. He was just in time. I found myself. And I found "they" had overlooked a piece of paper in my pocket. Strangely, a broken stump of pencil, overlooked, lay on the soiled mattress. I said, "Wait a second?" And scribbled a note.

"Take this to her they brought in here with me, will you?" And wrapping a fifty cent piece in the paper poked it through the bars to him. He put his finger to his lips, nodded his head, pushed back the fifty cent piece, took the note, and went away.

Next time around.

"Did she get it?"

"Sure," he said. "She's all right. The Missus is looking after her and the kids."

This fellow's sense of "duty" was remiss. He broke the devil's rules in hell.

And a little light came through.

I could breathe now.

It would be morning some time. It always was. My sense of humor was on its way back.

What remained of the night I sat up on the one clean corner of the mattress. Pacing the few steps to and fro—to rest—in my stocking feet so as not to wake the neighbors.

At daylight a clanging began in the distance. It came toward me with an increasing roar until the tumult seemed to rock the very jail and it must fall of its own insane weight. The door to the cell suddenly flew open with a reverberating clang following all the others by electrical release. The tumult died in echoes.

The narrow paved passage connecting my cage with other cages was there in front. I could go out into that.

A tin cup of Brown's liquid appeared at a little door set in the bars—a piece of Brown's bread beside it. I tasted his liquid and swallowed a bit of his bread. Without choking.

After a while my comrade next door came to say hello. He had the morning paper. It gets to the cells.

There were our pictures.

"Say," he said, "you got a swell girl. She sure stands by you."

"Yes, she sure does."

"Well," he said, "it's something not to be in here for nothing. You got something to tie to."

"Trouble is she's tied up here too."

"Aw, they won't do nothing to her though. They'll let them go all right."

"Will they?" I said. "I wonder why? The sheriff said he couldn't do anything for his own mother in the circumstances."

"Yeah!"

"What are you in here for?" I asked.

"Me? Sellin' a little likker. Second time.

"Wisconsin State Journal," October 21, 1926.

"Say, I got a swell girl myself," he went on. "Do you know what she done?"

"No, what did she do?"

"You see that place out there where visitors come to see us fellows?"

I looked and saw a broad space with a shower on one side where an inmate might go, stand up, and converse through a screen wire with someone standing in the outer space. You could have pushed a pencil through the screen but that is about as big as anything that would go through.

"You see, she hears that I'm in from the papers. She comes up out there and they calls for me. Then I goes out to see her. She watches the warden go away. 'Stand up close, Jimmy,' she says. I stands up close. Say! She unbuttons the bosom of her dress and what do you think she's got in there between 'em? Guess?"

"I couldn't."

"A quart, by God! A quart!"

"The warden goes by and she waits. Then she slips me three straws out of her pocket. 'Go to it, Jimmy,' she says, 'go to it. It'll do you good, besides helpin' you.' And I slips them straws into the stuff and I takes it all. Say! Can you beat that?"

"No," I said, "I don't believe anybody could beat that."

I stepped out into the gangway to walk a little way but ran into another prisoner. There was room for only one in the width of the avenue.

"Hello," said this one. "You look funny in here."

"Yes, I feel funny," I said.

"I read the papers about you and her this morning. Say I had a bigger spread than that when they got me in here." He pulled out a greasy clipping and proudly showed it to me.

"I'm in for the bogus bail racket. Trial coming up soon. But, I've got a good lawyer. Nash! The best in the state. He'll see me through, all right."

"Nash is his name?"

"Nash," he said.

"How can I see him? They won't let me call anyone."

"I'm going out to see him today and I'll tell him to come in and call you out to see him."

That is how I got another lawyer to add to the collection.

Nash, too, was a good lawyer.

He soon found out I was in jail for no reason that anybody knew except a telegram from some bailiff in Sauk County, Wisconsin, that a warrant had been sworn out for my arrest there. This telegram had reached Brown. Confirmation was lacking. Who sent it? We were all in jail on suspicion so far as the beneficent Brown was concerned.

Not so the newspapers. I was taken out by Brown to be interviewed by them that morning.

And we were formerly released in another public court scene, when the authorities at Baraboo, Wisconsin, appealed to, to go ahead refused to persecute.

The case, such as it was and whatever it was, was dropped. The thing had been set for late enough at night so that no correction or relief was possible without "going to jail," for "copy."

But the law in the hands of any professional blackmailer is a mean instrument of revenge with many angles, all fertile "points." We were not free to go. No, not yet.

The federal authorities had meanwhile been seen. We were to be held in jail pending appearance before an arm-chair federal, famous in the Northern Baptist-Belt for "moral" tendencies. He had grown to the chair with comparative affluence. I forget his name.

We went before this august limb of the Federal law on the charge of having violated that malign instrument of revenge diverted from its original purpose to serve just such purposes as this for many years past: the Mann Act. Mr. Mann and his wife used to sit across the aisle from me at my uncle's church, All Souls. His law was dead letter so far as public sentiment went. But a law for ulterior purposes just the same. Instead of walking, we had ridden across the state-line.

So, accompanied by the press-gallery and cameras, we went through the streets to the federal hearing together with the American public invited by the announcement in the enterprising press.

I had successfully shielded my little family from both press and camera until this episode. For twelve months I had beaten the reporters at their own game at every turn although my little daughter had to go out of the Union Station three days old at her mother's breast to get away from them. I had saved Olgivanna from a single "interview." Now it all ended in this "triumph" for them, rag, tag, and bobtail.

Bail was fixed in the sum of fifteen thousand dollars for us both. A separate count was lodged against each by Lafayette French, a resourceful, politically ambitious young prosecuting attorney, with a flair for salacious detail, as appeared at the investigation.

Bigger and Better publicity!

Our case now seemed serious. Far too serious for our friends. And they began to protest publicly. It seemed serious enough to us all by this time.

Nothing could keep my sister Jane from rushing down from Philadelphia to Minneapolis to reassure herself concerning us. And Maginel called attorney Nash from New York for such reassurance as he could give her.

We were released on bail after this second public appearance—the public again invited—after another night in jail for us all on account of this new ruse.

The second night in Hennepin County Jail was not so bad as the first.

I had not been allowed to see Olgivanna except in court. The children not at all. But I now knew from her they were well, and Olgivanna, though ready to drop, was facing it all like the thoroughbred she is. Tomorrow we would all be together again.

Meantime after the new "case" was lodged and before my new attorney, Nash, could get to Olgivanna, a federal officer had insinuated himself to get her "story." She had no more sense of wrongdoing than I had, in the Porto Rico matter, and told him everything. Which he duly recorded—with the matron's kind assistance to supply missing details. No detail was omitted, stated in terms Olgivanna did not at all understand. It all seems to be a game of "points"—or at simplest a game of hide and seek.

Thus the "confession" was complete. We were now involved with "Immigration."

Nash raged against the exploit of the federal. But that was that. The federals, too, are resourceful. I guess they have to be to get enough "points."

Our "Porto Rico" sojourn for two months after the birth of Iovanna to try and get peace and restore Olgivanna's health was another "violation" of the complex immigration-law, because Porto Rico was the United States but without grace of legal technicality as such. It was still a foreign country.

So, by the moral virtue of technicality, "they" said we had "entered the country" for immoral purposes. And the federals could do with us as they pleased.

We made it all as simple for them as that. The law is an implement. Technique is the lawyers.

Going back to jail I found Brown had sent in a clean mattress. The water closet was cleaned.

I lay on the clean mattress that second night getting the sense of "jail" the prisoners told me they got—a sense of protection. At least nothing could happen to you in jail. And, after the evening feeding of the animals through the trap-doors in the bars, some in the upper animal cages began to sing—one or two taking turns leading—fine manly baritone voices. Other caged-animals picked up the familiar songs and joined in. It was tremendous. They sang familiar song after song. Some popular, some religious. Were there hundreds of the sinners singing? Reverberations, I suppose. Twenty-five or thirty, maybe more at times. And they kept singing up to nine o'clock. Everyone then must be silent. A splendid sense of unity in their misery.

They made me feel ashamed of my shame.

The little chap, second cage over, in for bogus bailing, had gone out to his trial this day. I heard him come in late. He was whistling a popular tune softly. I wrapped a little on the bars to let him know I wasn't asleep.

"How now?" I whispered.

"Twenty years," he hissed back and went on whistling. Soon he was asleep. I heard him snore. Callous? Or was this fortitude?

Next morning I saw him in the corridor.

"Nash will get it cut," he said.

He gave me the details of his game. These illegal details were as complicated as the legal details to which we were subjected and almost as ingenious. A crook has technique too. This fellow had professional pride in a scientific piece of work. Initial direction gone wrong, that's all, and gone wrong for such curious, haphazard reasons. He had turned left instead of right.

After court opening at ten o'clock, my turn came to go up and be dismissed. I asked Brown for permission to "set up" porkchops and mashed potatoes to the singers of the night before and all their listeners.

"Sorry," said Brown, "against the rules."

The "boys" themselves bade me good luck. Their jailers all shook hands, warmly, they had done their best for me. Even so had Brown. But a man no bigger than his job has no right to have a job where humanities are concerned even though he makes himself a gift to the job.

A few days afterward I was sitting in Cleaver Thayer's car near the railway station waiting for Cleaver.[22] A Ford suddenly stopped by the curb opposite.

A man got out, grinning, rushed across the street, hand held out to me: "Hello, Mr. Wright, Hello! Say—my wife is in the car over there. And I want her to meet you. Can I bring her over?"

It took a second or two to recognize the warden. His uniform changed him—or was it the other way around?

"No," I said. "Let her stay where she is. I'll come over with you to meet her."

She was pleased to meet me.

He had a "nice girl," too.

But after it all was over it took some time longer to get permission to leave the state. Some kink in the coil of Law. I forget what kink or what coil of what law but the state was Minnesota.

The Thayers and Devines had been kind.

Cleaver put me up at his club. Both families were at the jail, early, to see Olgivanna and took the children for an airing.

I don't know how they ever got them out.

Brown must have been having his photograph taken.

Cleaver was fine all the time. He coined a phrase that pleased him continuously. "From Who's Who to the Hoosegow."

His father signed our bail bond.

Another flood of publicity had gone over the dam.

While marking time in Minneapolis awaiting the prosecuting attorney's permission to leave the state came a demand from the bank to "pay up."

A little surprised I wrote the bank reminding them of the circumstances of their mortgage.

No reply to this. The circumstances were unfit for record or publication it seems. Only another technicality out of line with technicalities. The classification is minute and the differentiation arbitrary but the consequences amazing.

My situation, in view of this Federal action, I suppose, looked bad to the bank. So the bank threatened foreclosure and insisted upon the immediate sale of the print collection I had placed in New York in Mitchell Kennerly's hands to be, sometime, sold!

It was a bad time to sell. But the bank insisted. The block of rare prints were disastrously sold for $42,000. And Kennerly took a "commission" of nearly thirty-five per cent, which didn't help. I had understood it would be fifteen.

During the months that followed the Minneapolis debacle in the Northern "Baptist Belt," we were in New York.

My sister Maginel took us in.

We had some respite, because my little sister and her home are charming. She did everything in her power—and she is resourceful—to mitigate the desperation of our circumstances. And we were together—to fight it all.

But the resources of the ultra legal publicity persecution were not yet exhausted. A deportation story got into the papers.

And "they" were now after Olgivanna.

She was formally arrested by immigration officials at the door to my sister's home and I gave a Liberty Bond—the last one—to be posted for bail.

This latest aggression added to our other woes was a cup, full. The sense of humor began to fade.

The immigration service is seldom kind. It cannot afford to be merciful. It too is a machine.

So is a bank a machine.

The bank now stirred again to action by all this impending disaster, pressed harder and harder for money.

I had nothing to give the bank because everything I had was in its hands. The bankers knew this.

Under pressure of these desperate circumstances I conceived the idea of incorporating myself—selling myself to such friends and clients as would "buy me" in order to raise the money to rid Taliesin and such collections as remained in the bank of the claims of the pressing bank itself, and allow me to work again. The proceeds of work would then be safe from suits that were sure to be brought by the persecution were I to earn anything at all.

With this scheme in mind soon subscribed to by the bank itself—we returned to Taliesin. But owing to that "blanket mortgage" we were liable to eviction at the bank's pleasure unless we "paid up."

And now began the process of incorporating what looked like a lost cause.

Darwin D. Martin liked the idea. He subscribed and his lawyer drew up the first papers.

I took them to others. My client, Mrs. Avery Coonley, subscribed. My friend, Dr. Ferdinand Schevill, Joe Urban, my sister Jane, too, among a number of others who could ill afford to subscribe. Finally I had seventy-five thousand dollars subscribed. Alexander Woolcott helped at this crucial time in more ways than one. Charlie McArthur did what he could—to keep a smile on my face.

Phil La Follette now stepped in, sympathetic.

"Frank, you have had bad legal advice."

"I have, Phil. And I have taken it far worse than the advice itself. Suppose you help?"

"All right," he said, "but not to take the case directly. Leave Jim (Judge Hill) where he is. And I'll do what I can from the side lines."

He went to see Ferdinand Schevill and Mr. Martin to see if they would stand by me.

Their response was satisfactory.

Things had quieted down. The figure head of the persecution, the outraged wife, was in Hollywood without funds. Her lawyers were without funds. The press was suffering time-lag. The story was dragging for them.

The corporation if now executed as originally designed would keep them outside of funds entirely and no "news" until prepared to treat fairly and reasonably in the circumstances. A drive along this line would have been effective. The various creditors pressing for settlement were proposing fair terms.

But Phil reversed the plan of procedure.

He began negotiating for divorce.

To get this we must go into court with "clean hands" as the choice phrase runs in legal circles. To do this he advocated the voluntary deportation of Olgivanna. And eventually handed a thousand dollars of corporation money to me for the purpose.

Phil took Levi's ground: district Attorney Knudson could not stand against popular prejudice moved by the press. Phil said he knew district attorneys. But attorneys do not seem to know each other very well. They, too frequently surprised each other.

"But," I said, "he has stood up pretty straight for what he sees right. I don't believe they can stampede him. Let me go to see him myself."

"Keep away from him," said Phil. "You will only compromise him and tie his hands if you go near him."

This looked reasonable.

"Frank, there is only one way. Send Olgivanna and the children away for a year, or with her defective passport the government is going to send her, anyway. There is no way that feature of your case can be fixed up. Go to work and make some money meantime. Then you can go over 'like a man' and get them back. A year after you get your divorce you can live a regular life."

"How long to get the divorce on your revised plan?" I asked.

"Don't know. Say six months."

"A year and six months for Olgivanna and the children with no home at all? And little, if any money? No, Phil," I said. "Your plan is 'no good'"

But again Phil and his partner—Rogers—put me into the sweat box.

"You are unfair to Olgivanna because they'll arrest you both, sure. And then what? One of the provincial juries around here? What chance would you have?"

Said Phil, "You're thinking more of yourself than of the woman. You might stand this—she can't. Frank, you are vain and selfish in all this. Take care of her now as you should have done long ago and send her away. Your courage is commendable but your cause is illegal."

This "high moral" tone offended me.

This "high-hat" did not seem to me like his father's son.

"Phil," I said, "you may be 'legal' but neither human nor radical. Your idea of taking care of Olgivanna would put an end to her and Iovanna. Yes, I am selfish. I started all this, apparently, in selfishness. I might as well end it that way. I'll take my chances, all standing together where we are, at home. We'll fight this thing out—and take what comes."

Then came more pressure. My legal advisers brought in my friends who were contributing money to untangle our affairs and give us protection. The advice I was now getting was really their contribution, too. This was cited.

Well, I gave in—took the money and the embarrassed parent went home to his little family and broke the news.

"Get ready," I said. "We're going to Washington."

On the way to New York I thought I'd try my own hand as a last chance. And I took Olgivanna to headquarters. Laid the cards on the table . . . the unvarnished truth of the case as it stood supported by the affidavits from Judge Hill and Svetlana's father, I already had.

Of course Olgivanna, by all moral standards, was my wife: the mother of a desired child born in our country. Her daughter, Svetlana, was the child of a naturalized father. We had all been legally tangled up in a coil of legal rope—legally trapped! The truth was continually ignored in order that we might continually be exploited for "news." The law was being used as a cat's paw to pull chestnuts out of the fire for an irresponsible woman urged to unseemliness and indiscretion by a free-for-all-press, not an unfamiliar form of persecution to the department at Washington it seemed.

Superior officialdom is not minor officialism. At last, intelligent responsibility.

"Could we have a respite to straighten out?"

"How long?"

"Six months."

We could.

I wired Phil no need to carry out the "plan."

We were coming home.

Indignant letter from him. I had broken down on an agreement made with him. "On no account come back to Taliesin."

But we came. There was nowhere else to go and no money to go there with. "Clean hands" or no "clean hands."

Without funds, and her attorney's now pressing her for settlement, having already confiscated her many "things" Miriam Noel came into court for separate maintenance and eventually sold the divorce she had already agreed to and signed two years and some months previously for exactly the same price she had agreed to then but plus the ruination she had planned and wrought by the false and sentimental appeal of "outraged-wife."

But that Wisconsin divorce, desirable as it seemed, was a divorce with a curse on it. The Wisconsin law forbade re-marriage within one year after the divorce, though the divorce was—in the language of the judge—"absolute."

I had thought this divorce was to end our difficulties. I had heard the word "absolute" from Judge Hoffman's own lips.

But the curtain had only been "rung up" by divorce. "Legality" now wiped out personality, character, courage, common sense. We were playing a legal game of tag—of legal hide and legal seek.

If I was caught in any "immoral situation"—in other words with my little family—during the year to follow, the "absolute" divorce was null and void, so Phil now informed me.

Lawyers know only the legal aspects of cases. It is for that they are lawyers.

Clarence Darrow had given me some good advice—long before. He said, "Your case is not a legal case, Frank. What you need is the advice of some wise man of the world who will be your friend and will see you through. Keep away from lawyers."

No doubt Phil was all right as life ran popularly or regularly or legally.

But as Clarence said, the case never was a legal one, except in certain superficial aspects of the whole matter.

Well . . . no sooner was the money divorce-settlement paid over to her than the "outraged wife" and a group of reporters were besieging the truly upright and independent young district attorney of our country. The "case" so far as the press was concerned was still more "game" now. There was more cheap drama. Scene after scene. Staged by the resourceful as news. The "outraged wife" was still played to the absurd limit by them all.

Divorce "absolute!"

We were at Taliesin standing our ground and at the same time trying to work. Several projects were in hand.

But the course of the corporation had changed. This was not what the subscribers had anticipated. The bank was not satisfied. My creditors were not satisfied. If my friends could pay $35,000 to end a clear case of persecution with no better effect than was now visible, they could be made to "pay up" all down the line . . . legality was a success. It has many diverse legal forms.

If only they would go after me hard enough, why anybody wait longer for their money? And the bank itself refused to stand by its subscription to the corporation. Several other subscribers, none too warm, learning this and that my sole property now consisted in a divorce—that left me more than ever at the mercy of unscrupulous exploitation—cancelled their subscriptions.

The corporate money paid in had gone to Miriam Noel and her lawyers.

So the creditors stiffened up and I was powerless.

The situation was now out of hand so far as the man in it was concerned. He was written off and the case was no longer a matter of live and let live, but a mare's nest of legal "troubles," that each and every one involved and demoralized life, and added costs to costs.

So, one afternoon during our absence, the bank president came up to Taliesin and hired our help to remain there in the bank's employ. They were told we "were going away." I learned this from a faithful young apprentice in the studio, John Davis, who had heard it from the help and thought I ought to know it myself.

Next day, by way of the bank, we received a long legal notice from Judge Hoffman's court in Madison to the effect that the premises were being used for immoral purposes—the mortgager was outraged—and the mortgagee objecting . . . we were asked to leave.

I called Phil at once.

No surprise to him. "Well?" he said, "I don't see what we can do about it."

"Do you mean to say I shall have to take this, too, lying down?"

"I don't see what *we* can do about it, Frank!"

So we got to Chicago to see what I could do. Nothing.

We went adrift.

The day before I had received a telegram from Albert McArthur: "Can you come out to Phoenix?" It seemed providential.

You see, the corporation was an unfinished fragment . . . helpless now, in these or any other circumstances.

We had the coveted divorce but not clean hands! And we were homeless and penniless. We got to Arizona. I went to work with Albert on the new Arizona Biltmore Hotel.[23]

The bank entered into legal possession of Taliesin as a whip to enforce collection of the sum due them, now augmented by attorneys' fees, court proceedings, foreclosure suits, interest on interest. Interest on a $25,000 mortgage given them as general security for current loans and held by them seven years, was charged into the sums due, when judgment was entered. Forty-three thousand dollars had become fifty-seven or eight thousand.

Legality was supreme!

Strange how legally right any man may be and how utterly wrong and outside all decency and equity! Legal Might now makes Right.

What went on hereafter was in my client Darwin D. Martin's hands. La Follette worked with the bank, at Mr. Martin's request to effect a fair settlement. Law and Money were now at deadlock.

Meantime, to whip my friends into line over my shoulders, the bank went through the business of auctioning Taliesin equipment, furnishings, and collections. The bank had thrown Taliesin into the street. Whereupon many saw it who otherwise would never have seen it. But the bank changed its mind when a few bids came in.

Then Money tried to sell the whole place, whole.

No one wanted to buy it. For various reasons. Some of them humane as I afterward learned.

Finally in September a compromise was effected. A telegram from Mr. and Mrs. Martin reached us at La Jolla—"Taliesin open for your return." After all the harrowing circumstances of nearly four years past, words that set us all madly rejoicing. The same real friend and client, Darwin D. Martin, for whom I had been building a Summer home on Lake Erie when we agreed to leave for parts unknown. I had sent John to Mr. Martin to finish up the work. "No," said Mr. Martin, "there can be no substitute for Frank Lloyd Wright. We will wait till he is out of his troubles."

I could help him, a little now. The Bank accepted substantially what had been offered and due in settlement before I had been forced to leave Taliesin and legal machinery had begun to pile up waste motion in ruinous legalities.

The bank vacated the premises which it had used during the summer as a rendezvous and as it pleased, to the detriment of the place.

But we were now free to return. A settlement, too, had been meantime made with the creditors. Darwin D. Martin, Ferdinand Schevill, and Ben Page were the substantial means by which this settlement was finally effected.

Many stories of this incorporation of my self appeared.

An idea gained credence that my financial troubles were over. That I could now work with no financial harassments or restrictions. The reports had me taken over and managed by Capital so that my usefulness might be indefinitely extended. Later the original corporation was somewhat extended by Harold McCormick and Mr. George Parker. And Charlie Morgan came forward, as a volunteer, and interested others.

But I wouldn't have liked the sound of this immunity on such terms if it were true.

As a matter of fact, a few staunch friends, Mr. Martin at their head, had invested what money they could and some of them at a sacrifice to themselves, to save me for any future usefulness at Taliesin, merely using "incorporation" as a legitimate means to secure their loans by owning my earning-capacity. They owned the corporation's preferred stock. I owned the common stock which could have no value until the preferred stock was paid.

The corporation was paid up, non assessable, had no capital whatever, nor any means of getting any, except as my earning capacity could produce it. And unless I could carry on from this point of "incorporation" there was no point whatever in incorporation. I, and mine, would starve and the stockholders lose their money.

Now appeared a singular reaction. I could get no life insurance anywhere. Sound and acceptable in every physical requirement, but—"too much publicity."

But before the final return to Taliesin was effected, one more act in the cheap drama of legality—"divertissement." We were located by the persecution in our cottage by the beach at La Jolla. In our absence the "outraged wife" from whom I had "absolute" divorce for nearly a year, invaded the premises. Smashed up the interior. Appropriated what she liked.

She then went into court at San Diego in the practiced role of "outraged wife," "absolute" divorce notwithstanding, and swore out a warrant for "immoral purposes" on the part of "her husband."

Another story went broadcast. And by the present arrangement of "absolute" divorce I was legally financing these various legal "strangle holds," and public entertainments and other insane private aggressions to entertain readers of the daily newspapers.

Instead of allowing me to use my reputation as an architect, myself, in order to earn my living, publishers were capitalizing it in headlines for "news."

If it profited them, the fact that I had made a reputation as an architect was all but ruining me in the circumstances.

Were I obscure or a nonentity I should have been left in peace. So, after all, I was being "shown up" and plucked because of what I had by painstaking labor, myself built up with some degree of success during a stormy twenty-two years.

Shortly after my marriage to Olgivanna which took place following the year of "probation" which in turn had followed the absolute divorce this sort of exploitation ended with a final move of the persecution . . . at Milwaukee.

Miriam Noel, on her way to Paris, reached Milwaukee encouraged to start suit to keep the trust fund established in her behalf, up to level. My earning capacity having been cut off by her, the trust fund established by me in her behalf had been drawn down by monthly payments to her as agreed upon, to a balance of some eleven thousand dollars. This suit started, she fell seriously ill. Her malady of long standing was aggravated by an operation in a Milwaukee hospital and she became unmanageable. A long distance call from the friend she had made in Milwaukee told me of this. And I confirmed it.

Several months later, having been removed in a state of coma from the asylum to a private sanitarium, without regaining consciousness, she died.

Her several children, two married daughters and unmarried son, were near her at the time. The mother was buried with no assistance from them.

And what was left of a remarkably vital high-spirited woman, who for fifteen years—psychopathic—had been going up in flame, seldom knowing real rest unless by some artificial means, had found it.

A mercy to herself and to all who had ever cared for her.

As her own children refused to touch anything that was hers, the Milwaukee woman who claimed her as a friend and her Milwaukee lawyer became the unfortunate Miriam Noel's "estate."

AUTUMN

The scarlet sumach runs like a forest fire along the hills.

All nature is visible song.

The seeds of the future lie perfected in fruits that have hung or still hang from boughs—tempting the present.

Acorns drop from the oak to the mold below to be sought and carried far. Bright berries, long

Taliesin III, living room. 1926. FLLW Fdn FA#2501.0058

since devoured by birds and beasts, have been carried to new ground.

By appeasing hunger and desire—the species assures the future.

Another life by way of veins and arteries has added stature to the trees, and given consequence to shrubs, flowers, and the grass.

Flaming creeper wreathes the singing bough. The leaves themselves taking on hues of the bloom that was their choicest moment—until now.

Gentle touches of coming frost bring natural response to inner rhythm. Work done, the trees, shrubs, flowers, and the grass begin to return the precious sap to the root.

To sleep.

In the little chapel under the mass of dark green firs—the family. Singing.

"Step by step since time began, we see the steady gain of man."

The gray old heads. The not so old. The not so young. The young and the very young. All together—the false, falsetto, and the flat, again lift the same old assurance to the boards of the chapel ceiling to go out through open windows and fade away across the many-colored hills.

The boy is standing. Singing, as the human exaltation, fervor all about him flood the masses of gold and purple plundered from the roadsides wreathing the pulpit with the purple cloth. The flaming woodbine pulled from trees. Branches of scarlet sumach broken from the wood.

The family sits down and the gray heads, those not so gray, those not so young, furtively wipe their tears away.

The boy wonders why they always cry? And they cry most when everything is best.

The Book lies open on the purple, edges flashing gold.

The preacher for today—the boy's Aunt Jane—rises behind the book.

Her text: "The time of Grace has come." Gratitude!

"Freely we have received."

Freely give."

"Grace! The gift of Freedom to the free soul.

"The time of grace has come: grace to others."

"Living up to life—man loves Beauty."

"So, does beauty love man."

"Beauty loves man" sinks into the boy-mind.

Tenderness for all life suffuses his thought with happy feeling.

He forgets to listen more.

"Beauty loves man."

He sees beauty all about. Again—a little—by his work, within the chapel door.

Boygaze wanders to the many-colored hills—sweeps the yellow rolling stubble fields from which the grain is garnered now—the glittering herd of black and white grazing the broad, still green meadows, and drifts to day-dreams.

All of beauty, all of life come crowding into his heart, beat in his pulse, open him wide to a flood of being.

Not gratitude. Fulfillment!

And the flood carries him, a song on its tide, over the colored hills afield in the farthermost spaces of the gleaming crystal sky.

WORK AGAIN

It is now 1927. Creative urge has gathered energy, once more. Objectives dimly felt, gropingly sought, are coming clearer now: confusion and disgraceful turmoil have ended. Sanity. The normal. Yes, it is the basis of all Freedom. Taliesin had been stripped: the house and workshop plundered and abused by curiosity as the Hillside Home School buildings had been defaced and all but destroyed. The place is grown over, and the rented fields grown up with weeds.

But the sky clearing, familiar signs and portents encourage—"bringing it all back" again.

There is more encouragement from Europe. How grateful I should be! I am.

The last work done at Taliesin was some further work on the cantilever glass and metal office building for Mr. Johnson and a study for an automobile objective for Gordon Strong.

The several young couples recently come from abroad to work with me were there then: Kameki and Nobu Tsuchiura from Tokyo; Werner and Sylva Moser from Zurich; Richard and Dione Neutra from Vienna.

The faithful William Smith from Ottawa was in his ninth year at stormy Taliesin.

That life at Taliesin has gone to other fields.

MEMORABILIA

At this time, to join the earlier publications of my work by Wasmuth in Germany, in 1910, Holland, in 1925, contributed by way of the art publication, *Wendingen*, a splendid volume. I had never expected anything like it, nor ever seen anything like it. I suspect no architect alive or dead, ever did.[1]

Wendingen is a Dutch-English-German fine art publication, the organ of a group of some nineteen architects, sculptors, and painters of Holland and Belgium, edited by the distinguished architect Th. J. Widejveld. There are now other publications. Four in German, two in Japanese, two in French, one in Czecho-Slovakian. None

yet in my own country.

Honorary membership in Academie Royale d'Anvers came as another surprise, a Flemish academic institution of the fine arts. This appreciation from European contemporaries reached me at a time when for several years I had walked the streets of many cities, Usonian exile with a worm's-eye view of Usonian society.

Now, after four years of exile from Taliesin—and from architecture, it is the same thing—I began work again on more definite plans for the cantilever office building, the gas-station, San Marcos In The Desert, and St. Mark's Tower, the mutilated box appears in the offing offering itself as "new!"

The ideal of an organic architecture, gone abroad, comes back, deformed and, turned up edgewise, seeks to be the "International Style." So it names itself. As though any "style" were not . . . offensive, now.

A certain narrow emulation along the meager lines of this "Style" begins to show itself. Propagandists begin to push another offshoot mode by propaganda à la mode. Little groups are forming within the group, trading upon narrow margins and concealing origins, all pushing each other aside and all as alike as peas in a pod . . . denying the pod and the vine.

Poor Usonia.

Prone to all this, beyond all other lands?

Why has she allowed herself to know nothing about architecture?

As for . . .

THE BOX

"Modernity," Usonia is now invited to suppose, is "international" matter of the cardboard box for boxing up space. Box, sans ornament, *sans souci, sans culotte*. Such legs as the stark boxment may have are naked. Steel.

So far, good. Boxes may be set up on posts. Boxes may be well to put something into. I like beautiful boxes. But the box idea of a building seems as childish to me now as it did twenty-seven years ago.

When holes are cut in a box such beauty as the

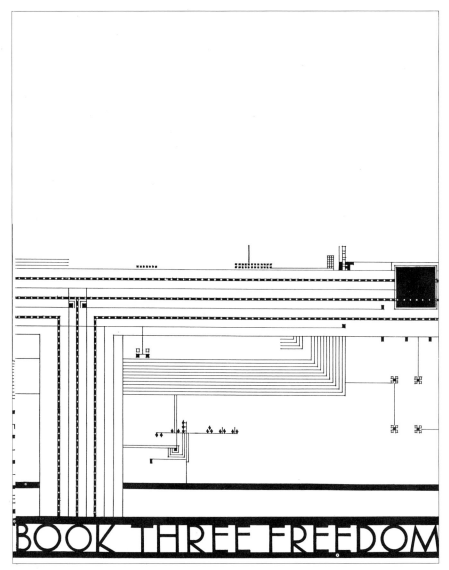

BOOK THREE FREEDOM

Divider page for "Book Three" from the original edition of *An Autobiography,* designed by FLLW. 1932

box has is gone. It is no longer simple.

The box idea is the reverse of free.

Violence must always be done upon the box in order to live in it. The box is divorced from nature by nature. The boxment must be attached to, fixed upon set in stuck on or "put over" on environment.

The box as building is an offense to any developed architectural sense of whole.

An architect's work should "click" with environment or nothing has happened except more effigies of the mutilated box in the offing. So more box buildings at the present time are the Expedient once again as ever before, however disguised as a new "aesthetic."

Ideas without technique or with bad technique are abortions.

ARIZONA

While anxiously waiting at Phoenix and La Jolla for the *"Yakamashii"* to clear away at Taliesin, the unit-block system, with my help, built another building—the Arizona Biltmore Hotel near Phoenix, Arizona.

Albert McArthur, one of my boys in the Oak Park workshop, was commissioned to build the building. Albert, at the psychological moment, appealed to me for help to establish the block system in the plans for the project. A wanderer myself, I turned into quarters at Phoenix and worked six months with Albert. The plans were finally made, but Albert encountered the usual opposition to the unusual in design and construction; he was unable to stem the co-lateral tide of suggested changes in technique which soon robbed the system of all economic value and left it standing as a novel and beautiful outside for an unintelligent engineer inside, whereas great technical economy was first and foremost a feature of the system had it been naturally allowed to work.

Having no authority myself beyond bullying or by way of "suggestion" I was powerless to prevent the tragic waste. In the building of the hotel cottages, however, the details of the system itself were better followed with better results.

But the story of the "Arizona Biltmore" Albert himself should tell. It would be a valuable warning and a reward. He is too near to it and too personally involved in its implications to tell it for another ten years.

Meantime the reunion with the McArthurs, old friends of my family—mother and three sons living in a group of beautiful homes in Phoenix. Their hospitality made our exile more bearable. If Phoenix had not had the McArthurs, it would have had no Arizona Biltmore.

While working with Albert I met Dr. Alexander Chandler of Chandler, Arizona. Chandler, his own town, is on the mesa about twenty-two miles from Phoenix. Already in that decent little town and in other serviceable ways he had built himself into that region. It had taken him thirty years but it was to good purpose.

A dream of Dr. Chandler's was an undefiled "desert resort" for wintering millionaires. He wanted to build this resort on a tract of several hundred acres of pure desert, in the Salt Range ten miles from his town of Chandler.

Learning I was in the neighborhood he came to see me and invited my little family and myself to come and see him at his pleasant "San Marcos."

Dr. Chandler had definite ideas concerning this new desert resort. They were good ideas, or better than that, I thought. But he had waited ten years before planning the building because he knew no one, he said, who could give him what he wanted, unless I could and he smiled his beautiful smile as he said this. There is only one more beautiful smile than his and that is his wife's.

So, together we went to see the spot, the inimitable black, Harris, driving. Harris too is an artist. And there is only one Harris!

There could be nothing more inspiring on earth than that spot in the pure desert of Arizona, I believe. Here was the time, the place, and here was the man in Dr. Chandler. He looked like the man of independent power and judgment always necessary to characterize thoroughbred undertakings—in building or anything else.

I liked him and I went to work *for* him and *with* him making the first sketches while at La Jolla in exile waiting to return to Taliesin. I showed them to him on the way home. The design pleased him. During the winter of the next year he wanted to build.

We had been back at Taliesin again and at work on this project for four or five months, when word came from the Doctor to come out and make the plans for the new resort there in Arizona, itself.

Joyful news. We were housebound at Taliesin in a blizzard, twenty-two degrees below zero, nevertheless we broke out in a blowing snowstorm.

The household and workshop at Taliesin closed and a trek by automobile to Arizona began, fifteen of us in all.

As I saw this desert resort it was to embody all that was worthwhile that I had learned about a natural architecture. First it was to be a better than

Arizona Biltmore Hotel, in construction. 1929. Phoenix, Arizona. FLLW Fdn FA#2710.0016

thoroughly practical "lay-out" or plan for the purpose. It was to grow up out of the desert as the Sahuaro grew, and the Sahuaro should be the motif that inspired its style.

Yes, at last, creation long denied, here came opportunity, ideal site unspoiled, the man well up to the thing he wanted done I feel by now. This is the rarest and most fortunate occurrence in any architect's life, if the United States is to have a creative architecture.

Having been held off so long from active creation, I could scarcely wait to begin. I had succeeded with the sketches. Having pretty well mastered

"block technique." With a man like Dr. Chandler I felt certain of results.

We all arrived at Chandler to find that suitable quarters in which to live and work there would cost several thousand dollars for the rest of the winter, spring and summer. And we couldn't live there in summer.

I had always wanted to camp in that region.

Why not camp now? Why not spend the "rent" on a camp, comfortable and spacious enough to use not only in which to plan the building but from which it might be officered during construction. I took the idea to Dr. Chandler and said that if he would give me a site somewhere we would build the camp ourselves. He reached for his hat, led the way to the little gray Ford coupe which he drives around the mesa at an average of fifty or more miles an hour and we flew away toward the Salt Range.

He stopped ten miles away by a low, spreading, rocky mound rising from the great floor of the desert—well away from everywhere, from which the site of the new resort itself might be seen.

"How would this do?" said he.

"This—do you mean it—can I have this to build on?" I said.

He nodded.

"Marvellous!" said I, "what more could anyone ask?"

"But," he suggested, "let us go a little farther over toward the hotel site, you might like that better."

"Oh no—I couldn't—I'll take this."

It was all too good, but it was true.

The lumber began to arrive that afternoon. Boxboards (unluckily green) and two-inch battens.

I sat down in a cold, vacant office in the town to make the plans. The boys stood around shivering, watching, handing me the tools. We set up a drawing-board on boxes. And it was cold. They said in Chandler that it was the coldest season in thirty years. But the scheme was soon ready and next morning we started in to build. We ate breakfast at the campsite as the frost came out of the air and the great red sun disc rose over the sublime spectacle of desert and mountain.

That night one of my boys, Donald Walker, slept outside on a pile of lumber, rolled up in blankets. By the next night we had set up the first box-bottom and put cots in it for three. Next day there was room for all to sleep but my little family group of three and myself. Reluctantly we went back to town. But we came back for early breakfast in that wonderful dining-room sixty miles wide, as long as the universe. We were cold, shivering, yes. But singing happy.

This vast battleground of titanic natural forces will make the playground for these United States some day. But it is too soon yet. They would only

spoil it now, à la Hopi or Mexicano-Hispano or boxment.

Out here obvious symmetry soon wearies the eye, stultifies imagination, closes the episode before it begins. So, there should be no obvious symmetry in building in the desert, none in the camp—we later named it "Ocatilla" and partly for this reason—nor anything like obvious symmetry in the new San Marcos In The Desert, as we named the new structure, to be. Any sound constitution is pregnant with graceful reflexes. Now comes adventure in the desert.

"OCATILLA"

Victor Hugo said: "The desert is where God is and Man is not."

And that is Arizona desert.

But the Arizonian has got himself a Midwestern cottage or sometimes, more fortunate, he thinks, a Mexico-Mediterraneano palazzo. And, believe it or not, he has built a few skyscrapers on the mesa.

And, oh ye eclectics, the Yankee-Hopi house is a favorite just now: confession of impotence in frustrated endeavor to do something "appropriate" by way of *taste*.

In all this weird, colorful, wind-swept, wide-sweeping terrain nothing is so deciduous as Arizona buildings, unless it is the crows lighting on the irrigated fields only to fly away.

Unspoiled character should not be trifled with like this. Arizona needs its own architecture. The straight line and broad plane should come here—of all places—to become the dotted line, the textured, broken plane, for in all the vast desert there is not one hard undotted line! Arizona's long, low, sweeping lines, uptilting planes, surfaces patterned after such abstractions in line and color as find "realism" in the patterns of the rattlesnake, the Gila-monster, the chameleon, and the sahuaro, cholla, or staghorn—or is it the other way around—are inspiration enough. But there lie her great striated and stratified masses, too, noble and quiet. The great nature masonry rising from the mesa floor is all the noble architecture she has at present. Pattern of

Arizona Biltmore Hotel, Phoenix, Arizona. 1929. FLLW Fdn FA#2710.0033. Photograph by John Reed

future Arizona architecture? The sahuaro. The sahuaro itself is a perfect example of "reinforced" construction. With its interior vertical rods it holds upright the great columnar mass for six centuries or more. A truer skyscraper than the functioneer builds.

The desert shows a remarkable scientific building economy in these constructions. And the desert could teach any architect applying for lessons. He may see the reinforcing rod employed in the flesh of the sahuaro but he may see the lattice reed and welded tubular construction in the stalk of the cholla, the staghorn, the bignana. Even the flesh of the prickly pear is worth studying for structure. In most of the cacti she employs box to box or cellular construction. She makes it everywhere strongly effective without having to reduce the scheme to post and girder construction before she can "figure" it out. She has this great advantage of our very best engineers.

The engineers are often as silly as the architects.

Aridity? Well, terrible as it is to beings ninety per cent of water, it seems no bar at all to life on its own peculiar terms out here.

And we from the north court sunshine in Arizona for six months of the year for its own sake pure and simple, then run from it to cover.

Across the mesa from the camp are great low-lying mounds of black, burnt rock covered with picture writing scratched on the surface by the Indians who came there at sunrise to worship the sun, the greatest evidence of the Great Spirit they knew.

The desert is prostrate to the sun.

All life here is sun-life: and dies a sun-death. Evidence is everywhere.

Now the architect and his helpers working away to build an architect's "compound," we will call it, in this unmitigated quotidian wilderness unchangeably changing.

We need fifteen cabins in all. Since they will be temporary, call them ephemera. You will soon see them all like a group of gigantic butterflies— say—conforming to the crown of the outcropping of splintered rock gently rising from the desert floor. This rock mound itself decorated by cacti,

greasewood, and palos verde will rise between the fleet of surrounding cabins to give *a measure* of privacy to all. Otherwise there could be very little or none for anyone.

The cabins themselves will be connected together by a low "staggered" box-board wall, its horizontal zig zag lines completing the enclosure just referred to as a "compound."

The necessary openings in the canvas-topped box buildings? We will close them with canvas-covered wood frames or "wings" hinged with rubber belting to open and shut tight instead of doors and windows, of which, of course, there will be none.

And when these white canvas wings, like sails, are spread, the buildings—the butterfly simile aside—will look like "desert ships." The group will look like some kind of desert fleet, so it seems to me as I work at it.

And with cold-water paint we paint the horizontal board walls continuing around and connecting the buildings about the mound the color of dry rose to match the light on the desert floor. The one-two triangles seen made by the mountain ranges around about the site will be seen reflected in the gables of the camp. We will paint the triangles scarlet, make the cabins bloom with these scarlet one-two triangles like the one-two triangles of the ocatilla bloom itself.

So we call the camp "Ocatilla." All this impromptu effort, as you now see, is a human circumstance as appropriately "nature" in Arizona as Arizona cacti, rocks, and reptiles themselves.

And I found the white luminous canvas overhead afforded diffusion of light within so enjoyable I now feel more than ever oppressed by the thought of the opaque solid overhead of the heavy Midwestern house.

We pay too slight attention to making slight buildings beautiful? Usually spend too much to make buildings "last" as we say. They are still making canes! No longer necessary even here.

Why in any changing period of our relation to the soil are transient buildings not best? Yes, transitory box-boards, battens, and canvas, in Arizona— for a preliminary study? Why not? These slight means may catch and reflect divinity of idea quite as well as the great sahuaro, standing there erect, six centuries old. There beside the king of the cacti grows a tiny, little wild hollyhock blooming for three days in some crevice of the burnt rock.

Is the tiny thing of less consequence in the scheme of the whole? It reflects the idea no less.

This noble, ancient sahuaro blooms at the very top of its dignified columns. In season it puts on a small chaplet of voluptuous white flowers that it may continue? The white sahuaro blossom opens with the sunrise, obeys some mysterious inner-rhythm, for it closes afternoon at four o'clock, never to open again. Each white flower in due time becomes a small apple, sought by the birds and the Indians for the same end, to carry the seed afar and return it to the earth.

The sahuaro message to the future?

"Ocatilla"—the camp—is ephemera. To drop a seed or two, itself? Who knows?

My draughtsmen, Heinrich, Donald, Vladimir, Cy, and brave George Kastner, Will Weston and I, made most of the camp ourselves. We put it

Svetlana, Iovanna, Olgivanna, and Frank Lloyd Wright parked in front of Ocatilla. Chandler, Arizona. 1928. FLLW Fdn#6104.0005

Ocatilla, the architect's camp, in construction. Chandler, Arizona. February 1929. FLLW Fdn FA#2702.0016

together with nails, screws, hinges, and rigged it with ship cord, designed as carefully as any "permanent" building. Executed as well as we knew how with such technique and endurance as we had.

I never grieve long now that some work of mine has met its end; *has had short life,* even though it happens that a better one cannot take its place, consoled by the thought that any *design* has far-reaching effect, today, because our machine so easily gives it, as a design, to the mind's eye of all. "Ocatilla" was published in German magazines two months after it was finished.[2] Thank the machine, at least, for this ubiquity of publicity. Prevalence of the idea in some graphic thought-form—certainly one of the best things the machine has done for us in this age. Even in this "matter of record," those architects failing to establish so-called "permanence" may get free from any desire to do so. Take comfort in the thought that architecture, too, is a

flux, a rapidly changeable working of principle in the world's workshop—manifest in one form today, tomorrow in another.

But when *organic* architecture comes to us we shall have no senseless destruction of life as we see destruction going on now. If such striving for "establishment" as we now have could end, life would be more abundant for all, better in quality at any rate. These foolish little "differences" without a difference to which we so pridefully cling lead only to repetition of infinite insignificant resemblances.

And this is the evil of such philosophy as we have today; that it never goes to seed that can grow anything fresh *from our own soil.* Yet, that growth from the soil is the simple province of all art and culture today as it was yesterday, or there will be no tomorrow for us. So rather than ponderous blunders—why not ephemera as preliminary study?

Here we are, "preaching" again. And preaching out here in the desert where the supreme mis-

Ocatilla. Chandler, Arizona. February 1929. FLLW Fdn FA#2702.0059

tress of creation gives all her "works" to bristle in self-defense with extraordinary weapons. Stylish. And their designer also patterns the creature inhabitants of the desert for defense. And seduction, too, it seems. In style the creatures all resemble in one way or another—and by way of pattern—the braided, branded, triangular terrain itself. No less than cacti she provides her reptiles with deadly weapons. They get poison fangs for theirs. And where are our defenses? "Ocatilla" has mild shelter, but no defenses, except the low box-board wall for enclosure . . . A man might push that over. But reptiles—no.

Well—we find that, although ephemera, our "desert ships" are strong enough to meet the "desert devils" as they come whirling across, miniature cyclones, slender, whirling columns of dust passing along the ground rising high in the air, one or two to be seen somewhere all the time, going to and fro, far and near. The ephemera will all shudder when a "devil" comes along to grasp and shake them, but they will not give way.

The canvas windows and doors like ship-sails when open may be shut against the dust or may open to deflect the desert breezes into the interiors. Screened openings for cross ventilation are everywhere at the floor levels to be used during the heat of the day; closed at night. The long sides of the canvas slopes lie toward the sun to aid in warming the interiors in winter. This long side is to have additional cover of canvas, air blowing between the two sheets of canvas, if the camp is occupied in summer. We can add this later if we stay on in summer, and make it "belong."

Everywhere around us see this stern, armed, creeping cover of "*growth*"! Ocatilla, greasebush, palos verdes, mesquite, bignana, cholla, sahuaro. Eternal mysterious purpose desperately determined, continually seeking conquest, in due course, of this titanic, ancient battlefield. To what end?

And this inexorable grasp of vegetation on the earth itself is more terrifying to me here as a principle at work, as it is everywhere, than are all the others put together.

There seems to be no mortal escape, even in death, from this earth-principle— or is it sun-principle—of growth. This creative creature of the sun.

Death being necessary to this creative creature's increase, death was invented.

Is this extraordinary style and character here in the desert of extremely born of the desperate nature of the struggle in the sun to survive the sun? Every line and the very substance of the great sweeping masses of rock and mesa speak of terrific violence. All are scarred by conquest, marred by defeat of warring forces.

Yet, subsidence, as we may see now in the stream lives of these endless ranges of mountains coming gently down to the mesa, has in this geological period found comparative repose. To these vast, quiet, ponderable masses so made by Fire and laid by Water, both architects, now comes the sculptor—Wind. Wind ceaselessly eroding, endlessly working to quiet and harmonize all traces of violence until a glorious unison is bathed in light that is eternity.

After sundown, the air-tight sheet-iron stoves in each light shelter keep the inside warm, we wrap up in a roll of blankets to sleep on the army cots, lie there and listen to the coyotes crying in the hills. Weird crying coming closer each night, no very pleasant thing to hear, for the women. But, finally it goes away.

It is very cold about three in the morning and impossible to keep warm until we learned to put several layers of newspapers on the canvas of the cots under the mattresses.

Soon we become sun-worshippers ourselves. As the great morning breaks far off over the blue mountain ranges we stamp the board floors, rush out to catch the first warming rays, and see "Ocatilla" with its sahuaro sentinels bathed in golden light.

In two weeks time, we have made the architect's camp a transient liveliness. It is living now in the Arizona desert. The first of an "Arizona type" it might well be. Whatever it is, there on the hill, ten miles from Chandler, it will be gone soon. Modest illustration of a great theme, in passing.

To justify the adventure, it cost not much more than the rent asked for equivalent accommodations in Chandler or Phoenix for one season were the same number of persons at work to be provided for. The cost was about $200 per cabin. The labor was our own. We are the better for that! One and all look back on the experience, hardships too, as something constructive in our lives.

SAN MARCOS IN THE DESERT

The camp was "practically" finished January 19th, 1928. Something of human significance had come alive in the desert. Under the glow of the translucent canvas "overhead" of the draughting room we worked away upon San Marcos In The Desert, resort to be for the jaded millionaires who still loved beauty and sought solitude in beautiful surroundings. We worked there until the middle of the following May. Often working at night by gasoline light until we put in a Kohler plant and had all the night light we wanted.

We worked out a great system of intercommunicating terraces, three of them, each with its pools and gardens, one terrace rising above the other against the mountain side. A monomaterial building and the latest expression of the block-shell system. Reinforced masonry within and without.

The ravine leading to the gorge between the two great hills is the road leading to the entrance to the "resort." This entrance is back in the gorge itself under the building. An organ tower of copper and block shell rises like a giant sahuaro from the gorge at this entrance, behind the building itself, intended to give "voice" to the whole. Echo-organs are to be planted in the hills—Dr. Chandler's idea—for open-air concerts in the desert.

The dining room, a toplit glass and copper arbor at the top of the central mass, is connected to the hill slopes on either side by the terrace tops of the upper stories of the wings, so adjacent dwellers in the mountain cottages, to be built later on as a part of the whole, may reach it comfortably.

No smoke or noise of service is to mar the building. Service or servant accommodation and garage are provided for over the low hill range to the right and are to be made the gateway feature of entrance to the San Marcos resort itself.

In every respect the far-flung, long-drawn-out levels of the terraces afford each room, each bathroom, each closet, each corridor, sunlight. Every living portion of the building is free to the magnificent views and has the warm southern exposure that every winter resort covets.

The whole structure would be what we call "permanent," all appurtenance systems adequate.

Every straight horizontal line in San Marcos In The Desert is a dotted line. Every flat plane grosgrained like the sahuaro itself. The building itself an abstraction of cactus life in masonry shells made more cactus than any cactus. And none the less, but rather more, a human habitation to live in as long as the mountain lasts.

Completely equipped and appropriately furnished according to reliable estimates San Marcos In The Desert would have cost, thus completely furnished in character, $4000 per room, the principal features and service systems all large enough for double the number of guest rooms. The cottages and transients would eventually provide that many more.

Here was human habitation come in to stay decently where man is not, showing not only appreciation of Arizona's character but naturally qualified to become a native part of Arizona for so long as any building has ever endured.

The Arizona desert itself was architectural inspiration and actually the architect's workshop in this endeavor. Is this not what we mean by an "indigenous architecture"?

So, it was all too good to happen.

Sometimes I think it was all just a dream. There are the plans, the carefully studied details, the responsible estimates complete, and the camp itself—still remains.

But where is Dr. Chandler?

April heat was becoming the heat that made the desert, and keeps it what it is. The "season" passed, dormant desert life was coming alive.

The boys at the camp had already nine rattlers to their credit. Among these were several sidewinders; Donald caught a large rattler and put it into a box with a cover of screen wire and kept the box by the side of his cot in the dormitory.

The sidewinder is a smaller type of rattlesnake, more poisonous than the larger type. It throws itself sidewise in convolutions like the figure three and strikes like the crack of a whip. The boys, catching one alive, dropped it in the box beside Donald's rattler to see what would happen. There was a furious battle and the little sidewinder was killed. But next morning the big rattler was dead.

A tarantula was tumbled out of one of the clothes closets.

The weather was now so warm that no perspiration showed on the skin under any exertion. And to take a deep breath one was inclined to turn the head aside, and hold a hand over nose and mouth.

How we all drank water, gallons a day! A truck came with bottled spring water once a week.

Olgivanna herself had taken charge of the commissary, and herself oftentimes drove the green Dodge truck we had acquired to the village for supplies and back again. Camp life is strenuous life. All must take a hand. And we planned, worked, and drove about the region in a free sun-life of the wide spaces.

But the heat of the desert generally was so dry we found less discomfort at 110 degrees than at home at 90 degrees.

For the homeward drive we had acquired a used Packard sport phaeton open to the sky. Camp broken and contents stored against return the following winter, this car now stands by the gate to the compound, to begin the drive overland to Taliesin.

Our luggage having been stored, we climbed in.

Olgivanna and myself sat in front to take turns driving. Svetlana and Iovanna were in the tonneau behind the windshield. As we had no shelter but the windshield all wore dark goggles.

We waved goodbye to the gay camp and drove off to pick up Dr. Chandler who was going with us as far as Holbrook. We wanted to investigate a new natural cement found in that region, as perhaps an ideal material for block-making.

This material found as a drift in the mesa floor was white, set quickly and hard, and was waterproof. We had left a plaster model made of the actual block units I proposed to use for San Marcos In The Desert, standing white and brilliant in the center of the camp compound on the crown of the hill.

Now began a wonderful drive, the second with my little family, across Arizona, New Mexico, and Colorado mountains and plains, across the great midlands, through hundreds of American villages: farms and villages all alike even in such differences as might be seen. Our towns and villages are more alike in their "differences" than anything else.

Such fluidity of thought entering into the life of the States as action is remarkable in respect to this deadly uniformity. I hope "Usonian" is not merely going to mean such *uniformity*. How did it all become so much alike? A carpenter-built house in New England is a machine-built house in Iowa, even a machine-built house in California. A popular tune whistled on New York streets today is whistled, a popular tune, on Los Angeles streets twenty-four hours later. Is this proof of weakness in the quality of individuality or only facility without inspiration? Does the machine facility inevitably breed monotony? Mediocrity?

At any rate the little decorated plaster cavern of Los Angeles is already the little decorated plaster caverns of Minneapolis, Buffalo, and New York. The "IN AND OUT DECORATOR"—seen on a Ginza sign in Tokyo—has it all his own way—his papier-mâché is all the way across the continent. The architecture of the country wherever fashion-driven by selective taste is, undeniably, the decorators.

This reiteration in the States is to weariness. Eventual extinction of individuality by way of machine-made monotony? God forbid! But to and fro everything goes, saturate at once with any new tincture or color. No new elements. Life nowhere in it, and yet, all lived in seemingly happily enough. Other resources undoubtedly but how much missed and so little to go forward on. Relieved by growing greenery. Blessed be the man who plants a tree.

Chicago reached, the drive, full of incident and interest, continued on to New York City. I was to consult with Norman Guthrie, the brilliant Rector and his Vestry concerning a tall apartment building for St. Mark's-in-the-Bouwerie to be built for revenue, in the Church Park at Tenth Street and Second Avenue.[3]

Eastern cities and towns are like Western cities and towns in the same lack of resourceful individuality, except that there is less new construction. One had the feeling that the young men had left the East and gone West, and the towns, villages, and cities were all waiting for their young to come back home to help.

We drove through the new Holland Tunnel, into scenes of indescribable confusion. The village streets of New York were in turmoil of reconstruction—new subways, taller buildings.

But seen here in New York is the same architectural insignificance except bigger and better in every way than the insignificance we had seen all the way along. There is the same lack of integrity as to idea, the same genuine monotony in ambitious variety. The man-eating "Skyscrapers"—the Hollanders call them *wolkenkrabber*—were all seeking false monumental-mass for steel skeletons. This is a contradiction of structure and idea: the tenuous open steel frame is, in character, the reverse of mass. Lightness, openness, and strength combined are its characteristics. These should be associated, not with heavy stone or concrete, but with light covering metals and glass, so designed and insulated as to emphasize the pattern of the structure itself, not belie it. Masonry materials not only do belie structure, but are a threat to the life of the structure by adding enormous useless weight for the frame to carry. That human equation, "the factor of safety," was seriously at work behind all this crowded mass of pier-buildings with crenolated tops of heavy masonry, senseless feudal masses standing there on steel stilts to mask and belie the real purpose and character of the building. Functioneering. Looking behind the masonry mask . . . it was all . . .

Doheny Ranch Resort (Project). Los Angeles, California. 1923. Perspective. Pencil and color pencil on tracing paper, 30 x 13".
FLLW Fdn#2104.005

TO THE AMERICAN ENGINEER

A great engineer came to mind. I saw him, as was his wont, walking the floor. Walking up and down. His shaggy head, beetling brows over deep set eyes, lowered in anxiety. The great tower of the Auditorium building had begun perceptibly to go down and take the adjoining structure with it. Two more stories added to that solid masonry tower had cut down the "factor of safety" after the footings were already in, a chance Dankmar Adler took to please Louis Sullivan and, be it said, as he himself knew, improve the scheme as a whole. Temptation had no doubt been yielded to in many of these structures, for reasons no better if dissimilar.

And for years the penalty of yielding was imposed solely on him. To add to that distress, to please his clients, the unforeseen banquet hall was added above the trusses which spanned the great auditorium after the great trusses were in place— wide steel trusses that clear-spanned the great room for Opera from sidewall to sidewall. These sidewalls felt the added load, and they, too, began perceptibly to go down. The long rows of arched box fronts in the great room itself at the sides were one-piece iron castings, set between the ends of beams projecting into the room from the outer sidewalls and cantilevered over the columns at the back of these boxes. As settlement proceeded these beams acting as gigantic open shears closing at the extremity where the box fronts were set like teeth between jaws, would crush and crack the cast iron box fronts with reports like cannon going off.

The level lines of the balcony and foyer, where they reached the tower, took a downward course and plaster ornament began to crack and fall. For eleven years the inexorable movement, gradual as a glacial drift, continued, and the patching of plaster inside was kept up. The sidewalk in front of the tower had twice to be raised. Ultimately an elevation of the street itself was visible as the enormous weight of the stone tower squeezed the mud aside and up from beneath the footings. And the brilliant throngs all these years would pass in and out in evening dress concerned only with the gaiety of the occasion, taking all for granted.

They saw a great, golden hall flooded with light and inspiring sound. But somewhere there was the solemn figure of the master-builder, anxiety in his heart, his anxious watchfulness all that stood between them and doom, walking the floor. Every few days he resurveyed and weighed carefully the new evidence that might appear, ready himself to give warning and close the doors of his own building to the public, should it become necessary. No one had enough science to *know* what would happen now.

All that could be done was to wait, to watch and, if necessary, give warning in time.

Often I would go down to sit there and enjoy the peace and harmony of the great room, sometimes the room placid, vacant. Sometimes a gay scene enlivened with great audiences and Opera. And I would sit under those wide, bland elliptical arches knowing the banquet hall had strained the iron trusses above the pendent elliptical bands of the ceiling so the turnbuckles in the tension rods had twice been tightened to bring them up again to level. I sat there often, one of the few who knew and perhaps when the veteran constructor himself was at the moment pacing the floor at home in anxiety.

Always, I sat there with perfect faith in him. It may be that at no time was there immediate danger of collapse any more than now that the movement has finally ceased. But I knew what the master-builder, if ever there was one, was suffering. It killed him twenty years before his time, I think. His big generous nature, his indomitable courage, his vast experience, all were put to a terrible test by yielding to the importunities of his clients, Ferdinand Peck and his directors. They, too, had perfect faith in whatever he would consent to do.

And behind all this smiling, suave mask of pretended architecture, this façade-making of New York, behind these beautiful and expensive interior decorations, life hangs by that slender element—the "factor of safety." The factor itself is a confession of uncertainty: the factor upon which human life is suspended! Engineers' computation tables say this much steel in this shape will bear so much if held together by so many rivets. Then the fallible engineer says, "Yes, but all human processes are fallible. Let's reduce the chances of disaster by multiplying safety by three or four—we will take no risks to save an owner's money." So four times stronger it is. But if twice as strong is not safe, how will four times stronger be safer? If the factor of ignorance admittedly exists it can have no definite multiple or limit—you take it or leave it.

This "human" equation is always back of these pretentious architectural masks.

Just as the living equation is behind every car flying along the highway and every elevator hangs by it, so we sit at its mercy in any building whatsoever.

But any faith we place in the factor of ignorance we fatuously call the "factor of safety" is in any final analysis not where our faith is fixed. We have faith that faith will be kept with faith.

Let us go back of the masonry masks and the factor of ignorance. Let us try to see what illusions we are cherishing in these prisons for life that we have built, and then see what freedom is possible for us if we will take it. Or is this an interruption for you? If you feel that it may be, and you prefer the thread of narrative to autobiographical "ideas," skip the next thirty pages, I am turning first of all to a study of the make-believe that is . . . our bondage.

The more efficient his machines become, apparently the more insignificant the man becomes.

Hide from the fact how we may we shall fail in the end to find "our own" . . . by this "Picture" way.

Encouraging light, however, is in the fact that we cling to memorial relics here in this rendezvous with riches of all-the-races, and in the fact that we do try by imitation to see ourselves in it as a cherished even though a copied reflection of "Beauty."

This dangerous much we have done by mechanical hook and educational crook . . . But that is why in our culture so little that is purposeful is honest, and so little that is honest is purposeful.

But the day is coming when even "taste" may

see that "style" is not something invented by man and "put on": not pictorial except as incident.

Freedom is the title—or is it the banner?—of this final section of an autobiographical study of Life-as-Idea and Idea-as-Life. But Freedom how? Where? What Freedom?

In this prison-house for the soul, the city, we shall not find much of it. In this sentimentalizing that is the picture we shall not find it. Only by mastering the new technique of a new age and life shall we ever find it. And the city of the future, in such a life—what would it be like? What portents are on the horizon of our city today, for the unborn city of tomorrow?

THE USONIAN CITY

Is the great city, natural triumph of the herd instinct over humanity, temporal hangover from the infancy of the race, to be outgrown as the performance of humanity grows "modern"?

Civilization has seemed to need and feature the city. The city has expressed what the civilization that built it most cherished. So the city may be said to have served civilization.

But the civilization that built the city invariably died with it.

Did the civilization itself die *of* it?

Acceleration—history records the fact—always preceded such decay.

So in the streets and avenues of the great city, acceleration due to the skyscraper is similarly dangerous and to any life the city may have, even though its very own interests may fail to see it.

I believe the city, as we know it today, is to die.

In intensified urban activity we are only witnessing the acceleration that goes before dissolution; the ceaseless to and fro, in gainful occupations, of the army of white collarites, is an activity of parasites on various forms of artificial "rent." Rent is the fetish of an artificial economic system that now owns the city. That and money, coming alive as something in itself, working to make all work useless.

Yet our "modern" civilization may not only survive the great city but profit by it because the death of the city—it is conceivable—will be the greatest service the machine can ultimately render the human being if by means of the machine, man conquers.

What beneficent significance to humanity, otherwise, has the machine?

The city as artificiality has already outgrown and overgrown itself until its carcass is past redemption.

But, if the machine conquers Man, modern man, too, will remain to perish with his City. Because the city, like all minions of the machine, is grown up only in man's image, minus the living impetus that is man. The city is man—the machine. It is itself only the baleful shadow of the sentient man that once needed the city and built it and maintained it because he needed it. The city that once was a necessity.

Even at this hour—via *"cubisme"* and *"futurisme"*—comes philosophic assertion that machinery, in itself, is prophetic of a more citified and fortified city. Café philosophers draw plans, picture, and prophesy a future city more desirable—they say—than the old one now overgrown and in travail.

The pictures reduce everything to dead level raised to mean height, geometrically disposed and symmetrically spaced. Man entombed, at the mercy of his own appliances? This ideal is now realized.

This "ideal" city relegates the human individual to, say, pigeon-hole 337611—shelf 522, block F, avenue A, street 127. And there is nothing at which to wink an eye that could distinguish No. 336611—shelf 117 from No. 337610 or 27643, bureau D, intersection 118 and 9. Thus all strife is ended. The harmony of inertia obtains. Nolition has arrived! Innocuous desuetude.

Thus does the old-fashioned sentient individual human factor, stripped to the bone, become a new-fashioned numerical unit, disposed of in the cavernous recesses of ultimate monogoria. Mechanistic systems are here seen not merely prophetic preparation for man's ultimate extinction. No. He has been philosophically extinguished in order to build a city, a mechanical sty.

This "future" city is utilitarian mechanics along the line of march toward the ultimate triumph of the machine over man. To me it is all dire prophecy. And it is all false.

What built the cities that have invariably died? Necessity, primarily.

That necessity gone, only the dogged tradition, another name for sentimental-habit, can keep the great city alive for any length of time. Necessity built the city on the basis of "leg-work, fuel-consumption, food-distribution, and the necessity for communication then to be had only by personal contact."

No effective mobilization of the individual nor any electrified means of communication existed.

Various physical contacts in that earlier day needed a certain congestion to facilitate and stimulate communication. Then the ancient city naturally grew and existed as the great means of human intercourse.

The city became the immediate source of wealth and power by way of such human intercourse as was essential to social, industrial, and financial growth.

Only by congregating thus in aggregations, the vaster the aggregation the better, could these fruits of human living then be had.

In that day the real life of the city lay in the stress of individual ties, the contact of varieties encountering variety. The electric spark of curiosity and surprise was alive in the street, in public meetings, in the home.

Government, the city had. Fashions and fads. But the salt and savor of individual wit, taste, and character made the city a festival of life: carnival as compared with any city of today. And this human establishment is not quickly changed as the conditions of its existence change.

Architecture reflected this livelier human condition.

The common denominator had not then arrived with its machine.

Now? The common denominator has not only arrived but by, with, and of the Machine.

New power is rendering the old impotent and obsolete. And it is only natural that the release of this new power should at first be fearfully and selfishly held back to the old habits and new ulterior purposes.

But machine-prophecy shows, and it shows nothing else, that we are to deal with the fact and principle of machinery in its most dangerous form here among us. And shows that the sentimentality that tries to break new forces to old habits is become impotent to deal with this element of machinery. We will deal with it soon, however, or it will finally deal with our posterity, as dominator.

To deny inherent power of growth and virtue to the common-denominator or to the common-emancipator, the Machine would be absurd. But the eventual city the common-denominator will build with its common machine will be greatly different from the ancient city or the city of today. Or any other graveyard for individuality, as obliteration of man, in any "city of futurisme."

It is impossible to put a new outside upon any city. The carcass of the city is old and *fundamentally* wrong for the future.

The city has become helplessly inorganic, where the great new forces molding modern life are concerned. They are making it useless.

What once made the City the great and all powerful human-interest is now by force of circumstance being driven in, preparing—within—the reaction that will by natural laws of organic change drive the city somewhere into somewhat other and else.

The human-element in the equation may already be seen drifting or pushed—going blindly, it is true—but going in several different directions.

Congestion was no unmixed evil by way of communication, until electric power, electric intercommunication, individual mobilization, and ubiquitous "publicity" became common denominator agents. Add to these, the airship when it lays away its wings and becomes a self-contained mechanical unit.

Accepting these, everything changes.

Organic consequences of these changes unperceived at first now appear.

The freedom of human-reach and movement, therefore the human horizon as a sphere of action is, in a decade, enormously widened by new service rendered by the machine. Horizontality has received an impetus that will make human activity immeasurable.

Therefore, such need for concentration, as built the city is ended or nearing an end in super-concentration. Nevertheless, these new facilities, owing to new gifts, insisting upon organic changes, seem for a time only to have intensified the trend of the old activity. By habit.

This habit is human nature's greatest weakness.

Additional human city-pressure is thus senselessly caused, in a new age.

Unable to face the issue, we are really witnessing an internal collision between mechanical factors—and thoughtlessly we find release by piling high up into the air. Cowardly, human tendency in any such pressure is to "stay right there where we are." We do, with animal fear and human sentimentality. We "pig-pile," in consequence.

To meet this human weakness under economic pressure, the skyscraper was born. Mechanistic invention for twenty years has been trying to hold the profits of this super-concentration, looking for salvation to the engineer, the elevator and the skyscraper! But the skyscraper is now the landlord's ruse to have and hold the profits of super-concentration. In the skyscraper we now see the commercial expedient that has enabled the landlord to exploit the city to the limit and by ordinance.

And, so, greater freedom, the ability to spread out without inconvenience, the most valuable gift brought by the undreamed of power of these new servants—electrical intercommunication, the automobile, the telephone, the airship, the radio, and the press—by the twist of the wrist the skyscraper represents for the moment, perverts benefits of machine increment, diverts these benefits from the man himself to the skyscraper, to profit lucky reality. The realtor has risen. Super-concentration booms.

Let us admit the thrill in acceleration and super-concentration directly due, pro and con, to exaggeration of these new mechanistic facilities. As temperatures run high, no one seems to want to know whether the acceleration is the healthy excitement of normal growth or the fever of disease: whether the acceleration means human progress or is only a form of the commercial exploitation likely to make the machine age the swiftest and shortest-lived in history.

Forces are themselves blind. But—reading between the lines—history will show that human beings, unaccustomed to thought as organic, but involved with organic forces, also remain blind. And over long stretches of time. But—saving clause, today along with these new revolutionary mechanistic factors, there comes this new faculty of communication, amounting to a new human faculty—an ubiquitous publicity that often succeeds in getting done in a month what formerly may have drifted a decade. We have cut elapsed time in all forms of human intercommunication, a hundred to one. To be conservative, what took a century in human affairs now takes but ten years.

Fifteen years, in the twentieth century, is an epoch.

Thirty years an "age."

So the reactions to any human activity—notwithstanding a temporary control of this agency as of all other popular agencies by salesmanship—may now show to all men in less than one lifetime the wisdom or folly of the nature of any activity. Humanity may now call for correction before the affair has gone too far.

Publicizing organic educational influences, by way of information, may avert the organic disaster that overtook earlier civilizations. It may also precipitate disaster, be it said.

The traffic problem already forces economic attention to tyrannical super-building.

Economic attention is our very best attention, but the problem is unsolved because there is no solution. Yet the "call" for solution is increasing.

The metropolis started wrong for organic development as modern.

The gridiron originally laid out for the village now grown to the metropolis is already cause for human pain, economic waste, and constant danger. High blood pressure in the veins and arteries that were once the village-gridiron will become intolerable.

The pretended means of relief specified by the space makers for rent—the expedient skyscraper—now renders this human distress more acute. The same means of "relief" carried only somewhat further along and before it reaches its logical conclusion "relief by the experts" will have killed the patient—the city. Witness the splitting up of Los Angeles and Chicago into several "centers" each again to be split up into as many more. The decentralization of the big department stores, the mail order houses, the migration of the factories has already begun. The financial center, alone, holds.

And yet in such machine-prophecy as the cubistic future-city of *futurisme,* this tyranny of the skyscraper finds philosophy to fortify itself as an "ideal," proposing to get new cities built—*on the sites of the old ones.* Standardization up on stilts. Enormous exaggeration of avenues of traffic only making inter-communication utterly impractical, where the nature of circumstances is making it entirely unnecessary.

And we may see, made plain by "drawing-board architecture," how the humanity involved in the machine-city of the machine-future of a machine-humanity is to be "dealt" with by machine-aesthetics to preserve and render the human benefits of electricity, the automobile, the telephone, the airship, and radio into systematic herd exploitation, instead of rendering these agencies more free as benefits to individual human lives.

Along with such skyscraper "solution-by-picture" of downtown confusion worse confounded, there goes—yes—the problem of the "tenement." The housing of the poor.

The poor are, not only to be with us still, but multiplied. Multiplied they are to be built in as fixture of the future city of the great machine. The "poor" are to be accepted, confirmed, and especially provided for as factors therein. As seen in the plans, Catastrophe is to be made organic. Catastrophe is to be built in!

That the poor will benefit by increased sanitation is granted at a glance. Not only are the living quarters of the poor to be germ-proof, but life itself, wherever individual choice is concerned, is to be made antiseptic. If we trust our eyes.

The straight-line is to be tipped up endwise and the flat-plane tipped up edgewise to crucify, not liberate, humanity.

And the poor man is to become just as the rich man—No. 367222, block 99, shelf 17, entrance K.

The surface and mass architecture that extinguishes the poor man as human, has already extinguished even his landlord: therefore why should the poor man complain? Has the poor man not, still, his labor for his pains? And what has the rich man for his?

There he is, the poor man! No longer in a rubbish heap. NO. Mechanized unit in a mechanical system! But so far as he goes there he is, still a cog. Still, but two by twice. He has been toned down, but further plucked and tucked in. The "slum" has thus been cardboarded up.

Nor can the poor in the—surface and mass—of the future-city choose anything aesthetically alive to live with. At least so far as neighbors or landlords can see it. But the dirty rags of the poor have been covered by a clean cardboard smock.

The poor man in the hard, modernistic picture is exhibit B—cog 300,000,128 in the new model for the standardized city to come. Humanity, it seems, has but one choice—sentimental or senseless?

Observe the simple aspect! How easy it all is.

This indeed, is "the *Ne Plus Ultra*" of the "*E Pluribus Unum*" of machinery.

This "new" city where no need exists for any city is delightfully impartial. The new "ideal" distinguishes no one, nor anything except certain routine economies sacred to a business-man's civilization. These routine economies are to be shared with the ubiquitous-numericals who are the common-denominator, shared with them by the nominators of the system, the system here seen perfected as the Ideal! The economies shared fifty-fifty? Half to the initial nominator, half to the numerical? Fair enough—or—who can say?

The indistinguishable division of the benefits of this standardization in any case must be left, and no less, to the generosity of the initial nominators as always.

And yet humanity is here orderly. Again—

rank and file—in the great war. The common-denominator gratuitously officered, standardized like any army, marched not only to and fro, but up and down no less. Even more. The common de-nominator on these machine terms would be no more alive without the initial nominator than the machine would be without the human brain. No—they themselves are here become the machine itself.

"The Noble Duke of York, he had ten thousand men," they all go ten floors up and up ten floors again. And none may know just why they go, now narrowly up, up, up, and some narrowly down, down, down—instead of going freely in and out and comfortably around about among the beautiful things to which their lives are related on this green earth.

Is this not to reduce all but the mechanistic devisors who may live on the top floors—or those who may secure the privileges of the higher stories, to the ranks—of the poor?

A free country, democratic in the sense that our forefathers intended ours to be free means *individual* freedom on the ground for all rich or "poor." Or else democracy is only an expedient to enslave man to the machine and make him like it.

Let the straight line be *horizontally* extended: give us the flat plane expanded parallel to Earth, gripping all to the ground. The sense of interior space must break through to the sunlight and air. The cave? Vanishing as feudal-masonry.

The machine is then, by nature conqueror of the drudgeries and demoralization of this earth.

The margin of human leisure for every man who works will widen if the machine succeeds for man, and this widening margin should be spent on field and stream, in public or private gardens on great architectural roads. The highway is becoming the horizontal line of Freedom extending from ocean to ocean tying woods, streams, mountains, and plains together by way of the regional field for building. All human occupation expanding and adding beauty of feature to the great national environment into which one brings the children that will be the Usonia of tomorrow.

The great power of the Machine so used will enable all that was ever humanly desirable in any city to go out along the great highways to natural beauty and freer life and grow up with the ground.

Machine increment placed where it belongs is going to enable human life to be based squarely on fruitful ground—fruitful ground because Man is with the ground.

The better personal element will withdraw more and more from the city as time goes on, leaving it more and more to the dregs or the machine shop. The better elements already are so far withdrawn that gang-rule is hard to break in cities, the city infested by evil as a wharf is infested with rats.

Only when the city becomes thus frankly utilitarian, pure, and simple, can it have the order that is beauty, and the simplicity to which the machine in competent hands is entitled.

The only ideal machine seen as a city will be an entirely subordinate collateral affair until it disappears. Invaded at ten o'clock, abandoned at four, for three days of the week, it will be unused the other four days of the week, which will be devoted to the more or less joyful matter of living elsewhere under conditions natural to normal manhood.

Organic change defeating "establishment"! Centralization giving way to Integration.

Henry Ford said a good word for decentralization in his proposal for Muscle Shoals. Dividing lines between town and country are gradually disappearing. Conditions are reversing themselves. The country begins to re-absorb the life of the city. The city shrinks to the utilitarian purposes that alone now justify its existence.

And even that cityful concentration for utilitarian purposes just admitted may itself be the first to go as the result of impending decentralization of industry. It will soon become unnecessary to concentrate in great masses for any purpose whatever as the individual, as unit, in general sympathetic grouping on the ground will grow stronger in the hard-earned freedom, fought for and gained, at first, by that element of the city, not swamped by circumstance nor prostitute to the machine.

Even the small town is too large. It, too,

will gradually merge into the general non-urban development.

Ruralism as distinguished from *"Urbanisme"* for future machine-age development is the business of the modern architect. Truly democratic business.

The United States everywhere already affords increasingly great road-systems. Splendid highways. The telephone poles that everywhere mar these highways of the countryside are already obsolete. The roadside fence is no longer—as modern farming goes—essential. These great road-systems, hastening movement toward the city at first, will facilitate reaction toward the countryside.

The railroads, like the metallic lines of communication strung across the country, are growing useless. They will soon be turned into great concrete arteries for mobile, continuous uninterrupted traffic. Clumsy heavy coaches dragged along roaring on hard rails are obsolete. The present heavy railway already is too cumbersome and too slow for modern mobilization.

The country is rapidly adding new and greater road-systems, and more splendidly built. The roads themselves will be more and more architectural. As they may be.

Leading toward the city at first to gratify old life, great open roads will work the normal way and lead away from senseless congestion to new life in freedom.

Natural parks are becoming everywhere available in our country. And millions of individual building sites, large and small, easy of access along these great developing road-systems may be seen everywhere neglected—good for little else. Why—where there is so much idle land—in such circumstances should land longer be parceled out by realtors to families in strips 25 feet or even 100 feet wide? This imposition is survival of feudal thinking. Establishment is trying to preserve the traditions of the ancient city to perpetuate the social and economic crimes practiced by might upon the serf . . . An acre to the family should be the democratic minimum if this machine of ours is a success.

What stands in the way of liberation?

It is only necessary to compact the standardized efficiency of the machine, confine the concentration of its operation where it belongs, and distribute the benefits at large.

Machine benefits are human benefits or they are bitter fruit. Much bitter fruit already hangs in the City tree, rotted, alongside the good—to rot the whole. Only a small part of our enormous machine increment is where it naturally belongs.

An important feature of the coming decentralization of the Usonian City—one more advance agent of re-integration—may be seen in any and every roadside service station along the highways.

The roadside service station is future city-service distribution in embryo. Each station that happens to be naturally located will grow into a well-designed convenient neighborhood distribution center, that will develop naturally into a meeting place, restaurant, restroom, or whatever else will be needed as integration proceeds. And already by the hundreds of thousands they occupy the best places in town or near town.

We will eventually thus have a thousand city-equivalents detracting from every small town or great city we now have. Integration will overcome centralization.

Integration is modern.

Integration along an extending center line is the technique of freedom and modern.

Added to many of these minor service stations to become beautiful features will be larger traffic stations—really neighborhood centers, where there will be more specialized commerce and such special entertainments as are not yet available by a man's own fireside. But soon there will be little not reaching the man where he lives, coming to him by broadcasting, television, and publication. Cultural quality of these new means is steadily advancing in spite of the old commercial ideal of centralization. Already the neighborhood garage—the "eating" place—the auto camp are features of the service stations, all, in numbers and in scale, increasing rapidly.

Perfect distribution like the ubiquitous publicity that serves or destroys is a common capacity of the machine, by no means fully realized. Nor can it ever be realized in "centralization" such as the city now represents. This simple capacity of mobilization for distribution to mobilization, when it really begins to operate, will soon revolutionize our present arbitrary, unnatural, wasteful arrangements.

Chain merchandising linked to chain-servicing, decentralized but integrated, will give more direct and perfect machinery for all kinds of distribution and stores than ever could be had by old-fashioned centralization in cities.

This complete mobilization of the people is another natural asset of the machine seen fast approaching. Therefore the opportunity will come soon for the individual to pick up, by the wayside, anything in the way of food and supplies he may require as well as find a satisfactory temporary lodg-

ing. Anywhere in America the great highways are the arteries of the integrated but otherwise decentralized metropolis of the future.

Wayside interests, even entertainments of all kinds, will soon be commonplace. As importance increases and freedom, too, no doubt quality in these will improve. The luxurious motor-bus traveling over superb road systems is making travel and intercommunication interesting and universal. The ponderous railway is already only for the "long haul." The aeroplane remodeled as a self-contained mechanical unit, as it soon will be, will pick up and continue this surface traffic as super-traffic in the air. Routed anywhere on earth. And then, and not until then, the airport will develop as another integral feature of modern life.

A day's journey anywhere will soon be something to be enjoyed in itself, enlivened, serviced,

San Marcos-in-the-Desert, Resort Hotel (Project). Chandler, Arizona. 1927. Perspective, watercolor and watercolor wash on art paper, 65 x 23". FLL

and perfectly accommodated anywhere en route. No need to tangle up in spasmodic stop and go traffic in some wasteful trip to town nor to any "great" city for anything whatsoever except to "view the ruins." The "journey" "anywhere" will soon become the delightful modern circumstance, the various adventure within reach of everyone.

Cities are great mouths. New York the greatest mouth in the world. With generally perfect and economic distribution of food over the entire area of the countryside a vital element that helped to build the city has left it forever to spread out in direct relation to the soil from which it came. Local products would find a short haul direct whereas an expensive long haul to the city and then back again was a feature of centralization.

Within easy distance of any man's dwelling,

will be everything needed in the category of foodstuffs or factoralized products which the city itself can now supply. And many the city never dreamed of.

The "movies," talkies and all, will soon be better seen at home than in any promiscuous hall. Symphony concerts, opera, lectures will eventually be more easily taken to the circle gathered at home, and better heard, than the circle there could ever be taken to the great halls in old style. And heard at home in congenial company.

The home of the individual social unit will grow in richness and power, containing in itself, in free space, freedom of the ground and the freedom of privacy.

The individual home in the Usonian City will have all the ancient city heretofore afforded, plus intimate comfort and free individual choice in bewildering variety, in unity.

Schools will be smaller—more individualized. And become more varied and directly related to all the arts. Among the arts—the art of living will have more attention than the art of selling. All schools will be most charming features in the rural gardens, byways, and parks of every countryside. Our popular games will be features in the school-parks, available far and near to everyone.

To gratify what is natural and desirable in the get-together-instinct of the community natural places of great beauty of which we have so many—in mountains, seasides, prairies, forests—will be developed as automobile-objectives. And at such recreation grounds would center the planetarium, the race track, the great concert-hall, the various units of a national theater, museums, and art galleries. A hundred such places to any one we have now and each more worthy the character of a great modern civilization is inevitable.

There need be no privately owned theaters. But good plays and other entertainments could be seen at these automobile objectives from end to end of the country in various national circuits whenever a play showed itself popular or desired.

Such objectives, easily reached by everyone in universal comfort, would naturally compete with each other in interest and beauty, stimulate travel, and make mobilization a pleasure affording somewhere worthwhile to go. The entire countryside would then be a well developed park, buildings standing in it, tall or wide, with privacy and beauty for everyone.

The centralized "city of the future" may be a depot of some kind. Whatever it is, it is certain that it will be only a degraded mechanistic servant of the machine because man himself will have escaped to find all the city ever offered him plus privacy the city never had and is trying to teach him that he does not want: gone to seek and find the manlike freedom for himself and that a free democracy means to him. And beauty of life, his birthright where men are free, will be his because his country is truly a Free country.

Very well, with this as ideal of Freedom, how

to mitigate, meantime, the horror of human life held helpless or caught unaware in the machinery that is the city? How easiest and soonest assist the social-unit to escape the gradual paralysis of individual independence that is characteristic of the machine--made moron—a paralysis of the emotional-nature necessary to the ultimate triumph of the Machine over Man—and quicken the humanity necessary to Man's triumph over the Machine?

That is the architect's real problem as I see it.

Measured over great free areas the living human-interest should be persistently educated to lie in this contact of free-individuality with free-individuality in the freedom of sunlight and air and in the breadth of spacing with the ground. That *human* interest should now characterize our free land.

Again we need the stress of true varieties encountering variety, *not monotony in variety*—so God forbid the International Style—and on a scale and in circumstances worthy our ideal of democracy. We should make this new life more a part of External Nature than any ever before seen. More a part of Eternal Nature too because of new harmony with Interior-Nature.

We want the electric spark of popular curiosity and surprise to again come alive, but come alive along the network of highways and byways that make every acre of all the land, alive. In the superior integration in freedom of charming homes and schools and significant public gathering places we would see architectural beauty related to natural beauty. Art must become natural and itself be the joy of creating perfect harmony between ourselves and the birthright we have neglected. Or all but sold.

We may now dream of the time when there will be less government yet more ordered freedom. More generous human-spacing, we may be sure, will see to that.

When the salt and savor of individual wit, taste, and character in modern life will have come into its own and the countryside far and near becomes a festival of life—great life—then only will Man have succeeded with his Machine. The Machine will have become the Liberator of Human

Life. Centralization was fixture. Monarchic. Despotic. Arbitrary destruction, ultimately of every civilization whatever and anywhere.

Integration is the technique of the new freedom, and our architecture will reflect this newer ideal of Freedom.

ST. MARK'S TOWER

You want specific outlines? Facts? Fair enough. Here is "St. Mark's Tower," an individual modern building that, as a type, fulfills machine-age requirements, utilizes machine-age resources at work upon machine-age materials in a machine-age way![4] The straight line and flat plane of the machine age seen as significant outline instead of monumental mass. The constitution of whole emphasizing interior space in light.

The structure is light and strong—one third lighter and three times stronger than the heavy masonry-encrusted box frame of steel. In eighteen stories the equivalent of two floors are available to live in, instead of being thrown away to give place to useless destructive wall thickness and weight. There is but ten per cent more glass area as "exposure" than you may see in Gordon Strong's Republic Building down on State Street, corner of Adams, in Chicago.

The textile, a machine-age product of great value and beauty, here clothes interior space inside the glass and allows more light or less light, more or less privacy as desired under changing conditions. All members of the building except the central mass and floors, the supporting structure itself, are metal. Partitions and furniture are designed as one and fabricated in shops. Such conservation of space may be effected by this means that the equivalent of a five room apartment, cave style, may be had in two thirds of the space. Sunlight method.

Economy? Extraordinary here in any case. In any operation on large scale—enormous economy. Astonishing release from field "waste."

Beautiful? Naturally somewhat strange at first. But the kind of beauty we see in the liner, the plane, and the motor is seen here. Added to that is a graceful sense of harmony in the whole, an imaginative touch in the detail that makes all the parts sing in unison with the whole. Here is an apartment building more useful than ever.

Beautiful?

What is your beauty—and yours—and yours—yes, and yours—my savant! I can't hear you but I imagine your answer. It would simmer down to a mere matter of "taste," if you spoke the truth. And "taste" is usually a matter of ignorance, or a personal idiosyncrasy, cultivated—overmuch.

Come to terms eclecticism! None of the great architectures of the World ever grew up on any such flimsy basis as "taste." Even such rare taste as yours, my connoisseur. Nor was it calculated by aesthete philosopher or functionist. Great architecture grew up as this building is built—true to materials, method, and purpose—aimed at greatest human benefits by way of spontaneous individual insight inspiring more individuals to ever-increasing insight until a new technique of a new life is residue and individuality still free. This building is embodiment of human use and comfort as a satisfaction to the mind. I don't mean a satisfaction merely to the intellect for that would be as unsure as the satisfaction offered to the taste of this transitory-period. I mean satisfaction to the mind that is a mind and includes a heart.

The fact is this building gets fresh hold on beauty as a new sense of order. It recognizes beauty as something that can never come by putting anything on anything at all, but as a *quality* that must come out of the thing itself as reward for integrity of means to ends and individual love of nature—in no "exterior" sense.

To see one expression of the city as it might have been but for culture, or as it might be, still for a time but for further betrayal of machine increment:

Premise! Take this type of tall building. Imagine similar ones, though infinite in variety rising as gleaming shafts of light, as tall as you please from every court space in town, throw away the cumbersome masonry caverns standing to the streets, and plant the areas thus thrown back into the city streets, as green parks. Out of this varied mass of shade trees and flowering shrubs, see the spider—steel—spinning its web to enmesh glass—glass clear—glass translucent—glass in relief—glass in color. See the iridescent surfaces of this light fabric rising high against the blue out of the whole city, the city now seen as a park, the metal fabrication of the shafts themselves turquoise, gold, silver, bronze, the glass surfaces between the threads of the fabric shimmering with light reflected, light refracted—sparkling light broken into imaginative patterns—all buildings standing free of each other in natural greenery. The cost of all this sunlit space would be, all told, one half the cost of the stuffy cavern it replaces. Imagine the money thus saved put into ground to free the city of demoralizing congestion, to enable it to live and let live by spreading out into the country.

Imagine all these human benefits of freedom to have come alive again by means of machinery. And you will have a glimpse of the new machine age, where the man himself is more healthful and happy because of his machine.

Let us now seek art as much nature as Nature herself. We are developed enough to desire it as ultimate feature of "human nature."

We must ourselves make it . . . yes, artificers . . . all. But artificial only as humble means to a greater integrity of life with nature. This . . . the great atonement . . . possible to the human race. Without this atonement the race will die—and should die—and Usonia will never have been born.

BETRAYAL. And yet the very captain of industry who might aid in the release of the man to some such future by building appropriate background for modern life in a more practical, rational way is sentimentally gratifying his own perverse acquired taste by wasting machine-made millions in reproducing an antique Gothic Minister that never suited its purpose even in the original.

The captain at Detroit, too, exercising the business man's license of sentimentality is now busy spending millions of machine increment to extend a reproduction of Liberty Hall some thousands of feet to make space enough to take all the old glass chandeliers—fiddles and fiddlesticks or any other old

thing he can find that the Colonials had on them or the Pilgrim Fathers brought over here from England: things they brought over to this new ground, blessed by a new Freedom, just because they had none other or better to bring.

Thus—the greatest trustee—how can he be more—of the increment of machinery in these United States betrays his trust by way of his own futile sentimental taste. And I believe some architect "sold" him the idea.

The captain himself—then—turns his back upon the future of the man at the machine.

Becomes a play-boy to waste the increment of the machine of his own day, himself turning to exploit a badly overdone, handmade past for his own amusement. Our amazement?

The weakness of the present capitalistic system glares here with rather a sinister glare no sentimental, patriotic simper can hide.

Where do we go, now, for the allegiance due?

In the studio we are working away night and day to get ready an exhibition of the work of these past years. Some six hundred photographs, several hundred drawings, five models of later work. Getting it all ready to go to Europe in a "setting" we ourselves designed.

Several European Governments arranged for the expense of transport and will set the exhibit in official galleries. We have prepared a catalogue to be printed in three languages. A separate color for each language. It will be the first authentic catalogue of my work. English to be printed in conventional black. German in red. French in blue. And the past year or two, hard times holding buildings back, I have gone about lecturing a little. The bulk of the material included in this first foreign exhibit has gone about with me to a number of places. It was seen first at Princeton University and next at the Architectural League of New York. The League gave a dinner in honor and there were many speeches, mine included. A kind of homecoming it seemed to be but it made me wonder a number of times during the evening, as the assembled architects would rise and lay an artificial or a faded or a real flower or wreath on past performances of mine,

National Life Insurance Company (Project). Chicago, Illinois. 1924. Perspective. Pencil and color pencil on tracing paper, 42 x 50". FLLW Fdn#2404.041

if my home-grown colleagues were really no longer afraid of me. I wondered if they thought I had passed the period of activity where they were inclined to "blanket" me as in the past? Write me down as I have always given them free and fresh opportunity to do, as ego-antagonistic.

But no, I soon had occasion to know I was still to be kept out at any cost. And I was not sorry to be "kept out" to be free to continue to play what havoc I might with the quotidian enemy, this perennial "hangover" of eclecticism. This freedom is precious to me. I have paid a price for it. The price has not been too great. Although I have longed for and still long for the enlightened comradeship and the good will of my kind, I shall maintain this freedom.

Goethe once met the criticism of his fellows by a poem saying in substance, "When I ride through a village and the dogs begin to bark, the demonstration convinces me of just one thing . . . and that is that I am on horseback." But it is doubtful if Goethe could have done his great work of liberation in the age that glorifies salesmanship as the consummate art.

Finding myself occasionally in academic circles, I told the story several times that my young cousin, Dick Jones, told me. He had blown in from the University at Madison. We were at supper. Dick was hungry, but as he unfolded his napkin, he looked over at me.

"Cousin Frank, here's a hot one for you . . . Why does the American Flu-flu bird fly backward?"

"The Flu-flu bird, Dick? I never heard of the Flu-flu bird."

"Never mind," said Dick. "Your answer is that he flies backward to keep the wind out of his eyes."

"All right, Dickie, the American Flu-flu bird flies backward to keep the wind out of his eyes."

"Naw," from Dickie. "Naw . . . the Flu-flu bird flies backward because he doesn't give a darn where he's going, but he's just got to see where he's been!"

Laughter. Thanks, Dick. That counts you *one*. That *is* a good one for me.

JOURNEYMAN PREACHER

From the extraordinary state university at Eugene, Oregon, came a hand-lettered appeal for the exhibition signed by all the architectural students and their shepherd, Walter Willcox, and it touched me. I managed to go there with the exhibition and then on to Seattle. Two lectures had been given in Denver following six at Princeton, the Princeton lectures since then built into the published book, *Modern Architecture*.[4] Two more lectures and exhibition at Wisconsin. Two at Minneapolis—I hope Sheriff Brown came. He would have felt at home in the fashionable throng overflowing the Art Museum. Two lectures and exhibit at Chicago Art Institute, since published by the Institute. Some of these meetings so crowded by my fellow men and women have affected me—those at Chicago and Wisconsin especially, where warm welcome in places of long association aroused the sleeping sentimentalist in me, though not to the point of modifying my ideals of sentiment. But dangerously near their demoralization just the same!

"The man is still iconoclast!" Whispered indignation. Perhaps. But, I wish they would dub me "radical," and let me go home. A good word "radical"? How know life unless through knowledge of the "root"? But even "radical" on the academic tongue spells "red"! The hypocrite instinctively hates the radical.

Everywhere I found the halls overflowing, everywhere youth eager and questioning. Natural modernity has captured the imaginations of Usonian youth as I hope the modern will possess the heart, remaking culture on liberal terms and more enduring conceptions of natural law. Under the fire of intent and intelligent questioning by youth, I began to feel a younger "youth" myself, to take deeper breaths. I began to feel less alone in my work.

And at Chicago an echo of my own earlier youth. One afternoon in the gallery where the exhibition stood, a tall handsome woman came toward me smiling. A moment's hesitation and I recognized Catherine. She was happily married again—Mrs. Ben E. Page. I had not seen her in fifteen years. The years seemed to have dealt with her gently and she looked—frankly—young and happy, as she said she was. We went about the exhibition, noticing many a work that had grown up out of the "other half" of the Oak Park establishment. However ill-advised her attitude toward me, she had never been other than loyal to anyone she ever loved.

MILWAUKEE

These exhibitions over and the material itself again back at Taliesin, Charlotte Partridge, curator of the Layton Art gallery, Milwaukee's center of culture in the Arts, asked me to send the exhibition and give a lecture. She volunteered to raise whatever money was necessary if I would come.

The last place I could imagine interested in anything modern would be Milwaukee.

Therefore I agreed. Miss Partridge had her private troubles getting the necessary fund. But the exhibition went forward. I was busy directing the boys setting it up when Miss Partridge introduced a tall, fair, young person as "doing the show" for the *Journal*. She was much too good looking to know much about architecture, I thought. And I went on working. She was persistent, followed me about asking questions. I answered between moments here and there. Finally: "Mr. Wright, would you mind telling me what you think of our new nine million dollar courthouse?"

The new courthouse was a steel structure surrounded by three stories of vertical solid stone wall punctured by small windows. Above that, all around ran a tall stone classic order. Surmounting the whole a heavy stone cornice. A steel building inside, a stone building outside. I did not know who the architect was.

"The new court house will set Milwaukee back fifty years from any cultural standpoint," I said, not thinking of talking for "publication."

"Oh, I'm so glad to hear you say that!" She danced up and down with glee.

Then from her, conscientiously: "Would you mind if I put that in print?" This request was so considerate that I stopped, touched. Thought a minute. What did it matter? It was at least true. "No, you may quote me." The interview continued and I thought no more about it.

Home late that evening. Next morning early, a long distance call from Milwaukee. The *News* "The *Journal* out with statement (it is always a statement) headline quoting you: 'New court-house sets Milwaukee back fifty years from any standpoint of culture.' How about it?"

"All right," I said, "make it a hundred. I've been thinking it over."

The fight was on, the pottage began to boil. The other newspapers called up wanting confirmation. They got it. Came follow-up interviews by the journals with Milwaukee's leading architects. Reporters comment on this, "All afraid to express an opinion, not caring to incur shafts of radical architect's wit." This pleased me. One of their number, Tullgren, saying: "Wright was always twenty years ahead of the time." The inference being, and so "why worry." Albert Randolph Ross, the winner of the competition for the new courthouse, himself interviewed by the *Journal*, explained why his design was classical instead of modern. Here is his explanation:

Mr. Hoover, talking in Washington recently on the occasion of appropriations for public work, said it was a good thing to carry on the traditions as established in Washington.

When I went into the competition I considered whether to design a building in the modern and experimental trend for a great public courthouse. I made modern sketches, but in my opinion, they fell flat for this purpose. They were not typical and expressive of public work, so I turned to that type established by our forefathers.

Turning to a defense of the courthouse design, Mr. Ross said that it was chosen unanimously by three of the country's most brilliant architects as that plan which completely met the requirements of beauty, plan, and utility.

I have no quarrel with modern trends in architecture. I take a fling at it myself, even considered it for the courthouse. But it simply won't do for public buildings. It violates the dictates of a definite style built up through the one hundred and fifty years of our history.

A departure into modernism would not be suitable for a courthouse. We must be trained slowly to things violently new. The public's money cannot rightly be used to force experiments down its throat.

The aesthetic side of the courthouse, Mr. Ross contended, counts only ten percent. All that is needed in a building is a design that will arrest light in such a way as to give a pleasing effect. That he thinks has been accomplished. The plan of the courts, offices and corridors, and the building's utility are to him most vitally to be considered.

The point of view of the functioneer-eclectic is here completely expressed. But if the aesthetic design of the courthouse is an affair separate from the courthouse and estimated by Ross at "ten per cent," why spend fifty per cent on it as extravagant useless stone envelope?

Reply to Ross:

Milwaukee should look at Chicago's county building, twenty years ago the last word in "chosen" pseudo-classic, today manifest to all as economic crime. A ponderous curse on culture.

And I say that the Milwaukee building today is the

same crime, modified only by Ross' taste. Within a few years this will be manifest to all. The thought of the world is growing more sensible.

Milwaukee's architect says "he is unwilling to spend the hard-earned millions of Milwaukee's money on any experiment." This may sound good to Milwaukee. If so, it is one of the things that is the matter with Milwaukee and will leave her permanently a backwater in civilization.

Architect Ross says he is not willing to "experiment." But as an architect he is willing to "bet" nine millions of popular money on the narrow margin of the unsure taste of a transitory period, as he sees it.

Why, therefore, should the future have any more respect for the Milwaukee-lie than for the Chicago-lie? There was some excuse for the Chicago-lie. The age had not awakened to engineering architecture. For the Milwaukee structural-lie there is none.

Were Ross blind to the progress of the last decade in his own profession and in architectural circles the world over, then he might consider honest engineering architecture an "experiment."

The Milwaukee county buildings will stand as a late experiment in sentimental falsehood doomed to failure.

Since experiment the courthouse must be, why not experiment with sanity and truth?

Our forefathers not withstanding, "monumental stone mass" disappeared, as a truth, when steel in tension, clear glass, and ferro-concrete became the actual body of our machine age. To combine stone and steel, even in their name, is dangerous anachronism. Young men in architecture all over these United States see this fact today. And that means that every man who thinks will see it soon.

Why "bet" or "experiment" with sentimentality, Architect Ross? Why not know?

So much talk infuriated the official city fathers. They got together, argued the question as to whether or not I should be called before them to explain the disparaging remarks. A vote was taken. The vote stood—ten to ten. The opposition claiming I was a notoriety seeker and to call me down publicly would only add fuel to my flame. I was not called.

The press had a good time adding editorials to headlines.

Meantime children and students were pouring into the exhibition. Miss Partridge said nothing the gallery had ever given attracted so much interest among the young people.

The architects, all but a few, kept away. To be seen going into that show was too much for most of them. Merely to gratify a curiosity? And not much curiosity.

There was the lecture yet to come. I had to postpone it for several days, but the Friday of the week following the Wednesday the exhibit opened I got to Milwaukee about four o'clock to speak that evening. Charlie Morgan and I were at the Pfister Hotel . . . a bath and getting dressed for a little dinner Miss Partridge was giving . . . A knock on the door. Loud. Charlie opened it. The sheriff stepped in with a warrant for my arrest.

What charge?

A judgment entered against me to pay seven thousand dollars to the deceased Miriam Noel. Brought by her estate.

The payments due her by contract were all made from a trust fund deposited in a Madison Bank at the time of divorce. There was eleven thousand dollars still left in the fund when she died. The fund reverted to me at her death, so the charge was only "my failure to pay myself seven thousand dollars, to bring the trust fund up again to original standard."

Ridiculous? But it served the legal purpose. The attorney of the "estate," whoever and whatever "the estate" might be, had sworn to the document and I was taken into custody, entered in the record at the county jail, and carried over to the justice before whom I was to be tried, photographed all along the way as I went. All had been arranged. Camera men posted where they could do the worst good.

I understood the situation, angry enough that these things should be, but putting the best face possible on the whole matter and keeping my head up.

"Justice" asked questions. Got answers. The lawyer, having gratified the curiosity of the assembled press, then urged the "court" that I be kept in custody over night. (The lecture in mind, I suppose.)

But the "court" thought this might be carrying things too far, for he denied the motion. Cold feet at the last moment perhaps. He set me free.

So the "plan" only partially succeeded I imagine.

The evening papers were on the street with fresh headlines opening old sores as Charlie and I went back to the hotel.

Miss Partridge by now had been reproached by Milwaukee architects for bringing disgrace upon the city, by having me there. She didn't seem to care. She is something of a captain herself.

It was now six-thirty. Time for the little dinner. We got there. Charlie more raging and furious than I. We dined and reached the hall. I think none of us knew just what might happen next. And I remembered Olgivanna's reluctance to have me go to Milwaukee at all: her plea to cancel the lecture and stay away.

The place was overflowing. One of the courthouse commissioners was in the audience, so they told me. And there was a general feeling that when I came to talk I would modify the remark about the nine-million-dollar courthouse.

Instead of the "arrest" putting a damper on my spirits that evening, the dinner and kindness of all concerned, even of the complimentary sheriff himself restored them for as enthusiastic and appreciative an audience as I've ever had anywhere. They heard me through.

Then I stepped down to give them all the half hour I knew they expected.

Many questions came and were answered.

The commissioner got to his feet: "Mr. Wright, we had hoped you would retract your remarks concerning our new courthouse, or at least explain them. Will you do this?"

"I will," I said.

"Milwaukee's new nine-million-dollar courthouse belongs to the nineteenth not to the twentieth century. That great stone mass over steel is memorial to a backwater in civilization and can only advertise to posterity that Milwaukee was neither scholar nor gentleman. No scholar because Milwaukee was ignorant of the current of advanced thought abroad in the world at the time, and no gentleman because regardless of its duty to the future."

A steel building inside and a stone building outside is an anachronism inviting destruction.

The commissioner, strangely, seemed pleased. The audience no less so.

"Well then," said the commissioner, on his feet again, "well then, why not tell us just what kind of courthouse we should have had, were we "scholars and gentlemen."

And as it came to me I gave them a modern building as I saw it.

The preparation of solid masses of terraced stone or concrete mingled with gardens. Rising upon this "stylobate" an iridescent light-enmeshing fabric of steel and glass. All, within, luminous and brilliant. The whole light and strong, free of space, and economical of material, free in thought, an expression of our opportunity in our time. I carried it on into some detail and delivered the whole to them where they sat for about five million dollars.

I had made it so obvious, it seems, that the audience broke into applause, including the commissioner and his party. And the episode was ended so far as anybody but Ross was concerned.

So I wrote a note to Ross himself saying I hoped and believed no harm had been done him. I had meant none.

Unfortunately behind every pseudo-classic plate-glass window, however small the window, there is some fine, well-meaning individual to be hit by any brick thrown by anyone. It was the cause, however, in this case. Not the man. And Ross was intelligent enough to know it. I had never thrown a brick directly before at any classic performance. But now it seemed high time to make the matter public issue. The modern hat was in the pseudo-classic ring.

My note to Ross received a gracious reply, "No harm."

And saying, guardedly, that he envied the future its coming freedom.

The lawyer for the "estate" dismissed his fake "suit" with profuse and servile apologies, offering to pay all costs. He volunteered the information in the presence of Jim Hill, my own lawyer, that he hadn't wanted to go through with it but no less than "five leading citizens" of Milwaukee had insisted on his "going through."

Interesting to follow this up? I have the means. But like all the persecution by publicity, of what use? More publicity?

That always is the weapon, where publicity is not wanted. Where it is wanted? Well, it is for them to sell it or none whatever.

And this is fair enough?

A letter from Holland saying the exhibition was opened at Amsterdam in the State Museum by our American Ambassador, Swenson, who tried to say something about the show but could talk only of America and the flag. The president of the Architects Society of Holland got up and made the speech for him that he might have made if he had known at all what the exhibition was about and why. A cablegram: my Dutch colleagues congratulating me in so many words on my "consistency in a great cause."

The word "consistency!" It is seldom the word for the imaginative mind in action?

I am inclined to deny the allegation.

I sincerely don't believe I have been very "consistent." Off on holidays too often. But direction has never changed nor development hindered. And I've always returned from a holiday refreshed for the work in hand—having learned much more from every "aside" than from the "line" itself.

Is that consistency? Then I would plead guilty to the soft impeachment.

Next the exhibition goes to the "Akademie der Kunste" at Berlin. The first time, I believe the "Reich" has honored modern architecture? From there to Frankfurt, then to Stuttgart and to Belgium. Home again in October so that it may go to work in our own country where it is most needed, if not so much wanted. Once Eclectic forever Eclectic?

Meantime I went as journeyman preacher to a week of speaking in New York City.

A WEEK IN NEW YORK

This week as amateur preacher was interesting to me and had somewhat interesting, though passing, consequences.

The week began Tuesday evening by a talk— *ex tempore*—to the Twentieth Century Club at Brooklyn, a "closed" club. Some hundred or more were present.

When I accepted their invitation I thought of "Cooper Union," "Pratt Institute," etc.—expecting to speak to an audience in a hall somewhere.

I found myself in the old Pratt Mansion in Brooklyn surrounded by very dignified and beautifully dressed people with old New York names.

A rug had been put over a low box in the hall for me to stand on.

But I stuck my manuscript behind my back and kept to the floor beside the box to lay before them in outline the gospel of the modern as "Youth." A Professor from Yale rose to refute a murderous side-slip I had made toward prevailing "sentimentality"—urging the right to "the Past."

The company applauded him. But it was familiar ground to me and not hard to dispose of the question he raised.

It was evident to me that the Twentieth Century Club was happy to be "overcome."

Next, an amusing Wednesday evening. A dinner to "Modern Architecture" at the Women's University Club of New York. I was co-guest of honor with several prominent skyscraperites, together with Buckminster Fuller and the city planners of New York and Catherine Dreyer.

The hostess—Miss Verplanck.

I looked down the speakers' table wondering where the audience at the tables below would be when we had all finished.

I was a minority report likely to spoil that party so I asked to speak last.

Miss Verplanck graciously acceded to my request, though the skyscraper architects were her "prophets" this evening.

Buckminster has ideas and they are good. He also has wit. His points came through but he, finally, was a dripping rag.

The room was hot and everybody getting tired. It had already been heavy spread.

Then came the major *"wolkenkrabber"* prophet as salesman for the Fair. Beautifully dressed, he began by paying handsome tributes. He sold the

Dymaxion house to the guests. Paid me a compliment so he might qualify it with, "But Frank Lloyd Wright will not stay in line. Frank Wright has never stayed in line."

Then he went on to sell the Chicago World's Fair as the last word in modern architecture.

The evening had, nevertheless, been rather dull. I had suppressed a yawn or two, as I saw others doing. It seemed like cruelty to animals to talk further to that patient audience about anything in the world except going home at once. Moreover, every speaker had made some polite reference to me and my work. But, tired and bored is no mood in which to make a speech. So when my gracious introduction came from Miss Verplanck I, too, made some references to the speakers—the less said about the references the better. Then, "Ladies and Gentlemen, you have just been listening to the slickest architectural salesman in these United States. As I sat listening to him had I not known precisely what the Chicago Fair was, he might have sold that to me too. But we have all had so bountiful a spread of oratory already that it would be cruelty to go on with more." And I sat down. But the audience had only been dozing a little, and insisted that I go on.

I record this insistence on their part to show their share of the blame for what followed.

I had listened too long to too much in little. I began by questioning the sincerity of this dinner to modern architecture when only eclectics who put the mask on the skyscrapers of New York were invited and the men whose science made the buildings stand there, the engineers, were left out. So far as I could see the dinner was really given to the eclectic and his modernisticisms. And I got to the Fair as the latest expression of the New York eclectic modernism. Having seen the handwriting on the popular wall the New York eclectics were crowding to be first to be modern, now all in a huddle over a "cross section of something or other" that looked to them like modern architecture as they had seen it somewhere.

The Fair was being " sold" as the result of this huddle. Here, in the Fair, the "PseudoModern"!

Olgivanna was sitting near. I glanced at her.

She frowned and shook her head.

I looked down at my sister Maginel, at the table below. She looked as though she wished she could sink out of sight.

So, with the feeling that I had already said too much, I sat down. But they wouldn't have it as finished. The first-class audience seems to like a row. So seldom it gets anything sincere or honest, I suppose.

And I remember that for the first time I said what I thought and felt about the whole hypocritical mess being made by the eclectics arriving at modernism by the adventitious road: sincerely described the Fair as I saw that commercially degenerate performance, the opportune New York functioneers, *"wolkenkrabbers,"* climbing into the latest band-wagon, regardless, determined to hold or drive.

And I tried to be as sincere as I was hopeless about the whole circumstance passing show as modern: the Fair itself the eclectics' latest "dish of tripe."

Poor Miss Verplanck! Head bowed she worked away at the table cloth. Olgivanna was blushing now herself, as was Maginel . . . for me. "Well," I said finally, "you would have it. I knew I was a minority report that would spoil this party, so I asked to come last . . . all the grace I have coming to me in the circumstance."And the meeting broke up.

Miss Verplanck acknowledged my existence but turned her back on me to face, solicitously, toward her major skyscraperite prophet. Buckminster Fuller shook my hand with a nervous grip. I felt something of the chagrin I felt the day I went into the back room to box with Isbell, Gaylord, *et al.* I had lost my cause, if I had any, no less. At least I had given justification to all eclecticism's barking fears.

Going out, the major prophet, his very charming wife, and lovely daughter were standing there in the lobby. I went to them to say good night, but not to apologize.

Said the charming daughter: "Some woman in the audience almost in tears told me to take her greeting to my poor dear 'eclectic' father."

Next evening came the Town Hall meeting,

suggested, I imagine, by Douglas Haskell, but called by help of the Fifth Avenue pioneer Paul Frankl and able Lee Simonson by way of the American Union of Decorative Artists and Craftsmen—Audac. A meeting called to protest against my non-employment by the Fair!

Anti-climax.

Already I had given *plenty* of good reason for such non-employment and was ready to give more. It was surely better to have one architect, out of employment, in these parlous times, than the eight or ten or fifteen already employed on the Fair?

Another group entirely would have come in with me.

This town meeting was prefaced with a dinner at the Crillon to which a congenial exponent of the Fair was invited. He came over to shake hands before whatever it was that was coming.

I didn't know what was coming. And, I guess, by the way he looked, he didn't care.

The hall was packed. Alexander Woolcott in the chair. I have seen Alex bubble with wit in his lair by the river and in his seat at the Algonquin but that night he was efflorescence itself. At least living in New York City does keen the rapier and polish the thrust.

The meeting at once took on an air of laughing gaiety. That changed when Lewis Mumford got up to speak. With the essential manliness and nobility seen in the man as seen in his work he made no attempt to be apologetic or conciliatory. He was earnest and seriously wrote down the matter of the Fair where "modern architecture" was concerned more clearly and effectively into the record than I had done the evening before or could do.

Then Douglas Haskell spoke of his view of the models of the Fair, shown at the League. That intense and brilliant young man's sense of aesthetic right and aesthetic wrong is the life in him. But the whole meeting was unstudied, not arranged: a kind of "impromptu" to see just what would happen. But a definite feeling pervaded, as I have said, that it was post-mortem record.

It was so that Lewis Mumford spoke.

So Haskell spoke.

So spoke Alexander Woolcott.

As for me, I hastily decided to pay my respects to the Fair by building a fair or two—three in fact—of diverse character while the crowd listened.

It seemed to me this would be constructive criticism worth something to architecture and entertaining.

And the only interest I have had in the Fair since first hearing of it, or any hope of it, whatever, was to prevent any such catastrophe to our culture as occurred in 1893.

I hate to see careful, devoted sacrifice of so many faithful years building up a great cause played up by clever pictorializing and salesmanship to snatch the great cause to feather the architectural offices of a few New York and Chicago eclectic plan-factories—however much I might like, or be flattered by, the factors themselves.

So I was placed in awkward position by this meeting because it would seem—generally—that I was present and spoke because I resented being left out by the "commission." Whereas I resent only their quick turnover and pretentious scene-painting as unworthy modern architecture.

As I sat there to speak, several contrasting ideas of a fair that would be modern architecture because genuine to our new structural resources came to me and on my feet to speak the schemes developed as I talked.

THREE PROGRESS FAIRS FOR ONE

I had given the schemes no study—they are all spontaneous. *Modern Scheme One:* As skyscraperism characterizes the thought of the group characterizing the fair—and they had themselves idealized the fair in so many words, as "like New York seen from one of its own high buildings . . ."

Why not, then, the Fair itself the apotheosis of the skyscraper?

Build a great skyscraper in which the Empire State Building might stand free in a central interior court-space which would be devoted to all the resources of the modern elevator.

Instead of the old stage-props of the previous fairs, miles of picture buildings faked in cheap materials wrapped around a lagoon, a fountain or theatrical waterfall in the middle—butchered to make a Roman holiday—let there be, for once, a genuine modern *construction*.

If elevators could handle the population of New York, they could handle the crowds at the Fair. Handle the crowds directly from several expansive tiers of mechanized parking space as great terraces from which the true skyscraper itself would directly rise. The construction should be merely the steel itself designed as integral pattern in the framing. Then concrete slabs for floors projecting as cantilever balconies from floor to floor—garden floors intervening as restaurants.

Instead of glass for enclosure—some of our many light, transparent, glass substitutes might be used. The multitudinous areas thus created could be let to the various exhibitors. The entire feature of the top stories could be garden observatories, pleasure places. A vast auditorium might join at the base with a vast stadium in order to give stability and breadth of base to the skyscraper and handle such great aggregations of people on the ground. This tower construction of steel might rise from the triple decked parking terraces, one corner of the terraces projecting and extending into the lake two ways at right angles to make piers and harbors for water craft. Beneath the lake nearby where the reflections of the tower would fall, powerful jets of the lake itself rising by way of inserted power pumps to great height. All to be illuminated by modern light projecting apparatus projecting toward the tower and projecting from it. The lake thus at contingent points becoming a series of great fountains irradiated by light.

The Lake Front Park itself would thus become merely landscape adjunct to the great modern structure which might easily, and modestly, rise two hundred and forty-five stories. The total construction say two thousand five hundred feet above the lake level—or a half mile high.

The clouds might naturally or artificially drift across its summit. Or effects be created by aeroplanes laying down colored ribbons of smoke to drift across it.

Such a construction—the fake architecture of the New York functioneer omitted—today would be no impossible feat, financially or structurally. In fact, entirely within reach as safe and reasonable. Practical.

And it could stay thus, a feature of the Chicago Lake Front, beautiful as the Eiffel Tower never was. The Eiffel Tower would reach only well below its middle.

Every floor would be a practical resource for future affairs of every sort. The business of the city itself might move into it and all its minor branches. Still there would be room enough left for a mighty, continuous, never-ending industrial fair that would embrace the products of the entire civilized world in Chicago.

Something accomplished worthy of a century of progress? The beacons from the top would reach adjoining states: the radio from the antennae lifting from the tower-crown would be in touch with all the world.

But if not skyscraper minded and preferring to roam instead of to be lifted up on high . . . then

Modern Scheme Two: A characteristic weaving of this age of steel in tension. Accept from John Roebling his pioneer work—the message of the Brooklyn Bridge.

Build noble pylons—since the Fair commissioners seemed to like the word "pylon"—on the Lake Front Park 500 feet apart each way until enough park, including threading waterways, had been covered to accommodate all exhibitors on the park level and in one balcony level surrounding the enclosed area. This canopy to be anchored by steel cables to the outer series of appropriate pylons. Weave, in main and minor and intermediate cables, a network that would support transparent fabrications such as we have as modern glass substitutes in our day. And thus make an architectural canopy more beautiful and vast than any ever seen. The canopy could rise five hundred feet at the pylons to fall to one hundred and fifty feet above the park between them. The fabric should fall as a screen at the sides to close the space against the wind. The rain water, falling, would wash the roof slopes clean or they could be flushed from the pylon tops as fountains, the water dropping through openings at the low points of the canopy into fountain basins, features of the system of lagoons that would wind and thread their way through the greenery of the park beneath the canopy.

All trees, foliage, and waterways combined with moving walkways to reach the individual plots allotted to the individual exhibitors. Each individual exhibitor would thus be free to set up his own show and bally-hoo it how he pleased.

The old fair-spirit, exciting as of old—but, thus free to excite the sophisticated modern ego once more.

Well, this type of construction with appropriate illumination and hydro-electric effects would cost less in standardization thus extended and made beautiful than the petti-fogging, picture-making, privatistic individual buildings of many architects only interfering with exhibits and exhibitions in order to say exactly nothing. And say it in the same old way. Tagged—only tagged—as "new." And, at least, the great "pylons" might remain as lighting features of the Lake Front Park. Whereas the privatistic buildings faked in synthetic cardboard and painted would all have to be thrown away some day.

Or—more romantically inclined? Then:

Modern Scheme Three: There is the Chicago harbor already enclosed against the turbulence of Lake Michigan.

Why not use it for a genuine holiday? A gay festival for the eyes. Why not a pontoon fair?

Make sealed metal cylinders, air exhausted like those of the catamaran, these to be used for floating foundations. Fabricate light, thin tubes, some large and some not so large. Some slender and each in any length. Fabricate them in pulp in order to be very light. Soaked and stiffened in waterproofing. Use these "reeds" in rhythmic verticality, grouping them to get support for light roof-webbing. Again use the steel strand anchored to the metal drums to get roof cover.

Large pontoons. Tall buildings. Long buildings. Square buildings. All connected by interesting floating bridges. Floating gardens too, connected to the buildings—the whole ground plan of assembled units to be connected together by linking the units, themselves attractive features, so that all might be joined and yet undulate with no harm to any unit.

Introduce transparent colored glass tubing among the colored pulp tubing. Illuminate the glass, have for once the airy verticality as a sheer legitimate modern fabrication, only aimed at as "a charm of New York."

The parti-colored opaque and transparent verticality would be doubled by direct reflection in the water.

The water itself again to be thrown up by inserted force-pumps to great heights in enormous quantity, costing little but power. The whole illuminated—irradiating and irradiated by light—an iridescent fair of iridescent, opalescent, and opaque "reeds."

The whole a picturesque pleasurable "float."

Modern pageantry, this.

And a genuine thing in itself. Appropriate space could thus be easily created for specific purposes and adapted to suit each purpose: all these varied units linked together as a continuous, varied, brilliant modern circumstance.

After the Fair certain appropriate units could be detached and floated to an anchorage in the lagoons of the various parks and waterways to serve as restaurants and good-time places.

And I said that if there are these three ideas genuine and practical as Modern Architecture, be sure there were, as easily, three hundred to choose from.

Well I had done my best to get out of a trying situation. Of course I can hear the group of eclectics saying they had thought of all these schemes themselves and rejected them. To reject them would be their judgment and, no doubt, their necessity.

The exponent of the "Fair" group of eclectics, called up by Alex, came from his place in the audience to tell, in rebuttal, a little story. And in passing, here are

TWO CORRECTIONS

Correction the First concerns the little story: Shortly before, I had first met and visited the "Fair" exponent at his home. I greatly enjoyed the visit, for, it seemed, I had found a friend. We had but one, or was it two, cocktails, when the matter of architect and client came up. In answer to my friend's question, "How do you get your buildings built?" I said, "Well, I develop a general scheme and a plan according to the client's requirements. When satisfied I have the right thing, I show it to the client." Then in answer to his question, "But what if he wouldn't take it?" he said I had said—"Well, by God, he would *have* to take it."

My friend pounded the table to emphasize the "have to." Showing clearly, so he must have thought and wanted those present to think—and it was his point to show—my unfitness to work *with* anyone. This, as he remembered the conversation.

The affair is unimportant, but I am inclined to give the conversation between us as I remember it.

Ex: "Frank, I don't know how you feel about it. But I believe if a client wants a door here or a window there I give it to him. If he wants this or that room here or there or so big, he gets it and where he wants it. And after the thing is all together, if I can't make architecture out of the thing I camouflage the whole business. I am camouflaging a house now." (Next day in his office he showed me the model of that house, pink, blue, and green triangles cutting the masses of the house to pieces.)

W: "Easy enough, but on that basis, Ray, any contractor could do for your client all you do. Any fool decorator can camouflage. Where do you come in as an architect?"

Ex: "All right, then, how do you get your houses built? By telling the owner what he's got to do? Or do you hypnotize him?"

W: "Yes, I hypnotize him. There is nothing so hypnotic as the truth. I show him the truth about the thing he wants to do as I have prepared myself to show it to him. And he will see it. If you know, yourself, what should be done and get a scheme founded on sensible fact, the client will see it and take it, I have found."

Ex: "But suppose he *wouldn't* take it?"

W: "But, by God, Ray, he *would* take it."

Now this is the true story. A surety that a client *would is* not the same as saying he *must*.

No client must take anything he doesn't want from any architect whatsoever. To dictate to any client would be to lose the client.

Correction the Second concerns the other public reference to myself by another specific "Fair" exponent, the prophet of the evening before. "But Frank Lloyd Wright can't stay in line. Frank Wright never has stayed in line"—oratorical gesture apparently anticipating the gesture of the "little story."

Now I submit exponent-the-second never met me in his life before he came to the dinner—ostensibly in my honor—at the Architectural League in New York City last May, where and when all and sundry "broke down, wept, confessed" and seemed to enjoy a good time. Nor, for that matter, had the first. Both expressed themselves "surprised" to find me so agreeable and really "one of them," as they put it. Why—I don't know.

So what was really meant was that so far as known, I couldn't be bent out of line and stay bent that way.

Stay in line? The diplomatic remark entitles a glance at the record.

Six years "in line," willing pencil in the hand of a master with whom I often disagreed, serving him well. Still loyal to him. He, when he died, still loyal to me.

Every building I've built I have built *with* my client in the best sense of mutual appreciation, except three.

One hundred and seventy-nine of them in all. Single-handed. No protecting, prospecting partners.

And this: I have stayed "in line" with the principles of an ideal I believe true to my own country and worth a man's time for thirty-two years. While eclecticism ran from pillar pseudo-classic to postmodernism—I stayed "in line" with principle.

No, not in line with "salesmanship" in the age that is martyr to it. And does it really matter that work must come to me instead of my going out after work?

Am I taking all this too seriously?

Certainly. But it is typical of what I have met, and still meet and must go on meeting. I am reconciled. Really, I like the company of a number of clever and plausible eclectics. I merely resent gratuitous attempts to make me "difficult" in order to justify the eclectics' latest attempt to make modern architecture over to fit eclecticism. In this resentment lies such bitterness as I know. It will pass.

So far as architecture goes, I am sure, like Samuel Butler's "Festus Jones," eclectics haven't much artist-conscience and what little they have is guilty.

As the "Fair" exponent at the Town Hall meeting came forward to tell his little story he said that "he had come to the meeting to have his face lifted." In surprise Alex Woolcott, who had called him, said he didn't quite know what the gentleman meant by "coming to have his *face* lifted . . . because he had sent in word to have his seat saved."

This broke up the meeting and I had no chance to say then what I have written here.

Another characteristic "comeback" at the Town Hall meeting was the statement that more architects should be in evidence to pass judgment on the situation.

The remark aimed at Mumford, Haskell—both life-students of architectural results—and at Woolcott. The implication was that they could not, themselves, build a building. Architects could and should therefore be the better judges of architecture.

Later, the same question arising, Lewis Mumford's reply was, "He could not lay an egg either, but he could tell a good one by testing it!"

According to the exponents, you see, only the hen who laid the egg could tell whether it was a good egg or not.

The following evening—Thursday—I was posted to speak on Twentieth Century Architecture at the New School of Social Research on Twelfth Street, Dr. Alvin Johnson presiding.

Henry Churchill introduced me in the very satisfactory auditorium designed by big-hearted Jo Urban. Jo designed the building for the New School and I could not refrain from saying complimentary things about it. It seemed so remarkable that it should be there in New York at all. Jo Urban is one Viennese gift to the country that has not gone wrong. Jo's touch is as Mozartian as his character is Falstaffian. He is responsible for more lyrical beauty in our world of decoration than anyone I know. He was in Europe so I couldn't get him up on the stage to keep me company. But there was no room for him. The stage was filled. As I came in the street door, Doctor Johnson was turning several hundred away, asking them to come again some other time. It hurt me that anyone should really want to hear a serious lecture on architecture and not be able to get in to hear it.

Several appealed directly to me to let them in and I took them in with me.

Not willing to trust to extemporizing, I had carefully prepared a lecture on Twentieth Century Architecture for this occasion. To treat the subject adequately with best thought where real issues are at stake, a well-studied written discourse that may be read will always be best.

Since you have had no discourse from me on modern architecture as a whole, it is perhaps time to sum up in different terms my best thought on the subject matter of this book. Inasmuch as this lecture is a unit, I might take it out and make it a separate booklet. So this "lecture," too, may be "skipped." But since it contains, compact, the essence of work and life as philosophy of form, line, material, and symbol—here is the unit in itself.

TWENTIETH CENTURY ARCHITECTURE

Where architecture, as essentially human, once expressed former civilizations, as *Life,* in our great united experiment architecture finds popular expression as systems of eclectic "taste" in imitation. Fashionable emulation has made our architecture a decoration, our decoration a furbishing. The Germans call it "*Geschmacksschematismus.*"

American architecture? An entirely eclectic question. The question? What "style" do you elect? Or what style did you get?

Our three graces: Mrs. Plasterbilt, fashionable eclectic; Mrs. Gablemore, arch-conservative; and Miss Flat-top, more advanced, but all devotees of commonplace elegance, have definite partisan "tastes."

If they would have a "pure" style? There they have Dr. Cram as Gothicist, Dr. Bacon, Greco-Romanist, Dr. Platt, Italian—"pasticcio." Yesterday Stanford White was connoisseur and specialist in assorted Renaissance, Hunt, the best Château man of his day. Richardson—great emotionalist—reincarnated the Romanesque.

Hundreds of fashionable architects, "T" square and triangle in hand, are still standing by Thomas Jefferson's grave, intent to be as Georgian as he, but not with so good an excuse. He brought his Georgian with him as he did his clothes, because he had none other.

Or would you have, perhaps, Camden or "Collegiate Gothic"? The latter harks back to Oxford, so, very conservative, indeed, that it is Mrs. Gablemore's choice. Owing to special impetus from Yale it is elect.

Or, more romantically inclined, do you lean to the Mediterranean now? Or to Midi-Romanesque . . . by way of Father La Tour? Or still yearning for Spanish—it is as easily yours. The Spaniards, not Gothicized, got their Spanish from Italy. The Mexicans got theirs from Spain. We took ours from Mexico by way of Father Junipero. But all these varieties of Spanish, however mixed, may be had. Any decorating department of our dry goods store is competent mixture. All periods, "Spanish" or otherwise, gone a little confused. Stale, now? Maybe. The tide ebbs.

Nevertheless—dear Mrs. Plasterbilt and no less expensive Mrs. Gablemore, the makings to suit all or each choice aimed at in the quotidian assortment may still be had in American urban, even suburban antique shops, in the *original*. Or Grand Rapids exists to help you out.

Miss Flat-top, younger, more advanced, a little bold, perhaps, but star of our expectancy, prefers, at the moment, the "modernistic." It is the newest popular urban "taste" in these United States. Unfortunately the modern as "istic" is too soon on sale. It, too, sometimes in a good way, often in a sad way, is to be had in the department stores of the larger cities. And, in a bad way or in a better way, in the urban and suburban decorators' shops in the provinces. All because of the Paris market with madame, in general, but with you, especially, Miss Flat-top. And it is not to your discredit.

But beware! As the ornamental Columbian Fair of 1893–1925 had its clean-shaven propagandists for ornamentia (rest their souls in peace!) so now the straight line and flat plane, by way of the Paris Exposition of 1925, has its ornamentally bearded propagandists for ornaphobia, with another Progress fair coming along probably to add tired to tired and add it again.

Enough! With us it has been as you see: "Off with the Old Architecture, on with the New," in periodic cycles of twenty-seven years. The popular purveyors of these deciduous effects themselves change, or are changed, periodically, as our surface decoration changes: three new series of names arrive and three new series fade within the twenty-seven year cycles, spaced, on the average, about nine years O.C. That is to say, nine years on centers. New arrivals at the moment are happily making hay in haste while the eclectic's sun, it is usually "*Eclectic,*" shines "modernistic."

I imagine, however, that choice is seldom, if ever, the fashionable eclectic's own, except on rather illiberal terms, because either fashionable or academic eclectic is early and easily had by fad or fancy for any fashion, if only it is "being done."

I do not imagine this has changed.

At the moment it is the latest from Paris.

So the American fashionable and academic eclectic is "culture-curious," not yet "culture-conscious."

What our plain, or uncurious people get now is little better, since the carpenter gave up to the mill-man, the plasterer listened to the inferior desecrator, and the mason was instructed by the antiquarian. These honest mechanics were popular American architects before "culture" corrupted them too. By way of culture they fell from poetry—crushed into fakery.

Thus it is that America puts a shame upon heredity and a curse upon environment.

And now, gentle listeners, apologizing to Mrs. Plasterbilt, Mrs. Gablemore, and especially Miss Flat-top, who may or may not be the star of our expectancy, that is to say as she may be only another eclectic or may know what she is about and be genuine in her revolt, such depraved promiscuity, irresponsible, shameless borrowing—such as this—in the name of the equivocal-personal-idiosyncrasy called "taste" is exactly what never happened in the world before. No—not even in the next worse era, the dubiety of the Victorian Era in England. Such fatuous demoralization did not occur even when round arches began to grow pointed.

Certainly no such soul-depravity existed among any of those great peoples sending hundreds of thousands of competent representatives to flourish in this great United Experiment. At this moment we are all undoubtedly—here—delegates by succession or election from every nation on earth, each with his or her little matter of "taste," cultivated regardless, which is, after all, only a matter of ignorance. A matter of ignorance because "taste" is not individuality. "Taste" is, merely, personal idiosyncrasy, cultivated.

As a consequence, since the country is free and choice a license, "taste" means that the Anglo-American is apt to choose Rococo; the Franco-American to prefer Hopi, or Africano; the German-American, Georgian or Mexicano; the Italo-American to feel at home only in Parisian L'Art Nouveaux; the Russo-American, to be consistent, must prefer "modernistic"; the Jewish-American, unless a matter of synagogue, say, a little of the best of each or all together, please. And so the ubiquitous eclectics roam unvaried in the varieties while the one hundred percenters go to and fro as they please, to emerge with the "accidental" more or less modified as occidental. In architecture, the lid is off—Utopia—you see? No questions asked beyond the, "Madam, what do you prefer?"—in this popular "speak-easy" of the styles.

Well, Love itself began as Lust. Perhaps a free Architecture may evolve from License. Who knows?

But meantime, is it life?—No! Something *on* life, not *of* it, except as economic issue. Something for Mr. Plasterbilt, Mr. Gablemore, and Miss Flat-top to pay for on the installment plan.

Is it architecture? Yes—thrown away!

Is it characteristic? It is . . . all too characteristic. The "melting pot" has snatched and broken to tidbits the styles of the civilized world eaten all up piecemeal and flung the empty shells, its houses, together into a scrap-pile of modern opportunity, modern methods, and modern Ideas of modern Men. We call the eclectic's scrap-pile American architecture!

Since America became culture-curious, inimical choice has mutilated reason, destroying sanity in the name of "taste." Were true *variety* seen in all this, that, at least, would be something. But no. The monotony-in-variety of "monogoria" is net result of American eclecticism's attempts to be "different." This monotony of false pretense is academically defended as preferable to monotony in monstrosity.

The assumption is that monstrosity is what we would have had had we earlier taken up architecture seriously and tried to learn something. But unfortunately, since the forests have been cut down, and the lumber wasted in various carpenter-built make-shifts by the million, we have found permanent building materials to record much of this usurious, gratuitous insult to tradition, from which we have learned nothing.

No matter. All is yet experiment to the Great Experiment. Americans, although their vice is become the "device," are ruled more by ideas, when they have any, and less by traditions, than any other people of the world. Should true ideas concerning architecture become popular—truth may become popular?—the misdeeds of a day America can afford to throw away. How quickly all this we call "Architecture" comes to pass or comes to grief. The law of growth as organic is relentless and remorseless. The "device" we need now (since we are committed for life, all the life we have, to mechanical devices) is some mechanical device to speed up spiritual growth . . . But there, any device lies . . . useless, and our protected, pretty, conventional "things" are eventually, even now, at the mercy of the savage, implacable rhythms of the machine.

Let us then, for the purpose of this hour together, not regard this recession by way of eclecticism too seriously. Let it be as it is, architectural travesty, not tragedy. And as we proceed to pick up the latest issue in sight, Miss Flat-top has, innocently, perhaps hopefully, been calling it a bad name, the "modernistic," let us stop a moment to think . . . and reason a while, together.

Such licentious waste of ourselves as we have called "taste" in getting ourselves built becomes, at last, important. No eclectic affair whatever can see America through the struggle that is coming in the twentieth century. Out of the ground into the Light is the way of growth and not groping or two-stepping by way of more artificial background into complete darkness.

As Sheldon Cheney has truly said in his *New World Architecture,* we are, as a nation, standing at the beginning of a world slope in this obscured human interest called architecture. We, as a people, can descend no lower than we are, so, however steep or slow that slope for us, it can only be upward toward the time when it will be as natural for things to be genuine and grow beautiful as it is nowadays for things to be false and remain ugly. Art has always been inseparably connected with the full bloom of a country's life. Wherever art has declined—that is to say—got itself as antique, anybody's antique, I say, into the hands of the connoisseur or the dealer either going or coming the whole country never grows, or, having grown must soon degenerate.

A morally strong and simple-hearted people will bring forth, instinctively, a strong and healthy art. Let us, therefore, at the moment console ourselves with the thought that we cannot degenerate. We cannot degenerate because, in art, "generation" is something America has never known. This affair we call "taste" may pall and change—as it does. But it is not high enough as a quality to "degenerate."

Yes—America is still young, but unfortunately for the new architectural opportunities emerging as natural to her, all ancient "Classical" or "pseudo-classic" American architects have copied as architecture were a kind of sculpture. That is to say, all these buildings of pseudo-classic tradition were some great block-mass of some building material, "sculpted," that is to say, fashioned or modeled into desired features from the outside. Exterior therefore in idea and in sense. Always there was an "outside" as outside and an "inside" as inside. The two were quite separate and independent of each other. Holes were cut in the block-mass for a little light and

some air; the deeper the hole looked to be, that is, the thicker the sides of it were—architects called the sides the "reveal"—the better. Great attention was paid to rather a pretentious hole to get in or get out of . . . So, all more or less resembled fortifications and often were actual fortifications.

They had to be fortifications, for civilization itself was then frankly founded upon force. Usually the classical and feudal dwellings were little masonry caverns. If more pretentious, they were caves.

Viewed from the outside, we must conceive this sculptured block of building materials of this period as hollowed out within before we can imagine anyone living in the heart of the block. At least that is the essential aesthetic sense of the whole.

Now this honorable enough, ancient idea of a building as masonry-mass, ornamented as may be, is now a serious set-back for architecture in our civilization founded upon Freedom. Indeed, the survival of this "exterior" ideal, itself, is mostly what interferes with any hope for fruitful life in our own country today.

This ancient ideal of building may be seen to have received its final illumination, therefore ruination, in the Renaissance. Michaelangelo [*sic*], great sculptor that he was, crashed the ruin when he finally hurled the Pantheon on top of the Parthenon. They named the result of the great Italian's impulsive indiscretion, St. Peter's. The World called it a day, celebrating the great act ever since in the sincerest form of human flattery possible. As we well ought to know, being specialists ourselves, that form is *imitation.*

Buonarroti, himself a sculptor, naturally set about making the grandest statue he could conceive out of Italian Renaissance architecture. This great new church dome of his, St. Peter's, was empty of meaning, had no significance at all except as the pope's mitre has it. But, in fact, this dome was just the sort of thing temporal *authority* had been looking for as a symbol. And symbol of "authority," holy or unholy, the dome immediately became.

Before Michaelangelo turned architect, domes, both great and small, had their haunches, that is to say the "thrust" of the dome (for a dome is an arch) well down within the building itself

St. Sophia is a noble example of true doming, built when the Roman empire was Oriental.

But the sculptor divorced his dome from the building—got it up higher than all other domes. He got it way up in the air on stilts. That was better. Much more grand! But history records cracks seen opening in the base of the dome. The massive masonry arch—a dome is an arch—was pushing out on all sides, with nothing but air to push against. This threatened the dome itself and the stilts on which it stood. A desperate call was sent for the blacksmith. A grand chain was needed—links the thickness of your leg. Desperate the hurry at the forge, to keep this monumental grandeur up there long enough to do its deadly work.

The blacksmith's chain was finally fastened around the haunches of the great dome that had been lifted up out of its natural bearings, lifted to immortality by our hero, the great sculptor. Ah! as an architect, I can imagine the relief with which the sculptor crawled into bed when the obliging and competent blacksmith had made all secure, and slept for thirty-six hours without once turning over.

And yet, proceeding to our own national Capitol, and downward to the domes of our state capitols, then to the lesser domes of our county courthouses, and from then on down to the little domes of the city halls—there the accepted symbol, saved by the blacksmith, stands. It may now be seen in the great new country, dedicated to freedom, proclaiming its debt to an artist's impulsive indiscretion, as America's grandest heritage from the rebirth of architecture in Italy—the Renaissance. Our native grando-mania took that form, that is all.

Sir Christopher Wren on behalf of England had previously borrowed the dome from the sculptor, but wisely, beforehand, borrowed the chain for St. Paul's from the sculptor's blacksmith. Amusing record: canny Sir Christopher said his masonry dome would have stood without the chain! All the same he did not try it. His caution showed him more a man of sense than his remark showed him competent as an architect.

But, worshipping the dome, Usonia's architects were more shrewd, even, than Sir Christopher.

Our grand masonry domes are all blacksmith iron shells imitating the sculptor's masonry.

So the "blacksmith" has arrived and the architect has gone out, whether for a recess or a holiday, to return or never to return, who can say, unless he comes back converted to the kinetic energy of this age and true master of the blacksmith's ironwork as no imitation whatsoever.

Here, out of a great sculptor's sense of grandeur in an art not quite his own, we see a tyranny that might well make the tyrannical skyscraper—our own St. Peter's of the present hour—sway in its socket, sick with envy.

Yes . . . how dangerous imitation is. And how tragic to allow authority to usurp the functions of validity.

Thus paying our respects to the dome—no longer a dome, but complicated ironwork imitating the unnatural masonry of the original one—is only by way of emphasis of the fact that all ancient architecture of monumental character, the duomo, the temple, the palazzo, the minster, was sculp, sculpturesque, sculptorial, or sculptoretto. And also to insist that all artificiality, as such, is soon carried to excess. Hyper-artificiality invariably becomes commonplace "grando-mania" . . . a form of senility.

How ridiculous, when not dangerous or vicious, is all cowardly or extravagant senility, that would obliterate the living by sentimentalizing over dead!

Our country is now where she has to choose between such sentimental senility as official, academic stabilization . . . and progress. President Hoover has officially recommended—senility. Such folly is the political consequence of automatically constituting a pretty good executive, in some respects an authority in the Fine Arts. Authority is soon the enemy of validity.

To sum up: As the only order this ancient sculptorial order was honorable. Subsequently the old order became betrayal. Because of that hyper-artificiality called the "Renaissance" or "rebirth" it came to us. Eventually, in our eclectic rebirths of that eclecticism the ancient order becomes finally a cultural curse, an economic crime, and a public nuisance.

It was Schumann who said of Beethoven's Fifth Symphony that revolution could take place within the four walls of a symphony and the police be none the wiser. And, making its way through the widespread consequences of oblique surmise called good "taste": coming through orgiastic depravity by way of the straight line and the flat plane, came the clean, swift outlines of organic simplicity. A new sense of depth appeared that was, in itself, a demand for new integrity. We call this new sense a new dimension. This new dimension is no more than a spiritual interpretation of the third. Here was revolution! Abroad in the American town—and America was none the wiser. But this uncommonsense was coming to light at the beginning of the twentieth century on our own ground, never, I hope, to gain such "authority," nor any artificial "stabilization," such as came to us by way of the sculptor's papal dome.

As *new validity* here was revolutionary sense of architecture; entirely new sense of building sprouted in Usonian soil, parallel to truths of being found innate in the simplicities of Jesus of Nazareth: seen, now, as natural in the organic philosophy of the Chinese sage, Laotze. Yes, my functionalists, why attempt to rely on science and reason?

Why eradicate the force at the heart of the whole matter?

The world will weary of negation in whatsoever form. The moving world tires of the ambitious protestant however he may be disguised. Let us all willingly confess that Modern Architecture *is,* first of all, in the nature of a spiritual conviction—detail, curtail, appropriate, or falsify it how you may. If this primal spiritual insight *as conviction* is lacking, no more than reiteration of certain bald, machine-age commonplaces will be the barren result of any devotion, however aesthetic.

Unfortunately for Modern Architecture, the very machine itself, functioning as ubiquitous publicity, makes it unnecessary to build many buildings to become an architect. Manage to get one built, somehow, by help of some contractor, write a book about it, then write another book about that book. The machine, well managed, will soon make you an architect and contractors will go on building the buildings.

Already barren emulation, appearance made an aim instead of character made a purpose, *imitates* machinery in buildings. Future generations can only move such imitations down to the highway, set them up on the wheels on which they seem to belong, and send them on their way. Machine facility works both ways—for progress and against it. But let us believe with the greatest and most prophetic romanticist, "that all one does for the truth—or tries to do against it, in the end serves it equally well."

Taking shape in the noble realm of ideas as architecture today to make machine-age increment, that is to say, to make our machine power and our millions democratically beneficent, is one great new integrity—a sense of the within as reality—and four limitless new resources.

The first new resource is a super-material. Glass.

The second new resource is a new standard means. Tenuity.

The third new resource is a new sense of the Nature of Materials.

The fourth new resource is Pattern as Natural.

All five together create new grasp on building and are demanding new significance as architecture in this twentieth century. All five resources are not only bases for Modern Architecture in this century, but are altogether, no less, a lesson to be learned by Modern Life itself.

Because of new riches in materials, new power in work, and notwithstanding our present distraction, a deepening sense of life—all are at this moment modern.

But this significance and these resources are new, only because architecture as "rebirth," for five centuries, culminating in such febrile imitation of imitations as are seen in our Plasterbilt, Gablemore, and Flat-top "American" architecture, is significant of insignificance. Not architecture but economic crime. Not art but a pretentious curse.

And, if you will be patient for a little while—scientist Einstein asked us for three days to explain the far less pressing and practical matter of relativity—we will take each demand in order, as with the five fingers of the hand.

We will begin with the first great integrity—this sense of the "within" as reality—as with the thumb. Because it is important to the other four resources as the thumb is to the four fingers. And we will see in all, taken together, this capacity for new grasp on architecture.

The first great integrity is deeper, more intimate sense of reality than was ever pagan. Or than even now is Christian. This although it has been living for more than two centuries innate in the simplicities of Jesus and organic in the natural philosophy of Laotze.

Said Ong Giao Ki, Chinese sage, "Poetry is the sound of the heart."

Well . . . this new sense of architecture, like poetry, is the *nature,* if not the sound, of the "within."

Architecture, as modern, now becomes the expression of the liveable interior space of the room itself. *The room-space itself must "come through!"* The "room" must be seen as architecture, or we have none. No longer do we have outside as outside. Or inside as inside seen as two separate things. Now the outside may come inside, and the inside may go outside. They are *of* each other.

This interior-space concept is the first broad new integrity as the basis for general new significance. Add to this for the sake of brevity, though it might well stand alone, that it is in the nature of the modern building to grow from its site, come out of the ground into the light—the ground seen as component part of the building itself—and we have primarily a new ideal of building as organic: "dignified as a tree in the midst of nature."

A new ideal for architecture as for our general culture.

Thus the end of agglomeration is seen in this rise of organic-entity by way of this old yet new and deeper sense of reality. In this we recognize the natural. Faith in the natural is the faith we need to grow on in the coming age of our twentieth century.

We come now to the first of the four new resources, glass. This first resource is new and is a "super-material" because it holds new means for awakened sensibilities. It too is a qualification in itself. If known in ancient times, glass would have abolished

ancient architecture completely. This super-material—GLASS—as we now have it, is a miracle. Air in air to keep air out or keep it in. Light itself in light, to diffuse or reflect or refract light.

By means of glass, then, the first integrity may find prime means of realization. Open reaches of the ground may enter as the building and the building interior may reach out and associate with the ground. Ground and building will, thus, become more and more obvious as directly related to each other in openness to environment, realizing the far-reaching implications and effects of the first integrity—the organic interior-space concept. Realization in all the vast variety of characteristic buildings needed for life in this complex age.

By means of glass, then, something of the freedom of our arboreal ancestors in their trees becomes more likely precedent for the freedom of twentieth-century life, just as the savage animals that "holed in" for protection were more characteristic of life based on the might of feudal times or the now "classical" times based on the labor of the chattel slave. In a free country, ourselves free, we may come out into the light without animal fear.

Yes, more important, perhaps, than all beside, here, by way of glass, the sunlit space as reality may and does become a higher order of the human spirit. A sense of cleanliness directly related to living in sunlight is coming. And with the extended vistas gained by blending buildings with ground-levels, or slopes and gardens, this new sense will begin to move us in building all our buildings.

More and more we will desire the sun.

The more we desire the sun, the more we will desire the freedom of the ground.

New space-values will enter into our ideas of life, appropriate to the ideal that is our own. Congestion will no longer encourage the "space-makers for rent." The "space-maker for rent" will himself be—"for rent" or "vacant."

So, to liberate this new sense of appropriate interior space as reality, which I hope, and I foresee, will soon be at work in us in this machine age, is this new qualification called glass. A super-material qualified to qualify us not only to escape from the

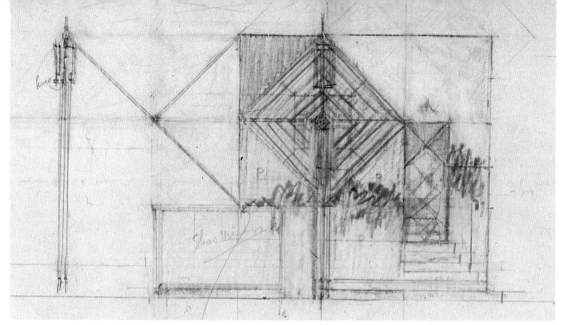

Standard Overhead Service Station (Project). 1932. Sketch elevation. Pencil and color pencil on tracing paper, 21 x 17".
FLLW Fdn# 3206.001

prettified cavern of our present domestic architecture as from the cave of our past, but waking in us active desire for such simplicity as will be seen as clear countenance of nature. Building again seen as nature of construction.

Construction itself now seen as nature pattern.

And this dawning sense of the *Within* as reality, seen as *Nature*.

Before long, by way of glass, the garden will be the building as much as the building is the garden. Walls are vanishing.

The cave is disappearing.

Walls themselves will become as windows, and windows as we know them will be seen no more. Ceilings will become as window-walls, too, often enough. The textile may now be used as a beautiful robe for space, an attribute of architecture instead of the decorator's camouflage. Modern mechanical heating, integral-lighting, and standardized-unit sanitation all make it reasonable as twentieth-century ideal to abolish building as either box-ment or borough.

Senseless elaboration and false mass have become insulting and oppressive. Senseless elaboration and false mass were tyrannical as conspicuous waste in all nineteenth century architecture wherever the American architect went. But now as second resource, resource essential to modern

architecture to cut down outrageous mass waste and mass lying in the principle of continuity. You must come with me for a moment, into "engineering," so called . . . an unavoidable strain upon your attention. You can't understand architecture as *modern* unless you do come.

Classic architecture knew only the post as *upright*, or column, knew only the beam as the "horizontal" resting upon the upright, or column. Two things, you see, one thing on top of another thing.

Ancient building science consisted simply in the various uses of these two things, but, really, it was just sticking up something in wood or stone and putting something in wood or stone on top of it: super-imposition, you see?

The Greeks developed this simple act of super-imposition pretty far in the way of refinement. The Roman builders, too, when they forgot the Greeks and brought the beam over as a curve by way of the arch, did something new of the same sort. But all architectural features made by any such "classic" agglomeration were killed, for us, by cold steel, though the corpses encumber American ground everywhere unburied. This simple principle of support and supported will always be valid, but both support and supported may now, by means of inserted or welded strands or filaments of steel, be united as one physical body.

So the new order wherever steel enters construction says: Weld these two things (post and beam) together by means of the steel strands buried and stressed within the mass material or electric-welded where steel meets steel.

Where beam leaves off and post begins is no longer seen because it no longer is. Steel in tension enables the support to slide into the supported, or the supported to grow into the support as a tree-branch into its tree-trunk. Therefrom arise a new series of interior physical reactions I here call "continuity." And as consequence the new aesthetic or appearance we call plasticity and call modern is no longer an appearance, but becomes the normal countenance of reality. The steel strands may so lie in an extended member, that the extension may be economical of material and be safe construction. There, as the branch, you may see the cantilever: the cantilever is one important phase of this second new structural resource demanding new significance.

Plasticity, modest new countenance in our architecture twenty-five years ago, but denied simple means, had eliminated all the separate identities of the post and beam architecture, known as pseudo-classic. But now, steel in tension enters eventually to arrive at actual, total plasticity if desired. And it now enters as physical *reality*.

To illustrate this magic simplifier we call "plasticity," see it as flexibility in the human hand. What makes any hand expressive? Flowing continuous line and continuous surfaces seen articulate of the structure of the hand as a whole. The line is seen as "hand" line. The plane seen as "hand" surface. Strip the hand to the separate identities of joined bones, and plasticity as an expression of the hand would disappear. We would be getting back to the joinings, breaks, jolts, and joints of ancient architecture. So plasticity is the reverse of agglomeration.

Already, plasticity in this sense, for twenty-seven years or more, has been unrecognized aesthetic ideal for such simplification as required by the Machine.

As significant outline and expressive surface,

this aesthetic of plasticity, as physical continuity, may now be supreme as the physical-body of our Architecture.

Of course, it is easier to cheat with plastic-simplicity than it is to cheat with naked structure. So, unluckily, here is the modernistic picture-maker's deadly facility for imitation at ease again.

But architecture is architecture only when plasticity is genuine expression of construction just as the articulate line and surface of the hand is articulate of the *structure* of the hand. My own later work, arriving at steel, first used continuity as actual stabilizing principle economizing building in the concrete ferro-block system I devised.

In the form of the cantilever or as horizontal continuity this new economy saved the Imperial Hotel in the great earthquake of 1922.

But in the new design for St. Mark's Tower, the principle of continuity economizes material, labor and space in a more developed sense and gives to the structure the significant outlines of remarkable stability. Instead of false masonry-mass comes significant outline and the pattern of structure.

Continuity realizes remarkable economy of labor and building materials and space.

Of course, in the ancient order, there was no thought of economy of materials. The more massive the whole looked, the better. But seen in the light of these new economic interior forces liberated by the tensile strength of a strand of steel in this machine age, the old order was weak with weight as the Buonarroti dome. Weak . . . because there could be no interrelation between the two elements of support and supported to reinforce each other.

So this tremendous new resource of *tenuity*—this quality of *pull* in a building—see it ushering in our new era in John Roebling's Brooklyn Bridge—was lacking in all ancient architecture.

The steel strand as a common material had not been born.

Today this element of continuity may cut down structural substance nearly one half. It may cut that half in two again by elimination of needless features due to the simplification called plasticity.

And by utilizing mass production in the factory in this connection, some idea of the remarkable new economies of modern architecture may be seen, approaching any well-built machine.

Involved as a matter of design in this mass production, however, are those involute reactions to which I have referred and that the building engineer yet knows little about. These, however, he is learning to calculate.

As the first great integrity and first two new resources appeared out of the interior nature of building, so, now—naturally interior to the nature of building—comes the third new resource, found in the nature of materials themselves.

As many different properties as there are different materials used to build the building will naturally qualify, modify, and even variously determine all architectural form whatever.

A stone building will no more *be* nor *look* like a steel building. A pottery, or terra-cotta building, will not be or look like a stone building. A wood building will look like none other, or it will glorify the stick. A steel and glass building could not possibly look like anything but itself. It will glorify steel and glass. And so on all the way down the long list of available riches in materials: Stone, Wood, Concrete, Metals, Glass, Textiles, Pulp, and Pigment; riches so great that no comparison with Ancient Architecture is at all sensible or in any way essential to Modern Architecture.

So, as you may see, in this resource architecture is going back to the natural source of all natural things.

To get this new Organic Architecture born, architects are forced to turn their backs upon the eclectic rubbish heaps that encumber our new ground. We are going to grow architecture up out of our own ground. And so far as architecture has gone, in my thought it is a character and a quality of *mind* that enters into human conduct, with social implications that might, at first, confound or astound you. The only basis for fear of them lies in the fact that they are all constructive.

Instinctively all forms of pretense fear reality.

The hypocrite must hate the radical.

This potent third new resource—the Nature of Materials—get at the common sense of the material and the thing to be done. It means the architect beginning at the very beginning according to nature, and sensibly going through with whatever material may be in hand for any purpose according to the methods and sensibilities of Man in this age. When I say "Nature," I mean *structure* seen as a matter of complete design within the thing itself, nature—pattern, that is. It is now this profound internal sense of materials that enters into building as third new resource, to captivate and hold the mind of the modern architect to his work.

Inevitable implication! This new machine age resource requires that all buildings do not resemble each other. The ideal does not require that buildings must be of steel, concrete, or glass. Idiotic waste.

Nor does it even *imply* that mass is no longer beautiful attribute of masonry materials genuinely used. We are entitled to vast variety in our buildings in our complex age.

But, this land richest of all earth in natural resources of new and old materials must now exercise imagination to see in each material, either natural or compounded, inherent style of its own. All beautiful.

Stick. Stone. Steel. Pottery. Concrete. Glass. Yes, pulp, too, as well as pigment. And since this dawning sense of the "within" as reality gives main *motif* for the building, so the uses of the materials of which the building is built will now go far to determine mass, outline, proportion, and character in the form of any and every building.

Strange! At this late day, it is modern architecture that wants modern life to learn to see life as life—because it must learn to see brick as brick, learn to see steel as steel, and glass as glass. Modern thought urges life to demand that a bank look like a bank and not depend upon false columns for credit, urges life to demand that an office-building look like an office-building, even if it should resemble a bee-hive. Life itself should insist that a hotel look and conduct itself like a hotel and not like an office-building. Life should declare that the railroad-station look the railroad station, not look like an ancient temple or monarchic palazzo. A place for opera like a place for opera—if we must have opera. Life should declare a filling station should stick to its work as a filling-station and look the part becomingly—not only like a Colonial diminutive or a pump. Life itself should demand the school as a generously spaced and thought built good time place, a story high—with some light overhead, for growing children in the sun. Modern architecture demands that life itself demand that a house look like the appropriate home of the man whose house it is, if we longer have any men in that connection.

Now this was all new type of common sense in our own architecture nearly thirty years ago. It grew in my own work as it must continue to grow in the work of the world. Insulting as it may seem to say so, it is still a novelty and only a little less strange today.

At last, as the fourth resource demanding new significance, we have arrived at integral ornament—the natural pattern of construction. Here, confessed as spiritual demand for finer significance, comes this subjective element so hard to understand that architects themselves least of all seem to understand.

And this last significance is really no matter for any but the most imaginative mind with some development in artistry. Certainly we must now go higher in the realm of imagination.

Many write good prose who cannot write poetry at all. Although specification is the fashion, as functionalist is the style in writing—poetic prose will always be desirable. But who condones prosaic poetry?

The fourth resource and the fifth demand for new significance is ornament *integral as poetry*.

Heretofore, I have used the word "pattern" instead of ornament to avoid confusion or timely prejudice. But here now the word ornament is in its place, meaning not only *surface qualified by human imagination*, but imagination giving natural pattern to structure itself. Perhaps this phrase says it all without fuller explanation. The resource—integral—ornament—meaning not only imagination qualifying surface—a valuable resource—but a greater means than that by way of *imagination giving natural pattern to structure itself*. A new significance, indeed. Long ago lost.

Evidently then, this expression of the structure as pattern and the nature of materials themselves may be taken further than bare need.

They may be as fully taken by machine, today, as ever by hand of old, into the higher realms of Imagination.

By this higher resource we may give greater structural entity and human significance to the expression of the whole building. This statement is heresy at the moment, so—taken how and taken when? You may well ask.

The Japanese have a word, *eda-buri,* untranslatable, but meaning the formative arrangement or growth habit of the stalk, stem, and leaf of a tree or a plant. The word means the special interior scheme or design—you see how many phrases I am using to render an equivalent for the single Japanese word that expresses the whole matter—that special interior scheme or design that grows pine character in the pine, willow character in the willow, gives peony character to the peony.

Let us in this connection repeat Ong's observation from the Chinese . . . "Poetry is the sound of the heart." Well, so in the same uncommon sense is integral ornament the developed sense or the *pattern-of-structure itself*. Integral pattern is *structure-pattern made visibly articulate*, as it is seen articulate in the trees, or in the peony. It is rhythm. Are we talking about Style? Probably. At any rate, we are talking now about *essential architecture* as distinguished from mere building.

Integral ornament is founded in organic simplicities, just as Beethoven's Fifth Symphony, that amazing revolution in tumult and splendor of sound, was built on four tones, based upon a rhythm a child could play on the piano with one finger. Imagination supreme reared the four tones repeated in the simple rhythms into a great symphonic poem that is probably the noblest thought built edifice in the world.

Concerning this higher development of a

building more completely to express a principle as significant and beautiful, let us say at once, by way of warning: It is better to die of Ornaphobia by the wayside than it is to build any more "ornamental" buildings, as such, and die any more ignoble deaths of "Ornamentia." All period and pseudo-classic buildings whatever, and (although the authors of their beings do not seem to know it) most protestant modernistic buildings, too, are wholly ornamental in this definitely objectionable sense. A plain flat surface cut to shape for its own sake, however large or plain, is, the moment it is so cut, no less ornamental than egg and dart. All such buildings are as objectionably ornamental as the old order because both such "New" and "Old" ignore the nature of the first great integrity. Both ignore the four resources and both neglect the *nature* of Machine methods. Both misjudge the nature of time, place, and the modern life of man.

Here, in this new emulation we have not the modern, but the "istic," ignoring all merely to get the "look" of the machine.

Here we have no organic architecture; we have again merely a new, superficial aesthetic.

But, if we can't have the fine buildings, I say we would better have more imitation machines until we can have organic architecture.

False and futile, the nineteenth century tried by the hook or crook it miscalled romance to sentimentalize our new life, in a world Romanized by would-be and should-be patriots.

And this, blind to the fact that for nearly three centuries Roman culture in the arts was itself dilute and emulate Greek. Roman culture, being borrowed, did not even know, for centuries, what to do with its own fine arch. Sham culture, such as Roman culture, let the new arch do the work behind, while in the form of Greek trabeation "culture" got itself out in front to be the "show." Thus, Roman culture was above the belt and beyond genius for "institution," barely artificial. Our pseudo-culture everywhere the pseudo-modern is now going is quite as busy doing to the great invention, steel, what Roman architecture did to its great invention, the arch. Why practical considera-

tions of structure become ugly whenever culture is borrowed is seen in the very nature of "borrowing." You see?

So we, too, clumsy brokers in the antique, strive to make this Machine Age beautiful by likewise lying to ourselves. We have cluttered up the country to cheat our posterity when we were trying to play the benefactor.

Where great wealth gives power, life is wasted with us in the same false sense as the sham culture of the Romans wasted and destroyed the Romans. Seen by such tangible proof as we have ourselves actually constructed, culture-curiosity as "Art" is a first mortgage at usurious interest on America's youth.

And, just for good measure, at the moment, it is well to know that the Greeks, themselves heroes of Roman "Culture," copied the marble forms of their own temples from the temples, built in wood and painted, that long before had preceded the marble temples—a form of senseless imitation prostitute to superstitious theocratic culture—when seen in the light of our modern ideal.

So the heroic Greek model itself, in this new light, is evident imitation of projecting wood beam ends, wooden pins and moldings, and the wooden cornice in the far nobler marble, a fine material with a noble life of its own undiscovered by them.

The Greeks then, to be in keeping with the precedent of painted wood, painted the noble new material entirely out of sight with gorgeous gold and color decoration, themselves, therefore, the original inferior-desecrators.

Therefore in the light of the ideal of an organic architecture the pure Greek model is far from suitable as intelligent or free. Greek architecture was sophisticated "exterior" refinement. As such, giving us beauty, in the sense that the "vase" itself is a thing of beauty. But the search for the "elegant solution" is far from the modern ideal of organic simplicity. An ideal kept alive for us by the innate simplicities of the Nazarene and by the organic philosophy of Laotze as it gradually comes to light. The ideal of organic simplicity as modern and natural might save the United States of America from Roman falsity.

Roman falsity means Roman fate.

There is a far greater power than slavery, even in such intellectual hands as the Greeks, back of these five demands for new machine-age significance: that stupendous and stupefying power is the machine itself. Yet as it is now set up in all its powers, the machine will confirm these new complicities in architecture at every point. It demands them all if we are to realize the finer significances demanded by modern architecture as of life itself. It is reasonable to believe that, in due course, life in our own country will be lived in full enjoyment of the new freedom of the horizontal line because the horizontal line becomes now the great architectural highway. The flat plane now becomes the regional field. And integral-pattern becomes "the sound of the American heart."

The extended horizontal line is the earth line of human life.

The broad expanded plane is freedom for man.

This new sense of pattern as integral is the spiritual awakening of these states to beauty, as the Usonian's horizon immeasurably extends by enlightened use of his machine in creative hands.

By way of these five new means *that are all "architecture"* this monster power awakened by the human brain will gradually come into humane use, instead of crucifying integrity by the eclectic's variety in monotony, and utterly wasting life by way of capitalized academic sham in the hands of captains of industry.

The captains seem to see machines only as engines of wealth founded upon convenient economic business systems: the captains themselves becoming in turn "culture-curious," turning traitor to machine-increment. Wasting it in bigger and better imitations of the already devastating antique.

At least, architecture, wearying of the shallow hokum of "taste," sees through academic lies at last. It looks and sees the aeroplane fly overhead, emancipated from make-believe, free to be itself and true to itself. Architecture looks and sees the steamship ride the seas, triumphant as the superb thing it is, for what it is; sees the motor-car becoming more the machine it should be, daily less like a coach, gradu-

ally acquiring the freedom to be itself for what it is. In all modern mobilizations or utensils whatsoever, architecture, awakening, sees the Machine Age more and more freely declaring for Freedom to express the simple facts of structure and be itself. And the purpose of its own being is but crudely seen in these true mechanical forms of its utensils.

In another ten years, so fast is American movement, twentieth-century architecture will look upon the monumental pier-masses for steel, devised by popular space-makers for rent, or the mutilated boxes of the modish modernist, again senility, offering itself as new to house the spirit of man.

By these new and valid economic standards in architecture which we have enumerated, at least, may be seen and measured eventual urban decay as the real service to be rendered twentieth-century mankind inspired by use of the principle of the machine. Up to and including the nineteenth century, mechanical forces placed a premium upon centralization.

Twentieth-century mobilizations—electrification in its multiple forms—are all advance agents of decentralization.

Man has only to get the machine into service of his imagination, get machine increment where it belongs—in his own hands. And the City is survival for burial: dead as a consequence of mechanical success and human excess. A finer ideal of machine age luxury, as primarily human, will bury the corpse.

But let us beware! Meantime, this group of ideas, now seen as one great demand for finer integrity of life, must repudiate any symbol it may itself create.

This new sense of reality should look any "made" "abstraction"—Greek, Hindu, Chinese, whatever its authority—full in the eye for the impostor it finally becomes.

This new demand for life as architecture—it is now a demand for architecture as life—must read its first lessons afresh in the book of creation itself, despising with the fervor of youth all that lives either ashamed or afraid to live as itself: afraid to live for what it is or to live because of what it may be or become because of its own nature.

Then life itself will carry these five significances as one great new integrity to full expression as the great architecture of a great life.

No need, America, to be afraid. "We may disregard the laws, but if we are for Nature—no . . . we are never lawless."

Finally let us add all four new resources to the first great integrity to make up one great new validity to take the place of senile authority: a quality of youth—and yet so ancient—to be realized by twentieth century manhood, whatever its years, powerfully working with great new forces, for your freedom and mine: our children's freedom in this dawning realm of living Ideas.

The Egyptians, for cultural symbol—the lotus.
The Greeks, for cultural symbol—the honeysuckle.
The Romans, for cultural symbol—the acanthus.
To our hoped for growth of organic culture in these United States—for cultural symbol—the tree.

Again; youth crowding about the speaker's table—eager faces, ten or more deep, around me pressing in until I could scarcely move, eagerly asking questions. Sensible questions.

They stood there, interesting me in trying to answer them until Dr. Johnson turned out the lights to get them to go home. They did not go.

And young men and young women were the great fact in these various lectures and were the circumstance that encouraged me in openly assuming the unpopular guise of the preacher, to lecture and send the exhibition of my work to various places at home and abroad. I have recounted some of the experiences of the congenital preacher here to show how the on-coming generation in our country is keen and coming along "clean" where the present generation has been stultified by the sentimentality of the Past . . . at least. The coming generation needs only to learn to differentiate between sentiment and sentimentality. Not so easy in times of reaction and high-power salesmanship.

But I believe from what I have already seen that the next generation will overturn the falsity and sentimentalities in which they were reared—and themselves on the road to Freedom give a fairer break to fine sentiment in the generation of which they become progenitors. That generation will have its need of action.

Henry Churchill finally came to carry me off to join Olgivanna at his charming apartment on the square. Congenial people were there in a congenial atmosphere. But I learned from my sister Maginel that my little daughter Catherine, whom I had not seen for several years, had been in the audience. She had waited and waited behind the group of eager young questioners to try to speak to her father. As she lived far away and her train was leaving she had to leave without his seeing her.

This Catherine was "Taffy," as I used to call the rogue at the studio door. And my faithful, blue-eyed daughter Frances, her home is far away. Lloyd is an architect in Los Angeles; John, an architect in Michigan. David is involved with a steel company. Llewellyn . . . a lawyer!

Svetlana?

Iovanna?

AUTOBIOGRAPHY

As I have been writing away, myself autobiographical, I see why all autobiography is written between the lines. It must be so.

No matter how skilled the writer or how spontaneous he may be, the implication outdoes his ability or undoes his intention. The law of change is at work as he writes and the circumstance flows from beneath the fixation at the point of his pen into endless other forms and significances, except as a single facet may catch the gleam of the reader's intelligence and he who reads writes the truth in between the lines for himself.

Autobiography is impossible except as implication.

I remember so many poignant experiences. They come crowding into my mind—press on my heart for utterance.

And when I have uttered them, they have gone away mocking.

Taliesin III. FLLW Fdn FA#2501.0274. Photograph by Bradley Storrer

Does the fluid nature of life itself allow nothing to be held? Is nothing to be arrested and directed in human experience—so far as the essential quality—the *life* in it *goes?* Is the writer as helpless as the surgeon with his anatomical study of the corpse on his dissecting table, helpless to put his hand, even for a moment, on what was the life of the corpse?

It seems so.

The sufferings of growth, the agony of the sentimentality that tries to hold life by "institution" and establishment and extend the fleeting hour until the simple inevitable becomes high tragedy—are they not all punishment for violation of the first simple law of Freedom: the law of organic change.

And yet, I remember and record and leave the rest to life.

I REMEMBER

The third week after I first left my first home in Oak Park the misery that came over me in a little café somewhere in Paris. Caring neither to eat nor drink, I was listening to the orchestra. It had been a long depressing rainy season, the Seine most of the time over its banks. And it was late at night.

The cellist picked up his bow and began to play Simonetti's Madrigale. Lloyd had played the simple antique melody often. I would sometimes play with him, on the piano.

The familiar strains gave me one of those moments of anguish when I would have given all that I had lived to be able to live again.

The remembered strains drove me out of the cafe into the dim streets of Paris with such longing and sorrow as a man seldom knows. I wandered about not knowing where I was going or how long I went, at daylight finding myself facing a glaring signboard—somewhere on the Boulevard St. Michel.

I remember:

When all was well at Taliesin, during my first two years of life there, whenever I would go to Chicago to keep track of my work I would go out to Oak Park, after dark, to reassure myself that all

Taliesin III. FLLW Fdn FA#2501.0608. Photograph by John Amarantides

was going well, too, with the children.

I would see the light streaming from open windows and hear their voices.

Perhaps playing the piano.

Perhaps singing.

Perhaps calling to each other. All cozy enough.

And I would turn away to town again. Relieved.

I remember:

Llewelyn would come down to stay with me at the Congress, bring his mandolin and play for me. It gave me pleasure to see him fold each garment neatly and put it carefully on a chair when he went to bed. And I would tuck him in. The "deserted" child.

I remember:

The little suppers at the Tip-Top Inn with Catherine and Frances. Young ladies . . . my deserted daughters. So much "young ladies," they were, that I was suspected by an acquaintance of mine of dereliction from the straight and narrow path of the devoted unconventional lover by conventional attentions to gay young things.

I remember: But this volume must reach seemly if untimely end, if not timely and seemly end.

So, I will remember to forget most of what I intended to write. And as with the stories of adventure in building I left out those I should have liked best to write, these pages lack the faces and names and places and times that would be most revealing and more significant than any I have recalled. But that mutability is the charm of life.

Live up to life bravely, sensitively, conscientiously, or philosophically how we may, this fleeting and becoming defies fixation.

Who can put his life into his own hands?

Unlucky he who could!

BACK TO TALIESIN III

Taliesin! When I am away from it, like some rubber band, stretched out but ready to snap back immediately the pull is relaxed or released, I get back to it, happy to be home again.

At sunrise last late September I stood, again with bare feet, on the hill-crown garden at Taliesin. Looking down toward the big dark-green clump of fir trees keeping the little family chapel company.

A little farther to the left rises the range of hills I sometimes walked along as a barefoot boy at night in search of peace, beauty, satisfaction, rest. A little over to the right, beyond, are the hills where I went to look for the cows: and where the surplus of the fervent hymns used to go. Below and beyond are the rolling fields where Uncle James used to call, "Come back, Frank, come back!"

Over the ridge nearby, lies—wasting away, a reproach and a sorrow to me—what is left of the Hillside Home School.

Romeo and Juliet still stands on the hill-crown to the right just above the school, a new wheel needed now. The third has been wrenched from the tower by severe northwest storms. The uncles and aunts, nephews and nieces—all gone elsewhere—or beyond. Occasionally, as in that boyhood time, come moments of abstraction. But I hear no one calling, "Frank, come back. Come back, Frank!" Only the free, long retrospect of Time, Place, and Otherwhere will come drifting through the present moment. Retrospect strung around the earth.

Not so many dreams of the future? Moments of anguish? Oh yes—but not of regret. I am enjoying more, day by day, the eternity that is now, realizing, at last, that it is now and that it only divides yesterday from tomorrow.

As though the mind itself is recording film in endless reel to go on perfecting and projecting pictures endlessly, seldom, if ever, the same. The same scene and the scheme shows itself from different angles as the point of view changes if informing principle, the *impulse* living in it all, stays fixed. Else the impotence of confusion. The chaos of madness. Imprisonment in the Past.

No—the several years since Taliesin settled down again for the third time to its work and its ideal have not been carefree. But—sad memories included—happy. Short. Hope never really dies. And life is richer than ever before, with "hard times," as we like to say—and must say—lying all around. And very near to Taliesin.

Olgivanna, Svetlana, Iovanna, and I were up at sunrise this particular September morning walking with bare feet in the thick white rime of the frosty dew. So cold was the rime that, every little while, we would have to stop to warm our feet in the hollows of our knees.

The tall, red-topped grass of the hill beyond the garden, in the slanting rays of the morning's sun, was everywhere hung with a covering of spider's webs of amazing size and brilliance. All were made sparkling by the myriad dewdrops that turned each strand of each web into a miracle of light: a construction that might well be ideal of this age. We might realize such beauty in Usonian buildings.

The German shepherd, Kave, as always leaping, nosing, and biting at our bare heels, we reached the melon-patch on the hillside below the reservoir. We gathered ripe melons, cool with the frosted morning dew, broke them across our knees and ate our fill of the watery sweetness of pink flesh decorated with black seeds. So many melons were lying there we ate only the hearts and threw the rest aside for the birds.

Fruit seeds were invented for birds, and animals too—but not for us this morning.

Kave sleeps by my bedside at night. Or by his mistress. If he is shut out his howls and protests are not to be borne. He gets in and lies there to wake us in the morning by brushing a cold nose on our faces or giving a warm tongue to the cheek at precisely a few moments before the ante-breakfast bell regularly rings on the hill. Then we all get up, go into the living room with the big expanse of waxed board floor, turn on some music, and have the morning frolic.

Winter nights—all in the white, outside—we love to build a wood fire in the big stone bedroom fireplace, close the inside wood shutters of the whole house, and lie story-telling or reading until we fall asleep. We sometimes take turns reading aloud, Iovanna's fairy-tales coming first. Carl's "The White-Horse Girl and the Blue Wind-Boy" is her favorite at the moment. And ours.

Taliesin scenes are homely scenes. These latter years—Iovanna is nearly six years old—have been a succession of changing hours made up of changing moments, each of which had its lovely picture among pictures. Curly heads and loving dark eyes, lithe supple bodies, eager minds, living life, make beautiful pictures and constant demands.

Life is not monotonous at Taliesin. The days are a continuous series of changing play and changing work. The landscape itself changes outside the windows as the sea changes, only more so.

There are no fixed habits, even good ones. Unless it is that breakfast bell. We avoid them.

Good company will sometimes find its way, as far away from the city as we are—but we are still pretty far away.

We live in quiet seclusion all over the house and workshops. Usually if the weather is severe, seven or eight great stone fireplaces are burning. Some of them burn most of the time at evening. The fireplaces have established a good market for cordwood in the neighborhood and "stabilize" it, although the fireplaces are for good measure because the whole place is heated by steam and lighted by our own hydro-electric plant. A pull on a switch-cord by the bedside lights the grounds about the house.

We love the snow.

In summer our range of activity widens somewhat, takes in the farm gardens, the hills, woods, fields, and roads. We plunder the roadsides for choice branches, bloom, and berries. And there is the broad, sand-barred Wisconsin River's changing flow in the broad bottomland below the house— for swimming. Our resources are constantly taxed. "Something is always happening in the country." We plan great things.

Music is essential to life at Taliesin.

A grand piano stands by the big living room fireplace, a cello resting against its hollow side, a violin on the ledge beside it. Olgivanna plays Bach, Beethoven, old Russian music. I play a few moments, while inspiration lasts, knowing nothing, feeling something out. And never can play any of the things, such as they are, a second time. Olgivanna says she likes to hear me play. Hers is a gentle, encouraging soul and she would not hurt even such pride as mine.

Svetlana plays, too, now. And Iovanna plays, with perfect style all the while. Her finger movements are perfect, but the notes she selects are not perfectly suited to each other. No matter, she plays, too.

My little five-year-old daughter and I, among constant inventions, have invented a game. She has many kinds and sizes of blocks, among them a set of well-made cubes about an inch square painted pure bright colors, red, blue, yellow, green, black, and white. Some of the cubes are divided on the diagonal in contrasting colors. Whoever deals deals seven blocks to each, two, diagonals. Iovanna's turn to play. She chooses a color-block (not fair to start with a diagonal) and places it square on the board floor. Then I select a color-block and put it, say, touching hers at the corner. Her turn. She studies a little, head one side, finally putting down a block in whatever way she chooses, but now making a decided geometrical figure. Imagination begins to stress the judgment.

Instead of extending the figure on the floor, she may now put a block on top of the one already "played" by me. She does so. The figure on the floor begins to look more and more interesting, as the "third dimension" enters and creeps up into the air. The block group begins to be a construction. I may follow up and down, too, or I may go crosswise with whatever color I have. But whatever I do, I will change the whole effect just as she will when her turn comes to play.

Sometimes she sees she has spoiled the figure with her "turn" and asks to change it.

All fourteen blocks in place we take in the result, critical or enthusiastic.

Always the little form and color exercises would make a good thesis in "Modern Art." In fact, that is what I intend them to be.

Yes . . . Taliesin life is one continuous round of movement, usually in a happy rhythm ending in sound sleep . . . to begin again with play and laughter, settling down into serious work.

We usually are together all the time and everywhere whether in work or in play. Iovanna does nearly everything we do. Her half bushel of gold-brown curls pile up on her head. They lie in ringlets there and look at you like eyes. Her name was made from her maternal Grandfather's—Ivan, or John, and her paternal Grandmother's—Anna. Literally John Anna, Johanna, or Iovanna, to go with Olgivanna, properly Olga Ivanovna. And the name of the charmingly disposed little daughter before we met, Svetlana, means, in Russian, "light."

Iovanna's own stories often astonish us.

Buddha, whom she sees all about in various forms, intrigues her imagination, and she romances with Buddha. But recently she has become interested in another great personality. Here is something concerning that new interest Olgivanna wrote down, word for word, changing nothing.

I am calling it Ave Maria. But I am, not in the least, sentimental?

AVE MARIA

"Go to bed now, you have run around enough. Come now," I said to my little daughter Iovanna.

"Wait, Mother. I must go and tell God 'goodnight.'"

I was surprised, as I heard this for the first time. I followed her into the living room. She stood there in the middle and said clearly, right into space, "Goodnight, God." We went back to the bedroom, I tucked her in bed.

"Stay with me, Mother, sit down—Mother, I would like to see God. Will you buy me some flying wings at Marshall Field's, so I can fly up into the sky to see him?"

"But God is not in the sky only. Remember what Papa told you in the church in New York, that God was in your heart?"

"Yes, Mother, I know, only I think my heart is too little for God. You see it is too little. When it gets cold, he gets cold in my heart and he goes up in the sky to build a big fire there to keep warm."

"But your heart is a fire. Your heart is love, it is like a flame, it keeps God warm."

"Oh, no, Mother, I told you, it is too little for God. He is big and my heart is little just like—well, you see just like a grain of sand."

"But think of all the hearts there are in the world: children's hearts and grown-up people's hearts, all together they make a great big fire for God to keep him warm."

"Oh, but he needs food, or he will get very hungry. We must give him something to eat. He is very kind you know. We must take care of him."

"He does not eat, he lives on love. He is never hungry if he has enough love."

"But, Mother, we should send him something

just the same. We should make a big bouquet of flowers for him, you know he loves flowers. And he loves shells. You see, all the shells of the sea come to him. They bring to him the food and the flowers and everything he needs. I want to send him something."

"Send him your love by being good, minding your Mother and Father. You should also work if you want to please God."

"Oh, I am working. I swept the sitting-room, I brushed Svetlana's dress for her, I rubbed Auntie Maginel's poor neck. I work very hard. Do you have to mind God too?"

"Certainly."

"And Papa?"

"Of course."

"Would God punish you if you and Papa were not good?"

"God never punishes, we punish ourselves."

"Would God punish me if I were not good?"

"No, but I would have to punish you if I could not make you good by being nice to you. I don't like to do it, but I have to, so that God can be warm in your heart. He is very cold and sad when you are not good."

"Is he warm right now?"

"Very."

"Mother, I wish I could see him."

It became very quiet in the room. In another moment she was asleep. I leaned over the little gold brown, curly head.

This book . . . To the Anna who is my mother. To the Ivan (John) whose daughter Olga Ivanovna, called Olgivanna, is Mother to Iovanna—little "John-Anna" . . . the last of that generation calling me father . . . And to Olgivanna herself. But for her this book were never written.

POSTLUDE

Here on this low hill in Southern Wisconsin, life and work are synonymous terms. In the retrospect is vast panorama of life as human experience; tapestry shot through with threads of gold as light gleams whenever truth was touched, wherever love rose worthy of noble selfhood, whenever life rose higher because of death.

The Valley from a terrace at Taliesin. FLLW Fdn FA#2501.0688 Photograph by John Amarantides.

Or where living faith justified defeat.

The original urge?

I say it is unchanged in all the quest.

Sincerely sought meantime, well loved, may be seen the principle, or is it the very quality of life itself—vaguely felt by the boy as "left out" in the early lesson preached by familiar feet in the snow in the Valley.

The order of change is limitless and profound.

And the nature of this order I have sought as a natural order. I have seen it as a quality. I am learning to see it as a principle.

So far as change is by law of natural growth, change is beneficent.

Organic change is not chance. No menace.

The inevitable is friend to natural order in any true culture founded on this reality. Age, then, becomes a desirable qualification.

Our life on earth should be blessed, not antagonized, by this beneficence of natural growth

. . . death a crisis of growth.

I have encountered violent breaks in the field of life and work, studying as normal this element not in the reckoning, as indicated in the graph of the harvest field. Reconciled to respect. Armed—not to establish but to foresee and forefend the flow that is human life.

Romance I have seen as Reality in this fluescent sense.

And I have been seeking ideal life and ideal building as, at the very beginning, I sought naked weed rising above blue arabesque, sunshot, on spotless white.

Thus, Life has been as it will be, a changing test of eternal principle.

Leading Life-adventure now is this keener romance of Time, Place, and Man flowing together to flow out into the making of a changing world so instituted as to be capable of natural change without constitutional disorder.

BOOK ONE:

1. German educator Friedrich Froebel (1782–1852) developed a method for mothers of educating young children, which he called "Kindergarten Gifts." Wright's most frequent references are to the geometric blocks that make up five of the first six "gifts."

2. William Wright filed for and was granted a divorce in 1885. Unless noted, biographical dates in this volume are from an unpublished chronology compiled by Robert L. Sweeney.

3. David R. Jones (1832–1915), a Welsh-born architect who practiced in Madison, 1870–1885. Information provided by Jack Holzheuter of the State Historical Society of Wisconsin.

4. Owen Jones (1807–1874) compiled the *Grammar of Ornament*, illustrating historic styles of ornament, 1856.

5. Wright and Catherine Tobin married June 1, 1889.

6. Frank Lloyd Wright, Jr., born 1890; John Lloyd Wright, born 1892; Catherine Lloyd Wright, born 1894; David Samuel Wright, born 1895; Frances Lloyd Wright, born 1898; Robert Llewellyn Wright, born 1903.

BOOK TWO

1. William Winslow House, River Forest, Illinois, 1893.

2. Nathan Moore House, Oak Park, Illinois, 1895. Redesigned by Wright and rebuilt after a fire in 1923.

3. "The Art & Craft of the Machine," delivered at Hull House, March 1901.

4. Ward Willits House, Highland Park, Illinois, 1901.

5. The "Master" is Louis Sullivan. Architectural historian Paul Sprague has identified Sullivan's first printed use of the expression "form follows function" in "The Tall Office Building Artistically Considered," published in *Lippincott's*, March 1896.

6. Wright's reference is to the earthquake of September 1923. He makes a similar error on p. 265, incorrectly dating it as 1924.

7. The Larkin Administration Building, Buffalo, New York, 1903.

8. Paul Mueller, a German-born engineer who worked with Wright on the Larkin Building, Unity Temple, and the Imperial Hotel.

9. Wright and Mamah Cheney left for Germany in the fall of 1909. Wright went ahead to Italy and was joined in Fiesole by Mrs Cheney in spring or early summer of 1910. (See Anthony Alofsin, *Frank Lloyd Wright: The Lessons of Europe,* University of Chicago, due 1993).

10. Before and after his return from Europe in 1910 Wright was attacked by newspapers and from pulpits for his scandalous conduct.

11. Alfonso Ianelli (1888–1965), Italian-born sculptor, collaborated with Wright on Midway Gardens. Richard Bock (1865–1949), German-born sculptor, worked with Wright on a number of projects prior to Midway Gardens.

12. August 15, 1914.

13. Henry Blackman Sell, journalist attracted to Chicago by the Little Theater in 1913. Kathryn Smith, "Frank Lloyd Wright, Hollyhock House, and Olive Hill, 1914–1924," *Journal for the Society of Architectural Historians*, March 1979, p. 18.

14. Tahoe Summer Colony (project), Lake Tahoe, California, 1922. Doheny Ranch Resort (project), Los Angeles, California, 1923.

15. Charles E. Roberts, influential supporter of Wright's, interceded on his behalf with the Unity Temple building committee. Also brought Wright the Kankakee, Illinois, commissions for B. Harley Bradley and Warren Hickox, both 1900. Leonard Eaton, *Two Chicago Architects and Their Clients* (Cambridge: MIT Press, 1969), pp. 77–78.

16. National Life Insurance Company (project), Chicago, Illinois, 1924. Wright dedicated this design to Louis Sullivan.

17. Miriam Noel left Wright in May 1924.

18. Taliesin II burned, April 1925.

19. Dankmar Adler died in 1900.

20. Anna Lloyd Wright died February 9, 1923.

21. Actually, October 21, 1926.

22. Cleaver Thayer, resident of Minneapolis, came to Wright's aid during this latest ordeal.

23. Following a request—in late 1927 or early 1928—from Albert Chase McArthur for permission to use Wright's concrete block system in the Arizona Biltmore Hotel, the Wrights went to Phoenix. (Robert L. Sweeney, *Wright in Hollywood: Visions of a New Architecture,* Architectural History Foundation/MIT, due 1993).

BOOK THREE

1. Wright must be referring to the extraordinary graphics of the *Wendingen* volume, a beautiful book, which he treasured above all other publications of his work.

2. Wright occupied Ocatilla for several months.

3. St. Mark's in the Bouwerie (project), New York, New York, 1929.

4. Reprinted in this volume.

INDEX

A

Addams, Jane (1860–1935), 152, 191
Adler, Dankmar (1844–1900), 168, 172, 173–174, *175,* 176, 296, 300
Adler and Sullivan, 103, 154, 164–176, 177, 178, 185, 186, 197, 198, 233, 296
Henry Allen House (1916), 289
All Souls Church, 145, 148, 150, 151, 153, 154, 186
American Institute of Architects (A.I.A.), 19, 43, 44, 189, 274, 283, 288
architecture:
  ancient vs. modern functions of, 47–49, 91–97
  block system in, 279–289, 327
  box idea in, 325–326
  cantilever construction in, 290–303
  commercialism of, 62–69, 94–95, 101, 182
  concrete in, 276–277
  of democracy, 49–51, 73–74, 91, 95–96, 203, 205, 293, 299, 340, 344, 345, 348
  desert in, 329–331, 335, 336
  egocentricity in, 83–84, 174
  glass in, 38–39, 350, 367
  light in, 89–90
  nature of materials in, 207–209, 369, 370
  pylon construction in, 359–360
  repose in, 58, 206
  residential, 36–37, 51–59, 84–85, 103, 199–209, 244–248, 279–290
  space in, 54–55, 69, 89–90, 358–359
  standardization in, 36, 68, 88, 291–293
  tenuity in, 367, 370–371
  urban disintegration and, 69–77
Arizona Biltmore Hotel (1929), 321, 327, *328, 330*
"Art and Craft of the Machine, The" (1901) (Wright), 191
Arts and Crafts movement, 30, 191–192, 218
Ashbee, C. R. (1863–1942), 218
Auditorium Building (1887–1890), 61, 154, 165, 172, 174, 233, 296, 299, 300–301
Autobiography of an Idea (Sullivan), 298

B

Bach, Johann Sebastian, 110–111, 128, 218, 267, 269
Bank of Wisconsin, 308–309, 318–321
Barnsdall, Aline (1882–1946), 70–71, 103, 267–276, 289
Aline Barnsdall Theatre, *70-71,* 270, 275
Beers, Clay and Dutton, 149, 153
Beethoven, Ludwig van, 111, 128, 218, 269, 367, 372
Blake, William (1757–1827), 59, 141, 227
Bock, Richard (1865–1883), 236–237

Broadacre City, 19
Brooklyn Bridge (1869–1883), 90, 359, 370
Burnham, Daniel H. (1846–1912), 187–189, 209, 218, 230
Burnham and Root, 164
Butler, Samuel (1835–1902), 121*n,* 362
Byrne, Frank, 278

C

Capitol Building (Madison, Wis.), 42–43, 125, 142–143
Capitol Building (Washington, D.C.), 59, 366
"Capitol Journal," *89*
"Cardboard House, The" (Wright), 19, 51–59
Carlyle, Thomas (1795–1881), 83, 93
cathedrals, 29, 66, 126
Centennial Exhibition (1876), 111
Chandler, Alexander, 327–329, 335
Cheney, Mamah Borthwick (1869–1914), 103, *221,* 239–240
Chicago Architectural Club, 33, 149
Cinema San Diego (1905), *74*
"City, The" (Wright), 19, 69–79
Columbian Fair (1893), 23, 176, 185, 188, 296, 363
concrete, 276–277
congestion, 62–64, 71
Conover, Allen D., 140, 141, 144
continuity, plasticity as, 87
Coonley House (1907), *18, 206,* 218, 229, 289
cornices, 42–51, 61
Corwin, Cecil, 150–154, *151,* 158, 159–163, 164, 165, 167, 171, 185–186, 190–191

D

Dana House (1900), 289
Darrow, Clarence (1857–1938), 320
decoration, definition of, 58–59, 98
Dictionnaire Raisonné de l'Architecture Française (Voillet-le-Duc), 43, 141, 154
Doheny Ranch Project (1923), 289, *338*
domes, 59–61, 365–366

E

Ecole des Beaux Arts, 24, 43, 66, 94, 170, 171, 173, 187, 188
Edelman, John (1852–1900), 172, 174, 300
Edelweiss Brewing Company, 238
Elmslie, George (1871-1952), 168, 170–171, 297, 299
Emerson, Ralph Waldo (1803–1882), 47, 113, 114
Endo Arata (1889-1951), *260,* 264
Ennis House (1923), 289

F

Fiesole, 220-221, *222, 223*
Ford, Henry (1863–1947), 50, 74, 77-79, 344
Fors Clavigera (Ruskin), 141
Francke, Kuno (1855-1930), 218–219

Frankl, Paul, 358
Fukuhara Country House (1917), 289
Fuller, Buckminster (1895–1983), 356-357
furniture, 56, 204–205

G

Gage Building, 174
Gannett, William C., 124
Getty Tomb, 300, 301
Gilbert and Sullivan, 129
Mrs. Samuel William Gladney House, *66, 96*
glassmaking, 38–39, 350, 367
Goethe, Johann Wolfgang von (1749-1832), 97, 144, 218, 252, 351
Gothic architecture, 23, 29, 60, 66
Graeco-Roman style, 30, 43, 46, 60, 67, 78, 373
Grammar of Ornament (Jones), 155, 165
Greece, ancient, 47–49, 188, 267, 373–374
gridiron plan, 64–65
Guaranty Building (1894–1896), 176, 296, 300
Gurdjieff Institute, 102, 306

H

Haskell, Douglas, 358, 362
Hayashi, Aisaku, 242–243, *244, 260,* 262, 264
W. R. Heath House (1905), 209
highways, 74–76, 90, 345
Hill, James, 294, 308, 309, 318, 319, 355
Hillside Home School (1902), 19, 192, 223, 289, 325, 378
Hitchcock, Henry-Russell (1903-1987), 15–17
Hollyhock House, 267–276, *268, 269,* 286, 289, 290
Hugo, Victor (1802–1885), 42–43, 47, 49, 52, 154–155, 156
Hull House, 22, 30, 191

I

Ianelli, Alfonso (1881–1965), 236
imagination, 33, 41, 84, 372
Imperial Hotel (1916–1922), 15, 87, 103, 207, 242, 250, *251, 257,* 258–266, *260,* 267, 271, 290, 293
industrial art, 40–41
International Style, 325, 348
In the Nature of Materials (Wright and Hitchcock), 15
"In the Realm of Ideas" (Wright), 82–91
Isaiah, 106–107, 108, 117, 294–295, 304

J

Japanese prints, 243, 251–252, 259
Japanese residences, 36–37, 244–248
Jefferson, Thomas (1743-1826), 46, 210, 222
Jesus Christ, 49, 58, 160–161, 367, 373
Johnson, A. M., 290–293, 325

Jones, David R. (Madison Capitol architect) (1832–1915), 143
Jones, Owen (1807–1874), 165

K

Kennerly, Mitchell, 317–318
Klimt, Gustav (1862–1918), 35

L

labor unions, 230, 236–237, 272
Lake Mendota, Wis. (1922), 114, 143
Lake Tahoe Project (1922), 289
"La Miniatura" Millard House (1923), 227, 279–289, *280, 281,* 290
Lamp, Robert, 125–126, 127, 129, 140
Lao-Tzu, 84, 367, 373
Larkin Administration Building (1903), 103, 209–210
Larkin Desk, *33*
liberty, 49–51, 73–74, 95–96, 203, 205
Lincoln, Abraham (1809–1865), 47, 61, 64, 299
Lloyd-Jones, Ellen (1845–1919) (aunt), 105, *120,* 127, 141, 192–197, *194*
Lloyd-Jones, Enos (1853–1941) (uncle), 105, 116, 117, *120,* 197
Lloyd-Jones, James (1850–1907) (uncle), 105, 114–123, *120,* 132, 135, 144, 146, 185, 195, 197, 219, 378
Lloyd-Jones, Jane (1848–1917) (aunt), 105, *120,* 127, 130, 141, 192–197, *194,* 324
Lloyd-Jones, Jenkin (1843–1918) (uncle), 105, *122,* 123–125, 145, 147, 151, 152, 156, 195, 197
Lloyd-Jones, John (1832–1908) (uncle), 105, 108, 125, 126, 197
Lloyd-Jones, Laura (aunt), 115, 116–117, 121
Lloyd-Jones, Mary (1836/37–1903) (aunt), 105
Lloyd-Jones, Mary (1808–1870) (grandmother), 105, 107–108, *118*
Lloyd-Jones, Nannie (1840/41–1844/45) (aunt), 105
Lloyd-Jones, Philip (uncle), 197
Lloyd-Jones, Richard (1873–1963) (cousin), 152–153, 352
Lloyd-Jones, Richard (1799–1885) (grandfather), 105–108, *118,* 125, 173, 223
Lloyd-Jones, Susan (aunt), 155
Lloyd-Jones, Thomas (uncle) (1830–1894), 104, 123, 124, 196
Lowell, James Russell (1819–1891), 109, 113
Luxfer Prism Company (1895), 197

M

McArthur, Albert (1881-1951), 321, 327
McArthur, Warren, 175, 178
"Machinery, Materials and Men" (Wright), 19-31, 32, 34
machines:
  art and architecture altered by, 21-31, 52, 341-343

machines (cont.)
    artistic uses of, 31-42, 68-69, 88-91, 97-100, 174, 191, 207-208, 293, 373-374
    urban change as regulated by, 74-77, 342-348
Martin, Darwin D., 209, 242, 289, 318, 321
Darwin D. Martin House (1904), 208, 209
Victor Metzger House (1901), 204
Metzner, Franz (1817-1919), 35
Michelangelo Buonarroti (1475-1564), 38, 59-60, 125, 365
Middle Ages, 20, 28
Midway Gardens (1914), 103, 229-239, 231, 277
Millard, Alice, 282-287
Millard House "La Miniatura," (1923), 282
Miserables, Les (Hugo), 141, 154-155
Modern Architecture (Wright), 352
modernism, 37, 77, 97-98
Modern Painters (Ruskin), 141
Momoyama period (Japan 1573-1615), 34-36
Monadnock Building (1889-1890), 61
Montgomery Ward (1891-1892), 23
Nathan Moore House (1895), 189-190, 209
Morris, William (1834-1896), 24
Moti (4-5th-c. B.C.), 43, 62
Mueller, Paul, 164, 167, 168, 169, 172, 173, 217, 230-231, 260, 262
Mumford, Lewis (1895-1989), 358, 362
Munch, Gottlieb, 115, 116, 121, 123, 135
Museum of Modern Art, 15
music, 45, 112, 127, 128-129, 150, 180, 267-274, 379

N

National Life Insurance Building (1924), 290-293, 325, 351
New School of the Middle West, 20, 53, 197
Elizabeth Noble Apartments (1929), 80-81, 85
Noel, Miriam (?1872–1930) (second wife), 102, 103, 248-249, 248, 250, 266, 293-294, 306, 308-321, 322, 354
Notre-Dame de Paris (Hugo), 42, 156

O

Oak Park, 82, 84, 89, 158, 159, 181, 189, 222, 223
    residence at, 157, 173, 175, 177, 179, 187, 376
    studio at, 197-198, 209, 210, 243, 277, 278
Ocatilla (1929), 329-335, 332, 333, 334
Okura, Baron Kihachiro, (1837-1928), 263-265
Olbrich, Josef M. (1867-1908), 35
Olive Hill, 269, 271, 275
Orchestra Hall Building, 229
organic simplicity, 17, 36, 48-50, 52, 56-59, 63, 85-88, 91, 96, 98-

101, 198, 203-204, 207, 209, 325, 333, 348-349, 371-373, 375

P

Palladio, Andrea (1508–1580), 23, 38, 44, 285
Pantheon, 23, 29, 59
Paris Exposition of 1925, 363
Parthenon, 23, 29, 47-48, 49, 59
"Passing of the Cornice, The" (Wright), 19, 42-51, 67
Perry, Commodore Matthew (1794-1858), 32, 253, 259
Phidias, 23, 48-49
Phi Gamma Delta Fraternity House (1924), 79
plasticity, 28, 34, 54, 79, 86-87, 174, 202, 206-207, 300, 301, 370
Prefabricated Farm Units (1932), 93
Princeton University, 19, 47, 87, 350, 352
pseudoclassicism, 23-29, 42-51, 60, 67, 78-79, 100, 182, 352-356, 363-366, 373
Puerto Rico (1888–1890), 306-308, 316
Pullman Building (Chicago 1883–1884), 149, 154, 298

R

Ravine Bluffs Bridge (1915), 235
realism, 233-234
Renaissance, 37, 39, 42-43, 52, 59-60, 156, 365
Residence B, 272
Richardson, H. H. (1838-1886), 172, 174, 188, 300, 302, 363
Roberts, Charles E., 211, 216-217, 289
Robie House (1906), 289
Roebling, John (1809-1869), 90, 359, 370
Romeo and Juliet tower (1896), 192-197, 193, 223, 378
Root, John Wellborn (1850-1891), 61, 172, 174, 187, 188, 300
Roycroft-Stickley-Mission style, 56, 203
Ruskin, John (1819-1900), 24

S

St. Mark's Tower (1929), 325, 349-350, 370
St. Peter's Basilica (1558-1564), 59, 60-61, 289
San Diego Exposition, 276, 282
San Marcos in the Desert (1928), 325, 329, 335-337, 346
Sartor Resartus (Carlyle), 141, 142
Schiller Building (1891), 182, 185
School of the Free Spirit (Tokyo, 1921), 289
Secession movement, 35
sentimentalism, 143, 161, 164, 172, 176, 270, 356, 366, 373
    see also pseudoclassicism
Seven Lamps of Architecture (Ruskin), 127
C. Thaxter Shaw House, remodeling (1906), 205
Shelley, Percy Bysshe (1792-1822), 141
Shintoism, 36-37, 244-248

Silsbee, J. L. (1848-1913), 148, 150, 151-152, 153, 154, 157, 158-159, 160, 163, 165-166, 174, 192, 299
"Skyscraper Regulation," 68
skyscrapers, 23, 59-69, 71, 73, 84, 290-293, 337, 342-344, 357, 358-359
Stones of Venice (Ruskin), 141
Strong, Gordon (1869-1954), 63, 325, 349
style, definition of, 24, 214-215
"Style in Industry" (Wright), 19, 31-42
Sullivan, Louis Henry (1856–1924), 35, 43, 61, 84, 86-87, 94, 103, 164-176, 175, 188, 190, 206, 208, 293, 296-303

T

Taliesin, Wis., 192, 197, 222-223, 278, 289
Taliesin I, 223-229, 239-241, 224, 225, 248, 270, 277, 296, 298, 299
Taliesin II, 240, 241-242, 242, 243, 244, 288, 290, 293-295, 303, 306
Taliesin III, 296, 303, 305, 308, 318, 320-321, 325, 327, 376, 377-381, 377
terra cotta, 28-29
Thoreau, Henry David (1817-1862), 113-114
"To the Young Man in Architecture" (Wright), 91-101
Transportation Building (Columbian Exposition 1893), 176, 300
"Twentieth Century Architecture" (Wright), 362-375
Two Lectures on Architecture (Wright), 82-101
"Tyranny of the Skyscraper, The" (Wright), 19, 59-69, 72

U

Unity Temple (1904), 89, 103, 209, 210-218, 211
"Usonian City, The" (Wright), 340-349
Usonians, 58, 70, 121, 140, 190, 217, 274, 325, 337, 363-366, 374

V

Vitruvius (90-20 B.C.), 20, 23, 38, 44
Vogelsang, John, 232-233, 237

W

Wagner, Otto (1841-1918), 35
Wainwright Building, 61, 69, 297, 300-301
Waller, Edward, Jr., 230-233, 237, 239
Waller, Edward C., 187-189, 218
Wasmuth, Ernst, 219, 242, 325
Weston, William, 228, 239, 332
Whistler, James Abbott McNeill (1834-1903), 29
White, Stanford (1853-1906), 302, 362

Whitman, Walt (1819-1892), 172, 219
Wilhelmmeister (Goethe), 141, 142
Ward W. Willits House (1901), 201
Winslow House (1893), 55, 88, 187, 189, 190, 197, 198, 202, 209, 289
Wisconsin, 102, 108, 224, 380
Wisconsin, University of, at Madison, 125, 136, 140-146, 154
Wisconsin River, 105, 378
Women's University Club, 356
Woollcott, Alexander (1887-1943), 318, 358, 362
World's Fair, Chicago (1893), 357, 358-362
Wren, Christopher (1632-1723), 366
Wright, Anna Lloyd-Jones (1839-1923) (mother), 104, 105, 108-114, 118, 122, 125, 127, 129, 130-131, 138, 139-140, 145-146, 161-163, 179, 241, 248, 266, 303
Wright, Catherine (1894-1979) (daughter), 177, 180, 181, 375, 377
Wright, Catherine Tobin (1871–1959) (first wife), 103, 155-157, 161-163, 164, 176-180, 187, 189, 190, 219, 249, 352
Wright, David (1895–)(son), 177, 180
Wright, Frances (1898-1959) (daughter), 177, 178-179, 180, 181, 217, 375, 377
Wright, Iovanna (1925–) (daughter), 102, 307, 308, 310, 311, 323, 332, 336, 375, 378, 379
Wright, Jane Lloyd (1869–1953) (sister), 110, 114, 125, 127, 140, 157, 316, 318
Wright, John Lloyd (1892–1972) (son), 177, 180, 236, 239-240, 312, 375
Wright, Robert Llewelyn (1903–1986) (son), 177, 178, 180, 375, 377
Wright, Frank Lloyd Jr. (1890–1978) (son), 177, 179-180, 266, 272, 277, 289, 375, 376
Wright, Maginel Lloyd (1877–1966) (sister), 114, 125, 128, 140, 157, 316, 318, 357, 375
Wright, Olgivanna Hinzenberg (1898–1985) (third wife), 15, 102-104, 295, 303-322, 307, 310, 332, 336, 355, 357, 375, 378-381
Wright, Svetlana Hinzenberg (1917–1946) (step-daughter), 102, 308, 312, 319, 332, 336, 375, 378, 379
Wright, William Russell Cary (1825–1904) (father), 62, 109-114, 118, 125-126, 127, 138-140, 161
Frank Lloyd Wright Studio Residence, 234

Y

Yahara Boathouse (1905), 45
Yedo, 250, 251, 252-258